Legal Foundations
of
Land Use Planning

Legal Foundations
of
Land Use Planning

Textbook/Casebook and Materials
on
Planning Law

Written and Edited by

Jerome G. Rose

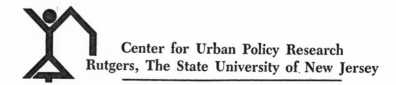

Center for Urban Policy Research
Rutgers, The State University of New Jersey

About the Author

Jerome G. Rose has a J.D. from Harvard Law School and is a member of the New York Bar. He is Professor of Urban Planning at Livingston College. Rutgers University and Editor-in-Chief of *Real Estate Law Journal*. He is author of *The Legal Advisor on Home Ownership* (1967); *Landlords and Tenants: A Complete Guide to the Residential Rental Relationship* (1973); *Legal Foundations of Environmental Planning: Cases and Materials on Environmental Law* (1974); *New Approaches To State Land Use Policies*, with Melvin R. Levin and Joseph S. Slavett (1974). *The Transfer of Development Rights* (1976); and *After Mount Laurel: The New Suburban Zoning* with Robert E. Rothman (1977).

Copyright, 1979, Rutgers - The State University of New Jersey
All Rights Reserved
Published in the United States by the
Center for Urban Policy Research
New Brunswick, New Jersey

Libary of Congress Cataloging in Publication Data

Rose, Jerome G
Legal foundations of land use planning.
Bibliography: p.
Includes index.
1. City planning and redevelopment law—United States—Cases. 2. Regional planning—Law and legislation—United States—Cases. I. Title.

KF5692.A4R67   346'.73'045   78-11527
ISBN O-88285-057-1

Acknowledgments

I am indebted to a number of people whose assistance made this book possible. Thomas Collins and Susan Kaplan, students in the joint degree program of the School of Law and the Department of Urban and Regional Planning, were helpful in assembling some of the materials and preparing the table of cases. Evelyn Kuhlman edited the new material written especially for this collection and Ann Daniel prepared the index. Daniel J. Sohmer skillfully guided the work through the publishing process. I am especially grateful to Dr. George Sternlieb, Director of the Center for Urban Policy Research, Rutgers University, who encouraged me to undertake this work and who made it possible by making available to me the talent and resources of the Center.

J.G.R.

Contents

Chapter Three   - EXCLUSIONARY ZONING AND MANAGED GROWTH

Chapter Seven - TRANSFER OF DEVELOPMENT RIGHTS

Table of Cases

Legal Foundations
of
Land Use Planning

Chapter One

The Law as an Instrument of Urban Planning

Urban planning is a process of analysis of the constraints within a community for the purpose of developing and implementing a plan for the achievement of the community's goals and objectives. In this process, planners use the skills of many disciplines including statistics, geography, economics, sociology, architecture and law. However, the law is only an instrument of urban planning; it is not a panacea; it is not a magic wand that can be waved to the accompaniment of mystic incantations to solve all urban problems or to meet all social needs. The ability of the legal system to implement the planning process is frequently limited by philosophical, historical and constitutional constraints.

A. PHILOSOPHICAL LIMITATIONS

Jurisprudence, the philosophy of law, is concerned with societal values and relationships that frequently limit the effectiveness of the law as an instrument of urban planning. For example, the relationship between certainty of the law and freedom of the individual raises the issue whether the laws of society enhance human freedom, or whether they overly restrict it. When law is definite and certain, freedom may be enhanced within the precise boundaries created by the law. Thus when the law is clear and certain, innovative planners may create new programs that utilize the full range of opportunities created by the law. On the other hand, the law may be very clear and certain, but nevertheless be so restrictive that freedom is limited or extinguished.

The goal of certainty in the law through consistency is embodied in the judicial principle of **stare decisis.** This doctrine of Anglo-American law imposes an obligation on courts to be guided by prior judicial decisions or precedents, and when deciding similar matters, to follow the previously established rule unless the case at bar is distinguishable because of the facts or because of changed social, political or economic conditions. The difficult question that arises is: At what point in time have social, political or economic conditions changed sufficiently to justify the modification or rejection of a previously established rule of law? This raises another issue of jurisprudence: namely, is justice enhanced by more flexibility or by more certainty in judicial determinations? Most lawyers and planners will have occasions to be on both sides of this issue at different times during their professional careers.

1

It should be clear that there are no "correct" answers to these and similar philosophical legal questions. In fact it frequently is not even possible to establish the "truth" of the premises on which decisions must be made. Lawyers and planners tend to become skeptics who become trained to evaluate both the quality and the quantity of data, facts and evidence. Lawyers usually think in terms of the "burden of proof," such as "beyond a reasonable doubt" for criminal matters and a "preponderence of evidence" for civil matters. Planners usually think in terms of accumulating and presenting data of sufficient quality and quantity to permit a prudent and reasonable person to make a decision.

In the excerpts set forth below, some well known legal scholars express their concern with some of these issues.

1. Certainty in the Law and Freedom

The end of the law is not to abolish or to restrain, but to preserve and enlarge freedom: for in all the states of created beings capable of law, where there is no law, there is no freedom.

John Locke, *Second Treatise of Government*, sec. 57

But, every man, when he enters into society, gives up a part of his natural liberty, as the price of so valuable a purchase; and, in consideration of receiving the advantages of mutual commerce, obliges himself to conform to those laws, which the community has thought proper to establish . . . . For no man, that considers a moment would wish to retain the absolute and uncontrolled power of doing whatever he pleases; the consequences of which is, that every other man would also have the same power; and there would be no security to individuals in any of the enjoyments of life.

Blackstone, *Commentaries*, Vol. III, 125

It is frequently remarked with great propriety, that a voluminous code of laws is one of the inconveniences necessarily connected with the advantages of a free government.

Alexander Hamilton, *The Federalist No 78* (1788)

For if there is any virtue in the Common Law whereby she stands for more than intellectual excellence in a special kind of learning, it is that Freedom is her sister, and in the spirit of freedom her greatest work has ever been done. By that spirit our lady has emboldened her servants to speak the truth before kings, to restrain the tyranny of usurping license, and to carry her ideal of equal justice and ordered right into every quarter of the world.

Sir Frederick Pollock, *The Genius of the Common Law* 124 (1912)

Absolute discretion is a ruthless master. It is more destructive of freedom than any of man's other inventions.

Douglas, J., *United States v. Wunderlich*, 342 U.S. 98, 101 (1951)

---

2. Certainty in the Law and Justice

I should be sorry that any opinion of mine should shake the authority of an established precedent; since it is better for the subject that even faulty precedents should not be shaken than that the law should be uncertain.

King v. Thompson, 2 T.R. 18,24 (1787)

It is better the law should be certain, than that every judge should speculate upon improvements in it.

Sheddon v. Goodrich, 8 Ves. 481, 497 (1803)

Precedents and rules must be followed unless flatly absurd or unjust.

Blackstone, *Commentaries* Vol. I, 70

The discretion of a Judge is the law of tyrants; it is always unknown. It is different in different men. It is casual, and depends upon constitution, temper, passion. In the best it is oftentimes caprice; in the worst it is every vice, folly and passion, to which human nature is liable.

Hindson v. Kersey, 8 How. St. Tr. 57 (1765)

Our common-law system consists in the applying to new combinations of circumstances those rules of law which we derive from legal principles and judicial precedents; and for the sake of attaining uniformity, consistency and certainty, we must apply those rules, where they are not plainly unreasonable and inconvenient, to all cases which arise; and we are not at liberty to reject them, and to abandon all analogy to them in those to which they have not yet been judicially applied, because we think that the rules are not as convenient and reasonable as we ourselves could have devised.

Mirehouse v. Rennell, 1 Cl & F. 527, 546 (1833)

I will look, your honor, and endeavor to find a precedent, if you require it; though it would seem to be a pity that the Court should lose the honor of being the first to establish so just a rule.

Rufus Choate, 1 Brown, *Works of Choate* 292 (1862)

It is revolting to have no better reason for a rule of law than that so it was laid down in the time of Henry IV. It is still more revolting if the grounds upon which it was laid down have vanished long since, and the rule simply persists from blind imitation of the past.

Oliver Wendell Holmes, "Path of the Law", *10 Harv. L. Rev. 457, 469 (1897)*

Precedents drawn from the days of travel by stage coach do not fit the conditions of travel today. The principle that the danger must be imminent does not change, but the things subject to the principle do change. They are whatever the needs of life in a developing civilization require them to be.

J. Cardozo, *MacPherson v. Buick Motor Co.*, 217 N.Y. 382, 391 (1916)

NEIDERMAN

v.

BRODSKY

436 Pa. 401, 261 A.2d 84 (1970)

The majority of the Pennsylvania Supreme Court changed a well established rule of negligence law that there can be no recovery for damages for negligence unless there is physical impact. In the following excerpt from the dissent Chief Justice Bell expressed his reasons why the established rule should not be changed:

* * *

Should we say to Stare Decisis, Quo Vadis? Or is Stare Decisis like Antaeus, who was lifted from but returned to the earth, or like Mohammed's coffin, which is suspended between Heaven and earth, with no one knowing when or which way it will fall? Or is it like Nineveh and Tyre, which were destroyed, but every now and then are restored to temporary glory? Today, no one knows from week to week or from Court session to Court session what the law is today or yesterday (retroactive decisions) or what it will be tomorrow. How can anyone know today what the law will be tomorrow, or what any-one's rights, privileges, powers, duties, responsibilities, limitations and liabilities are, or will be?

The basic principle of Stare Decisis which is the bedrock for all our Law is not as immutable as the law of the Medes and the Persians. It may be changed by the Legislature and, under some circumstances, it may be changed by the Courts. I would hold that the principle of Stare Decisis should always be applied, *irrespective of the changing personnel of this (or any Supreme) Court, except (1)* where the Supreme Court of Pennsylvania is convinced that prior decisions of the Court are irreconcilable: or (2) the application of a rule or principle has *undoubtedly* created great confusion: or (3) a rule of law has been only fluctuatingly applied: or (4) to correct a misconception in an occasional decision; or (5) in those rare cases where the Supreme Court is *convinced that the reason for the law undoubtedly no longer exists, and modern circumstances and Justice combine to require or justify a change, and no one's present personal rights or vested property interests will be injured by the change.* Change of circumstances or modern circumstances does not mean, nor has it ever heretofore been considered as the equivalent of change of personnel in the Court, or the substitution of the social or political philosophy of a Judge for the language of the Constitution or of a written instrument, or for well-settled principles of law.

Mr. Justice OWEN J. ROBERTS, Pennsylvania's most illustrious member of the Supeme Court of the United States, in a dissenting Opinion in Smith v. Allwright, thus aptly and strikingly expressed his views concerning the erosion or abolition of the principle of Stare Decisis: "The reason for my concern is that the instant decision, overruling that announced *about nine years ago,* tends to bring adjudications of this tribunal into the same class *as a restricted railroad ticket, good for this day and train only.* I have no assurance, in view of current decisions, that the opinion announced today may not shortly be repudiated and overruled by justices who deem they have a new light on the subject."

Mr. Justice FRANKFURTER, in his concurring Opinion in Green v. United States said: "To say that everybody on the Court has been wrong for 150 years and that that which has been deemed part of the bone and sinew of the law should now be extirpated is quite another thing. * * * The admonition of Mr. Justice Brandeis that we are not a third branch of the Legislature should never be disregarded."

Mr. Justice DOUGLAS, who is generally regarded as the leading opponent of Stare Decisis, in an article written for the Columbia Law Review of June 1949, Vol. 49, p. 735, said: "Uniformity and continuity in law are necessary to many activities. If they are not present, the integrity of contracts, wills, conveyances and securities is impaired. And there will be no equal justice under law if a negligence rule is applied in the morning but not in the afternoon. Stare Decisis provides some moorings so that men may trade and arrange their affairs with confidence. Stare Decisis serves to take the capricious element out of law and to give stability to a society. It is a strong tie which the future has to the past."

Mr. Justice EAGEN well expressed the same concern for Stare Decisis in the recent case of Commonwealth v. Woodhouse, (1960): "Unquestionably, in a republican form of government as we are privileged to enjoy, order, certainty and stability in the law are essential for the safety and protection of all. Stare Decisis should not be trifled with. *If the law knows no fixed principles, chaos and confusion will certainly follow.* * * * If it is clear that the reason for a law no longer exists and modern circumstances and justice require a change, and no vested rights will be violated, a change should be made."

What Chief Justice BLACK said for this Court in McDowell v. Oyer, (1853), concerning Stare Decisis, is presently most apposite, viz., "It is sometimes said that this adherence to precedent is slavish; that it fetters the mind of the judge, and compels him to decide without reference to principle. But let it be remembered that *stare decisis* is itself a principle of great magnitude and importance. It is absolutely necessary to the formation and permanence of any system of jurisprudence. Without it we may fairly be said to have no law; for law is a fixed and *established rule,* not depending in the slightest degree on the caprice of those who may happen to administer it."

Moreover, I may add that which is often forgotten by the Majority-it is one of the most important duties of an appellate Court to erect legal signposts with language inscribed thereon clearly, definitely, wisely and well that they who read may easily understand. This the Majority have likewise failed to do, in this case.

For the above reasons, I very strongly dissent.

B. HISTORICAL LIMITATIONS

The law has evolved slowly over the centuries in response to changing socio-economic circumstances. The law has grown incrementally with the result that historical concepts have been built into, and are still a part of our present legal system. For example, modern property law contains many concepts such as "landlord and tenant", **"title"** and **"real estate"** that are derived from the feudal system. The obligations of feudal lords, know as the **"incidents of feudal tenure"**, that arose by virtue of their "title" have evolved into the body of what we now know as property law, or real estate law. Two illustrations of feudal obligations of noble landlords that have evolved into significant modern concepts are **"taillage"** and **"relief"**. Taillage was the obligation of a landlord to give the king (or state) a cut of his substance. This obligation of a landlord to make an annual contribution of a part of his estate is the ancestor of both the property tax and the income tax. Relief was the obligation of an heir to make a contribution to the king as a precondition of his right to inherit his father's property. This feudal obligation is the historical source of inheritance taxes.

Another illustration of the effect of historical events upon the development of property law was the creation of **"equitable remedies"** during the feudal period. Historically, law courts had very limited authority to provide remedies for injustices arising out of transactions involving land. Because of the inadequacies of these remedies the noble landlords appealed to the conscience of the king to provide justice or **"equity"**. These applications were made with such frequency that the king appointed a special Chancellor who held court and created new "equitable remedies". Among these remedies, still used today, are **specific performance** of land contracts, **recision** of fraudulent contracts and the right of a debtor to **redeem** his mortgaged property when the mortgage debt is paid.

Knowledge of the historical development of the law is useful to planners because many concepts of land use regulation were shaped by historical events. This information can help planners determine if the historically created legal principles are still appropriate to modern conditions. If those principles are no longer appropriate, the planner may decide to argue for a change. In addition, historical knowledge can help the planner to understand the origin and nature of the powers of taxation, eminent domain and the police power, on which most programs of planning implementation are based.

Law in particular becomes then only a rational study when it is traced historically, from its first rudiments among savages, through successive changes, to its highest improvements in a civilized society.

Lord Kames, *Historical Law Tracts:Preface*

The law is what it is today because of what the law was yesterday; it cannot escape its ancestry, and it, too, must progress against the background of its history.

Alison Reppy, *"Common-Law Pleading," 2 N.Y.Law Forum* 1, 5 (1956)

_____

History, in illuminating the past, illuminates the present, and in illuminating the present, illuminates the future.

Benjamin Cardozo, *Nature of the Judicial Process* 53 (1921)

_____

The law is always approaching, and never reaching, consistency. It is forever adopting new principles from life at one end, and it always retains old ones from history at the other, which have not yet been absorbed or sloughed off. It will become entirely consistent only when it ceases to grow.

Oliver Wendell Homes, *Common Law* 36 (1881)

_____

One day through the primeval wood
A calf walked home, as good calves should;
But left a trail all bent askew,
A crooked trail, as all calves do. . .
And men two centuries and a half
Trod in the footsteps of that calf. . .
A hundred thousand men were led
By one calf near three centuries dead.
They followed still his crooked way,
And lost one hundred years a day;
For thus such reverence is lent
To well-established precedent.

Sam Walter Foss, *The Calf-Path*

_____

C. CONSTITUTIONAL LIMITATIONS

The United States Constitution embodies the fundamental values and principles that are the foundations of our legal system. Planners seeking to implement programs must be aware of the constitutional principles that limit, and others which promote their proposals. Thus, planners must have a basic understanding of the Constitution to anticipate challenges to their planning programs and to prepare possible defenses and alternatives. Without a knowledge of the constitutional limitations of the law as an instrument of the planning process, a planner might have a program declared unconstitutional because of a problem that could have been anticipated and resolved before any judicial challenge.

1. Federalism

Federalism is the division of power between the federal and state governments; it imposes many constraints on the use of the law to implement planning programs. The concept of federalism was used by the Founding Fathers to avoid a centralization of governmental power and to unify a group of thirteen autonomous sovereignties to achieve common objectives. The Constitution established the federal government as one of **limited and expressly enumerated powers.** Article I, Section 8 of the Constitution enumerates these powers, including the power of taxation and spending, the postal power, the power to regulate interstate commerce and others. The Tenth Amendement to the Constitution provides that any power not granted to the Federal Government and not prohibited to the states, will be held by the states. Thus, without using the word "federalism" in the document, the drafters established a federal system by implication. This system limits the jurisdiction of each state to the persons and property within its territorial boundaries. Consequently, large metropolitan areas like New York, have many enforcement and administrative difficulties arising from the fact that many urban problems such as transportation, air and water pollution extend beyond its jurisdictional boundaries.

The Founding Fathers could never have envisioned the jurisdictional handicaps of the New York metropolitan area, nor could they have foreseen the vast changes in the concept of federalism. For example, the Constitution does not grant the police power to the federal government. Nevertheless, the power to regulate interstate commerce has been so broadly interpreted that the federal government currently regulates the sale of land within state boundaries, as long as some minor instrumentality of interstate commerce, such as the telephone or the mails, is employed in the sale.

Federalism is very important to planners for a number of reasons: firstly because the states, rather than the federal government, have the **general police power.** Thus, the states and their local governments (through the state enabling legislation) have the power to adopt zoning legislation and other land use regulations. In addition, the states and local agencies administer public housing, urban renewal, community development programs and other programs with which planners are concerned. Secondly, the federal system assists in the process of municipal financing of capital improvements because the interest from municipal bonds is exempt from federal income taxes. This is the result of early tax cases that held that to protect the federal system, the federal government may not tax the instrumentalities of the state government (*Collector v. Day,* 11 Wall (U.S.) 113 (1871)) and the state government may not tax the instrumentalities of the federal government (*McCulloch v. Maryland,* 17 U.S. 316, 4 Wheat 316 (1819)).

> ## UNITED STATES
>
> v.
>
> ## CERTAIN LANDS IN CITY OF LOUISVILLE
>
> 78 F.2d 684 (6th Cir., 1935)

MOORMAN, Circuit Judge.

This is an appeal from a judgment of the District Court for the Western District of Kentucky dismissing the petition in a suit filed by the United States to condemn four city blocks within the city of Louisville for the construction of a low-cost housing and slum-clearance project under the provisions of title 2 of the National Industrial Recovery Act (48 Stat. 195). The petition alleged that the action was brought at the request of the Federal Emergency Administrator of Public Works, who, pursuant to and acting under authority vested in him by the National Industrial Recovery Act, had prepared a program of public works which included the construction of a low-cost housing and slum-clearance project in the city of Louisville, known as the Louisville housing project; that by virtue of the authority vested in him by the act the Administrator had found it necessary and advantageous to acquire an estate in fee simple in the lands described in the petition for the purpose of constructing a low-cost housing and slum-clearance project thereon; that acting through the Administrator pursuant to the provisions of the act the United States proposed to construct, erect, and build such a project on the lands; and that they were needed for a public use and purpose. Subsequent to the filing of the action, the government filed a written motion for the appointment of commissioners to assess the damage to the owners of the property sought to be condemned, but before commissioners were appointed one of the owners, Gernert, filed a demurrer to the petition. The trial court sustained the demurrer, and upon the failure of the government to plead further, dismissed the petition on the ground that it was not within the power of the government to condemn the property for the purposes for which it was designed. (D.C.) 9 F. Supp. 137.

Section 201 (a) of title 2 of the National Industrial Recovery Act (40 USCA § 401) (a) authorizes the President to create a Federal Emergency Administration of Public Works and to appoint a Federal Emergency Administrator. Section 202 (40 USCA § 402) authorizes the Administrator to prepare a comprehensive program of public works to include, among other things, "construction, reconstruction, alteration, or repair under public regulation or control of low-cost housing and slum-clearance projects." Section 203 (a) 40 USCA § 403 (a), quoted in the margin, authorizes the President, through the Administrator or through such other agencies as he may designate, to acquire, by the exercise of the power of eminent domain, any real of personal property in connection with the construction of any low-cost housing or slum-clearance project, and to sell any property so acquired, or to lease such property, with or without the privilege of purchase. Section 220 (40 USCA § 411) authorizes an appropriation of $3,300,000,000 to carry out the purpose of the act. By the Fourth Deficiency Act passed the same day (48 Stat. 274), Congress made the appropriation to carry into effect the provisions of the act.

* * *

We place our decision upon the second objection to the proceeding, viz., the lack of right in the government to exercise the power of eminent domain for the purposes contemplated by the act.

The government of the United States is one of delegated powers. There is no constitutional provision expressly authorizing it to exercise the power of eminent domain. It is nevertheless well settled that this power belongs to the government as an attribute of its sovereignty, see Kohl v. United States, Shoemaker v. United States. Equally well settled is it that the right can only be exercised where the property is to be taken for a public use. The contention of the government is that the property here sought to be condemned is to be devoted to a public use because, first, the construction of the project will relieve unemployment during the period of construction, and secondly, the leasing or selling of the new buildings at reasonable prices will give to persons of low incomes an opportunity to improve their living conditions. We do not think the first of these purposes, if made effective, could be said to constitute the use to which the property is to be put. While the act purports to authorize the construction with the view of relieving unemployment, it provides that the property when taken and after the project is constructed is to be leased or sold. The assertion that the taking of property to relieve unemployment and to improve living conditions among low-salaried workers is a taking for a public use rests upon the view that any taking which will advance the interest or well-being of a selected group of citizens will result in a benefit or advantage to larger groups or the entire community and must be regarded as a taking for a public use. * * *

Decisions dealing with condemnation proceedings are to be considered in the light of the powers possessed by the sovereign seeking to exercise the right. What is a public use under one sovereign may not be a public use under another. Clark v. Nash, supra. The state and federal governments are distinct sovereignties, each independent of the other and each restricted to its own sphere. Kohl v. United States, supra. Neither can invade or usurp the rightful powers or authority of the other. Hammer v. Dagenhart. In the exercise of its police power a state may do those things which benefit the health, morals, and welfare of its people. The federal government has no such power within the states. Green v. Frazier, supra, and Jones v. City of Portland, dealt with State legislation enacted pursuant to this power. In the latter case the court pointed out that it was not its function, under authority of the Fourteenth Amendment, "to supervise the legislation of the states in the exercise of the police power beyond protecting against exertions of such authority in the enactment and enforcement of laws of an arbitrary character." Thus in these and other cases involving state action the court dealt with the subject of public use as it pertained to the powers of the sovereign claiming the right to take. It must be similarly dealt with in the case at bar. As so considered with reference to the federal government, it does not, in our opinion, include the relief of unemployment as an end in itself or the construction of sanitary houses to sell or lease to low-salaried workers or residents of slum districts. The tearing down of the old buildings and the construction of new ones on the land here sought to be taken would create, it is true, a new resource for the employment of labor and capital. It is likewise true that the erection of new sanitary dwellings upon the property and the leasing or the selling of them at low prices would enable many residents of the community to improve their living conditions. It may be, too, that these group benefits, so far as they might affect the general public, would be beneficial. If, however, such a result thus attained is to be considered a public use for which the government may condemn private property, there would seem to be no reason why it could not condemn any private property which it could employ to an advantage to the public. There are perhaps many properties that the government could use for the benefit of selected groups. It might be, indeed, that by acquiring large sections of the farming parts of the country and leasing the land or selling it at low prices it could advance the interest of many citizens of the country, or that it could take over factories and other businesses and operate them upon plans more beneficial to the employees or the public, or even operate or sell them at a profit to the government to the relief of the taxpayers. The public interest that would thus be served, however, cannot, we think, be held to be a public use for which the government, in the exercise of its governmental functions, can take private property. The taking of one citizen's property for the purpose of improving it and selling or leasing it to another, or for the purpose of reducing unemployment, is not, in our opinion, within the scope of the powers of the federal government.

The judgment is affirmed.*

2. Separation of Powers

The concept of the **separation of powers** refers to the allocation of powers within the federal and state governments into legislative, executive and judicial branches. In framing this concept within the Constitution, the Founding Fathers made various assumptions. They assumed that power could be distributed to separate law-making, law-enforcing and law-adjudicating bodies. They presupposed that personnel should not work for more than one branch at the same point in time. They also assumed that once power is delegated to a branch, that branch should not re-delegate the power to another branch. The legislative branch does, of course, re-delegate some powers to the executive departments, but only after establishing sufficient standards that must be followed by the departments in establishing their regulations. A final and key as-

---

* But see Cleveland v. U.S. 329 (1945).

sumption upon which the doctrine of separation of powers is based is that the separation can prevent dictatorships through a system of checks and balances imposed upon each branch.

The **checks and balances** within the legislative branch include: the power of impeachment, the power of appropriation of funds, the power to affirm or deny the nomination of certain executive and judicial officers, the power to propose constitutional amendments, the power to override vetoes, and others. The executive branch holds various checks and balances including: the veto power, the power to nominate judges, the power of commander-in-chief, the ability to impound funds, and other powers. The judiciary's checks and balances include: the power to interpret and determine the constitutionality of legislative enactments, and the powers of **mandamus, injunction** and **certiorari. Mandamus** is the power of the court to order a government official to do an affirmative act; it is limited to mandatory or ministerial acts as opposed to discretionary ones. **Injunction** is the power of the court to order someone to stop what he or she is doing. Under certain circumstances mandamus and injunctions may be available against private citizens as extraordinary equitable remedies. **Certiorari,** which literally means "bring the papers forward," is a power of the courts to order a governmental official to come forward with documents to determine whether his actions were unreasonable, arbitrary, or capricious. The general rule holds that the official's act should be upheld by the court as long as there is any reasonable basis for the action.

The doctrine of separation of powers places many constraints on the planning process. For example many planning programs are held invalid or have their objectives emasculated by courts. Therefore, planners should be able to anticipate and attempt to avoid such occurrences. With a knowledge of the elements of the doctrine and the limits they impose on the planning process, planners can more effectively predict the likelihood of success of their programs and devise alternative methods of implementation. Lastly, planners should also realize that, as a consequence of the federal system, the federal government cannot control the organization of local governments and, consequently, there is no *direct* centralized federal planning of local governmental programs.

All legislative powers herein granted shall be vested in a Congress of the United States.
U.S.CONST., Art.I, sec. 1

The executive power shall be vested in a President of the United States of America.
U.S.CONST., Art.II, sec. 1

The judicial power shall be vested in one supreme Court, and in such inferior Courts as the Congress may from time to time ordain and establish.
U.S.CONST., Art.III, sec. 1

. . . and no Person holding any Office under the United States shall be a Member of either House during his Continuance in Office.
U.S.CONST., Art.I, sec. 6

THIBODEAUX

v.

COMEAUX

243 La. 468, 145 So.2d 1 (1962)

'. . . . It is a position of the defendants that the court does not have the authority to review all of the various facts affecting the feasibility of the proposed recreational project. This is true, it is asserted, unless the court rules that it has the power to substitute its discretion and judgment for that of the legislature, which passed the required resolution for amending the Constitution of the State of Louisiana authorizing recreational districts, and vesting them with the authority to hold elections and issue bonds; or, unless the court would substitute its discretion for that of both the electorate, which voted in favor of the constitutional amendment, and the Louisiana Legislature which has enacted LSA-R.S. 33:4562 et seq. (as amended) authorizing the creation of recreational districts, and conferring authority on those districts to incur debt and issue bonds under certain limitations which have not been exceeded here. Needless to say, we are cognizant of the doctrine which accords governmental subdivisions discretion in determining how to spend the money of which they have the administration. We recognize that such a prerogative should not be infringed upon by the courts; and, for the judiciary to meddle in such matters, save for the purpose of preventing injustice, fraud, oppression, or gross abuse of power, would be for it to invade the domain of other departments of the government in violation of the express prohibitions of the constitution for separation of powers. However, we are also aware that there is a point beyond which the legislative department, even when exercising the power of taxation, may not go and remain consistent with its obligation to recognize the citizen's right not to have his property taken without due process of law. The exaction from the owner of private property of the cost of the public improvement in substantial excess of the special benefits accruing to him is, to the extent of such excess, a taking, under the guise of taxation, of private property for the public use without compensation.

COMMONWEALTH, ex rel. CARROLL

v.

TATE

442 Pa. 45, 274 A.2d 193 (1971)

BELL, Chief Justice.

On June 16, 1970, President Judge Vincent A. Carroll, individually and on behalf of all of the Judges of the Court of Common Pleas of Philadelphia, instituted this suit by a Complaint in Mandamus to compel the Mayor and City Council of Philadelphia to appropriate the additional funds requested by them for the important and necessary administration of the Court of Common Pleas of Philadelphia for the fiscal year commencing July 1, 1970 and ending July 1, 1971.

We shall herinafter set forth the intricate facts involved in this suit, but, initially, we deem it important to focus on the fundamental questions involved: (1) whether the Judicial Branch of our Government has the inherent power to *determine* what funds are *reasonably necessary* for its efficient and effective operation; and (2) if the Judiciary has the power to determine what funds are reasonably necessary, does it then have the power to *compel* the Executive the Legislative Branches to provide such funds after the requested amount has been reduced in, or wholly or partially eliminated from, the budget proposed by the Executive Branch and approved by the Legislative Branch. * * *

Court's Inherent Power

It is a basic precept of our Constitutional form of Republican Government that the Judiciary is an independent and co-equal Branch of Government, along with the Executive and Legislative Branches. The line of separation or demarcation between the Executive, the Legislative and the Judicial, and their respective jurisdiction and powers, has never been definitely and specifically defined, and perhaps no clear line of distinction can ever be drawn. However, we must, of necessity, from time to time examine and define some of the respective powers within these undefined boundaries.

Because of the basic functions and inherent powers of the three co-equal Branches of Government, the co-equal independent Judiciary must possess rights and powers co-equal with its functions and duties, including the right and power to protect itself against any impairment thereof.

Expressed in other words, the Judiciary *must possess* the inherent power to determine and compel payment of those sums of money which are reasonable and necessary to carry out its mandated responsibilities, and its powers and duties to administer Justice, if it is to be reality a co-equal, independent Branch of our Government. This principle has long been recognized, not only in this Commonwealth but also throughout our

Nation. The very genius of our tripartite Government is based upon the proper exercise of their respective powers together with harmonious cooperation between the three independent Branches. However, if this cooperation breaks down, the Judiciary must exercise its inherent power to preserve the efficient and expeditious administration of Justice and protect it from being impaired or destroyed.

* * * The Court does not have *unlimited* power to obtain from the City whatever sums it would like or believes it needs for its proper functioning or adequate administration. Its wants and needs must be proved by it to be "reasonably necessary" for its proper functioning and administration, and this is always subject to Court review.

Mr. Chief Justice Marshall said in McCulloch v. Maryland, "* * * the power to tax involves the power to destroy; * * *" A Legislature has the power of life and death over all the Courts and over the entire Judicial system. Unless the Legislature can be compelled by the Courts to provide the money which is reasonably necessary for the proper functioning and administration of the Courts, our entire Judicial system could be extirpated, and the Legislature could make a mockery of our form of Government with its three co-equal branches—the Executive, the Legislative and the Judicial.

We have carefully considered all of the defendants' contentions, as well as all of the Court's contentions, but deem further discussion therof unnecessary.

We agree with Judge Montgomery's conclusion that "the amount recommended by Mayor Tate and approved by Council is inadequate to meet the reasonable needs of the Court [of Common Pleas] for the present fiscal year." We also agree with his Order of September 30, 1970, allowing the Court $2,458,000. This represents his allowance and specific allocation of certain of the amounts requested by the Court and his disallowance of certain items which the Court had requested. Judge Montgomery's award was based upon nine months remaining in the City's fiscal year, July 1, 1970 to July 1, 1971. We accordingly reduce the award to reflect the amount of time remaining in this fiscal year (five months from February 1, 1971) and award the Court of Common Pleas the sum of $1,365,555.

Judgment, as modified, is affirmed.

---

3. Impairment of the Obligation of Contracts

The Federal Constitution provides:. . . "No state shall. . .pass any. . .law impairing the Obligation of Contracts." U.S. Constitution, Article I, Sec. 10. This statement was included in the Constitution because the framers, who were predominantly landed aristocrats and merchants, feared that state governments might attempt to limit the proprietary rights arising out of their contracts. The term "contract" for this purpose may be defined as a legally enforceable agreement to do, or to refrain from doing, a specific thing. The phrase **"obligation of contract"** refers to the law or duty that binds parties to perform their agreements.

The following hypothetical situation may help to illustrate how the obligation of a contract could be impaired. Suppose that B agrees to sell specified goods to A and deliver them in six months. In consideration, A promises to pay to B $2,000, the market price at the time of the agreement. In six months, however, the market price drops to $1,800 and A refuses to take and pay for the goods. A court would require A to pay B $200 in damages, the difference between the agreed price and the price at which B can sell the goods on the market. (Usually a court would not compel A to take the goods and pay the $2,000. Such a remedy is called **"specific performance"** and is available only when the contract concerns a sale of land or a sale of something that may be shown to be "unique.") If a state law were enacted providing that... "no action may be brought to recover monies due and owing for the breach of a contract for the sale of goods...", then B would lose his contractual right under the obligation of contracts to recover the $200. This law would impair the obligation of his contract and would be held unconstitutional.

However, not all laws that impair contract obligations violate the Constitution. For example, statutes that regulate prostitution prevent the enforcement of agreements regarding the sale of sexual services. These laws do not violate the Constitution because such agreements are not enforceable because they are unlawful. The **Statute of Frauds** and the **Statute of Limitations** both impair the obligation of contracts. The Statute of Frauds bars the enforcement of certain classes of contracts, such as land sale contracts, unless they are in writing. The Statute of Limitations requires that law suits such as actions to recover on a contract be brought within a specified period (e.g., six years after the breach occurs). These and other statutes impair the obligation of contracts but are valid because they are considered reasonable impairments of private contractual rights imposed to promote the general welfare. In conclusion, planners should realize that the "obligation of contracts" clause can be an important limitation on planning programs, and that the test of the validity of the impairment will be one of reasonableness and balancing of private rights against public needs.

UNITED STATES TRUST CO.

OF NEW YORK

v.

NEW JERSEY

97 S.Ct. 1505, 52 L.Ed. 2d 92 (1977)

Mr. JUSTICE BLACKMUN delivered the opinion of the Court.

This case presents a challenge to a New Jersey statute, Laws 1974, c. 25, as violative of the Contract Clause of the United States Constitution. That statute, together with a concurrent and parallel New York statute, Laws 1974, c. 993, repealed a statutory covenant made by the two states in 1962 that had limited the ability of The Port Authority of New York and New Jersey to subsidize rail passenger transportation from revenues and reserves.

The suit, one for declaratory relief, was instituted by appellant United States Trust Company of New York in the Superior Court of New Jersey, Law Division, Bergen County. Named as defendants were the State of New Jersey, its Governor, and its Attorney General. Plaintiff-appellant sued as trustee for two series of Port Authority Consolidated Bonds, as a holder of Port Authority Consolidated Bonds, and on behalf of all holders of such bonds.

After a trial, the Superior Court ruled that the statutory repeal was a reasonable exercise of New Jersey's police power, and declared that it was not prohibited by the Contract Clause or by its counterpart in the New Jersey Constitution, Art. 4, § VII, ¶3. Accordingly, appellant's complaint was dismissed. The Supreme Court of New Jersey, on direct appeal and by *percuriam* opinion, affirmed "substantially for the reasons set forth in the [trial court's] opinion". We noted probable jurisdiction.

I

BACKGROUND

A. *Establishment of the Port Authority.* The Port Authority was established in 1921 by a bistate compact to effectuate "a better co-ordination of the terminal, transportation and other facilities of commerce in, about and through the port of New York." The compact, as the Constitution requires, received congressional consent.

The compact granted the Port Authority enumerated powers and, by its Art. III, "such other and additional powers as shall be conferred upon it by the Legislature of either State concurred in by the Legislature of the other, or by Act or Acts of Congress." The powers are enumerated in Art. VI. Among them is "full power and authority to purchase, construct, lease and/or operate any terminal or transportation facility within said district." "Transportation facility" is defined, in Art. XXII, to include "railroads, steam or electric. . . .for use for the transportation or carriage of persons or property."

The Port Authority was conceived as a financially independent entity, with funds primarily derived from private investors. The preamble to the compact speaks of the "encouragement of the investment of capital," and the Port Authority was given power to mortgage its facilities and to pledge its revenues to secure the payment of bonds issued to private investors.

See generally E. Bard, The Port of New York Authority (1942).

B. *Initial Policy Regarding Mass Transit.* Soon after the Port Authority's inception, the two States, again with the consent of Congress, agreed upon a comprehensive plan for the entity's development. This plan was concerned primarily, if not solely, with transportation of freight by carriers and not with the movement of passengers in the Port Authority district. The plan, however, was not implemented. The New Jersey Legislature at that time declared that the plan "does not include the problem of passenger traffic," even though that problem "should be considered in co-operation with the port development commission." The Port Authority itself recognized the existence of the passenger service problem.

In 1927 the New Jersey Legislature, in an act approved by the Governor, directed the Port Authority to make plans "supplementary to or amendatory of the comprehensive plan . . . as will provide adequate interstate and suburban transportation facilities for passengers." The New York Legislature followed suit in 1928, but its bill encountered executive veto. The trial court observed that this veto "to all intents and purposes ended any legislative effort to involve the Port Authority in an active role in commuter transit for the next 30 years."

C. *Port Authority Fiscal Policy.* Four bridges for motor vehicles were constructed by the Port Authority. A separate series of revenue bonds was issued for each bridge. Revenue initially was below expectations, but the bridges ultimately accounted for much of the Port Authority's financial strength. The legislatures transferred the operation and revenues of the successful Holland Tunnel to the Port Authority, and this more than made up for the early bridge deficits.

The States in 1931 also enacted statutes creating the general reserve fund of the Port Authority. Surplus revenues from all Port Authority facilities were to be pooled in the fund to create an irrevocably pledged reserve equal to one-tenth of the par value of the Port Authority's outstanding bonds. This level was attained 15 years later, in 1946.

In 1952, the Port Authority abandoned the practice of ear-marking specific facility revenues as security for bonds of that facility. The Port Authority's Consolidated Bond Resolution established the present method of financing its activities; under this method its bonds are secured by a pledge of the general reserve funds.

D. *Renewed Interest in Mass Transit.* Meanwhile, the two States struggled with the passenger transportation problem. Many studies were made. The situation was recognized as critical, great costs were envisioned, and substantial deficits were predicted for any mass transit operation. The Port Authority itself financed a study conducted by the Metropolitan Rapid Transit Commission which the States had established in 1954.

In 1958, Assembly Bill No. 16 was introduced in the New Jersey Legislature. This would have had the Port Authority take over, improve, and operate interstate rail mass transit between New Jersey and New York. The bill was opposed vigorously by the Port Authority on legal and financial grounds. The Port Authority also retaliated, in a sense, by including a new safeguard in its contracts with bondholders. This prohibited the issuance of any bonds, secured by the general reserve fund, for a new facility unless the Port Authority first certified that the issuance of the bonds would not "materially impair the sound credit standing" of the Port Authority. App. 812. Bill No. 16 was not passed.

In 1959, the two States, with the consent of Congress, created the New York-New Jersey Transportation Agency to deal "with matters affecting public mass transit within and between the 2 States."

Also in 1959, the two States enacted legislation providing that upon either State's election the Port Authority would be authorized to purchase and own railroad passenger cars for the purpose of leasing them to commuter railroads. Bonds issued for this purpose would be guaranteed by the electing state. New York so elected, New York Const., Art. X § 7, effective January 1, 1962, and approximately $100 million of Commuter Car Bonds were issued by the Port Authority to purchase about 500 air-conditioned passenger cars and eight locomotives used on the Penn Central and Long Island Railroads.

E. *The 1962 Statutory Covenant.* In 1960 the takeover of the Hudson & Manhattan Railroad by the Port Authority was proposed. This was a privately owned interstate electric commuter system then linking Manhattan, Newark and Hoboken through the Hudson tubes. It had been in reorganization for many years, and in 1959 the Bankruptcy Court and the United States District Court had approved a plan that left it with cash sufficient to continue operations for two years but with no funds for capital expenditures. A special committee of the New Jersey Senate was formed to determine whether the Port Authority was "fulfilling its statutory duties and obligations," App. 605. The committee concluded that the solution to bondholder concern was "[l]imiting by a constitutionally protected statutory covenant with Port Authority bondholders the extent to which the Port Authority revenues and reserves pledged to such bondholders can in the future be applied to the deficits of possible future Port Authority passenger railroad facilities beyond the original Hudson & Manhattan Railroad system." And the trial court found that the 1962 New Jersey Legislature "concluded it was necessary to place a limitation on mass transit deficit operations to be undertaken by the Authority in the future so as to promote continued investor confidence in the Authority."

The statutory covenant of 1962 was the result. The covenant itself was part of the bistate legislation authorizing the Port Authority to acquire, construct and operate the Hudson & Manhattan Railroad and the World Trade Center. The statute in relevant part read:

"The 2 States covenant and agree with each other and with the holders of any affected bonds, as hereinafter defined, that so long as any of such bonds remain outstanding and unpaid and the holders thereof shall not have given their consent as provided in their contract with the port authority. (a) . . . and (b) neither the States nor the port authority nor any subsidiary corporation incorporated for any of the purposes of this act will apply any of the rentals, tolls, fares, fees, charges, revenues or reserves, which have been or shall be pledged in whole or in part as security for such bonds, for any railroad purposes whatsoever other than permitted purposes hereinafter set forth." * * *

F. *Prospective Repeal of the Covenant.* Governor Cahill of New Jersey and Governor Rockefeller of New York in April 1970 jointly sought increased Port Authority participation in mass transit. In November 1972 they agreed upon a plan for expansion of the PATH system. This included the initiation of direct rail service to Kennedy Airport and the construction of a line to Plainfield, N.J., by way of Newark Airport. The plan anticipated a Port Authority investment of something less than $300 million out of a projected total cost of $650 million, with the difference to be supplied by federal and state grants. It also proposed to make the covenant inapplicable with respect to bonds issued *after* the legislation went into effect. This program was enacted, effective May 10, 1973, and the 1962 covenant was thereby rendered inapplicable, or in effect repealed, with respect to bonds issued subsequent to the effective date of the new legislation.

G. *Retroactive Repeal of the Covenant.* It soon developed that the proposed PATH expansion would not take place as contemplated in the Governors' 1972 plan. New Jersey was unwilling to increase its financial commitment in response to a sharp increase in the projected cost of constructing the Plainfield extension. As a result the anticipated federal grant was not approved. App. 717.

New Jersey had previously prevented outright repeal of the 1962 covenant, but its attitude changed with the election of a new governor in 1973. In early 1974, when bills were pending in the two States' Legislatures to repeal the covenant retroactively, a national energy crisis was developing. On November 27, 1973, Congress had enacted the Emergency Petroleum Allocation Act. In that Act Congress found that the hardships caused by the oil shortage "jeopardize the normal flow of commerce and constitute a national energy crisis which is a threat to the public health, safety, and welfare." This time, proposals for retroactive repeal of the 1962 covenant were passed by the legislature and signed by the governor of each State.

On April 10, 1975, the Port Authority announced an increase in its basic bridge and tunnel tolls designed to raise an estimated $40 million annually. This went into effect May 5 and was, it was said, "[t]o increase [the Port Authority's] ability to finance vital mass transit improvements."
* * *

II

At the time the Constitution was adopted, and for nearly a century thereafter, the Contract Clause was one of the few express limitations on state power. The many decisions of this Court involving the Contract Clause are evidence of its important place in our constitutional jurisprudence. Over the last century, however, the Fourteenth Amendment has assumed a far larger place in constitutional adjudication concerning the States. We feel that the present role of the Contract Clause is largely illuminated by two of this Court's decisions. In each, legislation was sustained despite a claim that it had impaired the obligations of contracts.

Home Building & Loan Assn. v. Blaisdell, (1934), is regarded as the leading case in the modern era of Contract Clause interpretation. At issue was the Minnesota Mortgage Moratorium Law, enacted in 1933, during the depth of the Depression and when that state was under severe economic stress, and appeared to have no effective alternative. The statute was a temporary measure that allowed judicial extension of the time for redemption; a mortgagor who remained in possession during the extension period was required to pay a reasonable income or rental value to the mortgagee. A closely divided Court, in an opinion by Mr. Chief Justice Hughes, observed that "emergency may furnish the occasion for the exercise of power" and that the "constitutional question presented in the light of an emergency is whether the power possessed embraces the particular exercise of it in response to particular conditions." It noted that the debates in the Constitutional Convention were of little aid in the construction of the Contract Clause, but that the general purpose of the Clause was clear: to encourage trade and credit by promoting confidence in the stability of contractual obligations. Nevertheless, a State "continues to possess authority to safeguard the vital interests of its people. . . . This principle of harmonizing the constitutional prohibition with the necessary residuum of state power has had progressive recognition in the eecisions of this Court." The great clauses of the Constitution are to be considered in the light of our whole experience, and not merely as they would be interpreted by its Framers in the conditions and with the outlook of their time.

This Court's most recent Contract Clause decision is *El Paso v. Simmons.* (1965). That case concerned a 1941 Texas statute that limited to a five-year period the reinstatement rights of an interest-defaulting purchaser of land from the State. For many years prior to the enactment of that statute, such a defaulting purchaser, under Texas law, could have reinstated his claim to the land upon written request and payment of delinquent interest, unless rights of third parties had intervened. This Court held that "it is not every modification of a contractual promise that impairs the obligation of contract under federal law." It observed that the State "has the 'sovereign right . . .' to protect the . . . general welfare of the people' " and " 'we must respect the "wide discretion on the part of the legislature in determining what is and what is not necessary," ' " The Court recognized that "the power of a State to modify or affect the obligation of contract is not without limit," but held that "the objects of the Texas statute make abundantly clear that it impairs no protected right under the Contract Clause."

Both of these cases eschewed a rigid application of the Contract Clause to invalidate state legislation. Yet neither indicated that the Contract Clause was without meaning in modern constitutional jurisprudence, or that its limitation on state power was illusory. Whether or not the protection of contract rights comports with current views of wise public policy, the Contract Clause remains a part of our written Constitution. We therefore must attempt to apply that constitutional provision to the instant case with due respect for its purpose and the prior decisions of this Court.

III

We first examine appellant's general claim that repeal of the 1962 covenant impaired the obligation of the State's contract with the bondholders. It long has been established that the Contract Clause limits the power of the States to modify their own contracts as well as to regulate those between private parties. Yet the Contract Clause does not prohibit the States from repealing or amending statutes generally, or from enacting legislation with retroactive effects. Thus, as a preliminary matter, appellant's claim requires a determination that the repeal has the effect of impairing a contractual obligation. * * *

The trial court recognized that there was an impairment in this case: "To the extent that the repeal of the covenant authorizes the Authority to assume greater deficits for such purposes, it permits a diminution of the pledged revenues and reserves and may be said to constitute an impairment of the states' contract with the bondholders."

Having thus established that the repeal impaired a contractual obligation of the States, we turn to the question whether that impairment violated the Contract Clause.

IV

Although the Contract Clause appears literally to proscribe "any" impairment, this Court observed in *Blaisdell* that "the prohibition is not an absolute one and is not to be read with literal exactness like a mathematical formula." Thus, a finding that there has been a technical impairment is merely a preliminary step in resolving the more difficult question whether that impairment is permitted under the Constitution. In the instant case, as in *Blaisdell*, we must attempt to reconcile the strictures of the Contract Clause with the "essential attributes of sovereign power, necessarily reserved by the States to safeguard the welfare of their citizens". Id.,at 434-440. * * *

The Contract Clause is not an absolute bar to subsequent modification of a State's own financial obligations. As with laws impairing the obligations of private contracts, an impairment may be constitutional if it is reasonable and necessary to serve an important public purpose. In applying this standard, however, complete deference to a legislative assessment of reasonableness and necessity is not appropriate because the State's self-interest is at stake. A governmental entity can always find a use for extra money, especially when taxes do not have to be raised. If a State could reduce its financial obligations whenever it wanted to spend the money for what it regarded as an important public purpose, the Contract Clause would provide no protection at all. * * *

V

Mass transportation, energy conservation, and environmental protection are goals that are important and of legitimate public concern. Appellees contend that these goals are so important that any harm to bondholders from repeal of the 1962 covenant is greatly outweighed by the public benefit. We do not accept this invitation to engage in a utilitarian comparison of public benefit and private loss. Contrary to Mr. Justice Black's fear, expressed on sole dissent in *El Paso v. Simmons*, the Court has not "balanced away" the limitation on state action imposed by the Contract Clause. Thus a State cannot refuse to meet its legitimate financial obligations simply because it would prefer to spend the money to promote the public good rather than the private welfare of its creditors. We can only sustain the repeal of the 1962 covenant if that impairment was both reasonable and necessary to serve the admittedly important purposes claimed by the State.

The more specific justification offered for the repeal of the 1962 covenant was the States' plan for encouraging users of private automobiles to shift to public transportation. The States intended to discourage private automobile use by raising bridge and tunnel tolls and to use the extra revenue from those tolls to subsidize improved commuter railroad service. Appellees contend that repeal of the 1962 covenant was necessary to implement this plan because the new mass transit facilities could not possibly be self-supporting and the covenant's "permitted deficits" level had already been exceeded. We reject this justification because the repeal was neither necessary to achievement of the plan nor reasonable in light of the circumstances.

The determination of necessity can be considered on two levels. First, it cannot be said that total repeal of the covenant was essential; a less drastic modification would have permitted the contemplated plan without entirely removing the covenant's limitation on the use of Port Authority revenues and reserves to subsidize commuter railroads. Second, without modifying the covenant at all, the States could have adopted alternative means of achieving their twin goals of discouraging automobile use and improving mass transit. Appellees contend, however, that choosing among these alternatives is a matter for legislative discretion. But a State is not completely free to consider impairing the obligations of its own contracts on a par with other policy alternatives. Similarly, a State is not free to impose a drastic impairment when an evident and more moderate course would serve its purposes equally well. In *El Paso v. Simmons*, the imposition of a five-year statute of limitations on what was previously a perpetual right of redemption was regarded by this Court as "quite clearly necessary" to achieve the State's vital interest in the orderly administration of its school lands program. In the instant case the State has failed to demonstrate that repeal of the 1962 covenant was similarly necessary.

We also cannot conclude that repeal of the covenant was reasonable in light of the surrounding circumstances. In this regard a comparison with *El Paso v. Simmons*, again is instructive. There a nineteenth century statute had effects that were unforeseen and unintended by the legislature when originally adopted. As a result speculators were placed in a position to obtain windfall benefits. The Court held that adoption of a statute of limitation was a reasonable means to "restrict a party to those gains reasonably to be expected from the contract" when it was adopted.

By contrast, in the instant case the need for mass transportation in the New York metropolitan area was not a new development, and the likelihood that publicly owned commuter railroads would produce substantial deficits was well known. As early as 1922, over a half century ago, there were pressures to invole the Port Authority in mass transit. It was with full knowledge of these concerns that the 1962 covenant was adopted. Indeed, the covenant was specifically intended to protect the pledged revenues and reserves againt the possibility that such concerns would lead the Port Authority into greater involvement in deficit mass transit.

During the 12-year period between adoption of the covenant and its repeal, public perception of the importance of mass transit undoubtedly grew because of increased general concern with environmental protection and energy conservation. But these concerns were not unknown in 1962, and the subsequent changes were of degree and not of kind. We cannot say that these changes caused the covenant to have a substantially different impact in 1974 than when it was adopted in 1962. And we cannot conclude that the repeal was reasonable in the light of changed circumstances.

We therefore hold that the Contract Clause of the United States Constitution prohibits the retroactive repeal of the 1962 covenant. The judgment of the Supreme Court of New Jersey is reversed.

MR. JUSTICE BRENNAN, with whom MR. JUSTICE WHITE and MR. JUSTICE MARSHALL, join, dissenting.

Decisions of this Court for at least a century have construed the Contract Clause largely to be powerless in binding a State to contracts limiting the authority of successor legislatures to enact laws in furtherance of the health, safety, and similar collective interests of the polity. In short, those decisions established the principle that lawful exercises of a State's police powers stand paramount to private rights held under contract. Today's decision, in invalidating the New Jersey Legislature's 1974 repeal of its predecessor's 1962 covenant, rejects this previous understanding and remolds the Contract Clause into a potent instrument for overseeing important policy determinations of the state legislature. At the same time, by creating a constitutional safe haven for property rights embodied in a contract, the decision substantially distorts modern constitutional jurisprudence governing regulation of private economic interests. I might understand, though I could not accept, this revival of the Contract Clause were it in accordance with some coherent and constructive view of public policy. But elevation of the clause to the status of regulator of the municipal bond market at the heavy price of frustration of sound legislative policy-making is as demonstrably unwise as it is unnecessary. The justification for today's decision, therefore, remains a mystery to me, and I respectfully dissent. * * *

The Court today dusts off the Contract Clause and thereby undermines the bipartisan policies of two states that manifestly seek to further the legitimate needs of their citizens. The Court's analysis, I submit, fundamentally misconceives the nature of the Contract Clause guarantee.

One of the fundamental premises of our popular democracy is that each generation of representatives can and will remain responsive to the needs and desires of those whom they represent. Crucial to this end is the assurance that new legislators will not automatically be bound by the policies and undertakings of earlier days. In accordance with this philosophy, the Framers of our Constitution conceived of the Contract Clause primarily as protection for economic transactions entered into by purely private parties, rather than obligations involving the State itself. See Gunther, Constitutional Law 604 (1975); Schwartz, A Commentary On the Constitution of the United States, pt. 2, The Rights of Property 274 (1965); Wright, The Contract Clause and the Constitution 15-16

(1938). The Framers fully recognized that nothing would so jeopardize the legitimacy of a system of government that relies upon the ebbs and flows of politics to "clean out the rascals" than the possibility that those same rascals might perpetuate their policies simply by locking them into binding contracts. * * *

Given that this is the first case in come 40 years in which this Court has seen fit to invalidate purely economic and social legislation on the strength of the Contract Clause, one may only hope that it will prove a rare phenomenon, turning on the Court's particularized appraisal of the facts before it. But there also is reason for broader concern. It is worth remembering that there is nothing sacrosanct about a contract. All property rights, no less than a contract, are rooted in certain "expectations" about the sanctity of one's right of ownership. Compare *ante,* at 19 n. 17, with J. Bentham, Theory of Legislation chap. VIII (1911). And other constitutional doctrines are akin to the Contract Clause in directing their protections to the property interests of private parties. Hence the command of the Fifth Amendment that "private property [shall not] be taken for public use, without just compensation" also "remains a part of our written Constitution." And during the heyday of economic due process associated with *Lochner v. New York,* (1905), and similar cases long since discarded, this Court treated "the liberty of contract" under the Due Process Clause as virtually indistinguishable from the Contract Clause. Gunther *supra,* at 603-604; Hale, The Supreme Court and the Contract Clause, 57 Harv. L.Rev.852,890-891 (1944). In more recent times, however, the Court wisely has come to embrace a coherent, unified interpretation of such constitutional provisions, and has granted wide latitude to "a valid exercise of [the states'] police powers," even if it results in severe violations of property rights. If today's case signals return to substantive constitutional review of States' policies, and a new resolve to protect property owners whose interest or circumstances may happen to appeal to Members of this Court, then more than the citizens of New Jersey and New York will be the losers.

I would not want to be read as suggesting that the States should blithely proceed down the path of repudiating their obligations, financial or otherwise. Their credibility in the credit market obviously is highly dependent on exercising their vast lawmaking powers with self-restraint and discipline, and I, for one, have little doubt that few, if any, jurisdictions would choose to use their authority "so foolish[ly] as to kill a goose that lays golden eggs for them." But in the final analysis, there is no reason to doubt that appellant's financial welfare is being adequately policed by the political processes and the bond marketplace itself. The role to be played by the Constitution is at most a limited one. For this Court should have learned long ago that the Constitution—be it through the Contract or Due Process Clause—can actively intrude into such economic and policy matters only if my Brethren are prepared to bear enormous institutional and social costs. Because I consider the potential dangers of such judicial interference to be intolerable, I dissent.

In re DEPARTMENT OF BUILDINGS

14 N.Y. 2d 291, 251 N.Y.S. 441, 200 N.E.2d 432 (1964)

FULD, Judge.

Acting under the authority of the so-called 1962 Receivership Law (Multiple Dwelling Law, § 309, as amd. by L1962, ch. 492), the Department of Buildings of the City of New York, the respondent here-in, petitioned for and obtained an order from the Supreme Court designating the Commissioner of Real Estate as receiver of the rents, issues and profits of the premises located at 221 West 21st Street. The Appellate Division unanimously affirmed, and the appellants, the owner and mortgagee of the premises involved, appeal as of right, urging, primarily, that the statute is unconstitutional.

Section 309 of the Multiple Dwelling Law was amended in 1962, as the Legislature itself declared (L.1962, ch. 492, § 1), to afford "additional enforcement powers" (1) to compel the correction of conditions it found existed in deteriorated or deteriorating dwellings which "may cause irreparable damage * * * or endanger the life, health or safety of [their] occupants, or the occupants of adjacent properties or the general public" and (2) "to increase the supply of adequate, safe and standard dwelling units, the shortage of which constitutes a public emergency and is contrary to the public welfare."

To effectuate these objectives, the Legislature prescribed a detailed and fairly elaborate procedure. Whenever the Department of Buildings certifies to the existence of a "nuisance"—defined in paragraph a of subdivision 1—which "constitutes a serious fire hazard or is a serious threat to life, health or safety," the department may issue a written order to the owner directing removal of the nuisance within the time specified, ordinarily, not less than 21 days after service of the order (subd. 1, par.e). If the order is not complied with, the department may apply to the Supreme Court for the appointment of a receiver to remove or remedy the condition and for a lien in favor of the Department of Real Estate to secure repayment of the costs incurred by the receiver in so removing or remedying such conditions (subd. 5, par. c, cl. 1). If after notice to the owner and any mortgagee, the court determines that a nuisance does exist, it shall appoint the New York City Commissioner of Real Estate as receiver of the rents, issues and profits of the property. However, upon application of the owner or mortgagee, the court may permit such applicant (upon certain specified conditions) to perform the work, within the time fixed by the court, in lieu of appointing a receiver and, if the owner or mortgagee fails to complete such work within the time allowed, the receiver shall then be appointed (subd. 5, par. c, cl. 3).

The receiver, expressly vested with "all of the powers and duties of a receiver appointed in an action to foreclose a mortgage," is to proceed "with all reasonable speed" to remove the nuisance "constituting a serious fire hazard or a serious threat to life, health or safety" and apply the rents which he is to collect from the property to the cost of "removing or remedying such nuisance, to the payment of expenses reasonably necessary to the proper operation and management of the property * * * and to unpaid taxes, assessments" and other charges (subd. 5, par. d. cl. 1). If the income from the property proves insufficient, the Department of Real Estate shall advance to the receiver—"from a fund to be known as the multiple dwelling section three hundred nine operating fund" (subd., 9)—any sums necessary to cover such cost and shall have a lien against the property for the sums so advanced (subd. 5, par. d, cl. 1). This lien, the statute goes on to recite (subd. 4, par. a), "shall have priority over all other liens and encumbrances except taxes, assessments and mortgages recorded previously to the existence of such lien," except as otherwise provided in subdivision 5. And that subdivision in paragraph e, declares that the lien in favor of the department "shall be subject to any [previously recorded] mortgage or lien * * * and the rights of the holders of such mortgages or liens shall not in any way be impaired by the appointment of a receiver. * * * or by the existence of such lien; provided, however, that no such mortgagee or lienor who has been duly served with the notice (as prescribed elsewhere in subd. 5) * * * shall be entitled to any of the rents, issues and profits of the property, nor, in any action to foreclose his mortgage or lien, to a discharge of the receiver * * * until the lien of the receiver in favor of the department of real estate shall have been fully paid and satisfied" (subd. 5, par. c).

The statute further provides that a mortgagee or lienor who at his own expense removes the nuisance shall have a lien "equivalent" to the lien granted to the receiver and that a mortgagee or lienor who, following the appointment of a receiver, reimburses the receiver and the department for costs and charges incurred shall be entitled to an assignment of the lien granted to the receiver (subd. 5, par. g). The receiver shall be discharged—upon rendering "a full and complete accounting to the court"—when the nuisance has been removed, the cost of such removal paid from the rents and income of the dwelling and the surplus money, if any, paid over to the owner or mortgagee as the court may direct. In addition, the owner, mortgagee or any other lienor, upon the removal of the nuisance, may apply for the discharge of the receiver upon payment of all sums expended by the receiver which were not paid out of the rents and income of the dwelling. * * *

It is the appellants' position (1) that the statute is unconstitutional in that it impairs the rights of appellant mortgagee under his prior mortgage contract (U.S. Const. art. I, § 10); (2) that they were denied a proper hearing; and (3) that, in any event, the facts failed to warrant the appointment of a receiver.

The legislation before us was enacted to accomplish the two-fold purpose of eliminating intolerable and dangerous housing conditions in multiple dwellings, for the most part in slum areas, and of increasing the supply of safe and adequate housing accommodations. As already noted, in passing the amendatory act, the Legislature expressly found (1) that there existed, in the cities to which its provisions apply, deteriorated or deteriorating dwellings which contain conditions constituting a threat to life, health and safety and (2) that there was a shortage, constituting a public emergency, of habitable dwelling units.

Confronted with such conditions—and we know from the cases which have been before us over the years that these findings are not without basis—the Legislature was warranted in attempting, by an exercise of its police power, to take remedial steps to promote the public interest in the maintenance of an adequate supply of safe and sanitary housing accommodations. * * * If the legislation before us "is addressed to a legitimate end and the measures taken are reasonable and appropriate to that end", it may not be stricken as unconstitutional, even though it may interfere with rights established by existing contracts. It is "fundamental", we wrote in the Durham Realty Corp. case that "the state may establish regulations reasonably necessary to secure the general welfare of the community by the exercise of its police power, although the rights of private property are thereby curtailed and freedom of contract is abridged." Accordingly, when, as here, housing accommodations are in short supply and multiple dwellings become unfit for use and a source of danger, the State may enact legislation reasonably aimed at correcting the situation and promoting the public welfare, even though the means devised to accomplish that result may impair the obligation of the mortgagee's contract with his mortgagor.

To this extent, the private interests embodied in contracts, are made subservient to the interests, of the public for whose benefit the State exercises its "continuing and dominant protective power". In other words, "contracts are made subject to this exercise of the [protective] power of the State when otherwise justified. * * *

Whether this protective power of the State be treated as "an implied condition of every contract and, as such, as much part of the contract as though it were written into it" or as " 'an exercise of the sovereign right of the government to protect the * * * general welfare of the people * * * paramount to any rights under contracts between individuals' " it is " 'settled law' " that " 'the interdiction of statutes impairing the obligation of contracts does not prevent the state from exercising such powers as * * * are necessary for the general good of the public, though contracts previously entered into between individuals may thereby be affected.' "

The appellants seek to overcome the trust of these principles by pointing to this court's decision (in 1938) in Central Sav. Bank v. City of New York. * * *

We had, the year before deciding that case, sustained the constitutionality of a subdivision (numbered subd. 4, par. a) of section 309 of the Multiple Dwelling Law which provided that, if an owner of an old law (pre-1901) tenement house desired to continue the structure as a tenement or multiple dwelling, he was obliged to make those changes in the building found necessary for the public health and welfare and that, if the owner refused to make the alterations, the city was authorized to do so, the cost becoming a lien upon the property subject to taxes, assessments and prior mortgages. (See Adamec v. Post, 273 N.Y. 250, 7 N.E.2d 120, supra.) A year later, as just noted, the court was called upon, in the Central Sav. Bank case to consider the effect of a 1937 amendment (to the statute sustained in Adamec) which declared that the cost of the alterations was to be assessed against the property and that the assessment was to be a lien upon the property having "priority over all other liens and encumbrances, including [previously recorded] mortgages". In holding that the provision rendered the statute unconstitutional insofar as the mortgagee was concerned, the court stated that his property was "taken without the process of law * * * and the obligation of his contract with the mortgagor impaired."

The court found the statute procedurally defective in that the mortgagee was given no opportunity to be heard and could not even question the amount of the lien placed ahead of his mortgage. Compelled to "it idly by" while the value of his lien was being diminished, the mortgagee, the court took pains to point out, "is given no opportunity for a hearing and cannot question the reasonableness or the amount of the expense (incurred for repairs). * * * The result of this procedure is that the (mortgagees) pay for all the improvements and alterations without having been given their day in court or afforded any hearing".

The 1962 amendatory act fully remedied the procedural deficiencies remarked in the Central Sav. Bank case. As the statute now reads, it provides that the receiver's lien shall have priority over an existing mortgage only if the mortgagee is given notice of the Building's Department's order directing removal of the nuisance as well as notice of the department's application for the appointment of a receiver. Instead of being relegated to the sidelines, to "sit idly by", the mortgagee has an opportunity to participate in the proceedings from beginning to end. More specifically, not only does he have the right to enforce his lien by an action to foreclose his mortgage but he has the opportunity of contesting the department's charge that a nuisance exists; and, if that issue is found against him, he may either do the required work himself—securing a lien against the rents—or, after the work is performed by the receiver, reimburse the latter in his expenditures and obtain an assignment of his lien. Finally, the mortgagee may, when the receiver renders his account to the court, question the reasonableness of the expenses incurred by him and reflected in his lien.

It is evident, therefore, that the due process objection leveled by the court against the 1937 amendment has been completely obviated by the Legislature in enacting the 1962 law.

It is likewise clear—turning to the second of the constitutional defects noted in the earlier statute—that the Central Sav. Bank decision may not be relied upon to invalidate the 1962 statute on the ground that it effects an unconstitutional impairment of the mortgagee's contractual rights. We assess the property and reasonableness and, by that token, the validity of an exercise of the police power in light of the conditions confronting the Legislature when it acts, and it can hardly be questioned that the situation, in terms of the shortage of safe and adequate dwelling units, which prompted the 1962 amendment (L.1962, ch. 492, § 1) presented a far more serious emergency than that existing in 1937.

Quite apart from this, the impairment wrought by the 1937 statute was far more severe and drastic than that resulting from the 1962 legislation. The priority now provided for is not an absolute priority, as granted by the earlier law, but a limited one. In other words, whereas the former statute created a prior lien in favor of the receiver against the property itself and enabled him, if the moneys expended by the municipality for repairs were not repaid, to foreclose on the property and thereby wipe out the mortgage and destroy the mortgagee's lien, the 1962 provision gives the receiver a prior right only to the rents of the property. Thus, paragraph c of subdivision 5, after explicitly reciting that the lien of the receiver "shall be subject to any (previously recorded) mortgage", goes on to state that the mortgagee shall not be entitled "to any of the rents" or "to a discharge of the receiver" until the cost of repairs and alterations has been satisfied.

When weighed against the vital public purposes sought to be achieved, the interference with the mortgagee's rights resulting from the present law may not be said to be so unreasonable or oppressive as to preclude the State's exercise of its police power. It is worth remarking that, if the mortgagee's lien may not be subordinated to the extent provided—that is, by postponing his right to collect rents from the property or to effect a discharge of the receiver until the cost incurred by the receiver (on behalf of the municipality) in removing the dangerous conditions has been repaid—the result would be that the State must permit slum conditions to continue unabated or, alternatively, either condemn unsafe buildings and thereby aggravate the acute housing shortage or continue making improvements with, however, only a lien subordinate to previously recorded mortgages. To insist upon the last course not only would result in a gratuitous addition to the security of prior encumbrancers but would undoubtedly render the operation financially impossible.   * * *

Concluding, as we do, that the statute is constitutional, * * * the order appealed from should be affirmed, with costs.

4. Search and Seizure

> The right of the people to be secure in their persons, houses, papers, and effects, against unreasonable searches and seizure, shall not be violated, and no Warrants shall issue, but upon probable cause, supported by Oath or affirmation, and particularly describing the place to be searched, and the persons or things to be seized.
>
> U.S. CONST. Amendment IV

The **Fourth Amendment** of the United States Constitution embodies a long history of concern for the protection of the sanctity, security and safety of one's person, home and possessions from intrusion by government officials. Its principles, like those of the other original nine amendments, were specifically designed to limit the power of the federal government. In *Mapp v. Ohio*, 367 U.S. 643, (1961), the U.S. Supreme Court held that the word "liberty" in the Fourteenth Amendment incorporates the protections of the Fourth Amendment. Consequently, since the Fourteenth Amendment applies to the state governments, the principles of the Fourth Amendment also limit the power of the state governments.

The words of the Fourth Amendment indicate some of its important principles. The *first* principle is that the people have the right to be secure. . ."against *unreasonable* searches and seizures." The issue of reasonableness of searches and seizures has been raised in many cases and various types of searches and seizures have been held to be *reasonable.* Some of these include; searches in emergency situations, searches incident to valid arrests *(U.S. v. Robinson,* 414 U.S. 218, 1973), searches in hot pursuit of suspects, searches conducted with the "knowing and intelligent consent" of the person involved, and others. The *second* principle is that. . . "no Warrants shall issue, but upon probable cause. . ." A search warrant is a judicial writ that permits government officials to conduct a search. "Probable cause" may be defined as a reasonable ground for suspicion, supported by circumstances sufficent to permit a prudent person to believe that the accused person has violated the law. The *third* principle is that the testimony upon which probable cause is based must be. . ."supported by Oath or affirmation." The *fourth* principle is that the warrant. . ."particularly describe the place to be searched and the persons or things to be seized." The remedy available if a search or seizure is held to be illegal is called the "exclusionary rule" because it calls for the exclusion from trial of any evidence gathered during an illegal search and seizure, or discovered by way of information derived from an illegal search.

The Fourth Amendment illustrates the inherent conflict in society between the desire to protect the fundamental freedoms of individuals (in this case the sanctity of one's home and possessions) and desire to protect the health, safety and welfare of the general public. Planners find it necessary to deal with the Fourth Amendment when they propose programs to preserve housing or to protect the environment. The decision of the United States Supreme Court in *Camara v. Municipal Court of the City and County of San Francisco,* 387 U.S. 523 (1967), is an illustration.

The Camara case involved a situation where an inspector was making a routine annual inspection for violations of the housing code. The building manager informed him that one of the tenants on the ground floor was using the back of a store as his personal residence. The inspector confronted the tenant and demanded he be allowed to inspect the premises claiming that the building's occupancy permit did not allow use of the ground floor as a residence. The tenant denied the inspector entry because he did not have a search warrant.

On two subsequent occasions the tenant refused to permit inspectors to enter because they did not have warrants. The tenant was thereafter charged with a violation of the housing code for refusal to permit a lawful inspection. He contended that the search would be a violation of his Fourth and Fourteenth Amendment rights in that the Code authorized municipal officials to enter a private dwelling without a search warrant. He argued futher that he could not be prosecuted for refusing to permit an unconstitutionally authorized inspection.

The United States Supreme Court held that the ordinance providing for a warrantless code enforcement inspection of his residence is invalid under the Fourth Amendment. The court said:

> "[T]he health and safety of entire urban populations is dependent upon enforcement of minimum fire, housing, and sanitation standards, and that the only effective means of enforcing such codes is by routine systematized inspection of all physical structures. Of course, in applying any reasonableness standard, including one of constitutional dimension, an argument that the public interest demands a particular rule must receive careful consideration. But we think this argument misses the mark. The question is not, at this stage at least, whether these inspections may be made, but whether they may be made without a warrant. * * * It has nowhere been urged that fire, health, and housing code inspection programs could not achieve their goals within the confines of a reasonable search warrant requirement. * * *

> * * * "[W]e hold that administrative searches of the kind at issue here are significant intrusions upon the interests protected by the Fourth Amendment, that such searches when authorized and conducted without a warrant procedure lack the traditional safeguards which the Fourth Amendment guarantees to the individual.* * *

In 1972, Congress enacted the Federal Environmental Pesticide Control Law, 86 Stat. 975, 7 U.S.C. § 136 et seq., that authorized the EPA Administrator to engage in warrantless searches of pesticide establishments "at reasonable times." Is this provision valid or will it be declared unconstitutional under the Fourth Amendment? There is reason to believe that this provision will be upheld because of the decisions of the United States Supreme Court in *Colonnade Catering Corp. v. United States*, 397 U.S. 72 (1970), upholding warrantless searches of retail liquor dealers and *United States v. Biswell*, 406 U.S. 311 (1972), upholding warrantless searches under the Gun Control Act of 1968, 82 Stat. 1213, 18 U.S.C. §921 et seq.

5. Due Process of Law

The **due process clause** is the most important, pervasive and frequently encountered constitutional principle that planners must understand. The due process clause imposes significant limitations on the law as an instrument of urban planning. It is this principle, more than any other in the constitution, that prescribes the limits of the ability of government to provide for the general welfare of the public.

The fundamental concept underlying due process of law was embodied in the Magna Carta in 1215, but the words, "due process of law" were not used until the Statutes of Edward III were enacted in 1355. The framers of the American Constitution incorporated this important phrase in the Fifth Amendment as a limitation on the power of the federal government. It was not until after the Civil War and the ratification of the Fourteenth Amendment that the phrase, "due process of law" was used to limit the actions of state governments. Many state constitutions also contain a "due process" clause.

The principle of due process contains two basic components: (1) **procedural due process** and (2) **substantive due process.** *Procedural due process* requires that before any person is deprived of life, liberty or property, he must be given a fair hearing or an opportunity to be heard and defend against proposed action to be taken against him. The principle of *substantive due process* requires that no person may be deprived of life, liberty, or property under circumstances that are unreasonable, arbitrary or capricious. This concept is essential to planners because it constitutes a major limitation on the police power of the states. The courts, through the principle of due process, have the power to review zoning, housing and other regulatory legislation to determine whether the enactments are reasonable. The extent to which courts will exercise this power is limited by an attitude of judicial restraint and by the principle of the presumption of the validity of legislative enactments.

These principles are applied quite dissimilarly by different judges and courts, and thus it is difficult to predict how far a court will venture to declare a law unreasonable and in violation of the due process clause. For example, a municipal ordinance requiring hot water supply, in all multiple dwelling buildings might seem reasonable. However, in 1970 a Florida court held that such a law was unreasonable and that the hot water requirement increased the owner's expenses and operated as a deprivation of his property without due process of law. *Safer v. City of Jacksonville,* 237 So.2d 8 (Fla. App. 1970). On the other hand, the New Jersey Supreme Court has held a municipal zoning ordinance invalid as a violation of due process of law because the municipal zoning ordinance failed to provide for the housing needs of the entire region. *Southern Burlington Co., NAACP v. Mount Laurel,* 67 N.J. 151, 336 A.2d 713 (1975). Thus, it is apparent that the due process clause may be used by an activist judge to interject his socio-economic philosophy into the planning process.

> No free man shall be taken or imprisoned or deprived of his freehold or his liberties or free customs, or outlawed or exiled, or in any manner destroyed, nor shall we come upon him, except by a legal judgment of his person or by the law of the land.
> MAGNA CARTA, Chapter 29 (1215)

> No man of what state or condition he be, shall be put out of his lands or tenements taken, nor disinherited, nor put to death, without being brought to to answer by due process of law.
> 28 Edw. III, Chapter 3 (1355)

> . . . nor shall any person . . . be deprived of life, liberty or property, without due process of law; . . .
> U.S.CONST. Amendment V

> . . . nor shall any State deprive any person of life, liberty or property, without due process of law; . . . .
> U.S.CONST. Amendment XIV

No person shall . . . be deprived of life, liberty or property without due process of law. . . .
MICH. CONST. Art. I, sec. 17

'Law of the land' guaranteed in the North Carolina constitution is synonymous with 'due process of law'.
State v. Hales, 256 N.C. 27, 122 S.E.2d 768

'Remedy by due course of law' as used in the Kansas Bill of Rights, Sec. 18 means 'ordered by a tribunal having jurisdiction in due course of procedure after a fair trial.'
Hanson v. Krehbiel, 68 Kan. 670, 75 P. 1041

In Southern Burlington County NAACP v. Township of Mount Laurel, 67 N.J. 151, 336 A.2d 713 (1975) the New Jersey Supreme Court held that the following provision of the state constitution contains the requirements of substantive due process and equal protection of the laws:

All persons are by nature free and independent, and have certain natural and unalienable rights, among which are those of enjoying and defending life and liberty, or acquiring, possessing, and protecting property, and of pursuing and obtaining safety and happiness.

---

5. Due Process (Continued)

a. Substantive Due Process

ARVERNE BAY CONSTRUCTION CO.

v.

THATCHER

278 N.Y. 222, 15 N.E.2d 587 (1938)

LEHMAN, Judge.

The plaintiff is the owner of a plot of vacant land on the northerly side of Linden boulevard in the borough of Brooklyn. Until 1928 the district in which the property is situated was classified as an "unrestricted" zone, under the Building Zone Resolution of the city of New York (New York Code of Ordinances, Appendix B). Then, by amendment of the ordinance and the "Use District Map," the district was placed in a residence zone. The plaintiff, claiming that its property could not be used properly or profitably for any purpose permitted in a residence zone and that, in consequence, the zoning ordinance imposed unnecessary hardship upon it, applied to the Board of Standards and Appeals, under section 21 of the Building Zone Resolution, for a variance which would permit the use of the premises for a gasoline service station. The application was denied, and, upon review in certiorari proceedings, the courts sustained the determination of the board.

Defeated in its attempt to obtain permission to put its property to a profitable use, the plaintiff has brought this action to secure an adjudication that the restrictions placed upon the use of its property by the zoning ordinance result in deprivation of its property without due process of law and that, in so far as the ordinance affects its property, the ordinance violates the provisions of the Constitution of the United States and the Constitution of the State of New York. U.S.C.A. Const. Amend. 14; Const.N.Y. art. 1, § 6. In this action it demands as a right what has been refused to it as a favor. The defendant challenges the right of the plaintiff to urge the invalidity of the zoning ordinance after denial of an application for a variance made under its provisions. At the outset, and before considering the merits of the plaintiff's cause of action, we must dispose of this challenge to the plaintiff's right to maintain this action.

The application for the favor of a variance is an appeal primarily to the discretion of the board, conferred upon it by the ordinance. It necessarily assumes the validity of the ordinance. A successful attack upon the validity of the ordinance destroys the foundation of any discretion conferred by the statute. To invoke the discretion of the board, an owner of property must show "unnecessary hardship." When that has been shown the board may grant "a special privilege" denied to others differently situated. Without such "special privilege," strict enforcement of a general rule restricting the use of all property within a district might work such hardship upon a particular owner that in effect it would deprive the owner of his property without compensation. The power to grant a variation might give such flexibility to the rule or its application that a property owner can without violation of its terms, make reasonable use of his property.

The rule established by that case is this: To sustain an attack upon the validity of the ordinance an aggrieved property owner must show that if the ordinance is enforced the consequent restrictions upon his property preclude its use for any purpose to which it is reasonably adapted. Thus it must appear either that the ordinance does not authorize a variation of the general rule which would admit of such use or that such variation has been refused by the administrative board in the exercise of a discretion which the ordinance confers upon it. Only two possible questions can be presented for decision upon an application for a variation: First, does the ordinance confer upon the administrative board power to grant the variation which is asked; second, if the board has power to grant it, does the exercise of a wise discretion call for the use of the power in the particular case? The issue whether without such variation the strict enforcement of the general rule would work such hardship as to constitute the taking of property without due process of law is not directly presented upon an application for a variation, and it follows that the denial of the application cannot be a binding adjudication that, without such variation, enforcement of the general rule will not deprive the applicant of his property without due process of law. True, where the board in the exercise of its discretion denies an application for a variation which it has *power* to grant, argument may be made that a refusal to exercise such discretion can legally, be based only upon a finding that even without such variation there is no unnecessary hardship, and that the enforcement of the general rule would not deprive the owner of his property or preclude a reasonable use of the property. Then the same considerations which induced the board to deny the application might constrain the court to decide that the statute is valid. None the less, the questions presented would not be identical and the denial of the application for a variance would not be a conclusive adjudication of the validity of the statute; and that would be true even though the courts had, upon review by certiorari, sustained the determination of the board. We proceed, then, to a consideration of the merits of the plaintiff's claim, and in our discussion it will appear that in this case the denial of the application for a variation may have been based upon considerations which cannot affect the judgment of the court in passing upon the validity of the ordinance in so far as it applies to the plaintiff's property.

The amendment to the zoning ordinance, about which complaint is made, changed from an unrestricted zone to a residential district the property abutting on Linden boulevard for a distance of four miles, with the exception of a small section at a railroad crossing. The district is almost undeveloped. There had been no building construction in that area for many years prior to the amendment. The chairman of the building zone commission which drafted the zoning ordinance, testifying as an expert witness for the defendant, described the district as in a "transition state from the farms as I knew them thirty and forty years ago south of this location." There are some old buildings used for non-conforming purposes, left from the days when the district was used for farming. There are only three buildings in Linden boulevard in a distance of about a mile. One of these buildings is a cow stable and a second building is used as an office in connection with the dairy business conducted there. A gasoline station erected on that boulevard would, it is plain, not adversely affect the health, morals, safety or general welfare of the people who now live in that neighborhood. Justification, if any, for the ordinance restricting the use of the property on Linden boulevard to residential purposes must be found in the control over future development which will result from such restrictions.

Without zoning restrictions, the self-interest of the individual property owners will almost inevitably dictate the form of the development of the district. The plaintiff claims, and has conclusively shown at the trial, that at no time since the amendment of the zoning resolution could its property be profitably used for residential purposes. The expert witness for the city, to whose testimony we have already referred and whose qualifications are universally recognized, admits that such a residential improvement would, even now after the lapse of ten years, be "premature." The property, then, must for the present remain unimproved and unproductive, a source of expense to the owner, or must be put to some nonconforming use. In a district otherwise well adapted for residences a gasoline station or other non-conforming use of property may render neighboring property less desirable for use as a private residence. The development of a district for residential purposes might best serve the interests of the city as a whole and, in the end, might perhaps prove the most profitable use of the property within such district. A majority of the property owners might conceivably be content to bear the burden of taxes and other carrying charges upon unimproved land in order to reap profit in the future from the development of the land for residential purposes. They could not safely do so without reasonable assurance that the district will remain adapted for residence use and will not be spoilt for such purpose by the intrusion of structures used for less desirable purposes.

"We are not required to say that a merely temporary restraint of beneficial enjoyment is unlawful where the interference is necessary to promote the ultimate good either of the municipality as a whole or of the immediate neighborhood. Such problems will have to be solved when they arise. If we assume that the restraint may be permitted, the interference must be no unreasonable, but on the contrary must be kept within the limits of necessity." People ex rel. St. Albans-Springfield Corporation v. Connell. The problem presented upon this appeal is whether or not the zoning ordinance as applied to the plaintiff's property is unreasonable.

Findings of the trial judge, sustained by evidence presented by the plaintiff, establish that, in the vicinity of the plaintiff's premises, the city operates an incinerator which "gives off offensive fumes and odors which permeate plaintiff's premises." About 1,200 or 1,500 feet from the plaintiff's land, "a trunk sewer carrying both storm and sanitary sewage empties into an open creek * * * The said creek runs to the south of plaintiff's premises and gives off nauseating odors which permeate the said property." The trial judge further found that other conditions exist which, it is plain, render the property entirely unfit, at present, for any conforming use. Though the defendant urges that the conditions are not as bad as the plaintiff's witnesses have pictured, yet as the Appellate Division has said: "It must be conceded, upon the undisputed facts in this case, that this property cannot, presently or in the immediate future, be profitably used for residential purposes."

We may assume that the zoning ordinance is the product of far-sighted planning calculated to promote the general welfare of the city at some future time. If the State or the city, acting by delegation from the State, had plenary power to pass laws calculated to promote the general welfare, then the validity of the ordinance might be sustained; for "we have nothing to do with the question of the wisdom or good policy of municipal ordinances." Village of Euclid, Ohio v. Ambler Realty Co. The legislative power of the State is, however, not plenary, but is limited by the Constitution of the United States and by the Constitution of the State. It may not take private property without compensation even for a public purpose and to advance the general welfare. "The protection of private property in the Fifth Amendment presupposes that it is wanted for public use, but provides that it shall not be taken for such use without compensation. A similar assumption is made in the decisions upon the Fourteenth Amendment. When this seemingly absolute protection is found to be qualified by the police power, the natural tendency of human nature is to extend the qualification more and more until at last private property disappears. But that cannot be accomplished in this way under the Constitution of the United States." Pennsylvania Coal Co. v. Mahon.

In the prevailing opinion in that case, Mr. Justice Holmes pointed out that "the general rule at least is that while property may be regulated to a certain extent, if regulation goes too far it will be recognized as a taking" (page 415, 43 S.Ct page 160). Whether a regulation does go too far is "a question of degree—and therefore cannot be disposed of by general propositions," and here Mr. Justice Holmes gave warning that "we are in danger of forgetting that a strong public desire to improve the public condition is not enough to warrant achieving the desire by a shorter cut than the constitutional way of paying for the change" (page 416, 43 S.Ct. page 160). The dissent of Mr. Justice Brandeis in that case is not based upon difference of opinion in regard to general principles, but upon different evaluation of the degree of the restrictions there challenged.

The warning of Mr. Justice Holmes should perhaps be directed rather to Legislatures than to courts; for the courts have not hesitated to declare statutes invalid wherever regulation has gone so far that it is clearly unreasonable and must be "recognized as taking," and unless regulation does clearly go so far the courts may not deny force to the regulation. We have already pointed out that in the case which we are reviewing the plaintiff's land cannot at present or in the immediate future be profitably or reasonably used without violation of the restriction. An ordinance which permanently so restricts the use of property that it cannot be used for any reasonable purposes goes, it is plain, beyond regulation, and must be recognized as a taking of the property. The only substantial difference in such case, between restriction and actual taking, is that the restriction leaves the owner subject to the burden of payment of taxation, while outright confiscation would relieve him of that burden.

The situation, of course, might be quite different where it appears that within a reasonable time the property can be put to a profitable use. The temporary inconvenience or even hardship of holding unproductive property might then be compensated by ultimate benefit to the owner or perhaps, even without such compensation, the individual owners might be compelled to bear a temporary burden in order to promote the public good. We do not pass upon such problems now, for here no inference is permissible that within a reasonable time the property can be put to a profitable use or that the present inconvenience or hardship imposed upon the plaintiff is temporary. True, there is evidence that the neighborhood is improving and that some or all of the conditions which now render the district entirely unsuitable for residence purposes will in time be removed. Even so, it is conceded that prognostication that the district will in time become suited for residences rests upon hope and not upon certainty, and no estimate can be made of the time which must elapse before the hope becomes fact.

During the nine years from 1928 to 1936, when concededly the property was unsuitable for any conforming use, the property was assessed at $18,000, and taxes amounting to $4,566 were levied upon it, in addition to assessments of several thousand dollars; yet, so far as appears, the district was no better suited for residence purposes at the time of a trial in 1936 than it was when the zoning ordinance was amended in 1928. In such case the ordinance is clearly more than a temporary and reasonable restriction placed upon the land to promote the general welfare. It is in substance a taking of the land prohibited by the Constitution of the United States and by the Constitution of the State.

We repeat here what under similar circumstances the court said in People ex rel. St. Albans-Springfield Corporation v. Connell, supra, "we are not required to say that a merely temporary restraint of beneficial enjoyment is unlawful where the interference is necessary to promote the ultimate good either of the municipality as a whole or of the immediate neighborhood." There the court held that the "ultimate good" could be attained and a "productive use" allowed by a variation of the zoning ordinance that "will be temporary and provisional and readily terminable." Here the application of the plaintiff for any variation was properly refused, for the conditions which render the plaintiff's property unsuitable for residential use are general and not confined to plaintiff's property. In such case, we have held that the general hardship should be remedied by revision of the general regulation, not by granting the special privilege of a variation to single owners. Perhaps a new ordinance might be evolved by which the "ultimate good" may be attained without depriving owners of the productive use of their property. That is a problem for the legislative authority, not for the courts. Now we hold only that the present regulation is applied to plaintiff's property is not valid.

The judgment of the Appellate Division should be reversed and that of the Special Term affirmed, with costs in this court and in the Appellate Division. _____

In some cases the court does not use the magic phrase, "due process of law." Instead it will use such phrases as, "unreasonable," **"constitutes a taking of property,"** or "no relationship to the objectives to be achieved." Take note of the language used by the Florida court in *Safer v. City of Jacksonville,* 237 So. 8 (Fla. App. 1970):

SAFER

v.

CITY OF JACKSONVILLE

237 So. 8 (Fla. App. 1970)

The primary question posed for consideration is whether the requirements that every rental unit contain a lavatory, convenience electrical outlets in each room, and a continuous supply of potable hot water are reasonably required in order to protect the health, safety, or welfare of the tenants occupying these units. To hold in the affirmative would do violence to the history of our country, in the early years of which hearty citizens were reared and grew to maturity under living conditions which included bathing in a bowl supplied by a water pitcher placed upon a washstand in the bedroom, and under which all hot water used by the family was heated in a kettle, pot, or tub on the kitchen stove. Research fails to reveal any substantial number of instances in which living under these conditions adversely affected the health, safely or morals of our forebears, or indeed many of the older generation living today. The paternalistic trend in government is gradually forcing a surrender of the living conditions commonplace in the 'good old days' for more modern concepts of living which frequently are influenced more by aesthetic considerations than those relating to health, safety, or welfare. To require the installation of lavatories, hot water heaters and convenience electrical outlets in all of the low rent dwellings units owned by appellants would not only be unreasonable but constitute a confiscation of appellants' property without compensation contrary to basic constitutional rights. The cost of compliance bears no reasonable relationship to the objects to be attained. * * *

---

5. Due Process (Continued)

b. Procedural Due Process

SHAUGNESSY

v.

MEZEI

345 U.S. 206, (1952)

In 1952 the U.S. Supreme Court upheld the validity of "preventative detention" of enemy aliens during the second world war. Justice Jackson *agreed that the detention of an alien would not be inconsistent with substantive* due process but dissented on the grounds that the alien was entitled to but did not receive *procedural* due process.

* * *

III. Procedural Due Process

Procedural fairness, if not all that originally was meant by due process of law, is at least what it most uncompromisingly requires. Procedural due process is more elemental and less flexible than substantive due process. It yields less to the times, varies less with conditions, and defers much less to legislative judgment. Insofar as it is technical law, it must be a specialized responsibility within the competence of the judiciary on which they do not bend before political branches of the Government, as they should on matters of policy which comprise substantive law.

If it be conceded that in some way this alien could be confined, does it matter what the procedure is? Only the untaught layman or the charlatan lawyer can answer that procedures matter not. Procedural fairness and regularity are of the indispensable essence of liberty. Severe substantive laws can be endured if they are fairly and impartially applied. Indeed, if put to the choice, one might well prefer to live under Soviet substantive law applied in good faith by our common-law procedures than under our substantive law enforced by Soviet procedural practices. Let it not be overlooked that due process of law is not for the sole benefit of an accused. It is the best insurance for the Government itself against those blunders which leave lasting stains on a system of justice but which are bound to occur on *ex parte* consideration. Cf. *Knauff v. Shaughnessy*, 338 U.S. 537, which was a near miss, saved by further administrative and congressional hearings from perpetrating an injustice. See Knauff, *The Ellen Knauff Story* (New York 1952).

Our law may, and rightly does, place more restrictions on the alien than on the citizen. But basic fairness in hearing procedures does not vary with the status of the accused. If the procedures used to judge this alien are fair and just, no good reason can be given why they should not be extended to simplify the condemnation of citizens. If they would be unfair to citizens, we cannot defend the fairness of them when applied to the more helpless and handicapped alien. This is at the root of our holdings that the resident alien must be given a fair hearing to test an official claim that he is one of a deportable class. *Wong Yang Sung v. McGrath*, 339 U.S. 33.

The most scrupulous observance of due process, including the right to know a charge, to be confronted with the accuser, to cross-examine informers and to produce evidence in one's behalf, is especially necessary where the occasion of detention is fear of future misconduct, rather than crimes committed.* * *

Congress has ample power to determine whom we will admit to our shores and by what means it will effectuate its exclusion policy. The only limitation is that it may not do so by authorizing United States officers to take without due process of law the life, the liberty or the property of an alien who has come within our jurisdiction; and that means he must meet a fair hearing with fair notice of the charges.

It is inconceivable to me that this measure of simple justice and fair dealing would menace the security of this country. No one can make me believe that we are that far gone.

In *American Oil Co. v. City of Chicago*, 331 N.E.2nd 67 (Ill. 1975), the court held that there was a violation of procedural due process where notice of a hearing to rezone property appeared only in a small newspaper and owners of the property were not given notice by mail even though their names and addresses where readily available from the recording office and the tax records.

See also *In re Department of Buildings*, supra, where the court upheld the New York receivership law after it was modified to overcome previous procedural due process objections.

6. Equal Protection of the Laws

The principle of **equal protection of the laws** does not appear in the original Constitution or in the Bill of Rights. The "equal protection of the laws" clause is contained in the Fourteenth Amendment of the federal Constitution and in many state constitutions. Consequently the equal protection applies *directly* only to the states. Two requirements of the principle of equal protection are: (1) no law may *unduly favor* one group over another; and (2) no law may impose a *hostile discrimination* on any particular group.

Most laws do not apply universally to all persons and groups and thus equal protection challenges are quite common. The issue in such cases usually involves the **reasonableness of the classification** by which one group is treated differently from another. The courts use one of two separate tests to resolve equal protection issues. The first test is based on whether there is a **rational basis** for the classification. When a court uses this test it will usually adhere to the principle of judicial restraint and attempt to avoid substituting its judgment for the judgment of the legislative body. Thus, if a court can find *any rational basis* for the classification then the law will usually be upheld.

The second test, called the "strict scrutiny" test, requires a much more careful examination by the court of the basis of the classification. The "strict scrutiny" test is applied only in cases involving either (1) an interference with **fundamental interest**, such as rights relating to criminal prosecution or the right to vote, or (2) a **suspect classification**, i.e., a classification based on a standard that is inherently suspect, such as classifications based on race. If neither a fundamental interest nor a suspect classification is found, then the rational basis test is applied. If, however, the court finds that a fundamental interest or a suspect classification is involved, then the classification will be upheld only if there is a "compelling state interest" sufficient to justify the difference in treatment of the groups involved.

It should be apparent that many planning programs make implicit and explicit classifications based on wealth, sex, age, and other standards. Consequently, it is important that planners develop an awareness of the principle of equal protection of the laws to avoid proposals that involve vulnerable or invalid classifications.

RHONDA REALTY CORP.
v.
LAWTON
414 Ill. 313, 111 N.E.2d 310 (1953)

DAILY, Justice.

This is an appeal from a judgment of the circuit court of Cook County which found subparagraph (2) of section 8 of the Chicago zoning ordinance (Municipal Code of Chicago, sec. 194A-8(2), to be unconstitutional and void. The trial court has certified that the validity of a municipal ordinance is involved and, that in its opinion, the public interest requires a direct appeal to this court.

The leading facts show that appellee, which is the Ronda Realty Corporation, applied to the commissioner of buildings of the city of Chicago, for a permit to remodel appellee's apartment building at 4201-15 North Sheridan Road, from twenty-one to fifty-three apartments. Accompanying the application was a certificate, by the secretary of the appellee, to the effect that on the premises there would be off-street facilities for parking eighteen automobiles. The commissioner issued the permit, whereupon thirteen tenants of the building, who are some of the appellants here, appealed to the zoning board of appeals seeking to reverse the action of the commissioner. The ground of the appeal was that the remodeling would result in the creation of fifty-three apartments; that section 194A-8(2) of the Municipal Code of Chicago requires an apartment building to provide off-street automobile parking facilities on the lot where the apartment building is maintained at the ratio of one automobile for each three apartments; that there is only space on appellee's lot for parking eight automobiles; that fifty-three apartments would require eighteen parking spaces and therefore the commissioner should not have issued the permit.

A hearing was held before the zoning board of appeals, which body, after hearing evidence and viewing the premises, concluded that there were not enough off-street parking facilities on appellee's property to comply with the ordinance and entered an order reversing the action of the commissioner and revoking the permit. Appellee then filed a complaint in the circuit court for review under the provisions of the Administrative Review Act (Ill. Rev. Stat. 1951, chap. 110, pars. 264-279) setting forth the facts and pleading the invalidity of the ordinance relied upon by the board. On the hearing for review, the court stated that it was deciding the case purely on a question of law and not on questions of fact, and entered its judgment that the section of the ordinance relied upon was unconstitutional and void in that it discriminated against appellee and deprived it of equal protection of the law. The order of the zoning board of appeals was reversed and the issuance of the building permit sustained. The tenants, the commissioner of buildings, the zoning board of appeals and the city of Chicago have perfected the appeal to this court.

The errors assigned in this court present but one decisive issue, namely, whether subparagraph (2) of section 8 of the zoning ordinance is invalid because it creates an unlawful classification, discriminatory in its nature. The complete provisions of section 8 of the ordinance are as follows:

"194A-8. (Section 8.) Apartment House Districts. Permitted uses in Apartment House districts are:

"(1) Any use permitted in a Family Residence district without restrictions except such as are applicable to auxiliary uses and any other use permitted in a Duplex Residence or Group House district;

"(2) Apartment house, provided that where there are more than two apartments in the building a private garage or automobile compound for the storage of one passenger automobile for each of 33 per cent of the

number of apartments shall be erected or established and maintained on
the lot used for the apartment house;

"(3) Boarding or lodging hourse, hotel, hospital, home for dependents
or nursing home;

"(4) Boarding school, vocational school, college or university, when not
operated for pecuniary profit;

"(5) Club, fraternity or sorority house, when not operated for pecuniary
profit;

"(6) Public art gallery, library or museum;

"(7) Auxiliary uses, subject to the following limitations;

"A sign may be maintained on any lot area or building, if the sign is not
more than 2 square feet in area and if it is located not nearer to the street
line than the building line and if it does not advertise anything except the
names and occupations of the occupants;

"A restaurant may be maintained in a hotel, if the public entrance to
the restaurant is from the lobby of the hotel and no sign advertising the
restaurant is visible to persons outside of the hotel."

The right of cities to enact zoning ordinances thereby imposing a
reasonable restraint upon the use of private property, and the rules of law
governing the validity of such ordinances are reasonably well settled. The
right which every property owner has to use his property in his own way
and for his own purposes is subject always to the exercise of police power
and it is in the exercise of this power that zoning ordinances are adopted.
To be a valid exercise of the police power, however, the ordinance must
bear a substantial relationship to the public health, safety, comfort or welfare. To those ends, legislative bodies may classify persons if the classification is based on some reasonable distinction having reference to the object of the legislation. Laws will not be regarded as special or class legislation merely because they affect one class and not another, provided they
affect all members of the same class alike. A classification which is not
purely arbitrary and is reasonably adapted to secure the purpose for
which it was intended will not be disturbed by the courts unless it can be
clearly seen that there is no fair reason for the distinction made. Also, in
this regard, we have held that even though a zoning ordinance be based
upon proper statutory authority and is reasonably designed to protect the
public health or safety, it cannot, in such guise, under the rights guaranteed by the Illinois and Federal constitutions, effect an arbitrary discrimination against the class on which it operates by omitting from its coverage
persons and objects similarly situated. Statutory classifications can only be
sustained where there are real differences between the classes, and where
the selection of the particular class, as distinguished from others, is
reasonably related to the evils to be remedied by the statute or ordinance.

Tested in the light of these established rules of law, we believe it is
manifest that subparagraph (2) of section 8 creates an unlawful classification, both arbitrary and discriminatory in its nature. Of all the different
types of structures upon which the section is made to operate, it is only
apartment buildings that are required to furnish off-street parking
facilities. The evils to be remedied on crowded city streets are well

known, but we do not see that the singling out of apartment buildings
from the other types of buildings embraced by the ordinance is reasonably
related to the elimination of those evils. Appellants urge that the classification is not discriminatory because it applies to all apartment buildings
equally and because it is apartment buildings, more than any other type
structure permitted, which contribute the most to street congestion
caused by parked automobiles. We see neither a fair nor reasonable basis
for such a classification nor its reasonable relation to the object and purpose of the ordinance. The street congestion problems created by boarding or rooming houses, hotels, and the like, are not essentially different
from those caused by apartment buildings. All are similarly situated in
their relation to the problems of congestion that are caused by parking
cars in the street, and all contribute proportionately to the evil sought to
be remedied. Indeed, we think it not unreasonable to say that the scope
and nature of the congestion may be greater in the case of large rooming
houses and hotels than in the case of apartment houses. First, due to the
comparative number of persons accommodated and, second, because the
apartment dweller suggests a resident of some permanency who would
seek to alleviate the problem of parking on the street, whereas the hotel
or rooming house guest suggests a transient who makes no effort to solve
his parking problem. It is our conclusion that the differences in kind between apartment buildings and numerous of the other structures upon
which the section is made to operate are not such as to warrant the distinction made by subparagraph (2). Relieving congestion in the streets is
not doubt a proper legislative purpose, but imposing the burden on one
kind of property, while excepting other kinds not significantly different, is
not a valid means for its accomplishment. A statute or ordinance cannot
be sustained which applies to some cases and does not apply to other
cases not essentially different in kind.

It follows that the circuit court was correct in holding subparagraph (2)
of section 8 of the ordinance invalid. The judgment of the circuit court is
therefore affirmed.

Judgment affirmed.

PROPERTY TAXES, SCHOOL FINANCING AND EQUAL PROTECTION

JEROME G. ROSE

2 *REAL ESTATE LAW JOURNAL* 486 (1973)

The cost of public education is the largest single local government expenditure for which property taxes are levied.[1] The significance of this
statistic to taxpayers is exacerbated by the additional fact that the property

tax is the primary source of local revenue for public school expenditures.[2] Taken together these facts explain why the real estate profession has followed the recent series of "school tax" decisions with particular interest.

The drama began at the end of the summer of 1971 when the California Supreme Court in *Serrano v. Priest*[3] held the California system of school financing invalid on the ground that it violated the equal protection clause of the Fourteenth Amendment of the United States Constitution. In California, as in most other states, revenue to support the public schools is derived from property taxes within the school districts. Districts with substantial tax ratables are therefore able to spend larger sums per pupil and still maintain a lower tax rate than districts with a lower ratio of ratables per pupil. The *Serrano* decision held that the equal protection clause is violated when the level of spending for education depends on the wealth of school districts.

Within a short time after the *Serrano* decision similar systems of school finance were held invalid in Texas by *Rodriquez v. San Antonio Independent School District*,[4] in New Jersey by *Robinson v. Cahill*[5] and in a number of other states.[6] The *Serrano* decision, and those that follow it, are based upon the following reasoning:

(1) The system of school financing discriminates on the basis of wealth[7] which is a "suspect classification" when it relates to a "fundamental interest;"

(2) Education is a "fundamental interest" because of its relation to individual success and the needs of a democratic society;

(3) A law based upon a "suspect classification" and relating to a "fundamental interest" can be justified only if the state can show that it has a "compelling interest which justifies the law [and] that the distinctions drawn by the law are *necessary* to further its purpose."[8]

(4) The present system of school finance is not necessary to accomplish any "compelling state interest."

After invalidating the system of school finance on the above reasoning, the California Supreme Court remanded the *Serrano* case to the trial court for additional evidence. In the meantime, the *Rodriquez* case was appealed to the United States Supreme Court. On March 21, 1973, the Supreme Court, in a 5 to 4 decision[9] rejected the *Serrano* reasoning adopted by the lower court in Rodriquez and held that the Texas system of school finance did not violate the equal protection clause because:

(1) The school finance system was *not* based upon a "suspect classification" because of "the absence of any evidence that the financing system discriminates against any definable category of 'poor' people. . . . "

(2) Education is *not* a "fundamental right" within the meaning of the equal protection clause of the Federal Constitution.

(3) Where the law is not based upon a "suspect classification" and does not involve a "fundamental interest" its validity does *not* depend upon a "compelling interest" but requires only that there be "some rational relationship to a legitimate state purpose." The court then found that such a rational relationship does exist between the system of school finance and a legitimate state purpose.

It seems clear that the court's decision was influenced by the realization that acceptance of the *Serrano* principle would have a great impact [10] upon the ability of local governments to maintain fiscal balance if they were required to provide equal distribution of municipal services. In reflecting upon this problem the court said: "Moreover, if local taxation for local expenditures is an unconstitutional method of providing for education then it may be an equally impermissible means of providing other necessary services customarily financed largely from local property taxes, including local police and fire protection, public health and hospitals and public utility facilities of various kinds. We perceive no justification for such a severe denigration of local property taxation and control as would follow from appellees' contentions. It has simply never been within the constitutional prerogative of this court to nullify statewide measures for financing public services merely because the burdens or benefits thereof fall unevenly depending upon the relative wealth of the political subdivisions in which citizens live." [11]

Within two weeks after the *Rodriquez* decision, the New Jersey Supreme Court expressed its own concern for the implications of the *Serrano* principle upon municipal finance. In *Robinson v. Cahill* [12] the court held that the New Jersey system of school finance does *not violate* the equal protection clause of the state constitution but does violate the state constitutional provision requiring a "thorough and efficient system of free public schools." [13] Thus the court affirmed the invalidity of the system of educational financing. However, by basing its decision on this narrower ground the court was able to limit the application of its ruling to the financing of education and without leading to a requirement of equalization of all municipal services.

Thus for a brief period during the interval from the Summer of 1971 to the Spring of 1973 it appeared as though the courts would establish a principle by which the equal distribution of municipal services might be included within the meaning of the federal and/or state equal protection clause. However, the United States Supreme Court and the New Jersey Supreme Court have both declined to so hold because of the potential "conclusive implications" of such a doctrine upon municipal home rule and because of the difficulties involved in the judicial administration of such a principle.

It may be argued that any decision resulting in a redistribution of the property tax burden throughout the state might also have "convulsive implications" upon the value of real estate affected thereby. One renowned authority has speculated that if the principle of the *Serrano* decision is extended, "the price of real estate on the 'right side of the tracks' will decrease in value, while it will increase on the 'wrong side of the tracks.'" [14] It may not be possible to predict such results with any certainty at this time. However, it does seem wise for real estate investors to continue to watch for judicial developments in this area.

NOTES

1. Bureau of the Census, U.S. Department of Commerce, 1967 Census of Governments, Compendium of Government Finances, Tables 3 and 8, (1969).

2. *Id.* Table 3.

3. Serrano v. Priest, 5 Cal. 3d 584, 96 Cal. Rptr. 601, 487 P.2d 1241 (1971).

4. Rodriquez v. San Antonio Independent School District, 337 F. Supp. 280 (W.D. Tex. 1971).

5. Robinson v. Cahill, 118 N.J. Super. 223, 287 A.2d 187 (1972).

6. E.g. Minnesota; Van Dusartz v. Hatfield, 334 F. Supp. 870 (D. Minn. 1971); Wyoming: Sweetwater County Planning Commission v. Hinkle, 491 P.2d 1234 (Wyo. 1971).

7. Discrimination in municipal services based on *race* is highly suspect and is subject to exacting judicial scrutiny. Hawkins v. Town of Shaw, 437 F.2d 1286 (1971). *See* Anderson, "Toward the Equalization of Municipal Services: Variations on a Theme by *Hawkins,*" 50 *Journal of Urban Law* 177 (1972).

8. Westbrook v. Hihlay, 2 Cal. 3d 765, 87 Cal. Rptr. 839, 471 P.2d 487 (1970).

9. San Antonio Independent School District v. Rodriquez (41 U.S.L.W. 4407, S. Ct., March 21, 1973).

10. *See* D. Hagman, "Property Tax Reform: Speculations on the Impact of Serrano Equalization Principle," 1 *Real Estate Law Journal* 115 (1972). *See also* W. Bateman and P. Brown, "Some Reflections on *Serrano v. Priest,*" 49 *Journal of Urban Law* 701 (1972).

11. *Supra* note 9 at 4423.

12. Robinson v. Cahill, No. A-58 (N.J. Sup. Ct., April 3, 1973).

13. N.J. CONST. Art. VIII, Sect. IV, para. 1.

14. Hagman, *supra*, note 10 at 120.

---

7. Private Enterprise

The United States has adopted an economic system that is usually characterized as "capitalistic" or based on the concept of **"private enterprise."** However, there is no specific provision in the Constitution that mandates the creation or the continuation of this type of economic system. It may be argued that a private enterprise system is implied in the Constitution in the due process clause, the clause prohibiting the impairment of the obligation of contracts and the clause prohibiting the taking of property without just compensation. Furthermore, it is apparent that the private enterprise system will remain the predominant economic system as long as a majority of the electorate believes that the benefits of individual freedom outweigh the inequities of a maldistribution of economic resources.

Planners frequently become enmeshed in this issue because planning proposals usually involve governmental intervention into activities previously left to private enterprise. Legal attacks upon such programs are usually directed to one of the constitutional provisions cited above. However, political opposition to planning programs frequently raise the private enterprise argument as though a constitutional mandate were involved.

> So great, moreover is the regard of the law for private property that it will not authorize the least violation of it; no, *not even for the general good of the whole community.*
> Blackstone, *Commentaries*, Vol. I, 139 (1782).

In a private enterprise economy, such as we have traditionally had in the United States, we rely on private initiative in search of profits or other income, to get the job done, within the framework of the 'free price system'. . . .

Under a private enterprise, free price system, consumers control what and how much shall be produced. The pricing process provides a way of registering consumer preferences through consumer money expenditures on various goods and services. The more consumers want something, the more money they will spend on it and the higher the price they will be willing to pay for it. The relative strength of consumer demand for various products is measured in the prices of the products and it is on the basis of this pattern of prices that the price system decides, so to speak, which are the most important goods and services to be produced.

Bowman and Bach, *Economic Analysis and Public Policy* pp 36-47 (1949)

Economic liberty (or laissez-faire as it traditionally is called) means simply that people are able to express their economic choices without interference from agencies or creatures of the state. Thus it leaves individuals free to choose the occupations they will enter, the ways in which they will invest their capital and the goods and services they will consume. . . . The theory assumes that people will choose to use their capacities and resources in ways which will yield them greatest satisfaction.

Taylor and Barger, *The American Economy in Operation* pp 8-12 (1949)

---

* * *

1. To what extent do the above quotations provide an accurate definition of "free enterprise"?

2. What is the relationship of the "free enterprise" system and the planning process?

* * *

Although this court favors the conduct of private enterprise over governmental, the people have permitted and allowed the government to usurp the field of building, developing, managing and operating airports and thus by custom and usage the same is in fact and law a public purpose.

City of Dayton v. Borchers, 13 Ohio Misc. 273,277-78, 232 N.E.2d 437, 440-41 (1967)

COURTESY SANDWICH SHOP, INC

v.

PORT OF NEW YORK AUTHORITY

12 N.Y.2d 379, 190 N.E.2d 402 (1963)

In *COURTESY SANDWICH SHOP, INC. v. PORT OF NEW YORK AUTHORITY*, 12 N.Y.2d 379, 190 N.E.2d 402 (1963) a taking for the World Trade Center was upheld as a "public use" although portions of the proposed structures were to be devoted to purposes to be used for the production of revenue for expenses of the port development project.

The following is an excerpt from the strong *dissent* of Van Voorhis, J:

This is not all a matter of policy for the Legislature. It is the function of courts to give effect to the Constitutions, State and Federal. It is the solemn duty of courts to enforce the constitutional limitation against taking private property by eminent domain except for public purposes. It is idle to suggest that respondents and others in like position are protected by condemnation procedures against taking for nonpublic purposes, inasmuch as the effect of the majority decision is to characterize the condemnation of any real estate in this 13-block area as being for a public purpose. What constitutes private property or public purposes changes from time to time, but the basic concept of private property does not change. If powers such as these be upheld to condemn property in good condition which is not potentially slum (cf. Cannata v. City of New York, 11 N.Y.2d 210, 227 N.Y.S.2d 903, 182 N.E.2d 395), without even paying for the good will, what may appear to be for the advantage of the New York City Chamber of Commerce or the Downtown Lower Manhattan Association or the New Jersey State Chamber of Commerce, or the Chambers of Commerce of Jersey City or Newark today may be turned against them tomorrow, as their counterparts learned in other countries to their sorrow and dismay after they had surrendered to the collectivist state. This ever-growing ascendency of government over private property and over free enterprise is no respecter of persons and cannot long be harnessed by those who expect to use it for private ends. As governmental ascendency is increasingly sanctioned by the constitutional law of our State, private capital is less likely to be invested to develop the Port of New York and more likely to fold its tents and silently move toward other States where government competition and expropriation are more restricted. As the cases show that have been previously cited, the power of government in these respects has been curbed by the courts of other States.

Disregard of the constitutional protection of private property and stigmatization of the small or not so small entrepreneur as standing in the way of progress has everywhere characterized the advance of collectivism. To hold a purpose to be public merely for the reason that it is invoked by a public body to serve its ideas of the public good, it seems to me, can be done only on the assumption that we have passed the point of no return, that the trade, commerce and manufacture of our principal cities can be conducted by private enterprise only on a diminishing scale and that private capital should progressively be displaced by public capital which should increasingly take over. The economic and geographical advantages of the City of New York have withstood a great deal of attrition and can probably withstand more, but there is a limit beyond which socialization cannot be carried without destruction of the constitutional bases of private ownership and enterprise. It seems to me to be the part of courts to enforce the constitutional rights of property which are involved here.

* * *

BOARD OF SUPERVISORS OF FAIRFAX COUNTY

v.

DeGROFF ENTERPRISES, INC.

214 Va. 235, 198 S.E.2d 600 (1973)

In September 1971 the Board of Supervisors of Fairfax County passed an amendment to the Fairfax County Zoning Ordinance which "requires the developer of fifty or more dwelling units in five zoning districts . . . to commit himself, before rezoning or site plan approval to build at least 15% of these dwelling units as low and moderate income housing. . . "

The trial court found that the Board of Supervisors had exceeded its authority under the zoning enabling act, that the Amendment was an improper delegation of legislative authority and was arbitrary and capricious. The Supreme Court of Virginia affirmed the lower court ruling stating:

"The amendment, in establishing maximum rental and sale prices for 15% of the units in the development, exceeds the authority granted by the enabling act to the local governing body because it is socio-economic zoning and attempts to control the compensation for the use of land and the improvements thereon.

"Of greater importance, however, is that the amendment requires the developer or owner to rent or sell 15% of the dwelling units in the development to persons of low or moderate income at rental or sale prices not fixed by the free market. Such a scheme violates the guarantee set forth in Section 11 of Article 1 of the Constitution of Virginia, 1971, that no property will be taken or damaged for public purposes without just compensation."

Chapter Two

Zoning

A. RELATIONSHIP TO COMMUNITY PLANNING

Zoning is one of a number of techniques of implementing the planning process. The relationship between zoning and planning should become clear from an analysis of the following definition of planning. "Planning" may be defined as a systematic, comprehensive, continuous, forward-looking process of analysis of a community's constraints for the purpose of formulating and implementing a plan for the achievement of the goals and objectives of the community. (See Chapin, *Urban Land Use Planning*, (1965)).

Planning is **continuous** in that it is an ongoing process by which a governmental entity seeks to update and modify its plans in response to changing sociological, economic and political information. The continuous nature of planning has been recognized by the New Jersey Municipal Land Use Law which requires the revision of the master plans of all New Jersey municipalities every six years. Planning is **forward-looking** because it entails thinking about the future and the problems of the future and because it is based on the philosophical assumption that the world of tomorrow can be improved by what we do today. Planning is a process of analysis that is used for the **purpose of achieving community goals and objectives**. One of the difficult problems of planning is that community goals change over time, as exemplified by the recent shift in many municipalities from goals of steady growth to slow or no-growth goals. Nonetheless, the planning process requires an attempt to formulate and articulate the communities goals and objectives. For example, the New Jersey Municipal Land Use Law requires every municipal master plan to have a statement of the basic goals, assumptions and policies of each municipality.

Part of the definition of "planning" directs attention to the fact that it is a **process of analysis** of various community **constraints**. These constraints act like the strands of a net; if one constraint is pushed or pulled, then many other constraints are greatly affected. To understand these community constraints, planners undertake an analysis of the demographic, environmental, economic, sociological and political forces in the community. **Demographic** studies can be used to approximate future population growth or decline. **Environmental** studies provide information relating to such factors as topography, soil, water and other ecological factors affecting the use of land. **Economic** studies are helpful and necessary to indicate the revenue and expenditure limitations on the plans of the community. **Sociological** studies illustrating the relative proportions of various groups in a community can be very valuable in planning to provide health, manpower training and other public service facilities. *Political* studies may point out the political constraints by portraying the decision-making forces at various levels of government which are likely to limit or to promote programs.

The first half of the planning process is designed to *formulate* a master plan for the achievement of community goals and objectives. A master plan, or comprehensive plan is composed of several elements. For example, in New Jersey, the enabling legislation (N.J.40:55D-28) requires every municipal master plan to contain a land use plan, a housing plan, a circulation plan, a utility service plan, etc. (See excerpts below).

The second half of the planning process is designed to *implement* the master plan. Among the techniques of planning implementation are: (1) zoning ordinances, (2) subdivision regulations, (3) official map ordinances, (4) eminent domain, (5) urban renewal or community development and (6) various social planning tools. A **zoning ordinance** is a legislative enactment of local government that divides the jurisdiction of the land into zones and prescribes regulations relating to (a) the "use" of the land, (b) the "bulk" or relationship of the building size to the land and (c) "height" or intensity of use. **Subdivision control** or regulation is implemented through local ordinances prescribing the procedures and standards that one must follow when dividing a large parcel of land into smaller parcels in preparation for development. An **official map** ordinance adopts a municipal map, showing proposed parks, streets and other facilities. The ordinances also provide that no building permits shall be issued for land located on the bed of any proposed streets or on the proposed location of any other facilities designated on the map. Eminent domain is the power of government to take property without the consent of the owner for a public use upon the payment of just compensation. **Urban renewal** or community development programs and social planning tools are other forms of planning implementation. Urban renewal or community development programs make it possible for a city or town to acquire existing structures, which are inappropriate for contemporary use, rehabilitate or demolish them and build new structures in their place. The technique is drastic and has been employed advantageously in some cases and disadvantageously in others.

From this discussion, it should be apparent that zoning law is one of a number of techniques of implementing the planning process to achieve the goals and objectives of the community.

The New Jersey Municipal Land Use Law provides a very good example of state enabling legislation provisions relating to the master plan:

NEW JERSEY MASTER PLAN

C. 40:55D-28 Preparation; contents; modification.

19. Preparation; contents; modification. a. The planning board may prepare and, after public hearing adopt or amend a master plan, or component parts thereof, to guide the use of lands within the municipality in a manner which protects public health and safety and promotes the general welfare.

b. The master plan shall generally comprise a report or statement and land use and development proposals, with maps, diagrams and text, presenting where appropriate, the following elements:

(1) A statement of objectives, principles, assumptions, policies and standards upon which the constituent proposals for the physical, economic and social development of the municipality are based;

(2) A land use plan element (a) taking into account the other master plan elements and natural conditions, including, but not necessarily limited to, topography, soil conditions, water supply, drainage, flood plan areas, marshes, and woodlands. (b) showing the existing and proposed location, extent and intensity of development of land to be used in the future for varying types of residential, commercial, industrial, agricultural, recreational, educational and other public and private purposes or combination of purposes, and (c) including a statement of the standards of population density and development intensity recommended for the municipality.

(3) A housing plan element, including but not limited to, residential standards and proposals for the construction and improvement of housing;

(4) A circulation plan element showing the location and types of facilities for all modes of transportation required for the efficient movement of people and goods into, about, and through the municipality;

(5) A utility service plan element analyzing the need for and showing the future general location of water supply and distribution facilities, drainage and flood control facilities, sewerage and waste treatment, solid waste disposal and provision for other related utilities;

(6) A community facilities plan element showing the location and type of educational or cultural facilities, historic sites, libraries, hospitals, fire houses, police stations and other related facilities, including their relation to the surrounding areas;

(7) A recreation plan element showing a comprehensive system of areas and public sites for recreation; and

(8) A conservation plan element providing for the preservation, conservation, and utilization of natural resources, including, to the extent appropriate, open space, water, forests, soil, marshes, wetlands, harbors, rivers and other waters, fisheries, wildlife and other natural resources; and

(9) Appendices or separate reports containing the technical foundation for the master plan and its constituent elements.

(c) The master plan and its plan elements may be divided into subplans and subplan elements projected according to periods of time or staging sequences.

D. The master plan shall include a specific policy statement indicating the relationship of the proposed development of the municipality as developed in the master plan to (1) the master plans of contiguous municipalities, (2) the master plan of the county in which the municipality is located and (3) any comprehensive guide plan pursuant to section 15 of P.L. 1961, c. 47 (C. 13:1B-15.52).

The following provisions from the state enabling legislation in California illustrate the concern of the legislators in that state with environmental problems:

CALIFORNIA MASTER PLAN

§ 65300.5 Construction of article

In construing the provisions of this article, the Legislature intends that the general plan and elements and parts thereof comprise an integrated, internally consistent and compatible statement of policies for the adopting agency.

§ 65302. Elements required to be included in plan

The general plan shall consist of a statement of development policies and shall include a diagram or diagrams and text setting forth objectives, principles, standards, and plan proposals. The plan shall include the following elements:

(a) A land-use element which designates the proposed general distribution and general location and extent of the uses of the land for housing, business, industry, open space, including agriculture, natural resources, recreation, and enjoyment of scenic beauty, education, public buildings and grounds, solid and liquid waste disposal facilities, and other categories of public and private uses of land. The land-use element shall include a statement of the standards of population density and building intensity recommended for the various districts and other territory covered by the plan. The land-use element shall also identify areas covered by the plan which are subject to flooding and shall be reviewed annually with respect to such areas.

(b) A circulation element consisting of the general location and extent of existing and proposed major thoroughfares, transportation routes, terminals, and other local public utilities and facilities, all correlated with the land-use element of the plan.

(c) A housing element, to be developed pursuant to regulations established under Section * * * 41134 of the Health and Safety Code, consisting of standards and plans for the improvement of housing and for provision of adequate sites of housing. This element of the plan shall make adequate provision for the housing needs of all economic segments of the community.

(d) A conservation element for the conservation, development, and utilization of natural resources including water and its hydraulic force, forests, soils, rivers and other waters, harbors, fisheries, wildlife, minerals, and other natural resources. That portion of the conservation element including waters shall be developed in coordination with any countywide water agency and with all district and city agencies which have developed, served, controlled or conserved water for any purpose for the county or city for which the plan is prepared. The conservation element may also cover:

(1) The reclamation of land and waters.

(2) Flood control.

(3) Prevention and control of the pollution of streams and other waters.

(4) Regulation of the use of land in stream channels and other areas required for the accomplishment of the conservation plan.

(5) Prevention, control, and correction of the erosion of soils, beaches, and shores.

(6) Protection of watersheds.

(7) The location, quantity and quality of the rock, sand and gravel resources.

The conservation element shall be prepared and adopted no later than December 31, 1973.

(e) An open-space element as provided in Article 10.5 (commencing with Section 65560) of this chapter.

(f) A seismic safety element consisting of an identification and appraisal of seismic hazards such as susceptibility to surface ruptures from faulting, to ground shaking to ground failures, or to effects of seismically induced waves such as tsunamis and seiches.

The seismic safety element fhall also include an appraisal of mudslides, landslides, and slope stability as necessary geologic hazards that must be considered simultaneously with other hazards such as possible surface ruptures from faulting, ground shaking, ground failure and seismically induced waves.

(g) A noise element, which shall recognize guidelines adopted by the Office of Noise Control pursuant to Section 39850.] of the Health and Safety Code, and which quantifies the community noise environment in terms of noise exposure contours for both near and long-term levels of growth and traffic activity. Such noise exposure information shall become a guideline for use in development of the land use element to achieve noise compatible land use and also to provide baseline levels and noise source identification for local noise ordinance enforcement.

The sources of environmental noise considered in this analysis shall include * * * but are not limited to the following :

(1) Highways and freeways.

(2) Primary arterials and major local streets.

(3) Passenger and freight on-line railroad operations and ground rapid transit systems.

(4) Commercial, general aviation, heliport, helistop, and military airport operations, aircraft overflights, jet engine test stands, and all other ground facilities and maintenance functions related to airport operation.

(5) Local industrial plants, including, but not limited to, railroad classification yards.

(6) Other ground stationary noise sources identified by local agencies as contributing to the community noise environment.

The noise exposure information shall be presented in terms of noise contours expressed in community noise equivalent level (CNEL) or day-night average level (L_{dn}). CNEL means the average equivalent A-weighted sound level during a 24-hour day, obtained after addition of five decibels to sound levels in the evening from 7 p.m. to 10 p.m. and after addition of 10 decibels to sound levels in the night before 7 a.m. and afer 10 p.m. L_{dn} means the average equivalent A-weighted sound level during a 24-hour day, obtained after addition of 10 decibels to sound levels in the night before 7 a.m. and after 10 p.m.

The * * * contours shall be shown in minimum increments of 5 db and shall continue down to 60 db. For * * * areas deemed noise sensitive, including but not limited to, areas containing schools, hospitals, rest homes, long-term medical or mental care * * * facilities, or any other land use areas deemed noise sensitive by the local jurisdiction, the noise exposure shall be determined by monitoring.

A part of the noise element shall also include the preparation of a community noise exposure inventory, current and projected, which identifies the number of persons exposed to various levels of noise throughout the community.

The noise element shall also recommend mitigating measures and possible solutions to existing and foreseeable noise problems. * * *

The state, local, or private agency responsible for the construction, * * * maintenance, or operation of those transportation, industrial, or other commercial facilities specified in paragraph 2 of this subdivision shall provide to the local agency producing the general plan, specific data relating to current and projected levels of activity and a detailed methodology for the development of noise contours given this supplied data, or they shall provide noise contours as specified in the foregoing statements.

It shall be the responsibility of the local agency preparing the general plan to specify the manner in which the noise element will be integrated into the city or county's zoning plan and tied to the land use and circulation elements and to the local noise ordinance. The noise element, once adopted shall also become the guideline for determining compliance with the state's noise insulation standards, as contained in Section 1092 of Title 25 of the California Administrative Code.

(h) A scenic highway element for the development, establishment, and protection of scenic highways pursuant to the provisions of Article 2.5 (commencing with Section 260) of Chapter 2 of Division 1 of the Streets and Highways Code.

(i) A safety element for the protection of the community from fires and geologic hazards including features necessary for such protection as evacuation routes, peak load and water supply requirements, minimum road widths, clearances around structures, and geologic hazard mapping in areas of known geologic hazards.

§ 65303. Elements permitted as part of plan

The general plan may include the following elements or any part or phase thereof:

(a) A recreation element showing a comprehensive system of areas and public sites for recreation, including the following, and, when practicable, their locations and proposed development.

(1) Natural reservations.

(2) Parks.

(3) Parkways.

(4) Beaches.

(5) Playgrounds.

(6) Other recreation areas.

(b) The circulation element provided for in Section 65302(b) may also include recommendations concerning parking facilities and building set-back lines and the delineations of such systems on the land; a system of street naming, house and building numbering; and such other matters as may be related to the improvement of circulation of traffic.

(c) A transportation element showing a comprehensive transportation system, including locations of rights-of-way, terminals, viaducts, and grade separations. This element of the plan may also include port, harbor, aviation, and related facilities.

(d) A transit element showing a proposed system of transit lines, including rapid transit, streetcar, motor coach and trolley coach lines, and related facilities.

(e) A public services and facilities element showing general plans for sewerage, refuse disposal, drainage, and local utilities, and rights-of-way, easements, and facilities for them.

(f) A public building element showing locations and arrangements of civic and community centers, public schools, libraries, police and fire stations, and other public buildings, including their architecture and the landscape treatment of their grounds.

(g) A community design element consisting of standards and principles governing the subdivision of land, and showing recommended designs for community and neighborhood development and redevelopment, including sites for schools, parks, playgrounds and other uses.

(h) A housing element consisting of standards and plans for the elimination of substandard dwelling conditions.

(i) A redevelopment element consisting of plans and programs for the elimination of slums and blighted areas and for community redevelopment, including housing sites, business and industrial sites, public building sites, and for other purposes authorized by law.

(j) A historical preservation element for the identification, establishment and protection of sites and structures of architectural historical, archaeological or cultural significance, including significant trees, hedgerows and other plant materials. The historical preservation element shall include a program which develops actions to be taken in accomplishing the policies set forth in this element.

Guidelines shall be developed by the Office of Planning and Research by February 1, 1976 in consultation with appropriate public and private organizations concerned with historical preservation.

(k) Such additional elements dealing with other subjects which in the judgement of the planning agency relate to the physical development of the county or city.

BAKER

v.

CITY OF MILWAUKIE

533 P.2d 772 (Oregon, 1975)

HOWELL, Justice.

This is an appeal from the dismissal of a writ of mandamus. The plaintiff sought to compel the City of Milwaukie to conform a zoning ordinance to its comprehensive plan, to cancel a variance approved by the Milwaukie Planning Commission, and to suspend the issuance of building permits in areas of the city where the zoning ordinance allows a more intensive use than that set forth in the comprehensive plan. The trial court sustained the City's demurrer to the alternative writ. The plaintiff refused to plead further and the court dismissed the writ. The Court of Appeals reversed the action of the trial court but on grounds not substantially in favor of the plaintiff, and plaintiff's petition for review to this court was allowed.

Basically, the petition for the alternative writ states that plaintiff is a landowner in the City of Milwaukie. On October 17, 1968, the City of Milwaukie adopted a zoning ordinance which designated plaintiff's land and the surrounding area "A 1 B" (residential apartment-business office). This category allowed 39 units per acre. On November 11, 1969, a comprehensive plan for the City of Milwaukie was adopted by the Planning Commission. This comprehensive plan designated plaintiff's land and the surrounding area as high density residential, allowing 17 units per acre. On January 12, 1970, the Milwaukie City Council passed a resolution adopting the above plan as the comprehensive plan for the City of Milwaukie.

On February 27, 1973, without public hearing and against staff recommendation, the Milwaukie City Planning Commission granted a variance authorizing a proposed 95-unit apartment complex near plaintiff's property with one and one-half parking spaces per unit rather than the required two.

Subsequent to the granting of the variance, an application was made for a building permit for the construction of a 102-unit apartment on property immediately adjacent to plaintiff's property. This 102—unit complex would result in 26 units per acre—less than the 39 units allowed by the zoning ordinance but substantially more than the 17 units allowed by the comprehensive plan.

After demand was made on the City Council and the Building Inspector to conform the zoning ordinance to the comprehensive plan, to cancel the variance previously granted, and to suspend the issuance of building permits where the zoning in the city did not conform to the comprehensive plan, the plaintiff brought this proceeding.

* * *

The Comprehensive Plan is the Controlling Land Use Planning Instrument for the City of Milwaukie.

The defendants argue that "the zoning ordinance would govern land use with a definite and precise requirement, and would control over the comprehensive plan." Thus the defendants contend that although the City has passed a comprehensive plan, there is no duty to effectuate it through the enactment of conforming zoning ordinance. They further argue that the present conflicting zoning ordinances remain in effect until the City decides to replace them with ordinances which are in accord with the comprehensive plan.

We agree with the plaintiff and the amici curiae that the position of defendants evidences a fundamental misunderstanding of the relationship between planning and zoning.

In order to answer the question of whether a city, once it has adopted a comprehensive plan, has a duty to zone in accord with that plan, it is first necessary to discuss the relationship between planning and zoning.

This court has recently recognized the controlling effect of the comprehensive plan on land use planning in a community:

"The basic instrument for county or municipal land use planning is the 'comprehensive plan.' * * * The plan has been described as a general plan to control and direct the use and development of property in a municipality.* * *" Fasano v. Washington Co. Comm.

Zoning, on the other hand, is the means by which the comprehensive plan is effectuated.

This servient relationship of zoning to planning was acknowledged in Oregon in 1919 with the passage of the requirement that municipal zoning be "in accord with a well considered plan." " 'Instead of being the city plan, for which it is so mistaken, * * * zoning is but one of the devices for giving effect to it.' " Haar, The Master Plan: An Impermanent Constitution, 20 Law & Contemp. Prob. 353, 362 (1955). *See also* Udell v. Haas.

Some writers have likened the comprehensive plan to a constitution. Thus it has been said that a comprehensive plan is a "constitution for all future development within the city." O'Loane v. O'Rourke.

"* * * If the plan is regarded not as the vest-pocket tool of the planning commission, but as a broad statement to be adopted by the most representative municipal body—the local legislature—then the plan becomes a law through such adoption. A unique type of law, it should be noted, in that it purports to bind future legislatures when they enact implementary materials. So far as impact is concerned, the law purports to control the enactment of other laws (the so-called implementary legislation) solely. It thus has the cardinal characteristic of a constitution. * * *" Haar, supra at 375.

While this analogy between a comprehensive plan and a constitution may be helpful in determining the relationship between planning and zoning, it must be remembered that the comprehensive plan is flexible and subject to change when the needs of the community demand. "[U]nlike [a constitution] it is subject to amendatory procedures not significantly different from the course followed in enacting ordinary legislation." Haar, supra at 375.* * *

Conclusion In summary, we conclude that a comprehensive plan is the controlling land use planning instrument for a city. Upon passage of a comprehensive plan a city assumes a responsibility to effectuate that plan and conform prior conflicting zoning ordinances to it. We further hold that the zoning decisions of a city must be in accord with that plan and a zoning ordinance which allows a more intensive use than that prescribed in the plan must fail.

B. PRE-ZONING LAND USE CONTROLS

The first comprehensive zoning ordinance was adopted in 1916, but prior to this time the use of land was regulated by several techniques. Starting in the Middle Ages, two techniques of land use regulation were developed that are still in effect today. These techniques are (1) judicial land use regulation through the **nuisance doctrine,** and (2) **private agreements** to regulate land use.

(1) Nuisance Doctrine

A **nuisance,** in the context of land use, may be defined as an unreasonable and substantial interference with the use or enjoyment of one's property without an actual physical trespass or unauthorized physical entry. The concept originated as an equitable remedy, and it is an important element of both the law of torts (i.e., private wrongs or injuries) and property law. If a nuisance is established, a court may enjoin the activities of the defendant that are the cause of the nuisance. The nuisance doctrine is alive and well today as exemplified by a number of recent cases involving complex technological and environmental problems. In addition, the nuisance doctrine operates concurrently with zoning regulations and thus, land uses that are allowed by zoning regulations may nevertheless be barred by the nuisance doctrine. N.J. CONST. Art. I, par. 1.

(A) Definition of Nuisance

An owner of property is entitled to enjoy its use without unreasonable interference by his neighbors. The nuisance issue arises when someone uses his property in a manner that causes annoyance, inconvenience, discomfort or damage to the owner of other property. It is possible for someone to inflict this harm without every crossing a boundary line or coming into personal contact. If one landowner creates noise or smells, or carries on any activity that is offensive or dangerous, and thus deprives another landowner of reasonable enjoyment of his property, the courts may call this activity a "nuisance" and provide a legal remedy.

(B) Examples of nuisance

i. Noise. Some noise is so annoying that it can appreciably diminish the enjoyment of an owner's property. In fact, noise can be so disturbing that it can effect the peace and health of persons subjected to its impact. For example, if someone habitually makes noise that is so loud and unusual in the neighborhood that other residents cannot sleep, read, concentrate, or converse normally until it stops, this noise is an unreasonable invasion of property rights and is a nuisance. Of course, if a house is in the center of a city, the owner cannot insist upon the quiet that he would expect in the country. Also, to be a nuisance the noise must be of such a nature as to disturb a person of normal sensitivity. If someone is sick or otherwise especially sensitive to sound he cannot impose his need for unusual quiet and stillness on his neighbors.

The question of whether any particular noise or sound constitutes a nuisance depends again upon the particular circumstances. In one case a court held that the ringing of church bells caused a substantial annoyance to the residents of the adjoining houses and that it was a nuisance. Another court ruled that the ringing of church bells in a heavily populated area was not a nuisance even though it did disturb a particular sick and sensitive person.

ii. Smells, smoke, and fumes. Every landowner is entitled to have in and around his property reasonably pure and wholesome air, consistent with the locality in which he lives. If someone carries on any activity or business that creates smells, smoke, or fumes which are offensive and make living uncomfortable, then such activity or business may constitute a nuisance.

Whether any particular smell or amount of smoke constitutes a nuisance depends upon the circumstances. The locality and surroundings must be considered. A smell may be objectionable in a residential area but common in a manufacturing area. Furthermore, the smell or smoke must cause an appreciable ámount of annoyance or discomfort. It is not enough for the plaintiff to claim that he is an unusually delicate or fastidious individual. One court held that the smell and smoke of burning leaves did not constitute a nuisance, but excessive smoke from burning rags and other offensive materials is a nuisance. Other courts have held that offensive cesspools and defective septic tanks constitute a nuisance. In various cases courts have held a fertilizer factory, a slaughter house, and a garbage plant to be nuisances because of the offensive odors which they produced.

iii. Dangerous or offensive conditions.

(a) Garbage. A landowner may create a nuisance if he deposits his garbage on his own property in such place and manner as to cause offensive odors or to invite vermin and rodents. However, in one case a court held that it is not a nuisance for a person to use his vacant lot to dump refuse when the only objection was that it is unsightly.

(b) Insects. In one case a court held that it is a nuisance to permit to exist, conditions which lead to the breeding of mosquitos, flies, or other disease-carrying insects.

(c) Cesspools and Septic Tanks. Cesspools and septic tanks which do not function properly, or are so constructed or maintained as to threaten or impair health, are nuisances.

(C) Legal Remedies Against Nuisance

If someone creates conditions that constitute a nuisance, the following legal remedies may be available:

(i) **Injunction.** Under some circumstances, a court will issue an injunction, ordering the offending landowner to cease the activity or remove the conditions creating the nuisance. The remedy of injunction is usually available where irreparable injury may result and where the nuisance is continuous or recurrent. In any case, the remedy is a matter of discretion of the court.

(ii) **Damages.** A landowner may sue to recover damages caused by the nuisance, no matter how slight or difficult to assess in monetary terms. If monetary damages are insignificant, he may be entitled to nominal damages. If the nuisance is willful or malicious, he may be entitled to punitive damages.

(iii) **Criminal Action.** A landowner may be subject to criminal penalties for creating a public nuisance. A public nuisance is an offense against the state. A condition which creates a hazard or annoyance to the public at large is a public nuisance.

(iv) **Self-Help.** Under limited circumstances, a landowner may resort to self-help to abate the nuisance, if he can do it without a breach of the peace.

(D) Objectionable Public Activities

Closely related to the problem of private nuisance caused by a private landowner, is the troublesome question of governmental activities which may interfere with, and disturb the quiet enjoyment of private property. In this situation, the activity itself is socially desirable or even necessary, but it creates noise, light, crowds, or other disturbance to residents in the immediate vicinity. Examples of this type of activity are airports, firehouses, schools, and churches.

(i) **Airports.** A landowner whose house is located in the immediate vicinity of an airport may be deprived of the peaceful enjoyment of his home by noise, vibration, dust, and light. Most homeowners whose houses are so situated do not have a legal remedy because the courts have held that the existence of an airport, in and of itself, is not a nuisance. To obtain help from the courts, a complaining homeowner must be able to prove that the airport is operated in an unreasonable manner that creates a nuisance. Some of the complaints which the courts have been asked to pass upon are excessive dust, low-flying planes, and noise.

(a) *Dust.* In one case a court held that the operation of a municipal airport was a nuisance because it created excessive amounts of dust which filtered into nearby houses and caused inconvenience, injury, and illness to the residents. In spite of this case, the general rule seems to be that a certain amount of dust and noise are incidental to the operation of an airport and they will not constitute a nuisance even though they cause discomfort and injury to residents nearby.

(b) *Low-Flying Planes.* Low-flying planes raise another interesting legal issue. Historically, the ownership of land has always included the right to all the land downward, indefinitely, and the right to all the airspace upward, indefinitely. With the development of the airplane, the right to the airspace above has been limited to only that space the owner reasonably needs. It is clear that an airplane which flies at a high altitude does not commit a trespass on the land below. However, if an airplane flies low enough, it will commit a trespass on the land below by flying through airspace which is the private property of the owner of the land. This legal issue has been raised in lawsuits against airports by owners of houses in the airport's immediate periphery, where planes pass close to rooftops when taking off and landing.

(c) *Noise.* The noise problem exists all year long, but becomes acute in warm weather when the windows of the house are open wide and the average homeowner spends more time on his patio or in his backyard. During this time of year, a homeowner who lives in or around a major city must expect the quiet and tranquility of his home to be jarred by the recurrent deafening roar of transcontinental jets. The demand for faster transportation has led to ever bigger and more powerful aircraft engines that only aggravate the noise problem. The technological development has raised legal questions which still have not been resolved.

The problem of aircraft noise is another interesting illustration of two political forces creating a legal conflict for which there is no easy solution. One political force consists of the local homeowners, who demand that aircraft use mufflers and other sound inhibitors to lessen noise; that aircraft be limited to flight patterns which avoid populated areas; and that in taking off they be required to gain altitude at a steep angle, rather than at a gradual angle and limit the area subject to noise disturbance. The other political force is represented by the various governmental agencies responsible for the safety of aircraft; they oppose any suggestion tending to increase the hazard to aircraft, pilots, or passengers.

(ii) **Schools, Firehouses, Hospitals, and Playgrounds.** No one can reasonably deny the need for, and desirability of, schools, firehouses, hospitals, and similar community facilities. However, most homeowners would also prefer to have these functions performed next to someone else's house rather than their own.

(iii) **Churches.** A church or other place of worship may be objectionable to the adjoining homeowner even if he is a member of that same congregation. The crowds, traffic, parked cars, and activity associated with church services and functions do impair the quiet enjoyment of a house. Restrictive covenants may prevent the building of a church. In a famous case in New York, the court held that where a restrictive covenant limited the use of the land to "dwellings," a church could not be built where the adjoining homeowner (who was a member of the same church) would not consent to it.

HULBERT

v.

CALIFORNIA PORTLAND CEMENT CO.

161 Cal. 239, 118 P. 928 (1911)

MELVIN, J. Petitioner has made an original application to this court to suspend the operation of a certain injunction until the decision of the appeals in two cases, in each of which the California Portland Cement Company, a corporation, is the defendant, on the ground that the property of the corporation would be so greatly damaged by the operation of the injunction pending the appeals that a judgment in defendant's favor would be almost fruitless; while it is contended the damage to plaintiffs is easily susceptible of satisfaction by a payment of money. Petitioner offers to furnish any bond this court may require, if the order which is prayed for shall be granted. As this was the first case in America, so far as this court knew, in which the operation of a cement plant had been enjoined because of the dust produced in the processes of manufacture, and as the showing which was made indicated that petitioner's loss would be very great if the injunction were enforced at once, an order was entered, temporarily staying its operation until both sides to the controversy could be heard. The court was moved somewhat to such action also because the trial court had made an order staying the operation of the injunction for 60 days, so that this court might have the opportunity of passing upon this application. Two principal questions are presented: (1) Has the Supreme Court the authority in aid of its appellate jurisdiction, under section 4 of article 6 of the Constitution, to suspend the operation of an injunction pending appeal? (2) If it have such power, is this a proper case for the exercise thereof? Owing to the conclusion which we have reached, it is unnecessary to answer the first question authoritatively, because, assuming a reply to it in the affirmative, we cannot say that the facts of this case warrant any other response to the second inquiry than a negative one.

The salient facts shown by the petitioner are that the California Portland Cement Company is engaged in the manufacture of cement on property situated nearly two miles from the center of the city of Colton, in the county of San Bernardino, but not within the limits of said city; that said manufactory is located at Slover mountain, where the substances necessary to the production of Portland cement are quarried; that long before the surrounding country had been generally devoted to the production of citrus fruits Slover mountain had been known as a place where limestone was produced; that quarries of marble and limestone had been established there; that lime kilns had been operated upon said mountain for many years; that in 1891 the petitioner obtained title to said premises, and commenced thereon the manufacture of Portland cement; that the said corporation has expended upon said property more than $800,000; that at the time when petitioner began the erection of the cement plant the land surrounding the plant was vacant and unimproved, except some land lying to the north. which had been planted to young citrus trees; that these trees were first planted about a year before the erection of the cement plant was commenced (but long after the lime kilns and the marble quarries had been operated) that subsequently other orange groves have been planted in the neighborhood; that the petitioner's plant on Slover mountain has a capacity of 3,000 barrels of cement per day; but that by the judgment of the superior court in two certain actions against petitioner, entitled Lillie A. Hulbert, Administratrix, etc., v. California Portland Cement Company, a Corporation, and Spencer E. Gilbert, plaintiff, v. Same Defendant, the corporation aforesaid was enjoined from operating its plant in such manner as to produce an excess of 88,706 barrels of finished cement per annum; that the regular pay roll of the company includes the names of about 500 men, who are paid about $35,000 a month; that the fixed, constant monthly expenses for supplies and materials amount to $35,000; that the California Portland Cement Company employs the best, most modern methods in its processes of manufacture, but that nevertheless there is an unavoidable escape into the air of certain dust and smoke; that petitioner has no other location for the conduct of its business at a profit; that the land of the Hulbert estate is located from 1,500 to 2,500 feet from petitioner's cement works, and that Spencer E. Gilbert's land is all within 1,000 feet therefrom; that petitioner has diligently sought some means of prepenting the excape of dust from its factories; that it has consulted the best experts and sought the best information obtainable, and that it is now and has been for a long time conducting experiments along the lines suggested by the most eminent engineering authorities upon this subject, and that as soon as any process can be evolved for preventing the escape of the dust, the petitioner will adopt such process in its works, and it is believed that a process now constructing with all diligence by petitioner will effectually prevent the escape of dust. Petitioner also alleges that it is easily possible to estimate the damages of the plaintiffs in money, while it is utterly impracticable to estimate the damages of the plaintiffs in money, while it is utterly impracticable to estimate the damage in money which will be caused to the petitioner by the closing of the plant, and that stopping the plant pending the appeals will cause financial ruin to the chief stockholders of the petitioner, and that the elements of loss averred are irreparable on account of the disorganization of petitioner's working force, loss of market, and deterioration of machinery.

The learned judge of the superior court, in deciding the cases in which petitioner here was defendant, described the method of manufacturing cement and the injury to the trees. He said, in part: "The output from these two mills at the present time is about 2,500 barrels of cement every 24 hours, and to produce this there is fed into the various kilns of the defendant, during the time mentioned, about 1,500,000 pounds of raw mix, composed of limestone and clay, ground as fine as flour and thoroughly mixed. This raw mix is fed into the tops of kilns, wherein the temperature varies from 1,800 to 3,000 degrees Fahrenheit, and through which kilns the heated air and combustion gases pass at the rate of many thousands of feet per minute. The result of this almost inconceivable draft is to carry out, in addition to the usual products of combustion, particles of the raw mix, to the extent of probably 20 tons per day or more, the greater part of which, without question, is carried up into the air by the rising gases, and thereafter, through the action of the winds and force of gravity, distributed over the surrounding territory." Speaking of the premises of the plaintiffs, he said that, because of prevailing westerly winds and on account of the proximity of the mills, said lands were almost continually subject to the deposit of dust. In this regard he said: "It is the fact incontrovertibly established by both the testimony of witnesses and personal inspections made by the court that a well-nigh continuous shower of cement dust, emanating from defendant's cement mills and caused by their operation, is, and for some years past has been, falling upon the properties of the plaintiffs, covering and coating the ground, filtering through their homes, into all parts. thereof, forming an opaque semi-cemented incrustation upon the upper sides of all exposed flowers and foliage, particularly leaves of citrus trees, and leaving ineradicable, yet withal plainly discernable, marks and evidence of dust, dusty deposits, and grayish colorings resulting therefrom, upon the citrus fruits. The incrustations above mentioned, unlike the deposits occasionally occurring on leaves because of the presence of undue amounts of road dust or field dust, are not dissipated by the strongest winds, nor washed off through the action of the most protracted rains. Their presence, from repeated observations, seems to be as continuous as their hold upon the leaves seems tenacious." The court further found that the deposit of dust on the fruit decreased its value; that the constant presence of dust on the limbs and leaves of the trees rendered the cultivation of the ground and the harvesting of the crop more costly than it would have been under ordinary conditions; and that said dust added to the usual and ordinary discomforts of life by its presence in the homes of the plaintiffs. The court also found that the operation of the old mill of the defendant corporation had occurred with the acquiescence of the plaintiffs, and that the defendant had acquired a prescriptive right to manufacture the maximum quantity of cement produced annually by that factory.

In view of such facts solemnly found by the court after trial, we cannot say that there is reason for a suspension by this court of the injunction, even conceding that we have power under proper circumstances thus to prevent a disturbance of existing conditions, pending an appeal. We are not insensible to the fact that petitioner's business is a very important enterprise; that its location is peculiarly adapted for the manufacture of cement; and that great loss may result to the corporation by the enforcement of the injunction. Even if the officers of the corporation are willing to furnish a bond in a sum equal to the value of the properties of Gilbert and of the Hulbert estate here involved, we cannot, under plain principles of equity, compel these plaintiffs to have recourse to their action at law only, and take from them the benefit of the injunctive relief accorded them by the chancellor below. To permit the cement company to continue its operations, even to the extent of destroying the property of the two plaintiffs and requiring payment of the full value thereof, would be, in effect, allowing the seizure of private property for a use other than a public one—something unheard of and totally unauthorized in the law. Nor may we say, as petitioner urges us to declare, that cement dust is not a nuisance, and therefore that the restraint imposed is illegal, even though this is one of the first cases, if not the very first, of its kind, in which the emission of cement dust from a factory has been enjoined, for we are bound by the findings of the court in this proceeding, and may not consider their sufficiency or lack of it until we take up the appeals on their merits. The court has found that the plaintiffs in the actions tried were specially damaged by a nuisance maintained by the cement company. This entitles the plaintiffs, not only to damages, but to such relief as the facts warrant, and the chancellor has determined that limiting the production in the manner selected is a proper form of protection to their rights. It is well settled in California that a nuisance which consists in pouring soot or the like upon the property of a neighbor in such manner as to interfere with the comfortable enjoyment of the premises is a private nuisance, which may be enjoined or abated, and for which, likewise, the persons specially injured may recover pecuniary damages. . . . The last-named case was one in which the operation of a gas factory had been enjoined, and the following language was used: "A gas factory does not constitute a nuisance per se. The manufacture in or near a great city of gas for illuminating and heating is not only legitimate, but is very necessary to the comfort of the people. But in this, as in any other sort of lawful business, the person conducting it is subject to the rule, "Sic utere tuo ut alienum non laedas," even when operating under municipal permission, or under public obligation to furnish a commodity. Nor will the adoption of the most approved appliances and methods of production justify the continuance of that which, in spite of them, remains a nuisance.

Petitioner contends for the rule that the resulting injuries must be balanced by the court, and that, where the hardship inflicted upon one party by the granting of an injunction would be very much greater than that which would be suffered by the other party if the nuisance were permitted to continue, injunctive relief should be denied. This doctrine of "the balance of hardship" and the associated rule that "an injunction is not of right but of grace" are the bases of petitioner's argument, and many authorities in support of them have been called to our attention. In petitioner's behalf are cited such cases as Richards' Appeal, where an injunction which had been sought to restrain defendant from using large quantities of bituminous coal to plaintiff's damage was refused, and the plaintiff was remitted to his action at law; the court saying, among other things: "Whatever of injury may have or shall result to his (the plaintiff's) property from the defendant's works, by reason of a nuisance complained of, is only such as is incident to a lawful business conducted in the ordinary way, and by no unusual means. Still, there may be injury to the plaintiff, but this of itself may not entitle him to the remedy he seeks. It may not, if ever so clearly established, be a cause in which equity ought to enjoin the defendant in the use of a material necessary to the successful production of an article of such prime necessity as good iron, especially if it be very certain that a greater injury would ensue by enjoining than would result by refusal to enjoin." The same rule was announced in Dilworth's Appeal, a case involving the building of a powder house near plaintiff, and in Huckenstine's Appeal. Petitioner admits that in the later case of Sullivan v. Jones & Laughlin Steel Co., supra, the Supreme Court of Pennsylvania reached a different conclusion, but contends that the opinion in that case merely defines the word "grace" as used in Huckenstine's Appeal: the real meaning of the expression "an injunction is a matter of grace" being that a high degree of discretion is exercised by a chancellor in awarding or denying an injunction. An examination of the case, however, shows that the court went very much further than a mere definition of the phrase "of grace." In that case the defendant had erected a large factory for the manufacture of steel on land purchased from one of the plaintiffs, but after many years defendant had commenced the use of "Mesaba" ore, which caused the emission of great quantities of fine dust upon the property of plaintiffs. The Supreme Court of Pennsylvania, in reversing the decree of the lower court, dismissing the bill, went into the matter of "balancing injuries" and "injunctions of grace" very thoroughly, and we may with propriety, I think, quote and adopt some of its language upon these subjects as follows:

"It is urged that, an an injunction is a matter of grace, and not of right, and more injury would result in awarding than refusing it, it ought not to go out in this case. A chancellor does act as of grace, but that grace sometimes becomes a matter of right to the suitor in its court, and, when it is clear that the law cannot give protection and relief—to which the complainant in equity is admittedly entitled—the chancellor can no more withhold his grace than the law can deny protection and relief, if able to give them. This is too often overlooked when it is said that in equity a decree is of grace, and not of right, as a judgment at law. In Walters v. McElroy et al. the defendants gave as one of the reasons why the plaintiff's bill should be dismissed that his land was worth but little, while they were engaged in a great mining industry, which would be paralyzed if they should be enjoined from a continuance of the acts complained of; and the principle was invoked that, as a decree in equity is of grace, a chancellor will never enjoin an act where, by so doing, greater injury will result than from a refusal to enjoin. To this we said: The phrase "of grace," predicated of a decree in equity, had its origin in an age when kings dispensed their royal favors by the hands of their chancellors; but, although it continues to be repeated occasionally, it has no rightful place in the jurisprudence of a free commonwealth, and ought to be relegated to the age in which it was appropriate. It has been somewhere said that equity has its laws, as law has its equity. This is but another form of saying that equitable remedies are administered in accordance with rules as certain as human wisdom can devise, leaving their application only in doubtful cases to the discretion, not the unmerited favor or grace, of the chancellor. Certainly no chancellor in any English-speaking country will at this day admit that he dispenses favors or refuses rightful demands, or deny that, when a suitor has brought his case clearly within the rules of equity jurisprudence the relief he asks is demandable ex debito justitiae, and needs not to be implored ex gratia. And as to the principle invoked, that a chancellor will refuse to enjoin when greater injury will result from granting than from refusing an injunction, it is enough to observe that it has no application where the act complained of is in itself, as well as in its incidents, tortious. In such case it cannot be said that injury would result from an injunction, for no man can complain that he is injured by being prevented from doing to the hurt of another that which he has no right to do. Nor can it make the slightest difference that the plaintiff's property is of insignificant value to him, as compared with the advantages that would accrue to the defendants from its occupation.' There can be no balancing of conveniences when such balancing involves the preservation of an established right, though possessed by a peasant only to a cottage as his home, and which will be extinguished if relief is not granted against one who would destroy it in artificially using his own land. Though it is said a chancellor will consider whether he would not do a greater injury by enjoining than would result from refusal, and leaving the party to his redress at the hands of a court and jury, and if, in conscience, the former should appear, he will refuse to enjoin (Richards' Appeal, supra), that 'it often becomes a grave question whether so great an injury would not be done to the community by enjoining the business that the complaining party should be left to his remedy at law' (Dilworth's Appeal, supra), and similar expressions are to be found in other cases, 'none of them, nor all of them, can be authority for the proposition that equity, a case for its cognizance being otherwise made out, will refuse to protect a man in the possession and enjoyment of his property, because that right is less valuable to him than the power to destroy it may be to his neighbor or to the public.' The right of a man to use and enjoy his property is as supreme as his neighbor's, and no artificial use of it by either can be permitted to destroy that of the other." . . .

Let the temporary order staying the operation of the injunction be dismissed, and the petition be denied.

But see *Boomer v. Atlantic Cement Co.*, 26 N.Y.2d 219, 309 N.Y. Supp. 2d 312, 257 N.E.2d 870 (1970), where the New York highest appellate court denied an injunction in a similar factual situation because of a finding that the socio-economic consequences of an injunction create problems that are more appropriately addressed by the legislature than the judiciary.

2. Private Agreements

Various types of **private agreements** can be used to restrict or control the use of land. Examples of such agreements are: covenants running with the land, conditions, easements, restrictions, and leases.

A **covenant running with the land** is more than a personal contract. A covenant is contractual in nature, but it is also enforceable by or against subsequent purchasers of the property from the original contracting parties as long as its burdens and benefits are found to "run with the land".

The requirements for a covenant to run with the land may become clear from the following illustrations: Suppose Beyer purchases land from Celler adjoining

Celler's property and in the deed promises to use the land only for a single family residence If Beyer decides not to build and sells the land to Builder who seeks to build a gas station on the property, can Celler or his successors enjoin the building of the gas station? A simplified answer is that if the restrictive covenant is duly recorded, subsequent purchasers will be charged with **"constructive notice"** of the covenant and may be enjoined from violating the covenant. **"Constructive notice"** means that the court imputes notice to purchasers of land if the deed is properly recorded or if there are sufficient facts to show that they should have known that there was a covenant restricting the use of the property. Restrictive covenants running with the land are enforced by the courts unless they are discriminatory in terms of race. See *Shelley v. Kramer*, 334 U.S. 1, 68 S.Ct. 836, 92L.Ed. 1161 (1948).

A **condition** is similar to a covenant but the resolution of a condition has more direct and dramatic consequences. For example, suppose Celler sells land to Beyer with a provision in the deed providing, "on the condition that said property be used only for the purposes of a single family residence . . . " The words "on the condition that" are key technical words that indicate that Beyer's ownership is subject to a condition subsequent. If the land is used for any purpose other than a single family residence, the condition has been broken and Celler, who holds a future interest called a power of termination, automatically regains title to the property.

An **easement** is a right of one person to use someone else's land for a limited purpose. Easements are created in one of the following ways: by agreement, by eminent domain, by implication, or by prescription. **Easements by agreement** are created by express grants by one party to allow another to use the grantor's land for a limited purpose. For example, A might expressly agree to allow B to walk across his property. The government may create easements by using the **power of eminent domain**, to acquire a right of way and to compensate the owner for the taking of that limited use. **Easements by implication** arise from circumstances surrounding the divison of one's land into two or more parcels and the conveyance of one parcel to another person. For instance, if Celler sells a piece of land to Beyer which is completely surrounded by Celler's property and the deed of conveyance does not mention any right of ingress and egress, then Beyer may seek a judicial remedy of an easement by implication for limited use of an existing driveway across Celler's property. An **easement by prescription** is a right to use someone else's property that arises from a continued use of that property. For example, if Owner permits Walker to cross his property on his way to work each morning, after a period of time Walker will acquire an easement by prescription that will give him the right to continue to use Owner's land. Easements by prescription arise in a manner similar to **adverse possession**. However, adverse possession gives the adverse user a right to *ownership,* whereas an easement by prescription only gives the adverse user a *limited right of use.* Both adverse possession and easements by prescription require that the possession or use be *adverse and hostile, open and notorious,* and *continuous.* The claim must be adverse and hostile to the owner's possession. The claimant need not be violent toward the owner. Rather his claim must be adverse in the sense that he must not have been given consent by the owner. The adverse claimant's possession or use must be such that the owner of the property has some opportunity to know that someone is making a claim on or using his land. The possession or use must be continuous for a period of time required by state statutes (usually from 10 to 2 years). To be continuous there must also be no break or interruption in the use or adverse possession of the land.

Restriction is a generic term that describes various land use limitations that are incorporated in subdivision plats (maps filed in subdivision proceedings) and in the deeds used to convey subdivision lots. For example, a developer might place restrictions in subdivision plats and deeds of conveyance setting minimum lot sizes to protect the value of the other properties bound by the same restrictions.

A **lease** is a common form of private agreement limiting the use of land. Some leases contain many very specific limitations and restrictions on the use of the land.

RHUE
v.
CHEYENNE HOMES, INC.
168 Colo. 6, 449 P.2d 361 (1969)

PRINGLE, Justice.

In the trial court, Cheyenne Homes, Inc., obtained an injunction prohibiting Leonard Rhue and Family Homes, Inc., hereinafter referred to as plaintiffs in error, from moving a thirty year old Spanish style house into a new subdivision which was about 80% improved and which contained only modern ranch style or split level homes.

At the time that the subdivision in which the plaintiffs in error seek to locate this house was platted, the owner placed upon the entire area certain restrictive covenants contained in a "Declaration of Protective Covenants," which was duly recorded. As recited in the document, these protective covenants were for the purpose of "protecting the present and future values of the properties located" in the subdivision. Admittedly, the house which the plaintiffs in error wish to put in the subdivision does not violate any of the few specific restrictions contained in the protective covenants. However, paragraph C-2 of the recorded protective covenants contains the following declaration:

"C-2 No building shall be erected, placed or altered on any lot until the construction plans and specifications and a plan showing the location of the structure shall have been approved by the architectural control committee * * * "

Plaintiffs in error failed to submit their plans to the architectural control committee, and the trial court, in entering its injunction, held (1) that such failure constituted a breach of the restrictive covenants, and (2) that the placing of the house would not be in harmony with the existing neighborhood and would depreciate property values in the area.

Plaintiffs in error contend that restriction C-2 is not enforceable because no specific standards are contained therein to guide the committee in determining the approval or disapproval of plans when submitted. We disagree.

It is no secret that housing today is developed by subdividers who, through the use of restrictive covenants, guarantee to the purchaser that his house will be protected against adjacent construction which will impair its value, and that a general plan of construction will be followed. Modern legal authority recognizes this reality and recognizes also that the approval of plans by an architectural control committee is one method by which guarantees of value and general plan of construction can be accomplished and maintained.

So long as the intention of the covenant is clear (and in the present case it is clearly to protect present and future property values in the subdivision), covenants such as the one before us have been upheld against the contention that they lacked specific restrictions providing a framework within which the architectural committee must act. In Kirkley v. Seipelt, supra, the plaintiff in error argued unsuccessfully that a covenant requiring approval of plans failed in the test of reasonableness because there were no standards to guide the approving party.

Nelson v. Farr, upon which plaintiffs in error solely rely, is not dispositive of the instant case. We were concerned there with the propriety of an injunction which imposed certain restrictions on land, even though there were no recorded instruments restricting the use of the affected land.

We have recognized in Colorado that restrictive covenants placed on land for the benefit of purchasers within a subdivision are valid and not against public policy, and are enforceable in equity against all purchasers. While we have here enunciated the proposition that the covenant requiring approval of the architectural committee before erection of a house in the subdivision is enforceable, we point out that there is a corollary to that proposition which affords protection and due process of law to a purchaser of a lot in the subdivison, namely, that a refusal to approve plans must be reasonable and made in good faith and must not be arbitrary or capricious. Kirkley v. Seipelt, supra; Winslette v. Keeler, supra; Hannula v. Hacienda Homes, supra.

Since two of the three committee members testified that they would disapprove the plans if they were presented to them, we examine the evidence to determine if such refusal is warranted under the rules we have laid down. There was testimony that the house was about thirty years old, and the other houses were no older than two years. The house of plaintiffs in error has a stucco exterior and a red tile roof. The other houses are commonly known as ranch style or split level, and are predominantly of brick construction with asphalt shingle roofs. There was further testimony that the style of the house would devalue the surrounding properties because it was "not compatible" with the houses already in place.

One member of the committee expressed concern that the house of plaintiffs in error would devalue surrounding property. The other added that he thought the covenant gave the architectural committee the authority to refuse approval to plans for property which would seriously affect the market value of other homes in the area. Clearly, a judgment of disapproval of the plans by the committee is reasonable and in good faith and in harmony with the purposes declared in the covenant.

The judgment is affirmed.

The City of Houston, Texas does not have a zoning ordinance but uses private agreements to regulate land use. See Comments, "Houston's Invention of Necessity—An Unconstitutional Substitute For Zoning?" 21 *Baylor L. Rev.* 307 (1969). Note, "Municipal Enforcement of Private Restrictive Covenants: An Innovation in Land Use Control," 44 *Texas L. Rev.* 741 (1966).

See generally, Berger, "Conflicts Between Zoning Ordinances and Restrictive Covenants: A Problem in Land Use Policy," 43 *Neb. L. Rev.* 449 (1964); Goldstein, "Rights of Entry and Possibilities of Reverter as Devices to Restrict the Use of Land," 54 *Harv. L. Rev.* 248 (1940).

Restrictions and private agreements can be used by planners when conveying government land or land obtained through eminent domain. Sometimes it is easier to implement desired goals through these types of agreements than through changes in zoning regulations. On the other hand, planners are more often concerned with how to remove various restrictions and agreements.

The courts have developed various principles by which these restrictions and agreements can be ignored or terminated. Under one principle that might be called "change in neighborhood," a court, upon a showing of vast and significant changes in a neighborhood, may refuse to enforce certain restrictions that no longer effectuate the goals they were designed to achieve. This equitable principle is often used to remove restrictions requiring residential use in areas that have become predominantly commercial. The courts will frequently refuse to enforce restrictions in cases where there have been numerous violations by many other people supposedly bound by the same agreements or restrictions. In other cases the courts will not enforce restrictions if they have already been violated by the plaintiff seeking to enforce them. Other courts have held that if a plaintiff had ample opportunity to enforce a restriction, but did not do so within a reasonable time then the restriction should be terminated. In one category of cases, the courts have created a judicial principle that since a covenant is a form of contract, after a long period of time, the obligations are substantially performed and need not be enforced any longer.

There are various non-judicial techniques for the removal of restrictions and agreements. Legislation in some states place time limitations on specific types of restrictions. **Blanket condemnation** through eminent domain proceedings is often used by urban renewal programs to insure that all rights derived from restrictions or agreements are terminated. Such blanket condemnation is often necessary to clear the title to a redevelopment area.

C. CONSTITUTIONAL ISSUES

Zoning regulations often raise one or more constitutional issues. The first issue is whether the *objectives sought to be accomplished by the zoning law are within the scope of the police power,* i.e., general purposes of protecting the health, safety, morality or welfare of the community. In recent years courts have begun to hold that this list of general purposes merely illustrate the scope of the police power and do not delimit it. In fact, the U.S. Supreme Court has stated that . . . "The concept of the public welfare is broad and inclusive . . . The values it represents are spiritual as well as physical, aesthetic as well as monetary." *Berman v. Parker,* 348 U.S. 28, 33 (1954).

A second type of constitutional issue is whether the *method selected to accomplish this objective is so harsh or unreasonable* that it violates the principles of due process of law. To meet the requirements of due process of law, the method selected to accomplish a valid objective must be reasonably calculated to do so without undue hardship. Thus, planners must be concerned with whether the laws used to effectuate a program are reasonably related to legitimate goals and whether they are overly harsh or cause undue hardship. If they are harsh, they will be declared unconstitutional. For example, this issue is raised in cases involving zoning ordinances that restrict the use of land to such an extent that the owner cannot make any reasonable use of his property.

The third type of constitutional issue involves the *equal protection clause* of the Fourteenth Amendment. To meet the requirements of equal protection, the application of the zoning law or regulation must be *non-discriminatory* and (in cases not involving suspect classifications or infringements of fundamental rights) there must be some *rational basis* for subjecting a particular group to the regulation. To meet this constitutional standard, the courts have held that zoning regulations must be in accordance with a comprehensive plan and that they must be comprehensive, i.e., all land within the jurisdiction must be regulated. See *Udell v. Hass,* 23 N.Y. 2d 463, 288 N.Y.S. 2d 888, 235 N.E.2d 897 (1968). Legislative enactments also require that zoning ordinances be comprehensive and in accordance with a comprehensive plan. Thus, the issue of comprehensiveness is both a constitutional and a legislative issue.

The United States Supreme Court decision in *Village of Euclid v. Ambler Realty Company* is the landmark decision in which the constitutionality of zoning laws was upheld. It is one of the few decisions that every student of planning law should know by name.

VILLAGE OF EUCLID

v.

AMBLER REALTY CO.

272 U.S. 365 (1926)

MR. JUSTICE SUTHERLAND delivered the opinion of the Court.

The Village of Euclid is an Ohio municipal corporation. It adjoins and practically is a suburb of the City of Cleveland. Its estimated population is between 5,000 and 10,000, and its area from twelve to fourteen square miles, the greater part of which is farm lands or unimproved acreage. It lies, roughly, in the form of a parallelogram measuring approximately three and one-half miles each way. East and west it is traversed by three principal highways: Euclid Avenue, through the southerly border, St. Clair Avenue, through the central portion, and Lake Shore Boulevard, through the northerly border in close proximity to the shore of Lake Erie. The Nickel Plate railroad lies from 1,500 to 1,800 feet north of Euclid Avenue, and the Lake Shore railroad 1,600 feet farther to the north. The three highways and the two railroads are substantially parallel.

Appellee is the owner of a tract of land containing 68 acres, situated in the westerly end of the village, abutting on Euclid Avenue to the south and the Nickel Plate railroad to the north. Adjoining this tract, both on the east and on the west, there have been laid out restricted residential plats upon which residences have been erected.

On November 13, 1922, an ordinance was adopted by the Village Council, establishing a comprehensive zoning plan for regulating and restricting the location of trades, industries, apartment houses, two-family houses, single family houses, etc., the lot area to be built upon, the size and height of buildings, etc.

The entire area of the village is divided by the ordinance into six classes of use districts, denominated U-1 to U-6, inclusive; three classes of height districts, denominated H-1 to H-3, inclusive; and four classes of area districts, denominated A-1 to A-4, inclusive. The use districts are classified in respect of the buildings which may be erected within their respective limits, as follows:

U-1 is restricted to single family dwellings, public parks, water towers and reservoirs, suburban and interurban electric railway passenger stations and rights of way, and farming, non-commercial greenhouse nurseries and truck gardening; U-2 is extended to include two-family dwellings; U-3 is further extended to include apartment houses, hotels, churches, schools, public libraries, museums, private clubs, community center buildings, hospitals, sanitariums, public playgrounds and recreation buildings, and a city hall and courthouse; U-4 is further extended to include banks, offices, studios, telephone exchanges, fire and police stations, restaurants, theatres and moving picture shows, retail stores and shops, sales offices, sample rooms, wholesale stores for hardware, drugs and groceries, stations for gasoline and oil (not exceeding 1,000 gallons storage) and for ice delivery, skating rinks and dance halls, electric substations, job and newspaper printing, public garages for motor vehicles, stables and wagon sheds (not exceeding five horses, wagons or motor trucks) and distributing stations for central store and commercial enterprises; U-5 is further extended to include billboards and advertising signs (if permitted), warehouses, ice and ice cream manufacturing and cold storage plants, bottling works, milk bottling and central distribution stations, laundries, carpet cleaning, dry cleaning and dyeing establishments, blacksmith, horseshoeing, wagon and motor vehicle repair shops, freight stations, street car barns, stables and wagon sheds (for more than five horses, wagons or motor trucks), and wholesale produce markets and salesrooms; U-6 is further extended to include plants for sewage disposal and for producing gas, garbage and refuse incineration, scrap iron, junk, scrap paper and rag storage, aviation fields, cemeteries, crematories, penal and correctional institutions, insane and feeble minded institutions, storage of oil and gasoline (not to exceed 25,000 gallons), and manufacturing and industrial operations of any kind other than, and any public utility not included in, a class U-1, U-2, U-3, U-4 or U-5 use. There is a seventh class of uses which is prohibited altogether. * * *

The enforcement of the ordinance is entrusted to the inspector of buildings, under rules and regulations of the board of zoning appeals. Meetings of the board are public, and minutes of its proceedings are kept. It is authorized to adopt rules and regulations to carry into effect provisions of the ordinance. Decisions of the inspector of buildings may be appealed to the board by any person claiming to be adversely affected by any such decision. The board is given power in specific cases of practical difficulty or unnecessary hardship to interpret the ordinance in harmony with its general purpose and intent, so that the public health, safety and general welfare may be secure and substantial justice done. Penalties are prescribed for violations, and it is provided that the various provisions are to be regarded as independent and the holding of any provision to be unconstitutional, void or ineffective shall not affect any of the others.

The ordinance is assailed on the grounds that it is in derogation of § 1 of the Fourteenth Amendment to the Federal Constitution in that it deprives appellee of liberty and property without due process of law and denies it the equal protection of the law, and that it offends against certain provisions of the Constitution of the State of Ohio. The prayer of the bill is for an injunction restraining the enforcement of the ordinance and all attempts to impose or maintain as to appellee's property any of the restrictions, limitations or conditions. The court below held the ordinance to be unconstitutional and void, and enjoined its enforcement. * * *

It is specifically averred that the ordinance attempts to restrict and control the lawful uses of appellee's land so as to confiscate and destroy a great part of its value; that it is being enforced in accordance with its terms; that prospective buyers of land for industrial, commercial and residential uses in the metropolitan district of Cleveland are deterred from buying any part of this land because of the existence of the ordinance and the necessity thereby entailed of conducting burdensome and expensive litigation in order to vindicate the right to use the land for lawful and legitimate purposes; that the ordinance constitutes a cloud upon the land, reduces and destroys its value, and has the effect of diverting the normal industrial, commercial and residential development thereof to other and less favorable locations. * * *

It is not necessary to set forth the provisions of the Ohio Constitution which are thought to be infringed. The question is the same under both Constitutions, namely, as stated by appellee: Is the ordinance invalid in that it violates the constitutional protection "to the right of property in the appellee by attempted regulations under the guise of the police power, which are unreasonable and confiscatory?" * * *

The ordinance now under review, and all similar laws and regulations, must find their justification in some aspect of the police power, asserted for the public welfare. The line which in this field separates the legitimate from the illegitimate assumption of power is not capable of precise delimitation. It varies with circumstances and conditions. A regulatory zoning ordinance, which would be clearly valid as applied to the great cities, might be clearly invalid as applied to rural communities. * * *

We find no difficulty in sustaining restrictions of the kind thus far reviewed. The serious question in the case arises over the provisons of the ordinance excluding from residential districts, apartment houses, business houses, retail stores and shops, and other like establishments. This question involves the validity of what is really the crux of the more recent zoning legislation, namely, the creation and maintenance of residential districts, from which business and trade of every sort, including hotels and apartment houses, are excluded. Upon that question this Court has not thus far spoken. The decisions of the state courts are numerous and conflicting; but those which broadly sustain the power greatly outnumber those which deny altogether or narrowly limit it; and it is very apparent that there is a constantly increasing tendency in the direction of the broader view. We shall not attempt to review these decisions at length, but content ourselves with citing a few as illustrative of all.

* * *

The decisions enumerated in the first group cited above agree that the exclusion of buildings devoted to business, trade, etc., from residential districts, bears a rational relation to the health and safety of the community. Some of the grounds for this conclusion are—promotion of the health and security from injury of children and others by separating dwelling houses from territory devoted to trade and industry; suppression and prevention of disorder; facilitating the extinguishment of fires, and the enforcement of street traffic regulations and other general welfare ordinances; aiding the health and safety of the community by excluding from residential areas the confusion and danger of fire, contagion and disorder which in greater or less degree attach to the location of stores, shops and factories. Another ground is that the construction and repair of streets may be rendered easier and less expensive by confining the greater part of the heavy traffic to the streets where business is carried on. * * *

The matter of zoning has received much attention at the hands of commissions and experts, and the results of their investigations have been set forth in comprehensive reports. These reports, which bear every evidence of painstaking consideration, concur in the view that the segregation of residential, business, and industrial buildings will make it easier to provide fire apparatus suitable for the character and intensity of the development in each section; that it will increase the safety and security of home life; greatly tend to prevent street accidents, especially to children, by reducing the traffic and resulting confusion in residential sections; decrease noise and other conditions which produce or intensify nervous disorders; preserve a more favorable environment in which to rear children, etc. With particular reference to apartment houses, it is pointed out that the development of detached house sections is greatly retarded by the coming of apartment houses, which has sometimes resulted in destroying the entire section for private house purposes; that in such sections very often the apartment house is a mere parasite, constructed in order to take advantage of the open spaces and attractive surroundings created by the residential character of the district. Moreover, the coming of one apartment house is followed by others, interfering by their height and bulk with the free circulation of air and monopolizing the rays of the sun which otherwise would fall upon the smaller homes, and bring, as their necessary accompaniments, the disturbing noises incident to increased traffic and business, and the occupation, by means of moving and parked automobiles, of larger portions of the streets, thus detracting from their safety and depriving children of the privilege of quiet and open spaces for play, enjoyed by those in more favored localities,—until, finally, the residential character of the neighborhood and its desirability as a place of detached residences are utterly destroyed. Under these circumstances, apartment houses, which in a different environment would be not only entirely unobjectionable but highly desirable, come very near to being nuisances.

If these reasons, thus summarized, do not demonstrate the wisdom or sound policy in all respects of those restrictions which we have indicated as pertinent to the inquiry, at least, the reasons are sufficiently cogent to preclude us from saying, as it must be said before the ordinance can be declared unconstitutional, that such provisions are clearly arbitrary and unreasonable, having no substantial relation to the public health, safety, morals, or general welfare. * * *

Under these circumstances, therefore, it is enough for us to determine, as we do, that the ordinance in its general scope and dominant features, so far as its provisions are here involved, is a valid exercise of authority, leaving other provisions to be dealt with as cases arise directly involving them. * * *

In the realm of constitutional law, especially, this Court has preceived the embarrassment which is likely to result from an attempt to formulate rules or decide questions beyond the necessities of the immediate issue. It has preferred to follow the method of a gradual approach to the general by a systematically guarded application and extension of constitutional principles to particular cases as they arise, rather than by out of hand attempts to establish general rules to which future cases must be fitted. This process applies with peculiar force to the solution of questions arising under the due process clause of the Constitution as applied to the exercise of the flexible powers of police, with which we are here concerned.

Decree reversed.

For an excellent review of the history of zoning laws and a detailed description of the circumstances leading up to the *Euclid* decision see Toll, *Zoned American* (1969).

In *Nectow v. City of Cambridge*, 277 U.S. 183, 48S. Ct, 447, 72 L.Ed. 842 (1928), the U.S. Supreme Court held a City of Cambridge zoning ordinance invalid as applied to the plaintiff's property upon a finding that "the health, safety, convenience and general welfare of the inhabitants of the part of the city affected will not be promoted by the disposition made by the ordinance of the locus in question."

SHEPARD

v.

SKANEATELES

300 N.Y. 115, 89 N.E.2d 619 (1949)

---

* * *"Zoning law, enacted as they are to promote the health, safety and welfare of the community as a whole. . ., necessarily entail hardships and difficulties for some individual owners. No zoning plan can possibly provide for the general good and at the same time so accommodate the private interests that everyone is satisfied. While precise delimitation is impossible, cardinal is the principle that what is best for the body politic in the long run must prevail over the interests of particular individuals. . . . There must however, be a proper balance between the welfare of the public and the rights of the private owner."

LA SALLE NATIONAL BANK

v.

COUNTY OF COOK

60 Ill.App.2d 39, 208 N.E.2d 430 (1965)

The Illinois Court upheld a zoning board decision refusing to permit the owner of land zoned for industrial use to use the land for a quarry operation. In its decision the court set forth a number of factors to be considered in balancing the interest of the public at large against the rights of a private owner:

A zoning ordinance is presumptively valid and this presumption may be overcome only by clear and convincing evidence. The burden of proof is on the plaintiffs. The validity of each zoning ordinance must be determined on the facts applicable to the particular case, but certain general lines of inquiry have been regarded as relevant, to-wit: (1) existing uses and zoning of nearby property; (2) the extent to which property values are diminished by the particular zoning restrictions; (3) the extent to which the destruction of property values of the plaintiffs promotes the health, safety, morals or general welfare of the public; (4) the relative gain to the public, as compared to the hardship imposed upon the individual property owner; (5) the suitability of the subject property for the zoning purposes; and (6) the length of time the property has been vacant as zoned, considered in the context of land development in the area in the vicinity of the property.

The fact that plaintiffs may suffer a loss in value is not sufficient to establish invalidity. It must also be shown that the public welfare does not require the restriction and resulting loss. All these factors with the exception of the loss to the plaintiffs if they are not allowed to build a quarry, have been considered in our discussion of plaintiffs' argument with respect to the alleged arbitrary action of the County Board.

* * *

After weighing the evidence relating to the public interest and the rights of the private owner of the property regulated the court may determine that the public interest is so slight or the deprivation of the owner is so great that the regulation is "unreasonable" under the circumstances and therefore invalid as a violation of substantive due process.

D. LEGISLATIVE ISSUES

Municipal governments are corporate entities (i.e., legal persons) that are created by the state governments for the purpose of administrating local affairs of a prescribed area. They are creatures of the state governments and have no constitutional right to exist under the federal constitution. In addition, a state legislature may, by general laws, regulate even the local affairs of municipalities. This is important in the context of zoning because all of the zoning powers of the municipality are prescribed, regulated and limited by **state enabling legislation.** Thus, since the enabling acts of most states require that municipal zoning regulations. . ."be in accordance with a comprehensive plan . . .", the question of comprehensiveness becomes a legislative issue. Furthermore, if a municipality's zoning ordinance is not within the powers granted by the state enabling act, then it is characterized as **ultra vires** and is invalid. The governmental power of most states would also permit the state legislature to reorganize the government structure of the municipalities into regional bodies. As a practical matter however, the state legislatures lack the political ability to effectuate such reorganization.

The following provisions from the California Code illustrate typical provisions found in state zoning enabling legislation:

CALIFORNIA CODE

§ 65850. Scope of power to regulate by ordinance

Pursuant to the provisions of this chapter, the legislative body of any county or city by ordinance may:

(a) Regulate the use of buildings, structures and land as between * * * industry, business, residents, open space, including agriculture, recreation, enjoyment of scenic beauty and use of natural resources, and other purposes.

(b) Regulate signs and billboards.

(c) Regulate location, height, bulk, number of stories and size of buildings and structures; the size and use of lots, yards, courts and other open spaces; the percentage of a lot which may be occupied by a building or structure; the intensity of land use.

(d) Establish requirements for offstreet parking and loading.

(e) Establish and maintain building setback lines.

(f) Create civic districts around civic centers, public parks, public buildings or public grounds and establish regulations therefor.

§ 65851. **Division of city or county into zones.** For such purposes the legislative body may divide a county, a city, or portions thereof, into zones of the number, shape and area it deems best suited to carry out the purpose of this chapter.

§ 65852. **Uniformity of zoning regulations.** All such regulations shall be uniform for each class or kind of building or use of land throughout each zone, but the regulation in one type of zone may differ from those in other types of zones.

It is important to note that the state enabling legislation authorizes a *local government* to adopt a zoning ordinance. Pursuant to this authority, each local government will enact its own individual ordinance. The following is the Table of Contents of the zoning ordinance adopted by the Borough of Princeton, New Jersey. It illustrates the scope of subject matter contained in a typical zoning ordinance.

PRINCETON CODE

ARTICLE 8. DEFINITIONS

E. REGULATION OF USE, BULK AND DENSITY

1. Regulation of Use

Zoning ordinances divide the jurisdiction into districts and prescribe regulations that limit the use of land in those districts to **residential, industrial and commercial purposes.** The following excerpt from the Zoning Ordinance of the City of Trenton, New Jersey illustrates how this is accomplished.

19-1.1 *Purpose.* Whereas, the city council of the City of Trenton deems it necessary to the promotion of health, safety, morals, and the general welfare of the City of Trenton to regulate therein the use, size and location of buildings and other structures; the size and location of yards and other open spaces in relation to buildings; and the use of land, the following districts are hereby created; and the following regulations are hereby established to accomplish that purpose and shall hereafter apply.

19-1.2 *Districts Created.*   For the purpose of this chapter the City of Trenton is divided into the following eight classes of districts:

Residence A-1 Districts
Residence A-2 Districts
Residence B Districts
Residence C Districts
Business A Districts
Business B Districts
Industrial A Districts
Industrial B Districts

The boundaries of these districts and classes of districts are hereby established on a map entitled "Revised Zoning Map for the City of Trenton," as amended by Ordinance No. 69-3 and Ordinance No. 69-7, which map accompanies and is hereby declared to be a part of this chapter.
* * *

19-2   Residence A-1 Districts.

19-2.1 *Permitted Buildings, Structures and Uses.* In Residence A-1 Districts no building or other structure shall be used or built, altered, or erected to be used, and no land shall be used for any purpose other than that of:

a. A single-family dwelling and its customarily accessory buildings, except no private garage or other outbuilding shall be used for storage of a commercial vehicle or for storage of any other vehicle not owned by a person residing on the premises and sheltering or feeding any person or persons for profit in a single-family dwelling shall not be permitted. For the purposes of this chapter a trailer or trailer cabin shall not be regarded as a dwelling. Accessory uses as herein defined shall not be permitted in Residence A-1 Districts.

    b.   Other buildings, structures and uses as provided by subsections 19-10.6 and 19-10.16.

    Most of the litigation under this topic involves questions relating to the alternative activities that may be carried on in a district designated for *residential* use. The following cases illustrate some of those questions.

a. Exclusion of Schools

UNION FREE SCHOOL DIST.

v.

VILLAGE OF HEWLETT BAY PARK

279 App.Div.618, 107 N.Y.S.2d 858 (1951)

MEMORANDUM BY THE COURT.

    Defendants appeal from a judgment which declares that as to the plaintiff, a Union Free School District, a provision of the zoning ordinance of the defendant village which prohibits the location of a public high school within the village is invalid, and enjoins the defendants from attempting to enforce said ordinance so as to prevent the location of such a high school in the defendant village.

    Judgment unanimously affirmed, with costs.

    The Village Law empowers villages to adopt zoning ordinances for "the purpose of promoting the health, safety, morals, or the general welfare of the community" § 175. Any regulations adopted must be designed to facilitate "the adequate provision of * * * schools" § 177. The Constitution of the State imposes the duty upon the Legislature to provide a system of free public education, and reserves to the Legislature full power in relation to the "maintenance, support or administration" of the system, notwithstanding the powers conferred by the Home Rule provisions of the Constitution. Art. XI; art. IX, § 13, subd. B. Board of Education of Union Free School Dist. No. 1 of Towns of Bethlehem, Coeymans, and New Scotland v. Wilson * * * In compliance with the direction of the Constitution, the Education Law has been enacted, and it imposes upon school districts or the boards of education therein the duty to locate schools and empowers them to secure sites by condemnation, if necessary (Education Law, §§ 404, 405). Plans for buildings such as the respondent has contracted to build must be and have been approved by the Commissioner of Education, § 408, who is empowered to hear appeals from the actions of school districts, § 310, and who cannot approve the plans in the absence of specific provision for the health and safety of the children, §§ 408, 409. In the absence of a specific grant of power, the defendant village cannot by a zoning regulation prevent the location of a school within its borders and thereby prohibit the performance by the school district of the duty imposed upon it by law.

b. Exclusion of Churches

CONGREGATION TEMPLE ISRAEL

v.

CITY OF CREVE COEUR

320 S.W.2d 451 (Mo., 1959)

HYDE, Presiding Judge.

Declaratory judgment action seeking a declaration that certain ordinances of the City of Creve Coeur were void (under which plaintiff was refused a permit to build a temple on its property); and asking that defendants be enjoined from enforcing these ordinances against plaintiff and from interfering with plaintiff in the use of its property for constructing a building to use for religious worship, Sunday School and other church purposes. The court entered a decree for plaintiff granting the relief sought and defendants have appealed.

Creve Coeur is one of the many cities of St. Louis County. In 1951, the City enacted a comprehensive zoning ordinance (No. 17) dividing the City into six use districts; A, B, C and D were single family dwelling districts, with lot sizes of one acre in A, 20,000 feet in B, 15,000 feet in C, and 7,500 feet in D; E was a multiple dwelling district and F was a commercial district. This original ordinance did not prohibit churches from being built in any district and as to the A district, among other matters, provided in Article IV:

"Section 2. Use Regulations: Except as otherwise provided, business and industry are specifically prohibited, and a building or premises shall be used only for the following purposes:

"1.   Single Family Dwellings.

"2.   Churches, but only when off-street parking space is provided upon the lot or within one hundred (100) feet thereof, which space is adequate to accommodate one (1) car for every eight (8) persons for which seating is provided in the main auditorium of the Church and exclusive of the seating capacity of Sunday School and other special rooms."

Article IV, Section 2, also permitted in the A district public and private schools, golf courses, private clubs, public parks and playgrounds, hospitals and institutions with certain provisions for size of site and parking space. On April 28, 1954, plaintiff made a contract to purchase from its owner a 23.66 acre tract, located in the A district of Creve Coeur. On June 1, 1954, the deed conveying this land to plaintiff was executed and recorded; and at that time no change in the zoning ordinance had been made. However, on May 12, 1954, a petition was presented at a meeting of the Board of Aldermen requesting amendment of the zoning ordinance. Thereafter, at a special zoning commission meeting, a public hearing was asked for on the petition requesting amendment; and publication of notice of a public hearing, to be held June 2, 1954, was made. A public hearing was held on that date, and amending ordinances were prepared. On June 23 another public hearing was held on proposed amending ordinances 104 and 105, and after this hearing these ordinances were adopted by the Board on that same date.

Ordinance 104 repealed all authorization for churches in any district in the City. Authorization for schools, public or private, golf courses, private clubs, public parks and playgrounds, and hospitals and institutions, was also repealed. Ordinance 105 provided that on written application for any of these uses the application should be forwarded to the City Zoning and Planning Commission "whose duty it shall be to promptly investigate, consider and make written report thereon to the Board of Aldermen." This ordinance further provided that a public hearing was required to be held; and that "after report by the City Zoning and Planning Commission, and after such public hearing, and subject to such protective restriction as it may deem necessary to protect the character of the surrounding property, the public health and the public welfare, the Board of Aldermen may issue a special permit authorizing the location, erection, reconstruction or structural alteration of any of the following land uses or structures in any district from which they are prohibited by this Ordinance; provided, however, in case of a protest against the granting of said application duly signed and acknowledged by the owners of ten (10) per cent or more of the area of the property located within an area determined by lines drawn parallel to and 1000 feet distant from the boundaries of the property sought to be devoted to such use, such permit shall not be issued except by the favorable vote of three-fourths of all the members of the Board of Aldermen." While this ordinance provides some standards for establishing protective restrictions when a permit is granted, it does not provide any standards for granting a permit as did the ordinance considered in State ex rel. Ludlow v. Guffey, cited by defendants.

Plaintiff's land is at the intersection of Ladue Road and Spoede Road, in the southeastern part of the City, near Lindbergh Boulevard, which in this section is on the boundary line between the cities of Creve Coeur and Ladue. On the east side of Lindbergh in Ladue are the Country Day School and the Mary Institute. Chaminade College is on the west side of Lindbergh south of Ladue Road in the southeast corner of Creve Coeur; and there is a church north of the College. The area adjoining plaintiff's land is correctly described by defendants, as follows: Ladue Road, which runs east and west, has a right-of-way 60 feet wide, and is paved with concrete 20 feet wide, while Spoede Road, which runs north and south, has a two-lane blacktop pavement. On Ladue Road, immediately east of plaintiff's tract, is located the Ranken-Jordan Home, a small institution for crippled children which existed there prior to the incorporation of the City, and is a nonconforming use under the comprehensive zoning ordinance. A portion of plaintiff's tract extends behind the Ranken-Jordan Home, and is bounded on the east by the Krey estate, consisting of a large home on a large tract of grounds, and by Country Fair Acres, a recent subdivision of one-half acre lots. Plaintiff's tract is bounded on the north by a subdivision known as Chilton Acres. To the west of plaintiff's tract, across Spoede Road and on the northwest corner of the intersection of that road with Ladue Road, is a six-pump Phillips 66 Service Station, also in existence prior to the incorporation of the City, and a nonconforming use under the zoning ordinance. North of this service station, along the west side of Spoede Road, are homes consistent with the others in the area. South of Ladue Road, across from plaintiff's tract and east of Spoede Road, is a large tract (about 15 acres) vacant except for a frame residence facing on Spoede Road. On the southwest corner of the intersection of Spoede and Ladue Roads, is a large subdivision of fine homes, known as Oak Park Estates. All of the area adjoining and surrounding plaintiff's tract, with the exception of Country Fair Acres which is in the B district, is in the A district under the zoning ordinances.

Plaintiff's congregation had 1340 members but only the head of a household was considered as a member. The temple was planned with a maximum seating capacity in the sanctuary of 1500 expected to be filled only on the two high holy days. Average weekly attendance was estimated at 200 to 300. There would be regular religious services weekly at 8:15 P.M. on Friday and 10:30 A.M. on Saturday (children's services for Sunday School) with special services for the five major Jewish festivals. Plaintiff's present temple is in the City of St. Louis but about 80 per cent of its members live in St. Louis County.

Plaintiff made an application which was denied, only one member of the Board of five being in favor of it. Plaintiff thereafter brought this suit and contends that these ordinances violate the First Amendment of the Constitution of the United States as applied to the states by the Fourteenth Amendment and also Sections 5, 7 and 10 of Article I of the Constitution of Missouri, V.A.M.S., claiming them to be laws prohibiting the free exercise of religion; that they violate the Fourteenth Amendment and Sections 10 and 13 of Article I of the Missouri Constitution because they lack adequate standards for issuance or denial of special permits, provide for unconstitutional delegation of legislative powers to adjoining landowners, violate the prohibition against ex post facto laws and laws retrospective in their operation, authorize the passage of special laws, and unlawfully discriminate against plaintiff in violation of the equal protection clause. Plaintiff further contends these ordinances are void because they fail to conform to and are not authorized by the Missouri enabling act authorizing zoning (Sections 89.010-89.140; statutory references are to RSMo and V.A.M.S.) saying there is no authority in the act for special permits, they were not adopted as a part of a comprehensive plan, and they fail to conform to the required purposes specified in the act, meet its requirement of uniformity or conform to its procedural requirements. Because of the view we take, it is not necessary to discuss all of these contentions.

This is true because we think this case comes within our ruling in State ex rel. St. Louis Union Trust Co. v. Ferriss, concerning the scope of the enabling act providing authority for zoning by cities. Section 89.020 provides: "For the purpose of promoting health, safety, morals, or the general welfare of the community, the legislative body of all incorporated cities, towns and villages is hereby empowered to regulate and restrict the height, number of stories, and size of buildings and other structures, the percentage of lot that may be occupied, the size of yards, courts, and other open spaces, the density of population, *and the location and use of buildings, structures and land for trade, industry, residence or other purposes.*" (Emphasis ours.) The italicized part of this section was construed in the Ferriss case, under the rule of ejusdem generis, as negating "implied authority to control the location of schools or other public buildings, because 'trade', 'industry' and 'residence' relate to private property only and the phrase 'other purposes' is not to be broadened to include a public use of property by the state in carrying out its constitutional mandate to establish and maintain free public schools." This ruling was in part based on our constitutional provision (Article IX, Section 1(a), that "the general assembly shall establish and maintain free public schools," and the statutes (165.100 and 165.370) enacted pursuant thereto, which would be nullified in part if the right to locate schools could be restricted by zoning ordinances. Clearly ordinances 104 and 105 are void, under this decision, insofar as they require a special permit for the location of schools. We think this is also true as to churches. Certainly churches do not come within the classification of trade, industry, residence or other similar purposes. . . . Furthermore, freedom of religion is one of the fundamental freedoms protected by the Bill of Rights, of both our federal and state constitutions. The provision of the First Amendment that "Congress shall make no law respecting an establishment of religion, or prohibiting the free exercise thereof" has been made applicable to the states by the Fourteenth Amendment. This is a stronger constitutional provision than that in our constitution concerning public schools and, in view of its absolute prohibition, we do not believe our legislature in using the language it did, in Section 89.020, had any intention of granting authority to municipalities to restrict location and use of buildings and land for churches. It certainly has not specifically stated any such authority as there is no mention of religious or church purposes either in the Act or its title. Therefore, the phrase "other purposes", as used in this context, should not be broadened by construction to include use of property for religious purposes by religious organizations whose rights to free exercise of religion are protected by such constitutional guaranties. Plaintiff and amici curiae cite many cases holding invalid zoning ordinances which have excluded churches or religious schools from residential districts, where no question of authority under an enabling act was raised. * * *

However, the United States Supreme Court has not yet passed upon the application of the First and Fourteenth Amendments to an ordinance excluding a church from a residential area. (But see Kunz v. People of

State of New York, 340 U.S. 290, 71 S.Ct. 312, 95 L.Ed. 280, holding invalid an ordinance requiring a permit to hold religious meetings on the streets, with no mention of the reasons for which such a permit could be refused.)

It is said in Bassett on Zoning, 1940, page 70: "When in 1916 the framers of the Greater New York building zone resolution were discussing what buildings and uses should be excluded from residence districts, it did not occur to them that there was the remotest possibility that churches, schools, and hospitals could properly be excluded from any districts. They considered that these concomitants of civilized residential life had a proper place in the best and most open localities." The author states the reasons why churches and schools were located in residence districts (near those who attend, open spaces available with good light and air, quiet locations, and their intimate connection with home life) and also states on page 200: "Practically all zoning ordinances allow churches in all residence districts. It would be unreasonable to force them into business districts where there is noise and where land values are high, or into dense residence districts (in cities which have established several kinds of such districts). Some people claim that the numerous churchgoers crowd the street, that their automobiles line the curbs, and that the music and preaching disturb the neighbors. Communities that are too sensitive to welcome churches should protect themselves by private restrictions." (See also Yokley, Zoning Law and Practice, Section 222; Rathkopf, The Law of Zoning and Planning, Vol. I, Chapter 19, page 259; for cases of private restrictions see Matthews v. First Christian Church of St. Louis, and cases cited.) Our act authorizing zoning was enacted in 1925. Laws 1925, p. 307. In view of the usual and customary location of churches in residence districts and the strong constitutional provisions for freedom of religious worship, we do not think our legislature had any intention of authorizing the exclusion of either churches or schools from residence districts and believe that the reasonable construction of the language of Section 89.020, hereinabove italicized, which was also used in the title to the act, is as hereinabove indicated. Therefore, upon the authority of State ex rel. St. Louis Union Trust Co. v. Ferriss, supra, we hold there is no such authority given to municipalities by our zoning act and ordinances 104 and 105 of the City of Creve Coeur are invalid as applied to both churches and schools.

Of course, as pointed out in the Ferriss case (304 S.W.2d loc. cit. 899), municipalities under the police power have the power of regulation of the facilities of public schools, and we hold the same thing is true of chruches, such as safety of boilers, smokestacks and similar facilities, sanitation, manner and type of construction for fire protection and certainly likewise off-street parking facilities, sewage disposal and other matters related to the public health, safety and welfare. Plaintiff concedes the validity of such requirements, states its intention to comply and has made provisions in its plans for more than the required off-street parking. As held in Cantwell v. State of Connecticut, supra (60 S.Ct.loc.cit.904), a case of solicitation of funds for religious purposes, "The state is likewise free to regulate the time and manner of solicitation generally, in the interest of public safety, peace, comfort or convenience. But to condition the solicitation of aid for the perpetuation of religious views or systems upon a license, the grant of which rests in the exercise of a determination by state authority as to what is a religious cause, is to lay a forbidden burden upon the exercise of liberty protected by the Constitution." (If it is believed to be necessary to regulate the location of churches, this is a matter for the legislature to provide with proper safeguards for the fundamental liberty of the free exercise of religion protected by the Constitution.) As stated, our conclusion is that the state by its zoning act has granted no authority to cities to prohibit building either churches or schools in residence districts and that the trial court reached the right result in holding these ordinances void.

The judgment is affirmed.

C. Accessory Uses

An **accessory use** is a use of property that is incidental to the use permitted as of right in the zoning ordinance. Most zoning ordinances permit accessory use in residential districts. A typical provision for accessory use will provide that the premises may be used for "professional offices and studios" or "by a professional person residing on the premises." The litigation that arises under these provisions usually involves questions of statutory interpretation to determine whether the proposed use is covered by the statutory language. For example, would dancing lessons or a photographer's studio be permitted under the above language? At what point would the activity of a doctor's office become so intensive that it would become more like a clinic or hospital and therefore no longer within the definition of an accessory use? Careful drafting of the definition of "accessory use" can avoid much of this ambiguity. The following provision of the City of Trenton zoning ordinance is an example of relatively restrictive definition.

TRENTON ZONING ORDINANCE

19-1.3 *Definitions.* Certain words and terms used in this chapter are defined for the purposes thereof, as follows:

Accessory Building—A building the use of which is customarily incidental to that of a dwelling and which is located on the same lot as that occupied by the main building.

Accessory Use—A use customarily incidental to the use of a building for dwelling purposes, and including:

a. The office or studio of a physician or surgeon, dentist, artist, musician, lawyer, architect, engineer, teacher, realtor, or other like professional person, residing on the premises, provided there are no more than two paid assistants and there is no advertising display, visible from the street, other than a small professional name plate.

b. Customary home occupations such as millinery and dressmaking, provided there is no display of goods visible from the street, no exterior advertising other than a small announcement sign, and such occupation is conducted in the main building, by a person or persons residing therein, without paid assistants, and does not occupy more than one-third of the total aboveground floor area thereof.

The types of activities that will be permitted as an accessory use are matters of legislative policy. If the zoning ordinance does not permit the proposed use as an accessory use the owner may apply for a variance. But as the following case illustrates, there is no assurance that this application will be approved.

PAUL

v.

BOARD OF ZONING APPEALS

142 Conn. 40, 110 A.2d 619 (1955)

WYNNE, Justice.

The defendant Development Sales Corporation, hereinafter referred to as the owner, appealed to the defendant board of zoning appeals of New Haven from the refusal of the building inspector to grant a building permit for the use of a portion of the basement of an apartment house for three suites of doctors' offices. The board overruled the inspector, and the plaintiffs, who are nearby residents and landowners, appealed to the Court of Common Pleas. From a judgment sustaining the appeal, the owner has appealed to this court.

Succinctly stated, the issue is whether the board of zoning appeals acted arbitrarily, illegally or in abuse of its discretion by granting a variance under the zoning ordinance of New Haven to permit doctors' offices in a residence zone.

The facts before the board may be stated as follows: This proceeding originated on December 3, 1953. The building inspector of New Haven had refused to grant a building permit to use a portion of the basement of an apartment house under construction at 570-576 Whitney Avenue for offices for three physicians. The apartment house is two stories high in front and has thirty-six apartments. It is in a residence AA zone, in which the zoning regulations do not expressly permit physicians' offices. With the exception of two offices maintained by a physician and a chiropractor in their private homes, there are no professional offices within a radius of approximately one-half mile in any direction. None of the apartment houses in the area contain professional offices.

Under § 1033(7) of the New Haven zoning ordinance, the board of zoning appeals may in an appropriate case, after notice and hearing and subject to appropriate conditions and safeguards, determine and vary the applications of the regulations in harmony with their general purpose and intent where there are practical difficulties or unnecessary hardships in the way of carrying out the strict letter of the ordinance or where the effect of the application of the ordinance is arbitrary. This can only be done in harmony with the general purpose and intent of the zoning ordinance so that the public health, safety and general welfare may be secured and substantial justice done. The owner did not specifically ask for a variance. On the face of its application for a permit, the ruling of the building inspector was correct because professional offices of the kind the owner sought permission for are not allowed in an AA residence district. New Haven Zon. Ordinance, §§ 1012, 1011 (1951). The case, however, has been treated as an application for a variance, and we shall consider it as such.

The plaintiffs' appeal from the action of the board in granting the variance must be sustained if it appears that the board acted arbitrarily or illegally or abused its discretion. We have repeatedly held that the power to grant a variance must be sparingly exercised. The record before the board is barren of any evidence of practical difficulty or unnecessary hardship upon the owner if the permit is not issued. A reasonable basis for a conclusion of difficulty or hardship is indispensable to the owner's case. The most that can be said is that the space in which the owner proposed to construct the professional offices will be unoccupied and useless unless the owner's request is granted and that, therefore, the owner will suffer a pecuniary loss. A pecuniary loss does not furnish the unnecessary hardship or practical difficulty contemplated by the zoning ordinance. The case at bar is very similar to Heady v. Zoning Board of Appeals. In that case we said, "It was to the defendant's financial advantage to convert his Cherry Street property into an office building. This did not warrant a relaxation of the zoning regulations on the ground of practical difficulty or unnecessary hardship."

The owner makes the claim that the provision of the ordinance empowering the board to grant a variance where the effect of the application of the ordinance is arbitrary is really controlling. The contention is made that because the ordinance does not provide for doctors' offices in residence zones, ready access to doctors is prevented in cases of emergency. "Arbitrary" means "[d]epending on will or discretion," that is, not governed by any fixed rules or standards. Webster's New International Dictionary (2d Ed.). Certainly the strict application of the rules set forth in a zoning ordinance could not be held to be arbitrary within the definition quoted. If provision should be made for the location of doctors' offices in residence zones, the question is one of legislative policy.

The trial court was correct in sustaining the plaintiffs' appeal from the action of the board.

There is no error.

In this opinion the other judges concurred.

D. Signs

The use of the zoning power to regulate the construction and installation of signs and billboards raises the issue of the extent to which the police power may be used to regulate matters that are substantially esthetic in nature. The earlier cases held that **esthetic considerations** are insufficient to justify the use of the police power. More recently the courts have tended to uphold the use of the police power to achieve esthetic objectives, but have done so by pointing up the relationship between esthetic considerations and economic, social and cultural objectives that have been traditionally included within the scope of the police power.

CROMWELL

v.

FERRIER

19 N.Y.2d 263, 279 N.Y.S.2d 22, 225 N.E.2d 749 (1967)

BREITEL, Judge.

Petitioner appeals from an order of the Appellate Division, Second Department. He brought this proceeding under article 78 of CPLR to review determinations of the respondents Building Inspector and Zoning Board of Appeals of the Town of Wallkill that two billboards on petitioner's land violated a town zoning ordinance. Special Term denied the application and the Appellate Division affirmed in a short memorandum by a divided court.

An important constitutional issue is involved. Petitioner concedes that the signboards violate the provisons of the local law in question but argues that the ordinance is unconstitutional.

Since 1961, petitioner has been the co-owner of a 200-acre parcel of land in the Town of Wallkill. The tract is bisected by a highway, Route 17, which passes through the parcel in a general north-south direction. Shortly after acquiring the land, petitioner constructed a service station and a diner upon a portion of the premises west of the highway.

The zoning ordinance was adopted March 14, 1963. In July, 1964 petitioner contracted with a display advertiser for the construction and installation of two signs, advertising petitioner's service station and restaurant. The signs were to be located on the portion of petitioner's land east of Route 17. Before the signs had been completed respondent Building Inspector served a stop order on petitioner on the ground that the signs violated the town zoning ordinance. Petitioner appealed to the Zoning Board which affirmed the action of the Building Inspector.

The ordinance contains a number of sections which set forth a comprehensive and detailed plan for the regulation of signs in the township. The town is zoned into a number of use districts (e.g., "business, highway commercial, industrial") and there are detailed provisions regulating the size, location and number of signs allowed in each district. The regulations, however, cover only signs which are "related to an establishment located on the same lot" ("accessory" signs) and "non-accessory" signs are implicitly prohibited throughout the township.

As the signs advertising petitioner's service station and restaurant are not on the same lot as the establishments they advertise, they are "nonaccessory" signs and, therefore, are excluded by the ordinance. Petitioner argues that the zoning ordinance, insofar as it prohibits the maintenance of nonaccessory signs anywhere within the township, is "arbitrary and unreasonable" and that its application results in "an unconstitutional deprivation of the property of Petitioner".

Special Term held that "The basic issue to be resolved is whether the Zoning Law regulates or prohibits billboards". The court dismissed the petition because the law "does not prohibit; it does regulate". On appeal, the majority in the Appellate Division came to the same conclusion as it regarded the ordinance "as reasonably regulating the erection of signs in the Town", and that the ordinance "promotes symmetry and protects the Town from becoming an eyesore". The two Justices who dissented concluded that the "flat prohibition of all advertising signs on all vacant land" was "unreasonable and confiscatory," citing Matter of Mid-State Adv. Corp. v. Bond.

On any realistic view, the ordinance involved in this case is indistinguishable in effect from the one ruled unconstitutional in *Bond* (supra). Consequently, a reexamination of the *Bond* case is required if the ordinance at issue is to be sustained as constitutional.

It is concluded that the decisional as well as the practical bases for the holding in *Bond* (supra) are either no longer valid or have changed so considerably that the case should be overruled. As Judge FINCH commented in his dissent in *Bond*: "The Constitution, it is true, does not change with the times, nor does an emergency or unusual circumstances warrant a disregard of constitutional provisons. A determination of what is due process, aside from procedural matters, however, depends upon the reasonableness of the legislation. Circumstances, surrounding conditions, changed social attitudes, newly-acquired knowledge, do not alter the Constitution, but they do alter our view of what is reasonable. Restrictions upon the use of property, which were deemed unreasonable in 1909, are regarded today as entirely reasonable and natural."

The question, then, is whether the rule in the *Bond* case (supra) reflects present conditions and understanding of present-day community conditions.

One important factor in the courts' increasingly permissive treatment of similar zoning ordinances has been the gradual acceptance of the conclusion that a zoning law is not necessarily invalid because its primary, if not its exclusive objective, is the esthetic enhancement of the particular area involved, so long as it is related if only generally to the economic and cultural setting of the regulating community. On this point, *People v. Stover* is now the leading case. In *Stover*, this court held that a city ordinance which prohibited the erection of clotheslines in certain areas of residential districts was not invalid even though the obvious purpose of the ordinance was almost exclusively esthetic. Writing for the majority, Judge FULD now Chief Judge, traced the history of the courts' treatment of zoning ordinances designed partly or primarily to satisfy esthetic objectives, commencing with the early cases such as People ex rel. Nineburgh Adv. Co. v. Murphy (195 N.Y. 126, 88 N.E. 17) which "had held that esthetic consderations alone would be insufficient to justify exercise of the

police power. But since 1930", Judge FULD noted that the question has
been an open one in New York. He then concludes: "Once it be conceded that aesthetics is a valid subject of legislative concern, the conclusion seems inescapable that reasonable legislation designed to promote
that end is a valid and permissible exercise of the police power."

This holding is important for present purposes not only because, realistically, the primary objective of any anti-billboard ordinance is an esthetic
one (Dukeminier, Zoning for Aesthetic Objectives: A Reappraisal, 20 Law
& Contemp. Prob. 218, 220) but also because it at least partially undermines the authority of *Bond* (supra). While the majority opinion in that
case held that the ordinance before it would be unconstitutional even if
"aesthetic reasons alone" could support such a legislative enactment, it is
significant that the first case cited by the court in support of its holding
was People ex rel. Wineburgh Adv. Co. v. Murphy upon which Judge
FULD commented in the *Stover* case (supra). Moreover, *Bond* also cited
People v. Rubenfeld and Perlmutter v. Greene, two decisions also cited
by *Stover* for its observation that the esthetic issue had been an open one
since 1930.

In the only other New York case cited by *Bond* (supra), People ex rel.
Publicity Leasing Co. v. Ludwig, the court held that an ordinance passed
by the Board of Aldermen of New York City limiting the height of signs
on roofs was not arbitrary and unreasonable.

Consequently, insofar as the *Bond* holding (supra) was predicated on
the now discarded notion that esthetic objectives alone will not support a
zoning ordinance, it may no longer be a valid precedent. But, as pointed
out in *Stover* (supra), the question remains whether such an ordinance
should still be voided because it constitutes an " 'unreasonable device of
implementing community policy'." Moreover, *Bond* is cited in *Stover* as a
case in which the legislative body (went) too far in the name of aesthetics.

In this respect, petitioner argues that the legislative distinction between
identification signs and nonaccessory signs is unreasonable and discriminatory. Neither *Bond* (supra) nor any other decision of this court has
dealt specifically with this point but numerous cases from other jurisdictions have had occasion to do so. In nearly all, zoning ordinances which
have distinguished between accessory and nonaccessory signs have been
upheld, providing that the distinctions were applied in a reasonable manner. The following excerpt from the opinion of Mr. Justice BRENNAN in
United Adv. Corp. v. Borough of Raritan is typical: "The business sign is
in actuality a part of the business itself, just as the structure housing the
business is a part of it, and the authority to conduct the business in a
district carries with it the right to maintain a business sign on the premises subject to reasonable regulations in that regard as in the case of this
ordinance. Plaintiff's placements of its advertising signs, on the other
hand, are made pursuant to the conduct of the business of outdoor advertising itself, and in effect what the ordinance provides is that this business
shall not to that extent be allowed in the borough. It has long been settled that the unique nature of outdoor advertising and the nuisances fos-
tered by billboards, and similar outdoor structures located by persons in
the business of outdoor advertising, justify the separate classification of

such structures for the purposes of governmental regulation and restriction."

In Norate Corp. v. Zoning Bd. of Adjustment (417 Pa. 397, 207 A.2d 890) the ordinance at issue prohibited all nonaccessory signs throughout the township. The Supreme Court of Pennsylvania, while recognizing the validity of the distinction between accessory and nonaccessory billboards, held that the ordinance nevertheless "does not attempt to regulate, but to prohibit" and that it must be declared invalid as "too general, too broad and unreasonable." On the other hand, in United Adv. Corp. v. Borough of Raritan, the Supreme Court of New Jersey upheld the constitutionality of a nearly identical statute. The opinion noted "It is enough that outdoor advertising has characteristic features which have long been deemed sufficient to sustain regulations or prohibitions peculiarly applicable to it" where the Supreme Court of Errors of Connecticut upheld in principle a similar statute but remanded the case to the trial court for further facts.

In concluding that the ordinance is constitutional and that the restrictive outlook of the *Bond* case (supra) should no longer be followed, it does not mean that any esthetic consideration suffices to justify prohibition. The exercise of the police power should not extend to every artistic conformity or nonconformity. Rather, what is involved are those esthetic considerations which bear substantially on the economic, social, and cultural patterns of a community or district. Advertising signs and billboards, if misplaced, often are egregious examples of ugliness, distraction, and deterioration. They are just as much subject to reasonable controls, including prohibition, as enterprises which emit offensive noises, odors, or debris. The eye is entitled to as much recognition as the other senses, but, of course, the offense to the eye must be substantial and be deemed to have material effect on the community or district pattern. Such limitations are suggested in the *Stover* case. No doubt, difficult cases will arise in which there will be the necessity for discrimination on very fine bases, but that is not a new difficulty for Legislatures, administrative agencies, or courts. This case does not involve, however, such a difficulty.

Accordingly, the order of the Appellate Division should be affirmed, with costs to respondents.

---

2. Regulation of Bulk

In addition to regulating the **use** of land, zoning ordinances regulate the **bulk** of the structures, i.e., the relationship of the size and shape of the structure to the parcel of land on which it is placed. There are a number of techniques by which the bulk of structures are regulated. Included are: percentage–of–buildable–area restrictions set-back requirements, floor area ratios, open space ratios and sky exposure plans. **Percentage-of-buildable area restrictions** prescribe the maximum percentage of lot area that may be covered with structures. For example the ordinance may provide that a house in a given residential district may not occupy more than 40 percent of the lot area. Such provisions are valid when reasonable. **Set-back requirements** establish the minimum distance from the street that a building may be built or lot boundaries. Set-back requirements are usually upheld except where the ordinance as applied to a particular property prevent any reasonable use of the land. The **floor area ratio** (FAR) is a device used to determine the *maximum floor area* that may be built upon a *given size lot*. For example, if the FAR is 6, and the lot area equals 10,000 square feet, then the maximum floor area allowed will be 60,000 square feet. The **open space ratio** is a device used to designate some portion of the zoning lot that must be open and unobstructed to the sky. For instance, upon determining that the floor area will be 60,000 square feet, the open space ratio is employed to find the percentage of the actual floor area that must be allocated to open space. Thus, if the open space ratio is 10, then 6,000 square feet of open space will be required. The **sky exposure plane** is a technique used to ensure sufficient light for city streets where high rise construction is permitted.

a. Set-back Requirements

The following excerpt from the zoning ordinance of the City of Trenton, New Jersey illustrates the modest set back requirements in a central city. In a suburban community the set-back requirements are usually very much greater.

TRENTON ZONING ORDINANCE

19-2.2 *Yard, Area and Height Provisions.*

a. *Front Yards.* No building or part of building other than steps, open porches for a distance not exceeding eight feet, over-hanging eaves and cornices, and similar fixtures shall extend nearer to a front street line than the average distance of setback of the nearest buildings, other than accessory buildings, within 200 feet on each side of said building and fronting on the same side of the street, except that in no instance shall a building be required by the above to be placed more than 20 feet back of the front main wall of the nearest building existing within 200 feet thereof. When only one building exists on the same side of the street with the building to be erected, and within 100 feet thereof, the building setback shall be the average between the setback of the existing building and 30 feet. When no building or buildings exist within 200 feet of and on the same side of the street with the building to be erected, the setback at the front shall be not less than 30 feet. In the case of a corner lot, any building other than a detached garage or other outbuilding may be placed to within 16 feet of the side-street property line.

Building setback lines specifically established otherwise for certain streets by subsection 19-10.13 of this chapter, or by special act of the city council; or by the city planning board incident to plot approval, shall have precedence over the above.

b. *Rear Yards.* There shall be a rear yard with a depth of not less than 35 feet. When a building extends through from street to street, the front yard restrictions shall be observed on both streets.

c. *Side Yards.* There shall be two side yards with a total width of not less than 16 feet except that for each foot a lot existing as of July 20, 1956 is less than 50 feet wide, the total width of the two side yards may be reduced by one foot to a total width of not less than 12 feet. The width of the narrowest of the two side yards shall not be less than six feet. For a nonresidential structure other than a garage or other outbuilding there shall be two side yards with a total width of not less than 50 feet and, for each foot the height of such a structure exceeds 35 feet, the total width of the two side yards shall be increased by two feet, and the narrower of the two side yards in relation to such structure shall not be less than one-third the total width of the two side yards.

ROBYNS

v.

CITY OF DEARBORN

341 Mich. 495, 67 N.W.2d 718 (1954)

DETHMERS, Justice.

Defendant appeals from decree enjoining enforcement of a zoning ordinance against plaintiffs' property because unreasonable and confiscatory as applied thereto.

Each of plaintiffs owns one of eight lots on the south side of Ford Road in the City of Dearborn across from the lots in Dearborn Township involved in Ritenour v. Township of Dearborn. Seven of the lots have a width of 20 feet and one 24.44 feet, fronting on Ford Road, with depths varying from 100 to 110 feet. Some of plaintiffs purchased their lots prior to, and some after, the adoption of the original ordinance which zoned the lots for Residence C use and some bought after adoption of an amendment changing the zoning to the present Residence A classification. Original building restrictions, since expired, limited use of some of the lots to business purposes and others to business or residential. Lots across the road in the township have been zoned light commercial since our holding in Ritenour and many are so used. Lots on the south side of Ford Road, immediately west of the lots here involved, are zoned Business B and those to the east, running for a considerable distance, are vacant. The ordinance in question provides "there shall be a minimum of ten feet between residences."

Plaintiffs prayed that the ordinance be decreed to be unconstitutional and void as applied to their lots, that they be decreed to be business property, that defendant be enjoined from enforcing the ordinance with respect thereto, and that a building permit for nonresidential purposes be required to issue as relates to one of the lots.

Defendant says the bill is multifarious. This it predicates in part on the fact that some plaintiffs acquired lots before, and some after, the ordinance and its subsequent amendment, suggesting that, on the authority of Hammond v. Bloomfield Hills Building Inspector, the rights of those who purchased before the ordinance differ, for that reason, from those who bought thereafter. Hammond does not so hold. Provisions of a zoning ordinance void as relates to a lot because unreasonable and confiscatory are not made valid with respect thereto by the transfer of title from the owner to another. * * *

Is the ordinance unreasonable and confiscatory as applied to plaintiffs' lots? It limits use to residences which, under its provisions, cannot be constructed on these lots at a width of more than ten feet, comparable, in this respect, to the situation in Ritenour. Other requirements of the ordinance with respect to area, minimum width of side yards, etc., cannot be complied with so as to permit construction of usable residences. Defendant's answer admits, in effect, plaintiffs' charge, that the provisions of the ordinance make use of the lots for residential purposes physically impossible, by alleging, in response thereto, that plaintiffs could comply by combining two or more lots for the building of residences thereon. We think the decision in Ritenour controlling here. Distinctions between that case and this in the respect that there the plaintiff acquired the property prior to enactment of the ordinance, that the property there involved had once been zoned for business purposes, and that the action there was brought by plaintiff within a year after adoption of the ordinance while here it was not brought until 22 years later, do not serve to alter the fact that the provisions of the ordinance would render plaintiffs' property here almost worthless. That the city may not do. Long v. City of Highland Park, supra. Transfer of title, or the lapse of 22 years, after adoption of the ordinance does not relieve the ordinance of its unreasonable and confiscatory character. It is invalid as applied to plaintiffs' lots. * * *

Affirmed, with costs to plaintiffs.

---

b. Floor Area Ratio

The **floor area ratio (FAR)** is used as the principal control on physical volume of buildings in New York City and other large central cities. FAR represents the relation between the floor area of the building and the area of a lot on which the building will be constructed. Expressed as a formula:

$$FAR = \frac{\text{Floor Area}}{\text{Lot Area}}$$

Thus a builder would look to the zoning ordinance to determine the floor area ratio limit to determine the maximum amount of floor space that could be contained in a proposed building. The following provision from the San Francisco City Planning Code illustrates how the FAR is used in that city.

SAN FRANCISCO CITY PLANNING CODE, SEC. 122

SEC. 122. Maximum Floor Area Ratio.

(a) The limits upon the floor area ratio of buildings, as defined in this Code, shall be as stated in this Section and Sections 122.1, 122.2, 122.3 and 122.4. The maximum floor area ratio for any building or development shall be equal to the sum of the basic floor area ratio for the district, as set forth in Section 122.1, plus any premiums, development bonuses and floor area transfers which are applicable to such building or development under Sections 122.2, 122.3 and 122.4.

(b) No building or structure or part thereof shall be permitted to exceed, except as stated in Section 107 of this Code, the floor area ratio limits herein set forth for the district in which it is located. *(Amended Ord. 136-68, approved 5-29-68)*

SEC. 122.1. Basic Floor Area Ratio.

(a) Except as provided in paragraphs (b), (c) and (d) of this Section, the basic floor area ratio limits specified in the following table shall apply to each building or development in the districts indicated.

TABLE 1

Basic Floor Area Ratio Limits

District	Basic Floor Area Ratio Limit
R-3, R-3.5	1.8 to 1
R-4	4.8 to 1
R-5	10.0 to 1
C-1, C-2	3.6 to 1
C-3-0	14.0 to 1
C-3-R	10.0 to 1
C-3-G	10.0 to 1
C-3-S	7.0 to 1
C-M	9.0 to 1
M-1, M-2	5.0 to 1

c. Open Space Ratio

The **open space ratio (OSR)** is used as a device to provide sufficient open space in relation to the intensity of development. OSR represents the relation between the open space on the lost and the total floor area of all the buildings on that lot. Expressed as a formula:

$$OSR = \frac{\text{open space X 100}}{\text{floor area}}$$

The definition of "open space" will vary in different municipal ordinances. It will usually be limited to those parts of the lot that are open and unobstructed to the sky and accessible to all residents of the building. Roof area might be included under prescribed circumstances; a prescribed percentage of open space may be used for off-street parking. Some ordinances provide for bonuses of additional floor area in return for additional open space than is otherwise required.

d. Sky Exposure Plane

The **sky exposure plane (SEP)** is used as a device to provide set back requirements for high rise buildings without prescribing a uniform system that would result in all high rise buildings having the same shape and proportions. The following diagrams illustrate the possibilities for varied building design available under the New York City provisions.

NEW YORK ZONING HANDBOOK

Sky Exposure Plane

In all Districts but R1 through R5, the "sky exposure plane" slopes up and back from an imaginary line above the street line, at a specified height. The "sky exposure plane" in Districts R1 through R5 begins above the front yard line.

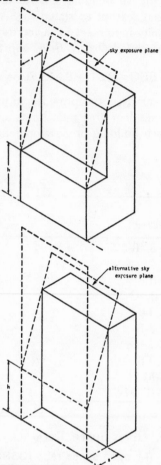

sky exposure plane

Alternate Provisions

In all Districts not governed by R1 through R5 bulk regulations, if a lot-width open area of specified depth ("depth of optional front open area") is provided, alternate regulations permit higher front walls, establish a steeper "alternate sky exposure plane" and prescribe no initial set-back distance. In R1 through R5 Districts, too, because front yards are mandatory, no initial setback distance is required.

alternative sky exposure plane

Tower Provisions

A tower is the portion of a building which penetrates a sky exposure plane. Thus, the regulations which govern towers are exceptions to the usual rules.

If towers are set back specified distances from the street line, they may, in certain Districts, rise to any height, provided the floor area ratio is not exceeded. On lots of over 20,000 square feet, permitted towers may cover no more than 40 per cent of their lots; but on lots under 20,000 square feet, they may cover a greater percentage of the lot—up to 50 per cent for lots of 10,500 square feet or less.

from: N.Y.C. *Zoning Handbook* pgs. 20,21

3. Density Regulations

Density regulations are designed to limit the number of people in a given area. The character of the community is directly related to the population density. For example, a rural area will have a population density of under 100 persons per square mile. A suburban community will have a typical density of approximately 2000 to 4000 persons per square mile. A zoning ordinance may contain one or more of several different forms of density regulations including minimum lot size requirements, minimum floor size limitations and maximum height limitations. **Minimum lot size** requirements may vary in size from 20 feet by 100 feet to five acres or more. Large lot zoning may be used to increase land costs and thereby discourage lower income residents. On the other hand, large lot zoning may be required to protect the public health in areas where water supply and sanitary disposal are dependent upon private wells and septic tanks. A **minimum floor size** requirement is a device that may be reasonable in some circumstances. However, this requirement tends to increase the cost of construction of new residences and may be used as an exclusionary device. **Maximum height limitations** simply limit the height of buildings in designated districts.

a. Minimum Lot Size

The following provision from the City of Trenton Zoning Ordinance is a typical zoning minimum land area requirement for a central city.

TRENTON ZONING ORDINANCE, SEC. 10-10.3

19-10.3 *Density Regulations, Minimum Land Area Per Dwelling Unit.* The minimum land area per dwelling unit in each of the several classes of districts shall be as follows:

a. *In Residence A-1 & A-2 Districts —*
6,000 square feet.

b. *In Residence B Districts —*
For single-family dwellings, 4,000 square feet.
For two-to-four family dwellings, 2,200 square feet.
For multi-family dwellings containing more than four dwelling units and for row houses, 2,000 square feet.

For any multi-family building containing more than four dwelling units and not exceeding four stories or 35 feet in height, Residence C District requirements may be substituted, provided that the following minimum requirements are met:
1. The building lot shall have a street frontage of not less than 120 feet.
2. The area of the building lot shall not be less than 15,000 square feet.

c. *In Residence C Districts —*
For all dwellings up to and including those containing 18 dwelling units and for row houses—the same as for Residence B Districts.
For any multi-family dwelling containing more than 18 dwelling units there shall be no limitation other than those imposed by the practical application of the other provisions of this chapter.

d. *In all other Districts —*
The same as for Residence C Districts.

The relatively low minimum lot size requirements in central cities do not raise serious legal problems. The difficult issues arise in suburban communities where the zoning ordinance may require a minimum lot of substantial size. As the minimum land area requirement increases in size, it tends to become suspect as an exclusionary zoning device. Nevertheless there are several cases where courts have upheld large lot zoning requirements. For example, in *Fischer v. Bedminister Township,* 11 N.J. 194, 93 A.2d 378 (1952), the New Jersey Supreme Court upheld a five acre minimum zoning requirement on the grounds that the plaintiff failed to sustain the burden of proving the requirement unreasonable under the circumstances. More recently, the federal court of appeals upheld a six acre minimum lot size requirements in a New Hampshire town. *Steel Hill Development Inc. v. Town of Sanbornton,* 469 F.2d 956 (1st Cir., 1973).

b. Minimum Building Size

LIONSHEAD LAKE

v.

WAYNE TOWNSHIP

10 N.J. 165, 89 A.2d 693. Appeal dismissed

344 U.S. 919, (1952)

In this well known New Jersey decision the court upheld the validity of a Wayne Township zoning ordinance providing minimum floor space requirements of 768 square feet for a one-story building and 1,200 square feet for a two-story building. The court said in part:

The Township of Wayne is still for the most part a sparsely settled countryside with great natural attractions in its lakes, hills and streams, but obviously it lies in the path of the next onward wave of suburban development. Whether that development shall be "with a view of conserving the value of property and encouraging the most appropriate use of land throughout such municipality" and whether it will "prevent the overcrowding of land or buildings" and "avoid undue concentration of population" depends in large measure on the wisdom of the governing body of the municipality as expressed in its zoning ordinance. It requires as much official watchfulness to anticipate and prevent suburban blight as it does to eradicate city slums.

Has a municipality the right to impose minimum floor area requirements in the exercise of its zoning powers? Much of the proof adduced by the defendant township was devoted to showing that the mental and emotional health of its inhabitants depended on the proper size of their homes. We may take notice without formal proof that there are minimums in housing below which one may not go without risk of impairing the health of those who dwell therein. One does not need extensive experience in matrimonial causes to become aware of the adverse effect of overcrowding on the well-being of our most important institution, the home. Moreover, people who move into the country rightly expect more land, and more freedom in their scale of living than is generally possible in the city. City standards of housing are not adaptable to suburban areas and especially to the upbringing of children. But quite apart from these considerations of public health which cannot be overlooked, minimum floor-area standards are justified on the ground that they promote the general welfare of the community and, as we have seen in Schmidt v. Board of Adjustment of the City of Newark, (1952), supra, the courts in conformance with the constitutional provisions and the statutes hereinbefore cited take a broad view of what constitutes general welfare. The size of the dwellings in any community inevitably affects the character of the community and does much to determine whether or not it is a desirable place in which to live. It is the prevailing view in municipalities throughout the State that such minimum floor-area standards are necessary to protect the character of the community. A survey made by the Department of Conservation and Economic Development in 1951 disclosed that 64 municipalities out of the 138 reporting had minimum dwelling requirements. In the light of the Constitution and of the enabling statutes, the right of a municipality to impose minimum floor-area requirements is beyond controversy.

With respect to every zoning ordinance, however, the question remains as to whether or not in the particular facts of the case and in the light of all of the surrounding circumstances the minimum floor-area requirements are reasonable. Can a minimum of living floor space of 768 square feet for a one-story building; of 1,000 square feet for a two-story dwelling having an attached garage be deemed unreasonable in a rural area just beginning to change to a suburban community? It is significant that the plaintiff admits that of the 100 houses in its development 30 met the minimum requirements when constructed and 20 more by voluntary additions of the owners to meet their individual needs have been enlarged to conform to the minimum requirements of the ordinance, and while this litigation has been pending 20 others have been constructed conforming to the ordinance. If some such requirements were not imposed there would be grave danger in certain parts of the township, particularly around the lakes which attract summer visitors, of the erection of shanties which would deteriorate land values generally to the great detriment of the increasing number of people who live in Wayne Township the year round. The minimum floor area requirements imposed by the ordinance are not large for a family of normal size. Without some such restrictions there is always the danger that after some homes have been erected giving a character to a neighborhood others might follow which would fail to live up to the standards thus voluntarily set. This has been the experience in many communities and it is against this that the township has sought to safeguard itself within limits which seem to us to be altogether reasonable.

OLIPHANT, J. (dissenting).

I find I must dissent from the philosophy and the result arrived at in the majority opinion. Zoning has its purposes, but as I conceive the effect of the majority opinion it precludes individuals in those income brackets who could not pay between $8,500 and $12,000 for the erection of a house on a lot from ever establishing a residence in this community as long as the 768 square feet of living space is the minimum requirement in the zoning ordinance. A zoning provision that can produce this effect certainly runs afoul of the fundamental principles of our form of government.

It places an unnecessary and severe restriction upon the alienation of real estate. It is not necessary, it seems to me, in order to meet any possible threat to the general health and welfare of the community.

It should be borne in mind that the threat to the general welfare and health of the community usually springs from the type of home that is maintained within the house rather than the house itself. Certain well-behaved families will be barred from these communities, not because of any acts they do or conditions they create, but simply because the income of the family will not permit them to build a house at the cost testified to in this case. They will be relegated to living in the large cities or in multiple-family dwellings even though it be against what they consider the welfare of their immediate families.

My difficulty with the provision in this ordinance is that it applies equally to every part of the 25½ square miles of this township and it applies without any regard to how the various districts of the community have been zoned. It applies to the districts classed Residence A and B, Business or Industrial Districts. While it is conceivable that some municipalities may be of such a cohesive and homogeneous character as to warrant the imposition of certain uniform regulations on the entire community, viz., the prohibition of any industrial plants in a purely residential community, (1949); the defendant township is certainly not of such character. It is sparsely settled and is made up of a group of widely separated communities or developments, and in some of these developments the minimum living space requirements imposed by the ordinance are easily met by all the existing dwellings while in other sections only a minority of the houses meet the standards imposed, and in the plaintiff's Lionshead Lake development only about 50% of the dwellings comply.

To impose identical living floor space minimums on all the sections of such a municipality is to fail completely to give any consideration whatever to the "character of the district and its peculiar suitability for particular purposes." While zoning regulations may legitimately be imposed in the district to serve the general welfare by "conserving the value of property and encouraging the most appropriate uses of land," such regulations are wholly unreasonable and beyond the zoning power and an unwarranted interference with private property rights if they are designed or operate to change completely, for better or for worse, the very character of the district. Any regulation imposed must bear a reasonable relation to the particular area subject thereto. Insofar as the minimum living floor space requirements of the ordinance under review apply to the entire community and to the plaintiff's properties in particular, they are clearly arbitrary and capricious and were very properly set aside by the trial court as an abuse of the zoning power.

My views on this particular phase of zoning do not prohibit minimum floor space in a house in particular districts or a proper correlation of minimum floor space in the house and the area of the lot or lots in question, but I cannot agree with the majority when they state with respect to this minimum square footage requirements that "whether it will 'prevent the overcrowding of land or buildings' and 'avoid undue concentration of the buildings' depends in large measure on the wisdom of the governing body of the municipality." This is clearly indicative of a lack of standard with respect to this particular phase of zoning in the Zoning Act itself and it assumes that the discretion of the zoning board or governing body of a municipality amounts to wisdom. To buttress their position the majority further states: "We may take notice without formal proof that there are minimums in housing below which one may not go without risk of impairing the health of those who dwell therein." In so stating they inferentially approve certain theories advanced to sustain this ordinance by text writers and certain reports of the Department of Conservation and Economic Development. But it seems to me that the decision as to what the minimum square footage in a particular house should be is essentially within the legislative province, and the Legislature not having spoken it is not within the power of this court or the Department of Conservation and Economic Development to attempt to supply the deficiency in the statute.

This decision was the cause of extensive debate in the law journals. See, Haar, "Zoning for Minimum Standards: The Wayne Township Case," **66 Harv.L.Rev.** 1051 (1953); Nolan & Horack, "How Small a House? - Zoning for Minimum Space Requirements," **67 Harv.L.Rev.** 967 (1954); Haar, "Wayne Township: Zoning for Whom? - In Brief Reply," **67 Harv.L.Rev.** 986 (1954); Williams & Wacks, "Segregation of Residential Areas Along Economic Lines: Lionshead Lake Revisited," 1969 **Wis.L.Rev.** 827.

The debate was revived a decade later when the New Jersey Supreme court upheld the validity of a Gloucester Township zoning amendment excluding trailer camps and trailer parks in an industrial district.

See *Vickers v. Township Committee of Gloucester Township*, 37 N.J. 232, 181 A.2d 129 (1962).

c. Height Regulations

The United States Supreme Court was called upon to determine the validity of an early Massachusetts statute limiting the height of buildings in Boston. In *Welch v. Swasey*, 214 U.S. 91 (1909) the Court made the following determinations:

> Whether a state statute is illegal because it delegates legislative power to a commission does not raise a Federal question.
> A statute limiting the height of buildings cannot be justified under the police power unless it has some fair tendency to accomplish, or aid in the accomplishment of, some purpose for which that power can be used; if the means employed, pursuant to the statute, have no real substantial relation to such purpose, or if the statute is arbitrary, unreasonable and beyond the necessities of the case, it is invalid as taking property without due process of law.
> In determining the validity of a state statute affecting height of buildings, local conditions must be considered; and, while the judgment of the highest court may not be conclusive, it is entitled to the greatest respect, and will not be interfered with unless clearly wrong.

Where the highest court of the State has held that there is reasonable ground for classification between the commercial and residential portions of a city as to the height of buildings, based on practical and not aesthetic grounds, and that the police power is not to be exercised for merely aesthetic purposes, this court will not hold that such a statute, upheld by the state court, prescribing different heights in different sections of the city is unconstitutional as discriminating against, and denying equal protection of the law to, the owners of property in the district where the lower height is prescribed.

Where there is justification for the enactment of a police statute limiting the height of buildings in a particular district, an owner of property in that district is not entitled to compensation for the reasonable interference with his property by the statute.

Chapters 333 of the acts of 1904 and 383 of the acts of 1905 of Massachusetts, limiting the heights of buildings in Boston and prescribing different heights in different sections of the city are, in view of the decision of the highest court of Massachusetts holding that the discrimination is based upon reasonable grounds, a proper exercise of the police power of the State, and are not unconstitutional under the equal protection and due process clauses of the Fourteenth Amendment.

193 Massachusetts, 364, affirmed.

In a more recent decision, a Florida Court was called upon to determine the validity of *minimum* height requirement for business buildings. In *City of North Miami v. Newsome*, 203 So.2d 634 (Fla.Dist.Ct.App. 1967) the court said, in part:

It was alleged the proposed building was designed and intended for a business use authorized for the area by the zoning ordinance; that it was in compliance with the building code; and that the permit was refused without legal or constitutional basis. Realtors charged that the respondent city was under a legal duty to permit the construction.

In response to the alternative writ of mandamus the city averred the basis for rejection of the realtor's application for the building permit was that the building as proposed did not comply with subsections (h) and (n) of section 29-40 of the Code of Ordinances of the City of North Miami which required, as to business buildings in that area, that "all main buildings or structures must have a minimum floor area of two thousand, five hundred (2,500) square feet," and that "all facades or false fronts of or to buildings shall be at least fifteen (15) feet in height." Upon the hearing there were presented copies of pertinent provisions of the ordinance and of minutes of the Board of Adjustment and of the City Council, which substantiated the above mentioned averment of the city's response.

The trial court granted judgment for the relators and ordered the issuance of a peremptory writ of mandamus commanding the respondent to issue the building permit. In the judgment the trial court stated:

"The Court is well acquainted with maximum and minimum sizes for dwelling structures and maximum heights for commercial buildings, but knows of no authority for minimum heights or sizes of structures in business districts. From the uses permitted in the said business district of said code (2-A commercial), the aforesaid subsection (h), on the face thereof, has no relationship to public health, safety, morals or welfare, has no relationship to lot area, is not necessary and is unreasonable, arbitrary, discriminatory, invalid and unconstitutional."

We have considered the contentions presented on behalf of the appellant in light of the record and briefs and find them to be without merit. The holding of the trial court, as quoted above, was not in error.

Zoning requirements specifying minimum height for business buildings have uniformly been held invalid, as arbitrary, unreasonable and having no relation to public health, safety, or welfare.

Regarding the city's zoning regulation requiring a minimum floor area of twenty five hundred square feet for business buildings, we hold the trial judge was not in error in declaring the provision of the zoning ordinance to be invalid. Although minimum floor area provisions with reference to *dwellings* in residential areas have generally been held to be valid as a proper exercise of police power (see Annot. 96 A.L.R.2d 1410), neither the briefs of the parties nor our independent search has revealed any decisions upholding such a zoning regulation with reference to business buildings.

The one decision which has come to our attention dealing with that question is a New Jersey case, Ridgeview Co. v. Board of Adjustment of Florham Park, in which a zoning stores was held to be clearly unreasonable, arbitrary and not designed to further the objectives of the zoning ordinance. Without holding or implying that validity would be conferred on such a regulation if imposed in relation to lot size, in the instant case we note, as did the trial judge, that the requirement for a minimum floor area of twenty five hundred square feet for business buildings was provided for in this zoning ordinance without any relation or regard to lot size or area. Compare City of West Palm Beach v. State ex rel. Duffey, wherein the Supreme Court of Florida affirmed a judgment in mandamus commanding the city to issue a building permit which the city had refused to issue for noncompliance with a zoning ordinance provision which there was held to be invalid, viz: "* * * (E)very new building or structure must substantially equal that of the adjacent buildings or structures in said subdivision in appearance, square foot area and height."

Accordingly, the judgment appealed from is affirmed.

F. ZONING ADMINISTRATION

Two competing constitutional principles create a tension in the administration of zoning laws. On one hand, the principle of equal protection of the laws requires **comprehensiveness** and **uniformity of application** of zoning laws to avoid having any group unduly favored or subjected to discrimination. On the other hand, the principle of due process of law requires departures from comprehensiveness and uniformity to avoid a harsh or unreasonable deprivation of the use of private property. To reconcile these competing legal principles, zoning enabling legislation authorizes several techniques that provide some escape from a literal and rigid enforcement of zoning laws and also create a governmental agency to administer the process by which these techniques are made available to landowners.

1. The Zoning Board of Adjustment

The Standard State Zoning Enabling Act, upon which most enabling legislation is based, provides for the creation of a **board of adjustment,** also known as a **zoning board of adjustment** or a **board of appeals.** This municipal body is usually given the following powers: (1) to hear and decide appeals where it is alleged that there is an error in any order or decision of an administrative official, e.g., a zoning officer or building officer; (2) to hear and decide **special exceptions;** (3) to authorize **variances** from the terms of the zoning law. In recent years some states have begun to develop variations on this theme. For example in New Jersey, the state enabling legislation gives the zoning board of adjustment the following powers: (a) hear and decide appeals; (b) hear and decide requests for **interpretation** of zoning laws; (c) grant **bulk variances** upon a showing of practical difficulties or undue hardship and (d) grant **use variances** upon a showing of special reasons. The New Jersey law also transfers the power to grant **special exceptions** from the zoning board to the planning board and changes the name of this technique from "special exception" to **"conditional use."** In most other states the power to grant special exceptions is retained by the zoning board.

The authority of a municipality or county to create a zoning board of adjustment is derived from the state legislature through enabling legislation. In most states, this authority is given to municipalities only. In some states, California for example, this power is given to county government as well. In most states, citizen members of the zoning board serve without compensation. In some states however, payment of compensation is authorized. The following excerpt from the California enabling legislation illustrates some of these variations.

CALIFORNIA STATUTES

§ 65900. **Creation of agencies; compensation of members.** The legislative body of a city or county may, by ordinance, create and establish either a board of zoning adjustment, or the office of zoning administrator or both. It may also, by ordinance, create and establish a board of appeals. Members of a board of zoning adjustment and members of a board of appeals may receive compensation for their attendance at each meeting of their respective boards in a sum to be fixed by the legislative body by which they are appointed. In addition, they may also receive reasonable traveling expenses to and from the usual place of business of such board to any place of meeting of the board within the county or city.

Applications to the zoning board are made at a public hearing at which neighbors and other interested persons are given the opportunity to be heard. To assure the opportunity for neighboring landowners to appear at such hearings the enabling legislation will usually prescribe a procedure for giving notice of forthcoming public hearings by the zoning board. The following excerpt from the California enabling legislation is one example of such provision.

§ **65905. Notice.** Whenever an application for a variance, or a conditional use permit or other permit, for revocation or modification of same or an appeal from the action taken thereon, is submitted to the body or person charged with conducting a public hearing thereon, notice of hearing shall be given by notice through the United States mails, with postage prepaid using addresses from the last equalized assessment roll, or alternatively, from such other records of the assessor or the tax collector as contain more recent addresses in the opinion of said body, or by both publication in a newspaper of general circulation in accordance with Section 65854 and posting said notice in conspicuous places close to the property affected. Procedure for mailing or posting of said notices shall be governed by the provisions of the local ordinance.

---

2. Variances

A **variance** is a grant of permission to depart from the literal enforcement of a zoning ordinance and allow the property to be used in a manner otherwise forbidden, upon findings by the zoning board, relating to standards prescribed in the zoning ordinance. There is ambiguity about the kinds of relief that may be granted under a variance because of the failure of the enabling legislation in most states to distinguish between **use variances** and **bulk variances.** The Standard State Zoning Enabling Act on which most legislation is based creates this ambiguity by the following provision:

> "To authorize upon appeal in specific cases such variance from the terms of the ordinance as will not be contrary to the public interest, where, owing to special conditons, a literal enforcement of the provisions of the ordinance will result in unnecessary hardship, and so that the spirit of the ordinance shall be observed and substantial justice done."

Compare the above provision with the following provisions from the New Jersey Municipal Land Use Law:

C. 40:55D-70 Powers.

Powers. The board of adjustment shall have the power to:

a. Hear and decide appeals where it is alleged by the appellant that there is error in any order, requirement, decision or refusal made by an administrative officer based on or made in the enforcement of the zoning ordinance;

b. Hear and decide in accordance with the provisions of any such ordinance, requests for interpretation of the zoning map or ordinance . . . . for decisions upon other special questions upon which such board is authorized to pass by any zoning or official map ordinance in accordance with this act;

c. Where by reason of exceptional **narrowness, shallowness or shape** of a specific piece of property, or by reason of exceptional topographic conditions, or by reason of other extraordinary and exceptional situation or condition of such piece of property the strict application of any regulation pursuant to article 8 of this act would result in peculiar and exceptional practical difficulties to, or exceptional and undue hardship upon the developer of such property, grant, upon an application or an appeal relating to such property, a variance from such strict application of such regulation so as to relieve such difficulties or hardship; provided, however, that no variance shall be granted under this subsection to allow a structure or use in a district restricted against such structure or use; and provided further that the proposed development does not require approval by the planning board of a subdivision, site plan or conditional use in conjunction with which the planning board shall review a request for a variance pursuant to subsection 47a. of this act.

d. Grant a variance to allow a structure or use in a district restricted against such structure or use in particular cases and for special reasons, but only by affirmative vote of at least two-thirds of the full authorized membership of the board.

No variance or other relief may be granted under the terms of this section unless such variance or other relief can be granted without substantial detriment to the public good and will not substantially impair the intent and purpose of the zone plan and zoning ordinance. An application under this section may be referred to any appropriate person or agency, including the planning board pursuant to section 17 of this act, for its report; provided that such reference shall not extend the period of time within which the zoning board of adjustment shall act.

Source:

R.S. 40:55-39 (as amended).

(a) The Standard State Enabling Act Provisions

In states with enabling legislation based upon the Standard State Enabling Act it is not clear whether variances may be granted to change the **use** to which the property may be used or whether variances are limited to changes dealing with the relationship of the bulk of the proposed structure to the lot. In either case, the **standard** prescribed by the legislation, upon which the zoning board must make findings, is that **"unnecessary hardship"** (or **"practical difficulties,"** in some legislation) will result from a literal enforcement of the terms of the ordinance. There have been numerous judicial decisions on the question of what constitutes "unnecessary hardship" or "practical difficulties." The decisions vary greatly on this issue. However, some principles are clear: (1) mere inconvenience is not sufficient; (2) reduction in value, alone, is not sufficient; (3) inability to put the property to its most profitable use does not constitute "unnecessary hardship or practical difficulties;" (4) the problem must be caused by the ordinance and not by the owner or some person; (5) a showing that the land could not be used for **any purpose** for which it is reasonably adapted does constitute "unnecessary hardship or practical difficulties."

In addition to the above findings, the zoning board must also find that the variance will "not be contrary to the public interest" and that "the spirit of the ordinance shall be observed and substantial justice done." This means that the applicant must show and the zoning board must find, that the granting of the variance will not be harmful to the public interest.

OTTO

v.

STEINHILBER

282 N.Y. 71, 24 N.E.2d 851 (1939)

FINCH, Judge.

The question presented on this appeal is whether, upon the record in this case, there are shown the requisite elements which would authorize the Board of Appeals to grant a variance in the application of the zoning laws upon the ground of unnecessary hardship.

The property in question fronts on the north side of Merrick road in the incorporated village of Lynbrook, Nassau county. The tract is an irregular plot of about five acres, with a frontage of 598.9 feet, a depth of 614 feet on the easterly side and of 495 feet on the westerly side. The rear is 237.9 feet. The area is approximately in the shape of a truncated triangle. Property on Merrick road is zoned for commercial purposes to a depth of 150 feet on either side of the road. The adjoining area is zoned for residential purposes. Thus the major portion of the land in question is within a class "A" residential zone. The only access to the residential portion of the tract is by way of crossing the portion within the commerical zone fronting on Merrick road. To the rear and sides of this block are the properties of the neighboring owners which front upon other streets. Intervener applied to the Board of Appeals for a variance (in the enforcement of the restrictions prevailing in the residential zone) so that he might erect a large roller skating rink upon both the commercial and the residential portions of his land. A roller skating rink is a permissible commercial use. The skating rink was to be set back fifteen feet from the property line and to face Merrick road. It was to have a width of 240 feet, a depth of 434 feet, and a height of 49 feet.

In the immediate residential area adjoining the proposed skating rink have been erected many family residences, the occupants of which allege that the erection of the skating rink and the attendance which it will bring will practically destroy the availability of the neighborhood for residential purposes. About 600 objectors have so protested.

The Board granted a variance on the ground of unnecessary hardship and, in its return to the order to review its determination, detailed as its reasons therefor these facts: (1) That the land lies within two zones, in one of which the requested use is available as of right under the zoning law; (2) that the only means of access to the residential portion is by crossing over the portion in the commercial zone; (3) that the intervener could erect the roller skating rink wholly within the commercial zone, but access to the rear portion would thereby be obstructed; (4) that if the roller skating rink is restricted to the commercial portion of the land, parking of automobiles of patrons will necessarily have to be in the streets in that vicinity, whereas if the roller skating rink is allowed to be erected in accordance with the variance granted by the Board of Appeals, the automobiles could be parked on the property and at the sides of the rink building, thereby obviating a potential traffic problem. In addition thereto, the intervener contends that he could not create a street over the commercial portion of his property outside of that to be occupied by the rink because of the width and grade required for a village street. Village Law, Consol. Laws, ch. 64, § 179-L.

The object of a variance granted by the Board of Appeals in favor of property owners suffering unnecessary hardship in the operation of a zoning law, is to afford relief to an individual property owner laboring under restrictions to which no valid general objection may be made. Where the property owner is unable reasonably to use his land because of zoning restrictions, the fault may lie in the fact that the particular zoning restriction is unreasonable in its application to a certain locality, or the oppressive result may be caused by conditions peculiar to a particular piece of land. In the former situation, the relief is by way of direct attack upon the terms of the ordinance. Nectow v. City of Cambridge. In order to prevent the oppressive operation of the zoning law in particular instances, when the zoning restrictions are otherwise generally reasonable, the zoning laws usually create a safety valve under the control of a Board of Appeals, which may relieve against "unnecessary hardship" in particular instances. This the statute accomplishes in the following language: "Where there are practical difficulties or unnecessary hardship in the way of carrying out the strict letter of such ordinance, the board of appeals shall have the power in passing upon appeals, to vary or modify the application of any of the regulations or provisions of such ordinance relating to the use, construction or alteration of buildings or structures, or the use of land, so that the spirit of the ordinance shall be observed, public safety and welfare secured and substantial justice done." Village Law, § 179-b. Cf. New York City Zoning Resolution, § 21. As a result of these provisions, "there has been confided to the board a delicate jurisdiction and one easily abused."

Before the Board may exercise its discretion and grant a variance upon the ground of unnecessary hardship, the record must show that (1) the land in question cannot yield a reasonable return if used only for a purpose allowed in that zone; (2) that the plight of the owner is due to unique circumstances and not to the general conditions in the neighborhood which may reflect the unreasonableness of the zoning ordinance itself; and (3) that the use to be authorized by the variance will not alter the essential character of the locality. Bassett, op. cit. supra, pp. 168, 169.

In the case at bar the applicant has failed to introduce any evidence whatever tending to show that the portion of his land which is located in the residential zone may not be reasonably employed in conformity with the zoning regulations governing Class "A" districts. The most which can be said for the cause of the intervener is that, if the variance were granted he could make an immediate profitable use of the entire tract. Intervener contends that the lack of access to the street from the rear portion constitutes an element showing unnecessary hardship. Intervener further contends that after the erection of the rink insufficient land will remain on either side to permit a street of the width required by the Village Law, § 179-1 for access to the residential portion of his property. This section, in so far as we are presently concerned, provides: "That the streets and highways shall be of sufficient width and suitable grade and shall be suitably located to accommodate the prospective traffic, to afford adequate light and air, to facilitate fire protection, and to provide access of fire-fighting equipment to buildings * * *." Intervener owns a frontage of virtually 600 feet upon Merrick road. He fails to show in any manner how the provisions of the statute quoted would prevent the creation of a right of way to the rear portion. For all that is shown, another use of the commercial property, or even a rearrangement of the rink building confined to the commercial portion, would seem to leave ample space for a village street. For the lack of any facts whatever from which it may reasonably be inferred that the zoning restrictions, requiring residential use of the rear portion of the land, would amount to an unnecessary hardship, a grant of a variance by the Board of Appeals was improper.

Furthermore, there is no evidence to show that the situation in which intervener finds himself, as a result of the fact that the commercial belt bordering the Merrick road extends to a depth of only 150 feet on either side of the road, is unique and distinct from that of the other owners whose properties front on the Merrick road. The provision for a commercial zone along the Merrick road is the result of the same situation which was involved in Dowsey v. Village of Kensington, supra, where this court held invalid a zoning ordinance in so far as it failed to allow commercial uses along the frontage of a main commercial highway. In the vicinity and back along both sides of the Merrick road lies a residential district. Because of the heavy traffic upon that highway it was but a reasonable regulation to permit commercial uses of the property fronting upon the highway. Obviously there have to be some limits to this commercial zone. The extent thereof is primarily a legislative question and has been resolved in the zoning law to be no more than 150 feet away from the Merrick road. For all that appears in the record, other property owners may also have rear portions without direct access to the streets in the residential area. If this be a hardship, then the vice is in the legislation itself and is not to be remedied by piecemeal exemption which ultimately changes the character of the neighborhood and creates far greater hardships than that which a variance may alleviate because of the obsolescence caused to property values created by those seeking residences in reliance upon the design of the zoning ordinance. Thus, the variance granted by the Board of Appeals does not comply with the remaining two of the three prerequisites mentioned above, that the hardship to be alleviated not only be one peculiar to the applicant, but also that the relief granted shall not alter the essential character of the neighborhood heretofore devoted to residential purposes. In that event the commercial zone would to all intents and purposes extend not 150 feet, but for several hundred feet beyond.

The grant of the variance to the intervener by the Board of Appeals, therefore, is improper upon this record, which does not set forth any proof of the three elements constituting unnecessary hardship within the meaning of the zoning laws.

The order of the Appellate Division, confirming the determination of the Board of Appeals, should be reversed, the determination of the Board of Appeals annulled, and the application of the intervener denied, with costs in all courts.

LEHMAN, J. (dissenting). Where the major part of a large parcel of land lies in a residence district but has access only to a street in a business district, the unnecessary hardship and practical difficulties of strict enforcement of the zoning ordinance seem to me obvious.

An issue that frequently arises in applications for a variance based upon hardship or practical difficulties, is whether the variance should be denied if the applicant knew of the zoning restrictions at the time that the property was purchased. Some courts have held that a hardship variance should not be granted where the applicant has purchased the property with knowledge of the zoning restriction. The difficulty with this position is that it penalizes the **current owner** of the property because of the effect of such a principle upon the market value of the property. Consequently, the courts in other states permit the purchaser of property to acquire whatever rights the seller had and thereby permit the decision to be based upon the merits of the particular case. See **Wilson v. Borough of Mountainside,** 42 N.J. 426, 201 A.2d 540 (1964). Compare with **Searles v. Darling,** 46 Del. 263, 83 A.2d 96 (1951).

(b) The New Jersey Land Use Law

In the New Jersey enabling legislation there are separate provisions for **bulk variances** and **use variances.** A *bulk* variance (i.e., exceptional narrowness, shallowness or shape of specific piece of property, or by reason of exceptional topographical conditions . . .) may be granted upon a showing of *peculiar and exceptional practical difficulties or undue hardship.* On the other hand, a *use* variance may be granted upon a showing of *special reasons.* In both cases the applicant must show and the zoning board must find, that the variance can be granted *"without substantial detriment to the public good and will not substantially impair the intent and purpose of the zone plan and ordinance."*

DESIMONE

v.

GREATER ENGLEWOOD HOUSING CORP. NO. 1.

56 N.J. 428, 267 A.2d 31 (1970)

HALL, J.

The basic case in this panoply of litigation is that involving the use variance. The background and setting of GEHC's Trumbull Park project is thoroughly elucidated in the voluminous testimony and extensive exhibits presented to the Board of Adjustment. From that mass of evidence the following picture emerges.

Englewood, like many others, is a city of striking contrasts. It is five square miles in area and lies on the western slope of the Palisades in eastern Bergen County. The population of about 28,000 is 20% to 25% black. It is one of the older suburban residential communities adjacent to New York City, its white population is generally affluent, and its Master Plan described it in 1959 as almost wholly built up, with an exceedingly low housing vacancy rate.

By far the greater part of the black population lives in the Fourth Ward (the southwestern quadrant of the city), literally and figuratively "on the other side of the tracks," and a very high percentage of the housing there is substandard, much of it not capable of rehabilitation. The trial judge found:

> * * * [F]or a considerable period the need for low and moderate income housing in the City of Englewood has not only been set forth and stated by government agencies and private citizens, but has been readily apparent to anyone viewing the Englewood scene. Down through the years an inevitable racial polarization of the inhabitants of Englewood has come into being. Of the City's four wards the First [northeast quadrant] and Second [southeast quadrant] are generally developed with expensive homes inhabited by Caucasians ranging from the more modest at the southern end of the Second Ward to inpressive estates as one goes northward into the First Ward.
> * * * [T]he Third Ward [northwest quadrant] can be generally characterized as one made up of modest one family structures on smaller lots predominately white with some degree of integration effected in recent years. The Fourth Ward, generally down hill from the First and Second Wards, is practically all black and can truly and accurately be characterized as a ghetto, a blighted and racially impacted area of the City. For some time the City of Englewood has passed resolutions and ordinances, it has conducted surveys and has issued reports in great number demonstrating the need for razing the ghetto area and building new housing.

(Plaintiffs expressly concede the need for low and moderate income housing in the Fourth Ward.)

Numerous prior efforts to provide some decent housing for the city's blacks have all failed. Not a single governmentally sponsored or assisted housing accommodation has been constructed. By reason of a racial disturbance in the city in July 1967, it became one of the communities scrutinized by the Governor's Select Commission on Civil Disorder. The Commission's "Report for Action" (February 1968) commented cogently on the housing situation, pointing out that prior efforts had foundered, in a sharply divided community, on the issue "whether to build within the Fourth Ward only, or whether to spread renewal beyond the ghetto." See discussion, op. cit. *supra* at pp. 63-64. It recommended:

> Englewood, which has the human and physical resources not only to solve its own problems but also to show the way to other communities, should consider reversing past decisions on its critical housing issue.

Political and community leaders, regardless of party, should work to unite all communities in support of solutions in accordance with public policy and the trend of the times toward residential integration. (op. cit. *supra*, at p. 169).

Obviously, the critical Englewood housing situation cries out for the active and continuous exercise of the highest responsible citizenship by all segments of the population and all governmental bodies. The governmental actions here under attack do represent the first indication of the reversal of past decisions. Sadly to relate, however, the objectors, despite all the legalisms in which this intense and pervading litigation is couched, in truth are not trying to vindicate the policy of the many statutes they invoke, but rather only in any way at all to oppose this project.

As has been indicated, the Trumbull Park site project in question is being undertaken by GEHC simultaneously with the Lafayette site project in the Fourth Ward. They will make possible redevelopment and renewal plans in the Fourth Ward by providing relocation homes for families to be displaced thereby. Construction of both is to be financed by an already committed $5.4 million 100% mortgage granted by the State Housing Financing Agency. Mortgage interest subsidy, as well as rent supplements to qualifying occupants, are to be provided by appropriate federal agencies. Federal regulations require, in such a situation, that new housing be built outside a ghetto area on at least a one for one basis with respect to that constructed within it. As the Board of Adjustment put it in its resolution recommending the use variance:

It is said, in short, that slum clearance cannot proceed without relocation housing; that low and/or moderate-income housing cannot be constructed without federal subsidies; that federal subsidies will not be forthcoming in the absence of provisions for balancing new units within the area of racial concentration with new units outside the area; * * *

The Board went on to remark that the Trumbull Park site is "the only available tract of suitable size in the City outside the racially-impacted area." * * *

The Variances

The one issue which is novel and important is the basis for the grant of the use variance.

The pertinent section of the zoning enabling act, N.J.S.A. 40:55-39(d) authorizes the grant of a use variance upon an affirmative finding of "special reasons" "in particular cases," together with the negative findings, applicable in all zoning relief situations, that the "relief can be granted without substantial detriment to the public good and will not substantially impair the intent and purpose of the zone plan and zoning ordinance."

It is long settled law in this state that this unique provision does not require that the particular premises cannot feasibly be used for a permitted use or that other hardship exists. "Special reasons" is a flexible concept; broadly speaking, it may be defined by the purposes of zoning set forth in N.J.S.A. 40:55-32, which specifically include promotion of "health, morals or the general welfare." Ward v. Scott, 11 N.J. 117, 93 A.2d 385 (1952). So variances have been approved for many public and semi-public uses because they significantly further the general welfare. See, e.g., Andrews v. Board of Adjustment of the Township of Ocean, 30 N.J. 245, 152 A.2d 580 (1959) (parochial school in residential zones); Black v. Montclair, 34 N.J. 105, 167 A.2d 388 (1961) (additional parochial school building in residential zone); Burton v. Montclair, 40 N.J. 1, 190 A.2d 377 (1963) (private school in residential zones); Yahnel v. Board of Adjustment of Jamesburg, 79 N.J.Super. 509, 192 A.2d 177 (App.Div.1963), cert. den. 41 N.J. 116, 195 A.2d 15 (1963) (telephone equipment building in residential zone); Kunzler v. Hoffman, 48 N.J. 277, 225 A.2d 321 (1966) (private hospital for emotionally disturbed in residential zone). Compare Kohl v. Mayor and Council of Borough of Fair Lawn, 50 N.J. 268, 234 A.2d 385 (1967); Mahler v. Board of Adjustment of Borough of Fair Lawn, 94 N.J.Super. 173, 227 A.2d 511 (App.Div.1967), aff'd o. b. 55 N.J. 1, 258 A.2d 705 (1969).

The conclusions of the Board of Adjustment and the governing body in this regard are fully supported by the very comprehensive proofs before the Board, and are worthy of full quotation. The Board said:

> Without regard, however, to any official federal or state requirements, the Board finds and concludes that the demand of public policy cannot be satisfied by continued confinement of non-white families in the Fourth Ward area, and that breaking the long-standing patterns of racial segregation in this city will promote the general welfare of the community. The Board further finds and concludes that the program in question will serve to alleviate urban blight; to promote the health, morals and general welfare of the residents of this City; and to encourage appropriate land use throughout the City. * * *

The Council adopted the Board's findings and added:

> 2. The Council of the City of Englewood further finds that the provision of low and moderate income housing by means of a governmentally financed housing program undertaken by the Greater Englewood Housing Corporation as a non-profit qualified housing sponsor which housing is limited to cluster-type units not exceeding two stories in height serves the general welfare of the City of Englewood which has for some time last past suffered from a desperate housing shortage for low and moderate income families residing within the City of Englewood and that the present condition of low and middle income families being forced to live in substandard, unsafe and unsanitary dwellings which are in need of major repairs or are unfit for residential use or are overcrowded constitute a condition detrimental to the health, safety, morals, welfare, and reasonable comfort of all of the people of the City of Englewood and that the amelioration of this condition will result from the granting of the requested variance and thereby promote the health, safety, morals and general welfare of the City of Englewood.
>
> 3. The Council of the City of Englewood further finds that the granting of the variance requested with respect to the aforemen-

tioned premises will together with the granting of the variance applied for in the companion application heretofore referred to, will result in a racially balanced housing program in that governmentally financed low and moderate income housing will be constructed both within and without the impacted area of the Fourth Ward of the City of Englewood and the Council further finds that freedom of choice of residents of the impacted area of the Fourth Ward to reside within or without said area in safe, decent and attractive housing that they can afford serves the community's interest in achieving an integrated, just and free society and promotes the general welfare of all citizens.

Also of importance in this connection is the legislative determination set forth in N.J.S.A. 55:16-2 of the statute under which GEHC was incorporated:

It is hereby declared that there is a severe housing shortgage in the State; that there are places in many municipalities of the State where dwellings lack proper sanitary facilities and are in need of major repairs or unfit for residential use; that these conditions are detrimental to the health, safety, morals, welfare and reasonable comfort of the people of the State; that these conditions reduce economic values and impair private investments and public revenues; that the improvement of these conditions requires the production of new dwellings at rents which the families who need housing can afford; that the creation of the agencies and corporations hereinafter described, is necessary and desirable for this purpose; that the provisions of housing to make possible and to assist the clearance, planning, development or redevelopment of blighted areas, as proposed in this act, is a public purpose and a public use for which public money may be spent and private property acquired; and that the necessity in the public interest for the provisions hereinafter enacted is hereby declared as a matter of legislative determination.

Plaintiffs challenge these conclusions as insufficient to constitute "special reasons." Judge Trautwein held that they were legally adequate and we thoroughly concur. We specifically hold, as matter of law in the light of public policy and the law of the land, that public or, as here, semi-public housing accommodations to provide safe, sanitary and decent housing, to relieve and replace substandard living conditions or to furnish housing for minority or underprivileged segments of the population outside of ghetto areas is a special reason adequate to meet that requirement of N.J.S.A. 40:55-39(d) and to ground a use variance.

Plaintiffs also challenge the agencies' findings that the negative criteria were not factually and legally met. The Board found that, "by reason of the location, topography and isolation of the tract in question, as well as the design and layout of the structures proposed to be erected, such adverse effect as the proposed multi-family use may have on nearby one-family uses will be minimal, and that the relief requested may, accordingly, be granted without substantial detriment to the public good and without substantial impairment of the intent or purpose of the zone plan or zoning ordinance." The governing body concluded that this finding was supported by the evidence. The trial court agreed and we think the conclusion is irresistible in the light of the proofs.

Indeed, we should observe, parenthetically, that courts rarely find land use cases where the evidence before local bodies is as comprehensive and as thoroughly presented and where, procedurally, hearings and other proceedings are as fairly, fully and meticulously conducted and resolutions and ordinances as well prepared as was done in the instant situation.

Finally, plaintiffs urge that the use variance is invalid as constituting rezoning without legislative action. Stress is laid on the 10 acre size of the tract. While a zoning amendment specifically changing the use of the site (some of the zoning ordinance's multi-family districts appear to be no larger) or providing for the use as a special exception under N.J.S.A. 40:55-39(b) would have been appropriate as well, the size of the site does not preclude a use variance under the circumstances. * * *

In sum, the use variance was properly granted. In fact, a denial of it under the circumstances and proofs could not well be sustained.

Little need be said about the bulk variance granted under N.J.S.A. 40:55-39(c), which authorizes a variance from yard, setback, height and similar restrictions caused by exceptional site situations or conditions which would otherwise result in peculiar and exceptional practical difficulties and hardship. There is some doubt whether it was required at all, since the use variance granted approval of the specific project, the full layout of which was before the Board of Adjustment on that occasion. The relief granted by the (c) variance was from requirements which fitted single-family dwellings but made no sense for a multi-family cluster-type project on a large, hilly, rocky site. If required at all, it was in fact essential by reason of the use variance previously allowed. We see nothing improper about it.

* * *

The judgments of the Law Division are affirmed.

---

3. Special Exception—Conditional Uses

A **special exception**, sometimes called a **special permit**, a **special use** or a **conditional use**, is a grant of permission to depart from the general provisions of a zoning ordinance, authorized by express provision by the ordinance, upon a finding of facts and the imposition of conditions prescribed by the ordinance. For example, the zoning ordinance may designate a district for single family use but provide that a hospital or school may be permitted by the zoning board upon a finding that such use would serve the public interest and subject to such conditions relating to parking, landscaping, etc. that would protect the interest of the nearby residents. Thus, there are four unique characteristics of a special exception: (1) the request use must be specified in the zoning ordinance; (2) an application must be made to and approved by the zoning board; (3) the zoning board must determine that the use, if permitted in the proposed site, would not be detrimental to the public good; and (4) the zoning board may attach such conditions as necessary to preserve such public good.

This ability to impose conditions to the approval is the reason why many planners, lawyers and an increasing number of statutes have begun to refer to

this technique as a **conditional use.** The New Jersey Municipal Land Use Law·
has adopted this terminology but has also gone one step further and transferred this power from the zoning board to the planning board.

KOTRICH

v.

COUNTY OF DU PAGE

19 Ill. 2d 181, 166 N.E.2d 601 (1960)

SCHAEFER, Justice.

This is a declaratory judgment proceeding which involves the validity of a "special use" permit granted by the defendant; the board of supervisors of Du Page County, to the defendant, Salt Creek Club, under the terms of the Du Page County zoning ordinance. The primary issues concern the statutory authority of the county to provide for "special uses" in its zoning ordinance, and, if the authority exists, the conditions that govern its exercise.

The defendant club is a not-for-profit corporation organized for social, educational, and athletic purposes. It owns the property in question, a six-acre parcel of land now zoned for R-2 single family residence use. On this land it proposes to build a clubhouse, a swimming pool, tennis courts and a parking area for use of its anticipated membership of 275 families.

The club applied to the zoning board for a special use permit under the county ordinance, to allow the construction of a private outdoor recreation center on the property. The board conducted a hearing and recommended to the county board that the special use permit be denied. Notwithstanding this recommendation, the county board passed a resolution granting the permit. The plaintiffs, who are adjacent property owners, commenced this suit in the circuit court of Du Page County to challenge the permit and the zoning ordinance under which it was granted. From a judgment sustaining the validity of the ordinance and the permit, they appeal directly to this court. The trial judge has certified that the validity of a county zoning ordinance is involved and that the public interest requires a direct appeal to this court. Ill.Rev.Stat.1959, chap. 110, par. 75.

The special use is a relatively new method of land use control. Zoning ordinances embodying this technique retain the usual residential, commercial, and industrial zones, specifying the uses permitted in each zone. For each zone, however, special uses are also established which are permitted within the zone only if approved by the zoning board or the governing legislative body. The Du Page County ordinance follows this general scheme, and it specifies private outdoor recreational facilities among the special uses which may be permitted in the R-2 single family residence zone. Among other special uses permitted in this zone are colleges and universities, public hospitals and sanitariums, planned developments of not less than 40 acres, and "public service uses" such as electric and telephone substations, filtration plants, and fire and police stations.

The first contention advanced by the plaintiffs is that the County Zoning Enabling Act (Ill. Rev. Stat. 1957, chap. 34 par. 152i et seq.) does not authorize counties to employ this method. In support of this contention they argue that since the special use technique is not mentioned in the act, and indeed did not exist at the time the act was adopted in 1935, the legislature could not have intended to authorize it. Their position is that the legislature must specifically grant counties the power to adopt special use provisions, as it has done in the case of variations and amendments, and as legislatures of some other States have done.

They note also that procedural safeguards limit the exercise of administrative and legislative discretion with respect to variations and amendments. Written findings of fact must accompany every variation, and any variation rejected by the zoning board of appeals can be approved only by a three-fourths majority of the legislative body. The same extraordinary majority is required to approve any amendment if 20% of adjacent landowners object. It is argued that the legislature has thus indicated its intention that deviations from the established zoning pattern should be permitted only by the procedurally restricted methods included in the act. * * *

Carl L. Gardner, a planning and zoning consultant, testified that the special use technique developed as a means of providing for infrequent types of land use which are necessary and desirable but which are potentially incompatible with uses usually allowed in residential, commercial and industrial zones. Such uses generally occupy a rather large tract of land. They connot be categorized in any given use zone without the danger of excluding beneficial uses or including dangerous ones. A typical example was presented in *Illinois Bell Telephone Co. v. Fox*, where this court affirmed a judgment ordering a special use permit to issue for construction of a telephone exchange in a residential district.

Instead of excluding such uses entirely from certain zones because of the harm they might cause, or, despite the potential harm, including them because of the benefits they will bring, the special use technique allows a more flexible approach. It contemplates that the county board may permit these uses when desirable and, if necessary, impose conditions designed to protect nearby property owners. This seems to be an effective method of dealing with a narrow but difficult problem of land use control. Approximately 25 municipalities and counties in Illinois have incorporated it in their zoning ordinances, and the record shows that its use is increasing.

It is true that the procedural restrictions prescribed for amendments and variations, as well as the standards prescribed for variations, evidence a legislative plan to guarantee property owners some protection from piecemeal changes in the general zoning scheme by *ad hoc* determinations with respect to particular pieces of property. And since granting a special use permit involves an *ad hoc* judgment which may affect surrounding property owners in the same way as a variation or an amendment, unlimited application of the special use technique to land uses that can readily be accommodated within the customary categories would undermine the protection contemplated by the statute. But unlimited application of the special use technique is not required to meet the problem it was designed to solve. Only those infrequent uses which are beneficial, but potentially inconsistent with normal uses in the various zones, need be included.

The statute authorizes the board of supervisors "to regulate and restrict the location and use of buildings, structures and land for trade, industry, residence and other uses which may be specified by such board, * * *; to divide the entire county * * * into districts of such number, shape, area and of such different classes, according to the use of land and buildings * * * as may be deemed best suited to carry out the purposes of this Act; to prohibit uses, buildings or structures incompatible with the character of such districts respectively; * * *." Ill.Rev.Stat.1957, chap. 34, par. 1521i. In our opinion, a residual category of those special uses which cannot, without distortion, be included in the customary classifications, is permissible as a means of implementing the powers conferred by the statute.

Applying these criteria, we think that a private country club such as that involved in the present case may properly be classified as a special use in a single family residence zone. Such uses of land are often found in residential areas. Proximity to a club may increase the desirability of land. On the other hand, a club may also produce increased noise from bathers, tennis players, social functions and automobiles. If the parking area is not properly designed, headlights may shine in neighboring houses; if it is not large enough, members' automobiles will overflow onto neighboring streets. Increased traffic may produce safety hazards. Whether these undesirable consequences will occur depends upon the design of the club's facilities and its location within the zone. In such a case, governmental supervision of each situation is justified.

The plaintiffs also contend that the ordinance providing for special uses is invalid because it does not specify standards by which the county board of supervisors is to judge whether a special use permit should be granted. Although the ordinance does not prescribe standards in so many words, it does state that special uses are established for the purpose of providing "for the location of special classes of uses which are deemed desirable for the public welfare within a given district or districts, but which are potentially incompatible with typical uses herein permitted within them * * *." It also empowers the board of supervisors to impose "such * * * conditions as it considers necessary to protect the public health, safety and welfare." A fair reading of the ordinance shows that it contemplates that the county board will weigh the desirability of the proposed use against its potential adverse impact. Since the board of supervisors is a legislative body, precise standards to govern its determination are not required. * * *

The judgment is affirmed.

For an interesting illustration of an attempt to use the "special-use" technique as a device for great zoning flexibility, see *Rockhill v. Chesterfield Township*,

23 N.J. 117, 128 A.2d 473 (1957). For an extensive discussion of this subject see, Note, "The Use and Abuse of the Special Permit in Zoning Law," 35 *Brooklyn L.Rev.* 258 (1969).

4. Amendments to the Zoning Ordinance—SPOT ZONING

After a comprehensive zoning ordinance is adopted, the governing body may find reason to modify its original enactment by an **amendment to the zoning law.** If the validity of the zoning amendment is challenged, the court will be concerned with the question of whether the amendment was adopted for the benefit of the public or whether the primary beneficiary is the private owner of the property. This judicial concern is limited by two fundamental principles of our governmental system: The first principle involves the **power of successive legislatures.** This means that no legislative session has any greater power than subsequent legislatures to adopt, repeal and amend laws. Consequently, subject only to constitutional restrictions, any governing body has the power to amend the zoning and other laws previously adopted. The second principle that limits the ability of courts to reject zoning amendments is the principle of **separation of powers.** Under this principle, it is not the function of the courts to review the wisdom of legislative determinations or to substitute its judgment for the policy decisions of the legislature.

In spite of these limitations, courts do strike down zoning amandments. Whether a zoning amendment will be upheld or invalidated is a factual question that depends upon the circumstances of the case. If the court finds that the zoning amendment was adopted for the benefit of a private person and not for the welfare of the community as a whole, the amendment will be called **"spot zoning"** and held invalid. Courts in different states have adopted different principles to determine the validity of zoning amendments. Some states have adopted the **mistake—change principle** by which it is presumed that the original zoning laws were based on comprehensive planning and were intended to be reasonably permanent. Under this principle, a zoning amendment is *invalid* unless it is shown that (1) conditions in the area have *changed,* or (2) there was a *mistake* made in the original zoning. This rule is considered to be unduly restrictive by the courts of other states because application of this rule would strike down a zoning amendment not based upon a mistake or change of circumstances, but instead is based upon a reevaluation of underlying goals or an unanticipated opportunity to achieve community objectives.

For this reason, the courts of other states have adopted the **comprehensive plan principle** to determine the validity of a zoning amendment. Under this principle, a zoning amendment is valid if it is in accordance with the comprehensive plan and is designed to promote the general welfare rather than the private interests of an individual. The Oregon court has refined this principle by holding that proof that the amendment does conform to the comprehensive plan should include evidence that (1) there is a *public need* for the change in question and (2) that the need is best served by changing the classification of the *particular piece of property* in question.

The issue of the validity of zoning amendments is further complicated by the fact that zoning changes can result in a *decrease* as well as an increase in value. If the zoning amendment results in a reduction of development density, such as a change from garden apartments to single family residence, the amendment will be characterized as **downzoning** and will usually be contested by the landowner.

The cases that follow illustrate the these principles.

FASANO

v.

COUNTY COMMISSIONERS OF WASHINGTON COUNTY

264 Or. 574, 507 P.2d 23 (1973)

The owner of vacant land zoned for single family residential use applied to the local governing body (Board of County Commissioners) for a zoning change to permit the construction of a mobile home park. The governing body amended the zoning ordinance to permit the mobile home use. The adjoining homeowners appealed that decision. The trial court held the zoning amendment invalid. In the opinion excerpted below, the Supreme Court of Oregon affirmed this decision.

* * *

The defendants argue that (1) the action of the county commissioners approving the change is presumptively valid, requiring plaintiffs to show that the commissioners acted arbitrarily in approving the zone change; (2) it was not necessary to show a change of conditions in the area before a zone change of conditions in the area before a zone change could be accomplished; and (3) the change from R-7 to P-R was in accordance with the Washington county comprehensive plan.

We granted review in this case to consider the questions—by what standards does a county commission exercise its authority in zoning matters; who has the burden of meeting those standards when a request for change of zone is made; and what is the scope of court review of such actions?

Any meaningful decision as to the proper scope of judicial review of a zoning decision must start with a characterization of the nature of that decision. The majority of jurisdictions state that a zoning ordinance is a legislative act and is thereby entitled to presumptive validity. This court made such a characterization of zoning decisions in Smith v. County of Washington. * * *

At this juncture we feel we would be ignoring reality to rigidly view all zoning decisions by local governing bodies as legislative acts to be accorded a full presumption of validity and shielded from less than constitutional scrutiny by the theory of separation of powers. Local and small decision groups are simply not the equivalent in all respects of state and national legislatures. There is a growing judicial recognition of this fact of life:

"It is not a part of the legislative function to grant permits, make special exceptions, or decide particular cases. Such activities are not legislative but administrative, quasi-judicial, or judicial in character. To place them in the hands of legislative bodies, whose acts as such are not judicially reviewable, is to open the door completely to arbitrary government." Ward v. Village of Skokie.

* * *

Ordinances laying down general policies without regard to a specific piece of property are usually an exercise of legislative authority, are subject to limited review, and may only be attacked upon constitutional grounds for an arbitrary abuse of authority. On the other hand, a determination whether the permissible use of a specific piece of property should be changed is usually an exercise of judicial authority and its propriety is subject to an altogether different test. An illustration of an exercise of legislative authority is the passage of the ordinance by the Washington County Commission in 1963 which provided for the formation of a planned residential classification to be located in or adjacent to any residential zone. An exercise of judicial authority is the county commissioners' determination in this particular matter to change the classification of A.G.S. Development Company's specific piece of property. The distinction is stated, as follows, in Comment, Zoning Amendments—The Product of Judicial or Quasi-Judicial Action, 33 Ohio St. L.J. 130 (1972):

"* * * Basically, this test involves the determination of whether action produces a general rule or policy which is applicable to an open class of individuals, interest, or situations, or whether it entails the application of a general rule or policy to specific individuals, interests, or situations. If the former determination is satisfied, there is legislative action; if the latter determination is satisfied, the action is judicial." 33 Ohio St. L.J. at 137.

We reject the proposition that judicial review of the county commissioners' determination to change the zoning of the particular property in question is limited to a determination whether the change was arbitrary and capricious.

In order to establish a standard of review, it is necessary to delineate certain basic principles relating to land use regulation.

The basic instrument for county or municipal land use planning is the "comprehensive plan." Haar, In Accordance with a Comprehensive Plan, 68 Harv.L.Rev. 1154 (1955); 1 Yokley, Zoning Law and Practice, § 3-2 (1965); 1 Rathkopf, The Law of Zoning and Planning, § 9-1 (3d ed. 1969). The plan has been described as a general plan to control and direct the use and development of property in a municipality.

In Oregon the county planning commission is required by ORS 215.050 to adopt a comprehensive plan for the use of some or all of the land in the county. Under ORS 215.110 (1), after the comprehensive plan has been adopted, the planning commission recommends to the governing body of the county the ordinances necessary to "carry out" the comprehensive plan. The purpose of the zoning ordinances, both under our statute and the general law of land use regulation, is to "carry out" or implement the comprehensive plan. 1 Anderson, American Law of Zoning, § 1.12 (1968).

Although we are aware of the analytical distinction between zoning and planning, it is clear that under our statutes the plan adopted by the planning commission and the zoning ordinances enacted by the county governing body are closely related; both are intended to be parts of a single integrated procedure for land use control. The plan embodies policy determinations and guiding principles; the zoning ordinances provide the detailed means of giving effect to those principles.

ORS 215.050 states county planning commissions "shall adopt and may from time to time revise a comprehensive plan." In a hearing of the Senate Committee on Local Government, the proponents of ORS 215.050 described its purpose as follows:

> "* * * The intent here is to require a basic document, geared into population, land use, and economic forecasts, which should be the basis of any zoning or other regulations to be adopted by the county. * * *"

* * *

We believe that the state legislature has conditioned the county's power to zone upon the prerequisite that the zoning attempt to further the general welfare of the community through consciousness, in a prospective sense, of the factors mentioned above. In other words, except as noted later in this opinion, it must be proved that the change is in conformance with the comprehensive plan.

In proving that the change is in conformance with the comprehensive plan in this case, the proof, at a minimum, should show (1) there is a public need for a change of the kind in question, and (2) that need will be best served by changing the classification of the particular piece of property in question as compared with other available property.

* * *

Because the action of the commission in this instance is an exercise of judicial authority, the burden of proof should be placed, as is unual in judicial proceedings, upon the one seeking change. The more drastic the change, the greater will be the burden of showing that it is in conformance with the comprehensive plan as implemented by the ordinance, that there is a public need for the kind of change in question, and that the need is best met by the proposal under consideration. As the degree of change increases, the burden of showing that the potential impact upon the area in question was carefully considered and weighed will also increase. If other areas have previously been designated for the particular type of development, it must be shown why it is necessary to introduce it into an area not previously contemplated and why the property owners there should bear the burden of the departure.

* * *

By treating the exercise of authority by the commission in this case as the exercise of judicial rather than of legislative authority and thus enlarging the scope of review on appeal, and by placing the burden of the above level of proof upon the one seeking change, we may lay the court open to criticism by legal scholars who think it desirable that planning authorities be vested with the ability to adjust more freely to changed conditions. However, having weighed the dangers of making desirable change more difficult against the dangers of the almost irresistible pressures that can be asserted by private economic interests on local government, we believe that the latter dangers are more to be feared.

* * *

When we apply the standards we have adopted to the present case, we find that the burden was not sustained before the commission. The record now before us is insufficient to ascertain whether there was a justifiable basis for the decision. The only evidence in the record, that of the staff report of the Washington County Planning Department, is too conclusory and superficial to support the zoning change. It merely states:

"The staff finds that the requested use does conform to the residential designation of the Plan of Development. It further finds that the proposed use reflects the urbanization of the County and the necessity to provide increased densities and different types of housing to meet the needs of urbanization over that allowed by the existing zoning. * * *"

Such generalizations and conclusions, without any statement of the facts on which they are based, are insufficient to justify a change of use. Moreover, no portions of the comprehensive plan of Washington County are before us, and we feel it would be improper for us to take judicial notice of the plan without at least some reference to its specifics by counsel.

As there has not been an adequate showing that the change was in accord with the plan, or that the factors listed in ORS 215.055 were given proper consideration, the judgment is affirmed.

BOARD OF SUPERVISORS OF FAIRFAX COUNTY

v.

SNELL CONSTRUCTION CORPORATION

214 Va. 655, 202 S.E.2d 889 (1974)

POFF, Justice.

This appeal presents our first opportunity to consider the standard to be applied in judicial review of the validity of a zoning ordinance, enacted on motion of the zoning authority, which effects a piecemeal reduction of permissible residential density (downzoning).

Under the 1964 Annandale Comprehensive Master Plan, a 26 acre tract of land lying south of State Route 236 between Backlick Road on the east and Ravensworth Road on the west in Annandale, now owned by Snell Construction Corporation and Preston Construction Corporation (landowners), was zoned for low residential density. On May 16, 1969, landowners filed an application for increased density on a 16 acre portion of the tract. At that time, the 1964 plan was being considered for revision.

On February 25, 1970, the Board of Supervisors of Fairfax County (the Board) adopted a new Annandale Master Plan. That plan, comprehending the entire Annandale complex, included two zoning districts affecting the 26 acre tract, one permitting high density and the other medium density.

Representing the southern boundary of the high density district, the dividing line between the two districts is shown on maps of the 1970 plan as a "collector" road running approximately parallel to Route 236 across landowners' property and connecting Backlick and Ravensworth. A dispute arose whether the eastern terminus of the dividing line was intended to be at Jayhawk Street 1300 feet south of Route 236 or at Falcon Street 1500 feet south. It was fixed in an undated errata sheet prepared by staff (never formally approved by the Board) at Falcon Street.

On December 28, 1970, at the express urging of the county land use staff, landowners filed an amended application requesting high density zoning in the northern portion of the 26 acre tract and medium density in the southern portion in accordance with the new Master Plan. Their application showed the eastern terminus of the dividing line at Falcon Street. The Planning Commission disapproved the amended application but recommended that the entire 26 acres be zoned to the density requested in the original application. On May 26, 1971 the Board declined the recommendation and adopted an ordinance granting landowners' amended application.

On April 17, 1972 a newly-elected Board of Supervisors, proceeding on its own motion, adopted an ordinance reducing the high density authorized by the old Board in the May 26, 1971 ordinance to medium density and fixing the eastern terminus of the southern boundary of the high density district at Jayhawk Street.

Landowners filed a motion for declaratory judgment praying that the trial court declare the April 17, 1972 ordinance void and the May 26, 1971 ordinance valid. By letter opinion dated November 14, 1972 and final decree entered November 24, 1972 the trial court granted landowners' prayer, ruling that "the defendants can change the zoning, provided there is a substantial change in circumstances or a mistake," finding that "the evidence does not support a finding of substantial change in circumstances or mistake as to merit the downzoning on April 17, 1972," and holding that "the action of Defendants . . . in downzoning the Complainant's property . . . (was) arbitrary, capricious and unreasonable and, therefore, illegal, invalid and void."

We look first to the policy and purposes of the zoning statutes adopted by the General Assembly, Code Title 15.1, Chapter 11. Read as a whole, the statutes strike a deliberate balance between private property rights and public interests.

"This chapter is intended to encourage local governments to improve public health, safety, convenience or welfare and to plan for the future development of communities to the end that transportation systems be carefully planned; that new community centers be developed with adequate highway, utility, health, educational, and recreational facilities; that the needs of agriculture, industry and business be recognized in future growth; that residential areas be provided with healthy surrounding for family life; and that the growth of the community be consonant with the efficient and economical use of public funds." Code § 15.1-427 (Repl. Vol. 1973).

The statutes recognize that public power over private property rights should be exercised judiciously and equitably. That policy springs not only from public respect for personal rights and individual integrity but also from enlightened public self-interest. The General Assembly has recognized that it is in the public interest that private land not required for public use be put to its optimum use to fulfill societal needs. One purpose of zoning ordinances is "to encourage economic development activities that provide desirable employment and enlarge the tax base," Code § 15.1-489 (Repl. Vol. 1973), and "(z)oning ordinances . . . shall be drawn with reasonable consideration for . . . the conservation of properties and their values . . ." Code § 15.1-490 (Repl. Vol. 1973).

Under the private enterprise system, land use is influenced by the profit motive. Profit flows from investments of time, talent, and capital. Landowners venture investments only when the prospects of profit are reasonable. Prospects are reasonable only when permissible land use is reasonably predictable. The Virginia landowner always confronts the possibility that permissible land use may be changed by a comprehensive zoning ordinance reducing profit prospects; yet, the Virginia statutes assure him that such a change will not be made suddenly, arbitrarily, or capriciously but only after a period of investigation and community planning.

We look next to general principles governing judicial review of zoning ordinances.

"The legislative branch of a local government in the exercise of its police power has wide discretion in the enactment and amendment of zoning ordinances. Its action is presumed to be valid so long as it is not unreasonable and arbitrary. The burden of proof is on him who assails it to prove that it is clearly unreasonable, arbitrary or capricious, and that it bears no reasonable or substantial relation to the public health, safety, morals, or general welfare. The court will not substitute its judgment for that of a legislative body, and if the reasonableness of a zoning ordinance is fairly debatable it must be sustained. (Citations omitted)." Board of Supervisors v. Carper.

These principles were articulated in a case involving a comprehensive amendment to a comprehensive zoning ordinance. All are sound. Insofar as apposite, we apply them here. But here, the April 17, 1972 ordinance is not a comprehensive zoning ordinance. Rather, it is a piecemeal zoning ordinance; one initiated by the zoning authority on its own motion; one selectively addressed to landowners' single parcel and an adjacent parcel; and one that reduces the permissible residential density *below* that recommended by a duly-adopted Master Plan.

Inherent in the presumption of legislative validity stated in *Carper* is a presumption of reasonableness. But, as Carper makes plain, the presumption of reasonableness is not absolute. Where presumptive reasonableness is challenged by probative evidence of unreasonableness, the challenge must be met by some evidence of reasonableness. If evidence of reasonableness is sufficient to make the question fairly debatable, the ordinance "must be sustained." If not, the evidence of unreasonableness defeats the presumption of reasonableness and the ordinance cannot be sustained.

With respect to the validity of a piecemeal downzoning ordinance such as that here involved, we are of opinion that when an aggrieved landowner makes a *prima facie* showing that since enactment of the prior ordinance there has been no change in circumstances substantially affecting the public health, safety, or welfare, the burden of going forward with evidence of such mistake, fraud, or changed circumstances shifts to the governing body. If the governing body produces evidence sufficient to make reasonableness fairly debatable, the ordinance must be sustained. If not, the ordinance is unreasonable and void.

The rule we have stated promotes the policy and purposes of the zoning statutes. While the landowner is always faced with the possibility of comprehensive rezoning, the rule we have stated assures him that, barring mistake or fraud in the prior zoning ordinance, his legitimate profit prospects will not be reduced by a piecemeal zoning ordinance reducing permissible use of his land until circumstances substantially affecting the public interest have changed. Such stability and predictability in the law serve the interest of both the landowner and the public.

The rule applied by the trial court is not inconsistent with the rule we have adopted. But the Board argues that the trial court should have found that the evidence satisfied the rule. It says that the action of the old Board in enacting the May 26, 1971 ordinance locating the collector road as shown in landowners' amended application at Falcon Street was a mistake within the meaning of the rule because the 1970 comprehensive plan intended it to be located at Jayhawk Street. We do not agree. Even if we assume that the 1970 plan intended the location to be at Jayhawk Street rather than Falcon Street (and the record does not resolve the dispute), it does not follow that the location fixed in the May 26, 1971 ordinance was a mistake. The statutes do not make the comprehensive plan a zoning ordinance but only a comprehensive guideline for zoning ordinances. The precise location of boundaries between zoning districts is a function of the zoning process, and in making a zoning judgment the governing body must consider not only the general boundary guidelines of the plan but also location of property lines, physical characteristics of the land, and other factors affecting optimum geographical alignment.

The trial court ruled that the evidence did not support a finding of substantial change in circumstances in the 11 month interval between adoption of the May 26, 1971 ordinance (which complied with the guidelines of the new Master Plan) and adoption of the April 17, 1972 piecemeal downzoning ordinance. In its brief the Board conceded that "(t)he testimony from all witnesses on the issues of both sewer and traffic consistently supported the conclusion that there had been no change in circumstances in the area". Indeed, with respect to sewer capacity and facilities for removing pollutants, two witnesses testified that circumstances had improved, and the fire chief testified that in addition to increased departmental manpower, two new fire stations serving the community were in the design stage.

The Board urges us to hold as a matter of law that a changed Board of Supervisors constitutes a "changed circumstance" within the meaning of the rule applied by the trial court. We must decline. As indicated above, the "changed circumstance" which justifies piecemeal downzoning is one substantially affecting the public health, safety, or welfare. Such a change should be objectively verifiable from evidence. A newly elected governing body is not such a change. While a new Board is not bound by the legislative acts of an old Board, in amending them the new Board is bound by rules of law.

Next, the Board argues in its brief that "a zoning action . . . is reasonably related to the health, safety and welfare . . . if the evidence renders the existence of such a relationship fairly debatable". But that principle must be read in context with the rule applied by the trial court. Proceeding consciously under that rule, the Board produced no probative evidence of mistake or fraud in the prior ordinance or of changed circumstances substantially affecting the public health, safety, or welfare. Reasonableness was, therefore, not fairly debatable, and the trial court's holding that "the action of the defendants on April 17, 1972 . . . was arbitrary, capricious and unreasonable and, therefore, illegal, invalid and void" was not plainly erroneous.

Finally, the Board contends that admission of testimony of legislative motive was prejudicial error. Since reasonableness was not fairly debatable and the ordinance was void, we need not consider whether testimony concerning legislative motive was prejudicial.

Finding no prejudicial error, we affirm the decree.

Affirmed.

---

5. Nonconforming Uses

A **nonconforming use** is a use of property that was lawful prior to the adoption or amendment of a zoning ordinance and is permitted to continue even though it fails to conform to the requirements of the ordinance. The justification for nonconforming uses is that it would be harsh and unreasonable, under most circumstances, to deprive an owner of the use of his property because of subsequent changes in the law. Thus, a previously existing laundry would be permitted to continue, as a nonconforming use, in a zoning district subsequently zoned for residential use.

In many instances, a nonconforming use is an aberration and an inconsistency in a zoning district that must be tolerated because of the due process requirements of the constitution. Nevertheless planners sometimes seek to eliminate them to protect the integrity of the neighborhood. Several techniques have been used to restrict and to eventually eliminate nonconforming uses: (1) **Statutory restrictions.** The zoning ordinance will usually contain provisions that restrict nonconforming uses by providing that (a) if destroyed it may not be rebuilt; (b) if discontinued it may not be restarted; (c) a different nonconforming use may not be substituted for the original nonconforming use; (d) substantial improvements or alterations may not be made; (2) **Termination as a nuisance.** The fact that the due process clause permits a nonconforming use to continue does not protect such use against the application of the *nuisance doctrine*.

Thus, a previously existing glue factory may be permitted to continue in a residential district as a nonconforming use but may be enjoined as a nuisance where its continuation would result in an unreasonable interference with the use and enjoyment of neighboring properties. (3) **Eminent domain.** A nonconforming use may be eliminated by government after the property is acquired by the exercise of the power of eminent domain; (4) **Amortization.** A nonconforming use may be prohibited after the expiration of a reasonable period of time during which the owner could recover the costs of his investment.

The following excerpt from the zoning ordinance of the City of Trenton, New Jersey illustrates some of the typical provisions dealing with nonconforming uses:

TRENTON ZONING ORDINANCE

19-10.9 Nonconforming Uses.

a. **Continuation Thereof.** All buildings, structures and uses not conforming to the regulations of the district in which they are located, as of July 20, 1956, shall be known and regarded as "nonconforming."

A nonconforming building or use may be continued and may be changed to another nonconforming use of the same or a more restricted classification, but no additions or extensions of such building or use shall be made, except on the same premises and exceeding 25 per cent of the occupied floor area; or 25 per cent of the cubical contents of the building or buildings as existing as of July 20, 1956; or 25 per cent of the service capacity of a use conducted all or partially in the open; and provided further, that subsequent to such extension or addition to a nonconforming building or use, there shall be no further additions or extensions except in accordance with the regulations of the district in which such building or use is located. Any extension of a nonconforming use or building made under a prior ordinance or by a variance granted by the board of adjustment prior to July 20, 1956, shall be considered applicable under this chapter and shall not again be allowable.

b. **Reversion Thereof.** If a nonconforming building or use is subsequently changed to a conforming use, it shall not again be altered or used except in accordance with the regulations of the district in which it is located. If a nonconforming building is destroyed or demolished by any cause or for any reason, it shall not be rebuilt or reconstructed except in conformity with the regulations of the district in which it is located. The vacation of a nonconforming building or use for a consecutive period of six months shall be regarded as a permanent vacation and, thereafter, the building shall nót be reoccupied except in conformity with the regulations of the district in which it is located, and the use may not be resumed.

c. **Nonconformance in Required Yard Spaces Only.** None of the above limitations shall apply to a building or other structure which is nonconforming only in respect to required yard spaces, or required area per dwelling unit, except that no building or other structure shall be altered, added to, or reconstructed to extend further into an already-deficient front, rear or side yard or to effect a further deficiency in area per dwelling unit.

TOWN OF SEABROOK v. D'AGATA

362 A.2d 182 (N.H. 1976)

GRIFFITH, Justice.

The town of Seabrook filed this petition in equity to enjoin the defendants, Salvatore J. and Carmeline D'Agata, from erecting or maintaining a structure allegedly in violation of the town's zoning ordinance.

* * *

The defendants' dwelling does not conform to the requirements of the plaintiff's zoning ordinance in three respects: it is situated on a lot which is less than the minimum prescribed size; it is not located a sufficient distance from the adjoining lot lines; and it contains three family units while located in an area zoned for single and two-family residences only. These conditions existed prior to the enactment of the zoning ordinance, however, and are therefore permitted to continue as a nonconforming use.

The defendants constructed an addition to their dwelling consisting of a twenty-eight by eight foot storage room in a formerly unoccupied area under the second floor of a portion of the building. Alterations consisted of the enclosure of a previously open carport and the pouring of a cement floor. The enclosed area, which contains no heat, electricity, water, or other amenities usually associated with a living-area, is suitable only for the use to which it is put, *i.e.*, the storage of various household items. This use is permitted by the town zoning ordinance in Zone 1, where the defendants' dwelling is located.

The plaintiff contends, however, that although such construction would be permissible in Zone 1 if the defendants' residence were a conforming structure, a nonconforming owner is not allowed to make such alterations. The basis for this argument is section VII:A of the ordinance, which states "A non-conforming use . . may not be changed subsequently to another non-conforming use of the same premises nor may the non-conforming use be expanded beyond that which existed at the adoption of this . . ." enclosure of the carport.

We do not agree that the defendants' constitutes "an expansion of the non-conforming use". We interpret that phrase to indicate an expansion in the non-conforming features of the dwelling, rather than an addition which entirely conforms to the zoning ordinance and which is in fact commonly found in the defendants' neighborhood. The defendants' storage room neither constitutes living quarters for another family nor does it affect the proximity of the dwelling to the sidelines. It does not enlarge the square footage of the dwelling so as to render the lot size proportionally more inadequate. To deny the defendants the right to build within the confines of their building a structure identical to that possessed by many of their conforming neighbors is in effect to penalize them for the nonconforming nature of their property.

Although the general policy of zoning is to carefully limit the extension and enlargement of nonconforming uses, a town may not interpret a use in such a way as to unlawfully reduce the original vested interest acquired by the owner. 2 A. Rathkopf, The Law of Zoning and Planning 58-18 (3d ed. 1972). "The fact that improved and more efficient or different instrumentalities are used in the operation of the use does not in itself preclude the use made from being a continuation of the prior nonconforming use providing such means are ordinarily and reasonably adapted to make the established use available to the owners and the original nature and purpose of the undertaking remain unchanged."

The plaintiff further contends that the defendants are required to secure a building permit by section VII:C of the ordinance, which specifies that such a permit must be obtained for the making of all structural alterations excepting those which increase the valuation of the principal structure by less than $500. The master's finding that the storage room increased the valuation of the defendants' dwelling by more than $500 is amply supported by the record and the defendants are required to obtain a building permit.

Exceptions sustained in part; denied in part; remanded.

All concurred.

CITY OF LOS ANGELES

v.

GAGE

127 C.A. 2d NN2, 274 P.2d 34 (1954)

VALLEE, Justice.

This appeal involves the constitutionality of the provisions of a zoning ordinance which require that certain nonconforming existing uses shall be discontinued within five years after its passage, as they apply to defendants' property.

Plaintiff brought this suit for an injunction to command defendants to discontinue their use of certain property for the conduct of a plumbing business and to remove various materials therefrom, and to restrain them from using the property for any purpose not permitted by the comprehensive zoning plan provisions of the Los Angeles Municipal Code. The cause was submitted to the trial court on admissions in the pleadings and a stipulation of facts. Defendants will be referred to as "Gage."

In 1930 Gage acquired adjoining lots 220 and 221 located on Cochran Avenue in Los Angeles. He constructed a two-family residential building on lot 221 and rented the upper half solely for residential purposes. He established a wholesale and retail plumbing supply business on the property. He used a room in the lower half of the residential building on lot 221 as the office for the conduct of the business, and the rest of the lower half for residential purposes for himself and his family; he used a garage on lot 221 for the storage of plumbing supplies and materials; and he constructed and used racks, bins, and stalls for the storage of such supplies and materials on lot 220. Later Gage incorporated defendant company. The realty and the assets of the plumbing business were transferred to the company. The case is presented as though the property had been owned continuously from 1930 to date by the same defendant. The use of lots 220 and 221 begun in 1930, has been substantially the same at all times since.

In 1930 the two lots and other property facing on Cochran Avenue in their vicinity were classified in "C" zone by the zoning ordinance then in effect. Under this classification the use to which Gage put the property was permitted. Shortly after Gage acquired lots 220 and 221, they were classified in "C-3" zone and the use to which he put the property was expressly permitted. In 1936 the city council of the city passed Ordinance 77,000 which contained a comprehensive zoning plan for the city. Ordinance 77,000 re-enacted the prior ordinances with respect to the use of lots 220 and 221. In 1941 the city council passed Ordinance 85,015 by the terms of which the use of a residential building for the conduct of an office in connection with the plumbing supply business was permitted. Ordinance 85,015 prohibited the open storage of materials in zone "C-3" but permitted such uses as had been established to continue as nonconforming uses. The use to which lots 220 and 221 was put by defendants was a nonconforming use that might be continued. In 1946 the city council passed Ordinance 90,500. This ordinance reclassified lots 220 and 221 and other property fronting on Cochran Avenue in their vicinity from zone "C-3" to zone "R-4" (Multiple dwelling zone). Use of lots 220 and 221 for the conduct of a plumbing business was not permitted in zone "R-4." At the time Ordinance 90,500 was passed, and at all times since, the Los Angeles Municipal Code (§ 12.23 B & C) provided: "(a) The nonconforming use of a conforming building or structure may be continued, except that in the 'R' Zones any nonconforming commercial or industrial use of a residential building or residential accessory building shall be discontinued within five (5) years from June 1, 1946, or five (5) years from the date the use becomes nonconforming, whichever date is later.
* * *

"(a) The nonconforming use of land shall be discontinued within five (5) years from June 1, 1946, or within five (5) years from the date the use became nonconforming, in each of the following cases: (1) where no buildings are employed in connection with such use; (2) where the only buildings employed are accessory or incidental to such use; (3) where such use is maintained in connection with a conforming building."
* * *

The business conducted by Gage on the property has produced a gross revenue varying between $125,000 and $350,000 a year. If he is required to abandon the use of the property for his business, he will be put to the following expenses: (1) The value of a suitable site for the conduct of its business whould be about $10,000; which would be offset by the value of $7,500 of the lot now used. (2) The cost incident to removing of supplies to another location and construction of the necessary racks, sheds, bins and stalls which would be about $2,500. (3) The cost necessary to expend to advertise a new location. (4) The risk of a gain or a loss of business while moving, and the cost necessary to reestablish the business at a new location, the amount of which is uncertain."

The noise and disturbance caused by the loading and unloading of supplies, trucking, and the going and coming of workmen in connection with the operation of a plumbing business with an open storage yard is greater than the noise and disturbance that is normal in a district used solely for residential purposes. * * *

A nonconforming use is a lawful use existing on the effective date of the zoning restriction and continuing since that time in nonconformance to the ordinance. A provision permitting the continuance of a nonconforming use is ordinarily included in zoning ordinances because of the hardship and doubtful constitutionality of compelling the immediate discontinuance of nonconforming uses. It is generally held that a zoning ordinance may not operate to immediately suppress or remove from a particular district an otherwise lawful business or use already established therein. 58 Am.Jur. 1022, § 148.

No case seems to have been decided in this state squarely involving the precise question presented in the case at bar. Until recently zoning ordinances have made no provision for any systematic and comprehensive elimination of the nonconforming use. The expectation seems to have been that existing nonconforming uses would be of little consequence and that they would eventually disappear. See 9 Minn.L.Rev. 593, 598. The contrary appears to be the case. 35 Va.L.Rev. 348, 352; Wis.L.Rev. (1951) 685; 99 Univ.Pa.L.Rev. 1019, 1021. It is said that the fundamental problem facing zoning is the inability to eliminate the nonconforming use. The general purpose of present-day zoning ordinances is to eventually end all nonconforming uses. There is a growing tendency to guard against the indefinite continuance of nonconforming uses by providing for their liquidation within a prescribed period. It is said, "The only positive method of getting rid of nonconforming uses yet devised is to amortize a nonconforming building. That is, to determine the normal useful remaining life of the building and prohibit the owner from maintaining it after the expiration of that time." Crolly and Norton, Termination of Nonconforming Uses, 62 Zoning Bulletin 1, Regional Plan Assn., June 1952.

Amortization of nonconforming uses has been expressly authorized by recent amendments to zoning enabling laws in a number of states. Ordinances providing for amortization of nonconforming uses have been passed in a number of large cities.[3] The length of time given the owner to eliminate his nonconforming use or building varies with the city and with the type of structure. In Austin v. Older, 283 Mich. 667, 278 N.W.727,730, it is said: "Certainly the maximum benefit of zoning ordinances cannot be obtained as long as nonconforming businesses remain within residential districts, and their gradual elimination is within the police power."

* * *

The theory in zoning is that each district is an appropriate area for the location of the uses which the zone plan permits in that area, and that the existence or entrance of other uses will tend to impair the development and stability of the area for the appropriate uses. The public welfare must be considered from the standpoint of the objective of zoning and of all the property within any particular use district. It was not and is not contemplated that pre-existing nonconforming uses are to be perpetual. The presence of any nonconforming use endangers the benefits to be derived from a comprehensive zoning plan. Having the undoubted power to establish residential districts, the legislative body has the power to make such classification really effective by adopting such reasonable regulations as would be conducive to the welfare, health, and safety of those desiring to live in such district and enjoy the benefits thereof. There would be no object in creating a residential district unless there were to be secured to those dwelling therein the advantages which are ordinarily considered the benefits of such residence. It would seem to be the logical and reasonable method of approach to place a time limit upon the continuance of existing nonconforming uses, commensurate with the investment involved and based on the nature of the use; and in cases of nonconforming structures, on their character, age, and other relevant factors.

Exercise of the police power frequently impairs rights in property because the exercise of those rights is detrimental to the public interest. Every zoning ordinance effects some impairment of vested rights either by restricting prospective uses or by prohibiting the continuation of existing uses, because it affects property already owned by individuals at the time of its enactment.

In essence there is no distinction between requiring the discontinuance of a nonconforming use within a reasonable period and provisions which deny the right to add to or extend buildings devoted to an existing nonconforming use, which deny the right to resume a nonconforming use after a period of nonuse, which deny the right to extend or enlarge an existing nonconforming use, which deny the right to substitute new buildings for those devoted to an existing nonconforming use—all of which have been held to be valid exercises of the police power.

The distinction between an ordinance restricting future uses and one requiring the termination of present uses within a reasonable period of time is merely one of degree, and constitutionality depends on the relative importance to be given to the public gain and to the private loss. Zoning as it affects every piece of property is to some extent retroactive in that it applies to property already owned at the time of the effective date of the ordinance. The elimination of existing uses within a reasonable time does not amount to a taking of property nor does it necessarily restrict the use of property so that it cannot be used for any reasonable purpose. Use of a reasonable amortization scheme provides an equitable means of reconciliation of the conflicting interests in satisfaction of due process requirements. As a method of eliminating existing nonconforming uses it allows the owner of the nonconforming use, by affording an opportunity to make new plans, at least partially to offset any loss he might suffer. The loss he suffers, if any, is spread out over a period of years, and he enjoys a monopolistic position by virtue of the zoning ordinance as long as he remains. If the amortization period is reasonable the loss to the owner may be small when compared with the benefit to the public. Nonconforming uses will eventually be eliminated. A legislative body may well conclude that the beneficial effect on the community of the eventual elimination of all nonconforming uses by a reasonable amortization plan more than offsets individual losses.

The ordinance in question provides, according to a graduated periodic schedule, for the gradual and ultimate elimination of all commercial and industrial uses in residential zones. These provisions require the discontinuance of nonconforming uses of land within a five-year period, and the discontinuance of nonconforming commercial and inndustrial uses of residential buildings in the "R" zones within the same five-year period. These provisions are the only ones pertinent to the decision in this case. However, it may be noted that other provisions of the ordinance require the discontinuance of nonconforming billboards and, in residential zones, the discontinuance of nonconforming buildings and of nonconforming uses of nonconforming buildings, within specified periods running from 20 to 40 years according to the type of building construction.

We have no doubt that Ordinance 90,500, in compelling the discontinuance of the use of defendants' property for a wholesale and retail plumbing and plumbing supply business, and for the open storage of plumbing supplies within five years after its passage, is a valid exercise of the police power. Lots 220 and 221 are several blocks from a business center and it appears that they are not within any reasonable or logical extension of such a center. The ordinance does not prevent the operation of defendants' business; it merely restricts its location. Discontinuance of the nonconforming use requires only that Gage move his plumbing business to property that is zoned for it. Such property can be found within a half mile of Gage's property. The cost of moving is $5,000, or less than 1% of Gage's minimum gross business for five years, or less than half of 1% of the mean of his gross business for five years. He has had eight years within which to move. The property is usable for residential purpose. Since 1930 lot 221 has been used for residential purposes. All of the land within 500 feet of Gage's property is now improved and used for such purposes. Lot 220, now unimproved, can be improved for the same purposes.

We think it apparent that none of the agreed facts and none of the ultimate facts found by the court justify the conclusion that Ordinance 90,500, as applied to Gage's property, is clearly arbitrary or unreasonable, or has no substantial relation to the public's health, safety, morals, or general welfare, or that it is an unconstitutional impairment of his property rights.

It is enough for us to determine and we determine only that Ordinance 90,500 of the city of Los Angeles, insofar as it required the discontinuance of Gage's wholesale and retail plumbing business on lots 220 and 221 within five years from the date of its passage, is a constitutional exercise of the police power.

For additional information on non-conforming uses see Anderson, "The Nonconforming Use—A Product of Euclidian Zoning," 10 *Syracuse L. Rev.* 214 (1959); Young, "Regulation and Removal of Non-Conforming Uses," 12 *Western Res.L.Rev.* 681 (1961); Mandelker, "Prolonging the Nonconforming Use: Judicial Restriction on the Power to Zone in Iowa," 8 *Drake L.Rev.* 44 (1958).

6. Vested Rights

Where an owner of land obtains a building permit based upon existing zoning laws and *expends substantial sums or incurs substantial liabilities in reliance thereon,* he obtains a *vested right* to complete construction in accordance with the terms of the permit even though the zoning ordinance is changed after the issuance of the permit. Once a landowner secures a vested right the government may not prohibit the construction even though it no longer complies with the zoning ordinance. Legal issues arise relating to whether the permit was issued lawfully, whether there was substantial commitment or expenditure, whether there was good faith and justifiable reliance upon the permit and the appropriateness of the remedy sought by the plaintiff.

COOPER

v.

CITY OF GREENSBURG

26 Pa. Commw. Ct 245, 363 A.2d 813 (1976)

CRUMLISH, Jr., Judge.

For the past nine years, Jared A. Cooper and the City of Greensburg (City) have been engaged in litigation over Cooper's right to construct a gasoline station on land which he owns in the City. Hopefully, this will be the last chapter in that struggle.

Presently before us is the City's appeal from an order of the Court of Common Pleas of Westmoreland County, sitting en banc, which dismissed the exceptions filed by the City and several of its residents (Intervenors) and which affirmed the decree nisi of the court which granted Cooper's petition for mandamus and ordered the issuance of the permits required for construction of Cooper's gasoline station. We affirm.

We will first summarize the facts and complicated litigation history of this case. In 1967, Cooper acquired 66.928 acres of land in the City. The land was part of territory which had been annexed by the City from a neighboring township in 1958. When the City annexed the territory, it had a zoning ordinance which provided that territory annexed to the City would automatically become zoned single-family residential (R-1). In June, 1967, Cooper applied for certain building permits for the portion of this newly annexed land which he had acquired from the City. One of the permits, the one with which we are here concerned, was for the construction of a gasoline service station on approximately 0.575 acres of the tract. The permit application was refused. After much litigation, this Court, in an opinion written by Judge Wilkinson, held invalid the City's automatic zoning ordinance and ordered the necessary certificates of compliance and occupancy to be issued. *Cameron v. Greensburg,* After this decision, Cooper, although he had lost a prospective tenant during the pendency of the litigation, began excavation work on his land in preparation for new tenants. However, prior to our decision in *Cameron* and prior to Cooper's starting the new excavation, the City enacted a new ordinance which zoned Cooper's lands as R-1. With regard to this new ordinance, we stated in *Cameron, supra,* that, although it was apparently validly enacted, it was not "pending" at the time of Cooper's 1967 application for certificates of compliance and occupancy and, therefore, it could not destroy Cooper's vested right to obtain the certificates. In the meantime, in April, 1969, the City had approved a subdivision plan submitted by Cooper which included the portion intended for the gasoline service station albeit with a slight variation in the metes and bounds description of the tract from that which was contained in Cooper's 1967 application. On February 16, 1973, Cooper entered into an option agreement with Boron Oil Company (Boron) for the sale of the 0.575 acre tract. Although Boron was not the same tenant contemplated by Cooper in his 1967 application, it also intended to use the land as a gasoline service station.

On June 14, 1973, acting upon directions given him by the City's zoning officer, Cooper applied for new compliance permits and certificates of occupancy in accordance with the provisions of the 1971 zoning ordinance. The application was refused for the reason that the use intended by Cooper was not permitted under the 1971 ordinance.

On October, 1973, Cooper filed a complaint in mandamus seeking to compel the City's zoning officer to issue the permits and certificates requested in the June 14, 1973 application. Approximately one hour after Cooper filed his complaint, the court below, on Cooper's motion, granted summary judgment in mandamus. The City's petition to open the judgment was dismissed. Once again, the City appealed to this Court. We vacated the lower court's order of summary judgment and remanded the mater for the making of a record. In an opinion written by Judge Kramer, we held that our decision in *Cameron v. Greensburg* gave Cooper a "vested right" to the permits requested in the 1967 application, not because he had purchased his property prior to the effective date of the 1971 zoning ordinance, but, rather, because the permits had been applied for before the 1971 zoning ordinance was "pending." In *City of Greensburg v. Cooper, supra,* we also held that there was an issue of fact as to whether Cooper's original compliance and building permits (the ones issued after our decision in *Cameron v. Greensburg*), had been abandoned because they had not been renewed. Apparently, the lower court did not have Cooper's 1973 application before it, only his 1971 application and the 1973 subdivision plan. Finding that the court below not only misinterpreted our decision in *Cameron v. Greensburg* but also failed to recognize the existence of issues of fact, we remanded the matter.

· In May, 1975, after hearings were held, the court below again ordered that the requested permits be issued. The City's exceptions were dismissed and the dismissal was affirmed by the court below sitting en banc. The City has again appealed to this Court.

It is well settled that mandamus is an extraordinary writ which lies to compel performance of a ministerial act or mandatory duty where there is a clear legal right in the plaintiff, a corresponding duty in the defendant, and a want of any other appropriate and adequate remedy. We are asked here to review the propriety of the granting of mandamus, rather than the propriety of granting summary judgment therefor. Therefore, we must determine whether the lower court abused its discretion or committed an error of law. Furthermore where, as here, a case has been previously remanded so that a particular finding can be made, we cannot substitute our findings for those of the lower court, but must determine only whether sufficient evidence supports the findings of the lower court.

We have held that one claiming a vested right in a building permit must establish that the application was made in good faith, that a substantial commitment or expenditure was made in justifiable reliance upon the granting of the permit, and that the permit was issued lawfully under zoning law then existing.

The court below found that Cooper had, at the time he filed the 1973 applications, met all of the requirements placed upon him by the City and therefore had a vested right to erect a service station on his lot. The City argues that Cooper abandoned the permits which were issued after our decision in *Cameron v. Greensburg, supra,* by not beginning construction or renewing them each six months as required by the City's zoning ordinance. However, the record amply supports the findings of the court below that Cooper had spent large sums of money for excavation of the land and at all times acted upon the instructions of the City's zoning officials as to the procedure for acquiring and maintaining permits.

Our careful review of the record reveals that the court below was justified in concluding that Cooper satisfied these requirements and, therefore, had a vested right to building permits for a gasoline service station on his tract.

Next, the City contends that mandamus is not the proper remedy for Cooper. This contention has no merit. In *Borough of Monroeville v. Effie's Ups & Downs,* (1974), we held that where a plaintiff has a clear legal right to the issuance of a building permit, mandamus is the appropriate remedy to compel its issuance.

Having concluded that Cooper had a vested right to the issuance of building and compliance permits and that mandamus is the appropriate remedy, we affirm the order of the court below.

ORDER

AND NOW, this 8th day of September, 1976, the order of the Court of Common Pleas of Westmoreland County is hereby affirmed.

MENCER, Judge (dissenting).
I respectfully dissent.

First: Mandamus is not Jared A. Cooper's (Cooper) proper remedy, and he should have appealed the zoning officer's refusal of his application to the zoning hearing board and thereafter taken a further appeal to the Court of Common Pleas if not satisfied by the board's action. Section 909 of the Pennsylvania Municipalities Planning Code, Act of July 31, 1968, P.L. 805, *as amended*, 53 P.S. § 10909, specifically so provides. It must be kept in mind that we are reviewing an application for a permit made in 1973 under a 1971 ordinance whose validity is not challenged in this litigation. The admitted validity of an existing and applicable zoning ordinance here is what makes *Borough of Monroeville v. Effie's Ups and Downs*, (1974), inapposite and not controlling in this case on the initial question as to whether or not mandamus is the appropriate remedy to compel the issuance of the permit sought.

Second: The majority concludes that Cooper has "a vested right to building permits for a gasoline service station on his tract." The basis for that conclusion is unclear to me. It surely could not be by virtue of our holding in *Cameron v. Greensburg*, (1971), by which we upheld a ruling which ordered the zoning officer to issue certificates of compliance and occupancy to Cooper. Those certificates were issued, and, if they have any remaining validity, what need did Cooper then have in 1973 for additional permits? However, because Cooper has changed somewhat the size of the lot in question and substituted another oil company as a prospective purchaser and the permits issued became null and void by a failure of Cooper to commence the authorized improvement within six months from the issuance date of the permits as provided by Section 1204-4 of the City of Greensburg's 1955 zoning ordinance, Cooper did need in 1973 to reapply and was subject to the 1971 zoning ordinance.

As we carefully pointed out in *City of Greensburg v. Cooper*, (1974), we did not decide in *Cameron v. Greensburg, supra*, that Cooper had the right to use the premises in question for a service station but only that Cooper was entitled to the permits he applied for on June 29, 1967. Those permits were issued and are not the subject matter of this mandamus action seeking issuance of permits applied for on June 14, 1973. The application in question here seeks a new compliance permit in accordance with the provisions of the 1971 zoning ordinance and is not controlled by our holding in *Cameron v. Greensburg, supra*.

A vested right to build in futuro a structure which violates a zoning ordinance can only be acquired by first securing a permit and *thereafter* expending substantial sums in reliance thereon. The record discloses that, since the issuance of the permits which were the subject of the *Cameron v. Greensburg, supra*, litigation, no action has been taken by Cooper to commence the erection of a gasoline service station on the subject property. The majority's reference to Cooper's having spent "large sums of money for excavation of the land" is in reference to grading and removal of an earthen bank on an adjacent lot sold by Cooper to the Church of the Open Door. These expenditures were for work completed in February 1972, less than two months after the completion of the litigation involving the 1967 permit applications and more than 16 months before the permit application which is the subject of this suit.

The only vested-right theory that has any comprehension to me on this record is the vested right, recognized in *Cameron v. Greensburg, supra,* that Cooper had to the issuance of the permits he sought by his applica‐ tion of June 29, 1967. We surely did not hold that he would have a vested right to any permit sought at any time thereafter.

Cooper is not here seeking utilization or renewal of the permits which were issued in accord with our discussion in *Cameron v. Greensburg, supra,* but rather the issuance of a new permit in 1973 under the zoning ordinance of 1971 which zoned the property in question R-1. If the major‐ ity's affirmance is based on the concept that the permits sought here are somehow merely renewals of those previously approved by this Court in *Cameron v. Greensburg, supra,* then it is granting relief in a mandamus action that is not responsive to the relief prayed for by Cooper. If the majority's affirmance is to authorize a permit to issue under the provisions of the 1971 zoning ordinance, as is sought by Cooper's 1973 application, then a commercial permit will issue contrary to the residential zoning provisions of the ordinance applicable to Cooper's property.

If this is, as the majority understandably hopes, the last chapter in the already over-protracted litigation which has befallen the property in ques‐ tion, it will not have an ending that coincides with my understanding of the applicable law.

G. DEVICES FOR ZONING FLEXIBILITY

The conventional zoning ordinance, based upon the Standard State Zoning Enabling Act and upheld in the landmark *Euclid* decision, provides for the de‐ lineation of designated zoning districts in which regulations relating to land use, lot size, bulk and density are applied uniformly throughout the district. This somewhat rigid form of land use regulation, facetiously referred to as **Eucli‐ dean zoning,** is based upon a number of assumptions that are not always true in fact. Among the assumptions of Euclidean zoning are: (1) that planners can predict the nature and quantities of the community's *needs* with some precision and exactitude; (2) that planners can, with accuracy, convert the quantification of community needs into an allocation and designation of land use; (3) that the economic and political forces within the community will respond compliantly with these designations; (4) that the very act of designation of specified zones for prescribed uses will not undermine the achievement of other community goals and objectives. Experience with the application of zoning laws indicates that when one or more of these assumptions is not correct, the effectiveness of Euclidean zoning is limited and one of the following devices for zoning flexibil‐ ity may become more appropriate.

1. Floating Zones

A **floating zone** is a "zone" created in a zoning ordinance for which regula‐ tions relating to use, bulk, density, etc. are prescribed, but the zone is not affixed to a specified parcel of land. The zone is permitted to "float" over the municipality until it is attached to a particular piece of land by application of the owner and pursuant to a prescribed procedure.

A floating zone in an ordinance may be challenged on any number of grounds: (1) **spot zoning**: if an amendment of the zoning ordinance is required, that amendment will be characterized as "spot zoning" and void; (2) **ultra vires**: if the zoning enabling legislation does not provide specifically for a floating zone, it will be argued that the zoning ordinance provision is outside the scope of the statutory authority and void; (3) **not in accordance with the comprehensive plan**: because the special provisions of the floating zone will eventually settle on to a parcel of land in a pre–existing zoned district, it will be argued that the changes are not in accordance with the comprehensive plan; (4) **violation of the uniformity clause**: when the special provisions of the floating zone are affixed to a specific parcel of land, that parcel will be governed by regulations that are different from other land in the zoned district and therefore in violation of the enabling act provision that "all such regulations shall be uniform for each class;" (5) **landowners' expectation of stability**: although the owners of property in the area do not have a vested right in current zoning classifications, nevertheless they are entitled to some degree of permanency.

The reactions of the courts to floating zone provisions have varied. The following two cases from New York and New Jersey illustrate the difference in judicial attitudes to different factual situations.

RODGERS

v.

VILLAGE OF TARRYTOWN

302 N.Y. 115, 96 N.E.2d 731 (1951)

FULD, Judge.

This appeal, here by our permission, involves the validity of two amendments to the General Zoning Ordinance of the Village of Tarrytown, a suburban area in the County of Westchester, within twenty-five miles of New York City.

Some years ago, Tarrytown enacted a General Zoning Ordinance dividing the village into seven districts or zones—Residence A for single family dwellings, Residence B for two-family dwellings, Residence C for multiple dwellings and apartment houses, three business districts and an industrial zone. In 1947 and 1948, the board of trustees, the village's legislative body, passed the two amendatory ordinances here under attack.

The 1947 ordinance creates "A new district or class of zone * * * [to] be called 'Residence B-B' ," in which, besides one- and two-family dwellings, buildings for multiple occupancy of fifteen or fewer families were permitted. The boundaries of the new type district were not delineated in the ordinance but were to be "fixed by amendment of the official village building zone map, at such times in the future as such district or class of zone is applied, to properties in this village." The village planning board was empowered to approve such amendments and, in case such approval was withheld, the board of trustees was authorized to grant it by appropriate resolution. In addition, the ordinance erected exacting standards of size and physical layouts for Residence B-B zones: a minimum of ten acres of land and a maximum building height of three stories were mandated; set-back and spacing requirements for structures were carefully prescribed; and no more than 15% of the ground area of the plot was to be occupied by buildings.

A year and a half after the 1947 amendment was enacted, defendant Elizabeth Rubin sought to have her property, consisting of almost ten and a half acres in the Residence A district, placed in a Residence B-B classification. After repeated modification of her plans to meet suggestions of the village planning board, that body gave its approval, and, several months later, in December of 1948, the board of trustees, also approving, passed the second ordinance here under attack. In essence, it provides that the Residence B-B district "is hereby applied to the [Rubin] property * * * and the district or zone of said property is hereby changed to 'Residence B-B' and the official Building Zone Map of the Village of Tarrytown is hereby amended accordingly [by specification of the various parcels and plots involved]."

Plaintiff, who owns a residence on a six-acre plot about a hundred yards from Rubin's property, brought this action to have the two amendments declared invalid and to enjoin defendant Rubin from constructing multiple dwellings on her property. The courts below, adjudging the amendments valid and the action of the trustees proper, dismissed the complaint. We agree with their determination.

While stability and regularity are undoubtedly essential to the operation of zoning plans, zoning is by no means static. Changed or changing conditions call for changed plans, and persons who own property in a particular zone or use district enjoy no eternally vested right to that classification if the public interest demands otherwise. Accordingly, the power of a village to amend its basic zoning ordinance in such a way as reasonably to promote the general welfare cannot be questioned. Just as clearly, decision as to how a community shall be zoned or rezoned, as to how various properties shall be classifed or reclassified, rests with the local legislative body; its judgment and determination will be conclusive, beyond interference from the courts, unless shown to be arbitrary, and the burden of establishing such arbitrariness is imposed upon him who asserts it. In that connection, we recently said Shepard v. Village of Skaneateles: "Upon parties who attack an ordinance * * * rests the burden of showing that the regulation assailed is not justified under the police power of the state by any reasonable interpretation of the facts. 'If the validity of the legislative classification for zoning purposes be fairly debatable, the legislative judgment must be allowed to control.' Village of Euclid v. Ambler Realty Co."

By that test, the propriety of the decision here made is not even debatable. In other words, viewing the rezoning in the case before us, as it must be viewed, in the light of the area involved and the present and reasonably foreseeable needs of the community, the conclusion is inescapable that what was done not only accorded with sound zoning principles, not only complied with every requirement of law, but was accomplished in a proper, careful and reasonable manner.

The Tarrytown board of trustees was entitled to find that there was a real need for additional housing facilities; that the creation of Residence B-B districts for garden apartment developments would prevent young families, unable to find accommodations in the village, from moving elsewhere; would attract business to the community; would lighten the tax load of the small home owner, increasingly burdened by the shrinkage of tax revenues resulting from the depreciated value of large estates and the transfer of many such estates to tax-exempt institutions; and would develop otherwise unmarketable and decaying property.

The village's zoning aim being clear, the choice of methods to accomplish it lay with the board. Two such methods were at hand. It could amend the General Zoning Ordinance so as to permit garden apartments on any plot of ten acres or more in Residence A and B zones (the zones more restricted) or it could amend that Ordinance so as to invite owners of ten or more acres, who wished to build garden apartments on their properties, to apply for a Residence B-B classification. The board chose to adopt the latter procedure. That it called for separate legislative authorization for each project presents no obstacle or drawback—and so we have already held. Whether we would have made the same choice is not the issue; it is sufficient that the board's decision was neither arbitrary nor unreasonable.

As to the requirement that the applicant own a plot of at least ten acres, we find nothing therein unfair to plaintiff or other owners of smaller parcels. The board undoubtedly found, as it was privileged to find, that garden apartments would blend more attractively and harmoniously with the community setting, would impose less of a burden upon village facilities, if placed upon larger tracts of land rather than scattered about in smaller units. Obviously, some definite acreage had to be chosen, and, so far as the record before us reveals, the choice of ten acres as a minimum plot was well within the range of an unassailable legislative judgment.

Nor did the board, by following the course which it did, divest itself or the planning board of power to regulate future zoning with regard to garden apartments. The mere circumstances that an owner possesses a ten-acre plot and submits plans conforming to the physical requirements prescribed by the 1947 amendment will not entitle him, *ipso facto*, to a Residence B-B classification. It will still be for the board to decide, in the exercise of a reasonable discretion, that the *grant* of such a classification accords with the comprehensive zoning plan and benefits the village as a whole. And—while no such question is here presented—we note that the board may not arbitrarily or unreasonably *deny* applications of other owners for permission to construct garden apartments on their properties. The action of the board must in all cases be reasonable and, whether a particular application be granted or denied, recourse may be had to the courts to correct an arbitrary or capricious determination.

The charge of illegal "spot zoning"—levelled at the creation of a Residence B-B district and the reclassification of defendant's property—is without substance. Defined as the process of singling out a small parcel of land for a use classification totally different from that of the surrounding area, for the benefit of the owner of such property and to the detriment of other owners; "spot zoning" is the very antithesis of planned zoning. If, therefore, an ordinance is enacted in accordance with a comprehensive zoning plan, it is not "spot zoning," even though it (1) singles out and affects but one small plot, or (2) creates in the center of a large zone small areas or districts devoted to a different use. Thus, the relevant inquiry is not whether the particular zoning under attack consists of areas fixed within larger areas of different use, but whether it was accomplished for the benefit of individual owners rather than pursuant to a comprehensive plan for the general welfare of the community. Having already noted our conclusion that the ordinances were enacted to promote a comprehensive zoning plan, it is perhaps unnecessary to add that the record negates any claim that they were designed solely for the advantage of defendant or any other particular owner. Quite apart from the circumstance that defendant did not seek the benefit of the 1947 amendment until eighteen months after its passage, the all-significant fact is that that amendment applied to the entire territory of the village and accorded each and every owner of ten or more areas identical rights and privileges.

By the same token, there is no basis for the argument that "what has been done by the board of trustees" constitutes a device for "the granting of a 'variance,'" opinion of CONWAY, J., 302 N.Y. p. 129, 96 N.E.2d 738. As we have already shown, the village's zoning aim, the statute's purpose, was not to aid the individual owner but to permit the development of the property for the general welfare of the entire community. That being so, the board of trustees followed approved procedure by changing the General Zoning Ordinance itself. See, e.g., Matter of Clark v. Board of Zoning Appeals, 301 N.Y. 86, 91, 92 N.E.2d 903, 905. Accordingly, when the board was called upon to consider the reclassification of the Rubin property under the 1947 amendment, it was concerned, not with any issue of hardship, but only with the question of whether the property constituted a desirable location for a garden apartment.

We turn finally to the contention that the 1947 ordinance is invalid because, in proclaiming a Residence B-B district, it set no boundaries for the new district and made no changes on the building zone map. The short answer is that, since the ordinance merely prescribed specifications for a new use district, there was no need for it to do either the one or the other. True, until boundaries are fixed and until zoning map changes are made, no new zone actually comes into being, and neither property nor the rights of any property owner are affected. But it was not the design of the board of trustees by that enactment to bring any additional zone into being or to affect any property or rights; the ordinance merely provided the mechanics pursuant to which property owners might in the future apply for the redistricting of their property. In sum, the 1947 amendment was merely the first step in a reasoned plan of rezoning, and specifically provided for further action on the part of the board. That action was taken by the passage of the 1948 ordinance which fixed the boundaries of the newly created zone and amended the zoning map accordingly. It is indisputable that the two amendments, read together as they must be, fully complied with the requirements of the Village Law and accomplished a rezoning of village property in an unexceptionable manner.

In point of fact, there would have been no question about the validity of what was done had the board simply amended the General Zoning Ordinance so as to permit property in Residence A and Residence B zones—or, for that matter, in the other districts throughout the village—to be used for garden apartments, provided that they were built on ten-acre plots and that the other carefully planned conditions and restrictions were met. It may be conceded that, under the method which the board did adopt, no one will know, from the 1947 ordinance itself, precisely where a Residence B-B district will ultimately be located. But since such a district is simply a garden apartment development, we find nothing unusual or improper in that circumstance. The same uncertainty—as to the location of the various types of structures—would be present if a zoning ordinance were to sanction garden apartments as well as one-family homes in a Residence A district—and yet there would be no doubt as to the property of that procedure. Consequently, to condemn the action taken by the board in effectuating a perfectly permissible zoning scheme and to strike down the ordinance designed to carry out the scheme merely because the board had employed two steps to accomplish what may be, and usually is, done in one, would be to exalt form over substance and sacrifice substance to form.

Whether it is generally desirable that garden apartments be freely mingled among private residences under all circumstances, may be arguable. In view, however, of Tarrytown's changing scene and the other substantial reasons for the board's decision, we cannot say that its action was arbitrary or illegal. While hardships may be imposed on this or that owner, "cardinal is the principle that what is best for the body politic in the long run must prevail over the interests of particular individuals." Shepard v. Village of Skaneateles, supra.

* * *

ROCKHILL

v.

CHESTERFIELD TP.

23 N.J. 117, 128 A.2d 473 (1957)

The zoning ordinance adopted by Chesterfield Township, New Jersey, designated all land in the township for "normal agriculture" and residential uses and also provided for "special uses" to be authorized by the planning board and the governing body where "investigation has shown that such structures and uses will be beneficial to the general development." Thus, a "floating zone" was created in the sense that the possibility that uses other than agriculture or residence existed for all land upon application to the planning board and showing that such use would be beneficial to the community. The New Jersey Supreme Court held this ordinance invalid in the decision excerpted below.

* * *

Zoning is in its essential policy and purpose a component of the reserve element of sovereignty denominated the "police power," the sovereign right so to order the affairs of the people as to serve the common social and economic needs, the principle that brought them together in civilized society for their mutual advantage and welfare, to which all property is subject; but whatever its quality and scope as an attribute of sovereignty, land use regulation in New Jersey is now controlled by Article IV, Section VI, paragraph 2 of the 1947 State Constitution, embodying and amplifying the amendment of the 1844 Constitution, Article IV, Section VI, paragraph 5, adopted at a special election held September 20, 1927, whereby the Legislature is empowered to enact "general laws" under which municipalities, other than counties, may adopt "zoning ordinances limiting and restricting to specified districts and regulating therein, buildings and structures, according to their construction, and the nature and extent of their use, and the nature and extent of the uses of land," an exercise of authority "deemed to be within the police power of the State." However broad the police power inherent in sovereignty to invoke measures conducive to the general good and welfare, the exercise of the zoning process must perforce conform to the constitutional regulation and the enabling statute.

The constitutional and statutory zoning principle is territorial division according to the character of the lands and structures and their peculiar suitability for particular uses, and uniformity of use within the division. And the legislative grant of authority has the selfsame delineation.

The local governing body is empowered to divide the municipality into districts of such number, shape, and area as may be deemed best suited to carry out the statutory policy, and to regulate and restrict the construction and use of buildings and other structures and the use of land within such districts, provided that "All such regulations shall be uniform for each class or kind of buildings or other structures or uses of land throughout each district, but the regulations in one district may be different from those in other districts." And such regulations shall be in accordance with a "comprehensive plan and designed" to subserve the public welfare in one or more of the enumerated particulars involving the public health, safety, morals, or the general welfare, and "shall be made with reasonable consideration, among other things, to the character of the district and its peculiar suitability for particular uses, and with a view of conserving the value of property and encouraging the most appropriate use of land throughout such municipality." And thus it is basic to the local exercise of the power that the use restrictions be general and uniform in the particular district, delimited in keeping with the constitutional and statutory considerations; otherwise, there would be the arbitrary discrimination at war with the substance of due process and the equal protection of the laws.

Classification to this end must be reasonably based in the public interest to be served. It is fundamental in our zoning policy that all property in like circumstances be treated alike. There cannot be invidious distinctions. And so it is that the use-district restraints are required to be general and uniform. All this, in virtue of the legislative grant itself, quite apart from constitutional zoning concept and the precepts for the fulfillment of basic civil liberties. Constitutional uniformity and equality demands that classification be founded in real and not feigned differences related to the purposes for which the classes are formed, i.e., zoning by districts according to the "nature and extent" of the use of land and buildings, to serve the statutory police considerations, some or all, the regulations to have reasonable regard to the "character of the district and its peculiar suitability for particular uses." "Spot zoning" would contravene the constitutional and statutory principle of zoning by districts in consonance with the character of the lands and structures and use suitability, and uniformity of use within the division. Moriarty v. Pozner, 21 N.J. 199, 121 A.2d 527 (1956). Such is the case here.

The scheme of the ordinance is the negation of zoning. It overrides the basic concept of use zoning by districts, that is to say, territorial division according to the character of the lands and structures and their peculiar use suitability and a comprehensive regulatory plan to advance the general good within the prescribed range of the police power. The local design is "normal agricultural" and residence uses and the specified "special uses" by the authority of the planning board and the local governing body, generally where "investigation has shown that such structures and uses will be beneficial to the general development," and "light industrial uses and other similar facilities having no adverse effect on surrounding property and deemed desirable to the general economic well-being of the Township," terms hardly adequate to channel local administrative discretion but, at all events, making for the "piecemeal" and "spot" zoning alien to the constitutional and statutory principle of land use zoning by districts and comprehensive planning for the fulfillment of the declared policy. The fault is elementary and vital; the rule of the ordinance is *ultra vires* and void.

Reserving the use of the whole of the municipal area for "normal agricultural" and residence uses, and then providing for all manner of "special uses," "neighborhood" and other businesses, even "light industrial" uses and "other similar facilities," placed according to local discretion without regard to districts, ruled by vague and illusive criteria, is indeed the antithesis of zoning. It makes for arbitrary and discriminatory interference with the basic right of private property, in no real sense concerned with the essential common welfare. The statute provides for regulation by districts and for exceptions and variances from the prescribed land uses under given conditions. The course taken here would flout this essential concept of district zoning according to a comprehensive plan designed to fulfill the declared statutory policy. Comprehensive zoning means an orderly and coordinate system of community development according to socioeconomic needs.

Duffcon Concrete Products, Inc., v. Borough of Cresskill is not to the contrary. There, the zoning ordinance excluded all industry from the municipality, a small residential community in Bergen County, in area 1,300 acres and in population 2,300. In an endeavor to maintain its residential character, the borough in 1941 adopted an ordinance establishing four zones, three entirely residential, and the fourth for "commercial districts for business centers." Chief Justice Vanderbilt said that what may be the most appropriate use of any particular property depends not alone on all the conditions, physical, economic and social, prevailing within the municipality and its needs, present and reasonably prospective, but also "on the nature of the entire region in which the municipality is located and the use to which the land in that region has been or may be put most advantageously," and the "effective development of a region should not and cannot be made to depend upon the adventitious location of municipal boundaries, often prescribed decades or even centuries ago, and based in many instances on considerations of geography, of commerce, or of politics that are no longer significant with respect to zoning," that is to say, the "direction of growth of residential areas" and of "industrial concentration" refuses to be "governed by such artificial lines;" that changes in "methods of transportation" and "in living conditions" have accentuated the "unreality" of dealing with zoning problems on the basis of the territorial limits of a municipality, and "[i]mproved highways" and "new transportation facilities" have made possible the "concentration of industry at places best suited to its development to a degree not contemplated in the earlier stages of zoning;" and that the advantages of the "existing and currently developing suburban and rural sections given over solely to residential purposes and local retail business services coextensive with the needs of the community" inure alike to "industry and residential properties and, at the same time, advance the general welfare of the entire region." Attention was directed to the "availability and use of the extensive bottom lands of the Hackensack River Valley within the region for industrial purposes," as indicating that the zoning scheme "comprehends, in the language of the statute, 'the most appropriate use of land throughout such municipality.' This rationale conforms to the basic principle of zoning by districts, and comprehensive regulation according to the given statutory considerations."

Zoning and planning are not identical in concept. Zoning is a separation of the municipality into districts for the most appropriate use of the land, by general rules according to a comprehensive plan for the common good in matters within the domain of the police power. And, though the landowner does not have a vested right to a particular zone classification, one of the essential purposes of zoning regulation is the stabilization of property uses. Investments are made in lands and structures on the faith of district use control having some degree of permanency, a well considered plan that will stand until changing conditions dictate otherwise. Such is the nature of use zoning by districts according to a comprehensive plan. The regulations here are in contravention of the principle.

The ordinance is vacated as *ultra vires* the enabling statute; and the cause is remanded for judicial action accordingly.

For additional information about floating zones, see Reno, "Non-Euclidean Zoning: The Use of the Floating Zone," 23 *Maryland L.Rev.* 105 (1963); Platt, "Valid Spot Zoning: A Creative Tool For Flexibility of Land Use," 48 *Ore. L. Rev.* 245 (1969).

2. Contract Zoning—Conditional Zoning

Contract zoning, or **conditional zoning,** as it is sometimes called, is the term used to describe zoning amendments that are adopted by a governing body providing for a change of land use in return for an agreement, or other form of consideration, provided by the owner of the property to be benefitted by the amendment. For example, an issue of contract zoning would arise if land is rezoned from residential use to commercial use in consideration for the owner's agreement to provide prescribed landscaping and other amenities. The legal objections to such an arrangement are similar to the legal objections to floating zones: (1) **spot zoning;** (2) **ultra vires;** (3) **not in accordance with the comprehensive plan;** (4) **violation of the uniformity clause;** (5) **inconsistent with the landowners' expectation of stability and continuation of existing land uses.** In addition, contract zoning is vulnerable to the argument that it is illegal because (6) **government cannot contract away its police power** to protect the health, safety and welfare of the public. This last argument becomes particularly persuasive if the government agrees to change the zoning permanently. As the following two cases indicate, the issue of contract zoning raises questions about which the courts are not in agreement.

CHURCH

v.

TOWN OF ISLIP

8 N.Y.2d 254, 203 N.Y.S. 866, 168 N.E.2d 680 (1960)

DESMOND, Chief Judge.

Neighboring property owners brought this declaratory judgment suit against the Town of Islip in Suffolk County and against its Town Board and the owners of the involved property to have declared unconstitutional and void a 1954 zoning change (from Residence A to Business) of defendants Housler's corner lot in Islip, irregular in shape and about 210 feet on Bay Shore Road and 230 feet on Udall's Road. The complaint charged that the amendment was not in conformity with a comprehensive plan, that it was passed arbitrarily after a contrary recommendation by the Town Planning Board, that it arbitrarily singled out this one tract for business zoning, and that it was illegal as "contract zoning" because the Town Board's consent to the change of zone was subject to the condition that defendants owners Housler agree to the following:

"1. The building shall not total more than 25% of the area.

"2. An anchor post fence, or equal, six feet high, is to be erected five feet within the boundary line of the property.

"3. Live Shrubbery, 3 feet high either within or outside of the fence is to be planted, and allowed to grow to the height of the fence and after that, to be maintained at the height of the fence.

"4. The above must be performed or put in operation before carrying on any retail business on the property."

* * *

We start with the proposition that this zoning being a legislative act (not a variance) is entitled to the strongest possible presumption of validity and must stand if there was any factual basis therefor. The Town Board's action in this instance was unanimous. Appellants do not seem to question the Appellate Division's fact findings. It is undisputed that Bay Shore Road has become a busy arterial highway, with a traffic light at this corner and that the very Town Planning Board which recommended against this zoning change recommended a shopping area (now established) only 600 feet from this parcel on Bay Shore Road. On the issue of arbitrariness, there was reliable testimony that all of Bay Shore Road would be eventually zoned for business and that this trend could not be stopped, that the subject property is more desirable for business use than for residential, and that there was nothing arbitrary, preferential or discriminatory about the Town Board action, unanimously voted after hearing and deliberation.

Appellants' arguments all revolve about the idea that this is illegal as "contract zoning" because the Town Board, as a condition for rezoning, required the owners to execute and record restrictive convenants as to maximum area to be occupied by buildings and as to a fence and shrubbery. Surely these conditions were intended to be and are for the benefit of the neighbors. Since the Town Board could have, presumably, zoned this Bay Shore Road corner for business without any restrictions, we fail to see how reasonable conditions invalidate the legislation. Since the owners have accepted them, there is no one in a position to contest them. Exactly what "contract zoning" means is unclear and there is really no New York law on the subject. All legislation "by contract" is invalid in the sense that a Legislature cannot bargain away or sell its powers. But we deal here with actualities, not phrases. To meet increasing needs of Suffolk County's own population explosion, and at the same time to make as gradual and as little of an annoyance as possible the change from residence to business on the main highways, the Town Board imposes conditions. There is nothing unconstitutional about it. Incidentally, the record does not show any agreement in the sense that the owners made an offer accepted by the board.

The judgment should be affirmed, without costs.

FROESSEL, Judge (dissenting).

I dissent and vote to reverse for the reasons stated in Presiding Justice Nolan's dissenting opinion below with respect to the Town Board's lack of power. The board is authorized by the Town Law to create districts subject to this condition: "All such regulations [within a district] shall be *uniform* for each class or kind of buildings, throughout such district" (§ 262), and "shall be made in accordance with a *comprehensive plan*" (§ 263; emphasis supplied). The purpose of a plan is to look ahead. Piecemeal, parcel by parcel, conditional zoning pending the adoption of a plan is unauthorized. Variances in appropriate situations may be granted by Zoning Boards of Appeal but only under prescribed safeguards (§§ 261,267). The power exercised by the Town Board is without warrant in law.

HOUSTON PETROLEUM CO.

v.

AUTOMOTIVE PRODUCTS CREDIT ASS'N.

9 N.J. 122, 87 A.2d 319 (1954)

An owner of property entered into an agreement with the City of Linden, New Jersey, by which the city reclassified the owner's property to light industrial in consideration for the owner's agreement to subject the property to deed restrictions that require a 75 foot setback that is to be seeded and planted. The property was subsequently sold to an owner who entered into a later agreement with the city to release some, but not all, of this land from the setback and planting agreement. The property was later subdivided and sold to different people. In a suit by one of the subsequent owners of part of the property to enforce the deed restriction, the question of the validity of the original contract with the city was brought into issue. In the decision excerpted below the New Jersey Supreme Court held that the original contract was invalid.

* * *

The defendant asserted below and asserts here among its questions involved on appeal that the covenants and restrictions sought by plaintiff to be enforced are invalid and unenforceable for the reason, *inter alia,* that the agreement of April 15, 1947, between Byrnes and the City of Linden constituted an abuse of the zoning power by the City, and was therefore *ultra vires,* illegal and void. With this contention we agree.

The latest exposition of the law applicable to the foregoing conclusion is contained in V. F. Zahodiakin, etc., Corp. v. Zoning Board of Adjustment of City of Summit. This court there held that the zoning power may not be exerted to serve private interests merely nor may the principle be subverted to that end, that a purported contract so made was *ultra vires* and all proceedings to effectuate it were *coram non judice* and utterly void.

The same principle is implicit in the decisions of this court in Beckmann v. Township of Teaneck, wherein the asserted authority of a municipality to contract for the exercise of legislative powers was denied by the court and Anschelewitz v. Borough of Belmar, wherein the court said: "A municipality cannot act as an individual does. It must proceed in conformity with the statutes, or in the absence of statute agreeably to the common law, by ordinance or resolution or motion. * * *Especially is this so where real property is concerned. * * *"

Contracts thus have no place in a zoning plan and a contract between a municipality and a property owner should not enter into the enactment or enforcement of zoning regulations. See Bassett on Zoning, p. 184 (1940). The covenants in question not only were imposed on the land for the purpose of obtaining rezoning of the Byrnes tract, but are themselves limited in duration to the period of time during which the premises remain zoned for light industry. Thus they seem related not to the benefit of individual portions of the tract but to zoning for the entire tract. In addition, the recorded agreement provides for release or modification of the covenants at any time by an agreement *to which the City of Linden is made a necessary party.* This again is referable to zoning, and is within the particular condemnation of the law as stated in the Zahodiakin case, supra. Thus it may be concluded that the covenants in themselves exhibit a plan in contravention of the public policy incorporated in the constitutional and statutory provisions relating to zoning. The former Supreme Court of this State in Sharp v. Teese held: "The attempt to contravene the policy of a public statute is illegal. Nor is it necessary to render it so that the statute should contain an express prohibition of such attempt. It always contains an implied prohibition; and to such attempt the principles of the common law are invariably and deadly hostile, not always by an interference between the parties themselves, or by enabling the one to recall from the other, where *in pari delicto*, what may have been obtained; but by at all times refusing the aid of the law to carry into effect or enforce any contract which may be the result of such intended contravention." And this court has reiterated the rule that a contract in contravention of the public policy of this State will not be enforced. Lobek v. Gross. We therefore conclude that the restrictive covenants in question, being violative of the public policy of this State implicit in our zoning laws, are illegal. The agreement establishing the covenants being illegal and void, the plaintiff is not entitled to their enforcement.

As the above case indicates, some states such as New Jersey, Florida, Maryland, North Carolina and Rhode Island have held conditional zoning illegal. On the other hand, New York, Washington, California, Wisconsin, Nebraska, Kansas, Massachusetts and Connecticut have upheld conditional zoning. See Miller, "Conditional Zoning," 12 **Municipal Attorney** 98 (1972); Comment, "The Use and Abuse of Contract Zoning," 12 **U.C.L.A. L.Rev.** 897 (1965); Shapiro, "The Case For Conditional Zoning," 41 **Temple L.Q.** 267 (1968).

---

3. Incentive Zoning

Incentive zoning is a term that is used to describe any type of zoning provision that offers an affirmative inducement to private developers to encourage them to develop the land in a manner that will achieve public objectives. For example, a developer may be permitted to increase the floor area of a proposed building if he provides a pedestrian plaza or arcade that will enhance the appearance of the area. The following provisions from the San Francisco City Planning Code illustrate the kinds of municipal amenities that may be encouraged by this technique.

SAN FRANCISCO CITY PLANNING CODE, SEC. 122.3

SEC. 122.3 Development Bonuses, C-3 Districts.

(a) In any C-3 district, the development bonuses specified in the following table, where applicable, may be added to the basic floor area ratio limit to determine the maximum floor area ratio for a building or development. Each building feature, and the unit of feature upon which the bonus is based, are more fully described in and limited by paragraph (b) below. Each separate bonus shall be credited where it applies; except that features 1 and 2 shall be mutually exclusive, and features 8 and 9 shall also be mutually exclusive. The basic allowable gross floor area in each case shall be as specified in Section 122.1 of this Code, and shall not include any development bonus specified herein or any transferred floor area as specified in Section 122.4 below.

The primary purposes of these development bonuses are: provision of good access to buildings, and improvement of access to properties, from the various forms of transportation serving the downtown area; improvement of pedestrian movement into and out of buildings, along streets and between streets; provision of pedestrian amenity by means of ground level open space; arrangement of buildings to provide light and air to streets and to other properties; and protection and enhancement of views.

(b) The following criteria shall apply to the building features listed in the table in paragraph (a) above, and to the unit of feature therein upon which each bonus is based.

1. *Rapid Transit Access.* The access shall be to a city or regional rapid transit system, leading directly to a station mezzanine of such system and conforming to the standards of the transit system, the Building Code and other applicable codes. The access shall be entered from a location within the lot lines of the subject lot, either within or outside a building, and shall be open during all business hours common in the area for use by the general public, marked for their use, and easily reached from a street or alley with a minimum sidewalk width of seven feet.

2. *Rapid Transit Proximity.* This bonus shall be available for any lot within 750 feet walking distance from a designated station mezzanine of a city or regional rapid transit system, and shall increase in proportion to the closeness of the lot to such mezzanine. The walking distance shall be measured along streets and alleys with a minimum sidewalk width of five feet, or along passageways conforming to the standards of features 1 above and 6 below. For this purpose, walking distance shall be taken as the shortest distance from any point along the station mezzanine, to any point along a lot line of the subject property from which there is general access to the subject building.

3. *Parking Access.* The access shall be from the subject building directly to an automobile parking structure located elsewhere than in the areas of concentrated development of the C-3-O and C-3-R districts. Such parking structure may be either part of or separate from the subject building, but if the parking structure is separate it shall be either in the same ownership as the subject building or part of a Planned Unit Development approved under Article 3 of this Code to include both the parking structure and the subject building. The access shall be open during all business hours for use by occupants of or visitors to the subject building and marked for their use, and shall provide a passage with a minimum width of five feet, separated from streets and alleys. A passageway that is proposed to bridge a street or alley or to occupy any other public area shall be reviewed by the Planning Commission subject to the criteria for Master Plan review under the City Charter and any other criteria that may be applicable. No parking space to which access is credited under this provision shall consist of a space actually required by this Code for any building use.

4. *Multiple Building Entrances.* This bonus shall be available where there is more than one major entrance to the subject building, open generally to occupants of the building for both entrance and exit and readily identifiable to them. All such major entrances shall be accessible from streets or alleys with a minimum sidewalk

width of five feet, and shall be located at least 50 feet apart along
such streets or alleys. Where a building face at ground level is
located more than 20 feet inside the lot line along such a street or
alley and contains at least one major doorway, each point at 50-
foot intervals along such lot line shall be considered a separate
major entrance to the building.

5. *Sidewalk Widening.* The sidewalk widening shall be along a
through street or through alley, shall consist of an arcade, can-
tilever, building setback or plaza, open at all times to the general
public, and shall run the full length of the lot along such street or
alley except for necessary interruptions by features required for
safety by other provisions of law, ordinance or the Municipal
Code. The widened area shall be directly accessible from the public sidewalk at both ends and along at least two-thirds of its
length, and if not fully open to such sidewalk shall have a
minimum clear width of seven feet. The widened area shall have
a minimum height of 10 feet, and although it may be occupied in
part by columns, building services, landscaping and other features, only areas capable of being walked upon shall be credited
in computation of the bonus. The maximum creditable depth of
the widened area from the lot line at the street or alley shall be
15 feet in the C-3-R district and 30 feet in the other C-3 districts,
or 50 feet from the curb, whichever is less.

Notwithstanding the requirements of this provision concerning
accessibility, continuity or horizontal dimensions, landscaped open
area located as herein provided at ground level, consistent with
the purposes of the bonus system and readily visible from a street
or alley or permanent public open space, may be credited as
sidewalk widening area within the scope of the 15 per cent
maximum permitted for the sidewalk widening bonus in Table 1A;
provided, that the bonus awarded shall be three square feet of
floor area for each creditable square foot of such open area.

6. *Shortening Walking Distance.* The shortening of walking distance
shall be computed by comparing walking distances along streets
and alleys having a minimum sidewalk width of five feet, with
distances along walkways through the subject lot that are open
during all business hours common in the area for use by the general public. Such a walkway may be either within or outside a
building, shall be readily identifiable from the public sidewalk,
and shall have a minimum width of 10 feet plus two feet for each
side which has shops, lobbies, elevator entrances or similar features along it. Where a walkway passes through two or more lots,
the bonus shall be prorated in proportion to the length of walkway
on each lot.

7. *Plaza.* The plaza shall be directly and conveniently accessible to
the general public during all business hours common in the area,
from either a street or alley with a minimum sidewalk width of
five feet, a feature conforming to the standards of 5 or 6 above, or
a permanent public open space. The creditable plaza area shall be

located at least 20 feet inside the lot lines separating the lot from streets and alleys, shall have a minimum entrance width of 10 feet, and shall be at least 30 feet in its horizontal dimensions. For the purpose of measuring such minimum horizontal dimensions, space occupied by a feature conforming to the standards of 5 above may be counted for up to one-third of any dimension; however, no area credited under 5 above shall also be credited as plaza area. Up to two-thirds of the surface of the creditable plaza area may be occupied by planting, sculpture, pools and similar features, and the balance shall be suitable for walking, sitting, and similar pursuits. Any building servicing requiring the presence of vehicles or goods in the plaza area shall be confined to times other than the business hours common in the area. Encroachments permitted by Section 126 of this Code for usable open space shall be permitted for the creditable plaza area.

Notwithstanding the requirements of this provision concerning accessibility or horizontal dimensions, landscaped open area located as herein provided at ground level, consistent with the purposes of the bonus system and readily visible from a street or alley or permanent public open space, may be credited as plaza area within the scope of the 15 per cent maximum permitted for the plaza bonus in Table 1A; provided, that the bonus awarded shall be three square feet of floor area for each creditable square foot of such open area.

8. *Side Setback.* The side building setback shall extend upward from a height of not more than 40 feet measured at the front of the setback, and shall also extend for the entire depth of the lot. The side setback shall be located either along a lot line which intersects a street or alley and does not itself separate the lot from a street or alley, or in an equivalent position between two buildings or building portions on the same lot exceeding 40 feet in height. The setback area shall be unobstructed to the sky and shall have a minimum width of 20 feet. Setback areas of irregular width may be credited, provided the minimum width of 20 feet is maintained and no part of the setback area to be credited is separated by a building from the street or alley which the setback intersects. The maximum creditable width of the setback area shall be 50 feet.

9. *Low Coverage at Upper Floors.* Each open area credited under this bonus shall extend upward unobstructed from a height of not more than 80 feet measured at the front of such open area, and shall also extend for the entire width or depth of the lot. The bonus shall be based upon reduction of both the over-all width and the over-all depth of the building by a minimum of 20 per cent of the respective lot dimensions, with additional bonus awarded as both such dimensions of the building are further reduced. Where the building is not located parallel to any of the lot lines, the over-all dimensions of the building shall be measured as appropriate to the specific siting of the building in relation to the lot and to streets and alleys.

10. *Observation Deck.* The observation deck or similar public space shall be located at or above the 20th story of the building and shall be of sufficient size to accommodate at least 50 persons at one time. Such space shall be advertised at ground level, and shall be open during the day and evening to the general public without the necessity of their doing business in the building other than paying an admission fee for the sole purpose of gaining access to the observation area.

(c) In application of the bonuses provided for in this Section, the Zoning Administrator shall follow such procedures, including placing of restrictions on the land records and other actions, as he may deem appropriate to assure the provision and retention of such building features as are credited in order to meet the requirements of this Code.

(d) In the C-3-O district, notwithstanding the development bonuses afforded by paragraphs (a), (b) and (c) of this Section, and in lieu of any and all such development bonuses, for a lot or portion thereof which is defined by this Code as a corner lot, a floor area premium may be added by increasing the area of the lot or portion, for purposes of determining the maximum floor area ratio for the building or development on such lot, by twenty (20) per cent. (*Amended Ord. 274-68, approved 9-16-68*)

For a discussion of the operation of the San Francisco zoning bonus system see Svirsky, "San Francisco: The Downtown Development Bonus System," *The New Zoning* (1970).

See also: Brooks, "Bonus Provisions in Central City Areas," (ASPO Advisory Services Report No. 257, May, 1970); Comment, "Bonus or Incentive Zoning—Legal Implications," 21 Syracuse L.Rev. 895 (1970).

---

4. Performance Zoning

Performance zoning is a term that is used to describe zoning provisions that prescribe the standards that must be met to permit a given use of the land. For example, industrial use may be permitted in a designated zone if the proposed use meets performance standards relating to noise, smoke, smell, etc. The same concept may be used to limit higher density residential use to proposals that meet performance standards relating to impervious cover ratio, open space ratio, proximity to water, sewer and other utilities, and the adequacy of schools, parks and other community facilities. One of the difficulties with this technique is the need to prescribe each of the performance standards with great detail and precision. The following provisions from a proposed zoning ordinance in Rome, New York, as cited in Anderson, *American Law of Zoning* Vol. 4, pp. 110-115 illustrate and detail that must be included in performance standard provisions.

Industrial Performance Standards

General Application

Where uses permitted in any M-District, and uses accessory thereto, are subject to the following performance standards and procedures. If the

Enforcement Officer or the Board of Appeals has reasonable grounds for believing that any other use will violate these performance standards, such use, existing or proposed, shall also be subject to these performance standards.

Performance Standards Procedure

a. *Prior to Construction and Operation.* Any application for a building permit for a use which shall be subject to performance standards, shall be accompanied by a sworn statement by the owner of subject property that said use will be operated in accordance with the performance standards set forth herein.

b. *Continued Compliance.* Continued compliance with performance standards is required and enforcement of continued compliance with these performance standards shall be enforced by the Enforcement Officer or Board of Appeals.

c. *Determination of Violation.* The Enforcement Officer shall investigate any purported violation of performance standards and, if there is reasonable ground for the same, shall notify the Board of Appeals of the occurrence or existence of a probable violation thereof. The Board shall investigate the alleged violation. If after public hearings on due notice, the Board finds that a violation occurred or exists, such violation shall be terminated as provided in paragraph d. following.

d. *Termination of Violation.* All violations, as ascertained in accordance with paragraph c. above shall be terminated within thirty (30) days of the decision of the Board or shall be deemed a separate violation for each day following and subject to fines as set forth herein, except that certain uses established before the effective date of this Ordinance and nonconforming as to performance standards shall be given a reasonable time in which to conform therewith as determined by the Board.

Regulation of Nuisance Elements

a. *Definition of Elements.* No land or building in any M-District which shall be used or occupied for manufacturing purposes shall be operated in such a manner so as to create any dangerous, injurious, noxious or otherwise objectionable fire, explosive or other hazard; noise or vibration, smoke, dust, dirt or other form of air pollution; electrical or other disturbance; glare; or other substance, condition or element in such amount as to adversely affect the surrounding area or premises (referred to herein as "dangerous or objectionable elements"); provided that any use permitted by this Ordinance may be undertaken and maintained in the M-Districts if it conforms to the regulations of this subsection limiting dangerous and objectionable elements at the specified point or points of the determination of their existence.

b. *Location Where Determinations are to be made for Enforcement of Performance Standards.* The determination of the existence of any dangerous and objectionable elements shall be made at:

1) The point or points where such elements shall be most apparent for fire and explosion hazards, for radioactivity and electrical disturbances, for smoke and other forms of air pollution.

2) The property lines of the use creating such elements for noise, for vibration, for glare, and for odors.

Standards to be Enforced

a. *Fire and Explosion Hazards.* All activities involving, and all storage of, inflammable and explosive materials shall be provided with adequate safety devices against the hazard of fire and explosion and adequate firefighting and fire suppression equipment and devices standard in this industry. Burning of waste materials in open fires is prohibited. The relevant provisions of State and local laws and regulations shall also apply.

b. *Radioactivity or Electrical Disturbance.* No activities shall be permitted which emit dangerous radioactivity or electrical disturbance adversely affecting the operation of any equipment other than that of the creator of such disturbance. All applicable Federal regulations shall be complied with.

c. *Noise.* At the points of measurement specified in Section 67, paragraph b. the maximum sound pressure level radiated in each standard octave band by any use or facility (other than transportation facilities or temporary construction work) shall note exceed the values for octave bands lying within the several frequency limits given in Table I after applying the corrections shown in Table II. The sound pressure level shall be measured with a Sound Level Meter and associated Octave Band Analyzer conforming to standards prescribed by the American Standards Association, Inc., New York, N.Y. (American Standard Sound Level Meters for Measurement of Noise and Other Sounds, 224.3-1944, American Standards Association, Inc., New York, N.Y., and American Standard Specification for an Octave-Band Filter Set for the Analysis of Noise and Other Sounds, 224.10-1953, or latest approved revision thereof, American Standards Association, Inc., New York, N.Y. shall be used.)

Table I

Frequency Ranges Containing Standard Octave Bands in Cycles Per Second	Octave Band Sound Pressure Level in Decibels re 0.0002 dyne/cm
20— 75	65
75— 150	55
150— 300	50
300— 600	45
600—1,200	40
1,200—2,400	40
Above 2,400	35

If the noise is not smooth and continuous and is not radiated between the hours of 10 p.m. and 7 a.m. one or more of the corrections in Table II shall be applied to the octave band levels given in Table I.

Table II

Type of Location of Operation or Character of Noise	Correction in Decibels
1. Daytime operation only	5
2. Noise source operates less than*	
a. 20% of any one-hour period	5
b. 5% of any one-hour period	10
3. Noise of impulsive character (hammering, etc.)............	–5
4. Noise of periodic character (hum, screech, etc.)...........	–5
5. Property is located in any M-District and is not within 200 feet of any R-District...............................	10

*Apply one of these corrections only.

d. *Vibration.* No vibration shall be permitted which is detectable without instruments at the points of measurement specified in Section 67 paragraph b.

e. *Glare.* No direct or sky-reflected glare, whether from floodlights or from high-temperature processes such as combustion or welding or otherwise, so as to be visible at the points of measurement specified in paragraph b. This restriction shall not apply to signs otherwise permitted by the provisions of this Ordinance.

f. *Smoke.* No emission shall be permitted from any chimney or otherwise, of visible grey smoke of a shade equal to or darker than No. 2 on the Power's Miscro-Ringlemann Chart, published by McGraw-Hill Publishing Company, Inc., and copyright 1954 (being a direct facsimile reduction of a standard Ringlemann Chart as issued by the United States Bureau of Mines), except that visible grey smoke of a shade equal to No. 3 on said chart may be emitted for 4 minutes in any 30 minutes.

g. *Odors.* No emission shall be permitted of odorous gases or other odorous matter in such quantities as to be readily detectable at the property line of the zone lot from which they are emitted without instruments.

h. *Other Forms of Air Pollution.* No emission of fly ash, dust, fumes, vapors, gases and other forms of air pollution shall be permitted which can cause any damage to health, to animal, vegetation, or other forms of property, or which can cause any excessive soiling.

For additional information on performance zoning see:

McDougal, "Performance Standards: A Viable Alternative to Euclidean Zoning?", 47 **Tul. L.Rev.** 255 (1973).
Hirsch, "Measuring the Good Neighbor: A New Look at Performance Standards in Zoning," 2 **Land Use Controls** 5 (Spring 1968).
Gillespie, "Industrial Zoning and Beyond: Compatibility Through Performance Standards," 46 **J. Urban L.** 723 (1969).

5. Special Districts—Mixed Use Districts

A **special district** is a zoning district that is created to restrict or to protect and promote a particular purpose. For example, a number of cities have adopted ordinances that either seek to restrict "porno shops" and "adult theaters" to limited areas, or to deconcentrate such activities to prevent the creation of skid-row neighborhoods. The validity of these special districts, facetiously called **"erogenous zones,"** has warranted the attention of the United States Supreme Court in *Young v. American Mini Theatres,* set forth below. On the other hand, other cities have created special districts to encourage certain activities. For example, New York City has a special theatre district in which developers are given bonus incentives to provide theatres and theatre facilities within a proposed building.

A **Mixed Use District (MUD)** is a form of special district in which several different land uses are permitted. Although it may be argued that a mixed use district is the antithesis of zoning, there are circumstances and places where a combination of different and distinct land uses in an integrated development may serve the needs of the community. Mixed use development may be particularly useful as part of a program to revitalize a downtown area of a central city by providing housing, commercial and recreational uses in a designated area.

(a) Erogenous Zones

YOUNG

v.

AMERICAN MINI THEATRES

427 U.S. 50, 97 S.Ct. 191, 49 L.Ed.2d 310 (1976)

Mr. Justice Stevens delivered the opinion of the Court.*

Zoning ordinances adopted by the city of Detroit differentiate between motion picture theaters which exhibit sexually explicit "adult" movies and those which do not. The principle question presented by this case is whether that statutory classification is unconstitutional because it is based on the content of communication protected by the First Amendment.

Effective November 2, 1972, Detroit adopted the ordinances challenged in this litigation. Instead of concentrating "adult" theaters in limited zones, these ordinances require that such theaters be dispersed. Specifically, an adult theater may not be located within 1,000 feet of any two other "regulated uses" or within 500 feet of a residential area. The term "regulated use" includes 10 different kinds of establishments in addition to adult theaters.

The classification of a theater as "adult" is expressly predicated on the character of the motion pictures which it exhibits. If the theater is used to present "material distinguished or characterized by an emphasis on matter depicting, describing or relating to 'Specified Sexual Activities' or 'Specified Anatomical Areas,' " * it is an adult establishment.**

The 1972 ordinances were amendments to an "Anti-Skid Row Ordinance" which had been adopted 10 years earlier. At that time the Detroit Common Council made a finding that some uses of property are especially injurious to a neighborhood when they are concentrated in limited areas. The decision to add adult motion picture theaters and adult book stores to the list of businesses which, apart from a special waiver, could not be located within 1,000 feet of two other "regulated uses," was, in part, a response to the significant growth in the number of such establishments. In the opinion of urban planners and real estate experts who supported the ordinances, the location of several such businesses in the same neighborhood tends to attract an undesirable quantity and quality of transients, adversely affects property values, causes an increase in crime, especially prostitution, and encourages residents and businesses to move elsewhere.

Respondents are the operators of two adult motion picture theaters. One, the Nortown, was an established theater which began to exhibit adult films in March 1973. The other, the Pussy Cat, was a corner gas station which was converted into a "mini theater," but denied a certificate of occupancy because of its plan to exhibit adult films. Both theaters were located within 1,000 feet of two other regulated uses and the Pussy Cat was less than 500 feet from a residential area. The respondents brought

---

*These terms are defined as follows:

"For the purpose of this Section, 'Specified Sexual Activities' is defined as:

"1. Human Genitals in a state of sexual stimulation or arousal;

"2. Acts of human masturbation, sexual intercourse or sodomy;

"3. Fondling or other erotic touching of human genitals, pubic region, buttock or female breast.

"And 'Specified Anatomical Areas' is defined as:

"1. Less than completely and opaquely overed: (a) human genitals, pubic region, (b) buttock, and (c) female breast below a point immediately above the top of the areoia; and

"2. Human male genitals in a discernibly turgid state, even if completely and opaquely covered."

**There are three types of adult establishments, book stores, motion picture theaters, and mini motion picture theaters, defined respectively as follows:

"Adult Book Store

"An establishment having as a substantial or significant portion of its stock in trade, books, magazines, and other periodicals which are distinguished or characterized by their emphasis on matter depicting, describing or relating to 'Specified Sexual Activities' or 'Specified Anatomical Areas,' (as defined below), or an establishment with a segment or section devoted to the sale or display of such material.

"Adult Motion Picture Theater

"An enclosed building with a capacity of 50 or more persons used for . . . presenting material distinguished or characterized by an emphasis on matter depicting, describing or relating to 'Specified Sexual Activities' or 'Specified Anatomical Areas,' (as defined below) for observation by patrons therein.

"Adult Mini Motion Picture Theater

"An enclosed building with a capacity for less than 50 persons used for presenting material distinguished or characterized by an emphasis on matter depicting, describing or relating to 'Specified Sexual Activities' or 'Specified Anatomical Areas,' (as defined below), for observation by patrons therein."

two separate actions against appropriate city officials, seeking a declaratory
judgment that the ordinances were unconstitutional and an injunction
against their enforcement. Federal jurisdiction was properly invoked and
the two cases were consolidated for decision.

The District Court granted defendants' motion for summary judgment.
On the basis of the reasons stated by the city for adopting the ordinances,
the court concluded that they represented a rational attempt to preserve
the city's neighborhoods. The court analyzed and rejected respondents'
argument that the definition and waiver provisions in the ordinances were
impermissibly vague; it held that the disparate treatment of adult theaters
and other theaters was justified by a compelling state interest and therefore did not violate the Equal Protection Clause; and finally it concluded
that the regulation of the places where adult films could be shown did not
violate the First Amendment.

The Court of Appeals reversed. The majority opinion concluded that
the ordinances imposed a prior restraint on constitutionally protected
communication and therefore "merely establishing that they were designed to serve a compelling public interest" provided an insufficient justification for a classification of motion picture theaters on the basis of the
content of the materials they purvey to the public. Relying primarily on
Police Department of Chicago v. Mosley, the court held the ordinance
invalid under the Equal Protection Clause. Judge Celebrezze, in dissent,
expressed the opinion that the ordinance was a valid "time, place, and
manner regulation," rather than a regulation of speech on the basis of its
content.

Because of the importance of the decision, we granted certiorari.

As they did in the District Court, respondents contend (1) that the
ordinances are so vague that they violate the Due Process Clause of the
Fourteenth Amendment; (2) that they are invalid under the First
Amendment as prior restraints on protected communication; and (3) that
the classification of theaters on the basis of the content of their exhibitions
violates the Equal Protection Clause of the Fourteenth Amendment. We
consider their arguments in that order.

* * *

A remark attributed to Voltaire characterizes our zealous adherence to
the principle that the Government may not tell the citizen what he may
or may not say. Referring to a suggestion that the violent overthrow of
tyranny might be legitimate, he said: "I disapprove of what you say, but I
will defend to the death your right to say it." The essence of that comment has been repeated time after time in our decisions invalidating attempts by the Government to impose selective controls upon the dis-
semination of ideas.

Thus, the use of streets and parks for the free expression of views on
national affairs may not be conditioned upon the sovereign's agreement
with what a speaker may intend to say. Nor may speech be curtailed
because it invites dispute, creates dissatisfaction with conditions the way
they are, or even stirs people to anger. The sovereign's agreement or

disagreement with the content of what a speaker has to say may not affect the regulation of the time, place, or manner of presenting the speech. * * *

We have recently held that the First Amendment affords some protection to commercial speech. We have also made it clear, however, that the content of a particular advertisement may determine the extent of its protection. A public rapid transit system may accept some advertisements and reject others. A state statute may permit highway billboards to advertise businesses located in the neighborhood but not elsewhere, and regulatory commissions may prohibit businessmen from making statements which, though literally true, are potentially deceptive. The measure of constitutional protection to be afforded commercial speech will surely be governed largely by the content of the communication.

More directly in point are opinions dealing with the question whether the First Amendment prohibits the state and federal governments from wholly suppressing sexually oriented materials on the basis of their "obscene character." In Ginsberg v. New York, the Court upheld a conviction for selling to a minor magazines which were concededly not "obscene" if shown to adults. Indeed, the Members of the Court who would accord the greatest protection to such materials have repeatedly indicated that the State could prohibit the distribution or exhibition of such materials to juveniles and unconsenting adults. Surely the First Amendment does not foreclose such a prohibition; yet it is equally clear that any such prohibition must rest squarely on an appraisal of the content of material otherwise within a constitutionally protected area.

Such a line may be drawn on the basis of content without violating the Government's paramount obligation of neutrality in its regulation of protected communication. For the regulation of the places where sexually explicit films may be exhibited is unaffected by whatever social, political, or philosophical message the film may be intended to communicate; whether the motion picture ridicules or characterizes one point of view or another, the effect of the ordinances is exactly the same.

Moreover, even though we recognize that the First Amendment will not tolerate the total suppression of erotic materials that have some arguably artistic value, it is manifest that society's interest in protecting this type of expression is of a wholly different, and lesser, magnitude than the interest in untrammeled political debate that inspired Voltaire's immortal comment. Whether political oratory or philosophical discussion moves us to applaud or to despise what is said, every schoolchild can understand why our duty to defend the right to speak remains the same. But few of us would march our sons and daughters off to war to preserve the citizens's right to see "Specified Sexual Activities" exhibited in the theaters of our choice. Even though the First Amendment protects communication in this area from total suppression, we hold that the State may legitimately use the content of these materials as the basis for placing them in a different classification from other motion pictures.

The remaining question is whether the line drawn by these ordinances is justified by the city's interest in preserving the character of its neighborhoods. On this question we agree with the views expressed by

District Judges Kennedy and Gubow. The record discloses a factual basis for the Common Council's conclusion that this kind of restriction will have the desired effect. It is not our function to appraise the wisdom of its decision to require adult theaters to be separated rather than concentrated in the same areas. In either event, the city's interest in attempting to preserve the quality of urban life is one that must be accorded high respect. Moreover, the city must be allowed a reasonable opportunity to experiment with solutions to admittedly serious problems.

Since what is ultimately at stake is nothing more than a limitation on the place where adult films may be exhibited, even though the determination of whether a particular film fits that characterization turns on the nature of its content, we conclude that the city's interest in the present and future character of its neighborhoods adequately supports its classification of motion pictures. We hold that the zoning ordinances requiring that adult motion picture theaters not be located within 1,000 feet of twoother regulated uses does not violate the Equal Protection Clause of the Fourteenth Amendment.

The judgment of the Court of Appeals is reversed.

Mr. Justice Powell, concurring.

Although I agree with much of what is said in the plurality opinion, and concur in Parts I and II, my approach to the resolution of this case is sufficiently different to prompt me to write separately. I view the case as presenting an example of innovative land-use regulation, implicating First Amendment concerns only incidentally and to a limited extent.

One-half century ago this Court broadly sustained the power of local municipalities to utilize the then relatively novel concept of land-use regulation in order to meet effectively the increasing encroachments of urbanization upon the quality of life of their citizens. Euclid v. Ambler Realty Company, (1926). The Court there noted the very practical consideration underlying the necessity for such power: "With the great increase and concentration of population, problems have developed, and constantly are developing, which require, and will continue to require, additional restrictions in respect of the use and occupation of private lands in urban communities." The Court also laid out the general boundaries within which the zoning power may operate: restrictions upon the free use of private land must find their justifications in "some area of the police power, asserted for the public welfare"; the legitimacy of any particular restriction must be judged with reference to all of the surrounding circumstances and conditions; and the legislative judgment is to control in cases in which the validity of a particular zoning regulation is "fairly debatable."

In the intervening years zoning has become an accepted necessity in our increasingly urbanized society, and the types of zoning restrictions have taken on forms far more complex and innovative than the ordinance involved in Euclid. In Village of Belle Terre v. Boraas, we considered an unusual regulation enacted by a small Long Island community in an apparent effort to avoid some of the unpleasantness of urban living. It restricted land-use within the village to single-family dwellings and defined "family" in such way that no more than two unrelated persons could inhabit the same house. We upheld this ordinance, noting that desires to avoid congestion and noise from both people and vehicles were "legitimate guidelines in a land-use project addressed to family needs" and that it was quite within the village's power to "make the area a sanctuary for people."

Against this background of precedent, it is clear beyond question that the Detroit Common Council had broad regulatory power to deal with the problem that prompted enactment of the Anti-Skid Row Ordinance. As the Court notes, the Council was motivated by its perception that the "regulated uses," when concentrated, worked a "deleterious effect upon the adjacent areas" and could "contribute to the blighting and down grading of the surrounding neighborhood." The purpose of preventing the deterioration of commercial neighborhoods was certainly within the concept of the public welfare that defines the limits of the police power. See Berman v. Parker, * * *

In these circumstances, it is appropriate to analyze the permissibility of Detroit's action under the four-part test of United States v. O'Brien, 391 US 367, (1968). Under that test, a governmental regulation is sufficiently justified, despite its incidental impact upon First Amendment interests, "if it is within the constitutional power of the Government; if it furthers an important or substantial governmental interest; if the governmental interest is unrelated to the suppression of free expression; and if the incidental restriction on . . . First Amendment freedoms is no greater than is essential to the furtherance of that interest." Ibid. The factual distinctions between a prosecution for destruction of a selective service registration certificate, as in O'Brien, and this case are substantial, but the essential weighing and balancing of competing interests are the same. Cf. Procunier v. Martinez.

There is, as noted earlier, no question that the Ordinance was within the power of the Detroit Common Council to enact. See Berman v. Parker, supra. Nor is there doubt that the interests furthered by this Ordinance are both important and substantial. Without stable neighborhoods, both residential and commercial, large sections of a modern city quickly can deteriorate into an urban jungle with tragic consequences to social, environmental, and economic values. While I agree with respondents that no aspect of the police power enjoys immunity from searching constitutional scrutiny, it also is undeniable that zoning, when used to preserve the character of specific areas of a city, is perhaps "the most essential function performed by local government, for it is one of the primary means by which we protect that sometimes difficult to define concept of quality of life." Village of Belle Terre v. Boraas (Marshall, J. dissenting).

The third and fourth tests of O'Brien also are met on this record. It is clear both from the chronology and from the facts that Detroit has not embarked on an effort to suppress free expression. The Ordinance was already in existence, and its purposes clearly set out, for a full decade before adult establishments were brought under it. When this occurred, it is clear—indeed it is not seriously challenged—that the governmental interest prompting the inclusion in the ordinance of adult establishments was wholly unrelated to any suppression of free expression. Nor is there reason to question that the degree of incidental encroachment upon such expression was the minimum necessary to further the purpose of the ordinance. The evidence presented to the Common Council indicated that the urban deterioration was threatened not by the concentration of *all* movie theaters with other "regulated uses," but only by a concentration of those that elected to specialize in adult movies. The case would present a different situation had Detroit brought within the ordinance types of theaters that had not been shown to contribute to the deterioration of surrounding areas. * * *

(b) Theatre Districts

Zoning Resolution of the City of New York, 1961, Special Theatre District, Sections 81-00,81-02,81-06

Chapter I Special Theatre District

81-00 General Purposes

The special theatre district established in this resolution is designed to promote and protect public health, safety, general welfare and amenity. These general goals include, among others, the following specific purposes:

(a) To preserve, protect and promote the character of the special theatre district area as the location of the world's foremost concentration of legitimate theatres—an attraction which helps the City of New York achieve pre-eminent status as a cultural showcase, an office headquarters center and a cosmopolitan residential community;

(b) To develop and strengthen a much-needed circulation network in order to avoid congestion arising from the movements of large numbers of people; including convenient transportation to, from and within the district, and provision of arcades, open space and subsurface concourses;

(c) To help insure a secure basis for the useful cluster of shops, restaurants and related amusement activities which have been attracted to the area based upon its past and present character.

(d) To retain and improve the special employment opportunities generated in the area which complement and enhance related City-wide employment generating activities and which might otherwise become scattered and diffused outside the City to its detriment;

(e) To provide an incentive for possible redevelopment of the area in a manner consistent with the aforegoing objectives which are an integral element of the Comprehensive Plan of The City of New York;

(f) To provide freedom of architectural design accommodating legitimate theatres and supporting activities within multi-use structures which should produce more attractive and economic development;

(g) To promote the most desirable use of land in this area in accordance with a well-considered plan, to promote the special character of the district and its peculiar suitability for uses related to the legitimate theatre and thus to conserve the value of land and buildings, and thereby protect the City's tax revenues.

81-02General Provisions

In harmony with the general purpose and intent of this resolution and the general purposes of the Special Theatre District and in accordance with the provisions of this Chapter, the City Planning Commission, by special permit after public notice and hearing and subject to Board of Estimate action, may grant special permits authorizing modifications of specified applicable district bulk regulations for any development in the Special Theatre District which contains a legitimate theatre or theatres.

In addition to meeting the requirements, conditions and safeguards prescribed by the Commission as set forth in this Chapter, each such development shall conform to and comply with all of the applicable district regulations on use, bulk, supplementary use regulations, regulations applying along district boundaries, accessory signs, accessory off-street parking and off-street loading, and all other applicable provisions of this resolution, except as otherwise specifically provided in this Chapter.

81-06

The Commission, by special permit after public notice and hearing, subject to Board of Estimate action, may authorize within the Special Theatre District an increase in permitted floor area ratio for any new building containing a legitimate theatre or theatres. The increase shall be in the discretion of the Commission and may range from the basic floor area ratio of the district up to but in no event exceeding the maximum limit set forth in Sections 33-120.5 and 43-120.5 (Maximum limit on floor area ratio) plus 20% thereof. In determining the precise extent of the increase the Commission shall take into consideration the following:

(a) Whether the legitimate theatre or theatres are of a size and type which the Commission deems appropriate under the circumstances pertaining at the time of the application, in order to achieve a balance of facilities responsive to the need of the district;

(b) Whether there are facilities to support legitimate theatre operations such as rehearsal, studio or storage space;

(c) Whether open spaces, arcades, subsurface concourses or subway connections are provided to ease congestion in the area by aiding in the circulation of pedestrians or vehicles;

(d) Whether restaurant facilities or other amenities useful to the Special Theatre District are provided; and

(e) Whether distribution of the bulk of the total development permits adequate access of light and air to surrounding streets and properties.

For a discussion of Special Districts see: Fonoroff, "Special Districts: A Departure from the Concept of Uniform Control," **The New Zoning** (1970).

For other examples of special district zoning see: City of Detroit Zoning Ordinance, Sec. A-13 (1968); Philadelphia Zoning and Planning Code, Sec. R14-2005 (1959).

---

6. Cluster Zoning

Cluster zoning is a term that is used to describe zoning ordinance provisions that permit the reduction in minimum lot sizes under circumstances that assure that the amount of land reduced from the minimum size of each lot in the development will be aggregated and set aside within the development as open space for recreational, conservation, or other historic or scenic purposes. Cluster zoning provisions may be used to achieve a number of purposes: (1) to lower the per lot cost for streets and utilities; (2) to reduce the total length of streets, thereby lowering the municipality's costs of service and maintenance; (3) to encourage the separation of vehicular and pedestrian traffic; (4) to provide for recreational facilities near the housing units; (5) to preserve natural ecological features of the community.

As the following excerpt from the Princeton Township, New Jersey ordinance illustrates, the circumstances under which a developer will be permitted to cluster must be prescribed with some care.

PRINCETON TOWNSHIP CODE § 23-31

(c) *Definitions.* As used in this section, the following definitions shall apply:

(1) *Cluster residential development.* Any major subdivision in zoning districts R-1, R-2, R-3, or R-4 employing the reduction in lot area provisions of paragraph (b)(1) of this section and approved as a cluster subdivision by the planning board under the provisions of chapter 20 of this Code.

(2) *Common open space.* The land set aside within a cluster residential development for use and enjoyment by all the residents of the subdivision or by the public at large, and which shall be preserved as open space and for open uses only.

(3) *Open space uses.* Any use of common open space for park or open, unroofed recreational purposes, conservation of land or other natural resources, or historic or scenic purposes.

(4) *Average lot area.* The sum of the area of all house lots, together with the area of all lots to be devoted to common open space, divided by the total number of house lots. (Ord. No. 645, § 2.)

Article IV. Special Permits.

Sec. 23-32. Jurisdiction of board of adjustment.

The board of adjustment shall hear and decide requests for special permits, in cases where special permits are authorized by this chapter, upon written application, in accordance with the procedure set out in this article. (Ord. No. 277, § 5:1).

Sec. 23-33. Determination of time and place of public hearing.

The board of adjustment, at its next regular meeting following the receipt of such application, or at a regular meeting of the board if the application is received thereat, shall determine the date, time and place for a public hearing on such application and shall notify the applicant thereof. (Ord. No. 277, § 5:1).

(3) Can be developed to encourage separation of vehicular and pedestrian traffic;

(4) Can be developed to include recreational facilities in appropriate relationship to places of residence;

(5) Can serve the needs of conservation by permitting the preservation of the natural ecological features of the community.

(b) *Space and bulk regulations.* The following adjustments in the Schedule of Regulations shall be permitted in cluster residential developments:

(1) Lot areas may be reduced to not less than twenty-two thousand and five hundred square feet per residential lot; provided, that:

a. The land area which would otherwise be required for house lots, but which is not so used under the permitted lot size reduction provisions of this section, shall be devoted instead to common open space.

b. The common open space so provided shall be not less than four acres in area.

c. The average lot area shall be not less than the minimum lot area otherwise required by the schedule of regulations for the zone district in which the development is located.

(2) If lot areas are reduced in accordance with paragraph (1), above, then:

a. Lot widths and lot depths may be reduced in the R-1 and R-2 Zones to a minimum of one hundred and fifty feet. Minimum lot widths and lot depths may not be reduced in the R-3 or R-4 Zones.

b. Front yards may be reduced to a minimum of twenty feet in the R-1 Zone, and fifteen feet in the R-2, R-3 and R-4 Zones; provided, that the cluster development design includes a separate pedestrian circulation system within the common open space and outside the street right-of-way.

c. Yard ratio to building height may be reduced to 1:1.

d. Floor area ratios for residential lots may be reduced to the following, subject to the limitations indicated:

R-1, forty per cent, but not to exceed 8,712 square feet of gross floor area.

R-2, thirty-seven and one-half per cent, but not to exceed 8,167 square feet of gross floor area.

Chapter Three
Exclusionary Zoning and Managed Growth

INTRODUCTION

Zoning ordinances have been used to prevent members of racial minorities and low-income families from moving from the central cities to suburban areas. The effect of such **exclusionary zoning laws** is to concentrate the poor and racial minorities in the cities and to restrict the use of the suburbs to middle- and upper-class residents. As a result, cities are required to undertake the higher social-welfare costs of the poor and thereby bear a greater proportion of the costs that, in all fairness, should be more equitably distributed throughout the state. In addition to the dangers inherent in geographic polarization by race and class, the socioeconomic imbalance created by exclusionary zoning tends to deny to the excluded groups the opportunity for better housing, better schools, greater employment opportunities, and better municipal services. Such exclusion may be regarded as contrary to the ideals of democracy and has been held to be contrary to the principles of the United States Constitution.

Legal scholars and planners have written at length on the subject of exclusionary zoning, analyzing the exclusionary effect of **large-lot zoning, multi-family dwelling prohibitions, bedroom restrictions, minimum floor space requirements, low income housing exclusions, building moratoria, refusals to provide municipal services, mobile home prohibitions and environmental impact impediments.** The most comprehensive compilation of this material is the Urban Land Institute's three volume series, entitled *Urban Land Institute, Management and Control of Growth: Issues-Techniques-Problems-Trends.* See also *National Commission Against Discrimination in Land Use.* (1974).

The issue of exclusionary zoning is an important one for planners because it directs attention to a dilemma that arises when planning takes place at a municipal level. On one hand, the planning process seeks to provide plans and programs to achieve the goals and objectives of the community through orderly growth and development that is consistent with the community's fiscal, environmental, social and political resources and limitations. On the other hand, the planned-for growth and development of any given municipality (or all municipalities) may not provide for the needs of people who reside in the larger region of which the municipality is a part. When zoning ordinances are used to implement municipal plans for limited growth and development and the opportunities for in-migration of non-residents is precluded, the validity of such

179

"exclusionary zoning" ordinances is called into question.

Those who defend the right of municipalities to use the zoning power for these purposes argue that a municipality has the right to regulate and manage the community's rate of growth and to regulate the socio-economic characteristics of the community. Those who attack municipal exclusionary zoning argue that exclusionary zoning practices violate provisions of the federal and/or state constitutions.

This chapter will examine the cases dealing with the issues of the validity of **programs of managed growth,** the control of the socio-economic composition of the population, and the special problems of racial, as distinguished from economic, discrimination. Then an indepth analysis will be made of the response of the New Jersey Supreme Court of this problem in the *Mount Laurel* and subsequent decisions.

A. THE RATE OF GROWTH OF THE COMMUNITY: TIMED SEQUENTIAL DEVELOPMENT

(1) Rate of Growth

As a first step in an analysis to determine whether the zoning power allows for **regulation of a community's growth rate,** it is useful to consider the scope of the typical zoning statute. Section 1 of the Standard State Zoning Enabling Act, on which most state enabling legislation is based, describes the zoning power as the authority,

> to regulate and restrict the height, number of stories, and size of buildings and other structures, the percentage of lot that may be occupied, the size of yards, courts, and other open spaces, the density of population, and the location and use of buildings, structures, and land for trade, industry, residence, or other purposes.

The authority to regulate, however, is not unchecked; the regulation must relate to the purposes of zoning. Under section 3 of the Standard Act, the purposes for which the zoning power may be exercised are expressly enumerated as follows:

> to lessen congestion in the streets; to secure safety from fire, panic, and other dangers; to promote health and the general welfare; to provide adequate light and air; to prevent the overcrowding of land; to avoid undue concentration of population; to facilitate the adequate provision of transportation, water, sewerage, schools, parks, and other public requirements....

Notwithstanding this limitation, the essence of the zoning as described in the standard enabling legislation, is its mandate to exclude and to restrict. From the explicit grant of power to zone for the purposes of preventing the overcrowding of land and the undue concentration of population, comes the clear implication that under the typical zoning act a municipality may regulate population growth to achieve these legitimate zoning objectives.

Of course, this finding does not preclude challenges to such regulation. Even if a municipal zoning ordinance is consistent with enabling legislation, it must nevertheless comply with federal and state constitutional limitations. An otherwise valid zoning regulation cannot stand if it is unreasonable, arbitrary or capricious, if it infringes upon freedom of religion, if it denies equal protection under the law, or if it constitutes an unlawful taking of property.

In addition to these traditional constitutional restrictions, courts have cited the constitutionally protected **right to travel** as a limitation upon the use of zoning laws to control municipal population growth. The right to travel has been recognized for many years in other contexts. It was first acknowledged as a constitutional principle in 1941 in the case of *Edwards v. California*, 314 U.S. 160, 62 S. Ct. 164, 80 L. Ed. 119 (1941), in which the United States Supreme Court struck down a California statute that imposed criminal liability on anyone bringing an indigent nonresident into the States. The Court held that such a restriction imposed an unconstitutional burden upon interstate commerce. In 1969 the Supreme Court in *Shapiro v. Thompson*, 394 U.S. 618, 89 S. Ct. 1322, 22 L. Ed. 2d 600 (1969), cited this constitutionally protected freedom to travel as the reason for invalidating a statute that conditioned eligibility for welfare assistance upon a one year residency requirement. The Court held that even though the residency requirement might not have operated as an actual deterrent to travel, the statute was nevertheless invalid if its purpose was to penalize the exercise of the right to travel, unless it could be shown to be necessary to promote a compelling governmental interest. In the 1972 case of *Dunn v. Blumstein*, 405 U.S. 330, 92 S. Ct. 995, 31 L. Ed. 2d 274 (1972), the Supreme Court cited the right to travel as one of the reasons for invalidating a one year residency requirement for voting.

In 1974 the Supreme Court reaffirmed the right to travel principle when it struck down an Arizona statute requiring at least one year's residence in a county as a condition of an indigent's eligibility to receive nonemergency hospitalization or medical care at the county's expense. *Memorial Hospital v. Maricopa County*, 415 U.S. 250 (1974). The Court found that the residency requirement violated the equal protection clause and infringed upon the constitutionally protected right to travel by denying newcomers a basic necessity of life. Because the law penalized indigents in the exercise of the right to travel, it could be justified only if it met the compelling state interest test. In an attempt to meet this standard, the state advanced numerous justifications for the statute: (1) the need to conserve the county's limited fiscal resources; (2) the desire to deter indigents from taking up residence in the county solely to utilize medical facilities; (3) the protection of the rights of long-time residents who have contributed to the community by the payment of taxes; (4) the need to maintain public support for the county hospital by assuring taxpayers that the tax revenues will be used primarily for their benefit; (5) the administrative convenience in establishing a clearcut criterion for bona fide residence; (6) the need to predict the scope of services to be rendered by the hospital for budget purposes. The Court nevertheless held that none of these reasons, singly or in combination, showed a state interest sufficiently compelling to outweigh the restriction on the right to travel.

Basing its decision upon this line of cases, a federal district court in California, in *Construction Industry Association v. City of Petaluma*, 522 F.2d 897 (9th Cir. 1975) held that a municipal ordinance designed to safeguard the community's small town character by keeping out newcomers unconstitutionally restricted the right to travel. The ordinance was part of a plan, known as the "Petaluma Plan;" its preamble declared:

"In order to protect its small town character and surrounding open spaces, it shall be the policy of the City to control its future rate and distribution of growth. . ." (emphasis added)

The plan consisted of a number of ordinances and policies that sought to achieve the following:

(1) Limit new housing construction to 500 units per year;

(2) Draw an "urban extension line" to indicate the geographical outer limits of the city's growth for the next twenty years or more;

(3) Within the boundary of the urban extension line, prescribe zoning densities to limit the city's population to 55,000;

(4) Establish a policy by which the city would refuse to annex or to extend city facilities outside the urban extension line;

(5) Establish a complicated "Catch 22" application procedure for building permits that would tend to discourage builders from applying for permits; and

(6) Although intended to last only to 1977, extend the plan at least to 1990 by official actions; e.g., the city entered into a contract with a water company until 1990, to provide sufficient water for a population of only 55,000.

The court described each of the components of the Petaluma Plan in an extensive statement of its findings of fact. The court also found that if the Petaluma growth limits were adopted throughout the region it would result in (1) a regionwide increase in the cost of housing; (2) a decline in the quality of housing stock throughout the region; (3) a loss of mobility of residents of the region, which would tend to keep people in the cities; (4) a regional increase in the percentage of substandard housing and a limitation of the choice of housing to persons with incomes under $14,000 per year.

Based upon these findings of fact the court then set forth its conclusions of law. At the outset, the court made it clear that the decision is based upon determinations by the United States Supreme Court in a long line of cases, that freedom to travel is a **"fundamental right"** protected by the Constitution, and this right includes the right to enter and live in any state or municipality in the Union. Having previously found that the express purpose and actual effect of the Petaluma Plan was to exclude substantial numbers of people who would otherwise have elected to immigrate to the city, the court determined that this limitation of population growth could be defended only insofar as it furthered a **"compelling state interest."**

The City of Petaluma had argued that there were three such compelling interests that would support the exclusionary measure. First, the City asserted that its sewage treatment facilities were inadequate to serve an uncontrolled population growth. However, the court found that the city's facilities for expansion were sufficient to meet the needs of a growing population. The court then suggested that, even if the facilities were inadequate, they could be increased. The court proposed further, in dicta that will probably be cited frequently, that even though courts will not order citizens to vote for expenditure of funds, "Neither Petaluma city officials, nor the local electorate may use their power to disapprove bonds at the polls as a weapon to define or destroy fundamental constitutional rights."

Second, the City had argued that its water supply was inadequate for enlarged population growth. However, the court found that the city purposefully calculated its water needs based on the restricted population projections and contracted for its water supply to meet the limited population. Such an alleged inadequacy of water supply was self-created, easily overcome by contracting for an enlarged supply and therefore, not a compelling interest that would justify a population limitation. Third, the City alleged that the zoning power gave it the right to control its own rate of growth and to protect the character of the community. In response, the court held that a municipality capable of supporting a natural population expansion may not limit growth simply because it does not prefer to grow at the rate which would be dictated by prevailing market demand. It based this decision on the Supreme Court cases holding that the right to travel is a "fundamental right," and on the reasoning adopted by Pennsylvania courts which invalidated zoning ordinances that sought to exclude newcomers. The court cited with approval the following excerpts from those cases:

> The question posed is whether the township can stand in the way of the natural forces which send out growing population into hitherto undeveloped areas in search of a comfortable place to live. We have concluded not. A zoning ordinance whose primary purpose is to prevent the entrance of newcomers in order to avoid future burdens, economic or otherwise, upon the administration of public services and facilities cannot be held valid. . . . *National Land & Inv. Co. v. Kohn*, 215 A.2d 597 at 612 (1966).

> The implication of our decision in National Land is that communities must deal with the problems of population growth. They may not refuse to confront the future by adopting zoning regulations that effectively restrict population to near present levels. It is not for any given township to say who may or may not live within its confines, while disregarding the interests of the entire areas. If Concord Township is successful in unnaturally limiting its population growth through the use of exclusive zoning regulations, the people who would normally live there will inevitably have to live in another community, and the requirement that they do so is not a decision that Concord Township should alone be able to make. *Appeal of Kit-Mar Builders*, 268 A.2d 765 at 768-769 (1970).

Based upon this analysis, the district court held that Petaluma's population growth limitations were not supported by any compelling governmental interest and were unconstitutional because they violated the right to travel. The court also declared that its decision is intended to encompass not only the limitation on the issuance of building permits but also "all other features of the plan which, directly or indirectly, seek to control population growth by any means other than market demands." To enforce its decision the court (1) enjoined implementation of the Petaluma Plan; (2) retained jurisdiction to prevent the city from circumventing the spirit of the holding; and (3) appointed a special master to supervise the enforcement of the order.

On July 12, 1974, Justice Douglas stayed this order pending appeal. In 1975 the United States Court of Appeals (Ninth Circuit) reversed for the reasons expressed in the opinion set forth below.

CONSTRUCTION INDUSTRY ASSOCIATION
OF SONOMA COUNTY

v.

THE CITY OF PETALUMA

522 F.2d 897 (9th Cir. 1975)

CHOY, Circuit Judge:

The City of Petaluma (the City) appeals from a district court decision voiding as unconstitutional certain aspects of its five-year housing and zoning plan. We reverse.

Statement of Facts

The City is located in southern Sonoma County, about 40 miles north of San Francisco. In the 1950's and 1960's, Petaluma was a relatively self-sufficient town. It experienced a steady population growth from 10,315 in 1950 to 24,870 in 1970. Eventually, the City was drawn into the Bay Area metropolitan housing market as people working in San Francisco and San Rafael became willing to commute longer distances to secure relatively inexpensive housing available there. By November 1972, according to un-official figures, Petaluma's population was at 30,500, a dramatic increase of almost 25 per cent in little over two years.* * *

To correct the imbalance between single-family and multi-family dwellings, curb the sprawl of the City on the east, and retard the ac-celerating growth of the City, the Council in 1972 adopted several resolu-tions, which collectively are called the "Petaluma Plan" (the Plan).

The Plan, on its face limited to a five-year period (1972-1977), fixes a housing development growth rate not to exceed 500 dwelling units per year. Each dwelling unit represents approximately three people. The 500-unit figure is somewhat misleading, however, because it applies only to housing units (hereinafter referred to as "development-units") that are part of projects involving five units or more. Thus, the 500-unit figure does not reflect any housing and population growth due to construction of single-family homes or even four-unit apartment buildings not part of any larger project.

The Plan also positions a 200 foot wide "greenbelt" around the City, to serve as a boundary for urban expansion for at least five years, and with respect to the east and north sides of the City, for perhaps ten to fifteen years. One of the most innovative features of the Plan is the Residential Development Control System which provides procedures and criteria for the award of the annual 500 development-unit permits. At the heart of the allocation procedure is an intricate point system, whereby a builder accumulates points for conformity by his projects with the City's general plan and environmental design plans, for good architectural design, and for providing low and moderate income dwelling units and various recreational facilities. The Plan further directs that allocations of building permits are to be divided as evenly as feasible between the west and east sections of the City and between single-family dwellings and multiple residential units (including rental units), that the sections of the City closest to the center are to be developed first in order to cause "infilling" of vacant area, and that 8 to 12 per cent of the housing units approved be for low and moderate income persons.* * *

Purpose of the Plan

The purpose of the Plan is much disputed in this case. According to general statements in the Plan itself, the Plan was devised to ensure that "development in the next five years, will take place in a reasonable, orderly, attractive manner, rather than in a completely haphazard and unattractive manner." The controversial 500-unit limitation on residential development-units was adopted by the City "(i)n order to protect its small town character and surrounding open space." The other features of the Plan were designed to encourage an east-west balance in development, to provide for variety in densities and building types and wide ranges in prices and rents, to ensure infilling of close-in vacant areas, and to prevent the sprawl of the City to the east and north. The Construction Industry Association of Sonoma County (the Association) argues and the district court found, however, that the Plan was primarily enacted "to limit Petaluma's demographic and market growth rate in housing and in the immigration of new residents."

Market Demand and Effect of the Plan

In 1970 and 1971, housing permits were allotted at the rate of 1000 annually, and there was no indication that without some governmental control on growth consumer demand would subside or even remain at the 1000-unit per year level. Thus, if Petaluma had imposed a flat 500-unit limitation on *all* residential housing, the effect of the Plan would clearly be to retard to a substantial degree the natural growth rate of the City. Petaluma, however, did not apply the 500-unit limitation across the board, but instead exempted all projects of four units or less. Because appellees failed to introduce any evidence whatsoever as to the number of exempt units expected to be built during the five-year period, the effect of the 500 *development-unit* limitation on the natural growth in housing is uncertain. For purposes of this decision, however, we will assume that the 500 development-unit growth rate is in fact below the reasonably anticipated market demand for such units and that absent the Petaluma Plan, the City would grow at a faster rate.

According to undisputed expert testimony at trial, if the Plan (limiting housing starts to approximately 6 per cent of existing housing stock each year) were to be adopted by municipalities throughout the region, the impact on the housing market would be substantial. For the decade 1970 to 1980, the shortfall in needed housing in the region would be about 105,000 units (or 25 per cent of the units needed). Further, the aggregate effect of a proliferation of the Plan throughout the San Francisco region would be a decline in regional housing stock quality, a loss of the mobility of current and prospective residents and a deterioration in the quality and choice of housing available to income earners with real incomes of $14,000 per year or less. If, however, the Plan were considered by itself and with respect to Petaluma only, there is no evidence to suggest that there would be a deterioration in the quality and choice of housing available there to persons in the lower and middle income brackets. Actually, the Plan increases the availability of multi-family units (owner-occupied and rental units) and low-income units which were rarely constructed in the pre-Plan days.

Substantive Due Process

Appellees claim that the Plan is arbitrary and unreasonable and, thus, violative of the due process clause of the Fourteenth Amendment. According to appellees, the Plan is nothing more than an exclusionary zoning device, designed solely to insulate Petaluma from the urban complex in which it finds itself. The Association and the Landowners reject, as falling outside the scope of any legitimate governmental interest, the City's avowed purposes in implementing the Plan—the preservation of Petaluma's small town character and the avoidance of the social and environmental problems caused by an uncontrolled• growth rate.

In attacking the validity of the Plan, appellees rely heavily on the district court's finding that the express purpose and the actual effect of the Plan is to exclude substantial numbers of people who would otherwise elect to move to the City. The existence of an exclusionary purpose and effect reflects, however, only *one* side of the zoning regulation. Practically all zoning restrictions have as a purpose and effect the *exclusion* of some activity or type of structure or a certain density of inhabitants. And in reviewing the reasonableness of a zoning ordinance, our inquiry does not terminate with a finding that it is for an exclusionary purpose. We must determine further whether the *exclusion* bears any rational relationship to a *legitimate state interest.* If it does not, then the zoning regulation is invalid. If, on the other hand, a legitimate state interest is furthered by the zoning regulation, we must defer to the legislative act. Being neither a super legislature nor a zoning board of appeal, a federal court is without authority to weigh and reappraise the factors considered or ignored by the legislative body in passing the challenged zoning regulation. The reasonableness, not the wisdom, of the Petaluma Plan is at issue in this suit.

It is well settled that zoning regulations "must find their justification in some aspect of the police power, asserted for the public welfare." The concept of the public welfare, however, is not limited to the regulation of noxious activities or dangerous structures. As the Court stated in *Berman v. Parker,* (1954):

The concept of the public welfare is broad and inclusive. The values it represents are spiritual as well as physical, aesthetic as well as monetary. It is within the power of the legislature to determine that the community should be beautiful as well as healthy, spacious as well as clean, well-balanced as well as carefully patrolled.

In determining whether the City's interest in preserving its small town character and in avoiding uncontrolled and rapid growth falls within the broad concept of "public welfare," we are considerably assisted by two recent cases. *Belle Terre*, and *Ybarra v. City of Town of Los Altos Hills*, each of which upheld as not unreasonable a zoning regulation much more restrictive than the Petaluma Plan, are dispositive of the due process issue in this case.* * *

Following the *Belle Terre* decision, this court in *Los Altos Hills* had an opportunity to review a zoning ordinance providing that a housing lot shall contain not less than one acre and that no lot shall be occupied by more than one primary dwelling unit. The ordinance as a practical matter prevented poor people from living in Los Altos Hills and restricted the density, and thus the population, of the town. This court, nonetheless, found that the ordinance was rationally related to a legitimate governmental interest—*the preservation of the town's rural environment*—and, thus, did not violate the equal protection clause of the Fourteenth Amendment.

Both the Belle Terre ordinance and the Los Altos Hills regulation had the purpose and effect of permanently restricting growth; nonetheless, the court in each case upheld the particular law before it on the ground that the regulation served a legitimate governmental interest falling within the concept of the public welfare: the preservation of quiet family neighborhoods (Belle Terre) and the preservation of a rural environment (Los Altos Hills). Even less restrictive or exclusionary than the above zoning ordinances is the Petaluma Plan which, unlike those ordinances, does not freeze the population at present or near-present levels. Further, unlike the Los Altos Hills ordinance and the various zoning regulations struck down by state courts in recent years, the Petaluma Plan does not have the undesirable effect of welling out any particular income class nor any racial minority group.

Although we assume that some persons desirous of living in Petaluma will be excluded under the housing permit limitation and that, thus, the Plan may frustrate some legitimate regional housing needs, the Plan is not arbitrary or unreasonable. We agree with appellees that unlike the situation in the past most municipalities today are neither isolated nor wholly independent from neighboring municipalities and that, consequently, unilateral land use decisions by one local entity affect the needs and resources of an entire region.

It does not necessarily follow, however, that the *due process* rights of builders and landowners are violated merely because a local entity exercises in its own self-interest the police power lawfully delegated to it by the state. *See Belle Terre, supra; Los Altos Hills, supra.* If the present system of delegated zoning power does not effectively serve the state interest in furthering the general welfare of the region or entire state, it is the state legislature's and not the federal courts' role to intervene and adjust the system. As stated *supra,* the federal court is not a super zoning board and should not be called on to mark the point at which legitimate local interests in promoting the welfare of the community are outweighed by legitimate regional interests. *See* Note, *supra,* at 608-11.

We conclude therefore that under *Belle Terre* and *Los Altos Hills* the

188   ZONING AND GROWTH

concept of the public welfare is sufficiently broad to uphold Petaluma's desire to preserve its small town character, its open spaces and low density of population, and to grow at an orderly and deliberate pace.
Reversed.

(2) Timed Sequential Development

The process of urban planning is complex because the community, for which plans are to be proposed, is rarely in a state of balanced equilibrium. Most communities are usually in a dynamic changing state. The forces of social, economic, political, and physical change constantly interact upon each other along a continuum of time. Today's placid and fallow fields may become a center of tomorrow's teeming activity. Today's neighborhood of well-built apartment houses may become tomorrow's core of urban decay.

The problem of dynamic community change is particularly acute in suburban areas where all components of the community structure do not grow and develop with equal and uniform progress. Houses, streets, utilities, water supply, schools, and recreational facilities do not emerge abruptly as a monolithic **community infrastructure** in the required proportions of a balanced community. The urban planning process is designed to provide plans and programs for rational and interrelated community growth. Zoning laws are enacted to allocate land to meet the projected community needs on which the plans are based. Until recently, zoning laws have not been devised to coordinate the **sequence of development** to maintain some degree of community balance during the process of development over a period of time.

In *Golden v. Ramapo* set forth below, the New York Court of Appeals was called upon to determine the validity of a zoning ordinance that permitted residential development to proceed only in accordance with such a plan for **sequential development and timed growth.** The zoning ordinance of the Town of Ramapo, in Rockland County, New York was designed to achieve the following policy of zoning and planning:

1. To economize on the costs of municipal facilities and services to carefully phase residential development with efficient provision of public improvements;
2. To establish and maintain municipal control over the eventual character of development;
3. To establish and maintain a desirable degree of balance among the various uses of land;
4. To establish and maintain essential quality of community services and facilities. . . .

The zoning ordinance was based upon a comprehensive master plan for future growth and upon a **Capital Budget** providing for the location and sequence of **capital improvements** for a period of eighteen years. Residential development is permitted only after obtaining a special permit, the issuance of which is conditioned upon the availability of five categories of facilities and services:

1. public sanitary sewers or approved substitutes
2. drainage facilities
3. improved public parks or recreation facilities, including schools

4. state, county, or town roads

5. firehouses.

Special permits for development would be issued only when the services and facilities were available. A point system was created to assign values to each such facility and a permit would be issued only when fifteen development points were applicable to the proposed development. A prospective developer could advance the date of development by agreeing to provide those improvements which would bring the proposed plat within the number of development points required by the ordinance. Thus, residential development becomes a function of the availability of municipal improvements and may proceed in accordance with the overall program of orderly growth incorporated into the eighteen year Capital Plan.

As you read the decision in the *Ramapo* case notice how the court responds to the issues raised by the complex problem involved in the conflict between the constitutional protection of the right to use private property, on one hand, and the public interest in providing for a system of orderly growth and development, on the other hand.

GOLDEN et al

v.

PLANNING BOARD OF the **TOWN OF RAMAPO**, et al.

30 N.Y. 2d 359, 334 N.Y.S.2d 138

285 N.E.2d 291 (1971)

SCILEPPI, Judge.

Both cases arise out of the 1969 amendments to the Town of Ramapo's Zoning Ordinance* * *

Experiencing the pressures of an increase in population and the ancillary problem of providing municipal facilities and services, the Town of Ramapo, as early as 1964, made application for grant under section 801 of the Housing Act of 1964 to develop a master plan. The plan's preparation included a four-volume study of the existing land uses, public facilities, transportation, industry and commerce, housing needs and projected population trends. The proposals appearing in the studies were subsequently adopted pursuant to section 272-a of the Town Law, in July, 1966 and implemented by way of a master plan. The master plan was followed by the adoption of a comprehensive zoning ordinance. Additional sewage district and drainage studies were undertaken which culminated in the adoption of a capital budget, providing for the development of the improvements specified in the master plan within the next six years. Pursuant to section 271 of the Town Law, authorizing comprehensive planning, and as a supplement to the capital budget, the Town Board adopted a capital program which provides for the location and sequence of additional capital improvements for the 12 years following the life of the capital budget. The two plans, covering a period of 18 years, detail the capital improvements projected for maximum development and conform to the specifications set forth in the master plan, the official map and drainage plan.

Based upon these criteria, the Town subsequently adopted the subject amendments for the alleged purpose of eliminating premature subdivision and urban sprawl. Residential development is to proceed according to the provision of adequate municipal facilities and services, with the assurance that any concomitant restraint upon property use is to be of a "temporary" nature and that other private uses, including the construction of individual housing, are authorized.

The amendments did not rezone or reclassify any land into different residential or use districts, but, for the purposes of implementing the proposals appearing in the comprehensive plan, consist, in the main, of additions to the definitional sections of the ordinance, section 46-3, and the adoption of a new class of "Special Permit Uses", designated "Residential Development Use." "Residential Development Use" is defined as "The erection or construction of dwellings or any vacant plots, lots or parcels of land" (§ 46-3, as amd.); and, any person who acts so as to come within that definition, "shall be deemed to be engaged in residential development which shall be a separate use classification under this ordinance and subject to the requirement of obtaining a special permit from the Town Board" (§ 46-3, as amd.).

The standards for the issuance of special permits are framed in terms of the availability to the proposed subdivision plat of five essential facilities or services: specifically (1) public sanitary sewers or approved substitutes; (2) drainage facilities; (3) improved public parks or recreation facilities, including public schools; (4) State, county or town roads—major, secondary or collector; and, (5) firehouses. No special permit shall issue unless the proposed residential development has accumulated 15 development points, to be computed on a sliding scale of values assigned to the specified improvements under the statute. Subdivision is thus a function of immediate availability to the proposed plat of certain municipal improvements; the avowed purpose of the amendments being to phase residential development to the Town's ability to provide the above facilities or services.

Certain savings and remedial provisions are designed to relieve of potentially unreasonable restrictions. Thus, the board may issue special permits vesting a present right to proceed with residential development in such year as the development meets the required point minimum, but in no event later than the final year of the 18-year capital plan. The approved special use permit is fully assignable, and improvements scheduled for completion within one year from the date of an application are to be credited as though existing on the date of the application. A prospective developer may advance the date of subdivision approval by agreeing to provide those improvements which will bring the proposed plat within the number of development points required by the amendments. And applications are authorized to the "Development Easement Acquisition Commission" for a reduction of the assessed valuation. Finally, upon application to the Town Board, the development point requirements may be varied should the board determine that such a variance or modification is consistent with the on-going development plan.

The undisputed effect of these integrated efforts in land use planning and development is to provide an over-all program of orderly growth and adequate facilities through a sequential development policy commensurate with progressing availability and capacity of public facilities. While its goals are clear and its purposes undisputed laudatory, serious questions are raised as to the manner in which these ends are to be effected, not the least of which relates to their legal viability under present zoning enabling legislation, particularly sections 261 and 263 of the Town Law. The owners of the subject premises argue, and the Appellate Division has sustained the proposition, that the primary purpose of the amending ordinance is to control or regulate population growth within the Town and as such is not within the authorized objectives of the zoning enabling legislation. We disagree.

In enacting the challenged amendments, the Town Board has sought to control subdivision in all residential districts, pending the provision (public or private) at some future date of various services and facilities. A reading of the relevant statutory provisions reveals that there is no specific authorization for the "sequential" and "timing" controls adopted here. That, of course, cannot be said to end the matter, for the additional inquiry remains as to whether the challenged amendments find their basis within the perimeters of the devices authorized and purposes sanctioned under current enabling legislation. Our concern is, as it should be, with the effects of the statutory scheme taken as a whole and its role in the propagation of a viable policy of land use and planning.

Towns, cities and villages lack the power to enact and enforce zoning or other land use regulations. The exercise of that power, to the extent that it is lawful, must be founded upon a legislative delegation to so proceed, and in the absence of such a grant will be held *ultra vires* and void. That delegation, set forth in section 261 of the Town Law, is not, however, coterminous with stated police power objectives and has been considered less inclusive traditionally. Hence, although the power to zone must be exercised under the aegis of the police power, indeed must inevitably find justification for its exercise in some aspect of the same, the recital of police power purposes in the grant, attests more to the drafters' attempts to specify a valid constitutional predicate than to detail authorized zoning purposes. The latter, "legitimate zoning purposes," are incorporated in accompanying section 263 and are designed to secure safety from various calamities, to avoid undue concentration of population and to facilitate "adequate provision of transportation, water, sewerage, schools, parks and other public requirements" (Town Law, § 263). In the end, zoning properly effects, and only in the manner prescribed, those purposes detailed under section 263 of the Town Law. It may not be invoked to further the general police powers of a municipality.

Even so, considering the activities enumerated by section 261 of the Town Law, and relating those powers to the authorized purposes detailed in section 263, the challenged amendments are proper zoning techniques, exercised for legitimate zoning purposes. The power to restrict and regulate conferred under section 261 includes within its grant, by way of necessary implication, the authority to direct the growth of population for the purposes indicated, within the confines of the township. It is the matrix of land use restrictions, common to each of the enumerated powers and sanctioned goals, a necessary concomitant to the municipalities' recognized authority to determine the lines along which local development shall proceed, though it may divert it from its natural course.

Undoubtedly, current zoning enabling legislation is burdened by the largely antiquated notion which deigns that the regulation of land use and development is uniquely a function of local government—that the public interest of the State is exhausted once its political subdivisions have been delegated the authority to zone. While such jurisdictional allocations may well have been consistent with formerly prevailing conditions and assumptions, questions of broader public interest have commonly been ignored.

Experience, over the last quarter century, however, with greater technological integration and drastic shifts in population distribution has pointed up serious defects and community autonomy in land use controls has come under increasing attack by legal commentators, and students of urban problems alike, because of its pronounced insularism and its correlative role in producing distortions in metropolitan growth patterns, and perhaps more importantly, in crippling efforts toward regional and State-wide problem solving, be it pollution, decent housing, or public transportation.

Recognition of communal and regional interdependence, in turn, has resulted in proposals for schemes of regional and State-wide planning, in the hope that decisions would then correspond roughly to their level of impact. Yet, as salutary as such proposals may be, the power to zone under current law is vested in local municipalities, and we are constrained to resolve the issues accordingly. What does become more apparent in treating with the problem, however, is that though the issues are framed in terms of the developer's due process rights, those rights cannot, realistically speaking, be viewed separately and apart from the rights of others "'in search of a (more) comfortable place to live.'"

There is, then, something inherently suspect in a scheme which, apart from its professed purposes, effects a restriction upon the free mobility of a people until sometime in the future when projected facilities are available to meet increased demands. Although zoning must include schemes designed to allow municipalities to more effectively contend with the increased demands of evolving and growing communities, under its guise, townships have been wont to try their hand at an array of exclusionary devices in the hope of avoiding the very burden which growth must inevitably bring. Though the conflict engendered by such tactics is certainly real, and its implications vast, accumulated evidence, scientific and social, points circumspectly at the hazards of undirected growth and the naive, somewhat nostalgic imperative that egalitarianism is a function of growth.

Of course, these problems cannot be solved by Ramapo or any single municipality, but depend upon the accommodation of widely disparate interests for their ultimate resolution. To that end, State-wide or regional control of planning would insure that interests broader than that of the municipality underlie various land use policies. Nevertheless, that should not be the only context in which growth devices such as these, aimed at population assimilation, not exclusion, will be sustained; especially where, as here, we would have no alternative but to strike the provision down in the wistful hope that the efforts of the State Office of Planning Coordination and the American Law Institute will soon bear fruit.

Hence, unless we are to ignore the plain meaning of the statutory delegation, this much is clear: phased growth is well within the ambit of existing enabling legislation. And, of course, it is no answer to point to emergent problems to buttress the conclusion that such innovative schemes are beyond the perimeters of statutory authorization. These considerations, admittedly real, to the extent which they are relevant, bear solely upon the continued viability of "localism" in land use regulation; obviously, they can neither add nor detract from the initial grant of authority, obsolescent though it may be. The answer which Ramapo has posed can by no means be termed definitive; it is, however, a first practical step toward controlled growth achieved without forsaking broader social purposes.

The evolution of more sophisticated efforts to contend with the increasing complexities of urban and suburban growth has been met by a corresponding reluctance upon the part of the judiciary to substitute its judgment as to the plan's over-all effectiveness for the considered deliberations of its progenitors.

Implicit in such a philosophy of judicial self-restraint is the growing awareness that matters of land use and development are peculiarly within the expertise of students of city and suburban planning, and thus well within the legislative prerogative, not lightly to be impeded. To this same end, we have afforded such regulations, the usual presumption of validity attending the exercise of the police power, and have cast the burden of proving their invalidity upon the party challenging their enactment.

Deference in the matter of the regulations' over-all effectiveness, however, is not to be viewed as an abdication of judicial responsibility, and ours remains the function of defining the metes and bounds beyond which local regulations may not venture, regardless of their professedly beneficent purposes.

The subject ordinance is said to advance legitimate zoning purposes as it assures that each new home built in the township will have at least a minimum of public services in the categories regulated by the ordinance. The Town argues that various public facilities are presently being constructed but that for want of time and money it has been unable to provide such services and facilities at a pace commensurate with increased public need. It is urged that although the zoning power includes reasonable restrictions upon the private use of property, exacted in the hope of development according to well-laid plans, calculated to advance the public welfare of the community in the future. The subject regulations go further and seek to avoid the increased responsibilities and economic burdens which time and growth must ultimately bring.

It is the nature of all land use and development regulations to circumscribe the course of growth within a particular town or district and to that extent such restrictions invariably impede the forces of natural growth. Where those restrictions upon the beneficial use and enjoyment of land are necessary to promote the ultimate good of the community and are within the bounds of reason, they have been sustained. "Zoning however is a means by which a governmental body can plan for the future—it may not be used as a means to deny the future." Its exercise assumes that development shall not stop at the community's threshold, but only that whatever growth there may be shall proceed along a predetermined course. It is inextricably bound to the dynamics of community life and its function is to guide, not to isolate or facilitate efforts at avoiding the ordinary incidents of growth. What segregates permissible from impermissible restrictions, depends in the final analysis upon the purpose of the restrictions and their impact in terms of both the community and general public interest. The line of delineation between the two is not a constant, but will be found to vary with prevailing circumstances and conditions.

What we will not countenance, then, under any guise, is community efforts at immunization or exclusion. But, far from being exclusionary, the present amendments merely seek, by the implementation of sequential development and timed growth, to provide a balanced cohesive community dedicated to the efficient utilization of land. The restrictions conform to the community's considered land use policies as expressed in its comprehensive plan and represent a bona fide effort to maximize population density consistent with orderly growth. True other alternatives, such as requiring off-site improvements as a prerequisite to subdivision, may be available, but the choice as how best to proceed, in view of the difficulties attending such exactions cannot be faulted.

Perhaps even more importantly, timed growth, unlike the minimum lot requirements recently struck down by the Pennsylvania Supreme Court as exclusionary, does not impose permanent restrictions upon land use. Its obvious purpose is to prevent premature subdivision absent essential municipal facilities and to insure continuous development commensurate with the Town's obligation to provide such facilities. They seek, not to freeze population at present levels but to maximize growth by the efficient use of land, and in so doing testify to this community's continuing role in population assimilation. In sum, Ramapo asks not that it be left alone, but only that it be allowed to prevent the kind of deterioration that has transformed well-ordered and thriving residential communities into blighted ghettos with attendant hazards to health, security and social stability—a danger not without substantial basis in fact.

We only require that communities confront the challenge of population growth with open doors. Where in grappling with that problem, the community undertakes, by imposing temporary restrictions upon development, to provide required municipal services in a rational manner, courts are rightfully reluctant to strike down such schemes. The timing controls challenged here parallel recent proposals put forth by various study groups and have their genesis in certain of the pronouncements of this and the courts of sister States. While these controls are typically proposed as an adjunct of regional planning, the preeminent protection against their abuse resides in the mandatory on-going planning and development requirement, present here, which attends their implementation and use.

We may assume, therefore, that the present amendments are the product of foresighted planning calculated to promote the welfare of the township. The Town has imposed temporary restrictions upon land use in residential areas while committing itself to a program of development. It has utilized its comprehensive plan to implement its timing controls and has coupled with these restrictions provisions for low and moderate income housing on a large scale. Considered as a whole, it represents both in its inception and implementation a reasonable attempt to provide for the sequential, orderly development of land in conjunction with the needs of the community, as well as individual parcels of land, while simultaneously obviating the blighted after math which the initial failure to provide needed facilities so often brings.

The proposed amendments have the effect of restricting development for onwards to 18 years in certain areas. Whether the subject parcels will be so restricted for the full term is not clear, for it is equally probable that the proposed facilities will be brought into these areas well before that time. Assuming, however, that the restrictions will remain outstanding for the life of the program, they still fall short of a confiscation within the meaning of the Constitution.

An ordinance which seeks to permanently restrict the use of property so that it may not be used for any reasonable purpose must be recognized as a taking: The only difference between the restriction and an outright taking in such a case "is that the restriction leaves the owner subject to the burden of payment of taxation, while outright confiscation would relieve him of that burden." An appreciably different situation obtains where the restriction constitutes a *temporary* restriction, promising that the property may be put to a profitable use within a reasonable time. The hardship of holding unproductive property for some time might be compensated for by the ultimate benefit inuring to the individual owner in the form of a substantial increase in valuation; or, for that matter, the landowner, might be compelled to chafe under the temporary restriction, without the benefit of such compensation, when that burden serves to promote the public good.

We are reminded, however, that these restrictions threaten to burden individual parcels for as long as a full generation and that such a restriction cannot, in any context, be viewed as a temporary expedient. The Town, on the other hand, contends that the landowner is not deprived of either the best use of his land or of numerous other appropriate uses, still permitted within various residential districts, including the construction of

a single-family residence, and consequently, it cannot be deemed confiscatory. Although no proof has been submitted on reduction of value, the
landowners point to obvious disparity between the value of the property,
if limited in use by the subject amendments and its value for residential
development purposes, and argue that the diminution is so considerable
that for all intents and purposes the land cannot presently or in the near
future be put to profitable or beneficial use, without violation of the restrictions.

Every restriction on the use of property entails hardships for some individual owners. Those difficulties are invariably the product of police
regulation and the pecuniary profits of the individual must in the long run
be subordinated to the needs of the community. The fact that the ordinance limits the use of, and may depreciate the value of the property will
not render it unconstitutional, however, unless it can be shown that the
measure is either unreasonable in terms of necessity or the diminution in
value is such as to be tantamount to a confiscation. Diminution, in turn, is
a relative factor and though its magnitude is an indicia of a taking, it does
not of itself establish a confiscation.

Without a doubt restrictions upon the property in the present case are
substantial in nature and duration. They are not, however, absolute. The
amendments contemplate a definite term, as the development points are
designed to operate for a maximum period of 18 years and during that
period, the Town is committed to the construction and installation of capital improvements. The net result of the on-going development provision
is that individual parcels may be committed to a residential development
use prior to the expiration of the maximum period. Similarly, property
owners under the terms of the amendments may elect to accelerate the
date of development by installing, at their own expense, the necessary
public services to bring the parcel within the required number of development points. While even the best of plans may not always be
realized, in the absence of proof to the contrary, we must assume the
Town will put its best effort forward in implementing the physical and
fiscal timetable outlined under the plan. Should subsequent events prove
this assumtpion unwarranted, or should the Town because of some unforeseen event fail in its primary obligation to these landowners, there
will be ample opportunity to undo the restrictions upon default. For the
present, at least, we are constrained to proceed upon the assumption that
the program will be fully and timely implemented.

Thus, unlike the situation presented in Arverne Bay Constr. Co. v.
Thatcher, the present amendments propose restrictions of a certain duration and founded upon estimate determined by fact. Prognostication on
our part in upholding the ordinance proceeds upon the presently permissible inference that within a reasonable time the subject property will be
put to the desired use at an appreciated value. In the interim assessed
valuations for real estate tax purposes reflect the impact of the proposed
restrictions. The proposed restraints, mitigated by the prospect of appreciated value and interim reductions in assessed value, and measured in
terms of the nature and magnitude of the project undertaken, are within
the limits of necessity.

In sum, where it is clear that the existing physical and financial resources of the community are inadequate to furnish the essential services and facilities which a substantial increase in population requires, there is a rational basis for "phased growth" and hence, the challenged ordinance is not violative of the Federal and State Constitutions. Accordingly, the order appealed from should be reversed and the actions remitted to Special Term for entry of a judgment declaring section 46—13.1 of the Town Ordinance constitutional.

For additional discussion of the *Ramapo* decision see, Note, "Time Controls on Land Use: Prophylactic Law for Planners," 57 *Cornell L. Rev.* 827 (1972); Finkler, "Nongrowth as a Planning Alternative: A Preliminary Examination of an Emerging Issue," Report No. 283 (American Society of Planning Officials, September, 1972) p.15; Comment, "Golden v. Town of Ramapo: Establishing a New Dimension in American Planning Law," 4 *The Urban Lawyer* ix (Summer, 1972).

(3) Obligations of a Public Utility

ROBINSON

v.

The CITY OF BOULDER

547 P.2d 228, (Colo. 1976)

DAY, Justice.

This is an appeal brought by appellant, City of Boulder (Boulder), seeking reversal of a trial court order mandating its extension of water and sewer service to appellees. We affirm.

Appellees (landowners) sought to subdivide approximately 79 acres of land in the Gunbarrel Hill area northeast of Boulder and outside of its city limits. The landowners proposed a residential development in conformity with its county rural residential (RR) zoning.

As a condition precedent to considering the question of development, the county required the landowners to secure water and sewer services; they were referred to the city for that purpose.

Boulder operates a water and sewer utility system. In the mid 1960's it defined an area beyond its corporate limits, including the subject property, for which it intended to be the only water and sewer servicing agency. The record reflects that this was accomplished in order to gain indirect control over the development of property located within the service area. Boulder contracted with and provided water and sewer service to the Boulder Valley Water and Sanitation District (the district), which is located within the service area. The subject property is immediately adjacent to the district. The contract between Boulder and the district vests in the former almost total control over water and sewer service within district boundaries. The latter functions in merely a nominal administrative capacity. For example, Boulder retains control over all engineering and construction aspects of the service as well as decision-making power over the district's authority to expand its boundaries. Pursuant to a city ordinance, the district cannot increase its service area without the approval of city council.

The landowners applied to the district for inclusion, and the application was accepted; however, Boulder disapproved the action on the grounds that the landowners' proposal was inconsistent with the Boulder Valley Comprehensive Plan and various aspects of the city's interim growth policy. The trial court found that:

> ". . . The City seeks to effect its growth rate regulation goals in the Gunbarrel Hill area by using its water and sewer utility as the means to accomplish its goals. . . ."

The decision was *not* based on Boulder's incapacity to supply the service or the property's remote location from existing facilities or any economic considerations.

The landowners then filed suit for declaratory relief, and the district court concluded that Boulder is operating in the capacity of a public utility in the Gunbarrel area. In terms of supplying water and sewer services, it must treat all members of the public within its franchise area alike—including these landowners. The court held that Boulder had unjustly discriminated against appellees by denying them service, while having previously approved service extensions to neighboring residential and industrial developments. The court concluded that Boulder can only refuse to extend its service to landowners for utility-related reasons. Growth control and land use planning considerations do not suffice. We agree.

I.

On appeal Boulder argues that its service program in Gunbarrel is not a public utility under the test which we enunciated in *City of Englewood v. Denver*, (1951):

> ". . . to fall into the class of public utility, a business or enterprise must be impressed with a public interest and that those engaged in the conduct thereof must hold themselves out as serving or ready to serve all members of the public, who may require it, to the extent of their capacity. The nature of the service must be such that all members of the public have an enforceable right to demand it. . ."

Boulder contends that it has never held itself out as being ready to serve all members of the public to the extent of its capacity. The trial court made findings to the contrary and the record amply supports them.* * *

Boulder relies on *City of Englewood, supra,* to support its position that it is not operating as a public utility within the area in question; that reliance is misplaced. The determination that Denver did not operate as a public utility in supplying Englewood with water was premised on an entirely different factual background. Denver's supplying of water to Englewood users was wholly incidental to the operation of its water system which was established for the purpose of supplying Denver inhabitants. Denver did not "stake out" a territory in Englewood and seek to become the sole supplier of water in the territory. Here, by agreements with other suppliers to the effect that the latter would not service the Gunbarrel area and by opposing other methods or sources of supply, Boulder has secured a monopoly over area water and sewer utilities. Further, as the trial court pointed out:

". . . The City of Boulder had dedicated its water and sewer service to public use to benefit both the inhabitants of Boulder and the residents of the Gunbarrel Hill area in the interest of controlling the growth of the area and to provide living qualities which the City deems desirable. . . ."

II.

Boulder argues that even if its program satisfies the tests of a public utility in the Gunbarrel area that it may use public policy considerations in administering its service program. It contends that the rules which apply to private utilities should not apply to a governmental utility authorized to implement governmental objectives, one of which is the adoption of a master plan of development.

Section 31-23-106(1), C.R.S.1973, in relevant part, states:

"*Master plan.* (1) It is the duty of the municipal planning commission to make and adopt a master plan for the physical development of the municipality, including any areas outside of its boundaries, *subject to the approval of the legislative or governing body having jurisdiction thereof*, which in the commission's judgment, bear relation to the planning of such municipality. Such plan, with the accompanying maps, plats, charts, and descriptive matter, shall show the commission's recommendations for the development of said territory including, among other things:

"(b) The general location and extent of *public utilities* and terminals, whether publicly or privately owned or operated, *for water*, light, *sanitation*, transportation, communication, power, and other purposes;

"(c) The removal, relocation, widening, narrowing, vacating, abandonment, change of use, or extension of any of the ways, grounds, open spaces, buildings, property, *utility*, or terminals referred to in paragraphs (a) and (b) of this subsection (1); . . ." (Emphasis added.)

To this end, the city of Boulder and Boulder County jointly developed and adopted the Boulder Valley Comprehensive Plan, one of the purposes of which is to provide a basis for the discretionary land use decisions which it must make. Boulder also cites section 31-23-109, C.R.S.1973, which states in relevant part:

"*Legal status of official plan.* When the municiple planning commission has adopted the master plan of the municipality or one or more major sections or districts thereof, no street, square, park or other public way, ground or open space, or public building or structure, or *publicly* or privately *owned public utility* shall be constructed or authorized in the municipality or in such planned section and district until the location, character, and extent thereof has been submitted for approval by the commission. In case of disapproval, the commission shall communicate its reason to the council, which has the power to overrule such disapproval by a recorded vote of not less than two-thirds of its entire membership. If the public way, ground space, building, structure, or utility is one the authorization or financing of which does not, under the law or charter provisions governing the same, fall within the province of the municipal council, then the submission to the planning commission shall be by the board, commission, or body having jurisdiction, and the planning commission's disapproval may be overruled by said board, commission, or body by a vote of not less than two-thirds of its membership. The failure of the commission to act within sixty days from and after

> the date of official submission to it shall be deemed approval." (Emphasis added.)

Boulder argues that its decision to deny the extension of services to the landowners in this case was based on the proposed development's noncompliance with growth projections outlined in the comprehensive plan. In the event of an alleged conflict between Boulder's public utility and land use planning duties we are asked to rule that the latter are paramount.

A municipality is without jurisdiction over territory outside its municipal limits in the absence of legislation. *See Pueblo v. Flanders*, 122 Colo. 571, 225 P.2d 832 (1950). We find nothing in the above-cited statutes which indicates a legislative intent to broaden a city's authority in a case such as the one before us. In our view, sections 31-23-106(1) and 31-23-109 place ultimate governmental authority in matters pertaining to land use in unincorporated areas in the county. In effect a city is given only an advisory role.

The record reflects that the proposed development would comply with county zoning regulations; and the county planning staff has indicated that it conforms with their interpretation of the comprehensive plan, though final consideration was put off pending a determination of whether the area would have adequate water and sewer facilities.

In view of the fact that it is the board of county commissioners—not Boulder—which must make the ultimate decision as to the approval or disapproval of the proposed development, we do not need to address the question of whether the Boulder Valley Comprehensive Plan relieves the City of Boulder of its duty to the public in its propriety role as a public utility.

In conclusion, we hold that inasmuch as Boulder is the sole and exclusive provider of water and sewer services in the area surrounding the subject property, it is a public utility. As such, it holds itself out as ready and able to serve those in the territory who require the service. There is no utility related reason, such as insufficient water, preventing it from extending these services to the landowners. Unless such reasons exist, Boulder cannot refuse to serve the people in the subject area.

Judgment affirmed.

B. THE SOCIAL AND ECONOMIC COMPOSITION OF THE COMMUNITY

In addition to the issue of the **rate and quantity** of population growth, there is the legal question whether it is within the zoning power to prescribe or regulate **socio-economic characteristics** such as the age, marital status, family size, or income, of the population. An analysis of the judicial decisions indicates that this question is still unresolved with respect to both **indirect** and **direct** forms of such regulation.

Many forms of zoning regulation have an **indirect effect** upon the social and economic characteristics of the community. **Minimum size lots, minimum floor space** requirements, **prohibition of or restrictions on apartments** and **exclusion of mobile home parks** are zoning devices that are frequently used to regulate, albeit *indirectly,* the social and economic composition of the community. Increases in minimum lot size and floor space requirements raise the costs of construction and thereby exclude residents with insufficient income. Restrictions on the construction of multiple dwellings and on the number of bedrooms therein tend to exclude single persons and larger families with lower income. Exclusion of mobile home parks has the same effect. Since a large proportion of low income families in urban areas are members of racial and ethnic minorities, these zoning restrictions fall most heavily upon minority groups and effectively exclude them from many suburban communities.

Initially such restrictions were approved by the courts as legitimate subjects for zoning regulation. In New Jersey, for example, a **minimum lot size** requirement of five acres was sustained on the grounds that it was an appropriate method of preserving the character of the community; *Fisher v. Township of Bedminister,* 11 N.J. 194, 205, 93 A.2d 378, 384 (1952), a **minimum floor space** requirement was upheld as a reasonable exercise of the zoning power; *Lionshead Lake, Inc. v. Township of Wayne,* 10 N.J. 165, 174-75, 89 A.2d 693, 697-98 (1952), appeal dismissed, 344 U.S. 919 (1953), and a **prohibition of mobile home** use within the jurisdiction was upheld on the basis of aesthetic considerations. *Vickers v. Township Comm. of Gloucester,* 37 N.J. 232, 248, 181 A.2d 129, 137 (1962), cert. denied, 371 U.S. 233 (1963). The Supreme Court itself has approved as a legitimate device of participation democracy a state constitutional provision requiring prior **referendum approval** for construction of subsidized housing. *James v. Valtierra,* 402 U.S. 137, 91 S. Ct. 1331, 28 L. Ea. 2a 678 (1971).

More recently, the courts in a number of states, particularly Pennsylvania, New Jersey and Michigan, have begun to reexamine the question of whether zoning regulations may be sustained without regard to the indirect consequences on the social and economic composition of the regulated community. The Pennsylvania Supreme Court struck down zoning ordinances prescribing minimum lot requirements of four acres; *National Land & Inv. Co. v. Easttown Township Board of Adjustment,* 419 Pa. 504, 533, 215 A.2d 597, 613 (1965), and three acres; *In re Kit-Mar Builders, Inc.,* 439 Pa. 466, 478, 268 A.2d 765, 770 (1970), as an arbitrary and unreasonable use of the zoning power in violation of the fifth and fourteenth amendments because their primary purpose was to "keep out people, rather than (to) make community improvements."; Id. at 474, 268 A.2d at 768 (reaffirming the decision in *National Land).* The same court has also invalidated a zoning ordinance that failed to provide multi-family dwelling use, except by a variance application. *In re Girsh,* 437 Pa. 237, 240, 263 A.2d 395, 396 (1970).

In the *Mount Laurel* decision (discussed at length in the Section C of this chapter) the New Jersey Supreme Court invalidated a zoning exclusion of mobile home parks when the effect of such prohibition would be to exclude a socioeconomic component of the population.

While the decisions of these courts may indicate a trend toward the invalidation of indirect regulation of social and economic composition of the population through zoning laws, the issue is still unresolved in most states. The issue is further complicated by the holding in some states that the only proper concern for zoning laws is the **physical use** of land and the structures thereon and that **socioeconomic objectives** are *not* within the zoning power.

The most explicit judicial prohibition of the use of the zoning power for the direct regulation of socioeconomic matters appears in *Board of Supervisors of Fairfax County v. DeGroff Enterprises, Inc.,* 214 Va. 235, 198 S.E.2d 600 (1973). In that case the Virginia Supreme Court struck down a **"mandatory percentage of moderately priced dwellings"** ordinance. The ordinance required a developer of fifty or more dwelling units to commit himself, before site plan approval to build at least fifteen percent of the units as low and moderate income housing. One of the grounds on which the Virginia court held the ordinance invalid was that it exceeded the authority granted by the statute to the local governing body because it was directed to socioeconomic objectives rather than to physical characteristics, as authorized by the state enabling statute. On the other hand, in *Village of Belle Terre v. Boraas,* set forth below, the United States Supreme Court upheld the validity of a municipal zoning ordinance specifically designed to exclude a component of society, i.e. groups of persons unrelated by blood or marriage, sometimes called "groupies." Compare the *Belle Terre* reasoning, written by Mr. Justice Douglas, with the reasoning of Justice Hall (author of the *Mount Laurel* decision) in the *Kirsch* case where a similar ordinance was held invalid. Then compare both of these decisions to the *Weymouth* case, written by Justice Pashman, where a zoning district for the exclusive use of the elderly (thereby excluding young marrieds and others) was upheld; then read the *Berger* case where a zoning ordinance was held invalid to the extent that it prohibited the use of a single family house for a group home for multi-handicapped, pre-school children.

After reading all of the above cases try to articulate a statement that describes the circumstances under which a court will uphold or invalidate a zoning ordinance that regulates the socioeconomic characteristics of the residents of the district.

(1) Exclusion of Unrelated Persons (Groupies)

VILLAGE OF BELLE TERRE

v.

BORAAS

416 U.S. 1, 94 S. Ct. 1536, 39 L. Ed. 2d 797 (1974)

MR. JUSTICE DOUGLAS delivered the opinion of the Court.

Belle Terre is a village on Long Island's north shore of about 220 homes inhabited by 700 people. Its total land area is less than one square mile. It has restricted land use to one-family dwellings excluding lodging houses, boarding houses, fraternity houses, or multiple dwelling houses. The word "Family" as used in the ordinance means. "One or more persons related by blood, adoption, or marriage, living and cooking together as a single housekeeping unit, exclusive of household servants. A number of persons but not exceeding two (2) living and cooking together as a single housekeeping unit though not related by blood, adoption, or marriage shall be deemed to constitute a family."

Appellees (Dickmans) are owners of a house in the village and leased it in December, 1971 for a term of 18 months to Michael Truman. Later Bruce Boraas became a colessee. Then Anne Parish moved into the house along with three others. These six are students at nearby State University at Stony Brook and none is related to the other by blood, adoption, or marriage. When the village served the Dickmans with an "Order to Remedy Violations" of the ordinance,[1] the owners plus three tenants[2] thereupon brought this action under 42 U.S.C. § 1983 for an injunction declaring the ordinance unconstitutional. The District Court held the ordinance unconstitutional and the Court of Appeals affirmed, one judge dissenting. The case is here by appeal, and we noted probable jurisdiction.

This case brings to this Court a different phase of local zoning regulations than we have previously reviewed. *Euclid v. Ambler Realty Co.,* involved a zoning ordinance classifying land use in a given area into six categories. Appellee's tracts fell under three classifications: U-2 that included two-family dwellings; U-3 that included apartments, hotels, churches, schools, private clubs, hospitals, city hall and the like; and U-6 that included sewage disposal plants, incinerators, scrap storage, cemeteries, oil and gas storage and so on. Heights of buildings were prescribed for each zone; also the size of land areas required for each kind of use was specified. The land in litigation was vacant and being held for industrial development; and evidence was introduced showing that under the restricted use ordinance the land would be greatly reduced in value. The claim was that the land owner was being deprived of liberty and property without due process within the meaning of the Fourteenth Amendment.

The Court sustained the zoning ordinance under the police power of the State, saying that the line "which in this field separates the legitimate from the illegitimate assumption of power is not capable of precise delimitation. It varies with circumstances and conditions." 272 U.S. at 387. And the Court added "A nuisance may be merely a right thing in the wrong place,—like a pig in the parlor instead of the barnyard. If the validity of the legislative classification for zoning purposes be fairly debatable, the legislative judgment must be allowed to control." *Id.*, at 388. The Court listed as considerations bearing on the constitutionality of zoning ordinances the danger of fire or collapse of buildings, the evils of overcrowding people, and the possibility that "offensive trades, industries, and structures" might "create nuisance" to residential sections. *Ibid.* But even those historic police power problems need not loom large or actually be existent in a given case. For the exclusion of "all industrial establishments" does not mean that "only offensive or dangerous industries will be excluded." *Ibid.* That fact does not invalidate the ordinance; the Court held:

> "The inclusion of a reasonable margin to insure effective enforcement, will not put upon a law, otherwise valid, the stamp of invalidity. Such laws may also find their justification in the fact that, in some fields, the bad fades into the good by such insensible degrees that the two are not capable of being readily distinguished and separated in terms of legislation." *Id.*, 388-389.

The main thrust of the case in the mind of the Court was in the exclusion of industries and apartments and as respects that it commented on the desire to keep residential areas free of "disturbing noises"; "increased traffic"; the hazard of "moving and parked automobiles"; the "depriving children of the privilege of quiet and open spaces for play, enjoyed by those in more favored localities." *Id.*, at 394. The ordinance was sanctioned because the validity of the legislative classification was "fairly debatable" and therefore could not be said to be wholly arbitrary. *Id.*, at 388.

Our decision in *Berman* v. *Parker*, 348 U.S. 26, sustained a land use project in the District of Columbia against a land owner's claim that the taking violated the Due Process Clause and the Just Compensation Clause of the Fifth Amendment. The essence of the argument against the law was, while taking property for ridding an area of slums was permissible, taking it "merely to develop a better balanced, more attractive community" was not, 348 U.S., at 31. We refused to limit the concept of public welfare that may be enhanced by zoning regulations.[3] We said:

> "Miserable and disruptable housing conditions may do more than spread disease and crime and immorality. They may also suffocate the spirit by reducing the people who live there to the status of cattle. They may indeed make living an almost unsufferable burden. They may also be an ugly sore, a blight on the community which robs it of charm, which makes it a place from which men turn. The misery of housing may despoil a community as an open sewer may ruin a river.

"We do not sit to determine whether a particular housing project is or is not desirable. The concept of the public welfare is broad and inclusive. . . . The values it represents are spiritual as well as physical, aesthetic as well as monetary. It is within the power of the legislature to determine that the community should be beautiful as well as healthy, spacious as well as clean, well-balanced as well as carefully patrolled." *Id.*, 32-33.

If the ordinance segregated one area only for one race, it would immediately be suspect under the reasoning of *Buchanan* v. *Warley*, 245 U.S. 60, where the Court invalidated a city ordinance barring a Black from acquiring real property in a white residential area by reason of an 1866 Act of Congress. 14 Stat. 27, 42 U.S.C. § 1982 and an 1870 Act, 16 Stat. 144, both enforcing the Fourteenth Amendment. *Id.*, 78-82. See *Jones* v. *Mayer Co.*, 392 U.S. 409.

In *Seattle Trust Co.* v. *Roberge*, 278 U.S. 116, Seattle had a zoning ordinance that permitted a "philanthropic home for children or for old people" in a particular district "when the written consent shall have been obtained of the owners of two thirds of the property within four hundred feet of the proposed building." *Id.*, at 118. The Court held that provision of the ordinance unconstitutional saying that the existing owners could "withhold consent for selfish reasons or arbitrarily, and may subject the trustee (owner) to their will or caprice." *Id.*, at 122. Unlike the billboard cases (*Cusack Co.* v. *City of Chicago*, 242 U.S. 526), the Court concluded that the Seattle ordinance was invalid since the proposed home for the aged poor was not shown by its maintenance and construction "to work any injury, inconvenience, or annoyance to the community, the district or any person." *Id.*, at 122.

The present ordinance is challenged on several grounds: that it interferes with a person's right to travel; that it interferes with the right to migrate to and settle within a State; that it bars people who are uncongenial to the present residents; that the ordinance expresses the social preferences of the residents for groups that will be congenial to them; that social homogenity is not a legitimate interest of government; that the restriction of those whom the neighbors do not like trenches on the newcomers' rights of privacy; that it is of no rightful concern to villagers whether the residents are married or unmarried; that the ordinance is antithetical to the Nation's experience, ideology and self-perception as an open, egalitarian, and integrated society.[4]

We find none of these reasons in the record before us. It is not aimed at transients. Cf. *Shapiro* v. *Thompson*, 394 U.S. 618. It involves no procedural disparity inflicted on some but not on others such as was presented by *Griffin* v. *Illinois*, 351 U.S. 12. It involves no "fundamental" right guaranteed by the Constitution, such as voting, *Harper* v. *Virginia Board*, 383 U.S. 663; the right of association, *NAACP* v. *Alabama*, 357 U.S. 449; the right of access to the courts, *NAACP* v. *Button*, 371 U.S. 415; or any rights of privacy, cf. *Griswold* v. *Connecticut*, 381 U.S. 479; *Eisenstadt* v. *Baird*, 405 U.S. 438, 453-454. We deal with economic and social legislation where legislatures have historically drawn lines which we respect against the charge of violation of the Equal Protection Clause if the law be "reasonable, not arbitrary" (quoting *Royster Guano Co.* v. *Virginia*, 253 U.S. 412, 415) and bears "a rational relationship to a (permissible) state objective." *Reed* v. *Reed*, 404 U.S. 71, 76.

It is said, however, that if two unmarried people can constitute a "family," there is no reason why three or four may not. But every line drawn by a legislature leaves some out that might well have been included.[5] That exercise of discretion, however, is a legislative not a judicial function.

It is said that the Belle Terre ordinance reeks with an animosity to unmarried couples who live together.[6] There is no evidence to support it; and the provision of the ordinance bringing within the definition of a "family" two unmarried people belies the charge.

The ordinance places no ban on other forms of association, for a "family" may, so far as the ordinance is concerned, entertain whomever they like.

The regimes of boarding houses, fraternity houses, and the like present urban problems. More people occupy a given space; more cars rather continuously pass by; more cars are parked; noise travels with crowds.

A quiet place where yards are wide, people few, and motor vehicles restricted are legitimate guidelines in a land use project addressed to family needs. This goal is a permissible one within *Berman* v. *Parker*, *supra*. The police power is not confined to elimination of filth, stench, and unhealthy places. It is ample to lay out zones where family values, youth values, and the blessings of quiet seclusion, and clean air make the area a sanctuary for people.

The suggestion that the case may be moot need not detain us. A zoning ordinance usually has an impact on the value of the property which it regulates. But in spite of the fact that the precise impact of the ordinance sustained in *Euclid* on a given piece of property was not known, 272 U.S., at 397, the Court, considering the matter a controversy in the realm of city planning, sustained the ordinance. Here we are a step closer to the impact of the ordinance on the value of the lessor's property. He has not only lost six tenants and acquired only two in their place; it is obvious that the scale of rental values rides on what we decide today. When *Berman* reached us it was not certain whether an entire tract would be taken or only the buildings on it and a scenic easement. 348 U.S., at 36. But that did not make the case any the less a controversy in the constitutional sense. When Mr. Justice Holmes said for the Court in *Block* v. *Hirsh*, 256 U.S. 135, 155, "property rights may be cutdown, and to that extent taken, without pay," he stated the issue here. As is true in most zoning cases, the precise impact on value may, at the threshold of litigation over validity, not yet be known.

Reversed.

KIRSCH HOLDING CO.

v.

BOROUGH OF MANASQUAN

59 N.J. 241, 281 A.2d 513 (1971)

HALL, J.

These cases, consolidated for argument on appeal, concern the validity of essentially identical zoning ordinance provisions of the Boroughs of Manasquan and Belmar prohibiting, *inter alia*, the "group rental" of seasonal seashore resort living accommodations.* * *

The background facts are matters of general knowledge in the section of the state bordering on the Atlantic Ocean and are not in dispute.[1] For generations the communities along the coast have during the hot summer months experienced a large influx of people from the cities and other inland areas seeking the benefits and pleasures of seashore sun, air and water, as well as the resort amusements and entertainment available. In most of the towns, this seasonal influx finds vacation living accommodations largely by ownership or rental of summer cottages designed for that purpose or even of more substantial homes constructed for all-year living, along with less frequent use of hotels, motels or rooming houses. Manasquan and Belmar are typical resort towns in this respect. Both also have, as do most of the seashore resort communities, a substantial all-year population, which has been increasing in recent years by reason of retired people taking up permanent residence and of the availability of the Garden State Parkway and other highways as a means of rapid automobile transportation to quite distant places of employment. In most communities these all-year homes are intermixed with dwelling units occupied only during the summer season. The structures are frequently close together on small lots.

Until fairly recent years summer dwelling occupancy has been largely by conventional family units, who generally rented the accommodations for a month or the entire season. With the increased mobility of the population and the ease of travel to other parts of the country, such lengthy family stays have very frequently decreased to a week or two, with the result that property owners desiring to rent their cottages or houses seasonally must find a succession of weekly or biweekly tenants.

The other side of the coin, which concerns us, is the proliferation of "group rentals" during the same period. This social phenomenon entails the rental of seashore cottages, houses or apartments for the season to a group of young unrelated adults, which ordinarily comprises a substantial number of individuals although the lease may be in the name of only one. Generally the renters are unmarried and of one sex, and some or all of them use the property full-time during work or school vacations or on weekends. These groups are not formally organized as clubs, fraternities, sororities and the like and have no internal or external head, supervision or control. Human biology being what it is, such a group attracts friends of the other sex, who may live on the premises from time to time as well as merely visit the occupants. One result is an almost continuous overcrowding of the sleeping, cooking and sanitary facilities available. From the owner's point of view, this type of rental is a financial bonanza. He will have only one letting for the entire season, and by reason of group participation in the rental, he can secure a much higher return than a conventional family is willing or able to pay.

The evil which the ordinance provisions in question seek to prevent relates to the uninhibited social conduct of many such group rental occupants within and without the buildings. Unquestionably, and regretably, excessive noise at all hours, wild parties, intoxication, acts of immorality, lewd and lascivious conduct and traffic and parking congestion often accompany these group rentals, making life not only unpleasant but practically unbearable to neighboring vacationers and permanent residents and having a general adverse effect on the whole municipality. In essence they constitute a public and private nuisance by not meeting the minimal standards of expected social conduct even in this rather permissive day and age. While conventional families, with a number of children and visiting friends and relatives, can be noisy and disturbing to some neighbors, the existence of parental or family supervision and control generally prevents their conduct from exceeding the bounds of the reasonable behavior tolerance necessarily resulting from the less formal character of vacation resort living.

The property owners here involved quite candidly admit the existence of the evil, but apparently are unwilling to assist in eradicating it by voluntarily refusing to rent to such groups, undoubtedly because of the greater economic advantage to them. They urge the problem can and should be met by police enforcement of existing general police power ordinances and criminal statutes relating to noise, disorderly and immoral conduct, vehicle and traffic control and the like rather than by zoning against these group uses.

This brings us to a consideration of the ordinance provisions challenged, which represent, through amendment, refinements of previous enactments. The design of the provision is to nip group rentals or use in the bud by prohibiting the practice and making the landlord (or the owner if he is a group user or gratuitously permits group use), the rental agent and the users subject to prosecution or injunction for violation of the prohibition. As we understand these zoning ordinances (complete copies have not been furnished us), the provisions apply in all zones of the municipalities where "one-family," two-family" or "multi-family" dwellings are permitted uses. The result is accomplished by the definition of "family" and by an express prohibitory section against group dwelling use.

Thus the Belmar ordinance defines "family," alternatively, as follows:
19-2.33 Family.

    a. One or more persons related by blood or marriage occupying a dwelling unit and living as a single, nonprofit housekeeping unit.

    b. A collective number of individuals living together in one house under one head, whose relationship is of a permanent and distinct domestic character, and cooking as a single housekeeping unit. This definition shall not include any society, club, fraternity, sorority, association, lodge, combine, federation, group, coterie, or organization, which is not a recognized religious order, nor include a group of individuals whose association is temporary and resort-seasonal in character or nature.

The prohibitory section of the Belmar ordinance reads:

19-3.4 Group Rentals. No house, dwelling, building, structure or enclosure, or any part of a house, dwelling, building, structure or enclosure, within any of the zones enumerated in section 19-3.1 preceding, shall be used, or be permitted to be used, or be rented for use, as living quarters or sleeping quarters or for living purposes or sleeping purposes, by or to any society, club, fraternity, sorority, association, lodge, combine, federation, group, coterie, or organization, or to any person or member on behalf of the same, or to any group or collection of persons who are unmarried or who do not qualify as a family as defined in subsection 19-2.33 of the within chapter. This subsection shall not apply to rooming houses, hotels, motels or other places of public accommodation in the Borough of Belmar, which places are duly licensed as such by the said borough, or to recognized religious orders, convents, rectories, or parish houses or manses utilized in conjunction with any church or synagogue or similar house of worship.

Appreciation of the full import and effect of the ordinance provisions requires that the definition and prohibitory sections be read and analyzed together. This task is not without its difficulties by reason of the obvious effort to be certain to bar obnoxious group rentals. It is plain that, in the effort to be certain to ban summer rentals by unruly groups of unrelated young adults, innocuous occupancies by other groups have been prohibited as well. A few instances will illustrate the point, without attempting to be complete.

By subsection a. of the definition section, any number of persons, so long as they are all related by blood or marriage and live as a single unit, constitute a "family" for zoning ordinance purposes, whether their dwelling occupancy be permanent or seasonal. This is obviously intended to cover one conventional "family," living together, whether it be composed of a spouse or spouses and children or of persons otherwise related. If the individuals are not so related, their joint occupancy of a dwelling is prohibited by alternative subsection b. unless it is of a permanent as distinct from a temporary and seasonal character. Thus two unrelated families of spouses and children cannot share an adequate cottage or house for the summer, nor could a small unrelated group of widows, widowers, older spinsters or bachelors—or even of judges. Likewise barred from seasonal use would be a perfectly respectable group or organization of older persons, unless (under the Belmar ordinance) they were all members of a recognized religious order. Such a non-religiously connected group would seem as innocuous as one with religious connections. Moreover, it appears that a violation would occur under subsection a. if the related family unit had house guests.

The extent of the prohibition becomes at least ambiguous and probably inconsistent when the prohibitory section is also brought into the picture. That section makes no distinction between permanent and season or temporary occupancy. It prohibits use, as well as rental, for living purposes to all the classes of organizations spelled out in definition subsection b., and any other groups or collections of persons who do not qualify as a family under the definition section. But in addition it goes on to extend the prohibition to use by any such group "who are unmarried." It is not clear whether the intended meaning is that each member of the group must be married to another person in the group, *i.e.*, requiring that the group be composed only of married couples all occupying the dwelling unit at the same time. It certainly would seem to modify or be inconsistent with the permission extended by subsection b. of the definition section to occupancy by a permanent group of unrelated individuals in requiring that the members thereof be married.

A panoramic view of these ordinance provisions indicates an effort to be certain to bar one offensive· dwelling use, which at the same time results in a prohibition of many which are non-obnoxious. Perhaps the prime difficulty is that of attemtping to define an unorganized group, to which a precise label cannot be affixed, without at the same time affecting other dwelling situations which present no sufficient evil. In reality the aim is to prevent anti-social conduct of a certain somewhat nebulous class of individuals by resort to prohibitions under the zoning power through a fragmentation of dwelling uses. The problem is one which has not previously reached this Court.

At the outset, it may well be questioned whether the zoning power, as delegated by the Legislature, legitimately extends so far. Justice Schaefer, speaking for a unanimous Illinois Supreme Court, felt that it did not in his thoughful opinion in City of Des Plaines v. Trottner, (1966). There the ordinance defined "family" as "one or more persons each related to the other by blood (or adoption or marriage), together with such relatives' respective spouses, who are living together in a single dwelling and maintaining a common household." Included within the definition as well were domestic servants and not more than one gratuitous guest residing with the "family." Convents, monasteries, rectories and parish houses were also expressly permitted in single-family residence districts. Four unrelated young men rented defendant's one-family house in a single-family residence district for common living quarters. The owner was charged with violation of the ordinance. Justice Schaefer, in reversing a prohibitory injunction, commented that the definition could hardly be regarded as an effective control upon the size of family units in prevention of the evils of intensity of use and concluded:

> The General Assembly has not specifically authorized the adoption of zoning ordinances that penetrate so deeply as this one does into the internal composition of a single housekeeping unit. Until it has done so, we are of the opinion that we should not read the general authority that it has delegated to extend so far. Such a reading would generate considerable questions of the kind [unreasonable classifica-

tion] suggested by the defendants, concerning which we express no opinion.

In the course of the opinion comment was made on the Essex County Court opinion in City of Newark v. Johnson, (1961). There the zoning ordinance similarly limited a "family" and single-family dwelling owners were convicted of ordinance violations because they had living within the homes unrelated children who were wards of the State Board of Child Welfare boarded with them by that agency. Justice Schaefer found the considerations advanced by the court to sustain the provision as not particularly persuasive. While we have similar doubts, we need express no definitive opinion because the factual situation there involved is now expressly covered by legislation. N.J.S.A. 40:55-33.2 (L.1962, c. 177) invalidates any zoning ordinance provision which discriminates between children who are members of a family by blood, marriage or adoption and foster children placed with such families by child care agencies. This enactment may be thought of as some indication of the legislative view that the zoning enabling act was not intended to confer power upon municipalities to limit a "family" to those biologically or legally related.

We prefer, however, to deal with the cases before us on the basis of unreasonableness and arbitrariness of these zoning provisions. It is elementary that substantive due process demands that zoning regulations, like all police power legislation, must be reasonably exercised—the regulation must not be unreasonable, arbitrary or capricious, the means selected must have a real and substantial relation to the object sought to be attained, and the regulation or proscription must be reasonably calculated to meet the evil and not exceed the public need or substantially affect uses which do not partake of the offensive character of those which cause the problem sought to be ameliorated. We think it clear that these "family" definitions and prohibitory ordinance provisions preclude so many harmless dwelling uses, as we have earlier pointed out by examples, in the effort to ban seasonal uses and rentals by unruly unrelated groups of young adults who indulge in anti-social behavior, that they must be held to be so sweepingly excessive, and therefore legally unreasonable, that they must fall in their entirety. To use the phrase expressed by the Law Division in Larson v. Mayor and Council of Borough of Spring Lake Heights, (1968), in striking down similar provisions in a general police power ordinance (see footnote (1)), "* * * municipalities should not 'burn the house to roast the pig.'"

We fully concur in the reasoning and conclusions of Judge Conford in Gabe Collins Realty, Inc. v. City of Margate City, (1970), which was held to be dispositive by the same court in *Schier*. While the zoning ordinance provision in *Gabe Collins*, aimed at the same evil, was more restrictive in some aspects and less in others than those in the cases at bar, his concluding comments are, in our opinion, equally applicable here:

> Upon a consideration of all of the foregoing, it is our judgment that a general municipal restriction of occupancy of dwelling units to groups of persons all of whom are related to each other by blood, marriage or adoption is unreasonably restrictive of the ordinary and

natural utility of such property as dwellings for people, and of the
right of unrelated people in reasonable number to have recourse to
common housekeeping facilities in circumstances free of detriment to
the general health, safety and welfare. * * Thus, even in the light of
the legitimate concern of the municipality with the undesirable concomitants of group rentals experienced in Margate City, and of the
presumption of validity of municipal ordinances, we are satisfied that
the remedy here adopted constitutes a sweepingly excessive restriction of property rights as against the problem sought to be dealt
with, and in legal contemplation deprives plaintiffs of their property
without due process.

Gabe Collins is the only reported appellate decision we know of which
deals with attempts to meet the type of seasonal group rental situation
involved here. As we indicated earlier, the evil arises because of the offensive personal behavior of many of these unrelated groups; group uses
by other unrelated segments of the summer resort population present no
problem. The practical difficulty of applying land use regulation to prevent the evil is found in the seeming inability to define the offending
groups precisely enough so as not to include innocuous groups within the
prohibition. Where that is possible in situations closest to those here involved, as, for example, college fraternities and sororities, such uses have
generally been successfully barred from residential districts in college
towns, on the basis that the frequently boisterous and overexuberant conduct of their members clashes with the general peace and good order
usual and expected in such zones. City of Long Beach v. California
Lambda Chapter of Sigma Alpha Epsilon Fraternity, (1967); City of
Schenectady v. Alumni Ass'n of Union Chapter, Delta Chi Fraternity, 5
(App. Div. 1957). Compare City of Baltimore v. Poe, (1961) (in which the
court said the proper remedy was not through zoning but by police action
or injunctive relief.) See Annot., "Application of Zoning Regulations to
College Fraternities or Sororities," 25 A.L.R.3d 921 (1969).

At oral argument counsel for the municipalities asked for some guidance
on how the problem might validly be handled if we found the zoning
ordinance provisions improper. We are entirely sympathetic to the community desire to prevent one segment of the summer population from so
adversely affecting other vacationers and permanent residents, as well as
the municipality as a whole, by their conduct. Ordinarily obnoxious personal behavior can best be dealt with officially by vigorous and persistent
enforcement of general police power ordinances and criminal statutes of
the kind earlier referred to. Zoning ordinances are not intended and cannot be expected to cure or prevent most anti-social conduct in dwelling
situations. When intensity of use, i.e., overcrowding of dwelling units and
facilities, is a factor in that conduct (as it well may be here on the theory
that, pragmatically speaking, fewer people make less noise and disturbance), consideration might quite properly be given to zoning or housing
code provisions, which would have to be of general application, limiting
the number of occupants in reasonable relation to available sleeping and
bathroom facilities or requiring a minimum amount of habitable floor area
per occupant. The latter type of regulation was upheld in Nolden v. East

Cleveland City Comn'n, (C.P. Cuyahoga County 1966), on the basis that fire safety, health, crime prevention and maintenance of property, neighborhood and community—all matters of public welfare—are thereby served. See also Haar, Zoning for Minimum Standards: The Wayne Township Case, 66 Harv. L. Rev. 1051, 1061 (1953); Haar, Wayne Township: Zoning for Whom?—In Brief Reply, 67 Harv. L. Rev. 986, 989 (1954).

The judgment of the Law Division in A-135 is reversed and the cause is remanded to that court for the entry of a judgment consistent with this opinion. The judgment of the Appellate Division in A-140 is affirmed. No costs in either case.

Can the decisions in the *Belle Terre* case and the *Kirsch* case be reconciled? What legal argument did the court in *Belle Terre* address itself to when it upheld the validity of the ordinance? On what legal argument did Justice Hall base his decision that the ordinance was invalid?

Would it be possible to draft an anti-grouper ordinance that would be valid in New Jersey in light of the *Kirsch* decision?

(2) Exclusion of Non-elderly

TAXPAYERS ASSOCIATION
OF WEYMOUTH TOWNSHIP, INC., et al.,

v.

WEYMOUTH TOWNSHIP

71 N.J. 249, 364 A.2d 1016 (1976)

PASHMAN, J.

This appeal raises the question whether a zoning ordinance may create a district in which one of the permitted uses is a mobile home park for the exclusive use of the elderly. The Appellate Division disagreed with the determination of the Law Division that such zoning is valid. Because this pattern of zoning developed in a rather roundabout way, it is helpful to state the following chronology and the content of the relevant municipal legislation:

Prior to the adoption in 1971 of Ordinances Nos. 172-1971 ("No. 172") and 171-1971 ("No. 171"), whose validity we deal with here, the general zoning ordinance of Weymouth Township, Ordinance No. 144, adopted in 1966, established six zoning districts, one of which was designated "T-Trailer and Mobile Districts." In that district, property was permitted to be used for any use allowed in an R-A Rural Residence District and also for "trailer camps." The ordinance contained specific regulations concerning such camps and the specifications of lots on which mobile homes or trailers could be placed * * *

No. 172 is an unusual ordinance. Although its title indicates that it is merely a regulatory ordinance concerning the parking, location and licensing of "mobile home parks," it actually functions as a zoning ordinance as well. Specifically, it prohibits "trailer parks . . . generally" within the township. However, it then provides that, upon recommendation of the planning board and approval by the township committee, mobile home parks may be established on tracts exceeding 140 acres. Moreover, each home site must be at least 5,000 square feet in area (section VI(b)), and no more than 20% of all mobile homes in any park may contain more than two bedrooms. Section XXII. Most important, the ordinance restricts occupancy of all mobile home parks to "elderly persons" or "elderly families." Section XXIII. Elderly persons are defined as persons 52 years of age or over, and elderly families as those "the head of which, or his spouse is 52 years of age or over." Section II. Occupancy of a mobile home or trailer outside an approved mobile home park is prohibited. Section XVII. Only three licenses for a mobile home park are permitted to be outstanding at any one time. Section XXI.

No. 172 also contains a "Declaration of Policy and Purpose," reciting the need for decent, safe and moderately priced housing for the elderly, the suitability of mobile home parks to satisfy this need and the necessity for regulation of such parks by the detailed regulatory and licensing provisions contained in the ordinance * * *

The net effect of these ordinances is that defendant property owner's land now constitutes a zoning district which is restricted to use for mobile home parks (whose occupancy is limited exclusively to elderly persons or elderly families), or to any use permissible in an R-A Rural Residential District. Moreover, mobile homes or trailers are not permitted as residences anywhere in the municipality except as homes for the elderly or elderly families.

In July 1971, defendant property owner filed applications for a Mobile Home Park license and for a site plan review with the township committee and the township planning board as required by section V of No. 172. These applications were accompanied by the appropriate tender of fees. Because of the pendency of the instant litigation, no official action has been taken on these applications.

In October 1971, the Taxpayers' Associations of Weymouth Township and several of its members who are individual property owners in Weymouth Township filed a joint complaint in lieu of prerogative writ challenging Ordinances Nos. 171 and 172 on a variety of grounds. Essentially, plaintiffs alleged that the ordinances were enacted improperly, have an unconstitutional effect on the rights of children, resulted from an unlawful conspiracy among the defendants and constituted illegal "spot zoning." After trial, the court ruled for defendants on all counts and dismissed the complaint with prejudice.

The Appellate Division reversed in a reported opinion and held that the age limitation of No. 172 was beyond the powers delegated to municipalities by the zoning enabling act, N.J.S.A. 40:55-30 *et seq.* The court also found the ordinance to be an unreasonable exercise of the police power and violative of the equal protection clause of the fourteenth amendment to the federal constitution. We granted the municipality's petition for certification and joined the case for oral argument with *Shepard v. Woodland Tp. Comm.*, 71 N.J. 230, 364 A.2d 1005 (1976), also decided today, to consider the validity and constitutionality of planned housing developments for the elderly.

The more important issues presented in this case were addressed by the Appellate Division in its opinion: whether the ordinances are beyond the authority delegated to municipalities by N.J.S.A. 40:55-30 *et seq.* and whether they violate principles of substantive due process or equal protection of the law.

A

The Zoning Power

Zoning is inherently an exercise of the State's police power. Consequently, municipalities have no power to zone except as delegated to them by the Legislature. In this regard, zoning powers are granted to municipalities by the zoning enabling act, N.J.S.A. 40:55-30 *et seq.*

Ordinances enacted under this grant of power, like other municipal ordinances, are accorded a presumtpion of validity which can only be overcome by an affirmative showing that the ordinance is arbitrary or unreasonable. Nevertheless, municipalities which exercise this power must observe the limitations of the grant and the standards which accompany it.

Thus, ordinances adopted under the zoning enabling act must bear a real and substantial relationship to the regulation of land within the municipality.

They must also advance one of the several purposes specified in the enabling statute. N.J.S.A. 40:52-32. Among these purposes is to "promote . . . the general welfare," a capacious phrase which appears to encompass all the others.

The concept of the general welfare in land use regulation has been given an expansive interpretation by both this Court and the United States Supreme Court. In this regard, the term is mutable and reflects current social conditions. In today's economic and social setting, the term clearly encompasses the concerns of housing and related needs. * * *

The question therefore arises whether the ordinances under review serve to "promote . . . the general welfare." The relationship which the Weymouth ordinances bear to the general welfare can only be appreciated when viewed against the background of larger demographic and social changes that have recently occurred both in New Jersey and in the nation at large.

The United States is experienceing a sharp demographic shift. As a consequence of declining birth rates and longer life expectancies, the elderly are increasing both in absolute numbers and in relative proportion to the total population. In 1950, there were approximately 12.3 million persons over the age of 65 in the United States, comprising 8.2% of the total population. By 1970, these numbers had risen to approximately 20 million, and 9.9% of the total population. *U.S. Bureau of the Census, 1970 Census of the Population, Characteristics of the Population: United States Summary* 1-276 (1973). More recent figures show that this age-group now includes more than 22 million people. If current trends continue, demographers project that there will be more than 29 million Americans over the age of 65 by the year 2000. *Hearings on Specialized Housing and Alternatives to Institutionalization before a Subcomm. of the House Comm. on Gov't Operations*, 93rd Cong., 2d Sess., at 2 (1974). Though the total population grew by one-third between 1950 and 1970, the number of elderly citizens in this country increased by nearly two-thirds. *Ibid.* In the next two decades, it is expected that the number of people between the ages of 65 and 74 will increase by an additional one-third and those 75 years of age and older will increase by 64%. Neugarten, "Age Groups in American Society and the Rise of the Young-Old," *The Annals of the American Academy of Political and Social Sciences* 193 (Sept. 1974). These national trends are reflected in the changing demographic composition of New Jersey as well. In 1950, New Jersey had approximately 394,000 residents over the age of 65, comprising 8.2% of its total population. By 1970, this number had grown to 697,000, and 9.7% of the population.

The rapid increase of the elderly population has brought increasing public recognition of the special problems confronting this age group. Among these problems are the special house needs of the elderly. The lack of housing specially designed to meet the needs and desires of the elderly is a matter that has generated increasing public concern at both the national and state levels.

In part the need of the elderly for specialized housing results from the fixed and limited incomes upon which many older persons are dependent. In 1970, 82.3% of households in New Jersey with persons over the age of 65 had incomes of less than $10,000 and 62.1% had incomes of less than $5,000. *N.J. Office on Aging, Detailed Housing and Income Information on the Elderly of New Jersey* 2 (1973). By comparison, the median income for all families in New Jersey at that time was $11,407. Because many of the elderly derive their incomes from pensions, social security or other government benefit programs, or from interest on savings or income-producing securities, they are among those hardest hit by inflation and the current statewide housing shortage.

Because of these special demands and the demographic trends discussed above, there now exists a critical shortage of housing suitable to meet the needs and desires of the elderly * * *

Both the state and federal governments have attempted to solve these problems by legislative enactment. *See, e.g.*, 12 U.S.C.A. §§ 1701h-1 (establishing an advisory committee on housing for the elderly), 1701q (providing loans for rental housing), 1701s (authorizing rent supplements for the elderly), 1701z-6 (establishing a research program), 1715v (providing for insurance of mortgages on rental housing); 42 U.S.C.A. §§ 1485 (assistance for rural housing), 3012(a)(4) (research program), 3028(a)(1) (demonstration projects); N.J.S.A. 55:141-1 *et seq.* (granting tax exemptions to nonprofit corporations constructing housing for elderly).

The Weymouth Township ordinances attempt to meet some of these same needs at the local level of government. The ordinances permit use of some land in the community for planned mobile home parks for the elderly. The role which mobile home developments can play in satisfying the special needs of the State's senior citizens is evident. First, mobile homes provide a relatively inexpensive form of housing at a time when the demand for such housing is great and its availability is limited:* * * Second, mobile developments afford the elderly the age-homogeneous environment which many older persons now seek and desire. Finally, the size of mobile homes is ideal for older persons with both physical and financial limitations: * * *

Therefore, while mobile homes have traditionally been a disfavored form of development among local zoning authorities, their inexpensiveness, compact size and easy maintenance give them special and growing appeal among older citizens who are in need of housing. Studies of elderly persons living in mobile home parks indicate that they are generally satisfied with this form of housing. Between 1960 and 1970, the percentage of senior citizens owning mobile homes increased from 1% to 4%; in addition, the percentage of those renting mobile homes rose from .4% to 1%. Thus, the future use of mobile home parks to provide specialized housing for the elderly seems to be neither unreasonable nor impractical. Moreover, as noted above, the concept of the "general welfare" in land use regulation is quite expansive, and encompasses the provision of housing for *all categories of people,* including the elderly.

We therefore conclude, for all the above reasons, that the Weymouth Township ordinances clearly promote the general welfare and hence fall well within the purview of the zoning enabling act. N.J.S.A. 40:55-32* * *

Admittedly, zoning is not a panacea for all social, cultural and economic ills especially where they are unrelated to the use of land. Furthermore, zoning ordinances which bear too tenuous a relationship to land use will be stricken as exceeding the powers delegated to municipalities by the enabling act. Thus, zoning may not be used to regulate family life, to protect local commercial establishments from undesired competition, or to prevent whole classes of people from residing within a community. The point at which the relationship between the principal purpose of a zoning ordinance and the regulation of land use becomes so tenuous as to place the ordinance beyond the limits of the zoning power cannot readily be determined in the abstract; it must be determined within the factual context of each case. We have no doubt, though, that the ordinances at issue in this case do bear a real and substantial relationship to land use.

We first observe that as a conceptual matter regulation of *land use* cannot be precisely dissociated from regulation of *land users.* Restrictions upon the use of land frequently restrict those who may utilize it. Thus, ordinances which regulate use by regulating identified users are not inherently objectionable* * *

B

Equal Protection

In addition to satisfying the requirements of N.J.S.A. 40:55-30 *et seq.*, a zoning ordinance must also satisfy the due process and equal protection requirements of the state and federal constitutions.

We first consider the equal protection issue. The Appellate Division held that the Weymouth ordinances were violative of the fourteenth amendment to the federal constitution on the ground that they unlawfully discriminate on the basis of age.

The federal equal protection clause does not require that government treat all persons identically. It requires only that differences in treatment of persons similarly situated be justified by an appropriate state interest; such distinctions may not be irrational or discriminate invidiously. Under the conventional "two-tiered" analysis applied by the United States Supreme Court, the burden is on the party attacking the classification to show that it lacks a rational relationship to a legitimate state objective. The notable exception to this test occurs in situations where the classification involves "suspect" criteria or impinges upon "fundamental" rights. In these cases the burden is on the state to show that the classification serves a "compelling state interest."

The only rights which are "fundamental" in this regard are those expressly guaranteed or clearly implied by the federal constitution. The Supreme Court has expressly rejected the contention that housing is a "fundamental" right protected by the fourteenth amendment. The high Court has also rejected the assertion that age is a "suspect" criterion.

Since neither "fundamental" rights nor "suspect" criteria for classification are implicated in the present matter, plaintiffs have the burden of demonstrating that the classification herein lacks a rational basis. Such classification must be sustained if it can be justified on any reasonably conceivable state of facts. It does not matter that the classification may be mathematically imperfect or that ir results in some inequities in practice.

Plaintiffs have not demonstrated that the age limitations in the Weymouth Township ordinances lack a rational basis. Similar age restrictions on housing occupancy have been upheld in various contexts in other jurisdictions.

The choice of 52 as the cutoff age for occupancy is necessarily somewhat arbitrary. That some minimum age must be designated is inherent in the concept of a planned housing development for the elderly. Any choice of a specific figure inevitably excludes some persons who might plausibly be admitted and includes others who might plausibly have been excluded. The specification is a legislative judgment which ought not be disturbed by the judiciary unless it exceeds the bounds of reasonable choice.

The point was aptly stated by Mr. Justice Holmes nearly 50 years ago:

> When a legal distinction is determined, as no one doubts that it may be, between night and day, childhood and maturity, or any other extremes, a point has to be fixed or a line has to be drawn, or gradually picked out by successive decisions to mark where the change takes place. Looked at by itself without regard to the necessity be-

hind it, the line or point seems arbitrary. It might as well or nearly as well be a little more to one side or to the other. When it is seen that a line or point there must be, and that there is no mathematical or logical way of fixing it precisely, the decision of the Legislature must be accepted unless we can say that it is very wide of any reasonable mark.

Though the elderly are commonly defined as those persons approximately 65 years old, it cannot be said that 52 is unreasonable or without a factual basis. As we have already noted, many persons who reach this age experience a decline in their net income. In addition, the median age at which men and women become grandparents is now only 57 and 54 respectively. Finally, an increasing number of Americans are retiring from active employment while they are still in the 50's. *Id.* at 14. Therefore, we cannot say that the age limit in this particular case is so unreasonable that it violates principles of equal protection.

Neither plaintiffs nor the Appellate Division have suggested that the principles of equal protection under the New Jersey Constitution require a different result.

As noted above, we have accorded the right to decent housing a preferred status under our State Constitution. Therefore, any governmental action which significantly impinges upon the ability of some class of individuals to obtain this necessity of life deserves close judicial scrutiny. Nevertheless, we are persuaded that the ordinances in question here satisfy the requirements of equal protection even when subjected to such scrutiny. The classification selected by the municipality is based upon real factual distinctions, and also bears a real and substantial relationship to the ends which the municipality seeks to accomplish by that classification.

C

Due Process

Plaintiffs also challenge the Weymouth Township ordinances on the grounds that they violate principles of substantive due process. The constitutional guarantee of substantive due process requires only that the operation of a particular regulation not be unreasonable, arbitrary or capricious, and that the means selected bear a real and substantial relationship to a permissible legislative purpose. In this particular case, the claim that the ordinances violate the due process clause is little more than a restatement of the contention that they contravene principles of equal protection. The same considerations which led us to conclude that the ordinances satisfy the latter constitutional requirement also warrant our conclusion that they do not offend principles of substantive due process. As we have already found, the age and occupancy provisions of the Weymouth Township ordinances do bear a real and substantial relationship to the ends sought, *i.e.*, the creation of a planned community for housing the elderly.

Although the foregoing discussion disposes of all the issues raised by the parties or examined by the trial court, another issue requires consideration. This matter concerns the question whether senior citizen housing has an impermissible exclusionary effect. In this regard, the Public Advocate, appearing as *amicus curiae*, suggests that because zoning for senior citizen housing does pose such a threat, it should be sustained only within a comprehensive plan which specifically provides for a balanced housing stock. In addition, the Public Advocate urges that the case be remanded so that Weymouth Township may demonstrate that the ordinances in question are part of such a comprehensive plan.

The question of exclusionary zoning also implicates the effect of the Municipal Land Use Law, L.1975, c. 291, N.J.S.A. 40:55D-1 *et seq.* upon this litigation. This law, which went into effect on August 1, 1976, contains the following provisions relative to zoning for senior citizen housing:

Section 2:

. . . It is the intent and purpose of this act: . . .

(1) To encourage senior citizen community housing construction consistent with provisions permitting other residential uses of a similar density in the same zoning district. . . .

Section 65:

. . . A zoning ordinance may: . . .

(g) Provide for senior citizen community housing consistent with provisions permitting other residential uses of a similar density in the same zoning district.

We requested the parties to file supplemental briefs on the effect which the new law has on these cases. Having reviewed their responses, we consider here whether the law casts light, by analogy, on the considerations involved in the issue of exclusionary zoning and, in Part IV *infra*, whether the statute operates to bar implementation of the local zoning provisions with respect to the property involved in this litigation. * * *

Nothing stated above warrants the conclusion that zoning for planned housing developments for the elderly is presumptively invalid as exclusionary. It may be used for improper exclusionary purposes, but it also has valid nonexclusionary uses. Our decision in *Mt. Laurel* requires developing municipalities to provide, by their land use regulations, the opportunity for an appropriate variety and choice of housing for all categories of persons who may desire to live there.

This task would be impossible if the municipality could not design its land use regulations to provide for the unsatisfied housing needs of specific, narrowly defined categories of people. While we were specifically concerned in *Mt. Laurel* with the needs of younger families with children, the elderly are also a segment of the population whose needs and desires are appropriate considerations for municipal land use planning. Therefore, to the extent that such needs exist, planned housing developments for the elderly may serve an inclusionary, rather than exclusionary function.

Furthermore, as suggested above, the true character of this zoning device must be assessed against the background of general land use regulation by the municipality. If it substantially contributes to an overall pattern of improper exclusion, the fact that the ordinance may also benefit the elderly is neither an excuse nor a justification to sustain a challenge to a zoning provision. In the present case, though, plaintiffs have not attacked the overall pattern of land use regulation adopted by Weymouth Township as improperly exclusionary. They did not try the case on any such theory, nor have they argued it on appeal before this Court. Indeed, the trial testimony of several individual plaintiffs suggests that their true objection to the ordinances may be that they are not sufficiently exclusionary. The record reveals little about the character of Weymouth Township, its present state of development, the extent of the unsatisfied housing needs in the municipality and the region at large, or the nature of its current land use regulations. We cannot say that plaintiffs have, even inadvertently, established a *prima facie* case of exclusionary zoning which would shift the burden to the municipality to justify its existing land use regulations. In so holding, we express no opinion as to whether the Weymouth Township zoning ordinances could survive such a challenge.

To avert any misunderstanding, though, we reemphasize our concern about the exclusionary potential which zoning for senior citizen housing possesses. A pattern of exclusionary land use regulation cannot be rendered invisible to the judicial eye by camouflaging it with invocations of the legitimate needs of the elderly. The Court's failure to probe more deeply into the possible exclusionary effect of similar ordinances should not be understood to be the product of blindness to their potentially exclusionary character, but only the consequence of plaintiffs' decision not to try the case on that legal theory. * * *

In summary, we hold that in zoning for planned housing developments for the elderly, Weymouth Township did not exceed the authority granted it by the zoning enabling act, N.J.S.A. 40:55-30 *et seq.*, and did not violate constitutional principles of due process or equal protection. We also hold that plaintiffs, on the present record, have not proven the existence of spot zoning, an illegal conspiracy or a pattern of illegally exclusionary practices. * * *

We therefore reverse the judgment of the Appellate Division.

---

(3) Exclusion of the Handicapped

BERGER, et al.,

v.

The STATE OF NEW JERSEY

71 N.J. 206, 364 A.2d 993 (1976)

MOUNTAIN, J.

This case presents the question of whether a group home for multi-handicapped, pre-school children must cease its operation either because of restrictive covenants in deeds of record or because of zoning provisions limiting the area to single family dwellings.

By deed dated July 9, 1973 William and Florence A. Graessle conveyed their premises in the Borough of Mantoloking as a gift to the New Jersey State Department of Institutions and Agencies. The deed specified that the premises, on which were located a well-maintained, 12 room ocean-front house and three-car garage, were to be known as the Graewill House and were to be devoted exclusively to the care of disadvantaged pre-school children under the age of nine. If the property were not so used, it would revert to the grantors. Moreover, the deed specified that the conveyance was subject to easements, covenants and restrictions of record as well as to the Borough's zoning provisions.

Pursuant to these conditions, the State formulated plans to utilize the property. The State intended that 8 to 12 multi-handicapped, pre-school children, most of whom would be wards of the State, would reside in the home with a married couple having 22 years of experience as foster parents. This arrangement would enable the children, who would otherwise be confined to hospitals, to grow and develop in a family environment. Supportive services would be provided by an educational specialist, two paraprofessionals, a cook-housekeeper and a maintenance man, none of whom would reside on the premises* * *

Four couples owning property either adjacent or in close proximity to the Graessle premises instituted this action on October 30, 1973 to restrain the use of the facility proposed by the State. Named as defendants were the State of New Jersey, Maurice G. Kott, Acting Commissioner of the Department of Institutions and Agencies, William and Florence A. Graessle, and the Borough of Mantoloking. Plaintiffs predicated their challenge on two bases: first, that the intended use of the Graessle premises would constitute a clear violation of the negative reciprocal covenants contained in deeds of record establishing a neighborhood scheme of single family residences, and second, that the proposed use would contravene Mantoloking's zoning ordinance restricting the area to single family dwellings.

Plaintiffs' application for a preliminary injunction was denied on November 29, 1973. At approximately the same time, the State officially began using Graewill House to care for handicapped children in the manner set forth above, a use which presently continues. Cross motions for summary judgment were made by the parties, culminating in a decision rendered July 26, 1974 denying plaintiffs' motion and granting summary judgment to defendants. The trial court's decision was based upon findings that the restrictive covenants regulated only the type of structure, not the occupancy or use of the premises, and that in any event the house was being used as a dwelling. It was also held that the zoning ordinance was invalid and that the State enjoyed immunity from its provisions. We certified plaintiffs' appeal prior to argument in the Appellate Division. For reasons hereinafter set forth we affirm.

Plaintiffs' first contention is that the use of the Graessle premises as a group home violates restrictive covenants in deeds of record establishing a neighborhood scheme of single family residences. Title to the premises of the plaintiff's and the Graessles, as well as title to much other adjoining land, derives from a common grantor, Bayhead-Mantoloking Land Co.

(Bayhead). About the year 1925, Bayhead plotted a large tract of land into numerous lots and filed a map of the tract as plotted. In conveying the lots, Bayhead included restrictions in each deed limiting the permissible structures on the premises to dwelling houses with private garages and prohibiting manufacturing or any dangerous, noxious or offensive use. Plaintiffs allege Graewill House fails to conform to these restrictions.

Analytically, these covenants impose three types of restriction. First, they prohibit the use of the property for certain non-residential purposes. Secondly, except for a private garage, no building may be erected that is not a dwelling house. Finally, the number of buildings (dwelling houses) that may be built on each lot is limited—apparently to a single such structure, with or without private garage. It will be noted that the covenants do not restrict the usage of the buildings to *one-family* residences. This being so, our decisional law holds that multi-family occupancy will not violate the covenant* * *

While in some instances the protections such covenants afford probably increase the value of property and may enhance marketability, they do nonetheless raise title problems and impair alienability. We adhere to the view that they must be strictly construed. Such covenants have, or may have, a very important effect upon land use. The limitations and prohibitions they impose may be felt over a very long period of time. It is not too much to insist that they be carefully drafted to state exactly what is intended—no more and no less* * *

It is also urged that the language utilized in the restrictive covenants here in issue manifests an intent to limit permissible structures to those used for *private residential living*. Accepting this contention *arguendo,* we do not agree that the present use of Graewill House violates the covenants. On the contrary, we look upon the present use as being that of a private residence for a limited number of children and their foster parents* * *

Plaintiffs further assert that the covenants in question require not only residential living but also occupancy by a single family. As we have seen above, there is nothing in the express language of the covenants to support this contention. In furtherance of this proposition, however, they rely on statements of Mr. Otis C. Strickland, the Secretary-Treasurer of the common grantor, Bayhead-Mantoloking Land Co., who prepared most of the deeds from Bayhead during 1925 and 1926. According to Mr. Strickland, the purpose of the covenants was "to create and impose a neighborhood scheme of single family residential living" in order "to preserve the family residential nature of the area." Moreover, he stated that the term dwelling house "was intended to establish the private residential scheme in accordance with the meaning and use of said term in 1925" and that "places of accommodation, such as boarding houses" were intended to be excluded.

Again conceding, for the sake of argument only, that single families may have been envisioned by the common grantor, we are unable to perceive in the avowed intent of Bayhead any design to restrict the use of the affected premises to single families comprised exclusively of related members. There is simply nothing to suggest that the relationship of the persons within a dwelling was of any concern to the common grantor. Rather, it is reasonable to conclude that its predominant interest was to preserve a family style of living, that is, a style characterized by fairly stable, rather than transient relationships, a single household headed by adults who both control and guide such children as may reside with them* * *

In light of the above, we find that the use of the Graessle premises as Graewill House does not violate the restrictive covenants of record nor does it contravene the neighborhood scheme. To the contrary, the use of the premises as a group home for handicapped children is clearly within the use contemplated by the term "dwelling house" and in conformity with, rather than in derogation of, the purported neighborhood scheme of residential living.

The other basis for plaintiffs' attack is that the use of the Graessle premises as a group-care home violates the zoning ordinance of the Borough of Mantoloking, which provides for only two zones within the municipality, a business zone and a residential zone. The latter zone, which encompasses 95% of the land of the Borough and includes the Graessle tract, is restricted to "single family dwellings," defined as "detached building[s] designed for, or occupied exclusively by, one family in one dwelling unit." "Family" is defined as

one person living alone or two or more persons related by blood, marriage or adoption and living together as a single unit in one house or within one curtilage and under one head (pater or mater familias); domestic servants, one companion, one housekeeper and occasional nonpaying guests may be included but no other person.

It is readily apparent that the residents of Graewill House do not constitute a family as defined by the above quoted section of the ordinance. We are, however, for reasons discussed below, unable to accept plaintiffs' argument that the operation of Graewill House should therefore be enjoined.

Initially, it should be noted that state agencies are generally immune from the zoning ordinance provisions of a municipality. While there are no precise criteria by which to determine the existence or scope of such immunity, we have recognized that the test is basically one of legislative intent—i.e., whether the Legislature intended the particular governmental unit to be immune with respect to the particular enterprise. As we indicated in *Rutgers v. Piluso, supra,* legislative intent is to be gleaned from a number of factors, including "the nature and scope of the instrumentality seeking immunity, the kind of function or land use involved, the extent of the public interest to be served thereby, the effect local land use regulation would have upon the enterprise concerned and the impact upon legitimate local interests." Considerations of these factors in the instant case compels the conclusion that the State is immune from the Mantoloking zoning ordinance.

The Department of Institutions and Agencies, a principal department in the executive branch of the State government, is entrusted with the responsibility of providing care for children whose needs cannot be adequately met in their own homes. To advance the public policy of providing adequate care and supervision for dependent children, the Legislature has proscribed discrimination in zoning regulations as between children in a conventional family setting and children in a group home—defined as any single family dwelling used in the placement of 12 or fewer children and recognized as such by the Department of Institutions and Agencies. From these enactments, it is clear that the Legislature intended to immunize the Department of Institutions and Agencies from the operation of local zoning provisions which prohibit the establishment of a group home* * *

It is fundamental, however, that any assertion of immunity must be reasonable so as not "to arbitrarily override all important legitimate local interests." Plaintiffs assert that the failure of the State to consider the objections of the community prior to establishing Graewill illustrates its unreasonableness. To support their position they rely on *Long Branch Division of United Civil & Taxpayers Org. v. Cowan,* wherein the Appellate Division held that the State Department of Health was immune from local zoning provisions thus permitting the establishment of a residential narcotic rehabilitation and treatment center in a residential zone of Long Branch. Nevertheless, the court took cognizance of the widespread opposition registered by the community with respect to the site selection and remanded the matter for a hearing on the issue of whether the Department had acted unreasonably or arbitrarily in selecting the location of the center.

We are not persuaded that the instant case merits the same disposition. We see nothing to suggest that the State acted arbitrarily in deciding to utilize the Graessle premises as a residential home for handicapped children, a use which is markedly different from a drug treatment center. The State negotiated with officials of Mantoloking to assure that Graewill House would continue to be compatible in appearance with the neighborhood and met with concerned residents of the town. The fact that many of the residents voiced opposition to Graewill House does not, in and of itself, mean that the State acted unreasonably in proceeding with its plans. Rather, the reasonableness of its action must be evaluated in terms of the effect Graewill has on the surrounding area. We find nothing to convince us that Graewill has such a detrimental effect as to warrant judicial interference, and have no difficulty in concluding that the State, acting reasonably, is immune from the Mantoloking zoning provisions restricting single family dwellings to persons related by blood, marriage or adoption.

That Graewill has been established as a group home gives rise to an equally compelling reason for one finding the zoning restriction to be without effect. Municipalities must look to legislation to determine the scope of their zoning powers. These are as comprehensive or as restrictive as the relevant statutes determine. The New Jersey Legislature has expressly prohibited municipalities from discriminating in their zoning ordinances governing single family dwellings between children residing therein by virtue of their relationship by blood, marriage or adoption and children residing therein by virtue of their placement in a group home. These two statutes were each amended to confirm and clarify the status of group homes for children as being single family units. This clearly evidences the Legislature's desire to accord the same protections to children placed in group homes as had been previously extended to foster children. Moreover, it may be interpreted as indicative of the Legislature's position that the zoning enabling act was not designed to empower municipalities to restrict a family to those biologically or legally related. *Kirsch Holding Co. v. Borough of Manasquan,* (1971). In summary, the Legislature has defined "group home" to include the kind of dwelling arrangement we are considering here, and has further declared that any municipal effort to treat such an arrangement as in any way different than a biological family unit will result in a declaration of invalidity.

Plaintiffs also contend that neither N.J.S.A. 30:4C-26 nor 40:55-33.2 validates the use of the Graessle premises as Graewill House because it is not being used as either a foster or group home. Plaintiffs seem to perceive Graewill as a non-residential facility in a single family residential area. While it may differ from the conventional foster or group home in that the children do not become active participants in the community and do require educational and medical services within the home, this is hardly sufficient to justify plaintiffs' characterization of Graewill. It is, both in essence and in operation, a family home and fully within the meaning of group homes as defined in the applicable legislation. As such, it is clear that N.J.S.A. 30:4C-26 and 40:55-33.2 invalidate so much of Mantoloking's zoning ordinance as restricts single family dwellings exclusively to persons related by blood, marriage or adoption.

The above statutory ground demonstrably disposes of plaintiffs zoning argument. However, because the matrix of this case is the extent to which the residential character of a neighborhood may be preserved by covenant and ordinance, we deem it advisable to speak further on the right of a municipality to zone to achieve that objective* * *

Nevertheless, while municipalities are free to zone in such a way as will best attain these values, and to prohibit from such areas any use which threatens to erode such values or destroy the residential character of the area, all restrictions must, at the same time, satisfy the demands of due process. Substantive due process requires that zoning regulations be reasonably exercised; they may be neither unreasonable, arbitrary nor capricious. The means chosen must have a real and substantial relation to the end sought to be achieved. Moreover, the regulation must be reasonably designed to resolve the problem without imposing unnecessary and excessive restrictions on the use of private property.

When the Mantoloking ordinance defining "family" as those persons related by blood, marriage or adoption is measured against the demands of due process, it is clear that the regulation must fall. It so narrowly delimits the persons who may occupy a single family dwelling as to prohibit numerous potential occupants who pose no threat to the style of family living sought to be preserved. As such, we cannot conclude that the definition of "family" is reasonable.

New Jersey courts have consistently invalidated zoning ordinances that were unreasonably restrictive in delineating permissible occupants. For example, in *Kirsch Holding Co. v. Borough of Manasquan, supra,* we struck down regulations which restrictively defined "family" and prohibited group rentals in two seashore communities. Finding that the ordinances precluded many harmless uses in the attempt to avoid rentals to unruly unrelated groups, we concluded, in reasoning that we reaffirm today, that they were sweepingly excessive and thus legally unreasonable* * *

While we have not hesitated to strike down zoning ordinances that fail to satisfy the demands of substantive due process, we are not unmindful of the problem confronting many municipalities which desire to maintain a prevailing family environment. Their need is to enact ordinances that will both withstand judicial scrutiny, and at the same time exclude uses that may impair the environment. We believe a satisfactory resolution of this problem would result, were local governments to restrict single family dwellings to a reasonable number of persons who constitute a *bona fide* single housekeeping unit. If such a requirement were incorporated into zoning ordinances, it would not only perpetuate the stability, permanence and other beneficial attributes long associated with single family occupancy but also preclude uses closely approximating boarding houses, dormitory and institutional living. Such an enactment—if carefully drawn—would be both reasonably related to the end of maintaining a peaceful family residential style of living—an end we uphold as a legitimate goal of zoning—and yet be neither excessive nor overreaching in its sweep.

Courts have similarly broadened the definition of family by focusing on whether a single housekeeping unit is involved. Illustrative of this approach is *City of White Plains v. Ferraioli*, (1974), where the court determined that a group home consisting of a married couple, their two children and 10 foster children constituted a single family within the meaning of the ordinance. The zoning ordinance defined family in these terms: "A 'family' is one or more persons limited to the spouse, parents, grandparents, grandchildren, sons, daughters, brothers or sisters of the owner or the tenant or of the owner's spouse or tenant's spouse living together as a single housekeeping unit with kitchen facilities." The court emphasized the significance of the fact that the home functioned as a single housekeeping unit and in every outward respect, was a "relatively normal, stable and permanent family unit." It concluded in reasoning pertinent here, that

> an ordinance may restrict a residential zone to occupancy by stable families occupying single-family homes, but neither by express provision nor construction may it limit the definition of family to exclude a household which in every but a biological sense is a single family. The minimal arrangement to meet the test of a zoning provision, as this one, is a group headed by a householder caring for a reasonable number of children as one would be likely to find in a biological unitary family.

Inherent in the above well-reasoned passage is an awareness of the fact that "[t]he concept of a one family dwelling is based upon its character as a single housekeeping unit." We adopt this reasoning and conclude that by its force, without resort to the protective legislation concerning group homes, that portion of the Mantoloking ordinance imposing what we find to be an unduly restrictive definition of the concept of "family," must fall.

It is our judgment that Graewill House need not cease its operation; that it violates neither restrictive covenants of record, nor the Borough's zoning provisions, the latter, to the extent indicated above, having been held invalid. Accordingly all forms of relief sought be plaintiffs are denied.

Judgment is affirmed.

C. THE MOUNT LAUREL DECISION AND ITS PROGENY

(1) Analysis of the Decision and the New Legal Issues

SOUTHERN BURLINGTON COUNTY N.A.A.C.P.

v.

TOWNSHIP OF MOUNT LAUREL

67 N.J. 151, 336 A.2d 713 (1975)

The Southern Burlington County NAACP and other plaintiffs representing minority group poor (black and Hispanic) filed a suit challenging the system of land use regulation by defendant Township of Mount Laurel on the ground that it unlawfully excluded low and moderate income families. Mount Laurel is a sprawling township of approximately 22 square miles (14,000 acres) in area and located about 7 miles from the city limits of Camden, N.J. In 1950, the township had a population of 2,817, but by 1960 the population had almost doubled to 5,249 and by 1970 had more than doubled again to 11,221.

Under the township zoning ordinance 29 percent of the land was zoned for industry, 1.2 percent was zoned for retail business use, and the remainder was zoned into four residential districts. These districts permitted only single family detached dwellings on single lots. Specifically, the R-1 district required minimum lot area of 9,375 square feet, a minimum lot width of 75 feet at the building line, and a minimum dwelling floor area of 1,100 square feet if a one story building and 1,300 square feet if one and one-half stories or higher. The R-2 district required a minimum floor area of 900 square feet for one story dwellings, a minimum lot size of 11,000 square feet, otherwise the requirements were the same as in the R-1 district. The R-3 district contained most of the remaining undeveloped land (4,600 acres). However, the ordinance's requirements for the R-3 district were substantially higher in that minimum lot size was increased to 20,000 square feet (one-half acre). The minimum lot width at the building line was 100 feet and the minimum floor area was the same as the R-1 district. Finally, the ordinance provided for an R-1D district or "cluster" zone and for a R-4 district or "Planned Adult Retirement Community".

HALL, J.

The legal question before us, as earlier indicated, is whether a developing municipality like Mount Laurel may validly, by a system of land use regulation, make it physically and economically impossible to provide low and moderate income housing in the municipality for the various categories of persons who need and want it and thereby, as Mount Laurel has, exclude such people from living within its confines because of the limited extent of their income and resources. Necessarily implicated are the broader questions of the right of such municipalities to limit the kinds of available housing and of any obligation to make possible a variety and choice of types of living accommodations.

We conclude that every such municipality must, by its land use regulations, presumptively make realistically possible an appropriate variety and choice of housing. More specifically, presumptively it cannot foreclose the opportunity of the classes of people mentioned for low and moderate income housing and in its regulations must affirmatively afford that opportunity, at least to the extent of the municipality's fair share of the present and prospective regional need therefor. These obligations must be met unless the particular municipality can sustain the heavy burden of demonstrating peculiar circumstances which dictate that it should not be required so to do.

We reach this conclusion under state law and so do not find it necessary to consider federal constitutional grounds urged by plaintiffs. We begin with some fundamental principles as applied to the scene before us.* * *

It is elementary theory that all police power enactments, no matter at what level of government, must conform to the basic state constitutional requirements of substantive due process and equal protection of the laws. These are inherent in Art. I, par. 1 of our Constitution, the requirements of which may be more demanding than those of the federal Constitution. It is required that, affirmatively, a zoning regulation, like any police power enactment, must promote public health, safety, morals or the general welfare. (The last term seems broad enough to encompass the others.) Conversely, a zoning enactment which is contrary to the general welfare is invalid. Indeed these considerations are specifically set forth in the zoning enabling act as among the various purposes of zoning for which regulations must be designed. N.J.S.A. 40:55-32. Their inclusion therein really adds little; the same requirement would exist even if they were omitted. If a zoning regulation violates the enabling act in this respect, it is also theoretically invalid under the state constitution. We say "theoretically" because, as a matter of policy, we do not treat the validity of most land use ordinance provisions as involving matters of constitutional dimension; that classification is confined to major questions of fundamental import. We consider the basic importance of housing and local regulations restricting its availability to substantial segments of the population to fall within the latter category.* * *

This brings us to the relation of housing to the concept of general welfare just discussed and the result in terms of land use regulation which that relationship mandates. There cannot be the slightest doubt that shelter, along with food, are the most basic human needs. "The question of whether a citizenry has adequate and sufficient housing is certainly one of the prime considerations in assessing the general health and welfare of that body." The same thought is implicit in the legislative findings of an extreme, long-time need in this state for decent low and moderate income housing, set forth in the numerous statutes providing for various agencies and methods at both state and local levels designed to aid in alleviation of the need.* * *

It is plain beyond dispute that proper provision for adequate housing of all categories of people is certainly an absolute essential in promotion of the general welfare require in all local land use regulation. Further the universal and constant need for such housing is so important and of such broad public interest that the general welfare which developing municipalities like Mount Laurel must consider extends beyond their boundaries and cannot be parochially confined to the claimed good of the particular municipality. It has to follow that, broadly speaking, the presumptive obligation arises for each such municipality affirmatively to plan and provide, by its land use regulations, the reasonable opportunity for an appropriate variety and choice of housing, including, of course, low and moderate cost housing, to meet the needs, desires and resources of all categories of people who may desire to live within its boundaries. Negatively, it may not adopt regulations or policies which thwart or preclude that opportunity.

It is also entirely clear, as we pointed out earlier, that most developing municipalities, including Mount Laurel, have not met their affirmative or negative obligations, primarily for local fiscal reasons.* * *

In sum, we are satisfied beyond any doubt that, by reason of the basic importance of appropriate housing and the longstanding pressing need for it, especially in the low and moderate cost category, and of the exclusionary zoning practices of so many municipalities, conditions have changed, and consistent with the warning in *Pierro, supra,* judicial attitudes must be altered from that espoused in that and other cases cited earlier, to require, as we have just said, a broader view of the general welfare and the presumptive obligation on the part of developing municipalities at least to afford the opportunity by land use regulations for appropriate housing for all.

We have spoken of this obligation of such municipalities as "presumptive." The term has two aspects, procedural and substantive. Procedurally, we think the basic importance of appropriate housing for all dictates that, when it is shown that a developing municipality in its land use regulations has not made realistically possible a variety and choice of housing, including adequate provision to afford the opportunity for low and moderate income housing or has expressly prescribed requirements or restrictions which preclude or substantially hinder it, a facial showing of violation of substantive due process or equal protection under the state constitution has been made out and the burden, and it is a heavy one, shifts to the municipality to establish a valid basis for its action or non-action. The substantive aspect of "presumptive" relates to the specifics, on the one hand, of what municipal land use regulation provisions, or the absence thereof, will evidence invalidity and shift the burden of proof and, on the other hand, of what bases and considerations will carry the municipality's burden and sustain what it has done or failed to do. Both kinds of specifics may well vary between municipalities according to peculiar circumstances.

We turn to application of these principles in appraisal of Mount Laurel's zoning ordinance, useful as well, we think, as guidelines for future application in other municipalities.

The township's general zoning ordinance (including the cluster zone provision) permits, as we have said, only one type of housing—single family detached dwellings. This means that all other types—multi-family including garden apartments and other kinds of housing more than one family, town (row) houses, mobile home parks—are prohibited. Concededly, low and moderate income housing has been intentionally excluded. While a large percentage of the population living outside of cities prefers a one-family house on its own sizeable lot, a substantial proportion do not for various reasons. Moreover, single-family dwellings are the most expensive types of quarters and a great number of families cannot afford them.[13] Certainly they are not pecuniarily feasible for low and moderate income families, most young people and many elderly and retired persons, except for some of moderate income by the use of low cost construction on small lots.* * *

Mount Laurel's zoning ordinance is also so restrictive in its minimum lot area, lot frontage and building size requirements, earlier detailed, as to preclude single-family housing for even moderate income families. Required lot area of at least 9,375 square feet in one remaining regular residential zone and 20,000 square feet (almost half an acre) in the other, with required frontage of 75 and 100 feet, respectively, cannot be called small lots and amounts to low density zoning, very definitely increasing the cost of purchasing and improving land and so affecting the cost of housing. As to building size, the township's general requirements of a minimum dwelling floor area of 1,100 square feet for all one-story houses and 1,300 square feet for all of one and one-half stories or higher is without regard to required minimum lot size or frontage or the number of occupants. In most aspects these requirements are greater even than those approved in Lionshead Lake, Inc. v. Township of Wayne, *supra,* almost 24 years ago and before population decentralization, outer suburban development and exclusionary zoning had attained today's condition. Again it is evident these requirements increase the size and so the cost of housing. The conclusion is irresistible that Mount Laurel permits only such middle and upper income housing as it believes will have sufficient taxable value to come close to paying its own governmental way.

Akin to large lot, single-family zoning restricting the population is the zoning of very large amounts of land for industrial and related uses. Mount Laurel has set aside almost 30% of its area, over 4,100 acres, for that purpose; the only residential use allowed is for farm dwellings. In almost a decade only about 100 acres have been developed industrially. Despite the township's strategic location for motor transportation purposes, as intimated earlier, it seems plain that the likelihood of anywhere near the whole of the zoned area being used for the intended purpose in the foreseeable future is remote indeed and that an unreasonable amount of land has thereby been removed from possible residential development, again seemingly for local fiscal reasons.

Without further elaboration at this point, our opinion is that Mount Laurel's zoning ordinance is presumptively contrary to the general welfare and outside the intended scope of the zoning power in the particulars mentioned. A facial showing of invalidity is thus established, shifting to the municipality the burden of establishing valid superseding reasons for its action and non-action. We now examine the reasons it advances.

The township's principal reason in support of its zoning plan and ordinance housing provisions, advanced especially strongly at oral argument, is the fiscal one previously adverted to, *i.e.*, that by reason of New Jersey's tax structure which substantially finances municipal governmental and educational costs from taxes on local real property, every municipality may, by the exercise of the zoning power, allow only such uses and to such extent as will be beneficial to the local tax rate. In other words, the position is that any municipality may zone extensively to seek and encourage the "good" tax ratables of industry and commerce and limit the permissible types of housing to those having the fewest school children or to those providing sufficient value to attain or approach paying their own way taxwise.

We have previously held that a developing municipality may properly zone for and seek industrial ratables to create a better economic balance for the community *vis-a-vis* educational and governmental costs engendered by residential development, provided that such was "* * * done reasonably as part of and in furtherance of a legitimate comprehensive plan for the zoning of the entire municipality." We adhere to that view today. But we were not there concerned with, and did not pass upon, the validity of municipal exclusion by zoning of types of housing and kinds of people for the same local financial end. We have no hesitancy in now saying, and do so emphatically, that, considering the basic importance of the opportunity for appropriate housing for all classes of our citizenry, no municipality may exclude or limit categories of housing for that reason or purpose. While we fully recognize the increasingly heavy burden of local taxes for municipal governmental and school costs on homeowners, relief from the consequences of this tax system will have to be furnished by other branches of government. It cannot legitimately be accomplished by restricting types of housing through the zoning process in developing municipalities.* * *

By way of summary, what we have said comes down to this. As a developing municipality, Mount Laurel must, by its land use regulations, make realistically possible the opportunity for an appropriate variety and choice of housing for all categories of people who may desire to live there, of course including those of low and moderate income. It must permit multi-family housing, without bedroom or similar restrictions, as well as small dwellings on very small lots, low cost housing of other types and, in general, high density zoning, without artificial and unjustifiable minimum requirements as to lot size, building size and the like, to meet the full panoply of these needs. Certainly when a municipaliry zones for industry and commerce for local tax benefit purposes, it without question must zone to permit adequate housing within the means of the employees involved in such uses. (If planned unit developments are authorized, one would assume that each must include a reasonable amount of low and moderate income housing in its residential "mix," unless opportunity for such housing has already been realistically provided for elsewhere in the municipality.) The amount of land removed from residential use by allocation to industrial and commercial purposes must be reasonably related to the present and future potential for such purposes. In other words, such municipalities must zone primarily for the living welfare of people and not for the benefit of the local tax rate.

We have earlier stated that a developing municipality's obligation to afford the opportunity for decent and adequate low and moderate income housing extends at least to "* * * the municipality's fair share of the present and prospective regional need therefore." Some comment on that conclusion is in order at this point. Frequently it might be sounder to have more of such housing, like some specialized land uses, in one municipality in a region than in another, because of greater availability of suitable land, location of employment, accessibility of public transportation or some other significant reason. But, under present New Jersey legislation, zoning must be on an individual municipal basis, rather than regionally. So long as that situation persists under the present tax structure, or in the absence of some kind of binding agreement among all the municipalities of a region, we feel that every municipality therein must bear its fair share of the regional burden. (In this respect our holding is broader than that of the trial court, which was limited to Mount Laurel-related low and moderate income housing needs.)

The composition of the applicable "region" will necessarily vary from situation to situation and probably no hard and fast rule will serve to furnish the answer in every case. Confinement to or within a certain county appears not to be realistic, but restriction within the boundaries of the state seem practical and advisable. (This is not to say that a developing municipality can ignore a demand for housing within its boundaries on the part of people who commute to work in another state.) Here we have already defined the region at present as "those portions of Camden, Burlington and Gloucester Counties within a semicircle having a radius of 20 miles or so from the heart of Camden City." The concept of "fair share" is coming into more general use and, through the expertise of the municipal planning adviser, the county planning boards and the state planning agency, a reasonable figure for Mount Laurel can be determined, which can then be translated to the allocation of sufficient land therefor on the zoning map. * * *

There is no reason why developing municipalities like Mount Laurel, required by this opinion to afford the opportunity for all types of housing to meet the needs of various categories of people, may not become and remain attractive, viable communities providing good living and adequate services for all their residents in the kind of atmosphere which a democracy and free institutions demand. They can have industrial sections, commercial sections and sections for every kind of housing from low cost and multi-family to lots of more than an acre with very expensive homes. Proper planning and governmental cooperation can prevent over-intensive and too sudden development, insure against future suburban sprawl and slums and assure the preservation of open space and local beauty. We do not intend that developing municipalities shall be overwhelmed by voracious land speculators and developers if they use the powers which they have intelligently and in the broad public interest. Under our holdings today, they can be better communities for all than they previously have been.

III

The Remedy

As outlined at the outset of this opinion, the trial court invalidated the zoning ordinance *in toto* and ordered the township to make certain studies and investigations and to present to the court a plan of affirmative public action designed "to enable and encourage the satisfaction of the indicated needs" for township related low and moderate income housing. Jurisdiction was retained for judicial consideration and approval of such a plan and for the entry of a final order requiring its implementation.

We are of the view that the trial court's judgment should be modified in certain respects. We see no reason why the entire zoning ordinance should be nullified. Therefore we declare it to be invalid only to the extent and in the particulars set forth in this opinion. The township is granted 90 days from the date hereof, or such additional time as the trial court may find it reasonable and necessary to allow, to adopt amendments to correct the deficiencies herein specified. It is the local function and responsibility, in the first instance at least, rather than the court's, to decide on the details of the same within the guidelines we have laid down. If plaintiffs desire to attack such amendments, they may do so by supplemental complaint filed in this cause within 90 days of the final adoption of the amendments.

We are not at all sure what the trial judge had in mind as ultimate action with reference to the approval of a plan for affirmative public action concerning the satisfaction of indicated housing needs and the entry of a final order requiring implementation thereof. Courts do not build housing nor do municipalities. That function is performed by private builders, various kinds of associations, or, for public housing, by special agencies created for that purpose at various levels of government. The municipal function is initially to provide the opportunity through appropriate land use regulations and we do have spelled out what Mount Laurel must do in that regard. It is not appropriate at this time, particularly in view of the advanced view of zoning law as applied to housing laid down by this opinion, to deal with the matter of the further extent of judicial power in the field or to exercise any such power. See, however, Pascack Association v. Mayor and Council of Township of Washington, 131 N.J.Super. 195, 329 A.2d 89 (Law Div.1974), and cases therein cited, for a discussion of this question. The municipality should first have full opportunity to itself act without judicial supervision. We trust it will do so in the spirit we have suggested, both by appropriate zoning ordinance amendments and whatever additional action encouraging the fulfillment of its fair share of the regional need for low and moderate income housing may be indicated as necessary and advisable. (We have in mind that there is at least a moral obligation to a municipality to establish a local housing agency pursuant to state law to provide housing for its resident poor now living in dilapidated, unhealthy quarters.) The portion of the trial court's judgment ordering the preparation and submission of the aforesaid study, report and plan to it for further action is therefore vacated as at least premature. Should Mount Laurel not perform as we expect, further judicial action may be sought by supplemental pleading in this cause.

The judgment of the Law Division is modified as set forth herein. No costs.

THE MOUNT LAUREL DECISION:
IS IT BASED ON WISHFUL THINKING?
4 REAL ESTATE LAW JOURNAL 61 (Summer, 1975)
JEROME G. ROSE

In Southern Burlington County NAACP v. Mt. Laurel, *the New Jersey Supreme Court struck down municipal zoning ordinances that exclude poor- or moderate-income families by such devices as prohibiting apartments or requiring single-family homes to be built on large lots. The court ruled that every developing municipality in the state has to provide for a fair share of the housing requirements of its surrounding region.*

In its brief life-span, this decision has become a landmark, criticized by some, hailed by others. Professor Rose, the editor-in-chief of Real Estate Law Journal, *examines the decision's components and analyzes the very fundamental questions of the judiciary's role in local matters raised by* Mount Laurel.

"The people of New Jersey should welcome the result reached by the Court in this case, not merely because it is required by our law, but more fundamentally, because the result is right and true to the highest American ideals." With these words, Justice Pashman, in his concurring opinion, set forth the New Jersey Supreme Court's underlying assumption in its decision to make the validity of municipal zoning dependent upon a new and complex standard. First, I will analyze the components of this newly created judicial standard of validity of municipal zoning; then I will examine the issue of whether its chances of success will be limited by political realities that conflict with the noble ideals upon which the decision is based.

Components of the Decision

The majority opinion, written by Justice Hall as his swan song after a brilliant career on the New Jersey Supreme Court, contains a contrived and carefully written collection of principles of planning and land-use law. Although all the principles are related to the extent that they seek to achieve a common objective, they are nevertheless separable into individual, distinct components, each of which is significant by itself and each of which may very well create a life of its own in the line of decisions certain to follow.

The Concept of "Fair Share"

The court has adopted the concept of "fair share" for allocating municipal responsibility for low- and moderate-income housing. There are at least four different criteria for defining "fair share":

(1) Allocation of an *equal share* of the obligation to each municipality;

(2) Allocation of responsibility for housing based upon *need;*

(3) Allocation of housing to achieve *economic and racial integration;* and

(4) The *suitability* of the jurisdiction to accommodate the housing.[1]

Although the court does not reject the possible use of any of the other three criteria of "fair share," it does require that at least the regional *need* for housing be considered. What the result may be where the regional *need* for housing in a given municipality conflicts with the *suitability* of that municipality to accommodate that need remains an unanswered question.

The Concept of "Region"

Municipal responsibility for housing goes beyond its own boundaries and includes the "**region**." The court does not define "region" except to say that its meaning will vary from situation to situation and that confinement of "region" to the county appears not to be realistic. By this determination, the Supreme Court has adopted the principle suggested by Judge Furman in the *Oakwood at Madison*[2] case that each municipality has a responsibility to meet the need for housing, not only for its own citizens but also for nonresidents living within the region who would like to move into the municipality. However, the Supreme Court has not adopted Judge Furman's suggestion that region be defined in terms of "the area from which in view of available employment and transportation, the population of the township would be drawn absent invalidly exclusionary zoning. . .", i.e., trip time to work.[3]

The Specific Municipal Act Required:
"To Affirmatively Afford an Opportunity"

Municipal attorneys and officials will be asking the question, "What does the court require us to do?" The court's answer to this question is, "Adopt a zoning ordinance that 'affirmatively affords an opportunity' for low- and moderate-income housing to be built within the jurisdiction." The court readily concedes that "courts do not build housing nor do municipalities." However, municipalities do have the responsibility to "make realistically possible the opportunity" for a variety and choice of housing for all categories of people who may desire to live there, including those with low and moderate incomes. The decision lists some of the requirements and proscriptions of a zoning ordinance that fulfills this responsibility: A valid zoning ordinance *must* permit multi-family housing; it *must* allow small dwellings on very small lots; it *must* permit high density zoning. A valid zoning ordinance *may not* impose bedroom or similar restrictions on multifamily housing; it *may not* impose "artificial and unjustifiable" minimum requirements as to lot size, building size; it *may not* zone for the benefit of the local tax rate (i.e., fiscal zoning is prohibited).

The Test of "Present and Prospective Regional Need"

A valid zoning ordinance must seek to meet the "**present and** *prospective* **regional need**" for low- and moderate-cost housing. The *present* need for low- and moderate-cost housing can be estimated reasonably accurately from existing date relating to population size, family income, number of existing units, vacancy rate, etc. However, the prediction of *prospective* (i.e., future) housing need is much more difficult. The accepted technique, adopted by Rutgers Center for Urban Policy Research[4] and the National Association of Housing and Redevelopment Officials[5] requires an initial prediction of the amount and type of commerce and industry that will move into the area. The income distribution of new residents is then based on the expected wage and salary levels of the jobs to be created by those employers. The number of housing units needed and the rent and cost range is, in turn, based upon that determination of income distribution. Even assuming that all of these calculations are performed with precision and accuracy, the final computation of *prospective housing need* can be no more accurate than the original prediction of the amount and type of commerce and industry that will move into the area. This prediction would seem to be a flimsy and debatable premise to base the validity of a municipal zoning ordinance.[6]

Requirement of a Relationship Between Residential and Industrial/Commercial Zones

For many years, proponents of open housing have argued that there is a municipal obligation to permit the construction of housing for the employees of the industries that provide the ratables. This argument was rejected in a recent federal district court decision that is presently being appealed.[7] The *Mount Laurel* decision, however, adopted this argument and determined that when a municipality zones for industry and commerce, it must zone to permit adequate housing for the employees who will work there. The difficulty with this concept is similar to the previous problem of predicting future housing needs. Both projections are dependent upon the accuracy of the prediction of the amount and type of industry and commerce that will in fact move into the area. However, as the officials of developing communities know well, the mere fact that land is zoned for commerce and industry is no assurance that such land will be used for those purposes within any foreseeable period of time. Does the obligation to permit housing arise upon the adoption of the ordinance designating industrial and commercial uses or does this obligation arise only when such land is *in fact* put to such uses? There are significant planning implications in either case, but this question is not answered by the decision.

State Constitutional Basis for the Decision

The majority opinion basis its decision upon state constitutional law, i.e., the state constitutional requirements of substantive due process and equal protection of the laws inherent in Article I, paragraph 1 of the New Jersey Constitution[8] and in the constitutional requirement that all police power regulations must promote the "general welfare." The state constitutional basis for the decision has two legal consequences: (1) It minimizes the possibility of appeal to the United States Supreme Court. It is possible, but unlikely, that the United States Supreme Court would determine that a federal question arises because of the interpretation of the meaning of "due process' and "equal protection," both of which are concepts originating in the United States Constitution. (2) It forecloses the possibility of having the decision overridden by the state legislature. If the decision were based upon a statutory interpretation of "general welfare,"[9] the New Jersey legislature, which is responsive to its substantially suburban constituency, could by simple majority supersede the decision by amending the zoning enabling legislation. This strategy, by which the court substitutes its political judgment in the place of the elected legislature, raises a fundamental issue to be discussed later in this article.

The Judicial Remedy

Although the high court sustained the trial court's ruling that the municipal ordinance is invalid, it modified the trial court's judgment in two important respects: (1) The court did not declare the zoning ordinance invalid *in toto*. Only those provisions of the zoning ordinance that are inconsistent with the opinion are invalid. The apparent purpose of this modification is to avoid a state of zoning anarchy that could put the municipality at the mercy of "voracious land speculators and developers." However, as each application for a building permit is made for construction which is not consistent with the zoning provisions, a litigable issue will arise whether the zoning provision in issue is or is not consistent with the opinion. (2) The court specifically vacated the trial court's judgment ordering the municipality to prepare and submit a housing study, and it thereby withdrew the judicial power, at this time, from the process of enforcing the above principles.[10] The court left compliance up to the municipality, initially, with the unexpressed threat of judicial intervention at a later stage if required.

Moral and Political Bases of the Decision

The eloquent opinions of Justices Hall and Pashman are based upon moral and political judgments that American ideals of equal opportunity and equality before the law are more than catchy platitudes to be resurrected and recited at quadrennial inaugural ceremonies and bicentennial independence celebrations. Both opinions have assumed that the suburban electorates and their municipal and state elected officials have forgotten these principles. Therefore, they need only be reminded by the judiciary of the historical and constitutional commitment to these principles and they will, with diligence—if not fervor—renounce their former transgressions and reaffirm these ideals. Simply put, the court has assumed that the suburban electorate—many of whom, at great cost and expense, have fled from the perceived and real dangers of city living to find relative safety and comfort in their socially homogeneous communities—will respond to the judicial mandate with the question, "What do we have to do to comply with this decision?"

Undoubtedly, there will be many who will respond in this manner. The judiciary performs the dual role of articulator of prevailing morality and at the same time is a formulator of emerging moral principles. In both roles, it imposes its principles with authority and persuasion in a law-abiding society. Many suburban communities will indeed respond sincerely and diligently with efforts to comply with this decision.

However, to much of the suburban community, the stakes are high, the perceived risks are great, and the impact of this decision is personal and direct. It remains to be determined what proportion of suburban residents will ask *not*, "How do we comply?" but rather, "How do we postpone, avoid, or even defy this decision?" This group will seek and find devices and techniques to protect its self-interest by avoiding the intended result of economic and racial integration.

It is much too soon to compile an exhaustive list of techniques that may be used to frustrate the goals of the *Mount Laurel* decision. However, a number of devices are self-evident.

Statistical Warfare

The implementation of this decision requires studies and reports based upon interpretations of such indeterminate and ambiguous concepts as "fair share," "region," "future housing need," and "presumptively realistic efforts to make possible an appropriate variety and choice of housing." Each concept must be quantified, for each municipality, in terms of numbers of housing units. This computation will be based upon underlying premises and theories of extrapolation about which competent and honest professional planners may differ. These differences in professional judgment can cause a wide disparity in the proposed number of housing units necessary to meet the requirements of the decision. It will be possible for a municipality to argue that with a minimum contribution of new housing, its zoning ordinance has met the prescribed standard of validity. A developer restricted by the ordinance will disagree, and the statistical issues will be joined and argued in the courts. The process of litigation has rarely been an inducement to housing construction.

Abetting Economic Realities

One of the many economic obstacles to the construction of housing for low- and moderate-income families is the fact that the land most appropriate for such residents is land that ideally should be within walking distance of shopping and public transportation. In developing communities, this land is frequently expensive because of these characteristics. However, even without such amenities, once an area is zoned for high-density development, its market value will rise to reflect its development potential. By careful and adroit planning and zoning, it would be possible to meet the requirements of the decision but at the same time designate land for multifamily dwelling use that becomes too expensive to build housing for low-and moderate-income families without substantial outside subsidies.

Ineffectual Efforts to Obtain Subsidies

At some stage of every discussion of the effect of "exclusionary zoning" upon the supply of housing for low- and moderate-income people, it becomes necessary to recall the fact that the removal of land-use restrictions alone will not result in the construction of such housing. Under prevailing costs of land, materials, labor, and financing, it is not possible in many areas to build housing that low-and moderate-income families can afford without some form of federal or state subsidy. The amount of funds available for these subsidies has traditionally been extremely limited and requires dedicated, diligent, and persistent efforts on the part of municipal officials to succeed in each application. Even after an application for funds is made and a "presumptively realistic effort to make possible an appropriate variety and choice of housing" is evidenced, that effort may fail as a result of an imperceivable (and difficult to prove) reduction in the diligent processing of the application. How long a period of failure in applications will be necessary before a court can conclude that a municipality's efforts have not been "presumptively realistic"?

Subterfuge and Cunning

The validity of a zoning ordinance of a developing community will depend upon evidence of its efforts to make low- and moderate-cost housing possible within the community. One recent proposal to provide such housing *without an outside subsidy* is the mandatory percentage of moderately priced dwelling (MPMPD) ordinance.[11] By the provisions of this type of ordinance, a developer is given a bonus in zoning density in return for his agreement to build a proportion of the units within the range of the moderate- and low-income market. Adoption of this type of ordinance would appear to be evidence of the kind of affirmative effort required by the decision. However, by skillful and crafty adjustment of the details of this program, it would be possible to raise the percentage of subsidized units, lower the income level of eligible tenants, provide for effective rent control of future leases, and otherwise administer the program in such a manner that would foreclose any possibility that the program will be utilized by any developer whose incentives include profit and investment protection.

Ecological Constraints

The opportunity for the use of ecological or environmental factors to justify limitations of housing development arises from the equivocal statements on the subject that appear in the opinion. On one hand, Justice Hall found that the environmental factors in Mount Laurel did not provide a sufficient excuse in itself to limit housing to single-family dwellings on large lots. But then he added, "This is not to say that land-use regulations should not take due account of ecological or environmental factors or problems. Quite the contrary. Their importance, at last being recognized, should always be considered." The state of the art of analysis and presentation of ecological and environmental evidence is at an early stage in its development. Professional planners are just now perfecting techniques and standards to describe the impact of various kinds of development on flooding, water supply, water pollution, air pollution and which cause other damage to the environment. This type of ecological information will provide the basis of arguments by idealistic and responsible members of the community for opposition to proposed housing construction.

Timed Growth Delays

A plan by which the sequential development of a community is programmed is not, per se, a device to frustrate the goals of the *Mount Laurel* decision. In fact, in the *Ramapo* decision in which a timed growth plan was upheld, the New York high court specifically found that the program was not intended to exclude population growth. However, the system does provide a device which can be used to postpone housing development until completion of capital improvement programs intended to serve the needs of future residents. Further extensions of time could be expected upon a showing of unanticipated problems. Ultimately, if low- and moderate-cost housing is not in fact produced, the program might be declared invalid or otherwise abandoned. But a substantial period of time could have elapsed before that happens, and the purposes of its advocates will have been served.

The availability of these and other devices that can be used to out-maneuver the judicial process suggests that the solution of this problem must come from an instrumentality of government other than the judiciary. What is needed is a responsive administrative mechanism that can issue regulations that remove ambiguities and close loopholes. This administrative agency would have to be empowered to define the "region," to determine "fair share," and to prescribe the range of land-use choices of each municipality. This agency would have to derive its authority from the state legislature, which is the only legitimate and effective instrumentality of government that has the mandate to make the kinds of policy judgments on which the *Mount Laurel* decision is based. If the state legislature is unable to create a workable consensus by the political processes of negotiation and accommodation of conflicting interests to resolve the underlying policy issues, then it is fair to ask whether the underlying goals of the *Mount Laurel* decision are presently achievable or whether they are based upon the wistful hopes of an idealistic but credulous court.

---

[1] For a discussion of the problems created by each of these criteria for defining "fair share," see Rose, "Some Unresolved Issues of Exclusionary Zoning and Managed Growth," 6 Rutgers Camden L.J. 689 (Spring 1975).

[2] Oakwood at Madison, Inc. v. Madison Township, 117 N.J. Super. 11, 283 A.2d 353 (1971), *on remand* 127 N.J. Super. 438, 320 A.2d 223 (1974), *appeal docketed.*

[3] For a discussion of some of the problems involved in using the "trip-time to work" definition of "region," see Rose, note 1 *supra.*

[4] See James & Hughes, *Modeling State Growth: New Jersey 1980* (Rutgers Center for Urban Policy Research 1973).

[5] See Alexander & Nenno, *A Local Housing Assistance Plan: A NAHRO Guidebook* 27 (National Association of Housing and Redevelopment Officials 1974).

[6] For a discussion of some of the problems involved in the methodology for the computation of prospective housing need, see Rose, note 1 *supra.*

[7] Metropolitan Housing Dev. Corp. v. Arlington Heights, 373 F. Supp. 208 (N.D. Ill. 1974), *appeal docketed.*

[8] It is interesting to note that this provision of the New Jersey Constitution does not expressly contain the phrases "due process" or "equal protection of the laws." The section referred to by the court provides as follows:

> All persons are by nature free and independent, and have certain natural and unalienable rights, among which are those of enjoying and defending life and liberty, of acquiring, possessing, and protecting property, and of pursuing and obtaining safety and happiness.

N.J. Const. Art. I, ¶ 1.

[9] Justice Mountan wrote a short concurring opinion in which he said that he reaches the same conclusion as the majority but he bases his decision on the interpretation of "general welfare" as it appears in the zoning enabling legislation, rather than on the state consitution.

[10] Justice Pashman wrote a long concurring opinion in which he said that he differs with the majority only in that he would have preferred to have the Court implement the principles contained in the majority opinion.

[11] For a discussion of this technique see Rose, "The Mandatory Percentage of Moderately Priced Dwelling Ordinance (MPMPD) Is the Latest Technique of Inclusionary Zoning," 3 Real Estate L.J. 176 (1974).

(2) A Partial Retreat From Mount Laurel

OAKWOOD AT MADISON, INC., et al.
v. THE TOWNSHIP OF MADISON
72 N.J. 481, 371 A.2d. 1192 (1977)

The opinion of the Court was delivered by CONFORD, P.J.A.D. (temporarily assigned).

We today review the decision of Judge Furman invalidating the 1973 amendatory zoning ordinance of defendant Township of Madison. That determination culminated an action instituted by plaintiffs in November 1970 challenging the validity of a zoning ordinance adopted by the township in September 1970 to replace a previous one in effect since 1964. Judge Furman had invalidated the 1970 ordinance in *Oakwood at Madison, Inc. v. Tp. of Madison,* but at the same time rejected an attack by plaintiffs on the constitutionality of the enabling zoning statute, N.J.S.A. 40:55-30 *et seq. Id.* at 16 * * *

Oral argument was originally heard by the court on March 5, 1973, and additional argument was requested for January 8, 1974. However, on October 1, 1973 Madison Township adopted a major amendment to the 1970 ordinance. Consequently, on January 8, 1974, while retaining jurisdiction, we remanded the action to the trial court for a trial and ruling on the ordinance as amended, with the result stated above * * *

Plaintiffs herein comprise two groups. Oakwood at Madison, Inc. and Beren Corporation (hereinafter "corporate plaintiffs"), both New Jersey corporations, were developers owning a tract of vacant developable land of some 400 acres, the disputed Oakwood-Beren tract. Six individuals were low income persons acknowledged by the trial judge as "representing as a class those who reside outside the township and have sought housing there unsuccessfully." *Oakwood at Madison Inc. v. Tp. of Madison.* Plaintiffs alleged, *inter alia,* (a) that the exclusionary nature of the ordinance rendered it unconstitutional; (b) that the enabling legislation was unconstitutional in its failure to provide adequate standards for municipal exercise of the zoning power; and (c) that the restrictive effect of the ordinance as applied to corporate plaintiffs' property rendered it confiscatory * * *

While the 1973 amendatory ordinance transferred substantial areas from large lot to smaller lot zoning, made more land available for multi-family development and provided for planned unit development (PUD) and "cluster" zones, the evidence in the case convinced the court that the municipality still was not satisfying its obligation to "provide its fair share of the housing needs of the region," particularly in relation to the low-income and moderate-income population. The amended ordinance was therefore again struck down in its entirety. *Ibid.*

The main lines of the Law Division opinion striking down the 1973 ordinance may be summarized as follows. A crisis in housing needs continues, most serious for those of low and moderate income. The region, whose housing needs must reasonably be provided for by such municipalities as Madison, is not necessarily coextensive with Middlesex County. "Rather, it is the area from which, in view of available employment and transportation, the population of the township would be drawn, absent invalidly exclusionary zoning."* * *

The court assessed Madison Township's obligation to provide its fair share of regional housing needs as follows:

> Without the rigidity of a mathematical formula this court holds that Madison Township's obligation to provide its fair share of the housing needs of its region is not met unless its zoning ordinance approximates in additional housing unit capacity the same proportion of low-income housing as its present low-income population, about 12%, and the same proportion of moderate-income housing as its present moderate-income population, about 19%. The amended zoning ordinance under review falls palpably short and must be struck down in its entirety. *Id.* at 447.

The court did not specify any absolute numerical quota of low and moderate income units the ordinance would be expected to render possible, but found that annual needs "into the 1980's were 750 to 1000 units, 500 to 600 of those low and moderate income." * * *

In the absence of legislation providing for regional zoning authorities, while municipalities are empowered to zone individually, they must nevertheless (if of the "developing" category described in *Mount Laurel*), by their zoning regulations serve and not impede the general welfare represented by satisfaction of the housing needs of lower income people throughout the region.

I

Outline of Major Issues

The judgment of the trial court, the intervention of our decision in *Mount Laurel* and the nature of the record and briefs before us combine to cast the issues for determination as follows:

1. Is the Madison 1973 zoning ordinance exclusionary, i.e., whether or not so intended, does it operate in fact to preclude the opportunity to supply any substantial amounts of new housing for low and moderate income households now and prospectively needed in the municipality and in the appropriate region of which it forms a part?

2. If, as we have concluded, the affirmative response to the foregoing question by the trial court should be sustained, is it incumbent upon the courts, pursuant to *Mount Laurel*, to demarcate a pertinent region and to fix a specific number of lower-cost housing units as the "fair share" of the regional need therefor to be made possible by the Madison ordinance?

3. If, as we have concluded, the foregoing question should be answered

in the negative, what kind of an order should be made to assure Madison's compliance, as a developing municipality, with *Mount Laurel's* mandate that its zoning ordinance "afford the opportunity" for at least "the municipality's fair share of the present and prospective regional need" for "decent and adequate low and moderate income housing"?

II
"Fair Share" and "Region"
Preliminary Considerations

As noted above, the prime question before us, in *Mount Laurel* terms, is whether the trial court has correctly found that Madison's zoning ordinance does not provide the opportunity to meet a fair share of the regional burden for low and moderate income housing needs* * *

However, we deem it well to establish at the outset that we do not regard it as mandatory for developing municipalities whose ordinances are challenged as exclusionary to devise specific. formulae for estimating their precise fair share of the lower income housing needs of a specifically demarcated region. Nor do we conceive it as necessary for a trial court to make findings of that nature in a contested case. Firstly, numerical housing goals are not realistically translatable into specific substantive changes in a zoning ordinance by any technique revealed to us by our study of the data before us. There are too many imponderables between a zone change and the actual production of housing on sites as zoned, not to mention the production of a specific number of lower cost units in a given period of time. Municipalities do not themselves have the duty to build or subsidize housing. Secondly, the breadth of approach by the experts to the factor of the appropriate region and to the criteria for allocation of regional housing goals to municipal "subregions" is so great and the pertinent economic and sociological considerations so diverse as to preclude judicial dictation or acceptance of any one solution as authoritative. For the same reasons, we would not mandate the formula approach as obligatory on any municipality seeking to correct a fair share deficiency* * *

III
Madison—Its Growth and Development

Madison Township consists of approximately 42 square miles, or 25,000 acres, in the southeast corner of Middlesex County, of which almost 40% is vacant developable land. Its location with the gap between the metropolitan centers of New York and Philadelphia is a strategic one: this "Atlantic urban region" gap is expected to be bridged within the next 25 years, with a concomitant population increase of 75%. The Tri-State Regional Planning Association (covering counties in New York, New Jersey and Connecticut and including Middlesex) predicts that Middlesex will be one of four counties to experience the greatest rates of growth in the tri-state area from 1970 to 2000 * * *

Madison is an archetypal "developing" municipality within the contemplation of the *Mount Laurel* specifications. During the past 25 years, it has experienced explosive growth. Its population increased over two decades by 561%, from 7,366 in 1950 to 48,715 in 1970. This boom has continued, with the population climbing to 50,000 by the time of the first trial and 55,000 by the second in 1974. With the growth and concomitant municipal problems came a steady rise in tax rates * * *

Thus the overall pattern of land use confronting Madison Township planners and officials in 1970 was one of substantial but scattered residential growth, with little industrial and commercial development. The 1970 ordinance was a hurried effort to slow population growth and the accompanying rise in the tax rate and largely to confine new population to designated areas.

IV
The Zoning Ordinances
A. The 1970 Ordinance

For present purposes the salient provisions of the 1970 ordinance are adequately summarized in the first opinion of the trial court. The patent intent and effect of the ordinance was to prevent construction of a substantial number of homes or apartments, particularly at low-cost. Most of the land area was zoned for one-or two-acre single family homes—uses not only beyond the reach of 90% of the general population but also responsive to little if any existing market. *Ibid.* It goes without saying that the ordinance was clearly violative of the principles later enunciated in *Mount Laurel.* Judge Furman properly condemned it as pure "fiscal zoning," not taking into consideration "[h]ousing needs of the region" and failing to promote "reasonably a balanced and well ordered plan for the entire municipality".

B. The 1973 Ordinance

The 1973 ordinance extensively revised the land use restrictions of the prior ordinance. The amount of land zoned nonresidential (commercial, office and industrial) was decreased by 760 acres from 19.80% to 16.70% of the total. A new "open space" zone–RP or Recreation-Preservation–was created * * *

Although the fact was not stressed at trial, Madison has placed more than 4,000 acres in zones restricted to industrial and office uses despite the fact that only some 600 acres have ever been devoted to that use. By comparison, we criticized Mount Laurel for zoning 4,100 acres industrial although only 100 acres had ever been so used.

The 1973 ordinance considerably increased the facial housing potential of the prior ordinance. It enlarged the total acreage available therefor by 800 acres and the potential housing capacity, inclusive of existing housing, by 16,000 units or 46,000 persons. These figures, supplied by the Madison Township Housing Study, may be misleading, as they assume all acreage zoned residential is or will be developed to its maximum permissible density whereas some of it is already developed, either non-residential or below permissible density, or is undevelopable * * *

Madison Township relies heavily on provisions in the 1973 ordinance for PUDs (planned unit developments) and clustering to satisfy its obligation with respect to low and moderate income housing. On the evidence, that reliance is illusory * * *

The cluster provisions (a PUD variation, not including commercial uses) apply to any lands in the R-40 or R-80 zones not alternatively designated PUD. Under the cluster provisions, a developer is allowed to build at increased densities if he preserves a proportion of his land as open space, public purpose space or donated public purpose space * * *

The credible proofs indicate that the clustering provisions are unlikely to have a significant impact on the cost of housing as the low densities and limits on numbers of attached units make significant economies of scale unlikely, and therefore, according to plaintiffs' experts, cluster development may not occur at all. Yet even under the cluster provisions costs would be prohibitive to most lower income families * * *

The distribution of vacant and developable acreage (and total acreage) among the various zones under the ordinance shows that low density, middle and high income residential uses are strongly-favored. Only a maximum of 2.37% of the town's vacant developable residential acreage is zoned for multi-family apartments (AF), and the correct figure may be as low as 1.02% or 0.84%. An additional 2% is zoned R-7 for small lot attached double houses. Though 9.9% is zoned for PUD development, the location of two of the three PUD tracts makes their development highly unlikely. Using the township planner's estimates of the potential future building capacity under the 1973 ordinance, the R-7 and AF zones account for a maximum of 16% of all housing units. By contrast, the R-80, R-40 and open space zones account for over 71% of the vacant developable residential acreage and over 41% of the housing units. If the R-15 and R-20 zones are counted, the large-lot single-family acreage figure increases to 82% and the unit figure to almost 50% * * *

V
"Least Cost" versus "Low and Moderate Income" Housing * * *

To the extent that the builders of housing in a developing municipality like Madison cannot through publicly assisted means or appropriately legislated incentives (as to which, see *infra*) provide the municipality's fair share of the regional need for lower income housing, it is incumbent on the governing body to adjust its zoning regulations so as to render possible and feasible the "least cost" housing, consistent with minimum standards of health and safety, which private industry will undertake, and in amounts sufficient to satisfy the deficit in the hypothesized fair share. * * *

Nothing less than zoning for least cost housing will, in the indicated circumstances, satisfy the mandate of *Mount Laurel*. While compliance with that direction may not provide *newly constructed* housing for all in the lower income categories mentioned, it will nevertheless through the "filtering down" process referred to by defendant tend to augment the total supply of available housing in such manner as will indirectly provide additional and better housing for the insufficiently and inadequately housed of the region's lower income population * * *

It will be apparent from our survey of the facts and the discussion hereinafter that the 1973 ordinance under review not only fails to provide directly for Madison's fair share of the region's low and moderate income housing needs but also is not geared to satisfy such a share in terms of "least cost" housing in the sense just described. The failure will be seen to be both quantitative and qualitative. Insufficient areas are zoned to permit such housing, and the zoning restrictions are such as to prevent production of units at least cost consistent with health and safety requirements.

VI
Incapacity of the 1973 Ordinance to
Effect Adequate Lower Income Housing

In summation of this point, the 1973 Ordinance is shown not to provide the opportunity for a substantial amount of new housing which could be available to the lower income segments of the population. This failure arises from both (a) the inadequacy or non-existence of areas zoned for homes on very small lots or for multi-family housing; and (b) the undue cost-generating features inherent in the ordinance which raise the expense of purchasing or renting new housing units above the reach of the great majority of the lower income population * * *

VIII
"Fair Share" and "Region"
—General Consideration

Of primary significance is the difference between the situation of an administrative planning agency functioning under authorizing legislation and that of a court dealing with an attack by litigation on the adequacy of the zoning ordinance of an isolated municipality. The former is dealing with a comprehensive, predetermined region and can render or delegate the making of allocations with relative fairness to all of the constituent municipalities or other subregions within its jurisdiction. Moreover, it presumably has expertise suited to the task. The correlative disadvantages of a court adjudicating an individual dispute are obvious.

The formulation of a plan for the fixing of the fair share of the regional need for lower income housing attributable to a particular developing municipality, although clearly envisaged in *Mount Laurel* 189-190, involves highly controversial economic, sociological and policy questions of innate difficulty and complexity. Where predictive responses are called for they are apt to be speculative or conjectural. These observations are supported not only by the published literature but by the proofs and comprehensive briefs supplied us by the parties and *amici*.

Some of the problems catalogued above were touched upon in *Mount Laurel*, e.g., "region," 190; incidence of subsidized construction in contemplation, sources of reliance for "fair share" guidance, quantity of needed housing reasonably expectable under proper zoning. We take this occasion to make explicit what we adumbrated in *Mount Laurel* and have intimated above—that the governmental-sociological-economic enterprise of seeing to the provision and allocation throughout appropriate regions of adequate and suitable housing for all categories of the population is much more appropriately a legislative and administrative function rather than a judicial function to be exercised in the disposition of isolated cases. Fortuately, the other branches of government are giving the matter their attention. But unless and until other appropriate governmental machinery is effectively brought to bear the courts have no choice, when an ordinance is challenged on *Mount Laurel* grounds, but to deal with this vital public welfare matter as effectively as is consistent with the limitations of the judicial process * * *

We thus proceed to formulation of our position as to the concept of region in the context of an *ad hoc* application of *Mount Laurel* principles to a single litigated ordinance, having in mind our determination in II, *supra*, that it would not generally be. serviceable to employ a formulaic approach to determination of a particular municipality's fair share. We conclude that, in general, there is no specific geographical area which is necessarily the authoritative region as to any single municipality in litigation. Different experts may quite reasonably differ in their concepts of the pertinent region. But in evaluating any expert testimony in terms of the *Mount Laurel* rationale, weight should be given to the degree to which the expert gives consideration to the areas from which the lower income population of the municipality would *substantially* be drawn absent exclusionary zoning. (Evidence of the historical sources of a municipality's population, among other indicia, is relevant thereto.) This is broadly comparable to the concept of the relevant housing market area, to which there has been prior reference herein * * *

Harking back to our statement in II as to why we proposed in this opinion to discuss the concepts of fair share and region notwithstanding that we would not, nor would we require the trial court to specify a pertinent region or fix a fair share housing quota for Madison, we summarize the observations in VII and VIII as follows:

1. Based upon our analysis and findings in IV and VI, the 1973 ordinance is clearly deficient in meeting Madison's obligation to share in providing the opportunity for lower cost housing needed in the region, whether or not the specific fair share estimates submitted by defendant are acceptable. Those estimates are, in any event, defective at least in not including prospective need beyond 1975.

2. The objective of a court before which a zoning ordinance is challenged on *Mount Laurel* grounds is to determine whether it realistically permits the opportunity to provide a fair and reasonable share of the region's need for housing for the lower income population.

3. The region referred to in 2 is that general area which constitutes, more or less, the housing market area of which the subject municipality is a part, and from which the prospective population of the municipality would substantially be drawn, in the absence of exclusionary zoning.

4. Fair share allocation studies submitted in evidence may be given

such weight as they appear to merit in the light of statements 2 and 3 above. But the court is not required, in the determination of the matter, itself to adopt fair share housing quotas for the municipality in question or to make findings in reference thereto.

IX
Environmental Considerations

As noted above, a considerable amount of vacant acreage in Madison borders certain streams or comprises important acquifer storage and discharge areas. Depositions and counter-depositions were taken by defendant and plaintiffs, respectively, bearing upon the effect of development of varying kinds on such areas as Burnt Fly Bog, the Old Bridge Sands, Raritan Bay beachfront, the salt marshes behind Raritan Bay and the four streams flowing into South River. Defendant offered the depositions at the trial to establish that certain areas zoned R-80, R-40 and RP were so sensitive to flood, water contamination and related problems that they should be kept from development at all or restricted to very low residential density. The trial judge declined to consider this evidence on the ground that considerable other land, free from such ecological considerations, and amenable to higher density development, was available within the township with which it could meet its fair share obligation for its own and the region's housing needs.

Plaintiffs' experts testified on depositions that the answer to the ecological problems posed was not prohibition or regulation of the density of development *per se* but careful use of the land, with adequate controls in respect of construction, sewerage, water control and treatment, sufficient open space per structure and other services.

Ecological and environmental considerations were also advanced by the municipality in *Mount Laurel* to justify large lot zoning throughout the township. We pointed out given consideration in zoning "the danger and impact must be substantial and very real (the construction of every building or the improvement of every plot has some environmental impact)—not simply a makeweight to support exclusionary housing measures or preclude growth * * *

Notwithstanding the foregoing, we conclude the trial court erred in not receiving in evidence and giving consideration to the environmental depositions mentioned.

X
"Affirmative Action" for Lower
Income Housing

Plaintiffs and supporting *amici* press for a judicial mandate that developing municipalities be required affirmatively to act for creation of additional lower income housing in more ways than by eliminating zoning restrictions militating against that objective. Of the devices which have been suggested to this end, tax concessions and mandatory sponsorship of or membership in public housing projects must be summarily rejected. Tax concessions would unquestionably require enabling legislation and perhaps constitutional amendment. While we have described the sponsorship of public housing projects as a moral obligation of the municipality in certain specified circumstances, we have no lawful basis for imposing such action as obligatory. It goes without saying, however, that the zoning in every developing municipality must erect no bar or impediment to the creation and administration of public housing projects in appropriate districts. * * *

XII
Relief for Corporate Plaintiffs

The corporate plaintiffs contend that the 1973 ordinance is invalid not only generally, as exclusionary of lower income housing, but specifically as to their own tract of land because of zoning restrictions which are confiscatory. They therefore ask that the court specifically order the township to place their property in an appropriate multi-family or PUD zone to be created—in effect, to grant them a permit to build the kind of moderate-to-middle income housing they have in mind * * *.

A consideration pertinent to the interests of justice in this situation, however, is the fact that corporate plaintiffs have borne the stress and expense of this public-interest litigation, albeit for private purposes, for six years and have prevailed in two trials and on this extended appeal, yet stand in danger of having won but a pyrrhic victory. A mere invalidation of the ordinance, if followed only by more zoning for multi-family or lower income housing elsewhere in the township, could well leave corporate plaintiffs unable to execute their project. There is a respectable point of view that in such circumstances a successful litigant like the corporate plaintiffs should be awarded specific relief * * *

Such judicial action, moreover, creates an incentive for the institution of socially beneficial but costly litigation such as this and *Mount Laurel* and serves the utilitarian purpose of getting on with the provision of needed housing for at least some portion of the moderate income elements of the population. We have hereinabove referred to the indirect housing benefits to low income families from the ample provision of new moderate and middle income housing.

The foregoing considerations have persuaded us of the appropriateness in this case of directing the issuance to the corporate plaintiffs, subject to the conditions stated *infra*, of a permit for the development on their property of the housing project they proposed to the township prior to or during the pendency of the action, pursuant to plans which, as they originally represented, will guarantee the allocation of at least 20% of the units to low or moderate income families. This direction will be executed under the enforcement and supervision of the trial judge in such manner as to assure compliance with reasonable building code, site-plan, water, sewerage and other requirements and considerations of health and safety.

An express condition of this holding, moreover, is that the trial court, after consideration of the ecological and environmental proofs referred to in IX, *supra*, determine that the plaintiff's land is environmentally suited to the degree of density and type of development plaintiffs propose. Subject to these conditions it is our purpose to assure the issuance of a building permit to corporate plaintiffs within the very early future.

XIII
Remedy and Remand

We herewith modify the judgment entered in the Law Division to hold, as we did in *Mount Laurel* as to the ordinance there involved, that the 1973 zoning ordinance is invalid, not *in toto*, but only "to the extent and in the particulars set forth in this opinion." For the reasons elaborated above the ordinance is presumptively contrary to the general welfare and beyond the scope of the zoning power in the particulars mentioned. The municipality has not borne its consequent burden of establishing valid reasons for the deficiencies of the ordinance. It is obvious that a revision of the residential provisions of the ordinance is called for in order to provide the opportunity for that amount of least-cost housing in the township which will comply with the directions contained in this opinion.

In *Mount Laurel* we elected not to impose direct judicial supervision of compliance with the judgment "in view of the advanced view of zoning law as applied to housing by [the] opinion". The present case is different. The basic law is by now settled. Further, the defendant was correctly advised by the trial court as to its responsibilities in respect of regional housing needs in October 1971, over five years ago. It came forth with an amended ordinance which has been found to fall short of its obligation. Considerations bearing upon the public interest, justice to plaintiffs and efficient judicial administration preclude another generalized remand for another unsupervised effort by the defendant to produce a satisfactory ordinance. The focus of the judicial effort after six years of litigation must now be transferred from theorizing over zoning to assurance of the zoning opportunity for production of least cost housing.

The trial court on remand shall execute the directions in IX and XII above and render its findings thereon with the reasonable dispatch appropriate to the age of this litigation. It shall become the obligation of the defendant, within 90 days thereafter, unless more time is allowed by the trial court, to submit to the trial court for its approval a revised ordinance.

The revision shall zone, in the manner specified in this opinion, to create the opportunity for a fair and reasonable share of the least cost housing needs of Madison's region, the 'concept of "region" to be understood as generally set forth in II and VIII hereinabove. While no formulaic determination or numerical specification of such a fair and reasonable share is required, we do not preclude it if the municipal planning advisors deem it useful. The revision shall, as *minima:* (a) allocate substantial areas for single-family dwellings on very small lots; (b) substantially enlarge the areas for dwellings on moderate sized lots; (c) substantially enlarge the AF district or create other enlarged multi-family zones; (d) reduce the RP, R-80 and R-40 zones to the extent necessary to effect the foregoing, subject to the directions in IX, *supra;* (e) modify the restrictions in the AF zones and PUD areas discussed hereinabove which discourage the construction of apartments of more than two bedrooms; (f) modify the PUD regulations to eliminate the undue cost-generating requirements specified above; and (g) generally eliminate and reduce undue cost-generating restrictions in the zones allocated to the achievement of lower income housing in accordance with the principles of least cost zoning set forth in V hereinabove.

The trial court shall have discretion, in the event of undue delay in compliance with this opinion or of a finding by the court that any zoning revision submitted by defendant fails to comply with this opinion, to appoint an impartial zoning and planning expert or experts. Such expert may be directed to file a report or to testify, as the court may deem appropriate, as to a recommendation for the achievement by defendant of compliance with this opinion or with any further directions by the court pursuant thereto. * * *

Judgment modified, and affirmed as modified; no costs.

**OAKWOOD AT MADISON: A TACTICAL RETREAT
BY THE NEW JERSEY SUPREME COURT
JEROME G. ROSE
13 URBAN LAW ANNUAL 3 (1977)**

After over six years of litigation, the New Jersey Supreme Court finally rendered its decision in *Oakwood at Madison v. Township of Madison*. In a 4 to 3 decision, written by Justice Conford and with separate opinions written by Justices Clifford, Mountain, Pashman and Schreiber, the court made a tactical decision to withdraw its troops (i.e. the trial courts) from the losing battle of "statistical warfare" involved in the legislative-administrative process of defining "region" and allocating a "fair share" of regional housing needs to municipalities which appeared to be required by *Southern Burlington County NAACP v. Township of Mount Laurel*.

Oakwood at Madison is the New Jersey Supreme Court's latest word in the litigation that gave rise to the concept of a municipal obligation to provide for a fair share of regional housing needs adopted by the court in *Mount Laurel*. The litigation started in September 1970 when the developer-plaintiff brought an action challenging the validity of the Madison Township zoning ordinance.

The trial court held the zoning ordinance invalid on the grounds that "it fail[ed] to promote reasonably a balanced community in accordance with the general welfare." The decision also said that in defining a "balanced community, a municipality must not ignore housing needs, that is, its fair proportion of the obligation to meet the housing needs of its own population and of the region." This decision was appealed to the New Jersey Supreme Court and was scheduled for argument in March, 1973 and again in January, 1974, together with oral argument in the *Mount Laurel* case. However, because Madison Township had adopted a major amendment to the zoning ordinance the New Jersey Supreme Court remanded the *Oakwood at Madison* case to the trial court for a ruling upon the effect on the amended ordinance. The Supreme Court then rendered a decision in the *Mount Laurel* case.

After a hearing on remand, the trial court held that the township's obligation to provide its fair share of the housing needs of its region is not met unless its zoning ordinance approximates in additional housing unit capacity the same proportion of low income housing as its present low income and moderate income population. The trial court found that the amended ordinance did not meet this test and the entire ordinance was therefore invalid. In defining "region," the housing needs of which must be met by the township, the trial court said that the region is not coextensive with the county, "rather it is the area from which in view of available employment and transportation the population of the township would be drawn absent invalidly exclusionary zoning."

Upon return of the appeal to the supreme court, oral argument was presented twice with emphasis placed upon the effect of the *Mount Laurel* decision that had been rendered in the intervening period. The New Jersey Supreme Court affirmed the judgment with modifications. In the majority opinion, written by Justice Conford, the legal issues of the case were broken down into three questions: (1) Is the zoning ordinance exclusionary? (2) Should the trial court demarcate the "region" and determine the "fair share" of regional need? and (3) What is the proper judicial remedy?

In answering the first question, whether the zoning ordinance is exclusionary, the court made it clear that a zoning ordinance is "exclusionary" if it "operates in fact to preclude the opportunity to supply any substantial amounts of new housing for low and moderate income households now and prospectively needed in the municipality and in the appropriate region" whether or not such effect was intended. Thus the New Jersey Supreme Court has taken a position that squarely contravenes the position taken by the United States Supreme Court a few weeks earlier in *Village of Arlington Heights v. Metropolitan Housing Development Corp.* In *Arlington Heights* the United States Supreme Court upheld the refusal of a municipality to zone to permit subsidized multifamily housing because there was insufficient evidence to show a racially discriminatory *intent* even though such a refusal had a racially discriminatory *effect*. In *Oakwood at Madison,* the New Jersey Supreme Court held that a zoning ordinance may be "exclusionary" without a showing of exclusionary *intent.*

The test established by the New Jersey Supreme Court is whether the zoning ordinance operates *in fact* to preclude the opportunity for the requisite share of low and moderate income housing to be built. Under this new test it is not necessary for the municipality "to devise specific formulae for estimating [a] precise fair share of the lower income housing needs of a specifically demarcated region." Nor is it necessary for a trial court to make such findings. What is necessary under the *Oakwood at Madison* test is a "bona fide" effort by the municipality toward the elimination or minimization of undue cost-generating requirements in the zoning ordinance. In the language of the court:

> To the extent that the builders of housing in a developing municipality like Madison cannot through publicly assisted means or appropriately legislated incentives . . . provide the municipality's fair share of the regional need for lower income housing, it is incumbent on the governing body to adjust its zoning regulations so as to render possible and feasible the "least cost" housing, consistent with minimum standards of health and safety, which private industry will undertake, and in amounts sufficient to satisfy the deficit in the hypothesized fair share.

Under this standard for evaluating the exclusionary effect of a zoning ordinance the court held the Madison ordinance invalid because (1) it designated insufficient areas for very small lots and multi-family housing; (2) it contained undue cost generating features such as requirements for roads and utilities; (3) it failed to provide for *prospective* regional need for lower cost housing beyond 1975.

The primary contribution of the *Oakwood at Madison* decision may be its admonition to the trial courts to withdraw from the process of "demarcating the region" and determining the "fair share" of the municipality. The court observed that this process "involves highly controversial economic, sociological and policy questions of innate difficulty and complexity. Where predictive responses are called for they are apt to be speculative or conjectural." In a statement that may have only limited significance, the court articulated the constitutional truism that this process "is much more appropriately a legislative function rather than a judicial function to be exercized in the disposition of isolated cases." Nevertheless, after indicating its awareness of the existence and importance of the fundamental principle of separation of powers in our legal system, the court stated:

> But unless and until other appropriate governmental machinery is effectively brought to bear the courts have no choice, when an ordinance is challenged on *Mount Laurel* grounds, but to deal with this vital public welfare matter as effectively as is consistent with the limitations of the judicial process.

These preliminary statements alone would have left unanswered the question of how the trial courts will deal with the concepts of "region" and "fair share" when the validity of a municipal zoning ordinance is challenged in an action before them. The opinion, however, continues and provides some guidelines. Generally, the court concluded that "there is no specific geographical area which is necessarily the authoritative region as to any single municipality in litigation." The objective of the trial courts is to determine whether the zoning ordinance "realistically permits the opportunity to provide a fair and reasonable share of the region's need for housing for the lower income population." The technical details of the basis for fair share allocations of regional goals among municipalities are not as important "as the consideration that the gross regional goal shared by the constituent municipalities be large enough fairly to reflect the full needs of the housing market of which the subject municipality forms a part." The court then indicated its approval of the trial court's definition of "region" as "the area from which, in view of available employment and transportation, the population of the township would be drawn absent exclusionary zoning." The court also reaffirmed the statement by Justice Hall in *Mount Laurel* that "confinement to or within a certain county appears not to be realistic, but restriction within the boundaries of the state seems practical and advisable." The opinion predicted that an official fair share housing study of a group of counties or municipalities conducted under the auspices of a regional agency pursuant to the governor's Executive Order No. 35 would be entitled to prima facie judicial acceptance.

On the question of the computation of the "fair share" allocation for the defendant municipality, the court was equally circumspect. The court noted that "because of the conjectural nature of such calculations, utilization of the court as the forum for determining a municipality's fair share may result in 'statistical warfare' between the litigants." Nevertheless, the court acknowledged that "fair share studies by expert witnesses may be of substantial evidential value to a trial court." The opinion then summarized the court's conclusion on this issue.

> Fair share allocation studies submitted in evidence may be given such weight as they appear to merit in the light of [our above conclusions]. But the court is not required, in the determination of the matter, itself to adopt fair share housing quotas for the municipality in question or to make findings in reference thereto.

After setting forth these general principles relating to the fair share allocation to municipalities, the court directed its attention to the specific issue of the relevance of ecological and environmental considerations in this process. Evidence had been offered at the trial relating to the adverse environmental impact of the proposed development upon the surrounding area. The trial court had declined to consider this evidence because there was a substantial amount of other land free from such environmental impact available in the municipality with which the fair share of its regional housing needs could be met. The supreme court ruled that the trial court had erred in not receiving in evidence and considering these environmental factors. The court said:

> It is not an answer to say there is ample other land capable of being deployed for lower income housing. The municipality has the option of zoning areas for such housing anywhere within its borders consistent with all relevant considerations as to suitability. . . .

To prevent future litigants from generalizing too broadly from this statement, the court repeated its statement in the *Mount Laurel* decision that although ecological and environmental factors may be considered in zoning "the danger and impact must be substantial and very real (the construction of every building or the improvement of every plat has some environmental impact)—not simply a makeweight to support exclusionary housing measures or preclude growth."

To prospective developers of higher density housing in suburban communities the most significant part of the *Oakwood at Madison* decision may be the order of the court directing the issuance of a permit for the development of the housing project proposed by the developer-plaintiff. The order, however, was made subject to the condition that the developer comply with its representation that it will guarantee the allocation of at least 20% of the units to low or moderate income families. However, the court did subject the enforcement of the order to the supervision of the trial court to assure compliance with local regulations and to determine whether the developer's land is environmentally suited to the degree and density and type of development proposed.

In addition, the court ordered the municipality to submit to the trial court for its approval a revised zoning ordinance that would, among other things, allocate more land for single family houses on small lots, allocate more land for multi-family units, eliminate provisions resulting in bedroom restrictions and eliminate undue cost-generating requirements. The trial court is specifically authorized, in its discretion, to appoint an impartial zoning and planning expert or experts, to assist in the process.

The full significance of an important judicial decision is seldom immediately discernible. It is often necessary for some time to elapse before the many complex ideas can be ascertained and interrelated with each other and with the realities of the world in which they will be applied. Some first impressions may be of interest:

The *Oakwood at Madison* decision reaffirms the *Mount Laurel* principle that the zoning ordinance of every developing municipality must afford the opportunity for the municipality's "fair share" of the present and prospective regional need for low and moderate income housing. Although the role of the trial courts is to be more constrained, the test of validity of a municipal zoning ordinance will continue to be based upon the answers to such questions as (1) What is the "region?" (2) What is "fair share?" (3) What is the present housing need?" (4) What is the prospective housing need?"

In *Oakwood at Madison* the New Jersey Supreme Court has paid homage to the constitutional principle of separation of powers and to the concept of judicial restraint. The court has recognized the impropriety of judges engaging in the legislative and administrative processes necessary to define "region" and calculate "fair share." The Court has at the same time, however, made it clear that it intends to retain such judicial power as is necessary to protect and preserve the integrity of the judicial process. Having found in *Mount Laurel* that exclusionary zoning violates the state constitution, the court does not intend to abandon the judicial power to enforce its ruling. The *Oakwood at Madison* decision should not be interpreted as a weakening of the court's resolve the outlaw exclusionary zoning. The decision is based instead upon a tactic designed to consolidate the judicial forces into a position which will be less vulnerable to direct attack.

It is also interesting to note that most of the admonition relating to the court's participation in the process of demarcating the region and computing "fair share" is more applicable to Judge Furman's decision in *Urban League v. Mayor & Council (Carteret)* than Judge Furman's decision in *Oakwood at Madison*. Although the *Urban League* case was not before the court there is little doubt that the court knew of its existence and the extent to which a trial judge can become enmeshed in the intricacies of the planning process.

Oakwood at Madison fails to provide an unambiguous standard for municipal officials to determine, with some assurance, whether their zoning ordinances will be upheld, short of completely abandoning all programs of rational and comprehensive community planning. On one hand the decision states that it is not necessary for a municipality whose zoning ordinance is challenged to devise specific formulae for estimating its precise share of the housing needs of the region. Rather, the municipalities and the courts should look to the *bona fide* efforts toward the elimination or minimization of undue cost generating requirements. On the other hand when a zoning ordinance is challenged, the court will evaluate "fair share" allocation studies submitted in evidence (although the court will not adopt a "fair share" housing quota for the municipality). Thus, it would appear that a municipality could make a bona fide effort toward the elimination of undue cost-generating requirements in the zoning ordinance but still be vulnerable to attack on the grounds that it has not fulfilled its "fair share" housing quota. Consequently each municipality and each developer-challenger of the zoning validity will have to prepare its own study to support its position and the statistical warfare will continue to be fought in the courtrooms. The only difference after *Oakwood at Madison* is that the trial court will remain aloof from the proceedings and only evaluate the alternative methodologies but will not prescribe one for the municipality.

When the court ordered the issuance of a building permit to the developer-plaintiff subject to the condition that the developer guarantee the allocation of at least 20% of the units to low or moderate income families, it did not deal with the complex problem of administering the procedure by which the benefits of low and moderate income housing units would be preserved over a period of time for succeeding generations of occupants. This issue creates a difficult dilemma. If no attention is given to the implementation of the mandatory percentage of moderately priced dwellings (MPMPD) requirement the first occupant of each of the 20% of the units will benefit from the court-ordered allocation imposed on the developer. As costs rise and property values increase, however, subsequent occupants will have to pay the increased nonsubsidized costs of occupancy. On the other hand, to avoid the short-lived benefits to only the first occupant, a system of administration would have to be established that would control the rents of apartments or control the selling prices of sales units. Either mechanism would subject the developer to a form of regulation that would constitute a significant disincentive to development.

The *Oakwood at Madison* decision recapitulated the misconception of *Mount Laurel* that the state of the art of the planning profession has been developed to the point where a competent, honest, and objective professional planner can, with or without the aid of electronic data processing devices, calculate objectively and accurately the numbers on which "fair share" allocations can be made. There is an assumption in both *Oakwood at Madison* and *Mount Laurel* that the disparity in testimony from competing expert planning witnesses is the result of the advocacy procedure and that planning truth can be found by the simple device of turning to an objective source of information and advice. This would appear to be the basis on which the court suggests that fair share housing allocations made by regional planning agencies (such as the Delaware Regional Planning Commission) would merit prima facie judicial acceptance. This assumption also appeared to be the basis for the authorization to the trial court to appoint an impartial zoning and planning expert or experts.

The difficulty with this assumption is that honesty, integrity, competence, and objectivity alone are insufficient to extrapolate, project, and predict the events upon which the future development of a region will depend. The planning process is designed to formulate plans and programs to achieve goals and objectives of the community it seeks to serve. Professional planners do not make basic policy decisions, such as whether the community seeks rapid growth, moderate growth, or slow growth. An "objective" planner would base his projections and calculations upon policy judgments of the appropriate community officials. For example, *predictions* of future housing need will depend upon policy decisions relating to desired rate of growth. *Actual* housing needs, in most regions, will depend upon the extent to which employment opportunities are generated *in fact* in the region. The science, methodology, and art of predicting the number of future jobs (i.e., industrial and commercial growth) in any given region have not yet been developed to the point where an impartial regional planning agency or an impartial court-appointed planner can provide calculations of sufficient reliability to determine the validity of a municipal zoning ordinance.

At some point in every comprehensive discussion of exclusionary zoning it becomes necessary to remind all participants that there are two separate and distinct questions that must be resolved if low and moderate income families are to have an opportunity to live in suburban communities. The first question is: Is land available in the community that can be used for "least cost" housing? The second question is: Are subsidies available to close the gap between the cost of housing construction and the amount that low and moderate income families can afford to pay? The *Oakwood at Madison* decision focused attention upon the duality of these issues and reaffirmed the principle that the state constitution requires each developing municipality to make land available for "least cost" housing. In response to the second question, however, the court was unwilling to impose an affirmative obligation on developing municipalities to help to subsidize construction costs. Although an amicus brief had suggested various forms of affirmative municipal action to help subsidize these costs, the New Jersey Supreme Court deferred this issue to another day.

The New Jersey Supreme Court is continuing its leadership in the exclusionary zoning field. *Oakwood at Madison* reaffirms the principles of the landmark *Mount Laurel* decision and goes so far as to grant specific relief to the plaintiff-developer. But municipal officials who had hoped that *Oakwood at Madison* would provide an unambiguous standard to determine the validity of their zoning ordinances may find this latest decision unsatisfactory.

A NEW TEST FOR EXCLUSIONARY ZONING:
DOES IT "PRECLUDE THE OPPORTUNITY" FOR
"LEAST COST" HOUSING?, JEROME G. ROSE
6 REAL ESTATE LAW JOURNAL (FALL, 1977)

The New Jersey, Pennsylvania, New York, Colorado, California, and federal courts, among others, have in the past few years rendered landmark decisions dealing with the validity of municipal land use regulations that tend to limit development and exclude people from suburban communities. More specifically, municipal ordinances that prohibit, or make no provisions for, multifamily housing, allocate insufficient land for housing on small lots, or impose cost-generating requirements for housing developments have been challenged as invalid, "exclusionary zoning." Prior issues of the *Real Estate Law Journal* have explored the questions raised by many of these decisions.

One of the troublesome legal questions involved in all these cases is which criteria should be used to determine whether a land use regulation is "exclusionary"—and therefore vulnerable to attack. In *Oakwood at Madison, Inc. v. Township of Madison,* the New Jersey Supreme Court has proposed a new test for making this determination: A land use regulation is "exclusionary" if it "operates in fact to preclude the opportunity to supply any substantial amounts of new housing for low and moderate income households now and prospectively needed in the municipality and in the appropriate region," whether or not such effect was intended.

This new judicial formula, couched in language that is more legislative than judicial in style, contains several elements, each of which raises new legal issues for further litigation to resolve. Among these issues are:

● What is the definition of "preclude the opportunity," and will the new test succeed in replacing the "fair share" test?

● Is it realistic to include new housing for *low*- as well as *moderate*-income persons in the test, and what is the definition of "least cost" housing to be provided for this purpose?

● Is it feasible to include *prospective* as well as *present* housing need in the test?

● Is the test of exclusionary *effect* rather than exclusionary *intent* too broad and inclusive?

● Does the test involve an evaluation that is within the scope of the judicial process?

"Preclude the Opportunity"— Will It Replace "Fair Share?"

The new test proposed by the New Jersey Supreme Court calls for evidence relating to whether the land use regulation will *preclude the opportunity* for the described types and amount of housing. This test is a great improvement over that previously prescribed by the court. Under the previous test, a developer could challenge a municipal zoning ordinance merely by showing that the land use regulations have not made *realistically possible* a variety and choice of housing—including low- and moderate-income housing. The burden of proof would then shift to the municipality to establish a valid basis for the law. But the old test was based on a misconception; in fact, land use regulations *do not and can not* make low- and moderate-income housing "realistically possible." However, land use regulations can and sometimes do "preclude the opportunity" for such housing to be built within a municipality, and consequently, the new test is a more accurate reflection of the economic realities of the housing-construction industry.

Although it was easy for the New Jersey Supreme Court to substitute the "preclude the opportunity" standard for the "realistically possible" standard, it is questionable whether the new standard will be able to replace the "fair share of regional housing needs" test of whether a municipal ordinance is exclusionary. One of the purposes of the "preclude the opportunity" test proposed in *Oakwood at Madison* is to extricate the trial courts from the process of "demarcating the region" and calculating the municipality's "fair share" of regional housing needs. The court correctly observed that this process "involves highly controversial economic, sociological and policy questions of innate difficulty and complexity. Where predictive responses are called for they are apt to be speculative or conjectural." The court also recognized (in a footnote) the danger that "because of the conjectural nature of such calculations, utilization of the court as the forum for determining a municipality's fair share may result in 'statistical warfare' between the litigants."

It would seem that one of the purposes of the new test is to enable a trial court to determine whether a municipal zoning ordinance is exclusionary without having to engage in the "controversial," "speculative or conjectural" calculations required to determine fair-share allocations of regional housing need. However, it seems unlikely that a trial court will be able to determine whether a given zoning ordinance precludes the opportunity for the required types and amounts of housing without evidence relating to fair share of regional housing needs. For example, would a municipal ordinance be characterized as "exclusionary" where evidence establishes that (1) there is a significant amount of existing housing for low- and moderate-income persons; (2) there are zoning districts in which some multifamily housing can be built; (3) there are districts in which some single-family housing can be built on small- and moderate-sized lots; (4) there are some districts in which cost-generating requirements are reduced; (5) the plaintiff-developer's land is not in any of the above districts; (6) there are other districts for which high-cost single-family dwellings are contemplated?

It is very likely that a trial court would not be able to determine whether such a zoning ordinance is exclusionary unless it receives evidence relating to the amounts and relative proportions of the types of housing possible under the existing ordinance. This information will have only limited significance unless the court also receives evidence relating to local and regional housing needs for each of the categories of housing authorized by the ordinance. Thus it remains to be seen whether it will be possible to determine whether a municipal zoning ordinance is exclusionary without implicating the trial courts in the statistical warfare involved in calculating the fair-share allocation of regional housing needs.

New Housing For Low- as Well as Moderate-Income Persons: "Least Cost" Housing

Under the new test, a land use regulation is exclusionary if it precludes the opportunity for *new* housing for *low-* as well as moderate-income persons. There are at least two debatable economic and public-policy issues assumed in this part of the test: (1) Is new housing economically feasible for low-income persons? (2) Is there an obligation for all (developing) municipalities to allocate land for low-income persons regardless of suitability of the municipality for low-income residents?

Whether it is realistic and economically feasible to provide new housing for low-income persons is debatable at best. The underlying difficulty with this principle is that current costs of housing construction in most areas of the country put the sales or rental prices of new housing far beyond the reach of low-income persons. To close the gap between the costs of new housing and the ability of low-income persons to pay, substantial subsidies to reduce the costs of housing and/or to supplement the income of low-income persons are necessary. Experience has indicated that the nation is prepared to allocate only a limited amount of its national resources to this purpose. For this reason, it may be argued that more low-income persons can be benefited if the limited subsidies are applied to the lower costs of *older* housing. A sense of the inequity of prescribing older and therefore a lower-standard housing for low-income persons, and other manifestations of socioeconomic philosophy, seem to have entered into the court's reasoning when it formulated this part of the new test.

The New Jersey Court has reponded to this issue by creating a new addition to the lexicon (and the litigable issues) of exclusionary zoning, called, "least cost" housing. Where builders of housing cannot, with public assistance and incentives, provide for the municipality's fair share of the regional housing need for lower-income housing, the court has declared that "it is incumbent on the governing body to adjust its zoning regulations so as to render possible and feasible the 'least cost' housing, consistent with standards of health and safety. . . ." In a footnote, the court explained that the concept of "least cost" housing does not contemplate the construction of housing that could easily deteriorate into slums. Health and safety standards should be maintained. However, innovation and economy in construction and the elimination of regulations that unnecessarily increase construction costs should be used to reduce housing construction costs as much as possible, consistent with those standards. The court stated expressly that nothing less than zoning for "least cost" housing will satisfy the judicial mandate.

After making this declaration, however, the court concede that compliance with this requirement may not provide new housing for *all* lower income persons. Nevertheless the "least cost" requirement would assist the lower-income population by increasing the total supply of housing available to it through the "filtering down" (also known as the "trickle down") process, defined as the movement of uppermoderate-, or middle-income families to newly constructed housing, leaving their former housing available for families lower in the income scale.

The second assumption made by the court in formulating the new test for exclusionary zoning is that *all* (developing) municipalities have an obligation to house low-income persons regardless of the suitability of the municipality for such persons. It can be argued that a municipality that has few jobs, no public transportation, insufficient educational, medical, and social services, and a high property tax, or a combination of the above, would be inappropriate for low-income persons and that the failure to provide for low-income housing should not be a reason to characterize the land use regulations as "exclusionary." In spite of this argument, any (developing) municipality whose land use laws preclude low-income housing will be characterized as "exclusionary" without regard to suitability.

Provision For Future Housing Needs

Land use regulations are exclusionary under the new test if they preclude the opportunity for housing needed in the *future* as well as at *present*. The requirement to provide for *future* housing needs is surprising in view of the court's interest in eliminating difficult, complex, conjectural and speculative calculations from the judicial process. Estimating the present housing needs of a municipality is difficult and conjectural but possible within an acceptable margin for error. Present need may be estimated by considering such factors as vacancy rates, extent of delapidation, extent of overcrowdedness, number of low-income families paying over 25 percent of income for housing, and then estimating the extent of overlap of the factors used in the computation.

The estimation of future housing needs of an area is much more speculative. Planning experts may select one of several alternate methodologies for this purpose. The following methodology was adopted by the New Jersey Division of State and Regional Planning:

Step 1. *Predict* the population for a given date in the future.

Step 2. *Predict* the average household size at that date.

Step 3. Divide the *predicted* population by the *predicted* average household size. The quotient is the *predicted* number of households at the given date.

Step 4. Subtract present number of households from *predicted* number of households. The difference represents the total household growth for the period.

Step 5. *Predict* the percentage of future households that will have low and moderate income.

Step 6. Multiply the *predicted* household growth for the period by the *predicted* percentage of low- and moderate-income households. The product is the *predicted* prospective housing needs for low- and moderate-income households at the given date in the future.

Although separate sub-methodologies are available for each of the predictions required in the above steps, critical policy decisions are involved in these methodologies. For example, in predicting future population growth, the New Jersey Department of Labor and Industry has proposed four different population projections for estimating future levels of growth. The projections make different assumptions relating to fertility-birth rates, mortality rates, and in-out-migration from the state. There are also different assumptions relating to long-term trends, economic events, and so on. The projections for each group of assumptions may be characterized as: (1) Slow growth; (2) Current trends; (3) Long-term trends; and (4) Maximum growth. Each of the assumptions differs significantly and the selection of one rather than another will have a significant effect on the prediction of future housing needs. Similar variations will result from the selection of other assumptions (e.g., future average household size) in the process of computation.

Thus the requirement that future housing needs be considered in the process of determining whether a municipality's land use regulations are exclusionary requires speculative and conjectural calculations and will involve the courts in battles of statistical warfare that the New Jersey Supreme Court had hoped to avoid.

Regional as Well as Local Housing Needs

The new test for exclusionary zoning raises the issue whether the municipal zoning ordinance precludes the opportunity for *regional* as well as *local* housing needs. Thus, under the test, a zoning ordinance that provides for land for housing to meet the needs of its own residents will nevertheless be characterized as exclusionary if it precludes the opportunity to provide for housing to meet the needs of persons living outside the municipality but within a "region." The difficulties with this test is that it becomes necessary to (1) "demarcate" the appropriate region, and (2) calculate the housing needs for that region. Where conflicting evidence is presented, a court will have to make a finding of fact on these issues.

The New Jersey Supreme Court has offered some suggestions to assist the trial courts. It indicated approval of Judge David Furman's definition of "region" as "the area from which, in view of available employment and transportation, the population of the township would be drawn absent exclusionary zoning." The court also reaffirmed the observation of Justice Frederick Hall that "confinement to or within a certain county appears not to be realistic, but restriction within the boundaries of the state seems practical and advisable." It should be readily apparent that neither definition is sufficiently precise to enable a trial court to select the appropriate region from among the many delineations of region that may be made and offered in evidence, within the vague guidelines of the two judicial statements.

The second part of the regional housing needs test makes it necessary to calculate the housing needs of the newly delineated region. This process can become extraordinarily complicated and conjectural, particularly where Judge Furman's definition is adopted. Under this definition the region will very frequently assume a shape resembling an amoeba with fingerlike protrusions along major highways. The size and shape of the region under this definition will also depend on a very basic but debatable assumption relating to the travel time to work. An assumption that the trip time to work should be one half hour will produce a very much smaller region than an assumption that many suburban residents are willing to and do in fact travel up to two hours each way to and from work. Many alternate sizes and shapes of regions are possible with other assumptions.

Because of the many serious problems involved in a judicial demarcation of a region, the courts of most states, other than New Jersey, New York and California have not adopted a regional test for the validity of municipal zoning. The federal courts, particularly, have avoided becoming involved in this issue, taking the position that "the federal court is not a super zoning board and should not be called on to make the point at which legitimate *local* interests in promoting the welfare of the community are outweighed by legitimate *regional* interest. . . ." (Emphasis added.)

Is the Test of Exclusionary Effect too Broad and Inclusive?

Under the new test, if a zoning ordinance has the effect of excluding low-income households, even though this effect was not intended, the ordinance is nevertheless characterized as exclusionary. It should be readily apparent that the burden of proving exclusionary *effect* is very much easier than the burden of proving a legislative *intent* to keep low-income persons out of the jurisdiction. The test also invites the temptation and risk of attributing to zoning laws the impact of the maladjustment of housing construction costs in the general economy that have the effect of precluding the opportunity of low-income persons to purchase or rent housing in most parts of the country.

The danger of adopting an effects test of exclusionary zoning is that it may be too broad and inclusive. In a complex economic system, many economic forces interact together to cause an effect; this test attributes to only one cause the impact of many causes. Further, zoning ordinances are particularly, but unfairly, vulnerable to an effects test because the primary purpose of zoning laws is to restrict and exclude.

For these and other reasons the U.S. Supreme Court and the Court of Appeals for the Ninth Circuit have rejected the effects test. In a case involving a similar issue, the Supreme Court has held that the refusal of a suburban municipality to change its zoning laws to permit low-income housing does not violate the provisions of the U.S. Constitution even though the *effect* of the municipal zoning ordinance is to exclude members of racial minorities from the community. In the Court of Appeals decision, the court held that even where the *express purpose* and actual effect is to exclude substantial numbers of people who would otherwise elect to move to that municipality, the zoning ordinance is not invalid. The court observed that "practically all zoning restrictions have as a purpose and effect the *exclusion* of some activity or type of structure or a certain density of inhabitants." (Emphasis in original.)

Is the Test Appropriate to the Judicial Process?

The proposed test is designed to establish the criteria by which a trial court may determine whether a municipal zoning ordinance is exclusionary. To make this determination, a trial court will have to hear evidence on such issues as: (1) What is the present housing need of the municipality? (2) What is the future housing need of the municipality? (3) What is the appropriate region of which the municipality is a part? (4) Is the region delineated by the municipality a reasonable one? (5) Is the region delineated by the plaintiff a better one? (6) What is the present housing need of the region? (7) What is the future housing need of the region? (8) What are the assumptions on which the region's growth is based? (9) What are the alternative assumptions on which regional growth may be predicted? (10) Is it economically feasible to build a new housing for low-income families? (11) What are the kinds and characteristics of "least cost" housing in the municipality and the region? (12) Is the allocation of land in the ordinance for multi-family housing reasonable or sufficient? (13) Is the allocation of land in the ordinance for single-family dwellings on small- and moderate-sized lots reasonable or sufficient? (14) Are the cost-generating requirements of the land use regulations reasonable in view of ecological and other factors? (15) To what extent should the suitability of low income housing in the defendant municipality be considered?

The evidence required for these and other issues of fact that must be determined under the test will tend to make the trial a long, drawn-out, and expensive procedure that will be based on "highly controversial economic, sociological and policy questions of innate difficulty and complexity." The evidence will be based on the testimony of "experts" whose responses are "apt to be speculative or conjectural." This is just the kind of process the New Jersey Supreme Court indicated that it would like to avoid.

The future of the new test is very much in doubt because of its questionable utility and because its administration would conflict with the purpose of the *Oakwood at Madison* decision to extricate the trial courts from a process involving policy decisions. The New Jersey Supreme Court cast additional doubt upon the viability of the new test within two months after its formulation. In March, 1977 the court rendered its decisions in the *Washington Township* and *Demarest* cases and made the following statements in dicta not required for either decision:

> "But the overriding point we make is that it is not for the courts to substitute their conception of what the public welfare requires by way of zoning for the views of those in whom the Legislature and the local electorate have vested responsibility. . . ."

> "In short [the judicial role] is limited to the assessment of a claim that the restrictions of the ordinance are patently arbitrary or unreasonable or violative of the statute, not that they do not match the plaintiff's or the court's conception of the requirements of the general welfare, whether within the town or the region. . . ."

> "We are, of course, not insensitive to the current social need for

larger quantities of affordable housing of all kinds for the general population. . . . A possibility of some relief in that regard is contained within the statutory special exception or variance process. . . . But insofar as review of the validity of a zoning ordinance is concerned, the judicial branch is not suited to the role of an *ad hoc* super zoning legislature, particularly in the area of adjusting claims for satisfaction by individual municipalities of regional needs, whether as to housing or any other important social need affected by zoning. . . ."

These statements of the New Jersey Supreme Court made so soon after the formulation of the test for exclusionary zoning in the *Oakwood at Madison* decision would seem to argue against the use of the judicial process for the administration of the test it had so recently created. If this is true, the prognosis for the successful implementation of the new test is very much in doubt.

AFTER THE RECENT NEW JERSEY SUPREME COURT CASES: WHAT IS THE STATUS OF SUBURBAN ZONING? JEROME G. ROSE 54 NEW JERSEY MUNICIPALITIES 16 (May, 1977)

Many municipal officials are confused about the law that will determine the validity of their zoning ordinances. Ever since the *Mount Laurel* decision in March, 1975, they have heard from attorneys, planners, developers, public advocates and others, that their zoning ordinance will be held invalid unless it provides for apartments and other forms of housing for low and moderate income persons. During the past two years many officials have become reconciled to the prospect of having to amend their zoning ordinance to provide for such housing or face the possibility of having their ordinance held invalid under the *Mount Laurel* principle.

However, during the past year, the New Jersey Supreme Court has handed down a number of decisions that have begun to create doubts about the impact and effectiveness of the *Mount Laurel* requirements. The first hint of things to come appeared in September, 1976 in the Court's decision in the *Weymouth Township* case. On its face, this decision held only that a municipal ordinance that created a mobile home park district for the elderly is valid. However, many legal eyebrows were raised because the net result of this decision (in spite of the elaborate judicial rationale) was that the court upheld a provision of a zoning ordinance that had the *effect* of excluding young married with children from the zoning district.

Then, in January 1977, the New Jersey Supreme Court decided the *Oakwood at Madison* case and determined that the trial courts will no longer engage in the process of "demarcating the region" or calculating the "fair share" of regional housing needs that the municipal zoning ordinance must provide for. There was also some hint of a changing judicial attitude in the Court's statements that controversial economic sociological and questions are more appropriately a legislative than a judicial function.

And while the municipal officials and attorneys were still reeling under the influence of the heady effects of the potential significance of the *Oakwood at Madison* decision, the New Jersey Supreme Court rendered two more decisions in the *Washington Township* and *Demarest* cases. In its narrowest sense, these cases held only that (1) the *Mount Laurel* principle applies only to "developing municipalities" (hardly a surprise to those who read the *Mount Laurel* decision carefully), and (2) there were sufficient grounds for the Demarest Board of Adjustment to deny a use variance for multi-family residential units. However, these decisions taken together, have begun to make many municipal officials begin to wonder whether the New Jersey Supreme Court has expressed something more important than the narrow holdings of those cases. There is reason to believe that there may be a change in the court's attitude about the propriety of judicial intervention in the planning and zoning process. It is difficult to ignore the potential import of such statements as the following that were included in the *Washington Township* decision:

> "But it would be a mistake to interpret *Mount Laurel* as a comprehensive displacement of sound and long established principles concerning judicial respect for local policy decisions in the zoning field. What we said recently in this regard in Bow and Arrow Manor v. Town of West Orange, 63 N.J. 335, 343 (1973), is worth repeating as continuing sound law: 'It is fundamental that *zoning* is a *municipal legislative function, beyond the purview of intereference by the courts* unless an ordinance is seen in whole or in application to any particular property to be clearly arbitrary, capricious or unreasonable, or plainly contrary to fundamental principles of zoning or the statute . . .'" (emphasis added)

> "But the overriding point we make is that it is not for the courts to substitute their conception of what the public welfare requires by way of zoning for the views of those in whom the Legislature and the local electorate have vested responsibility . . ."

> "In short (the judicial role) is limited to the assessment of a claim that the restrictions of the ordinance are patently arbitrary or unreasonable or violative of the statute, not that they do not match the plaintiff's or the court's conception of the requirements of the general welfare, whether within the town or the region . . ."

> "We are, of course, not insensitive to the current social need for larger quantities of affordable housing of all kinds for the general population . . . A possibility of some relief in that regard is contained within the statutory special exception or variance process . . . But insofar as review of the validity of a zoning ordinance is concerned, the judicial branch is not suited to the role of an *ad hoc* superzoning legislature, particularly in the area of adjusting claims for satisfaction by individual municipalities of regional needs, whether as to housing

or any other important social need affected by zoning . . ."

After evaluating the recent decisions in the light of these statements, municipal officials have begun to ask: What are the obligations of my municipality to provide for housing for low and moderate income persons? If there are insufficient zoning provisions for such housing will the ordinance be vulnerable to a use variance application?

To answer these questions with any sense of assurance, municipal officials, and their legal and planning advisers, are going to have to undertake a multistep analysis of their municipality and zoning ordinance. The following is an outline of the steps that should be useful in such an analysis:

Step One: Determine whether your municipality is a "developing municipality" within the meaning of the Mount Laurel decision.
  A. If the municipality is not a developing municipality, go directly to Step Three.
  B. If the municipality is a developing municipality go to Step Two and Step Three.

Step Two: Determine whether the zoning ordinance is "exclusionary."
  A. If the zoning ordinance is "exclusionary," consider the amendments necessary to change that characterization.
  B. If a challenge to the zoning under the *Mount Laurel* principle is expected, undertake the studies necessary to defend the validity of the ordinance.
  C. Go back to the primary question of Step Two and reconsider the conclusion in light of action taken under Step Two, A and B.

Step Three: Determine whether the zoning ordinance is vulnerable to a use variance application by a high density developer. To make this determination, answer the following questions:
  A. Is a regional need for multi-family housing a "special reason" for granting a use variance?
  B. Will a multi-family development impair the intent and purpose of the zone plan?

STEP ONE: IS YOUR MUNICIPALITY A "DEVELOPING MUNICIPALITY" WITHIN THE MEANING OF THE MOUNT LAUREL DECISION?

The *Mount Laurel* decision determined, and the *Washington Township* and *Demarest* decisions reaffirmed, that the obligation imposed by *Mount Laurel* (that a municipal zoning ordinance must provide for its fair share of the housing needs of the region) is limited to "developing municipalities." Thus, if a municipality is not a "developing municipality," its zoning ordinance will be upheld even if it does not provide for its fair share of the regional housing needs, unless it is arbitrary, unreasonable or results in a confiscatory taking of the owner's property. It therefore becomes essential for every municipality to determine whether it is, or is not, a "developing municipality." The *Mount Laurel* decision sets forth the criteria for this determination. Under the standards established in that decision, there would appear to be three categories of municipalities:
  1. **Developing** municipalities like Mount Laurel,

2. **Developed** municipalities like Washington Township and Demarest, and
3. **Undeveloped** municipalities that are still rural and likely to continue to be for some time yet.

To determine whether your municipality is a "developing municipality" or whether it fits into one of the other two categories, it will be necessary to examine each of the following characteristics of a "developing municipality."

Sizeable Land Area

A developing municipality is one that has "sizeable land area." Thus, it will become necessary to determine whether the land area in your municipality is, in fact, "sizeable." This determination will be based upon a comparative judgment after considering the relative size of the 567 municipalities in the state. The land area of New Jersey municipalities rantes from tiny Shrewsbury Township with only .09 square miles to Hamilton Township with over 113 square miles. The median size of municipalities in the state is 4.3 square miles. The average (arithmetical mean) size is 13.2 square miles. The court has determined that Mount Laurel's 22 square miles is sizeable; Washington Township's approximately 3 square miles and Demarest's approximately 2 square miles are not sizeable. It would be reasonable to argue that a municipality with land area substantially under the average of 13.2 square miles and certainly one with less than the median of 4.3 square miles is not sizeable. As the land area of a municipality approaches the arithmetical mean of 13.2 square miles in size it becomes susceptible to the characterization of having "sizeable land area."

Location Outside Central City and Older Built-up Suburbs

A developing municipality is one that is outside the central city and older built-up suburbs. There are a number of reasons why the Supreme Court adopted this characteristic as a standard. It seems clear that the court intended to exempt the central city and older built-up suburbs from additional responsibilities to provide for the housing needs of the region. Thus, the *Mount Laurel* obligation applies only to the newer and more recently developed or developing municipalities. This result is consistent with the underlying purpose of the decision: to open up the suburbs to migration by low- and moderate-income persons currently trapped within the central cities and older suburbs. Additional housing facilities within the central cities would help meet the housing needs of the region but would not help to achieve the court's other purpose of fostering economic and racial integration within the state.

Loss of Rural Characteristics

A developing municipality is one that has "shed its rural characteristics." This is a somewhat subjective criterion. However, there are at least two factors that are relevent when the question arises whether a formerly rural community has in fact changed its characteristics. Those factors are: (1) significant changes in population density; and (2) significant changes in land use. A report by the Regional Plan Association observed that at about 100 persons per square mile, the rural feeling begins to change to urban. A population of approximately 2,000 to 4,000 persons per square mile is a typical density of a suburban area.

The standards for comparison of the proportions of various land uses for a rural area are less precise. A typical rural community would have predominately agricultural or undeveloped land use with a minimum of commercial and industrial use. A municipality begins to shed its rural characteristics when it *begins to use* increasing proportions of its land for non-agricultural purposes. The *Mount Laurel* opinion seems to indicate that rural characteristics are also shed when the municipality begins to zone substantial amounts of its area for commercial and industrial uses. The basis for such a position would be that the designation of a large amount of area for commercial and industrial uses raises a suspicion that the municipality is under pressure for residential development and is trying to avoid its regional obligations by zoning an unrealistically large amount of its land for industrial purposes.

Great Population Increases
Since World War II

A developing municipality is one that has had great increases in population in the period since 1940. The significance of an analysis of population figures during this period may be to distinguish the three categories of municipalities, as follows:

1. **Developing municipalities.** The population in the 1940's will have been relatively small. During the period since 1940 the proportionate population increase will have been significant and the incremental trend will continue up to the time of analysis, providing evidence for a projection of continuing growth and development of the municipality.

2. **Developed municipalities.** The population during the period from 1940 to the present may or may not indicate significant growth but recent population count would indicate a slowing or a termination of previous growth. This category would include both those municipalities that had substantial population in the 1940's that have not grown substantially since that time and also those communities that have grown substantially during this period but have reached a peak and are no longer in a period of growth or development.

3. **Pre- or non-developing municipalities.** The population in the 1940's will have been relatively small. During this period there will have been relatively insignificant increases in population indicating that the municipality remains relatively small and undeveloped, and has a population growth that is not significant enough to use as a basis for projecting future population increases.

The significance of changing population growth statistics is subject to conflicting interpretation and will probably become the basis of future litigation. On one hand, it may be argued that a dramatic decrease in population growth is evidence that a municipality has reached its saturation point and therefore is no longer "developing." On the other hand it may also be argued that a decreased population growth rate is evidence of the exclusionary zoning practices that the *Mount Laurel* decision is intended to eliminate, and that if those exclusionary zoning obstacles were removed, the municipality would continue to develop.

Incomplete Development

A developing municipality is one that is not completely developed. In determining whether a municipality is completely developed it will be necessary to examine *both:* (1) the *amount* of land undeveloped and (2) the *characteristics* of that land. The amount of undeveloped land is significant in terms of both its relative size, i.e., its proportion of all of the land in the municipality (and possibly in the region) and its actual size. In the *Mount Laurel* case, 65% of the land in the municipality was undeveloped. In the *Demarest* case, approximately 3% of the land was undeveloped, and the court held that Demarest is not a developing municipality. The difficult cases will involve proportions between those figures.

However, the *quantity* of undeveloped land taken along could provide a misleading index of whether the municipality has reached its limits of development. The Appellate Division, in the *Washington Township* case astutely identified this issue when it characterized the *nature* of the land to be considered as "readily and quickly available for development." There are many reasons why some land remains undeveloped after most of the other land in the municipality has been developed. Among the reasons why some land is not "readily and quickly available for development" are: (1) land assembly problems, (2) agricultural use, (3) part of a large private estate, (4) part of public parks, playground, country clubs, camps, college campus, or other institutional use, (5) unavailability of water, sewer or other utilities, (6) soil, topography, drainage or other high-cost-of-development problem.

If, for any of the above, or other reasons, land in a municipality is not readily available for development, it is debatable (and litigable) whether such land should be included in the amount of land to be considered for the purpose of determining whether a municipality is "not completely developed" within the definition of a developing municipality.

Location in the Path of
Inevitable Future Growth

A developing municipality is one that is in the path of inevitable future residential, commercial, and industrial demand and growth. The concept of a "path of inevitable future growth" is even more imprecise, vague and amorphous than the concept of "region." The path of inevitable future growth, in the northeast region of the country, would include a huge swath from Boston to Washington, D.C. If so defined, the "path" would be too broad and inclusive to serve any useful purpose. On the other hand, if all of the many pockets and interstices of non-growth are to be excluded, the analysis will become too complex and intricate to serve any useful purpose. Nevertheless, the path of inevitable growth is one of the factors to be considered in determining whether a municipality is developing for the purpose of imposing the Mount Laurel requirements of zoning validity.

After applying the above standards, if a municipal official determines that his municipality is a "developing municipality" then it becomes necessary to proceed to the next step.

STEP TWO: IS YOUR MUNICIPAL ZONING ORDINANCE "EXCLUSIONARY" WITHIN THE MEANING OF THE OAKWOOD AT MADISON DECISION?

To determine whether your municipal zoning ordinance is "exclusionary" it is necessary to examine the ordinance and analyze its effect upon the ability of a developer to build "least cost" housing in the municipality. More specifically, it is necessary to apply the new test established in the *Oakwood at Madison* case, namely, does the zoning ordinance "operate in fact to preclude the opportunity to supply any substantial amounts of new housing for law and moderate income households now and prospectively needed in the municipality and in the appropriate region."

Although the application of this new test is difficult and complex, in many cases it may be possible to resolve the issue quickly by asking the following questions:

• Does the ordinance provide for substantial areas for single family dwellings on very small lots?

• Does the ordinance provide for substantial areas for single family dwellings·on moderate sized lots?

• Does the ordinance provide for substantial areas for multi-family swellings?

• Does the ordinance not discourage the construction of apartments with two or more bedrooms?

• Does the ordinance not create undue cost-generating requirements that would discourage "least cost" housing construction?

Unless the answer to all of the above questions is clearly and conclusively, "yes" there is a risk that the ordinance may be characterized as "exclusionary." Consequently, it will be necessary to amend the ordinance in an effort to eliminate the "exclusionary" characterization and/or undertake studies to defend the validity of the ordinance when it is challenged by a developer seeking the right to build housing at a location and at a density not in accordance with the zoned plan.

It would be advisable for every municipality that cannot, with assurance and certainty, answer "yes" to each of the above questions to direct its planning staff or consultant to find answers to the following questions:

1. **What is the present housing need of the municipality?**
   The report should include an analysis of such factors as vacancy rates, extent of delapidation, extent of overcrowdedness, number of low income families paying over 25% of income for housing and an estimate of the extent of overlap of the factors used in the computation.

2. **What is the future housing need of the municipality?**
   This report will include an analysis of population projections for a future date, household size, number of households and predictions of proportions of low and moderate income households in the municipality at that future date.

3. **What is the appropriate "region" of which the municipality is a part?**
   This report will include an analysis of each of the many possible demarcations of "region" that may arguably be appropriate for the municipality together with persuasive reasons for the adoption of the demarcation of "region" selected.

4. **What is the present housing need of the "region" selected?**
   The report will include the items discussed in question number 1 above.

5. **What is the future housing need of the "region" selected?**
   The report will include the items discussed in question number 2 above.

6. **What are the alternative assumptions upon which regional growth may be predicted?**
   The report will analyze the various assumptions upon which regional population projections may be based and will provide the reasons why the adopted rate of population growth was selected instead of alternate assumptions and theories.

7. **What are the types and characteristics of "least cost" housing that may be built in the municipality and region?**
   This report will contain an analysis of the various forms of least cost housing including methods of construction, size, lot size and will include an analysis of the costs of construction, maintenance costs, including property taxes and the amount of income required to maintain such housing.

8. **Is the allocation of land in the ordinance for multi-family housing reasonable or sufficient?**
   This report will make a "fair share" allocation of regional needs and provide the reasons to support the adopted theory of "fair share" allocation.

9. **Is the allocation of land in the ordinance for single family housing on small and moderate sized lots reasonable or sufficient?**
   This report will include items discussed in question number 8 above.

10. **Are the cost generating requirements of the land use regulations reasonable in view of ecological and other factors.**
    This report will analyze ecological, esthetic, fiscal and other constraints that may justify "cost generating" requirements.

To the municipal official who balks at the length, complexity, and expense of the reports required to answer the above questions, the most telling response is that if he/she fails to respond satisfactorily to these questions then the ordinance will be vulnerable to attack under the **Mount Laurel** and subsequent decisions.

To make matters even worse, a satisfactory response to all of the above questions does not guarantee that the legislative policy decisions about the character and development of the community will prevail. Even if the zoning ordinance withstands the attack of being "exclusionary" the zoned plan may be disrupted by the granting of a use variance application. To face up to the issues raised by this possibility, proceed to Step Three.

STEP THREE: IS YOUR ZONING ORDINANCE VULNERABLE TO A USE VARIANCE APPLICATION BY A HIGH DENSITY DE-VELOPER?

Under the New Jersey Municipal Land Use Law the zoning board of adjustment may grant a use variance to allow a structure of use in a district restricted against such structure or use upon a showing of "special reasons" therefore and upon a showing that such a variance can be granted "without substantial detriment to the public good and will not substantially impair the intent and purpose of the zone plan and zoning ordinance," i.e., the so-called "negative criteria." The two questions that arise from this provision are: (1) Is a regional need for multi-family housing a "special reason" within the meaning of the use variance provision? and (2) will the court uphold a finding that the granting of a use variance for multi-family housing in a single family district fails to meet the "negative criteria" requirement, because of substantial detriment and impairment of the intent and purpose of the zone plan?

A. Is a regional need for multi-family housing a "special reason?"

The question of what is a "special reason" that will justify the granting of a use variance is a complex one. In general, a "special reason" is one that promotes the health, morals or general welfare. Consequently, variances have been upheld for public and semi-public uses, such as parochial schools, telephone equipment, private hospitals and semi-public low income housing outside a ghetto area. However, since almost every legal use of property would in some way serve the "general welfare," the New Jersey Supreme Court has held that the mere showing that the proposed use would serve the general welfare is insufficient. In addition to serving the general welfare, a court will find that a "special reason" exists if the proposed use either (1) is one that "inherently" serves the general welfare, such as a school or a hospital, where the use *per se* constitutes a special reason for a variance, or (2) is *"peculiarly fitted to the particular location"* for which the variance is sought.

In applying the above principles the court has held that "variances to allow new nonconforming uses should be granted only sparingly and with great caution since they tend to impair sound zoning." In the *Demarest* case, the court recited criticism of a recent trial court decision that upheld a variance for construction of garden apartments on the grounds that such housing constitutes a special reason. The cited criticism argued that this decision "would lead to subverting rational land use planning" and "inevitably result in even greater misplanning in New Jersey suburbs."

The *Demarest* opinion also cited Justice Hall's statement in *Mount*

Laurel that "while the special exception method . . . is frequently appropriate for the handling of such uses, it *would indeed by the rare case* where proper 'special reasons' could be found to validly support a (use) variance for such privately built housing . . ." (emphasis added by the court).

After directing attention to this important issue and after raising the question whether a variance to provide private rental housing in a region that plainly needs it is "inherently" for the general welfare, the New Jersey Supreme Court, decided in the *Demarest* decision "to leave definitive resolution of this knotty problem to a future case which will compel it; the instant one does not."

Thus, after the latest word from the New Jersey Supreme Court, it is not possible for municipal officials to determine whether the courts will decide that an application for a variance for rental housing will meet the "special reasons" requirement for a use variance.

B. Will multi-family housing in a single family district meet the "negative criteria" requirements of a use variance?

The *Demarest* decision upheld the decision of the board of adjustment to deny the granting of a use variance for multi-family housing upon a finding that the grant would substantially impair the intent and purpose of the zone plan and zoning ordinance. The court recognized that the board of adjustment has authority to weigh all the evidence, consider the argument *pro* and *con* and then exercise its discretion in deciding whether to grant or deny a variance application. Consequently the courts will not disturb the variance decision of the board of adjustment as long as that determination is not arbitrary or capricious. Having found that there was substantial evidence for the determination of the board of adjustment, the court upheld the board's decision.

The lesson that municipal officials may learn from the *Demarest* case is that, if a decision to deny a use variance for a multi-family development is to be made by the board of adjustment and sustained by a court it will be necessary to provide evidence for the record that would support the denial. Such evidence may be provided by the testimony of a planning consultant retained by the planning board to analyze the issue and report the findings of such study. The failure to provide such evidence may result in a record that cannot support a denial of the variance.

Conclusion

After the recent New Jersey Supreme Court decision, the status of suburban zoning is still very much in doubt and subject to conflicting judicial principles and statements. On one hand, the State Supreme Court has reaffirmed the *Mount Laurel* principle that requires the zoning ordinance of a developing municipality to provide for its fair share of the regional housing needs for low and moderate income persons. On the other hand, the court has withdrawn the trial courts from the process of "demarcating the region" or calculating "fair share." In addition, the court has more recently expressed the need for judicial restraint and for judicial respect for the legislative and administrative processes. The court has held that the *Mount Laurel* requirements are limited to "developing municipalities" and that those principles apply only if the municipality's zoning ordinance is "exclusionary." The problem of how to determine whether or not the ordinance is "exclusionary" is still unresolved, as are the problems of "demarcating the region," calculating "fair share," determining "present housing need" and predicting "future housing need" for the municipality and the region.

There are enough unresolved issues to occupy the time and energies of municipal officials and courts for many years to come. However, it is very likely that the New Jersey Supreme Court will adopt a policy that will result in an abatement of the flurry of zoning decisions by the Supreme Court for a substantial period of time to provide the opportunity for the state and local policy making bodies to respond to the social, economic, political and constitutional requirements of the state.

An Alternative to the Mount Laurel "Fair Share" Approach

In the *Mount Laurel* decision, the New Jersey Supreme Court determined that the validity of the zoning laws of a developing municipality depends upon whether the land use laws of the municipality provide for its "fair share" of the local and regional housing needs of low and moderate income families. In the *Washington Township* decision, the New Jersey high court recognized the limited ability of the courts to administer this decision in such statements as "the judicial branch is not suited to the role of an ad hoc superzoning legislature, particularly in the area of adjusting claims for satisfaction by individual municipalities of regional needs, whether as to housing or any other important social need affected by zoning. . . .".

The above, and similar statements of the propriety of judicial restraint by the New Jersey court in the *Washington Township* decision, raise the question whether it will be possible for the court to enforce the principles of the *Mount Laurel* decision without violating the principles of the *Washington Township* decision. To a great extent, this judicial dilemma results from the adoption of the "fair share" test in *Mount Laurel* instead of the test of "reasonableness" that is more usually appropriate for the judicial process. More specifically, the *Mount Laurel* decision imposed an obligation on every developing municipality to provide for its "fair share" of the housing needs of the region. Evidence introduced to calculate "fair share" involves the litigants and the courts in a form of "statistical warfare" relating to planning concepts and methodology based upon legislative policy judgments. It will be very difficult, if not impossible, for a court to adhere to the *Washington Township* principles of judicial restraint and at the same time enforce a judgment based upon a determination of a municipality's "fair share" of regional housing needs.

On the other hand, it would be possible for the courts to avoid becoming a "superzoning legislature" if they abandon the "fair share" test and instead impose the standard that every municipality (whether developing or not) must make "reasonable" provision for local and regional housing needs. The New York highest appellate court has avoided the new Jersey dilemma by this most sensible solution of the problem of the role of the courts in conflicts between

managed municipal growth and exclusionary zoning. The principle was announced in *Berenson v. New Castle*, set forth below, in which the court established a two-fold test of the validity of a local ordinance that eliminates the
need for the New York courts to become involved in the statistical warfare of
the litigants in calculating a municipality's "fair share" of regional housing
needs.

BERENSON et al.

v.

TOWN OF NEW CASTLE

38 N.Y.2d 102, 378 N.Y.S.2d 67

341 N.E.2d 236 (1975)

JASEN, J. The plaintiffs in this declaratory judgment action attack the
validity of the Zoning Ordinance of the Town of New Castle in its entirety
on the ground that the ordinance excludes multifamily residential housing
from the list of permitted uses.

The Town of New Castle is a relatively quiet and undeveloped suburban community nestled in the hills of northern Westchester County. The
town is but 35 miles north of New York City, and this close proximity to a
major metropolitan center has placed it directly in the path of the post-
World War II rush to suburbia. Since 1950, New Castle has experienced
a three-fold increase in population; growing from 5,312 inhabitants to over
17,000. The town fathers, anxious to preserve as much of the rustic
township as they could, took steps to prevent the construction of both
apartment houses and small one-family homes in the town. Ever since the
first zoning ordinance was adopted by New Castle, the town has refused
to authorize or permit the development of any multiple-family dwellings
within the boundaries of the town. A few older apartment buildings were
built prior to the enactment of the ordinance and exist as nonconforming
uses.

The present zoning ordinance, which was enacted in 1971 to replace a
1945 version, provides for 12 types of districts. Four districts are restricted to residential use base on minimum lot size. Districts R-2A and
R-1A mandate two-acre and one-acre minimum lot sizes respectively,
while the other two residential classes call for one-half and one-quarter
acre lot development. Six districts are set aside for business development
and another two are earmarked for industrial uses. However, in terms of
surface area, most of the town is restricted to one- and two-acre residential development. In none of the 12 districts would the development of
multiple-family dwellings be permitted.

The plaintiffs, either individually or through corporations, had controlled or owned since 1955 a parcel of 50 acres situated on the southern
end of New Castle. Their land fronts on Bedford Road to the west and

Old Farm Road to the southwest and is zoned for one-acre residences. Indeed, the plaintiffs originally owned more land in the same parcel but subdivided it and constructed one-family houses, in conformity with existing zoning requirements. The properties adjoining the plaintiff's parcel on the west and east are zoned for one-half acre development. The property on the northern boundary is set aside for one-quarter acre lots. Just beyond the one-half acre zone to the west of the plaintiffs' property lies a relatively large retail, commercial and industrial zone.

In early 1972, the plaintiffs planned the construction of a large condominium development on their remaining property. The proposed improvements would include public water and sanitary sewers, a five-acre lake, and a recreational area (including swimming pools and tennis courts) of seven or eight acres. The condominium's community would be "age-oriented" and, with respect to married couples, either the husband or the wife would have to be at least 50 years of age. Mitchell Berenson, one of the plaintiffs, was informed by town officials that the requested zoning changes would not be made. Thereupon, this action was brought to declare the town's zoning ordinance unconstitutional. In denying cross motions for summary judgment, Special Term found that triable issues of fact existed—the principal question being whether the need for multiple-family housing in New Castle "is so compelling as to amount to a deprivation of the constitutional rights of those people, who are presently, or would if economically feasible, become residents of the Town," On cross appeals to the Appellate Division, that court stated its agreement with Special Term's delineation of factual issues and affirmed the order denying summary judgment. The Appellate Division granted leave to appeal to our court upon a certified question as to the correctness of its order of affirmance. We agree that factual issues remain to be resolved upon a plenary trial and that the motions for summary judgment were properly denied. Accordingly, we would affirm the order of the Appellate Division and answer the certified question in the affirmative. However, we disagree with the formulation of the issues by the lower courts. In view of the highly significant public policy considerations involved, it is necessary that we set forth our own views at some length in order that, upon the trial to be had in this case, the proper factual issues will be considered.

In determining under what circumstances, if at all, a zoning board may adopt a regulation that would prohibit entirely the construction of any new multiple residential housing within its borders, a review of the legislative and judicial history would be instructive. * * *

In determining the validity of an ordinance excluding multi-family housing as a permitted use, we must consider the general purposes which the concept of zoning seeks to serve. The primary goal of a zoning ordinance must be to provide for the development of a balanced, cohesive community which will make efficient use of the town's available land. By balanced, we do not mean to imply that a community must maintain a certain quantitative proportion between various types' of development. Clearly, such a requirement would rub against one of the basic purposes of zoning, which is to provide in an orderly fashion for actual public need for various types of residential, commercial and industrial structures.

Similarly, the town is free to set up various types of use zones. There is no requirement that each zone must contain some sort of housing balance. Our concern is not whether the zones, in themselves, are balanced communities, but whether the town itself, as provided for by its zoning ordinances, will be a balanced and integrated community. Thus, as in the Scarsdale case, if a district is set aside for multiple-dwelling development, there is no requirement that other portions of a town contain such developments.

While it may be impermissible in an undeveloped community to prevent entirely the construction of multiple-family residences anywhere in the locality, it is perfectly acceptable to limit new construction of such buildings where such units already exist.

The first branch of the test, then, is simply whether the board has provided a properly balanced and well ordered plan for the community. Of course, what may be appropriate for one community may differ substantially from what is appropriate for another. Thus, in this case, the court must ascertain what types of housing presently exist in New Castle, their quantity and quality, and whether this array adequately meets the present needs of the town. Also, it must be determined whether new construction is necessary to fulfill the future needs of New Castle residents, and if so, what forms the new developments ought to take.

Secondly, in enacting a zoning ordinance, consideration must be given to regional needs and requirements. It may be true, for example, that New Castle already has a sufficient number of multiple-dwelling units to satisfy both its present and future populations. However, residents of Westchester County, as well as the larger New York City metropolitan region, may be searching for multiple-family housing in the area to be near their employment or for a variety of other social and economic reasons. There must be a balancing of the local desire to maintain the *status quo* within the community and the greater public interest that regional needs be met. Although we are aware of the traditional view that zoning acts only upon the property lying within the zoning board's territorial limits, it must be recognized that zoning often has a substantial impact beyond the boundaries of the municipality. Thus, the court, in examining an ordinance, should take into consideration not only the general welfare of the residents of the zoning township, but should also consider the effect of the ordinance on the neighboring communities. While regional needs are a valid consideration in zoning, apart from any question as to the standing of persons outside the zoning jurisdiction to raise the issue, a town need not permit a use solely for the sake of the people of the region if regional needs are presently provided for in an adequate manner. Thus, for example, if New Castle's neighbors supply enough multiple-dwelling units or land to build such units to satisfy New Castle's need as well as their own, there would be no obligation on New Castle's part to provide more, assuming there is no overriding regional need. The second branch of the test is whether the town board, in excluding new multiple housing within its township, considered the needs of the region as well as the town for such housing. So long as the regional and local needs for such housing were supplied by either the local community or by other accessible areas in the community at large, it cannot be said, as a matter of law, that such an ordinance had no substantial relation to the public health, safety, morals or general welfare.

Zoning, as we have previously noted, is essentially a legislative act. Thus, it is quite anomalous that a court should be required to perform the tasks of a regional planner. To that end, we look to the Legislature to make appropriate changes in order to foster the development of programs designed to achieve sound regional planning. While the people of New Castle may fervently desire to be left alone by the forces of change, the ultimate determination is not solely theirs. Whether New Castle should be permitted to exclude high density residential development depends on the facts and circumstances present in the town and the community at large. Until the day comes when regional, rather than local, governmental units can make such determinations, the courts must assess the reasonableness of what the locality has done. That is what remains to be considered upon the trial in this case.

The order appealed from should be affirmed, with costs, and the certified question answered in the affirmative.

D. SPECIAL PROBLEMS OF RACIAL DISCRIMINATION

Although there are many similarities between exclusion based upon race and exclusion based upon class or wealth, the courts have nevertheless tended to treat *racial discrimination* differently from *discrimination against the poor*. A number of reasons have been proposed to explain this difference in judicial treatment: (1) race is an inherited characteristic, beyond the ability of a person to change; (2) poverty, unlike race, is more a matter of degree than of kind; (3) current morality permits acceptance of distinctions based on wealth more readily than distinctions based on race.

In spite of the differences between racial and economic discrimination, it seems very clear, as the Supreme Court has observed, that evidence is available to show that discrimination against low-income groups is, to a large extent, discrimination against racial minorities, thereby requiring the ordinance to be "scrutinized with great care." *Bolling v. Sharpe,* 347 U.S. 497, 499, (1954). It is also true that some zoning ordinances operate to exclude many middle-income class families from the suburbs as well, but as the court said on another occasion, "the reality is that the law's impact falls hardest on the minority." *Hunter v. Erickson,* 393 U.S. 385, 89S.Ct. 557, 21 L.Ed.2d 616 (1969). Thus an examination of the validity of laws excluding the poor is pertinent to the issue of racial discrimination. See *McDonald v. Board of Election Comm.,* 394 U.S. 802, 807 (1969).

However, it must be clearly understood that although there may be some question about the extent to which, and the circumstances under which, the Constitution prohibits discrimination against the poor, there is no question that the Constitution and laws of the United States prohibit discrimination on the basis of race. The Equal Protection clause of the Fourteenth Amendment prohibits discrimination by any state (or state agency) on the grounds of race. The Thirteenth Amendment prohibits slavery and involuntary servitude and gives Congress power to enforce this provision by appropriate legislation. Federal, state and local laws have been enacted that prohibit discrimination in housing based on race. It is clear that a zoning ordinance that is *intended* to discriminate against persons on the ground of race would violate these constitutional and statutory prohibitions. The cases and material that follow illustrate some of the issues that arise under these legal principles.

The Fourteenth Amendment: What is "State Action"?

The Fourteenth Amendment prohibits a *state* (or state agency) from denying a person due process of law or equal protection of the laws. This provision makes it unconstitutional for a *state* (or state agency) to discriminate against any person on the grounds of race unless the state can show a "compelling reason" for such discrimination. However, it is clear that the Fourteenth Amendment was not intended to, and does not in fact, prohibit *private* discrimination against a person on the grounds of race. Therefore, a private person could refuse to sell or lease a house to a member of racial minority without violating the Fourteenth Amendment. If, however, an agency of the state, such as a court, a police officer, a sheriff, etc., is called upon to enforce an act of private discrimination on the grounds of race, the issue arises whether there is sufficient "state action" to invoke the provisions of the Fourteenth Amendment.

The cases that follow explore this issue: *Shelley v. Kraemer* raises the question whether judicial enforcement of a racially discriminatory restrictive covenant is "state action" within the meaning of the Fourteenth Amendment; *Reitman v. Mulkey* deals with the question whether state constitutional protection of private discrimination violates the Fourteenth Amendment; the *Valtierra* and *City of Eastlake* cases respond to the question whether referendum requirements for zoning changes are the kinds of "state action" that violates the Fourteenth Amendment. When reading these cases ask yourself the following question: At what point does the relationship between private action and state participation become so entwined that the action of a private person should be considered "state action" within the meaning of the Fourteen Amendment? For example, state and local governments are involved in the construction of housing in many ways such as the provision of streets, water, sewer and electric utilities, by administering zoning, building and housing codes and even by providing police, fire, sanitation and education facilities, without which housing development would not be feasible. It has been argued that that the relationship between state and local government and housing developers is so close as to constitute "state action" within the meaning of the Fourteenth Amendment. To date, this argument has not had much success in the courts.

(1) Judicial Enforcement of Restrictive Covenants

SHELLEY

v.

KRAEMER

341 U.S. 1, 68 S.Ct. 836, 92 L.Ed. 1161 (1948)

MR. CHIEF JUSTICE VINSON delivered the opinion of the Court.

These cases present for our consideration questions relating to the validity of court enforcement of private agreements, generally described as restrictive covenants, which have as their purpose the exclusion of persons of designated race or color from the ownership or occupancy of real property. Basic constitutional issues of obvious importance have been raised.

The first of these cases comes to this Court on certiorari to the Supreme Court of Missouri. On February 16, 1911, thirty out of a total of thirty-nine owners of property fronting both sides of Labadie Avenue between Taylor Avenue and Cora Avenue in the city of St. Louis, signed an agreement, which was subsequently recorded, providing in part:

". . . the said property is hereby restricted to the use and occupancy for the term of Fifty (50) years from this date, so that it shall be a condition all the time and whether recited and referred to as (*sic*) not in subsequent conveyances and shall attach to the land as a condition precedent to the sale of the same, that hereafter no part of said property or any portion thereof shall be, for said term of Fifty-years, occupied by any person not of the Caucasian race, it being intended hereby to restrict the use of said property for said period of time against the occupancy as owners or tenants of any portion of said property for resident or other purpose by people of the Negro or Mongolian Race."

* * *On August 11, 1945, pursuant to a contract of sale, petitioners Shelley, who are Negroes, for valuable consideration received from on Fitzgerald a warranty deed to the parcel in question. The trial court found that petitioners had no actual knowledge of the restrictive agreement at the time of the purchase.

On October 9, 1945, respondents, as owners of other property subject to the terms of the restrictive covenant, brought suit in the Circuit Court of the city of St. Louis praying that petptioners Shelley be restrained from taking possession of the property and that judgment be entered divesting title out of petitioners Shelley and revesting title in the immediate grantor or in such other person as the court should direct. The trial court denied the requested relief on the ground that the restrictive agreement, upon which respondents based their action, had never become final and complete because it was the intention of the parties to that agreement that it was not to become effective until signed by all property owners in the district, and signatures of all the owners had never been obtained.

The Supreme Court of Missouri sitting *en banc* reversed and directed the trial court to grant the relief for which respondents had prayed. That court held the agreement effective and concluded that enforcement of its provisions violated no rights guaranteed to petitioners by the Federal Constitution. At the time the court rendered its decision, petitioners were occupying the property in question. * * *

Petitioners have placed primary reliance on their contentions, first raised in the state courts, that judicial enforcement of the restrictive agreements in these cases has violated right guaranteed to petitioners by the Fourteenth Amendment of the Federal Constitution and Act of Congress passed pursuant to that Amendment. Specifically, petitioners urge that they have been denied the equal protection of the laws, deprived of property without due process of law, and have been denied privileges and immunities of citizens of the United States. We pass to a consideration of those issues. * * *

It cannot be doubted that among the civil rights intended to be protected from discriminatory state action by the Fourteenth Amendment are the rights to acquire, enjoy, own and dispose of property. Equality in the enjoyment of property rights was regarded by the framers of that Amendment as an essential pre-condition to the realization of other basic civl rights and liberties which the Amendment was intended to guarantee. Thus, §1978 of the Revised Statutes, derived from § 1 of the Civil Rights Act of 1866 which was enacted by Congress while the Fourteenth Amendment was also under consideration provides:

> "All citizens of the United States shall have the same right, in every State and Territory, as is enjoyed by white citizens thereof to inherit, purchase, lease, sell, hold, and convey real and personal property."

* * *Since the decision of the Court in the *Civil Rights Cases*, 109 U.S. 3 (1883), the principle has become firmly embedded in our constitutional law that the action inhibited by the first section of the Fourteenth Amendment is only such action as may fairly be said to be that of the States. That Amendment erects no shield against merely private conduct, however discriminatory or wrongful.

We conclude, therfore, that the restrictive agreements standing alone cannot be regarded as violative of any rights guaranteed to petitioners by the Fourteenth Amendment. So long as the purposes of those agreements are effectuated by voluntary adherence to their terms, it would appear clear that there has been no action by the State and the provisions of the Amendment have not been violated. Cf. *Corrigan* v. *Buckley, supra.*

But here there was more. These are cases in which the purposes of the agreements were secured only by judicial enforcement by state courts of the restrictive terms of the agreements. The respondents urge that judicial enforcement of private agreements does not amount to state action; or, in any event, the participation of the State is so attenuated in character as not to amount to state action within the meaning of the Fourteenth

Amendment. Finally, it is suggested, even if the States in these cases may be deemed to have acted in the constitutional sense, their action did not deprive petitioners of rights guaranteed by the Fourteenth Amendment. We move to a consideration of these matters. * * *

That the action of state courts and judicial officers in their official capacities is to be regarded as action of the State within the meaning of the Fourteenth Amendment, is a proposition which has long been established by decisions of this Court. * * *

These cases demonstrate, also, the early recognition by this Court that state action in violation of the Amendment's provisions is equally repugnant to the constitutional commands whether directed by state statute or taken by a judicial official in the absence of statute. * * *

The short of the matter is that from the time of the adoption of the Fourteenth Amendment until the present, it has been the consistent ruling of this Court that the action of the States to which the Amendment has reference includes action of state courts and state judicial officials.

* * * We have no doubt that there has been state action in these cases in the full and complete sense of the phrase. The undisputed facts disclose that petitioners were willing purchasers of properties upon which they desired to establish homes. The owners of the properties were willing sellers; and contracts of sale were accordingly consummated. It is clear that but for the active intervention of the state courts, supported by the full panoply of state power, petitioners would have been free to occupy the properties in question without restraint.

These are not cases, as has been suggested, in which the States have merely abstained from action, leaving private individuals free to impose such discriminations as they see fit. Rather, these are cases in which the States have made available to such individuals the full coercive power of government to deny to petitioners, on the grounds of race or color, the enjoyment of property rights in premises which petitioners are willing and financially able to acquire and which the grantors are willing to sell. The difference between judicial enforcement and nonenforcement of the restrictive covenants is the difference to petitioners between being denied rights of property available to other members of the community and being accorded full enjoyment of those right on an equal footing. * * *

We hold that in granting judicial enforcement of the restrictive agreements in these cases, the States have denied petitioners the equal protection of the laws and that, therefore, the action of the state courts cannot stand.

* * * Upon full consideration, we have concluded that in these cases the States have acted to deny petitioners the equal protection of the laws guaranteed by the Fourteenth Amendment. Having so decided, we find it unneccessary to consider whether petitioners have also been deprived of property without due process of law or denied privileges and immunities of citizens of the United States.

For the reasons stated, the judgment of the Supreme Court of Missouri and the judgment of the Supreme Court of Michigan must be reversed.

(2) State Protection of Private Discrimination

REITMAN

v.

MULKEY

387 U.S. 369, 87 S.Ct. 1627, 18 L.Ed.2a 830 (1967)

Mr. Justice WHITE delivered the opinion of the Court.

The question here is whether Art. I, § 26, of the California Constituion denies "to any person * * * the equal protection of the laws" within the meaning of the Fourteenth Amendment of the Constitution of the United States. Section 26 of Art I, an initiated measure submitted to the people as Proposition 14 in a statewide ballot in 1964, provides in part as follows:

> "Neither the State nor any subdivision or agency therof shall deny, limit or abridge, directly or indirectly, the right of any person, who is willing or desires to sell, lease or rent any part or all of his real property, to decline to sell, lease or rent such property to such person or persons as he, in his absolute discretion, chooses."

The real property covered by § 26 is limited to residential property and contains an exception for state-owned real estate.

The issue arose in two separate actions in the California courts, *Mulkey v. Reitman* and *Prendergast v. Snyder*. In *Reitman*, the Mulkeys who are husband and wife and respondents here, sued under § 51 and § 52 of the California Civil Code alleging that petitioners had refused to rent them an apartment solely on account of their race. An injunction and damages were demanded. Petitioners moved for summary judgment of the ground that §§ 51 and 52, insofar as they were the basis for the Mulkeys' action, had been rendered null and void by the adoption of Proposition 14 after the filing of the complaint. The trial court granted the motion and respondents took the case to the California Supreme Court.

In the *Prendergast* case, respondents, husband and wife, filed suit in December 1964 seeking to enjoin eviction from their apartment; respondents alleged that the eviction was motivated by racial prejudice and therefore would violate § 51 and § 52 of the Civil Code. Petitioner Snyder cross-complained for a judicial declaration that he was entitled to terminate the month-to-month tenancy even if his action was based on racial considerations. In denying petitioner's motion for summary judgment, the trial court found it unnecessary to consider the validity of Proposition 14 because it concluded that judicial enforcement of an eviction based on racial grounds would in any event violate the Equal Protection Clause of the United States Constitution. The cross-complaint was dismissed with prejudice and petitioner Snyder appealed to the California Supreme Court which considered the case along with *Mulkey v. Reitman*. That court, in reversing the *Reitman* case, held that Art. I, § 26, was invalid as denying the equal protection of the laws guaranteed by the Fourteenth Amendment. For similar reasons, the court affirmed the judgment in the *Prendergast* case. We granted certiorari because the cases involve an important issue arising under the Fourteenth Amendment.

We affirm the judgments of the California Supreme Court. We first turn to the opinion of that court in *Reitman*, which quite properly undertook to examine the constitutionality of § 26 in terms of its "immediate objective," its "ultimate effect" and its "historical context and the conditions existing prior to its enactment." Judgments such as these we have frequently undertaken ourselves. * * *

First, the court considered whether § 26 was concerned at all with private discriminations in residential housing. This involved a review of past efforts by the California Legeslature to regulate such discrimiations. The Unruh Act, Civ. Code §§ 51-52, on which respondents based their cases, was passed in 1959. The Hawkins Act, formerly Health & Safety Code §§ 35700-35741, followed and prohibited discriminations in publicly assisted housing. In 1961, the legislature enacted proscriptions against restrictive covenants. Finally, in 1963,came the Rumford Fair Housing Act, Health & Safety Code §§ 35700-35744, superseding the Hawkins Act and prohibiting racial discriminations in the sale or rental of any private dwelling containing more than four units. That act was enforceable by the State Fair Employment Practice Commission.

It was against this background that Proposition 14 was enacted. Its immediate design and intent, the California court said, were "to overturn state laws that bore on the right of private sellers and lessors to discriminate," the Unruh and Rumford Acts, and "to forestall future state action that might circumscribe this right." This aim was successfully achieved: the adoption of Proposition 14 "generally nullifies both the Rumford and Unruh Acts as they apply to the housing market," and establishes "a purported constitutional right to *privately* discriminate on grounds which admittedly would be unavailable under the Fourteenth Amendment *should state action* be involved." * * *

Second, the court conceded that the State was permitted a neutral position with respect to private racial discriminations and that the State was not bound by the Federal Constitution to forbid them. But, because a significant state involvement in private discriminations could amount to unconstitutional state action, Burton v. Wilminton Parking Authority, the court deemed it necessary to determine whether Propositon 14 invalidly involved the State in racial discriminations in the housing market. Its conclusion was that it did. * * *

There is no sound reason for rejecting this judgment. Petitioners contend that the California court has misconstrued the Fourteenth Amendment since the repeal of any stature prohibiting racial discrimination, which is constitutionally permissible, may be said to "authorize" and "encourage" discrimination because it makes legally permissible that which was formerly proscribed. But as we understand the California court, it did not posit a constitutional violation on the mere repeal of the Unruh and Rumford Acts. It did not read either our cases or the Fourteenth

Amendment as establishing an automatic constitutional barrier to the repeal of an existing law prohibiting racial discriminations in housing; nor did the court rule that a State may never put in statutory form an existing policy of neutrality with respect to private discriminations. What the court below did was first to reject the notion that the State was required to have a statute prohibiting racial discriminations in housing. Second, it held the intent of § 26 was to authorize private racial discrimination in the housing market, to repeal the Unruh and Rumford Acts and to create a constitutional right to discriminate on racial grounds in the sale and leasing of real property. Hence, the court dealt with § 26 as though it expressly authorized and constitutionalized the private right to discriminate. Third, the court assessed the ultimate impact of § 26 in the California environment and concluded that the section would encourage and significanly involve the State in private racial discrimination contrary to the Fourteenth Amendment.

The California court could very reasonably conclude that § 26 would and did have wider impact than a mere repeal of existing statutes. * * *

The right to discriminate, including the right to discriminate on racial grounds, was now embodied in the State's basic charter, immune from legislative, executive, or judicial regulation at any level of the state government. Those practicing racial discriminations need no longer rely solely on their personal choice. They could now invoke express constitutional authority, free from censure or interference of any kind from official sources. * * *

This Court has never attempted the "impossible task" of formulating an infallible test for determining whether the State "in any way of its manifestations" has become significantly involved in private discriminations. "Only by sifting facts and wieghing circumstances" on a case-by-case basis can a "nonobvious involvement of the State in private conduct be attributed its true significance." * * *

Section 26 was intended to authorize, and does authorize, racial discrimination in the housing market. The right to discriminate is now one of the basic policies of the State. The California Supreme Court believes that the section will significantly encourage and involve the State in private discriminations. We have been presented with no persuasive considerations indicating that these judgments should be overturned.

Affirmed.

(3) Requirement of Zoning Referendum

JAMES

v.

VALTIERRA

402 U.S. 137, 91 S.Ct.1331, 28 L.Ed.2d 678 (1971)

MR. JUSTICE BLACK delivered the opinion of the Court.

These cases raise but a single issue. It grows out of the United States Housing Act of 1937, 50 Stat. 888, as amended, 42 U.S.C. § 1401 *et seq.*, which established a federal housing agency authorized to make loans and grants to state agencies for slum clearance and low-rent housing projects. In response, the California Legislature created in each county and city a public housing authority to take advantage of the financing made available by the federal Housing Act. See Cal. Health & Safety Code § 34240. At the time the federal legislation was passed the California Constitution had for many years reserved to the State's people the power to initiate legislation and to reject or approve by referendum any Act passed by the state legislature. Cal. Const., Art. IV, § 1. The same section reserved to the electors of counties and cities the power of initiative and referendum over acts of local government bodies. In 1950, however, the State Supreme Court held that local authorities' decisions on seeking federal aid for public housing projects were "executive" and "administrative," not "legislative," and therefore the state constitution's referendum provisions did not apply to these actions. Within six months of that decision the California voters adopted Article XXXIV of the state constitution to bring public housing decisions under the State's referendum policy. The Article provided that no low-rent housing project should be developed, constructed, or acquired in any manner by a state public body until the project was approved by a majority of those voting at a community election. *

The present suits were brought by citizens of San Jose, California, and San Mateo County, localities where housing authorities could not apply for federal funds because low-cost housing proposals had been defeated in

---

* "Section 1. No low rent housing project shall hereafter be developed, constructed, or acquired in any manner by any state public body until, a majority of the qualified electors of the city, town or country, as the case may be, in which it is proposed to develop, construct, or acquire the same, voting upon each issue, approve such project by voting in favor thereof at an election to be held for that purpose, or at any general or special election.

"For the purposes of this article the term 'low rent housing project' shall mean any development composed of urban or rural dwellings, apartments or other living accommodations for persons of low income, financed in whole or in part by the Federal Government or a state public body or to which the Federal Government

referendums. The plaintiffs, who are eligible for low-cost public housing, sought a declaration that Article XXXIV was unconstitutional because its referendum requirement violated: (1) the Supremacy Clause of the United States Constitution; (2) the Privileges. and Immunities Clause, and (3) the Equal Protection Clause. A three-judge court held that Article XXXIV denied the plaintiffs equal protection of the laws and it enjoined its enforcement. 313 F.Supp. 1 (ND Cal. 1970). Two appeals were taken from the judgment, one by the San Jose City Council, and the other by a single member of the council. We noted probable jurisdiction of both appeals. 398 U.S. 949 (1970); 399 U.S. 925 (1970). For the reasons that follow, we reverse.

The three-judge court found the Supremacy Clause argument unpersuasive, and we agree. By the Housing Act of 1937 the Federal Government has offered aid to state and local governments for the creation of low-rent public housing. However, the federal legislation does not purport to require that local governments accept this or to outlaw local referendums on whether the aid should be accepted. We also find the privileges and immunities argument without merit.

While the District Court cited several cases of this Court, its chief reliance plainly rested on *Hunter* v. *Erickson*, 393 U.S. 385 (1969). The first paragraph in the District Court's decision stated simply: "We hold Article XXXIV to be unconstitutional. *See* Hunter v. Erickson . . . ." The court below erred in relying on *Hunter* to invalidate Article XXXIV. Unlide the case before us, *Hunter* rested on the conslusion that Akron's referendum law denied equal protection by placing "special burdens on racial minorities within the governmental process." *Id.*, at 391. In *Hunter* the citizens of Akron had amended the city charter to require that any ordinance regulating real estate on the basis of race, color, religion, or national origin could not take effect without approval by a majority of those voting in a city election. The Court held that the amendment created a classification based upon race because it required that laws dealing with racial housing matters could take effect only if they survived a mandatory referendum while other housing ordinances took effect without any such special election. The opinion noted:

"Because the core of the Fourteenth Amendment is the prevention of meaningful and unjustified official distinctions based on race, [citing a group of racial discrimination cases] racial classifications are 'constitutionally suspect' . . . and subject to the 'most rigid scrutiny.' . . . They 'bear a far heavier burden of justification' than other classifications." *Id.*, at 391-392.

The Court concluded that Akron had advanced no sufficient reasons to justify this racial classification and hence that it was unconstitutional under the Fourteenth Amendment.

---

or a state public body extends assistance by supplying all or part of the labor, by guaranteeing the payment of liens, or otherwise. . . .

"For the purposes of this article only 'persons of low income' shall mean persons or families who lack the amount of income which is necessary (as determined by the state public body developing, constructing, or acquiring the housing project) to enable them, without financial assistance, to live in decent, safe and sanitary dwellings without overcrowding."

Unlike the Akron referendum provision, it cannot be said that California's Article XXXIV rests on "distinctions based on race." *Id.*, at 391. The Article requires referendum approval for any low-rent public housing project, not only for projects which will be occupied by a racial minority. And the record here would not support any claim that a law seemingly neutral on its face is in fact aimed at a racial minority. Cf. *Gomillion* v. *Lightfoot*, (1960). The present case could be affirmed only by extending *Hunter* , and this we decline to do.

California's entire history demonstrates the repeated use of referendums to give citizens a voice on questions of public policy. A referendum provision was included in the first state constitution, Cal. Const. of 1849, Art. VIII, and referendums have been a commonplace occurrence in the State's active political life. Provisions for referendums demonstrate devotion to democracy, not to bias, discrimination, or prejudice. Nonetheless, appellees contend that Article XXXIV denies them equal protection because it demands a mandatory referendum while many other referendums only take place upon citizen initiative. They suggest that the mandatory nature of the Article XXXIV referendum constitutes unconstitutional discrimination because it hampers persons desiring public housing from achieving their objective when no such roadblock faces other groups seeking to influence other public decisions to their advantage. But of course a lawmaking procedure that "disadvantages" a particular group does not always deny equal protection. Under any such holding, presumably a State would not be able to require referendums on any subject unless referendums were required on all, because they would always disadvantage some group. And this Court would be required to analyze governmental structures to determine whether a gubernatorial veto provision or a filibuster rule is likely to "disadvantage" any of the diverse and shifting groups that make up the American people.

Furthermore, an examination of California law reveals that persons advocating low-income housing have not been singled out for mandatory referendums while no other group must face that obstacle. Mandatory referendums are required for approval of state constitutional amendments, for the issuance of general obligation long-term bonds by local governments, and for certain municipal territorial annexations. See Cal. Const., Art. XVIII; Art. XIII, § 40; Art. XI, § 2 (b). California statute books contain much legislation first enacted by voter initiative, and no such law can be repealed or amended except by referendum. Cal Const., Art. IV, § 24 (c). Some California cities have wisely provided that their public parks may not be alienated without mandatory referendums, see, *e.g.*, San Jose Charter § 1700.

The people of California have also decided by their own vote to require referendum approval of low-rent public housing projects. This procedure ensures that all the people of a community will have a voice in a decision which may lead to large expenditures of local governmental funds for increased public services and to lower tax revenues. * It gives them a voice in decisions that will affect the future development of their own community. This procedure for democratic decisionmaking does not violate the constitutional command that no State shall deny to any person "the equal protection of the laws."

The judgment of the three-judge court is reversed and the cases are remanded for dismissal of the complaint.

Reversed and remanded.

MR. JUSTICE MARSHALL, whom MR. JUSTICE BRENNAN and MR. JUSTICE BLACKMUN join, dissenting.

By its very terms, the mandatory prior referendum provision of Art. XXXIV applies solely to

"any development composed of urban or rural dwellings, apartments or other living accommodations for persons of low income, financed in whole or in part by the Federal Government or a state public body or to which the Federal Government or a state public body extends assistance by supplying all or part of the labor, by guarante-eing the payment of liens, or otherwise."

Persons of low income are defined as

"persons or families who lack the amount of income which is neces-sary . . . to enable them, without financial assistance, to live in de-cent, safe and sanitary dwellings, without overcrowding."

The article explicitly singles out low-income persons to bear its burden. Publicly assisted housing developments designed to accommodate the aged, veterans, state employees, persons of moderate income, or any class of citizens other than the poor, need not be approved by prior re-ferenda.*

In my view, Art. XXXIV on its face constitutes invidious discrimination which the Equal Protection Clause of the Fourteenth Amendment plainly prohibits. "The States, of course, are prohibited by the Equal Protection Clause from discriminating between 'rich' and 'poor' *as such* in the for-mulation and application of their laws." *Douglas* v. *California,* (1963) (HARLAN, J., dissenting). Article XXXIV is neither "a law of general applicability that may affect the poor more harshly than it does the rich," *ibid.,* nor an "effort to redress economic imbalances," *ibid.* It is rather an explicit classification on the basis of poverty—a suspect classification which demands exacting judicial scrutiny, see *McDonald* v. *Board of Election,* (1969): *Harper* v. *Virginia Board of Elections,* (1966); *Douglas* v. *California, supra.*

The Court, however, chooses to subject the article to no scrutiny what-soever and treats the provision as if it contained a totally benign, technical

---

* Public low-rent housing projects are financed through bonds issued by the local housing authority. To be sure, the Federal Government contracts to make contributions sufficient to cover interest and principal, but the local government body must agree to provide all municipal services for the units and to waive all taxes on the property. The local services to be provided include schools, police, and fire protection, sewers, streets, drains, and lighting. Some of the cost is de-frayed by the local governing body's receipt of 10% of the housing project rentals, but of course the rentals are set artificially low. Both appellants and appellees agree that the building of federally financed low-cost housing entails costs to the local community. Appellant Shaffer's Brief 34-35. Appellees' Brief 47. See also 42 U.S.C. §§ 1401-1430.

economic classification. Both the appellees and the Solicitor General of the United States as *amicus curiae* have strenuously argued, and the court below found, that Art. XXXIV, by imposing a substantial burden solely on the poor, violates the Fourteenth Amendment. Yet after observing that the article does not discriminate on the basis of race, the Court's only response to the real question in these cases is the unresponsive assertion that "referendums demonstrate devotion to democracy, not to bias, discrimination, or prejudice." It is far too late in the day to contend that the Fourteenth Amendment prohibits only racial discrimination; and to me, singling out the poor to bear a burden not placed on any other class of citizens tramples the values that the Fourteenth Amendment was designed to protect.

I respectfully dissent.

CITY OF EASTLAKE et al.,

v.

FOREST CITY ENTERPRISES, INC.

426 U.S. 668, 96 S.Ct. 2358, 49 L.Ed.2d 132 (1976)

Mr. Chief Justice BURGER delivered the opinion of the Court.

The question in this case is whether a city charter provision requiring proposed land use changes to be ratified by 55% of the voters violates the due process rights of a landowner who applies for a zoning change.

The city of Eastlake, Ohio, a suburb of Cleveland, has a comprehensive zoning plan codified in a municipal ordinance. Respondent, a real estate developer, acquired an eight-acre parcel of real estate in Eastlake zoned for "light industrial" uses at the time of purchase.

In May 1971, respondent applied to the City Planning Commission for a zoning change to permit construction of a multi-family, high-rise apartment building. The planning Commission recommended the proposed change to the City Council, which under Eastlake's procedures could either accept or reject the Planning Commission's recommendation. Meanwhile, by popular vote, the voters of Eastlake amended the City Charter to require that any changes in land use agreed to by the Council be approved by a 55% vote in a referendum. The City Council approved the Planning Commission's recommendation for reclassification of respondent's property to permit the proposed project. Respondent then applied to the Planning Commission for "parking and yard" approval for the proposed building. The Commission rejected the application, on the ground that the City Council's rezoning action had not yet been submitted to the voters for ratification.

Respondent then filed an action in state court, seeking a judgment declaring the charter provision invalid as an unconstitutional delegation of legislative power to the people. While the case was pending, the City

Council's action was submitted to a referendum, but the proposed zoning change was not approved by the requisite 55% margin. Following the election, the Court of Common Pleas and the Ohio Court of Appeals sustained the charter provision.

The Ohio Supreme Court reversed. Concluding that enactment of zoning and rezoning provisions is a legislative function, the court held that a popular referendum requirement, lacking standards to guide the decision of the voters, permitted the police power to be exercised in a standardless, hence arbitrary and capricious manner. Relying on this Court's decisions in *Washington ex rel. Seattle Title Trust Co.* v. *Roberge,* (1928), *Thomas Cusack Co.* v. *Chicago,* (1917), and *Eubank* v. *Richmond,* (1912), but distinguishing *James* v. *Valtierra,* (1971), the court concluded that the referendum provision constituted an unlawful delegation of legislative power.

We reverse.

I

The conclusion that Eastlake's procedure violates federal constitutional guarantees rests upon the proposition that a zoning referendum involves a delegation of legislative power. A referendum cannot, however, be characterized as a delegation of power. Under our constitutional assumptions, all power derives from the people, who can delegate it to representative instruments which they create. See, *e.g.,* Federalist Papers, No. 39. In establishing legislative bodies, the people can reserve to themselves power to deal directly with matters which might otherwise be assigned to the legislature. *Hunter* v. *Erickson,* (1969).

The reservation of such power is the basis for the town meeting, a tradition which continues to this day in some States as both a practical and symbolic part of our democratic processes. The referendum, similarly, is a means for direct political participation, allowing the people the final decision, amounting to a veto power, over enactments of representative bodies. The practice is designed to "give citizens a voice on questions of public policy."

In framing a state constitution, the people of Ohio specifically reserved the power of referendum to the people of each municipality within the State.

> "The initiative and referendum powers are hereby reserved to the people of each municipality on all questions which such municipalities may now or hereafter be authorized by law to control by legislative action. . . ." Ohio Const. Art. II, § 1f (1955).

To be subject to Ohio's referendum procedure, the question must be one within the scope of legislative power. The Ohio Supreme Court expressly found that the City Council's action in rezoning respondent's eight acres from light industrial to high-density residential use was legislative in nature. Distinguishing between administrative and legislative acts, the court separated the power to zone or rezone, by passage or amendment of a zoning ordinance, from the power to grant relief from unnecessary hardship. The former function was found to be legislative in nature.

II

The Ohio Supreme Court further concluded that the amendment to the City Charter constituted a "delegation" of power violative of federal constitutional guarantees because the voters were give no standards to guide their decision. Under Eastlake's procedure, the Ohio Supreme Court reasoned, no mechanism existed, nor indeed could exist, to assure that the voters would act rationally in passing upon a proposed zoning change. This meant that "appropriate legislative action (would) be made dependent upon the potentially arbitrary and unreasonable whims of the voting public." The potential for arbitrariness in the process, the court concluded, violated due process.

Courts have frequently held in other contexts that a congressional delegation of power to a regulatory entity must be accompanied by discernible standards, so that the delegatee's action can be measured for its fidelity to the legislative will. Assuming, *arguendo,* their relevance to state governmental functions, these cases involved a delegation of power by the legislature to regulatory bodies, which are not directly responsible to the people; this doctrine is inapplicable where, as here, rather than a delegation of power, we deal with a power reserved by the people to themselves.

In basing its claim on federal due process requirements, respondent also invokes *Euclid v. Ambler Realty Co.,* (1926), but it does not rely on the direct teaching of that case. Under *Euclid,* a property owner can challenge a zoning restriction if the measure is "clearly arbitrary and unreasonable, have no substantial relation to the public health, safety, morals, or general welfare." If the substantive result of the referendum is arbitrary and capricious, bearing no relation to the police power, then the fact that the voters of Eastlake wish it so would not save the restriction. As this Court held in invalidating a charter amendment enacted by referendum:

> "The sovereignty of the people is itself subject to those constitutional limitations which have been duly adopted and remain unrepealed."

But no challenge of the sort contemplated in *Euclid v. Ambler* is before us. The Ohio Supreme Court did not hold, and respondent does not argue, that the present zoning classification under Eastlake's comprehensive ordinance violates the principles established in *Euclid v. Ambler.* If respondent considers the referendum result itself to be unreasonable, the zoning restriction is open to challenge in state court, where the scope of the state remedy available to respondent would be determined as a matter of state law, as well as under Fourteenth Amendment standards. That being so, nothing more is required by the Constitution. . . .

Neither *Eubank* nor *Roberge* involved a referendum procedure such as we have in this case; the standardless delegation of power to a limited group of property owners condemned by the Court in *Eubank* and *Roberge* is not to be equated with decision-making by the people through the referendum process. The Court of Appeals for the Ninth Circuit put it this way:

> "A referendum, however, is far more than an expression of am-

biguously founded neighborhood preference. It is the city itself legislating through its voters—an exercise by the voters of their traditional right through direct legislation to override the views of their elected representatives as to what serves the public interest." *Southern Alameda Spanish Speaking Organization v. City of Union City, California,* (1970).

Our decision in *James v. Valtierra,* (1971), upholding California's mandatory referendum requirement, confirms this view. Mr. Justice Black, speaking for the Court in that case, said:

"This procedure ensures that *all the people* of a community will have a voice in a decision which may lead to large expenditures of local governmental funds for increased public services . . . ."

Mr. Justice Black went on to say that the referendum procedure at issue here is a classic demonstration of "devotion to democracy . . . ." As a basic instrument of democratic government, the referendum process does not, in itself, violate the Due Process Clause of the Fourteenth Amendment when applied to a rezoning ordinance. Since the rezoning decision in this case was properly reserved to the People of Eastlake under the Ohio Constitution, the Ohio Supreme Court erred in holding invalid, on federal constitutional grounds, the charter amendment permitting the voters to decide whether the zoned use of respondent's property could be altered.

The judgment of the Ohio Supreme Court is reversed and the case is remanded for further proceedings not inconsistent with this opinion.

Reversed and ·remanded.

---

(4) Thirteenth Amendment: Badges of Slavery

JONES

v.

MAYER

392 U.S. 409, 88 S.Ct. 2186,20 L.Ed. 2a 1189 (1968)

MR. JUSTICE STEWART delivered the opinion of the Court.

In this case we are called upon to determine the scope and the constitutionality of an Act of Congress, 42 U.S.C. § 1982, which provides that:

"All citizens of the United States shall have the same right, in every State and Territory, as is enjoyed by white citizens thereof to inherit, purchase, lease, sell, hold, and convey real and personal property."

On September 2, 1965, the petitioners filed a complaint in the District Court for the Eastern District of Missouri, alleging that the repondents had refused to sell them a home in the Paddock Woods community of St. Louis County for the sole reason that petitioner Joseph Lee Jones is a Negro. Relying in part upon § 1982, the petitioners sought injunctive and other relief. The District Court sustained the respondents' motion to dismiss the complaint, and the Court of Appeals for the Eighth Circuit affirmed, concluding that § 1982 applies only to state action and does not reach private refusals to sell. We granted certiorari to consider the questions thus presented. For the reasons that follow, we reverse the judgment of the Court of Appeals. We hold that § 1982 bars all racial discrimination, private as well as public, in the sale or rental of property, and that the statute, thus construed, is a valid exercise of the power of Congress to enforce the Thirteenth Amendment.

I

At the outset, it is important to make clear precisely what this case does *not* involve. Whatever else it may be, 42 U.S.C. § 1982 is not a comprehensive open housing law. In sharp contrast to the Fair Housing Title (Title VIII) of the Civil Rights Act of 1968, Pub. L. 90-284, 82 Stat. 73, the statute in this case deals only with racial discrimination and does not address itself to discrimination on grounds of religion or national origin. It does not deal specifically with discrimination in the provision of services or facilities in connection with the sale or rental of a dwelling. It does not prohibit advertising or other representations that indicate discriminatory preferences. It does not refer explicitly to discrimination in financing arrangements or in the provision of brokerage services. It does not empower a federal administrative agency to assist aggrieved parties. It makes no provision for intervention by the Attorney General. And, although it can be enforced by injunction, it contains no provision expressly authorizing a federal court to order the payment of damages.

* * *We begin with the language of the statute itself. In plain and unambiguous terms, § 1982 grants to all citizens, without regard to race or color, "the same right" to purchase and lease property "as is enjoyed by white citizens." As the Court of Appeals in this case evidently recognized, that right can be impaired as effectively by "those who place property on the market" as by the State itself. For, even if the State and its agents lend no support to those who wish to exclude persons from their communities on racial grounds, the fact remains that, whenever property "is placed on the market for whites only, whites have a right denied to Negroes." So long as a Negro citizen who wants to buy or rent a home can be turned away simply because he is not white, he cannot be said to enjoy "the same right . . . as is enjoyed by white citizens . . . to . . . purchase [and] lease . . . real and personal property." 42 U.S.C. § 1982. (Emphasis added.)

On its face, therefore, § 1982 appears to prohibit *all* discrimination against Negroes in the sale or rental of property—discrimination by private owners as well as discrimination by public authorities. Indeed, even the respondents seem to concede that, if § 1982 "means what it says"—to use the words of the respondents' brief—then it must encompass every racially motivated refusal to sell or rent and cannot be confined to officially sanctioned segregation in housing. Stressing what they consider to be the revolutionary implications of so literal a reading of § 1982, the respondents argue that Congress cannot possibly have intended any such result. Our examination of the relevant history, however, persuades us that Congress meant exactly what it said. * * *

In light of the concerns of the debates that preceded its passage, it is clear that the Act was designed to do just what its terms suggest: to prohibit all racial discrimination, whether or not under color of law, with respect to the rights enumerated therein—including the right to purchase or lease property. * * *

The remaining question is whether Congress has power under the Constitution to do what § 1982 purports to do: to prohibit all racial discrimination, private and public, in the sale and rental of property. Our starting point is the Thirteenth Amendment, for it was pursuant to that constitutional provision that Congress originally enacted what is now § 1982. The Amendment consists of two parts. Section 1 states;

> "Neither slavery nor involuntary servitude, except as a punishment for a crime whereof the party shall have been duly convicted, shall exist within the United States, or any place subject to their jurisdiction."

Section 2 provides:

> "Congress shall have power to enforce this article by appropriate legislation."

As its text reveals, the Thirteenth Amendment "is not a mere prohibition of State laws establishing or upholding slavery, but an absolute declaration that slavery or involuntary servitude shall not exist in any part of the United States." *Civil Rights Cases*, 109 U.S.C. 3, 20. It has never been doubted, therefore, "that the power vested in Congress to enforce the article by appropriate legislation," *ibid.*, includes the power to enact laws "direct and primary, operating upon the acts of individuals, whether sanctioned by State legislation or not." *Id.*, at 23.

Thus, the fact that § 1982 operates upon the unofficial acts of private individuals, whether or not sanctioned by state law, presents no constitutional problem. If Congress has power under the Thirteenth Amendment to eradicate conditions that prevent Negroes from buying and renting property because of their race or color, then no federal statute calculated to achieve that objective can be thought to exceed the constitutional power of Congress simply because it reaches beyond state action to regulate the conduct of private individuals. The constitutional question in this case, therefore, comes to this: Does the authority of Congress to enforce the Thirteenth Amendment "by appropriate legislation" include the power to eliminate all racial barriers to the acquisition of real and personal property? We think the answer to that question is plainly yes.

"By its own unaided force and effect," the Thirteenth Amendment "abolished slavery, and established universal freedom." *Civil Rights Cases*, 109 U.S. 3, 20. Whether or not the Amendment *itself* did any more than that—a question not involved in this case—it is at least clear that the Enabling Clause of that Amendment empowered Congress to do much more. For that clause clothed "Congress with power to *pass* all laws necessary and proper for abolishing all badges and incidents of slavery in the United States." Ibid. (Emphasis added.) * * *

Negro citizens North and South, who saw in the Thirteenth Amendment a promise of freedom—freedom to "go and come at pleasure" and to "buy and sell when they please"—would be left with "a mere paper guarantee" if Congress were powerless to assure that a dollar in the hands of a Negro will purchase the same thing as a dollar in the hands of a white man. At the very least, the freedom that Congress is empowered to secure under the Thirteenth Amendment includes the freedom to buy whatever a white man can buy, the right to live wherever a white man can live. If Congress cannot say that being a free man means at least this much, then the Thirteenth Amendment made a promise the Nation cannot keep. * * *

The judgment is *Reversed.*

---

(5) Fair Housing Laws

Racial discrimination in housing is illegal under two major federal laws and **fair housing laws** adopted by approximately 18 states and over 30 municipalities.

The Civil Rights Act of 1866 provides that: "All citizens of the United States shall have the same right, in every State and Territory, as is enjoyed by white citizens thereof to inherit, purchase, lease, sell, hold, and convey real and personal property."

In *Jones v. Mayer,* set forth above, the U.S. Supreme Court held that the 1866 law prohibits "all racial discrimination, private as well as public, in the sale or rental of property."

In Title VIII of the Civil Rights Act of 1968 (the Fair Housing Law), Congress declared a national policy of providing fair housing throughout the United States. This law makes discrimination based on race, color, religion or national origin illegal in connection with the sale or rental of most housing and any vacant land offered for residential construction or use.

The Federal Fair Housing Law provides protection against the following acts, if they are based on race, color, religion or national origin:

- Refusing to sell or rent to, deal or negotiate with any person (Section 804(a)).
- Discriminating in terms or conditions for buying or renting housing (Section 804(b)).
- Discriminating by advertising that housing is available only to persons of a certain race, color, religion or national origin (Section 804(c)).
- Denying that housing is available for inspection, sale or rent when it really is available (Section 804(d)).
- **"Blockbusting"**—for profit: persuading owners to sell or rent housing by telling them that minority groups are moving into the neighborhood (Section 804(e)).
- Denying or making different terms or conditions for home loans by commercial lenders, such as banks, savings and loan associations and insurance companies (Section (805).

● Denying to anyone the use of or participation in any real estate services, such as brokers' organizations, multiple listing services or other facilities related to the selling or renting of housing (Section 806).

The Federal Fair Housing Law does not apply to all housing. The prohibitions of this legislation apply only to some, but not all, single family housing and to some, but not all, multi-family housing. Single family housing *owned by private individuals* is covered by the Federal Fair Housing Law only if:

    * a broker or other person in the business of selling or renting dwellings is used, or

    * discriminatory advertising is used.

In addition, single family housing is covered if the housing unit is not owned by a private individual or if owned by a private individual who owns more than three such housing, or who, in any two-year period, sells more than one in which he was not the most recent resident.

Multi-family housing is covered if the structure contains five or more units, or if it contains four or fewer units and the owner does not reside in one of the units.

The Federal Fair Housing Law of 1968 does *not* cover the following acts:

    1. The sale or rental of single-family houses owned by a private individual owner of three or fewer such single-family houses if:

    * A broker is not used,

    * Discriminatory advertising is not used and no more than one house in which the owner was not the most recent resident is sold during any two-year period.

    2. Rentals of rooms or units in owner-occupied multi-dwelling for two to four families, if discriminatory advertising is not used.

    3. Limiting the sale, rental, or occupancy of dwellings which a religious organization owns or operates for other than a commercial purpose to persons of the same religion, if membership in that religion is not restricted on account of race, color or national origin.

    4. Limiting to its own members the rental or occupancy of lodging which a private club owns or operates for other than a commercial purpose.

Although the above acts are not covered by the Federal Fair Housing Act of 1968 it should be kept in mind that the Civil Rights Act of 1866 prohibits *all* acts of racial discrimination in the sale or rental of property. In addition the fair housing laws of some states and municipalities may prohibit acts of racial discrimination not covered by the Federal Fair Housing Act of 1968.

(6) Discriminatory Effect Without Discriminatory Intent

When a court is called upon to determine the validity of a zoning ordinance alleged to be exclusionary or racially discriminatory, the first question it must decide is the *standard of validity.* If the test of validity is that the challenged ordinance is invalid, if but only if it was the *intent* of the ordinance to discriminate against racial minority groups residing in the region who would like to find housing in the municipality, then it becomes very difficult to overturn an exclusionary municipal ordinance. If, on the other hand, proof of discriminatory *intent* is not necessary and it is only necessary to show that the zoning ordinance has a discriminatory *effect*, then it becomes very much easier for a court to invalidate a municipal zoning ordinance that fails to meet the housing needs of racial minorities.

In Village of *Arlington Heights v. Metropolitan Housing Development Corp.*, set forth below, the United States Supreme Court held that the refusal of a municipality to change its zoning laws to permit low income housing does not violate the provisions of the United States Constitution even though the *effect* of the zoning decision is to exclude members of racial minorities from the community. Under the standard of validity adopted by the Supreme Court, **proof of racially discriminatory intent or purpose** is required to show a violation of the equal protection clause. The court suggested that discriminatory intent may be shown by an inquiry into direct and circumstantial evidence that may be available.

After reading the *Arlington Heights* case, reread the *Oakwood at Madison* decision where the New Jersey Supreme Court adopted a position that squarely contravenes the decision in *Arlington Heights*. The test established in *Oakwood at Madison* is that a zoning ordinance is invalid if it *operates in fact* (i.e., has the "effect") to preclude the opportunity to supply substantial amounts of new housing for low and moderate income families in the region, whether or not such effect was intended. Thus, under the New Jersey test of validity, it is significantly easier to invalidate a municipal zoning ordinance on the grounds that it is "exclusionary" than it would be under the Supreme Court test where proof of discriminatory intent would be required.

The difficulty with the New Jersey "effects" test is that, within the complex housing construction industry, many economic forces interact to preclude the opportunity for construction of housing for low and moderate income families in the region. The "effect" of no new housing for low and moderate income families in a municipality to meet regional needs may be the result of such factors as high construction and financing costs. This would preclude the opportunity for such housing even if zoning ordinances presented no obstacle. Consequently, by applying the "effects" test, a New Jersey court may invalidate a municipal zoning ordinance and nevertheless fail to achieve the objective of providing housing for low and moderate income persons.

VILLAGE OF ARLINGTON HEIGHTS

v.

METROPOLITAN HOUSING DEVELOPMENT CORPORATION

429 U.S. 252, 97 S.Ct. 555, 50 L.Ed. 2d 450 (1977)

MR. JUSTICE POWELL delivered the opinion of the Court.

In 1971 respondent Metropolitan Housing Development Corporation (MHDC) applied to petitioner, the Village of Arlington Heights, Ill., for the rezoning of a 15-acre parcel from single-family to multiple-family classification. Using federal financial assistance, MHDC planned to build 190 clustered townhouse units for low and moderate income tenants. The Village denied the rezoning request. MHDC, joined by other plaintiffs who are also respondents here, brought suit in the United States District Court for the Northern District of Illinois. They alleged that the denial was racially discriminatory and that it violated, *inter alia*, the Fourteenth Amendment and the Fair Housing Act of 1968, 42 U.S.C. § 3601 *et seq.* Following a bench trial, the District Court entered judgment for the Village, 373 F. Supp. 208 (1974), and respondents appealed. The Court of Appeals for the Seventh Circuit reversed, finding that the "ultimate effect" of the denial was racially discriminatory, and that the refusal to rezone therefore violated the Fourteenth Amendment. We granted the Village's petition for certiorari, and now reverse.

I

Arlington Heights is a suburb of Chicago, located about 26 miles northwest of the downtown Loop area. Most of the land in Arlington Heights is zoned for detached single-family homes, and this is in fact the prevailing land use. The Village experienced substantial growth during the 1960's, but, like other communities in northwest Cook County, its population of racial minority groups remained quite low. According to the 1970 census, only 27 of the Village's 64,000 residents were black.

The Clerics of St. Viator, a religious order (the Order), own an 80-acre parcel just east of the center of Arlington Heights. Part of the site is occupied by the Viatorian high school, and part by the Order's three-story novitiate building, which houses dormitories and a Montessori school. Much of the site, however, remains vacant. Since 1959, when the Village first adopted a zoning ordinance, all the land surrounding the Viatorian property has been zoned R-3, a single-family specification with relatively small minimum lot size requirements. On three sides of the Viatorian land there are single-family homes just across a street; to the east the Viatorian property directly adjoins the back yards of other single-family homes.

The Order decided in 1970 to devote some of its land to low and moderate income housing. Investigation revealed that the most expeditious way to build such housing was to work through a nonprofit developer experienced in the use of federal housing subsidies under § 236 of the National Housing Act, 12 U.S.C. § 1715z-1.

MHDC is such a developer. It was organized in 1968 by several prominent Chicago citizens for the purpose of building low and moderate income housing throughout the Chicago area. In 1970 MHDC was in the process of building one § 236 development near Arlington Heights and already had provided some federally assisted housing on a smaller scale in other parts of the Chicago area.

After some negotiation, MHDC and the Order entered into a 99-year lease and an accompanying agreement of sale covering a 15-acre site in the southeast corner of the Viatorian property. MHDC became the lessee immediately, but the sale agreement was contingent upon MHDC's securing zoning clearances from the Village and § 236 housing assistance from the Federal Government. If MHDC proved unsuccessful in securing either, both the lease and the contract of sale would lapse. The agreement established a bargain purchase price of $300,000, low enough to comply with federal limitations governing land acquisition costs for § 236 housing.

MHDC engaged an architect and proceeded with the project, to be known as Lincoln Green. The plans called for 20 two-story buildings with a total of 190 units, each unit having its own private entrance from the outside. One hundred of the units would have a single bedroom, thought likely to attract elderly citizens. The remainder would have two, three or four bedrooms. A large portion of the site would remain open, with shrubs and trees to screen the homes abutting the property to the east.

The planned development did not conform to the Village's zoning ordinance and could not be built unless Arlington Heights rezoned the parcel to R-5, its multiple-family housing classification. Accordingly, MHDC filed with the Village Plan Commission a petition for rezoning, accompanied by supporting materials describing the development and specifying that it would be subsidized under § 236. The materials made clear that one requirement under § 236 is an affirmative marketing plan designed to assure that a subsidized development is racially integrated. MHDC also submitted studies demonstrating the need for housing of this type and analyzing the probable impact of the development. To prepare for the hearings before the Plan Commission and to assure compliance with the Village building code, fire regulations and related requirements, MHDC consulted with the Village staff for preliminary review of the development. The parties have stipulated that every change recommended during such consultations was incorporated into the plans.

During the Spring of 1971, the Plan Commission considered the proposal at a series of three public meetings, which drew large crowds. Although many of those attending were quite vocal and demonstrative in opposition to Lincoln Green, a number of individuals and representatives of community groups spoke in support of rezoning. Some of the comments, both from opponents and supporters, addressed what was referred to as the "social issue"—the desirability or undersirability of introducing at this location in Arlington Heights low and moderate income housing, housing that would probably be racially integrated.

Many of the opponents, however, focused on the zoning aspects of the petition, stressing two arguments. First, the area always had been zoned single-family, and the neighboring citizens had built or purchased there in reliance on that classification. Rezoning threatened to cause a measurable drop in property value for neighboring sites. Second, the Village's apartment policy, adopted by the Village Board in 1962 and amended in 1970, called for R-5 zoning primarily to serve as a buffer between single-family development and land uses thought incompatible, such as commercial or manufacturing districts. Lincoln Green did not meet this requirement, as it adjoined no commercial or manufacturing district.

At the close of the third meeting, the Plan Commission adopted a motion to recommend to the Village's Board of Trustees that it deny the request. The motion stated: "While the need for low and moderate income housing may exist in Arlington Heights or its environs, the Plan Commission would be derelict in recommending it at the proposed location." Two members voted against the motion and submitted a minority report, stressing that in their view the change to accommodate Lincoln Green represented "good zoning." The Village Board met on September 28, 1971, to consider MHDC's request and the recommendation of the Plan Commission. After a public hearing, the Board denied the rezoning by a 6-1 vote.

The following June MHDC and three Negro individuals filed this lawsuit against the Village, seeking declaratory and injunctive relief. A second nonprofit corporation and an individual of Mexican-American descent intervened as plaintiffs. The trial resulted in a judgment for petitioners. Assuming that MHDC had standing to bring the suit, the District Court held that the petitioners were not motivated by racial discrimination or intent to discriminate against low income groups when they denied rezoning, but rather by a desire "to protect property values and the integrity of the Village's zoning plan." 373 F. Supp., at 211. The District Court concluded also that the denial would not have a racially discriminatory effect.

A divided Court of Appeals reversed. It first approved the District Court's finding that the defendants were motivated by a concern for the integrity of the zoning plan, rather than by racial discrimination. Deciding whether their refusal to rezone would have discriminatory effects was more a disproportionate impact on blacks. Based upon family income, blacks constituted 40% of those Chicago area residents who were eligible to become tenants of Lincoln Green, although they comprised a far lower percentage of total area population. The court reasoned, however, that under our decision in *James v. Valtierra*, (1971), such a disparity in racial impact alone does not call for strict scrutiny of a municipality's decision that prevents the construction of the low-cost housing.

There was another level to the court's analysis of allegedly discriminatory results. Invoking language from *Kennedy Park Homes Association v. City of Lackawanna*, (1970), the Court of Appeals ruled that the denial of rezoning must be examined in light of its "historical context and ultimate

effect." Northwest Cook County was enjoying rapid growth in employment opportunities and population, but it continued to exhibit a high degree of residential segregation. The court held that Arlington Heights
could not simply ignore this problem. Indeed, it found that the Village
had been "exploiting" the situation by allowing itself to become a nearly
all-white community. The Village had no other current plans for building
low and moderate income housing, and no other R-5 parcels in the Village
were available to MHDC at an economically feasible price.

Against this background, the Court of Appeals ruled that the denial of
the Lincoln Green proposal had racially discriminatory effects and could
be tolerated only if it served compelling interests. Neither the buffer policy nor the desire to protect property values met this exacting standard.
The court therefore concluded that the denial violated the Equal Protection Clause of the Fourteenth Amendment.

II

(In section II the Court found that respondents MHDC and Ransom
met all standing requirements.)

III

Our decision last Term in *Washington v. Davis*, (1976), made it clear
that official action will not be held unconstitutional solely because it results in a racially disproportionate impact. "Disproportionate impact is not
irrelevant, but it is not the sole touchstone of an invidious racial discrimination." Proof of racially discriminatory intent or purpose is required to
show a violation of the Equal Protection Clause. Although some contrary
indications may be drawn from some of our cases, the holding in *Davis*
reaffirmed a principle well established in a variety of contexts. *E.g., Keyes
v. School District No. 1*, (1973) (schools); *Wright v. Rockefeller*, (1964)
(election districting); *Akins v. Texas*, (1945) (jury selection).

Davis does not require a plaintiff to prove that the challenged action
rested solely on racially discriminatory purposes. Rarely can it be said that
a legislature or administrative body operating under a broad mandate
made a decision motivated solely by a single concern, or even that a particular purpose was the "dominant" or "primary" one. In fact, it is because legislators and administrators are properly concerned with balancing
numerous competing considerations that courts refrain from reviewing the
merits of their decisions, absent a showing of arbitrariness or irrationality.
But racial discrimination is not just another competing consideration.
When there is a proof that a discriminatory purpose has been a motivating
factor in the decision, this judicial deference is no longer justified.

Determining whether invidious discriminatory purpose was a motivating factor demands a sensitive inquiry into such circumstantial and direct
evidence of intent as may be available. The impact of the official action—whether it "bears more heavily on one race than another,"
Washington v. Davis, may provide an important starting point. Sometimes a clear pattern, unexplainable on grounds other than race, emerges

from the effect of the state action even when the governing legislation appears neutral on its face. *Yick Wo v. Hopkins*, (1886); *Guinn v. United States*, (1915); *Lane v. Wilson*, (1939); *Gomillion v. Lightfoot*, (1960). The evidentiary inquiry is then relatively easy. But such cases are rare. Absent a pattern as stark as that in *Gomillion* or *Yick Wo*, impact alone is not determinative, and the Court must look to other evidence.

The historical background of the decision is one evidentiary source, particularly if it reveals a series of official actions taken for invidious purpose. The specific sequence of events leading up to the challenged decision also may shed some light on the decisionmaker's purposes. *Reitman v. Mulkey*, (1967); *Grosjean v. American Press*, (1936). For example, if the property involved here always had been zoned R-5 but suddenly was changed to R-3 when the town learned of MHDC's plans to erect integrated housing, we would have a far different case. Departures from the normal procedural sequence also might afford evidence that improper purposes are playing a role. Substantive departures too may be relevant, particularly if the factors usually considered important by the decisionmaker strongly favor a decision contrary to the one reached.

The legislative or administrative history may be highly relevant, especially where there are contemporary statements by members of the decisionmaking body, minutes of its meetings, or reports. In some extraordinary instances the members might be called to the stand at trial to testify concerning the purpose of the official action, although even then such testimony frequently will be barred by privilege. See *Tenney v. Brandhove*, (1951); *United States v. Nixon*, (1974); 8 Wigmore, Evidence § 2371 (McNaughton rev. ed. 1961).

The foregoing summary identifies, without purporting to be exhaustive, subjects of proper inquiry in determining whether racially discriminatory intent existed. With these in mind, we now address the case before us.

IV

This case was tried in the District Court and reviewed in the Court of Appeals before our decision in *Washington v. Davis*, *supra*. The respondents proceeded on the erroneous theory that the Village's refusal to rezone carried a racially discriminatory effect and was, without more, unconstitutional. But both courts below understood that at least part of their function was to examine the purpose underlying the decision. In making its findings on this issue, the District Court noted that some of the opponents of Lincoln Green who spoke at the various hearings might have been motivated by opposition to minority groups. The court held, however, that the evidence "does not warrant the conclusion that this motivated the defendants."

On appeal the Court of Appeals focused primarily on respondents' claim that the Village's buffer policy had not been consistently applied and was being invoked with a strictness here that could only demonstrate some other underlying motive. The court concluded that the buffer policy, though not always applied with perfect consistency, had on several occasions formed the basis for the Board's decision to deny other rezoning proposals. "The evidence does not necessitate a finding that Arlington

Heights administered this policy in a discriminatory manner." The Court of Appeals therefore approved the District Court's findings concerning the Village's purposes in denying rezoning to MHDC.

We also have reviewed the evidence. The impact of the Village's decision does arguably bear more heavily on racial minorities. Minorities comprise 18% of the Chicago area population and 40% of the income groups said to be eligible for Lincoln Green. But there is little about the sequence of events leading up to the decision that would spark suspicion. The area around the Viatorian property has been zoned R-3 since 1959, the year when Arlington Heights first adopted a zoning map. Single-family homes surround the 80-acre site, and the Village is undeniably committed to single-family homes as its dominant residential land use. The rezoning request progressed according to the usual procedures. The Plan Commission even scheduled two additional hearings, at least in part to accommodate MHDC and permit it to supplement its presentation with answers to questions generated at the first hearing.

The statements by the Plan Commission and Village Board members as reflected in the official minutes, focused almost exclusively on the zoning aspects of the MHDC petition, and the zoning factors on which they relied are not novel criteria in the Village's rezoning decisions. There is no reason to doubt that there has been reliance by some neighboring property owners on the maintenance of single-family zoning in the vicinity. The Village originally adopted its buffer policy long before MHDC entered the picture and has applied the policy too consistently for us to infer discriminatory purpose from its application in this case. Finally, MHDC called one member of the Village Board to the stand at trial. Nothing in her testimony supports an inference of invidious purpose.

In sum, the evidence does not warrant overturning the concurrent findings of both courts below. Respondents simply failed to carry their burden of proving that discriminatory purpose was a motivating factor in the Village's decision. This conclusion ends the constitutional inquiry. The Court of Appeals' further finding that the Village's decision carried a discriminatory "ultimate effect" is without independent constitutional significance.

V

Respondents' complaint also alleged that the refusal to rezone violated the Fair Housing Act. 42 U.S.C. § 3601 *et seq.* They continue to urge here that a zoning decision made by a public body may, and that petitioners' action did, violate § 3604 or § 3617. The Court of Appeals, however, proceeding in a somewhat unorthodox fashion, did *not* decide the statutory question. We remand the case for further consideration of respondents' statutory claims.

Reversed and remanded.

MR. JUSTICE STEVENS took no part in the consideration or decision of this case.

MR. JUSTICE MARSHALL, with whom MR. JUSTICE BRENNAN joins, concurring in part and dissenting in part.

I concur in Parts I-III of the Court's opinion. However, I believe the proper result would be to remand this entire case to the Court of Appeals for further proceedings consistent with *Washington* v. *Davis*, 426 U.S. 229 (1976), and today's opinion. The Court of Appeals is better situated than this Court both to reassess the significance of the evidence developed below in light of the standards we have set forth and to determine whether the interests of justice require further District Court proceedings directed towards those standards.

MR. JUSTICE WHITE, dissenting.

The Court reverses the judgment of the Court of Appeals because it finds, after re-examination of the evidence supporting the concurrent findings below, that "respondents failed to carry their burden of proving that discriminatory purpose was a motivating factor in the Village's decision." *Ante.* p. 17. The Court reaches this result by interpreting our decision in *Washington* v. *Davis*, 426 U.S. 229 (1976), and applying it to this case, notwithstanding that the Court of Appeals rendered its decision in this case before *Washington* v. *Davis* was handed down, and thus did not have the benefit of our decision when it found a Fourteenth Amendment violation.

The Court gives no reason for its failure to follow our usual practice in this situation of vacating the judgment below and remanding in order to permit the lower court to reconsider its ruling in light of our intervening decision. The Court's articulation of a legal standard nowhere mentioned in *Davis* indicates that it feels that the application of *Davis* to these facts calls for substantial analysis. If this is true, we would do better to allow the Court of Appeals to attempt that analysis in the first instance. Given that the Court deems it necessary to re-examine the evidence in the case in light of the legal standard it adopts, a remand is especially appropriate. As the cases relied upon by the Court indicate, the primary function of this Court is not to review the evidence supporting findings of the lower courts. See *e.g.*, *Wright* v. *Rockefeller*, 376 U.S. 52, 56-57 (1964); *Akins* v. *Texas*, 325 U.S. 398, 402 (1945). A further justification for remanding on the constitutional issue is that a remand is required in any event on respondents Fair Housing Act claim, 42 U.S.C. § 3601 *et seq.*, not yet addressed by the Court of Appeals. While conceding that a remand is necessary because of the Court of Appeals' "unorthodox" approach of deciding the constitutional issue without reaching the statutory claim, *ante*, p. 18, the Court refuses to allow the Court of Appeals to reconsider its constitutional holding in light of *Davis* should it become necessary to reach that issue.

Even if I were convinced that it was proper for the Court to reverse the judgment below on the basis of an intervening decision of this Court and after a re-examination of concurrent findings of fact below, I believe it is wholly unnecessary for the Court to embark on a lengthy discussion of the standard for proving the racially discriminatory purpose required by *Davis* for a Fourteenth Amendment violation. The District Court found that the Village was motivated "by a legitimate desire to protect property values and the integrity of the Village's zoning plan." The Court of Appeals accepted this finding as not clearly erroneous, and the Court quite properly refuses to overturn it on review here. There is thus no need for this Court to list various "evidentiary sources" or "subjects of proper inquiry" in determining whether a racially discriminatory purpose existed.

I would vacate the judgment of the Court of Appeals and remand the case for consideration of the statutory issue and, if necessary, for consideration of the constitutional isse in light of *Washington v. Davis.*

E. FEDERAL FUNDING AND EXCLUSIONARY ZONING

Objection to the granting of federal financial assistance has become the new battleground on which the conflict between municipal managed growth and exclusionary zoning will take place with increased frequency. The legal issue in this encounter is whether any federal constitutional or statutory principle is violated if a federal grant to a municipality fails to meet the housing needs of low income people in the region. Various aspects of this issue have begun to come before the federal courts.

In *Hills v. Gautreaux* 425, U.S. 284, 96 S.Ct, 1538, 47 L.Ed 2d 792 (1976), the United States Supreme Court held that the Department of Housing and Urban Development (HUD) violated the Fifth Amendment and the Civil Rights Acts by providing financial assistance to the Chicago Housing Authority (CHA) even though responsible officials at HUD knew that it was the policy of CHA to avoid placing black families in white neighborhoods. The court considered the fact that an Illinois statute permitted the CHA to operate three miles beyond the city limits where no other city or incorporated municipality had jurisdiction; therefore HUD could be required to take remedial action outside the city limits of Chicago.

However, the court took pains to emphasize that "the remedial decrees would neither force suburban governments to submit public housing proposals to HUD nor displace the rights and powers accorded local government entities under federal or state housing statutes or existing land use laws." The opinion pointed out that under the § 8 Lower-Income Housing Assistance program HUD may contract directly with private owners to make leased housing units available to eligible lower income persons. Under the § 8 program local governmental approval is not explicitly required as a condition of the program's applicability to a locality. But the court specifically directed attention to the fact that:

> "Use of the § 8 program to expand low-income housing opportunities outside areas of minority concentration would *not* have a coercive effect on suburban municipalities. For under the program, the local governmental units retain the right to comment on specific assistance proposals, to reject certain proposals that are inconsistent with their approved housing assistance plans, *and to require that zoning and other land use restrictions be adhered to by builders.* (Emphasis added).

These statements make it clear that the United Sates Supreme Court did not intend the *Gautreaux* decision to be a general mandate to require federal funding to be used to impose regional obligations upon local governments.

In *City of Hartford v. Hills,* the United States Court of Appeals upheld a district court decision that enjoined HUD from awarding community development block grant funds to suburban municipalities in the vicinity of Hartford, Connecticut. The action was brought by the City of Hartford and individual low income and minority residents of Hartford alleging that HUD officials abused their discretion when they approved applications for community development funds under the Housing and Community Development Act of 1974 in violation of statutory policy to achieve spatial deconcentration of lower-income groups, particularly from the central cities. More specifically, plaintiffs argued that the suburban communities were ineligible for the federal community development block grants because they failed to comply with the **Housing Assistance Plan (HAP)** condition of eligibility for such grants. One of the elements of a HAP is that the applicant for a community development grant must estimate the housing needs of low income persons **"expected to reside" (ETR)** within its borders. Six of the defendant towns had their grants approved by HUD although they estimated "zero" as the number of low income persons **"expected to reside"** within their borders. HUD regulations provide that ETR estimates are to be based upon existing and estimated employment facilities. It was argued that an estimate of "zero" was not an accurate estimate of the housing needs of such persons. The Court of Appeals held that HUD improperly waived the ETR requirement of the HAP.

The implications of this decision are significant and far reaching. The *Hartford* decision directs attention to the fact that Congress has made a policy decision to seek spatial deconcentration of lower-income persons, particularly from the central cities. To achieve this policy objective, Congress has required suburban communities to consider *regional* housing needs when requesting federal community development funds. This type of legislative judgment is entirely appropriate for Congress to make. The legislative policy is also consistent with the principles of sound planning as long as the estimate of low income persons "expected to reside" is based upon the number of jobs currently existing and reasonably expected to be available in the area. The converse of this principle is equally sound, namely, that where there is no reasonable expectation of jobs for low income persons there is also no reason to require a municipality to provide for housing for such persons.

The third recent case involving an attack upon federal funding of a suburban municipality is the decision of the United States Court of Appeals (Second Circuit) in *Evans v. Lynn* 537 F. 2d 571 (2nd Cir. 1976). In *Evans*, the court held that a group of central city residents did not have standing to challenge the validity of a federal grant for sewers and recreational development. In spite of the argument that the federal financial assistance to an exclusive and wealthy community would tend to perpetuate a pattern of economic segregation, the court held that plaintiffs did not have standing because they could not show that the sewer or park construction would cause any direct injury to them. It is interesting to note that the same court, in the *Hartford* case held that the low income non-resident plaintiffs there did have a **standing to sue.** They were **injured in fact** as a result of the failure to consider an amount of low income persons "expected to reside" in the defendant communities, which in turn, reduced the chances of plaintiffs to move to the suburbs.

The importance of these three decisions in the outcome of the conflict between managed municipal growth and exclusionary zoning varies greatly. The

Gautreaux decision has only limited long range significance. This decision was based upon the peculiar facts of that case, namely, that (1) HUD had, over a long period of time, acquiesced in a racially discriminatory practice; and (2) the state enabling legislation authorized the city housing authority to operate in a prescribed area outside the geographic boundaries of the city. It is unlikely that both of these facts will occur in other cases with any frequency. The *Hartford* decision, on the other hand, is particularly important because it expresses a judicial determination to enforce a Congressional mandate to seek spatial deconcentration of low income persons when making community development block grants. To the extent that suburban communities are required to estimate the number of low income non-residents "expected to reside" in the community, to that extent they will be required to consider the housing needs of the *region* as a condition of eligibility for community development funding. The *Evans* decision is significant because, in the absence of specific Congressional requirements, such as HAP, the availability of the federal courts is severely limited as a forum in which regional obligations may be imposed upon suburban municipalities. Consequently, the attempt to impose a regional obligation upon individual municipalities, in the absence of specific Congressional mandate, will require judicial and/or legislative action in each individual state.

Editor's note:

In 1977 the U.S. Court of Appeals reheard the *City of Hartford* case (under the name, *City of Hartford v. Towns of Glastonbury*, 561 F.2d 1032 (1977). On rehearing, the Court of Appeals reversed and remanded with instructions to dismiss the complaint. The court found that the plaintiffs did not have standing because the alleged unlawful act, the failure to estimate properly the number of low income persons expected to reside within the community, did not injure the plaintiffs. The plurality opinion emphasized the fact that the ETR figure does not represent a community goal or obligation but merely a *prediction* of future growth patterns. See Rose, "Conflict Between Regionalism and Home Rule: The Ambivalence of Recent Planning Law Decisions," 31 *Rutgers Law Review* 1 at 4 (1978).

Chapter Four

Subdivision Regulation

A. INTRODUCTION

Subdivision regulation is one of the techniques for implemention of the planning process. **Subdivision ordinances** establish the standards and procedure under which a developer or owner of land may divide that land into two or more parcels for sale or development. A procedure is established in which a governmental agency, usually the planning board, determines the conditions that must be met by the subdivider for approval of his plan for subdivision. The developer's plan will be described on a **plat,** or map. The blocks and lots are described in surveyed metes and bounds dimensions, together with the streets, sidewalks, utilities and other requirements of the subdivision ordinance. The developer may be required to dedicate land for streets and to install roads, sidewalks, utilities and other improvements as a condition of subdivision approval.

At first glance it might appear that the refusal to permit an owner to subdivide his property unless he dedicates part of his land and provides public improvements is an onerous restriction on the use of private property. And perhaps it is. However the impact of subdivision development upon the community is so great as to justify this restriction. Local government is interested in the subdivision process for a number of reasons: (1) the design of the street pattern will have a long time effect upon traffic and vehicular congestion; (2) the design and width of the streets must consider the need for fire department equipment to reach all houses; (3) there must be satisfactory provision for water supply and sewage disposal; (4) the additional storm water run-off must be channelled to minimize down-stream flooding; (5) each lot must be described with precision to avoid boundary disputes and title defects; (6) the relationship between the costs of services needed and the revenue produced by the new development will have an impact upon the tax rate paid by all the residents. For a detailed discussion of this subject, see Melli, "Subdivision Control in Wisconsin," 1953 *Wis. L. Rev.* 389.

In addition to the public interest in the substantial impact of the subdivision process on the community, there are two well established common law principles that help to justify the significant limitations of the rights of private property. The first principle is the rule of the **implied easement.** This principle, from the law of conveyancing, imposes an easement of ingress and egress upon the property of a seller to assure the buyer of a parcel in the subdivision that he will have access to his new purchase. With this principle firmly established in the law it was an easy step to require a subdivider to dedicate land to provide *access to all the lots* in the subdivision. The second principle involves the concept of **special assessments.** This principle, from the law of local taxation and finance, imposes the cost of a public improvement on the property owners who benefit directly and whose property value is enhanced thereby. Consequently, if the subdivider dedicates the land for a road to each of the lots but does not pave the road, the costs of paving would be borne by each of the adjoining property owners when the government improves the road. It is apparent, therefore, that the purchasers of each of the lots in a subdivision will have to pay for the costs of improvement of the area. Either the subdivider will pass on his costs of roads, sidewalks, water and sewer utilities and other costs of subdivision in the selling price of each of the lots, or the government will impose these costs by a special assessment.

As the subsequent discussion will reveal, the subdivision approval process is frequently time consuming and expensive. For this reason a carefully drawn subdivision enabling statute will exclude some subdivisions from the regulatory process. For example, the New Jersey statute excludes the following types of subdivision from the approval procedure if no new streets are created: (1) divisions of agricultural land into parcels of five acres or larger; (2) divisions of property by testamentary, etc., provisions; (3) divisions of property by court order; and (4) conveyances to *combine* existing lots by deed. In addition, the New Jersey statute establishes a simple form of subdivision procedure for a classification of subdivision called a **minor subdivision,** defined as a subdivision of land that does not involve (1) the creation of more than a limited number of lots (usually two or three); (2) and new street; (3) any extension of off-tract improvement, or (4) planned unit development (PUD).

Subdivision regulation is only one step in the process of implementing the comprehensive plan. The *zoning ordinance* regulates the use of land and the density of development; the *official map ordinance* designates the proposed roads and sites for public improvements; the *subdivision ordinance* provides for the improvement of the roads, sidewalks, utilities and other services at the time of development; the *zoning ordinance* will be used again to regulate the placement of the houses on each of the lots; the *building codes* will prescribe the specifications for construction; the *housing code* will prescribe the minimum standards of use, maintenance and occupancy of housing units. If, over a period of time, the area deteriorates and becomes blighted the techniques of *urban renewal and community development* will be used to rehabilitate or redevelop the area. Each technique serves a specific and limited purpose in the process. The successful implementation of the planning process requires capable and diligent administration at each stage.

B. THE PLANNING BOARD—PLANNING COMMISSION

Subdivision regulation is administered by an agency of local government called the **planning board or planning commission.** The powers of the planning board will be authorized by the state enabling legislation and prescribed by the local ordinance. Among the typical powers of a planning board are: (1) subdivision administration; (2) site plan review; (3) preparation of the master plan; (4) preparation of the official map; (5) preparation of the zoning ordinance; (6) preparation or review of the capital improvement program; (7) preparation or review of urban renewal or community development programs.

C. THE SUBDIVISION PROCEDURE

The procedure by which a developer or subdivider seeks governmental approval of his proposal to subdivide his land is broken down into three distinct steps: (1) **Pre-application discussion;** (2) **Preliminary plat approval;** and (3) **Final plat approval.** The following description of this procedure is derived from *Suggested Land Subdivision Regulations* published by Housing and Home Finance Agency.

1. Pre-application Discussion

The purpose of the **pre-application discussion** is to save time and money by giving the subdivider an opportunity to consult with the planning board before preparing the preliminary plat and before making formal application for its approval. The subdivider will gather data and information about his parcel of land and will consider various site development possibilities. The proposal(s) will be prepared in **sketch form** and submitted to the planning board for advice and assistance. The pre-application plans and data should include the following:

● **General Subdivision Information** should describe or outline the existing conditions of the site and the proposed development as necessary to supplement the drawings required below. This information may include data on existing covenants, land characteristics, and available community facilities and utilities; and information describing the subdivision proposal such as number of residential lots, typical lot width and depth, price range, business areas, playgrounds, park areas, and other public areas, proposed protective covenants and proposed utilities and street improvements.

● **Location Map** will show the relationship of the proposed subdivision to existing community facilities which serve or influence it. Included will be the development name and location; main traffic arteries; public transportation lines; shopping centers; elementary and high schools; parks and playgrounds; principal places of employment; other community features such as railroad stations, airports, hospitals and churches; title; scale; north arrow; and date.

● **Sketch Plat** on topographic survey will show in simple sketch form the proposed layout of streets, lots, and other features in relation to existing conditions. The sketch plat may be a free-hand pencil sketch made directly on a print of the topographic survey. In any event the sketch plat will include either the existing topographic data or such of these data as the planning board determines is necessary for its consideration of the proposed sketch plat.

The planning board will review the **sketch plat** and other information and will consider their relationship to the community comprehensive plan, the design standards and improvement requirements and will discuss the results of this review and evaluation with the subdivider.

2. Preliminary Plat Approval

The subdivider will arrive at some preliminary conclusions after the sketch plat discussion and will prepare a preliminary plat for submission to the planning board with his application for **preliminary approval.** The plats and data submitted will include the following:

● **Topographic Data** required as a basis for the preliminary plat, will include existing conditions as follows:

a. *Boundary lines:* bearings and distances.

b. *Easements:* location, width and purpose.

c. *Streets on and adjacent to the tract:* name and right-of-way width and location; type, width and elevation of surfacing; any legally established center-line elevations; walks, curbs, gutters, culverts, etc.

d. *Utilities on and adjacent to the tract:* location, size and invert elevation of sanitary, storm and combined sewers; location and size of water mains; location of gas lines, fire hydrants, electric and telephone poles, and street lights; if water mains and sewers are not on or adjacent to the tract, indicate the direction and distance to, and size of nearest ones, showing invert elevation of sewers.

e. *Ground elevations of the tract,* based on a datum plane approved by the City Engineer: for land that slopes less than approximately 2 percent show spot elevations at all breaks in grade, along all drainage channels or swales, and at selected points not more than 100 feet apart in all directions; for land that slopes more than approximately 2 percent either show contours with an interval of not more than 5 feet if ground slope is regular and such information is sufficient for planning purposes, or show contours with an interval of not more than 2 feet if necessary because of irregular land or need for more detailed data for preparing plans and construction drawings.

f. *Subsurface conditions on the tract:* location and results of tests made to ascertain subsurface soil, rock and ground water conditions; depth to ground water unless test pits are dry at a depth of 5 feet; location and results of soil percolation tests if individual sewage disposal systems are proposed.

g. *Other conditions on the tract:* water courses, marshes, rock outcrop, wooded areas, isolated preservable trees one foot or more in diameter, houses, barns, shacks, and other significant features.

h. *Other conditions on adjacent land:* approximate direction and gradient of ground slope, including any embankments or retaining walls; character and location of buildings, railroads, power lines, towers, and other nearby nonresidential land uses or adverse influences; owners of adjacent unplatted land; for adjacent platted land refer to subdivision plat by name, recordation date, and number, and show approximate percent built-up, typical lot size, and dwelling type.

i. *Photographs,* if required by the planning board: camera locations, directions of views and key numbers.

j. *Zoning* on and adjacent to the tract.

k. *Proposed public improvements:* highways or other major improvements planned by public authorities for future construction on or near the tract.

l. *Key plan* showing location of the tract.

m. *Title and certificates:* present tract designation according to official records in office of appropriate recorder; title under which proposed subdivision is to be recorded, with names and addresses of owners, notation stating acreage, scale, north arrow, datum, benchmarks, certification of registered civil engineer or surveyor, date of survey.

● **Preliminary Plat** (Preliminary Subdivision Plan, General Subdivision Plan) should be at a scale of two hundred (200) feet to one (1) inch or larger. It should show all existing conditions required above in Topographic Data, and should show all proposals including the following:

a. *Streets:* names; right-of-way and roadway widths; approximate grades and gradients; similar data for alleys, if any.

b. *Other rights-of-way or easements:* location, width and purpose.

c. *Location of utilities,* if not shown on other exhibits.

d. *Lot lines, lot numbers* and *block numbers.*

e. *Sites,* if any, to be reserved or dedicated for parks, playgrounds, or other public uses.

f. *Sites,* if any, for multifamily dwellings, shopping centers, churches, industry or other nonpublic uses exclusive of single-family dwellings.

g. *Minimum building setback lines.*

h. *Site data,* including number of residential lots, typical lot size, and acres in parks, etc.

i. *Title, scale, north arrow,* and *date.*

● **Other Preliminary Plans.** When required by the planning board, the Preliminary Plat should be accompanied by profiles showing existing ground surface and proposed street grades, including extensions for a reasonable distance beyond the limits of the proposed subdivision; typical cross sections of the proposed grading, roadway and sidewalk; and preliminary plan of proposed sanitary and storm water sewers with grades and sizes indicated. All elevations should be based on a datum plane approved by the City Engineer.

● **Draft of Protective Covenants** whereby the subdivider proposes to regulate land use in the subdivision and otherwise protect the proposed development.

After reviewing the preliminary plat and other material submitted, the planning board will determine whether the application conforms to the subdivision standards prescribed by the enabling legislation and the subdivision ordinance. The board will negotiate with the subdivider on changes deemed advisable and the nature and extent of improvements to be made by him. The enabling legislation will usually require the planning board to come to a decision within a prescribed period of time. If approval is denied, the planning board will usually be required to state the reasons for disapproval. If the application is approved the board will set forth the conditions of such approval.

NEW JERSEY MUNICIPAL LAND USE LAW

(a) Effect of Preliminary Plat Approval

The enabling legislation will confer upon the subdivider a number of rights derived from preliminary plat approval upon which he may rely for a prescribed period of time. For example, the New Jersey enabling legislation confers the following rights for a 3-year period from the date of the preliminary approval:

C. 40:55D-49 Effect of preliminary approval.

Effect of preliminary approval. Preliminary approval of a major subdivision pursuant to section 36 of this act or of a site plan pursuant to section 34 of this act shall, except as provided in subsection d. of this section, confer upon the applicant the following rights for a 3-year period from the date of the preliminary approval:

a. That the general terms and conditions on which preliminary approval was granted shall not be changed, including but not limited to use requirements; layout and design standards for streets, curbs and sidewalks; lot size; yard dimensions and off-tract improvements; and, in the case of a site plan, any requirements peculiar to site plan approval pursuant to section 29.3. of this act; except that nothing herein shall be construed to prevent the municipality from modifying by ordinance such general terms and conditions of preliminary approval as relate to public health and safety;

b. That the applicant may submit for final approval on or before the expiration date of preliminary approval the whole or a section of sections of the preliminary subdivision plat or site plan, as the case may be; and

c. That the applicant may apply for and the planning board may grant extensions on such preliminary approval for additional periods of at least 1 year but not to exceed a total extension of 2 years, provided that if the design standards have been revised by ordinance, such revised standards may govern.

d. In the case of a subdivision of or site plan for an area of 50 acres or more, the planning board may grant the rights referred to in subsections a., b., and c. above for such period of time, longer than 3 years, as shall be determined by the planning board to be reasonable taking into consideration (1) the number of dwelling units and nonresidential floor area permissible under preliminary approval, (2) economic conditions, and (3) the comprehensiveness of the development. The applicant may apply for thereafter and the planning board may thereafter grant an extension to preliminary approval for such additional period of time as shall be determined by the planning board to be reasonable taking into consideration (1) the number of dwelling units and nonresidential floor area permissible under preliminary approval, and (2) the potential number of dwelling units and nonresidential floor area of the section or sections awaiting final approval, (3) economic conditions and (4) the comprehensiveness of the development: provided that if the design standards have been revised, such revised standards may govern.

3. Final Plat Approval

After receiving preliminary plat approval, the subdivider will make the expenditures necessary to survey and stake out the tract, install the roads, sidewalks, etc. on which preliminary plat approval was conditioned, or will post a certified check or bond to guarantee completion of the improvements stipulated. He will then prepare a final plat and other documents as follows:

The final plat must comply with the Map Filing Law and should contain the following elements:

a) Date of submission, name and location of the subdivision, name of the owner, graphic scale and reference meridian.

b) Tract boundary lines, street right-of-way lines, street names, easements (and, other rights-of-way), land to be dedicated to public use, lot lines and other site lines, bearings or deflection angles, and radii, arcs and central angles of all curves.

c) Designation of the purpose of any easement or land set aside for public use, and a notation of proposed use of any non-residential sites.

d) Designation of zoning of all adjacent lands.

e) Numbers for all blocks and all of the lots within each block which shall be consecutive beginning with the number one. (The block and lot numbering should conform with the numbering system of the tax plates.)

f) Minimum building set-back line on all lots and other sites.

g) Location and description of all monuments.

h) Names of the owners of adjoining unsubdivided land.

i) Certification that the map has been approved by the appropriate local, county or state agencies.

The final plat should be accompanied by the following documents:

a) Certification by a licensed engineer or surveyor with respect to the accuracy of the details of the plat.

b) Certification that the applicant is the owner of the land or his properly authorized agent, or that the owner has given consent under an option agreement.

c) Cross section and profile drawings of streets which must be approved by the municipal engineer.

d) Plans and profiles of storm and sanitary sewers and water mains.

e) Certification from the tax collector that all taxes are paid to date.

The final plat should show a five-foot contour interval for slopes of ten per cent or more and a two-foot interval for lesser slopes.

To comply with the Map Filing Law, the plat shall be one of four standard sizes as measured from cutting edges, viz:

8½ x 13 inches
15 x 21 inches
30 x 42 inches
34 x 36 inches

In addition, there shall be endorsements by a licensed land surveyor attesting to the accurate setting of monuments, and by the municipal engineer certifying that the plat conforms with the Map Filing Law and municipal ordinances applicable to the subdivision. Signature lines for the mayor, municipal clerk, and planning board chairman should be provided.

After reviewing the final plat and other material submitted, the planning board will inform the subdivider what is lacking to obtain approval and upon compliance by the subdivider will grant **approval of the final plat.** The state enabling legislation will usually prescribe a time limit within which the planning board must come to a decision. In some states it may be necessary to seek approval from a county planning board, or in some limited circumstances, from a state regulatory agency.

After approval, the planning board will return the original plat to the subdivider and file copies with a number of governmental officials such as the municipal clerk, municipal engineer, building inspector, tax assessor, zoning officer, municipal school board, board of health and county planning board. The subdivider will file the plat in the county recording office within a prescribed period of time. Failure to file the plat within that prescribed time could cause the approval to expire.

- **Effect of Final Plat Approval**

The legal effect of final plat approval will be prescribed in the state enabling legislation. A typical provision, e.g., N.J.S.A. 40:55D-52, will assure the developer that the conditions of preliminary plat approval and the zoning requirements applicable to the subdivision will not be changed for a prescribed period after the date of final approval, providing that the developer records the plat within the prescribed time.

- **Public Hearing for Subdivision Approval**

The state enabling legislation will require the planning board to hold a public hearing at the time that the preliminary plat is being considered. The statute will usually require notice to be published in the local newspapers and notice mailed to adjoining property owners and property owners within a prescribed distance from the subdivision. The statute may also require notice of the hearing to be sent to the clerk of any adjoining municipality within a prescribed distance of the proposed subdivision.

- **Appeal of Aggrieved Parties**

The state enabling legislation will provide for the opportunities for appeal by the subdivider or by adjoining landowners. The statute may permit an aggrieved party to appeal to the governing body. There is a difference of opinion among planners and municipal attorneys whether the governing body should devote its time to the review of subdivision applications. In any event, the opportunity for appeal to the courts will usually be available.

● Vested Rights After Final Plat Approval

Final plat approval certifies that the developer has complied with the requirements of the subdivision ordinance. No new subdivision conditions may be imposed for the period of time specified in the subdivision ordinance. However, it may still be possible for the appropriate governing body to change the zoning ordinance or other requirements of land development. As a general rule, if a property owner has performed substantial work or incurred substantial liabilities in good faith reliance upon a building permit, he acquires a **vested right** to complete construction in accordance with the terms of the permit. Once a landowner has secured a vested right, the government may not, because of a change in the zoning law, prohibit construction authorized by the permit on which he relied.

However, if a developer fails to apply for and receive a building permit after receiving final plat approval, he runs the risk of not securing a vested right even though he subsequently expends substantial sums in reliance upon subdivision approval. In *Avco Community Developers, Inc. v. South Coast Regional Comm.,* 132 Cal. Rptr. 386, 553 P.2d 546 (1976) the Supreme Court of California held that a developer had not obtained vested rights after expending over two million dollars for utility installation and other land improvements in reliance upon subdivision approval. The court held that in spite of subdivision approval, it was necessary for the developer to comply with the California Coastal Zone Conservation Act of 1972 that had become effective before a building permit was issued.

ILLUSTRATIONS OF SKETCHES AND
PLAT IN SUBDIVISION PROCEDURE

(From *Control of Land Subdivision* (N.Y. State Office of Planning Coordination, 1968)).

1. *Sketch Plat*

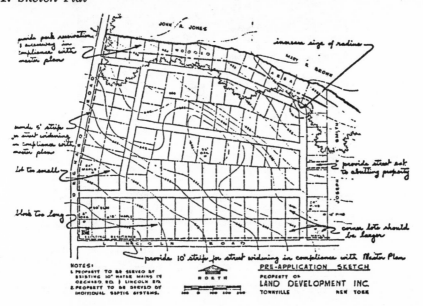

2. Preliminary Plat

3. Final Plat

D. QUESTIONS TO BE CONSIDERED IN SUBDIVISION REVIEW

The issues to be considered in the process of subdivision approval will vary with each application. However there are several fields of inquiry that should be made in most applications to make sure that the subdivision will serve the best interests of the community. The following questions have been suggested by the New Jersey Department of Community Affairs in *Administrative Guide to Subdivision Regulations:*

N.J. ADMINISTRATIVE GUIDE TO SUBDIVISION REGULATION

1. General Questions

a) What is the contemplated character of the proposed subdivision with respect to quality and price of houses and lots?

b) Will the subdivider construct the houses or have any control over construction?

c) Would a subdivision of this character substantially benefit the community?

d) Is there a reasonable market in the community for a subdivision of this type?

2. Physical Limitations

a) Is the topography suitable (below 10 degree slope) for a development of the proposed density and character?

b) Are there swamps, creeks or saturated areas in the subdivision which might be an obstacle to development?

c) Will subsurface conditions–(underlying rock, water table, etc.) safely permit development at proposed density?

d) Are there any surface or subsurface irregularities (rock outcrops, pockets of clay, abrupt changes of terrain, etc.) which should be accounted for in the design and layout of the subdivision?

e) Are there any periodic irregularities or hazards (floods, rockslides, etc.) which would limit development?

3. Location

a) Would the proposed subdivision be compatible with the neighboring areas?

b) Is the proposed subdivision reasonably accessible by road?

c) Will the proposed subdivision place an undue burden upon the municipal street system?

d) Is the proposed subdivision too close to other traffic-generating land uses?

e) Is the proposed subdivision safely removed from or shielded against heavy highway traffic?

f) If the proposed subdivision borders another municipality, is it compatible with that municipality's land use?

4. Legal and Financial Restrictions

a) Has title been cleared to all of the lands within the proposed subdivision?

b) Have taxes been paid up to date on all of the lands in the proposed subdivision?

c) Are there any liens against the property?

d) Does the proposed subdivision conform to the zoning ordinance?

e) Does the proposed subdivision fit in with the general plan of the municipality and carry out its objectives?

f) Does the proposed subdivision abide by the administrative requirements of the municipal subdivision regulations?

g) Is the proposed subdivision in accord with the municipal building, health, plumbing and sanitation codes and other local, county or state regulations?

h) Is there reasonable financing available for the project?

i) What previous experience has the developer had in this field?

5. Roads

a) Do the roads fit in reasonably well with the topography and drainage of the area?

b) Do the proposed roads fit in conveniently with the existing road pattern?

c) Is the street design for the subdivision convenient and safe?

d) How wide will the roads be and what kind of paving will be used?

e) Does the street pattern take full advantage of the topographical potential of the site?

f) Are there any conditions in the streets and roads which could cause flooding or otherwise aggravate other natural hazards?

g) Is the street pattern orderly enough to avoid confusion and facilitate purely local traffic?

h) Does the street pattern discourage heavy through traffic?

i) Are there any dangerous or concealed entrances onto heavily traveled highways?

j) Are there any hazards (odd-angle curves, "dog-leg" jogs, unduly steep grades, hairpin curves, discrepancies in width, blind alleys, etc.) within the street pattern of the proposed subdivision?

6. Utilities

a) Are sub-surface conditions such that individual wells and septic systems can be safely used at the population density level of the proposed subdivision?

b) Is there any written guarantee that the necessary water and sewer systems will be provided?

c) Will the utilities for the proposed subdivision tie in with existing utilities?

d) Are the proposed facilities so placed as to insure proper drainage?

e) Have adequate precautions been taken against pollution of neighboring bodies of water, streams or other developments?

f) Will there be adequate water pressure to insure a supply for domestic use and adequate fire protection?

g) If an outside source must be used for water, where will the supply come from?

h) Who will construct, operate, and maintain the necessary water and sewage pumping stations and/or treatment plants?

i) Has the proposed water supply and water allocations been approved by the State Water Policy and Supply Council?

7. Block and Lots

a) Are the blocks reasonably long (between 500 to 1,500 feet)?

b) Do the extra long blocks provide for pedestrian crosswalks?

c) Are the lots laid out in a regular order along the streets?

d) Are there any irregularities ("landlocked lots", odd-shaped lots, double frontage lots, etc.) in the design of the proposed subdivision?

e) Are the lots and houses so sited as to take advantage of the amenities of the area?

f) Are there any natural wooded, rock or swampy areas which should be used, or set aside, as park or open space rather than built upon?

g) Will all of the residents of the proposed subdivision have access to the beaches, lakes, parks or recreation areas of the development?

h) Is the lot and block design compatible with that of neighboring developments?

8. Parks and Landscaping

a) Are provisions made for parks and landscaping?

b) Are there provisions for saving large, well-grown trees on the site?

c) Will the landscaping obscure motorists' view or create a hazard to safe driving?

d) Are there any provisions for use of hedges or trees to screen against undesirable views or to act as a buffer to absorb unwanted glare?

e) Have landscaping plans been furnished with the plats?

f) Are the proposed park areas of a useful size and shape, and well located?

g) Can the proposed park areas be operated and maintained economically by the municipality?

9. Public Services

a) Have provisions been made to take care of the extra school children who will be brought in by the proposed subdivision?

b) Will the community be reasonably able to provide the services which the inhabitants of the proposed subdivision will require?

c) Will the anticipated revenue be enough to pay for the municipal services which must be rendered?

10. Special Considerations

a) Do areas subject to erosion, flood or other chronic natural hazards, have special measures to cope with the situation?

b) Where such protective works are necessary, who has designed and recommended them?

c) Where waterfront lagoons or coves are used, have suitable measures been taken to insure that these will be self-flushing and free of pollution and debris?

d) Are clubhouses, docks, swimming pools or other amenities provided in the subdivision?

e) Are there any special covenants in the area or provided for in the proposed subdivision to regulate landscaping, building or use of amenities?

f) Where amenities are provided, what arrangements have been made with respect to their use, operation and maintenance?

E. ENFORCEMENT OF SUBDIVISION REGULATIONS

The state enabling legislation will provide for several methods of enforcing subdivision regulations:

1. Building Permit Requirement

A typical provision for **building permits** will require that the building lot abut an existing street or a street on an approved subdivision plat. Such provision would allow the owner of a large tract to obtain a building permit for a house on an existing street, but would require him to obtain subdivision approval before he could obtain a building permit for construction on other lots within the tract.

2. Recording Requirement

The enabling legislation will usually provide that the county recording officer may not accept for filing any map unless it has been approved by the appropriate municipal officer. Such approval would not be forthcoming unless the map complies with the subdivision law and has been approved by the planning board. If the map is not recorded it will not be possible to obtain a building permit.

3. Criminal Penalties

The state enabling legislation will usually provide for a criminal penalty of fine and imprisonment for a subdivider who subdivides and sells land without complying with the law.

4. Administrative Remedies

To avoid loss to an unsuspecting purchaser from an unscrupulous subdivider who engages in the sale of subdivided property without subdivision approval, the state enabling statute will usually authorize the municipality to seek an injunction and to seek a judicial order setting aside any contract or conveyance of land that is not in compliance with the subdivision regulations.

5. Performance Bonds

The legal restrictions on the ability of a subdivider to sell lots within a development before final approval are so effective that, without some relaxation of the regulations, a developer would not be able to sell any lots, and the houses built on them, until he receives final plat approval. This would mean that no sales could take place until all the roads, sidewalks, curbs, utilities, street lights, and all other improvements were installed. Such a delay in sales would impose an onerous financial burden on the developer, who must invest vast sums of money for these improvements, if he could not replenish these expenditures with income from the sale of lots during the development process. State enabling legislation responds to this economic reality by provisions that permit final plat approval before the completion of all required improvements if the developer is able to furnish a guarantee of performance in the form of cash, securities or a **performance bond**.

A **performance bond** is a bond or guarantee from an insurance company, or other acceptable financial institution, that provides assurance to the municipality that the conditions of plat approval will be fulfilled by the subdivider, or in case if his default, by the insurance company. By filing a performance bond the developer is able to obtain final plat approval and start selling his lots so that he can obtain income to pay for the costs of the improvements. The bonding company will issue its bond upon payment of a fee by the developer if the bonding company is persuaded that the developer is a good risk. Among the factors that the bonding company will consider to determine its risk are: (1) the liquid assets of the developer; (2) the developer's prior record of success; (3) an appraisal of the housing market and other indicators of possible success of the development.

Among the issues that arise from the use of performance bonds are such questions as (1) the amount of the bond; (2) the duration of the period of liability; (3) methods of reduction of the amount of liability; (4) provisions for release of the obligation. The following provisions from the New Jersey Municipal Land Use Law illustrate one statutory method of addressing these issues:

N.J. MUNICIPAL LAND USE LAW

C. 40:55D-53 Guarantees required; surety; release.

41. Guarantees required; surety; release. a. Before recording of final subdivision plats or as a condition of final site plan approval or as a condition to the issuance of a zoning permit pursuant to subsection 52 d. of this act, the approving authority may require and shall accept in accordance with the standards adopted by ordinance for the purpose of assuring the installation and maintenance of on-tract improvements:

(1) The furnishing of a performance guarantee in favor of the municipality in an amount not to exceed 120% of the cost of installation for improvements it may deem necessary or appropriate including: streets, grading, pavement, gutters, curbs, sidewalks, street lighting, shade trees, surveyor's monuments, as shown on the final map and required by the "Map Filing Law," P.L. 1960, c. 141 (C. 46:23-9.9 et seq.), water mains, culverts, storm sewers, sanitary sewers or other means of sewage disposal, drainage structures, erosion control and sedimentation control devices, public improvements of open space and, in the case of site plans only, other on-site improvements and landscaping.

(2) Provision for a maintenance guarantee to be posted with the governing body for a period not to exceed 2 years after final acceptance of the improvement, in an amount not to exceed 15% of the cost of the im-

provement. In the event that other governmental agencies or public utilities automatically will own the utilities to be installed or the improvements are covered by a performance or maintenance guarantee to another governmental agency, no performance or maintenance guarantee, as the case may be, shall be required by the municipality for such utilities or improvements.

b. The amount of any performance guarantee may be reduced by the governing body, by resolution, when portions of the improvements have been certified by the municipal engineer to have been completed. The time allowed for installation of the improvements for which the performance guarantee has been provided may be extended by said body by resolution.

c. If the required improvements are not completed or corrected in accordance with the performance guarantee, the obligor and surety, if any, shall be liable thereon to the municipality for the reasonable cost of the improvements not completed or corrected and the municipality may either prior to or after the receipt of the proceeds thereof complete such improvements.

d. When all of the required improvements have been completed, the obligor shall notify the governing body in writing, by certified mail addressed in care of the municipal clerk of the completion of said improvements and shall send a copy thereof to the municipal engineer. Thereupon the municipal engineer shall inspect all of the improvements and shall file a detailed report, in writing, with the governing body, indicating either approval, partial approval or rejection of the improvements with a statement of reasons for any rejection. If partial approval is indicated, the cost of the improvements rejected shall be set forth.

e. The governing body shall either approve, partially approve or reject the improvements, on the basis of the report of the municipal engineer and shall notify the obligor in writing, by certified mail, of the contents of said report and the action of said approving authority with relation thereto, not later than 65 days after receipt of the notice from the obligor of the completion of the improvements. Where partial approval is granted, the obligor shall be released from all liability pursuant to its performance guarantee, except for that portion adequately sufficient to secure provision of the improvements not yet approved. Failure of the governing body to send or provide such notification to the obligor within 65 days shall be deemed to constitute approval of the improvements and the obligor and surety, if any, shall be released from all liability, pursuant to such performance guarantee.

f. If any portion of the required improvements are rejected, the approving authority may require the obligor to complete such improvements and, upon completion, the same procedure of notification, as set forth in this section shall be followed.

g. Nothing herein, however, shall be construed to limit the right of the obligor to contest by legal proceedings any determination of the governing body or the municipal engineer.

F. STATUTORY AND CONSTITUTIONAL VALIDITY

1. General Principles

As a condition of subdivision approval a developer may be required to provide substantial and costly improvements. In most cases, these costs will not come as a surprise to the developer. He will be able to find out about the municipality's standards by examining the subdivision ordinance and by discussion with the planning board at a sketch plat conference. For this reason it is common practice for a developer to enter into an **option agreement** with the owner of land that will provide the opportunity to estimate the costs of subdivision improvement *before* buying the land. Developers frequently avoid those municipalities where subdivision improvement costs will make the selling cost of the houses too expensive to be sold easily. In addition, the "front-end" costs of land development are usually sufficiently high that a developer *cannot afford the costs of delay* incurred while he litigates the validity of an onerous subdivision condition up to the state's highest court. For this reason the number of judicial decisions on subdivision issues are comparatively limited.

Nevertheless, there are situations where a developer finds it necessary to appeal a planning board's decision to impose one or more conditions for plat approval. The judicial appeal will usually involve at least two legal issues: (1) statutory interpretation, and (2) the constitutionality of the condition. The statutory issue will involve the question whether the enabling legislation or the municipal ordinance authorizes the imposition of the conditions in issue. In response to this issue, some courts will adopt a *strict interpretation* and decide that the condition is *unauthorized* unless the statute provides *specifically* for its imposition. In other cases, the courts will decide that the condition is *valid* if it tends to achieve the general objectives of the subdivision statute and is *not specifically prohibited* by the statute.

The constitutional issues will involve (1) the *due process clause* and/or (2) the *eminent domain power*. The due process clause will be raised by the argument that the conditions for subdivision approval are so harsh and unreasonable as to be confiscatory and to deprive the developer of the reasonable use of the property. the eminent domain argument is similar to the due process argument in that it is alleged that the condition is so onerous and unreasonable as to constitute a "taking" of the property by government without the payment of just compensation.

Keep these issues in mind as you read all of the cases in this chapter. In addition, remember too that the costs of all subdivision improvements will be passed on to the purchasers of the lots and houses in the development. The more extensive and costly the improvements, the more costly will be the houses. The developer's primary interest in avoiding costly subdivision improvements is to keep the selling price of the houses lower for easier sale.

AYERS

v.

CITY COUNCIL OF CITY OF LOS ANGELES

34 Cal.2d 31, 207 P.2d 1 (1949)

SHENK, Justice.

This appeal is by the petitioner from a judgment denying relief in a mandamus proceeding brought to compel the respondent city council to approve a proposed subdivision map without certain imposed conditions.

A tentative map for the subdivision of thirteen acres owned by the petitioner in what is commonly known as the Westchester District in the city of Los Angeles was submitted in October 1944 to the city planning commission pursuant to the Subdivision Map Act, Stats.1937, p.1874, as amended, now Sec. 11500 et seq. Business & Professions Code. The planning commission attached four conditions to which the petitioner objected, whereupon he appealed to the city council. The matter was noticed for a hearing before that body, after which an order was made sustaining each of the conditions. The petitioner thereupon commenced the present proceeding in the superior court. Because of the inclusion in the petition of allegations tendering the issue of lack of a full hearing, the court in overruling the demurrer to the petition also ordered that the trial of other factual issues proceed on presentation and consideration of all material and relevant evidence. The trial consumed two weeks in the course of which the trial judge viewed the locality of the proposed subdivision. Findings were made and judgment entered upholding the lawfulness and reasonableness of the imposed conditions. The appeal involves the sufficiency of the evidence to support the findings and judgment.

The area known as Westchester District of which the proposed thirteen acre subdivision forms a part consists of 3023 acres. It is bisected in a northerly and southerly direction by Sepulveda Boulevard, and easterly and westerly by Manchester Boulevard. It extends one mile to the south of Manchester and a mile and a half to the north; and one mile on either side of Sepulveda. Before subdivision the land in the district was owned by Los Angeles Extension Company, Security-First National Bank of Los Angeles, and Superior Oil Company. The petitioner represented the latter as subdivider and selling agent. In 1940 the formation of a general plan of development of the district was commenced. The plan fixed the business area on Sepulveda Boulevard immediately south of Manchester Boulevard and the petitioner was placed in charge of development by the subdividers. The so-called cellular design of residence lot subdivision was employed so that the rear of residential lots abuts the principal thoroughfares, thus prohibiting access to the lots therefrom. Another purpose of this type of subdivision was to minimize the amount of land required for street purposes. This general plan had been followed in the Westchester district. Requirements insuring uniformity were imposed, among which were the dedication of a ten foot strip in the residence areas and a thirteen foot strip on each side in the business section for the widening of Sepulveda Boulevard, and the setting aside of a strip for planting purposes varying in width at the rear of lots in the residence sections bordering the principal thoroughfares.

The petitioner's thirteen acre tract, the last of the subdivisions in the district, is a long narrow triangle. Its northerly boundary is less than 500 feet in length, and the southerly point of the triangle about 2400 feet from the northerly line. Arizona Avenue runs along the westerly line. Sepulveda Boulevard, the principal thoroughfare and heavily trafficked artery, borders the easterly line. These highways converge and form the southerly point of the triangle. Sepulveda Boulevard, from a point a short distance north of the convergence to the north line of the tract, is 100 feet wide but south of that point is 110 feet wide. Seventy-Seventh Street enters Arizona Avenue from the west approximately opposite the center of the tract, and the proposed subdivision map shows the extension of that street through the tract. Seventy-ninth Street enters Arizona Avenue from the west a short distance north of the southerly point of the tract. An extension of that street through the subdivision would leave a triangular tip of land about 12½ feet wide by 75 feet to the southerly point. The proposed subdivision would include ten residence lots north of the Seventy-Seventh Street extension fronting on Arizona Avenue with 80 foot frontages and depths to Sepulveda Boulevard varying from 312 to 462 feet. Entrance to the residence lots would be from Arizona Avenue exclusively. The lot immediately north of and adjoining the Seventy-Seventh Street extension is proposed to be used for business drive-in and the lot south of Seventy-Seventh Street for religious purposes.

The four conditions imposed by the planning commission and approved by the city council and the trial court are:

1. That a ten foot strip abutting Sepulveda Boulevard be dedicated for the widening of that highway.

2. That an additional ten foot strip along the rear of the lots be restricted to the planting of trees and shrubbery for the purpose of preventing direct ingress and egress between the lots and Sepulveda Boulevard.

3. That the extension of Seventy-Seventh Street be dedicated to a width of eighty instead of sixty feet.

4. That the area which would be covered by an extension of Seventy-Ninth Street and south of the point of the triangle be dedicated for street use for the purpose of eliminating it as a traffic hazard.

The petitioner objected to the foregoing conditions on the ground that they were not expressly provided for by the Subdivision Map Act nor by city ordinance; that conditions 1, 2 and 4, and condition 3 in so far as it required dedication in excess of 60 feet in width, bear no reasonable relationship to the protection of the public health, safety or general welfare, and amount to a taking of private property for public use without compensation.

Article VIII, Secs. 94 to 99½, of the Los Angeles City Charter deals with the Department of City Planning. By section 94 the department is given all the powers and duties which are granted to or imposed upon city planning commissions or departments by state law, and as provided by city ordinance, subject to Article VIII. Pursuant thereto and to the Planning Act of 1929, Stats. 1929, p. 1805, as amended, Gen. Laws, Act 5211b, there is functioning in the City of Los Angeles a planning commission and a director of planning appointed by it who acts as the advisory agency of the commission. Section 95 of the charter requires the director of planning to prepare a master plan for the physical development of the city, and vests in him the powers and calls for discharge of the duties in relation to proposed subdivisions as required by the Subdivision Map Act and as may be imposed by ordinance. By section 96½ the planning commission is required to hold hearings on the master plan or parts thereof and consider and adopt the same.

Section 11525 of the Subdivision Map Act vests control of the design and improvement of subdivisions in the governing bodies of cities and counties, subject to review as to reasonableness by the superior court in and for the county in which the land is situated.

Section 11526 provides that the design, improvement and survey data of subdivisions and related matters, including procedure in securing official approval, are governed by the provisions of the Subdivision Map Act and by the provisions of local ordinances regulating the design and improvement of subdivisions.

Section 11538 makes it unlawful for any person to offer for sale or to sell any subdivision lot until the filing of a final map in compliance with the Act and local ordinances. The conveyance of any part of a subdivision by lot or block number is not permitted until a final map has been recorded. Sec. 11539. Section 11550 declares that the initial action is the preparation of a tentative map with data as specified in the local ordinances and the Map Act.

Section 11551 states that if there is a local ordinance regulating the design and improvement of subdivisions the subdivider shall comply with its provisions before the map may be approved; but if there is no such ordinance the governing body as a condition precedent to approval may require streets and drainage ways properly located and of adequate width but may make no other requirements.

Section 11552 provides that if the subdivider is dissatisfied with the initial action regarding the tentative map he may appeal to the governing body which upon a noticed hearing shall take testimony as to the character of the neighborhood in which the subdivision is to be located, the kinds, nature and extent of improvements, the quality or kinds of development to which the area is best adapted and any other phase of the matter it may desire to inquire into, at the conclusion of which the governing body may make such findings as are not inconsistent with the provisions of the Act or local ordinances.

The words "Design" and "Improvement" as used in the Act are defined. Section 11510 provides that "Design" refers to street alignment, grades and widths, alignment and widths of easements and right of ways for drainage and sanitary sewers and minimum lot area and width. Section 11511 defines "Improvement" as only such street work and utilities to be installed, or agreed to be installed, by the subdivider on the land to be dedicated for streets, highways, etc., as are necessary for the general use of the lot owners in the subdivision and local neighborhood traffic and drainage needs.

Ordinance No. 79,310 of the City of Los Angeles, as amended, prescribes the rules and regulations governing the platting and subdividing of lands and the filing and approval of subdivision maps. The ordinance adopts the definitions for "Design" and "Improvement" as declared in the Subdivision Map Act. Specifically treated are such subjects as Primary and Secondary Streets, which are to conform to the Master Plan of traffic arteries, Alignments, Street Widths, Grades, Curves and Tangents, Intersections, Dead-ends, Rounding Block Corners, Private Streets, Alleys, Size, Frontage and Side Lines of Lots, Blocks, Sewer and Drainage Grades and Facilities, Existing Improvements, Dangerous Areas, Easements, Walkways, and the like. Under "Conditions of Acceptance" it is provided that the city engineer may refuse to accept any final map which does not conform to the provisions of the Subdivision Map Act, the provisions of the ordinance, or the conditions of approval of the tentative map. It is also provided that upon recommendation of the advisory agency or the city engineer such variations may be made as in the exercise of sound, reasonable, judgment may be warranted or required because of the size, use, physical or other conditions of the property, or the type of subdivision, except that no variations may be made as to the requirements of the Subdivision Map Act.

It appears to be the petitioners contention that no condition may be exacted which is not expressly provided for by the Subdivision Map Act or the ordinance provisions not in conflict therewith; that at all events the requirements may deal only with streets to be laid out by the subdivider within the confines of the subdivision to take care of traffic needs therein, and that no dedication may be exacted for additions to existing streets or highways.

It must be obvious at the outset that this effect may not be drawn from the statute or from the city's organic law or ordinances. The foregoing review of those provisions does not indicate that the authority of the city planners is so circumscribed. The status of an autonomous city, Const. Art. XI, sec. 6; is recognized by express references to city ordinances in the Subdivision Map Act. Where as here no specific restriction or limitation on the city's power is contained in the Charter, and none forbidding the particular conditions is included either in the Subdivision Map Act or the city ordinances, it is proper to conclude that conditions are lawful which are not inconsistent with the Map Act and the ordinances and are reasonably required by the subdivision type and use as related to the character of local and neighborhood planning and traffic conditions. * * *

The Subdivision Map Act, Sec. 11552, and the city ordinances indicate that the matters for consideration in relation to the reasonableness of imposed conditions contemplate the character of the neighborhood, the kinds, nature and extent of improvements, the quality or kinds of development to which the area is best adapted, the traffic needs, and other phases, including the size, use physical or other conditions of the property, and the type of subdivision.

As to condition 1, that a ten foot widening strip be dedicated, the finding is that the widening of Sepulveda Boulevard had been in contemplation by the authorities whether or not the petioner intended to subdivde; but that the creation and the proposed uses of the subdivision would give rise to traffic and other conditions necessitating the widening of the boulevard; that the widening was necessary for and would benefit the lot owners, and that the requirement was reasonably related to the protection of the public health, safety and general welfare.

With regard to condition 2, that an additional ten feet be reserved for a planting strip, the court found that such a strip was already in contemplation, but that the creation of the subdivision necessitated the restricted use to confine ingress and egress to and from the lots away from Sepulveda Boulevard; to screen the lot owners from the traffic noises, fumes and views of the fast-moving traffic on the boulevard; to provide safety islands for residents crossing the boulevard on foot and waiting lanes for vehicular traffic, and that the imposition of the condition was reasonably related to the protection of the public health, safety and general welfare.

It was found that the foregoing pattern of subdivision, including the widening and planting strips in the development of Sepulveda Boulevard frontage, was in comformity with neighborhood plan and design, and had been carried out without objection by the petitioner and others in the district until the filing by petitioner of the tentative map for subdivision of his thirteen acres. Variations in some requirements, changes in or abandonment of others, delays in making improvements, incompleteness of the master plans or failure to indicate thereon the precise details, the court found to be minor, not unauthorized, and without adverse bearing on the lawfulness or reasonableness of the conditions imposed.

The finding as to condition 3, respecting the required eighty foot width of the Seventy-Seventh Street extension through the tract, was covered by the trial court's general conclusion that there was no unreasonable application of the Subdivision Map Act as to any of the conditions objected to by the petitioner.

Specifically as to condition 4, the dedication to eliminate the southerly tip of the triangle, it was found that without regard to the subdivision it had been the intention to project Seventy-Ninth Street either across the petitioner's tract or below it; also that the subdivision would give rise to and create traffic conditions and hazards necessitating the elimination of the tip for the proper control of traffic in the locality, would benefit the lot owners in the proposed subdivision, and was reasonably related to the protection of the public health, safety and general welfare.

All intendments must be indulged to sustain the findings and judgment. Consideration alone of the physical facts and conditions, remembering also that the trial judge viewed the locality, indicate sufficient support therefor.

The contentions respecting the required width of the Seventy-Seventh

Street extension will not be further discussed except to note that the proposed business and religious uses of the respective abutting lots and the fact that Seventy-Seventh is the only street to transverse the tract between Sepulveda Boulevard and Arizona Avenue, sufficiently support the conclusion that the required width is reasonably related to the potential traffic needs.

The petitioner does not quarrel with the conclusion that the other conditions are desirable and that their fulfillment will accomplish the ends stated. His more specific complaint is that the city contemplated taking the property for the purposes indicated in any event, that the benefit to the lot owners and the tract will be relatively small compared to the beneficial return to the city at large; therefore that the requirements amount to an exercise of the power of eminent domain under the guise of pursuing the authority of subdivision map-proceedings, and that the exercise thereof is unconstitutional unless compensation be paid.

In his arguments the petitioner appears to have lost sight of the particular type of lot subdivision and uniformity of neighborhood design and plan theretofore applied in the locality, including the requirement for strip dedication for widening purposes and strip restriction to planting use without dedication. As stated, consideration of these matters is not precluded by the provisions of the Subdivision Map Act, but on the contrary both the statutory provisions and the local law indicate that the subdivision design and use should conform to neighborhood planning and zoning requirements. Here the greater than average depth of the lots minimizes the land loss and street improvement cost. In fact it may be said that the petitioner's position would seem to be greatly improved by this type of subdivision and its related requirements in conformity with neighborhood planning and zoning. The regular design of subdivision, with ingress and egress to and from Sepulveda Boulevard, would have been out of harmony with the neighborhood plan and traffic needs. It would have required dedication and improvement by the petitioner of lateral service roads and lanes for diversion of the local traffic to and from the main artery which the evidence shows would have used more land than for the widening and planting strips, and would have increased the cost of the improvements to be installed by the petitioner. The record indicates that the so-called cellular design was generally adopted because it interfered less with the free flow of traffic, minimized the hazards on the main thoroughfares, and reduced land dedication and improvement expense. The petitioner and the lot owners in the subdivision will participate in these benefits and savings by the selection of and adherence to the particular design. In fact the petitioner makes no objection to that design as such. It is to be assumed that he prefers it with the resulting savings in land and cost. But he seeks in addition compensation for the fulfillment of the conditions which make this type of lot subdivisions feasible. Similar observations apply to the dedication of the southerly tip of the triangle. The petitioner could reasonably be required to provide for the dedication and improvement of the extension of Seventy-Ninth Street through the tract to provide safe turning for traffic to and from the subdivision and incidentally to eliminate as a traffic hazard the practically useless remainder of the tip. He has lost nothing by the requirement for dedication and is benefited by being relieved of the burden of improvement. The conclusion is justifiable that the widening and planting strips and the elimination of the hazardous tip are as much a part of design and improvement within the proposed subdivision as would the lateral and transverse service roads and lanes had the regular or non-cellular design been selected.

Questions of reasonableness and necessity depend on matters of fact. They are not abstract ideas or theories. In a growing metropolitan area each additional subdivision adds to the traffic burden. It is no defense to the conditions imposed in a subdivision map proceeding that their fulfillment will incidentally also benefit the city as a whole. Nor is it a valid objection to say that the conditions contemplate future as well as more immediate needs. Potential as well as present population factors affecting the subdivision and the neighborhood generally are appropriate for consideration. Nor does the fact that master plans are incomplete; or that the specific details are not shown thereon, affect the result. It was in evidence that the city had been working toward the formulation of a complete and entire master plan, although all the elements or part thereof were not as yet in the final stage of completion. The contention that the requirements for a master plan or some over-all plan must be approved and adopted before authority vests in relation to the conditions here imposed is without merit since in any event the charter contemplates that portions thereof may be adopted. It is inconceivable that a master plan including all essential factors for a growing city could be completed in a short period of time. The trial court correctly concluded that delay in the adoption of the final master plan or plans had no material bearing on the controversial issues in this proceeding. The reasonableness of the conditions and the authority to impose them do not necessarily depend upon their inclusion in the official master plan for the district. As noted, subdivision design and improvement obviously include conformance to neighborhood planning and zoning, and it may properly be said that the formulation and acceptance of the uniform condition in the development of the district constitute the practical adoption of a master plan and zoning requirements therefor. Nor is there merit in the petitioner's contention that a uniform plan is lacking because of some discrepancies in uniformity or delays in enforcement or fulfillment of the conditions. Time, funds and manpower are requisites to execution, and lack of speed in accomplishment, or some changes because of differing circumstances as to use or otherwise, cannot defeat the otherwise uniform and reasonable application of the imposed conditions in a growing community.

The petitioner may not prevail in his contention that, since the use of the land for the purposes stated was contemplated in any event, the dedication and use reservation requirements in this proceeding are unconstitutional as an exercise of the power of eminent domain. A sufficient answer is that the proceeding here involved is not one in eminent domain nor is the city seeking to exercise that power. It is the petitioner who is seeking to acquire the advantages of lot subdivision and upon him rests the duty of compliance with reasonable conditions for design, dedication, improvement and restrictive use of the land so as to conform to the safety and general welfare of the lot owners in the subdivision and of the public. The well-considered observations in Mansfield & Swett v. Town of West Orange, 120 N.J. L. 145, 193 A. 225, also involving a subdivision proceeding, are pertinent in this connection. The court there recognized the distinction between the exercise of the sovereign power of eminent domain and the non-compensatory nature of reasonable restrictions in respect to private interests when they must yield to the good of the community. That these general principles apply in subdivision map proceedings is also demonstrated in the cases of *Ridgefield Land Co.* v. *City of Detroit,* and *Newton* v. *American Sec. Co.,* where the distinction was made between the exercise of authority in such proceedings and the exercise of the power of eminent domain. In each of those cases it was held that the requirement for the dedication of land to the widening of existing streets was not a compulsory taking for public use; but that where it is a condition reasonably related to increased traffic and other needs of the proposed subdivision it is voluntary in theory and not contrary to constitutional concepts. * * *

No sufficient reasons have been advanced which would justify this court in overturning the findings of the trial court as to the authority for and the reasonableness of the conditions imposed.

The judgment is affirmed.

GIBSON, C. J., and EDMONDS, TRAYNOR, and SPENCE, JJ., concur.

WALD CORP.

v.

METROPOLITAN DADE COUNTY

338 So.2d 863 (Fla. App. 1976)

NATHAN, Judge.

The appellant in this case, Wald Corporation, is challenging a required dedication of canal rights-of-way and maintenance easements which was imposed by the appellee, Metropolitan Dade County, as a condition of approval of appellant's plat for a proposed subdivision. Wald refused to dedicate, and instead filed a complaint in Dade County Circuit Court, seeking a declaration of the unconstitutionality of those sections of the Code of Metropolitan Dade County which required dedication of land for canal purposes as a condition for plat approval.

The trial court granted the County's motion for summary judgment, holding that the subdivision requirements relating to drainage would be upheld as a matter of law under either of the two prevailing standards of review. While we essentially agree with the decision of the trial court, we feel that it is advisable for us to review the applicable law in the area of subdivision dedication requirements.

There are two distinct standards which have generally been applied by the various state courts when confronted with mandatory dedication. The first was initially proposed by the California Supreme Court in the leading case of *Ayres v. City Council*, (1949). In that case, the city planning commission conditioned approval of a proposed subdivision plat upon the dedication of an eighty feet wide strip of land which was to be used for the extension of a nearby cross street. Despite the fact that the existing street was only sixty feet wide, the *Ayres* court upheld the dedication requirement, noting that the facts of the case sufficiently supported the conclusion "that the required width is *reasonably related* to the potential traffic needs." *Id.* at 39, 207 P.2d at 6. (Emphasis added.)

THIS "reasonable relation" requirement has been applied in a number of other jurisdictions. Unfortunately, however, the language of *Ayres* often seems to be cited in cases with markedly different fact patterns, to the extent that the original test pronounced in *Ayres* may be rendered virtually unrecognizable.

The confusion surrounding application of the *Ayres* test may be evidenced through reference to several cases which were decided by the Illinois Supreme Court. In the first, *Rosen v. Village of Downers Grove*, (1960), the high court of Illinois held that a municipality lacked statutory authority to exact cash payments in lieu of dedicating land for educational purposes. Although compulsory dedication itself was not in issue, the *Ayres* opinion was cited:

> "The provisions of the statute . . . appear to be based upon the theory that the developer of a subdivision may be required to assume those costs which are *specifically and uniquely attributable* to his activity and which would otherwise be case upon the public. It is upon this theory that we sustain the requirement that a subdivider provide curbs and gutters in *Peterson v. City of Naperville*."
>
> *   *   *
>
> "The distinction between permissible and forbidden requirements is suggested in *Ayres v. City Council of City of Los Angeles*, which indicates that the municipality may require the developer to provide the streets *which are required by the activity within the subdivision* but can not require him to provide a major thoroughfare, the need for which stems from the total activity of the community." *Rosen*, (emphasis added.)

As noted above, the *Ayres* court had upheld a dedication requirement which was "reasonably related" to the needs of the municipality, yet it was suggested in *Rosen* that such requirements had to be "specifically and uniquely attributable" to the activity of the subdivider.

In a subsequent decision, *Pioneer Trust & Savings Bank v. Village of Mount Prospect*, (1961), the Illinois Supreme Court was directly confronted with an issue of mandatory dedication. Although the court noted that *Rosen* had not decided the dedication question, it quoted the "specifically and uniquely attributable" language of the *Rosen* case to distinguish between permissible and forbidden requirements. Like the earlier *Rosen* case, *Pioneer Trust* also cited *Ayres* as support for this standard of review. But while *Ayres* ruled that mandatory dedication requirements would be upheld where "reasonably related" to municipal needs, *Pioneer Trust* ruled that such requirements would be invalid unless "specifically and uniquely attributable" to the subdividers activity.

Although the *Pioneer Trust* decision cited *Ayres* as precedent, it would seem that the two cases proposed entirely different standards for the review of subdivision dedication requirements. The *Ayres* standard of "reasonable relation" puts a heavy burden on the developer to show that the required dedication bears no relation to the general health, safety and welfare. In this regard, it is couched in traditional police power language:

"It is the [developer] who is seeking to acquire the advantages of lot subdivision and upon him rests the duty of compliance with reasonable conditions for design, dedication, improvement and restrictive use of the land so as to conform to the safety and general welfare of the lot owners in the subdivision and of the public."

Thus, the *Ayres* standard of "reasonableness" defers to the legislative judgment that there is or will be a threat posed to the welfare of both lot owners and the general public if the required dedication is not made.

Pioneer Trust, on the other hand, shifts the burden of proving the validity of subdivision exactions to the municipality; mandatory dedication is only to be upheld where the discerned needs are directly and solely attributable to the proposed subdivision. The presumptions of validity which are usually attendant police power measures are undermined, if not ignored altogether, thus affording little deference to the judgment of the lcoal legislative authority.

Both of these standards have their relative strengths and weaknesses. The *Ayres* standard allows the municipality considerable flexibility in the formulation of comprehensive plans for future growth and development. It assurés the local legislature that its dedication requirements will be upheld short of gross abuse. But while such wide latitude is routinely accorded in other areas of police power regulation, required dedication as a condition for approval for subdivision plats stands in derogation of constitutionally protected property rights. Thus, it is imperative that some sort of standard be imposed which will not allow virtually unbridled interference with private property. While we believe that a legislative authority may require dedication of land as a condition for subdivision plat approval, the constitutional validity of such requirements should not be tested merely for reasonableness. Such a method of review would allow local governbments almost unlimited discretion in the imposition of dedication requirements. For this reasons, we cannot accept the *Ayres* rule of "reasonable relation."

At the same time, the *Pioneer Trust* case created a standard which is unduly restrictive of local exercises of the police power. While it is possible to envision instances where potential problems will be "specifically and uniquely attributable" to the proposed subdivision, more often than not, local authorities are faced with situations which involve an entire community, including land owned by the complaining subdivider. The cause and effect approach advocated by *Pioneer Trust* disallows a formidable method of subdivision control, which is an integral part of comprehensive planning. And while it is important to guard against unbridled municipal discretion, it is equally important that those who propose to subdivide may be subjected to rational dedication requirements. For this reason, we also reject the "specifically and uniquely attributable" rule of *Pioneer Trust.*

In seeking to establish a moderate standard with which to review the actions of Dade County in the instant case, we have sought guidance from the Florida courts. One circuit court has adopted the "strictly and uniquely attributable" standard of *Pioneer Trust. Carlann Shores, Inc. v. City of Gulf Breeze,* (1966). As noted above, however, we choose not to adopt such a restrictive standard. The Fourth District Court of Appeal invalidated a mandatory dedication requirement in *Admiral Development Corp. v. City of Maitland,* (1975), but because the municipality had exceeded its charter authority. While the *Maitland* case did cite a Rhode Island decision which utilized the "specific and unique" language of *Pioneer Trust,* both of these cases are distinguishable to the extent that they were concerned with dedication requirements which were set at a fixed percentage by law. Such fixed percentage requirements were found to be arbitrary on their face.

Although no Florida appellate cases can be found on the point concerned herein, the Supreme Court of Florida has had occasion to limit exercises of the police power where private property rights were adversely affected without adequate justification. In ·a case concerning the regulation of outdoor advertising, the court held that private business could not be subjected to police power restrictions where there was "no reasonably identifiable rational realtionship between the demands of the public welfare and the restraint upon private business . . . " *Eskind v. City of Vero Beach,* (Fla.1963).

Although *Eskind* involved a business regulation, its standard of review may be readily appropriated for use in determining the validity of the subdivision exaction which is currently before us. The situations involved in the two cases are analogous. As was noted in a widely cited commentary on subdivision control requirements:

> The subdivider is a manufacturer, processor, and marketer of a product; land is but one of his raw materials. In subdivision control disputes, the developer is not defending hearth and home against the king's intrusion, but simply attempting to maximize his profits from the sale of a finished product. As applied to him, subdivision control exactions are actually business regulations.

John D. Johnston, Jr., *Constitutionality of Subdivision Control Exactions: The Quest for a Rationale,* 52 Cornell L.Q. 871, 923 (1967). While this statement displays the correlation between subdivision control and business regulation, it is also supportive of a critical distinction which must be drawn between the ordinary property owner and the subdivider.

Unlike one who merely reserves his property for personal use or sale as a single tract, the subdivider profits from the sale of lots within the subdivision to prospective home builders. The local government, in turn, must consider the welfare of the families who will be filling the development. It is eminently reasonable, therefore, to allow the municipality to impose certain conditions upon the developer so that it may provide for the needs of persons who would not otherwise have been a local concern. And in a very real sense, the subdivider profits from the conditions imposed upon him, since the provision of safety and health requirements benefits potential buyers, thus rendering the lots of the subdivision more attractive.

This same reasoning was utilized by the Supreme Court of Wisconsin to uphold a required dedication of land for school, park and recreational purposes. *Jordan v. Village of Menomonee Falls*, (1966). Using a police power rationale, the Wisconsin court found that there was a reasonable connection between the required dedication and the anticipated needs of the community. The court noted that it might be impossible to show at times that the required exaction would be necessary to meet a need which was solely attributable to one particular subdivision. Nevertheless, the local authorities might well be able to prove that continued approval of subdivisions over the years could result in dramatic increases in the amount of services and safeguards which the municipality would have to provide. Such proof would certainly justify the dedicatory requirement.

This "rational nexus" approach provides a more feasible basis for testing subdivision dedication requirements than the two methods of review discussed earlier. It allows the local authorities to implement future-oriented comprehensive planning without according undue deference to legislative judgments. It requires a balancing of the prospective needs of the community and the property rights of the developer. But above all, it treats the business of subdividing as a profit-making enterprise, thus drawing proper distinctions between the individual property-holder and the subdivider. While the former may not ordinarily have his property appropriated without an eminent domain proceeding, the latter may be required to dedicate land where the requirement is a part of a valid regulatory scheme.

The record in the instant action clearly demonstrates the need for proper drainage through the proposed subdivision. The Wald property is located in a "glade area" of Dade County which has been subject to periodic flooding. Although the subdivison parcel itself is slightly above flood level, other parts of the glade both upstream and downstream from the parcel are lower, and are thus subject to runoff from the Wald subdivision. In 1957, the Board of County Commissioners for Dade County adopted a plan for a secondary canal system which was intended to run through the Wald Property. This plan was tentative, according to an affidavit by F.D.R. Parks, the Water Control Engineer for the Dade County Public Works Department; it is revised and realigned as different tracts are developed. The latest revision to the water control plan was approved in 1972. Parks' affidavit notes that both upstream and downstream property will be adversely affected if flow-through drainage is not provided across the Wald subdivision. A further critical point is that the subdivision itself would be damaged by periodic flooding without flow-through drainage. These points are not refuted. To the contrary, Wald concedes that it will be benefited once the canal system is connected.

Although appellant belabors the fact that the canal system is not yet fully operable, this point is without merit, since it would otherwise be impossible to institute reasonable regulation and dedication requirements as part of comprehensive municipal planning. Whole areas of a community are often zoned before any actual development occurs. In fact, Florida Statutes §§ 163.160 and 163.195 specifically authorize the adoption of comprehensive plans for future development. Where such plans are adopted, zoning changes may not be implemented where the proposed change will not conform to the comprehensive plan, unless there is approval by the local governmental commission. It would seem illogical to foster intelligent prospective planning in the area of zoning, only to deny this same type of function in the area of subdivision control.

For these reasons, we find that Sections 28-13(a), (b) and (c) of the Code of Metropolitan Dade County are rationally connected to the goals which the County seeks to achieve. The rational nexus between intelligent planning which is designed to protect the health, safety and welfare of the citizens of Dade County and the disputed dedication requirement is sufficient to uphold the subject ordinances as a valid exercise of the police power.

Wald finally contends that Section 28-13 is unconstitutionally vague in that it allows for unlimited and unsupervised discretion in the determination of required dedications. We feel that this claim is unfounded. Chapter 28 of the County Code is replete with regulations and considerations concerning subdivisions and dedication. It contains more than adequate standards to be applied by the Department of Public Works so far as platting and subdivision requirements are concerned. While the Department is allowed some reasonable, warranted discretion, it is properly limited by Chapter 28 when read in conjunction with the County's Manual of Public Works Construction, Water Control Section, and the County Water Control Master Plan. Finally, the actions of the Dade County Plat Commission, are reviewable by the Zoning Appeals Board, which affirmed the Plat Committee's denial of approval for the Wald subdivision plat. We therefore find that Wald's claim of unbridled discretion is without merit. See *Thomas v. City of West Palm Beach*, 299 So.2d 11 (Fla.1974).

We hold that Sections 28–13(a), (b) and (c) of the Code of Metropolitan Dade County are constitutionally valid, both upon their face and as applied to the Wald subdivision. The trial court's order granting Dade County's motion for summary judgment is therefore affirmed.

Affirmed.

Schools and Parks

The typical subdivision enabling legislation and ordinance will authorize the planning board to require, as a condition of plat approval, the installation of streets, gutters, sidewalks, street lighting, sewers and other subdivision improvements required to protect the public interest. However, state statutes are usually silent on the question whether the subdivider may be required to **dedicate land** for *schools and parks*. The problem is further complicated by the fact that each new subdivision imposes an additional burden on the school system, the increased cost of which will tend to increase taxes for all the residents of the community. Consequently, attempts are made frequently to compel the developer to donate land for schools as a condition of subdivision plat approval. The courts are divided on the question of the validity of such a condition. Some courts have held that the obligation to build and maintain schools is a governmental responsibility that must be borne by the public at large and paid for by general taxes, and that the denial of the right to subdivide land on condition that the developer donate land for schools purposes is a violation of the due process clause. Other courts have held that such conditions are reasonable requirements for subdivision approval and are valid.

The issue may be clarified by statute. In New Jersey, for example the state enabling legislation authorizes the **reservation of land** for schools and parks for one year after approval of the final plat. During that period the municipality may either purchase the property, by negotiation or eminent domain, or thereafter the developer will not be bound by such reservation. As you read the following excerpt from the New Jersey Municipal Land Use Law, notice the provision for payment of compensation to the developer for the loss of use of his property during the period of temporary reservation of land for public areas:

NEW JERSEY MUNICIPAL LAND USE LAW
C. 40:55D-44 Reservation of public areas.

32. Reservation of public areas. If the master plan or the official map provides for the reservation of designated streets, public drainageways, flood control basins, or public areas within the proposed development, before approving a subdivision or site plan, the planning board may further require that such streets, ways, basins or areas be shown on the plat in locations and sizes suitable to their intended uses. The planning board may reserve the location and extent of such streets, ways, basins or areas shown on the plat for a period of 1 year after the approval of the final plat or within such further time as may be agreed to by the developer. Unless during such period or extension thereof the municipality shall have entered into a contract to purchase or institute condemnation proceedings according to law for the fee or a lesser interest in the land comprising such streets, ways, basins or areas; the developer shall not be bound by such reservations shown on the plat and may proceed to use such land for private use in accordance with applicable development regulations. The provisions of this section shall not apply to streets and roads, flood control basins or public drainageways necessitated by the subdivison or land development and required for final approval.

The developer shall be entitled to just compensation for actual loss found to be caused by such temporary reservation and deprivation of use. In such instance, unless a lesser amount has previously been mutually agreed upon, just compensation shall be deemed to be the fair market value of an option to purchase the land reserved for the period of reservation; provided that determination of such fair market value shall include, but not be limited to, consideration of the real property taxes apportioned to the land reserved and prorated for the period of reservation. The developer shall be compensated for the reasonable increased cost of legal, engineering, or other professional services incurred in connection with obtaining subdivision approval or site plan approval, as the case may be, caused by the reservation. The municipality shall provide by ordinance for a procedure for the payment of all compensation payable under this section. _____

The New Jersey Supreme Court has interpreted the previous enactment of this provision to express a legislative intent to *limit* municipal authority to the *reservation* of land for parks and schools for a limited period of time to permit the municipality to *purchase* the land. Consequently, a municipality could not require a developer to contribute to the support of education as a condition of subdivision approval. *West Park Ave. Inc. v. Township of Ocean*, 48 N.J. 122, 224 A.2d 1 (1966). On the other hand, the Illinois court, in the *Naperville* case, set forth below, concluded that a similar statutory provision for the **reservation of land** is in *addition* to the right of the municipality to require a **dedication of land** for schools as a condition to subdivision approval.

KRUGHOFF

v.

CITY OF NAPERVILLE

41 Ill. App. 3d 334, 354 N.E. 2d 489 (1976)

SEIDENFELD, Justice.

Whether the defendant, the City of Naperville, can, by its ordinance, (referred to as 72–20) require contribution of land, * * * to be used for school and park sites as a condition of approval of a plat of subdivision or planned unit development within defendant's boundaries or within 1½ miles therefrom is before us in this appeal.

The plaintiffs filed a class action for declaratory judgment to declare the defendant's ordinance 72–20 void as being beyond defendant's constitutional home rule powers, unauthorized by statute and violative of the Illinois and United States Constitutions. The trial court declared the ordinance valid, and the plaintiffs appeal.

The plaintiffs, O. L. Krughoff and James Kroughoff, doing business as the K Company, acquired property within 1½ miles of defendant's boundaries suitable for subdividing into residential lots. They submitted a final plat of subdivision which the defendant refused to approve without the dedications or donations required by ordinance 72–20. The Krughoffs did not comply and claim that as a consequence they were not able to proceed with their plans. The plaintiffs, Paul W. Hoffman, Harold E. Moser, the Oliver-Hoffman Corporation and The Macom Corporation (hereinafter referred to collectively as "Oliver-Hoffman") acquired land within the City of Naperville to subdivide and sell as residential lots. They were required to contribute $37,650 to be held in trust for acquisition of a school site, and they agreed in writing to contribute a lot for the Naperville Park

District's use. These plaintiffs seek return of the money and nullification of the agreement, should the ordinance be declared invalid.

* * *

There was evidence from planning studies that the City of Naperville has experienced a rapid population increase, from 12,933 in 1960 to 28,610 by the end of 1973. The city's population was projected to continue to increase to between 42,000 and 52,000 in 1980 and between 66,000 and 81,000 in 1990.

Ordinance 72–20, enacted by the city on June 19, 1972, imposes certain conditions precedent to the approval of a plat of subdivision or planned unit development within the city's jurisdiction. In accordance with existing standards establishing the optimum accessibility of different types of parks and recreational areas for every resident, the ordinance requires the dedication of land within the devlopment for park and recreational purposes. The amount to be dedicated is 5.5 acres per 1000 of ultimate population in a proposed development. In recognition of the fact that private recreational areas within the development, such as swimming pools, may reduce the demand for comparable public facilities, the ordinance provides that credit may be given for the furnishing of private recreational areas.

The ordinance also requires the dedication of land to be used as school sites pursuant to criteria for optimum capacity, location, and site size of elementary, junior high, and high schools to serve the population of the development. Ultimate population is determined by reference to a table, incorporated in the ordinance, which estimates the number of persons and the age distribution of children who will occupy various types of new living units. A subdivider or developer has the option of submitting his own demographic study showing the additional estimated population to be generated if he objects to the use of the table in the ordinance.

* * *

Section 11–12–8 provides, as material here:

> "*Compliance of plat with map—Designation of public lands—Approval—Bond—Order—Failure to act upon plat.* The corporate authorities of the municipality shall determine whether a proposed plat of subdivision or resubdivision complies with the official map. To secure such determination, the person requesting the subdivision or resubdivision shall file four copies of plat thereof with the clerk of the municipality, and shall furnish therewith four copies of all data necessary to show compliance with all applicable municipal regulations and shall make application for preliminary or final approval of the proposed plat.
>
> Whenever the reasonable requirements provided by the ordinance including the official map shall indicate the necessity for providing for a school site, park site, or other public lands within any proposed subdivision for which approval has been requested, and no such provision has been made therefor, the municipal authority may require that lands be designated for such public purpose before approving such plat. Whenever a final plat of subdivision, or part thereof, has

been approved by the corporate authorities as complying with the official map and there is designated therein a school site, part site or other public land, the corporate authorities having jurisdiction of such use, be it a school board, park board or other authority, such authority shall acquire the land so designated by purchase or commence proceedings to acquire such land by condemnation within one year from the date of approval of such plat; and if it does not do so within such period of one year, the land so designated may then be used by the owners thereof in any other manner consistent with the ordinance including the official map and the zoning ordinance of the municipality.

The corporate authorities may by ordinance provide that a plat of subdivision may be submitted initially to the plan commission for preliminary approval. The application for preliminary approval * * * shall indicate * * * proposed dedication of public grounds, if any, * * * but need not contain specifications for proposed improvements. * * *"

These provisions of Section 11–12–8 of the Illinois Municipal Code with respect to school and park sites do not appear to have been construed by any court (although this section was noted in *Bd. of Ed. v. Surety Developers, Inc.*, supra, in the dissent of Justice Schaffer). The developer contends that this section was added to the Municipal Code for the purpose of limiting to designation and reservation rather than dedication the means by which school and park sites may be obtained. The city, however, contends that the dedications and donations required by ordinance 72–20 are authorized under the Municipal Code, citing *Pioneer* and *Surety*. It contends that Section 11–12–8 merely authorizes an additional means of obtaining the necessary public grounds.

The provisions of Section 11–12–8 could arguably be viewed as a legislative response to the court decisions in *Rosen* and *Pioneer* and as establishing the statutory policy that a municipality is prohibited from requiring that a subdivider dedicate and donate school or park sites at no cost to the public. However, the fact that this section was in effect at the time of the decision in *Surety Developers*, supra, did not prevent the majority of the court from reaffirming the tests enunciated in *Pioneer* and *Rosen* and from holding that reasonable requirements for school and park dedications may be imposed upon a developer. Presumably, the provisions of the statute, although not referred to in the majority opinion, were before the court inasmuch as the section was referred to in the dissenting opinion, inferentially, as changing the rule of *Pioneer Tr. & S. Bank v. Village of Mt. Prospect.*

Moreover, the provisions of 11–12–8 are not clear and unambiguous as plaintiffs contend. The plaintiffs would interpret the phrase "and no such provision has been made therefor," which relates to the necessity of providing school and park sites or other public lands, as referring to a situation in which no such provision has been made by the developer. The city argues with equal reason that it could as well refer to the *city's* failure to make provisions for such sites by failing to pass an ordinance in the nature of ordinance 72–20. The city contends with some reason that section 11–12–8 merely authorizes an additional power to require designation and reservation of public lands in instances where other provisions have not been made to obtain them or in instances in which the city needs a larger site within a particular subdivision than that which the subdivider may be required to dedicate under the ordinance.

We note that dedication requirements and reservation requirements are recognized as two different types of land development regulation. See Johnston, "Constitutionality of Subdivision Control Exactions: The Quest for a Rationale," 52 Cornell L.Q. 871, 904–24; 1967 U.Ill.L.F. 318; Model Land Development Code, §§ 2—103, 3–202 (Proposed Official Draft, 1975); Ark.Ann.Stat. § 19–2829 (1968). That the legislature recognized that the implementation of an official comprehensive plan and map may require a combination of land dedications and reservations is implicit, we believe, in the reference to "proposed, dedication of public grounds," in the third paragraph of section 11–12–8 and the retention, in section 11–12–5, of statutory language substantially similar to that construed in the earlier cases.

In view of these facts and the majority opinion in *Surety Developers,* we conclude that the provisions of section 11–12–8 were not intended as a limitation on the city's power to enact an ordinance which imposes "reasonable requirements for public streets, alleys, ways for public service facilities, parks, playgrounds, school grounds, and other public grounds." (See Ill.Rev.Stat.1959, ch. 24, pars. 53–2, 53–; see also Ill.Rev.Stat.1973, ch. 24, pars. 11–12–5, 11–12–12), but as an additional means by which a municipality may implement its plans for orderly growth.

* * *

We have concluded that the provisions of ordinance 72–20 are authorized by state statute. We further conclude that the ordinance is constitutional whether tested by state or federal constitutional standards.

The developers essentially mount their constitutional attack on ordinance 72–20 on the basis that it constitutes an exercise of a power of eminent domain, therefore violating several related provisions of the constitution requiring due process, compensation, and trial by jury; and that it constitutes an exercise of the power of taxation therefore violating related provisions of uniformity, special assessments and double taxation.

However, in Illinois the imposition of reasonable regulations as a condition precedent to the subdivision of land and recording of plats is to be tested by the law applicable to cases involving the exercise of police power. Also, in Illinois the question of the reasonableness of the regulation is dependent on the finding that the burden cast upon the subdivider is specifically and uniquely attributable to his activity.

Each of the parties has cited authorities from other jurisdictions which appear to provide conflicting results as to the constitutionality of ordinances requiring a subdivider to dedicate public lands or to pay fees for that purpose. Because of the different fact situations and the varying statutes, the outside authorities are not helpful except as they show a modern trend to uphold reasonable exactions, and to strike down those which are unreasonable. See, e.g., *East Neck Estates, Ltd. v. Luchsinger,* 61 Misc.2d 619, 305 N.Y.S.2d 922 (1969) (required dedication of shore front land which would decrease value of tract costing $208,000 by over $90,000 struck down as confiscatory); *Kessler v. Town of Shelter Island Plan. Bd.,* 40 A.D.2d 1005, 338 N.Y.S.2d 778 (1972) (refusal of a plat of subdivision on the ground that the entire area is a recreation or school site on the official map amounts to confiscation); *Frank Ansuini, Inc., v. City of Cranston,* 107 R.I. 63, 264 A.2d 910 (1970) (flat percentage dedication requirement held arbitrary as not shown to result from activities specifically and uniquely attributable to the development); *Aunt Hack Ridge Estates, Inc., v. Planning Com'n,* 27 Conn.Sup. 74, 230 A.2d 45 (1967) (provision that monies collected in lieu of land dedication not limited to uses directly benefiting a subdivision is invalid); *McKain v. Toledo City Plan Commission,* 26 Ohio App.2d 171, 270 N.E.2d 370 (1971) (requirement of dedication of a strip of land for the purpose of widening a main thoroughfare 700 feet away from and totally unrelated to the proposed subdivision held an improper exercise of the police power and unconstitutional).

*   *   *

The presumption of validity attaches to municipal enactments and regulations adopted under the police power and the burden of proving to the contrary is upon one who asserts the invalidity.

Here, the record shows that the acreage requirements were based on the formulae contained in the ordinance which were stipulated to be reasonable.

Moreover, the statutory scheme does not indicate an attempt to make developers pay for past inadequacies inasmuch as the city had approximately 10 acres per 1000 population in park and recreational lands and also had sufficient schools to accommodate the current enrollment and had acquired additional sites for schools which had not been built. Further, the trial court found that the requirements of the ordinance were "uniquely and specifically attributable to the development of the lands to which it is applicable." The detailed financial analysis presented by appellees tends to demonstrate that the city is not putting an impossible financial burden on the developers nor on the potential residents of subdivisions or planned unit developments.

The failure to apply the requirement to commercial and industrial uses does not establish an invalid classification since there is a reasonable basis for the differentiation. Although there was some testimony which indicated that the rapid population growth in the Naperville area was partially attributable to commercial and industrial development in the area, the city council certainly could conclude that the need for school and park sites was more reasonably related to the development of residential complexes than to the development of commercial complexes which could employ persons who resided outside its planning jurisdiction.

The judgment of the trial court is, therefore, affirmed.

Affirmed.

3. Cash Fee in Lieu of Dedication

Not every subdivision development contains land that is suitable for parks, schools, or other public uses. Nevertheless, every additional development of land increases the need for additional public facilities. In response to this problem, some municipalities have required developers to pay **cash fee in lieu of land dedication.** The ordinance requiring the cash fee may, or may not, provide for the creation of a trust fund to assure that the monies collected will be used for the designated purposes. The courts in different states have interpreted their state enabling legislation differently. In New York, and other states, the cash fee in lieu of dedication has been upheld. In New Jersey, and other states, the courts have held that the enabling legislation does not authorize a cash fee in lieu of dedication of land.

JENAD, INC.

v.

VILLAGE OF SCARSDALE

18 N.Y.2d 78, 271 N.Y.S.2d 955, 218 N.E.2d 673 (1966)

DESMOND, Chief Judge.

The Village of Scarsdale, pursuant to statute (Village Law, Consol. Laws, c. 64, § 179-k) has given its Planning Commission the authority to approve proposed plats for subdividing lands in the village. On this appeal the principal question of law, answered in the negative by the Appellate Division, is this: was it valid for the village to authorize its planning board to require, as a condition precedent to the approval of subdivision plats which show new streets or highways that the subdivider allot some land within the subdivision for park purposes or, at the option of the village planning board, pay the village a fee in lieu of such allotment? Our answer is in the affirmative. We hold, first, that section 179-*l* of the Village Law, empowering a village to require as to subdivision plats that there be set aside therein lands for parks, playgrounds or other recreational purposes, is valid and enforcible. Further, we hold that there is no constituional or statutory ban against section 2, article 12, of the Rules and Regulations of the Planning Commission of defendant Village of Scarsdale as approved by the village trustees on September 24, 1957. These rules and regulations give the commission power to direct that, in lieu of such dedication of land, a charge or fee of $250 per lot be collected by the village "and credited to a separate fund to be used for park, playground and recreational purposes in such manner as may be determined by the Village Board of Trustees from time to time."

The facts of the particular controversy between plaintiff and the village are set out in full in the dissenting opinion and need not be repeated. We add some generally pertinent items. In at least five counties of this State there are cities, towns or villages which make it possible to insit on developers' paying cash in lieu of setting aside areas in their developments for parks, playground and similar purposes (information supplied by the New York State Office for Local Government). In Westchester County alone 16 or more local governments (among them several villages including Scarsdale) have "monies in lieu of land" regulations (this data received from Westchester County Department of Planning). As we shall see later on when we cite recent cases from Wisconsin and Montana, such rules exist and are upheld by courts in other States. There is conflict between a 1956 opinion of the State Attorney-General that a city has no such power under section 33 of the General City Law, Consol. Laws, c. 21, and three separate opinions of the State Comptroller dated in 1954, 1961, and 1963 (1954 Op.St. Comp. No. 6836; 17 Op.St. Comp., 1961, p.79; 19 Op.St.Comp., 1963, p. 3) which state that towns and villages could exact such fees under section 277 of the Town Law, Consol. Laws, c. 62 and section 179-*l* of the Village Law.

We find in section 179-*l* of the Village Law a sufficient grant to villages of power to make such exactions. In specific terms the staute validates "in proper cases" requirements by village planning boards that a subdivision map, to obtain approval, must show "a park or parks suitably located for playground or other recreation purposes." There is, to be sure, no such specificity as to a village rule setting up a "money in lieu of land" system. However, section 179-*l* says that a village planning board, when the specific circumstances of a particular plat are such that park lands therein are not requisite, may "waive" provision therefor, "subject to appropriate conditions and guarantees." We agree with the above cited opinions of the State Comptroller that the phrase "appropriate conditions and guarantees" reasonably includes the kind of arrangement here made. That is, instead of allotting part of the subdivision itself for parks and play areas, the subdivider may be ordered to pay so much per lot into a separate village fund which is "to be used for park, playground and recreational purposes," in such manner as the village trustees may decide. * * *

Plaintiff (and *amicus curiae*) insist that what Scarsdale has imposed is an unconstitutional and unauthorized "tax" on plaintiff and others similarly situated, in that the payments are for general governmental purposes thus charged against subdivision developers. We think that this labeling distorts the purpose and meaning of the requirements. This is not a tax at all but a reasonable form of village planning for the genreal community good.

Scarsdale and other communities, observing that their vacant lands were being cut up into subdivision lots, and being alert to their responsibilities, saw to it, before it was too late, that the subdivisions make allowance for open park spaces therein. This was merely a kind of zoning, like setback and side-yard regulations, minimum size of lots etc., and akin also to other reasonable requirements for necessary sewers, water mains, lights, sidewalks, etc. If the developers did not provide for parks and playgrounds in their own tracts, the municipality would have to do it since it would now be required for the benifit of all the inhabitants.

But it was found, in some instances, that the separate subdivisions were too small to permit substantial park lands to be set off, yet the creation of such subdivisions, too, enlarged the demand for more recreational space in the community. In such cases it was just as reasonable to assess the subdividers an amount per lot to go into a fund for more park lands for the village or town. One arrangement is no more of a "tax" or "illegal taking" than the other.

In 1965 (*Jordon* v. *Village of Menomonee Falls,*) The Supreme Court of Wisconsin in a careful and convincing opinion upheld as against assertions of unconstitutionality a village ordinance or statute which, for present purposes, is identical with the one we are considering. The Wisconsin court noted that municipal planners agree that to create a good environment for dwellings there must be a minimum devotion of land to park and school purposes. It was held in the *Jordan* case that it was not necessary to prove that the land required to be dedicated for a park or school site was to meet a need solely attributable to the influx into the community of people who would occupy this particular subdivision. The court concluded that "a required dedication of land for school, park, or recreational sites as a condition for the approval of trhe subdivision plat should be upheld as a valid exercise of police power if the evidence reasonably establishes that the municipality will be required to provide more land for schools, parks, and playgrounds as a result of approval of the subdivision." As to the constitutionality of what was called an "equalization fee provision" the court said that the same reasons justify with equal force the land dedication requirement and the provision for an equalization fee, and that the equalization fee was not a tax imposed on the land as such but was a fee imposed on the transaction of obtaining approval of the plat. In 1964 the Montana Supreme Court in *Billings Props. Inc.* v. *Yellowstone County,* 144 Mont. 25, 394P.2d 182 passed on a State statute which required land to be dedicated for park and playground purposes as a condition precedent to approval of a subdivision plat and which statute authorized the county planning board to waive the requirement in appropriate cases. The Montana court remarked that: "Statutes requiring dedication of park and playground land as a condition precedent to the approval of plats are in force in one form or another in most all states." The court said this at page 33, 394, P.2d at page 187: "Appellant does not deny the need for parks and playgounds, however, it would require the city to purchase or condemn land for their establishment. But this court is of the opinion that if the subdivision creates the specific need for such parks and playgrounds, then it is not unreasonable to charge the subdivider with the burden of providing them."

Defendants make two other arguments against recovery back by plaintiff of these fees. They point to the fact that plaintiff paid without protesting, and to plaintiff's failure to comply with the time requirements of section 341-b of the Village Law for filing claims and bringing actions against villages. Since we are holding that the village acted within its rights in collecting these moneys from plaintiff, we need not consider these other points made by defendants.

The order appealed from should be reversed and defendants' motion for summary judgment dismissing the complaint granted, with costs in this court and in the Appellate Division.

WEST PARK AVE., INC.

v.

OCEAN TP.

48 N.J. 122, 224 A.2d 1 (1966)

WEINTRAUB, C.J.

Plaintiff sued to recover $17,700 which it paid defendants, allegedly under duress. The trial court found the payments were in fact made unwillingly but held they nonetheless were "voluntary" in law and therefore unrecoverable because plaintiff ought to have sued to restrain the defendant municipality from pressing its illegal demand. We certified plaintiff's appeal before argument in the Appellate Division.

I

Plaintiff acquired 60 lots from one Leon Massar, which lots were part of a subdivision plan. After completing a model home, plaintiff erected signs advertising its tract, whereupon plaintiff was told by municipal officials that it could not use a billboard or receive further building permits or certificates of occupancy unless it agreed to pay to the defendant Board of Education the sum of $300 per house.

As we have said, the trial court found that plaintiff yielded unwillingly to this imposition. That finding, we think, was inescapably correct. Plaintiff feared it could not survive if its project stood still during a period of litigation. It also sensed a danger of hostile enforcement of ordinances bearing upon the construction of homes. This was especially understandable because of the boldness with which the dollar demand was made, for the municipality did not so much as adopt an ordinance to give color to the exaction. Rather the demand was made at the administrative level by minor officials, who, pursuant to instructions from above, simply refused to obey their duties of office.

When plaintiff yeilded, counsel for the municipality prepared a writing, with a flimsy contractual overlay, calling for a payment of $300 "upon the closing of title and delivery of deed to a purchaser for each house and lot," said moneys to be placed "in a trust fund or sinking fund, to be established for capital improvements of said school system and the erection of additional or adequate school construction in the said Township of Ocean." There were two such agreements, one executed in February 1959 for some of the 60 lots and the other in April 1960 for the balance of them.

In point of time, those transactions followed close upon our decision in *Daniels* v. *Borough of Point Pleasant*, (1957), in which we struck down an ordinance which attemped to impose a tax for revenue purposes upon new construction. In form the ordinance increased the fees for building permits. We said (at p. 362, 129 A.2d p. 267):

"* * * Admittedly, the purpose of the ordinance was to raise revenue to defray the increased cost of school and other government services. The philosophy of this ordinance is that the tax rate of the borough should remain the same and the new people coming into the municipality should bear the burden of the increased costs of their presence. This is so totally contrary to tax philosophy as to require it to be stricken down; see *Gilbert* v. *Town of Irvington*, (1956). Admittedly, these fiscal problems confronting many of our rapidly growing municipalities are grave ones and would seem to call for legislative action; the remedy must come not from the municipalities nor from the courts but from the Legislature."

The Legislature has not been unaware of the overall problem. It dealt with it in its statute relating to subdivisions. N.J.S.A. 40:55-1.21 reads:

"Before final approval of plats the governing body may require, in accordance with the standards adopted by ordinance, the installation, or the furnishing of a performance guarantee in lieu thereof, of any or all of the following improvements it may deem to be necessary or appropriate: street grading, pavement, gutters, curbs, sidewalks, street lighting, shade trees, surveyor's monuments, water mains, culverts, storm sewers, sanitary sewers or other means of sewage disposal, drainage structures, and such other subdivision improvements as the municipal governing body may find necessary in the public interest."

But with respect to the impact of housing developments upon the educational scene, the Legislature went no further than to provide that the governing body or planning board "shall be permitted to reserve the location and extent of *school sites*, public parks and playgrounds shown on the master plan or any part thereof for a period of one year after the approval of the final plat or within such further time as agreed to by the applying party," but "Unless during such one-year period or extension thereof the municipality shall have entered into a contract to purchase or instituted condemnation proceedings according to law, for said school site, park or playground, the subdivider shall not be bound by the proposals for such areas shown on the master plan." N.J.S.A. 40:55-1.20. (Italics supplied.)

Thus the Legislature authorized the municipality to require a developer to install improvements which may be said to benefit peculiarly the land being developed. As to such improvements, it may be noted that if they were made by the municipality itself, it would be consistent with our general statutory thesis to recover the cost by special assessment upon the properties benefited. Hence the dollar burden upon the property is not significantly different whether the developer finances the improvement or pays for it after it is installed by the municipality. Moreover, when the developer finances the improvements, the initiative to go ahead remains with him., whereas if the municipality had to make the investment, it might not share the developer's optimism as to sales and might decline to act on that account.

But as to services which traditionally have been supported by general taxation, other considerations are evident. The dollar burden would likely be unequal if new homes were subjected to a charge in addition to the general tax rate. As to education, for example, the vacant land has contributed for years to the cost of existing educational facilities, and that land and the dwellings to be erected will continue to contribute with all other real property to the payment of bonds issued for the existing facilities and to the cost of renovating or replacing those facilities. Hence there would be an imbalance if new construction alone were to bear the capital cost of new schools while being also charged with the capital costs of schools serving other portions of the school district. And if new construction were required in like manner to contribute specially to other programs supported by general taxation, for example, police and fire protection, then a municipality, if its hands were wholly unguided, could so deal with new housing as to burden, perhaps intolerably, the right of every citizen to seek a better home.

It is not our purpose to prejudge the constitutional power of the Legislature to authorize municipalities to impose charges such as the one here involved. As to the subject, see Heyman and Gilhool, "The Constitutionality of Imposing Increased Community Costs on New Suburban Residents through Subdivision Exaction," 73 Yale L.J. 1119 (1964); Reps and Smith, "Control of Urban Land Subdivision," 14 Syracuse L.Rev. 405 (1963); Note, 66 Colum.L.Rev. 974 (1966); Rather our point is that the Legislature has not committed that authority to local government.

There being no statutory authorization, it is clear the municipality could not have lawfully exacted the charges here involved. At the oral argument before us, defendants conceded this to be so. We have no doubt the municipality was conscious of the illegality of what it did and for that reason refrained from adopting an ordinance, seeking instead to achieve its ends through the guise of "voluntary" contributions with spurious "agreements" to make them stick.

* * *

For these reasons we are satisfied that plaintiff is entitled to judgment. We note that this result is supported by decisions elsewhere. See Rosen v. *Village of Downers Grove,* 19 Ill.2d 448, 167 N.E.2d 230, 235 (Sup.Ct. 1960); *Gordon* v. *Village of Wayne,* 370 Mich. 329, 121 N.W.2d 823 (Sup.Ct. 1963); *Ridgemont Development Co.* v. *City of East Detroit,* 358 Mich. 387, 100 N.W.2d 301 (Sup.Ct.1960); cf. *Kelber* v. *City of Upland,* 155 Cal.App.2d 631, 318 P2d 561 (D.Ct.App.1958); *Haugen* v. *Gleason,* 226 Or. 99, 359 P.2d 108 (Sup.Ct.1961); *Theatre Control Corp.* v. *City of Detroit,* 370 Mich. 382, 121 N.W.2d 828 (Sup.Ct. 1963).

The judgment is reversed and the matter remanded to the trial court with directions to enter judgment in favor of plaintiff for $17,700 together with interest.

4. Offsite Improvements

The authority of local government to impose the cost of **on-site improvements** such as streets, sewer, and drainage on the subdivider is pretty well established in most enabling legislation. However, only a few states have thus far made provision for the contribution by the subdivider for a share of the cost of such facilities *located outside the property limits* of the subdivision but made necessary by development of the subdivision. The following provision from the New Jersey Municipal Land Use Law authorizes the local governing body to impose a pro-rata share of offsite improvements upon the developer:

NEW JERSEY LAND USE LAW

C. 40:55D-42 Contribution for off-tract water, sewer, drainage, and street improvements.

Contribution for off-tract water, sewer, drainage, and street improvements. The governing body may by ordinance adopt regulations requiring a developer, as a condition for approval of a subdivision or site plan, to pay his pro-rata share of the cost of providing only reasonable and necessary street improvements and water, sewerage and drainage facilities, and easements therefor, located outside the property limits of the subdivision or development but necessitated or required by construction or improvements within such subdivision or development. Such regulations shall be based on circulation and comprehensive utility service plans pursuant to subsections 19 b. (4) and 19 b. (5) of this act, respectively, and shall establish fair and reasonable standards to determine the proportionate or pro-rata amount of the cost of such facilities that shall be borne by each developer or owner within a related and common area, which standards shall not be altered subsequent to preliminary approval. Where a developer pays the amount determined as his pro-rata share under protest he shall institute legal action within 1 year of such payment in order to preserve the right to a judicial determination as to the fairness and reasonableness of such amount.

Chapter Five

Site Plan Review, Planned Unit Development and Official Map

A. SITE PLAN REVIEW

Site plan review is a process by which a proposed plan of development is submitted for approval by the planning board, or similâr governmental agency. It reviews the specific site development characteristics including the general form of the land before and after development, the spatial relationships of the structures and open spaces to existing and proposed land uses and the visual and environmental impact of the development on the community.

Site plan review is similar to subdivision review in many ways. However, site plan review is not limited to applications to divide the property into two or more lots. Site plan review may be required for industrial parks, recreational areas and shopping centers as well as residential uses, such as a number of apartment houses, where no subdivision into smaller lots may be required. A carefully drawn site review ordinance might apply to all of the following situations, where:

1. any structure is erected, relocated or externally altered
2. the use of any land is changed
3. a watercourse is diverted or its channel or flood plain dredged or filled
4. any open parking area is constructed or enlarged
5. any land is subdivided
6. any development permit or certificate of occupancy is granted.

However such an inclusive provision would probably have to exempt applications by an owner of a single family dwelling, minor subdivisions and similar situations where site plan review would be inappropriate.

(1) Criteria and Standards of Approval

Site plan review is not intended to inhibit a developer in the˙exercise of his creativity, invention and innovation. Nor is the process intended to permit a governmental agency to impose any architectural, style or design preferences upon the developer. The following excerpts from the Borough of Princeton,

New Jersey Land Use Ordinance (Sec. 17A-193) illustrate the kind of criteria and standards by which a site plan proposal would be evaluated:

PRINCETON, N.J. LAND USE ORDINANCE

(a) *Ecological considerations.* The development shall insofar as practicable:

(1) Result in minimal impairment of the regenerative capacity of aquifers and other ground water supplies;

(2) Result in minimal degradation of unique or irreplaceable land types and in minimal adverse impact upon the critical areas specified in paragraph (h) of section 17A-199;

(3) Conform with existing geologic and topographic features to the end that the most appropriate use of land is encouraged;

(4) Cause minimal interference with the natural functioning of plant and animal life processes.

(b) *Landscape.* The landscape shall be preserved in its natural state, insofar as practicable and environmentally desirable, by minimizing tree and soil removal. If development of the site necessitates the removal of established trees, special attention shall be given to the planting of replacements or to other landscape treatment. Any grade changes shall be in keeping with the general appearance of neighboring developed areas.

(c) *Relation of proposed structures to environment.* Proposed structures shall be related harmoniously to themselves, the terrain and existing buildings and roads in the vicinity that have a visual relationship to the proposed structures. The achievement of such harmonious relationship may include the enclosure of space in conjunction with other existing buildings or other proposed buildings and the creation of focal points with respect to avenues of approach, terrain features or other buildings.

Proposed structures shall be so sited as to minimize any adverse impact upon the surrounding area, and particularly upon any nearby residences, by reason of:

(1) Building location, height, bulk and shadows;

(2) Location, intensity, direction and times of use of outdoor lighting;

(3) Likelihood of nuisances;

(4) Other similar considerations.

Appropriate natural or artificial screening may be required to minimize any such adverse impact.

(d) *Scenic, historical, archaeological and landmark sites.* Scenic, historical, archaeological and landmark sites and features that are located on or adjacent to the proposed development shall be preserved and protected insofar as practicable.

(e) *Surface water drainage.* The proposed development shall provide for proper surface drainage so that removal of surface waters will not adversely affect neighboring properties or the public storm drainage system and will, so far as practicable, conserve the water resources of the area and avoid flooding, erosion and detrimental depositing of silt, gravel or stone. Surface water shall be removed from all roofs, canopies and paved areas and disposed of in an appropriate drainage system. Surface water in all paved areas shall be disposed of in a manner consistent with sound engineering and ecological practices. The drainage system shall be so designed that, except in unusual circumstances, the rate of runoff of surface waters from the site in the condition in which it is proposed to be developed will not exceed the rate of runoff from the site in its undeveloped or existing condition.

(f *Driveway connections to public streets.* All entrance and exit driveways to public streets shall be located with due consideration for traffic flow and so as to afford maximum safety to traffic on the public streets. All such entrances and exits shall be so located and designed as to:

(1) Conform with the municipal sight triangle requirements at corners;

(2) Achieve maximum practicable distance from street intersections and from existing and proposed access connections from adjacent properties;

(3) Minimize left-hand turns and other turning movements;

(4) Discourage the routing of vehicular traffic to and through local residential streets.

(g) *Traffic effects.* The site development proposal generally shall minimize adverse traffic effects on the road networks serving the area in question, either those existing or as included in the master plan.

(h) *Pedestrian safety.* Insofar as practicable, pedestrian and bicycle circulation shall be separated from motor vehicle circulation.

Safe and convenient pedestrian circulation, including appropriate sidewalks, shall be provided on the site and its approaches. The pedestrian circulation plan shall be designed to minimize adverse effects of vehicular traffic upon sidewalks and bicycle paths.

(i) *On-site parking and circulation.* The location width and layout of interior drives shall be appropriate for the proposed interior circulation. The location and layout of accessory off-street parking and loading spaces shall provide for efficient circulation and the safety of pedestrians and vehicles. Insofar as practicable, separate rows or aisles in parking areas shall be divided by trees, shrubbery and other landscaping devices. The location of parking areas shall not detract from the design of proposed buildings and structures or from the appearance of the existing neighboring buildings, structures and landscape.

Provision shall be made for access by police, fire and emergency vehicles.

(j) *Utility services.* Electric, telephone and other wire served utility lines and service connections shall be underground insofar as feasible and subject to state public utilities regulations. Any utility installations remaining aboveground shall be located so as to have a harmonious relation to neighboring properties and to the site.

(k) *Disposal of wastes.* There shall be adequate provision for the disposal of all solid, liquid and gaseous wastes and for the avoidance of odors and other air pollutants that may be generated at the site. All applicable federal, state and local pollution control standards shall be observed.

(l) *Noise.* All applicable federal, state and local regulations dealing with the control of outside noise expected to be generated at the site shall be complied with.

(m) *Advertising features.* The size, location, height, design, color, texture, lighting and materials of permanent signs and outdoor advertising structures or features shall not detract from the design of proposed buildings and structures or of the surrounding properties.

(n) *Special features.* Outside storage areas, service and machinery installations, service areas, truck loading areas, utility buildings and structures, and similar accessory areas and structures shall be subject to such setbacks, screenplantings or other screening methods as shall reasonably be required to prevent any adverse effect upon the environment or nearby property.

---

(2) Application Procedure

The site plan review ordinance should provide for a procedure for site plan approval. The applicant should be afforded the opportunity to seek an **early review** in **sketch plan** form to provide an informal and free exchange of ideas. This provides the opportunity to make modifications in the site development with a minimum expense. The Princeton, New Jersey Site Plan Ordinance goes even further in trying to reduce the applicant's expense, where possible, by providing for a procedure for a classification of the development as a "minor" or "major" development and requiring only minimum documentation for a "minor" development.

The application for site plan approval will include site plans and building drawings as specified by the ordinance. The Princeton, New Jersey ordinance contains the following provisions specifying the contents of site plans:

PRINCETON, N.J. LAND USE ORDINANCE

Sec. 17A-197. Contents of site plans.

The required site plans shall consist of an accurate plot plan, drawn to a scale of not less than one inch equals fifty feet, or as large as feasible in relation to the size of the project, showing the tax map section, block and lot number, dimensions, orientation and acreage of each lot or plot to be built upon or otherwise used and showing the following existing and proposed features:

(a) All existing physical features, including streams, watercourses, bodies of water, rock outcroppings and, in areas to be affected by proposed construction, trees greater than eight inches D.B.H. caliper, significant soil conditions affecting the site and an outline of tree masses on the site, with an indication whether such masses are evergreen or deciduous and their approximate height;

(b) The size, shape and location of buildings, and their relation to surrounding properties and buildings thereon and on both sides of adjacent streets;

(c) The location, layout and dimensions of parking and loading areas, with an indication of the areas to be paved;

(d) All parking spaces, driveways and access points to public streets;

(e) Contours at intervals not exceeding five feet;

(f) Sanitary sewer and water facilities and connections;

(g) Location and type of catch basins or suface water detention basins and other surface drainage facilities;

(h) Electric, telephone, gas and other utilities;

(i) Landscaping plan including location, height and types of plantings and screenings;

(j) All required setback lines;

(k) Rights-of-way and easements;

(l) Location and height of fences, retaining walls and railings;

(m) Location, height, size and design of exterior signs and advertising features;

(n) Location of exterior lighting, area of illumination and height and type of standards;

(o) Location and layout of sidewalks, bicycle paths, curbs, and interior walkways;

(p) Key map showing entire project and its relation to surrounding areas, roads and watercourses.

For convenience and clarity, the foregoing information may be shown on one or more separate drawings or on the plot plan.

The site plan application and supporting documents will be reviewed by the appropriate municipal administrative officer, the municipal engineer and by a site plan committee, all of whose reports are sent to the planning board. The planning board then reviews the application, upon notice and public hearing, and either denies or grants **preliminary site plan approval.** Preliminary approval may contain conditions, relating to the prescribed criteria and standards, reasonably designed to promote the purposes of the ordinance.

The applicant who received preliminary site plan approval may proceed with the development in accordance with the plan and conditions contained in the preliminary approval. Upon completion of the development the applicant applies for **final site plan approval.** If the planning board finds, upon report from the municipal engineer, that the applicant has complied with the requirements of the approved plan, it will grant final site plan approval.

(3) Legal Issues

The first legal issue to be resolved is the question whether the state enabling legislation expressly or impliedly authorizes the municipality to adopt a site plan review ordinance. In some states, the zoning or other land use enabling legislation specifically authorizes such regulation. In other states, it is not clear whether municipalities have authority to adopt a site plan review ordinance.

Even if express statutory authority for a site plan review ordinance exists, a developer may nevertheless challenge the site plan review decisions of the planning board on such grounds as vagueness of the ordinance, unreasonableness of the conditions, or a failure to comply with the prescribed procedure. The *City of Pittsburgh* and the *Town of Bloomfield* cases, that follow, illustrate these issues.

SUN OIL COMPANY,

v.

ZONING BOARD OF ADJUSTMENT
OF THE CITY OF PITTSBURGH.

403 Pa. 409, 169 A.2d 294 (1961)

BENJAMIN R. JONES, Justice.

Sun Oil Company (Sun) is the equitable owner of a tract of land located at the corner of Saw Mill Run Boulevard and Edgebrook Avenue in Pittsburgh. This tract extends 151 feet along the northerly side of Saw Mill Run Boulevard and 50 feet along the westerly side of Edgebrook Avenue and is within a district zoned as "M-1" Limited Industrial District wherein an automobile and gasoline service station is a permissive use.[1] Saw Mill Run Boulevard, a four-lane highway, is a major traffic approach to downtown Pittsburgh and bears very heavy vehicular traffic.

Proposing to use this land as the site of an automobile and gasoline service station, on June 3, 1959 Sun submitted a "site plan application" to the Department of City Planning of Pittsburgh and, on July 17, 1959, Sun was notified that its application had been disapproved because the proposed distance between vehicular "access points on the land" represented too great a departure from the requirements of section 2401-6, article 24 of the zoning ordinance which provides, inter alia, that "vehicular access points shall be limited, where possible, to intervals of not less than three hundred (300) feet when on a *major traffic thorofare*."

On August 28, 1959, Sun applied to the Superintendent of Building Inspection for a building and occupancy permit which application was denied because the "site plan application" had been disapproved. On August 31, 1959 Sun appealed to the Board of Adjustment (Board). After a hearing, the Board upheld the denial of the permit and from that decision Sun appealed to the County Court of Allegheny County which on March 26, 1960 remanded the matter to the Board for the taking of further testimony. After taking additional testimony, the Board again upheld the denial of this permit and, without taking any further testimony, the County Court of Allegheny County entered an order which sustained the Board's decision and dismissed Sun's appeal. From that order this appeal has been taken.

Sun contends both that section 2401-6, Article 24, of the zoning ordinance is unconstitutional and that the Board abused its descretion in the denial of a permit.

Section 2401-6 of the ordinance requires that applicants must submit to the Planning Commission a "site plan" upon which must be shown, inter alia, "the location of vehicular access onto the site". The focal point of Sun's attack is the second paragraph of section 2401-6 which provides: "In considering any site plan hereunder, the *Commission* shall endeavor to assure safety and convenience of traffic movement, both within the site covered and in relation to access *streets*, and harmonious and beneficial relationship of *structures* and uses on the site as well as contiguous properties. In so doing, vehicular access points shall be limited, where possible, to intervals of not less than three hundred (300) feet when on a *major traffic thorofare*".

Sun attacks the constitutionality of this provision upon two grounds: *subjectively*, in that the requirement of a 300-foot distance between "access points" bears no reasonable relationship either to the safety or to the general welfare of the public and, *objectively*, in that the provision is vague, indefinite and capricious.

To be valid a provision in a zoning ordinance must bear a reasonable relationship to the protection of the health, safety, morals or general welfare of the public. That this particular provision of the ordinance which requires a 300-foot distance between "access points" of a site located upon an admittedly major traffic thorofare bears a direct and reasonable relationship to the safety and general welfare of the public travelling upon this particular vehicular artery is beyond question. As Judge Beck well stated in the court below: Saw Mill Run Boulevard is a major public highway carrying a heavy volume of motor vehicular traffic and the parties to this case treated the problem involved as of neccessity requiring some type of reasonable regulation in the interest of public safety and the general welfare. (Sun's) real complaint is that the requirement in the ordinance of a frontage of approximately 300 feet between access points on major traffic thorofares, as applied by the City Planning Commission to gasoline service stations, is economically not feasible because (Sun) would be required to make a larger investment in land than its business would justify, and thus (Sun) would be at a competitive disadvantage with other gasoline station operators. This position, if adopted, would negative any effort by municipal action to meet and solve safety and general welfare problems as they arise and plan for the future in urban areas. * * *

"In its zoning ordinance the City of Pittsburgh has undertaken to regulate vehicular access points of ingress and egress with respect to property abutting major traffic thoroughfares for the purpose of assuring safety and convenience of traffic movement. Maintaining the continuous flow of traffic without undue delays is a proper concern in promoting safety and serving the general welfare in the use of public highways. The layout and design of gasoline service station access points, including the distance between the point where a motor vehicle enters a station, and where, after being serviced, leaves the station, is substantially related to preserving and promoting safety on major traffic thoroughfares. Adequate distance between access points tends to avoid the likelihood of congestion on the station driveways, and to prevent situations where vehicles waiting to enter protrude into the highway traffic lanes. Such regulations contribute to maintaining a continuous flow of traffic and the avoidance of the collision of motor vehicles on the highways, and are neither unreasonable nor arbitrary and are within the legitimate purposes of the police power." Sun's claims of invalidity of this provision in this respect is without merit.

Sun next urges that the provisions of the ordinance are vague, indefinite and capricious. If a legislative enactment is vague and indefinite so that courts are unable to determine with any reasonable degree of certainty the intent of the legislative body or so incomplete, conflicting and inconsistent in its provisions that it cannot be executed, such enactment will be deemed invalid. An examination of the provision of the ordinance leaves no doubt as to the legislative intent, i.e., the protection of the safety and general welfare of the public using Saw Mill Run Boulevard. Sun claims that the phrase "vehicular access points" is vague and that "access points" mean either vehicular *entrances* to or vehicular *exits* from a major traffic thoroughfare but that they cannot mean both. With this we disagree. "Access" is * * * the right which an abutting owner has of ingress to and egress from his premises * * *." Black Law Dictionary (4th ed.) p. 28. As employed in this ordinance, it is clear that "access points" clearly mean both the approach *from* the land *to* the major traffic artery and the approach *from* the major traffic thoroughfare *to* the land.

Sun next argues that the manner of measurement between the "access points" is likewise vague. Sun, however, is in nowise harmed by the manner of measurement because even if the measurement was made between the *outside* points of the approaches—the points most favorable to Sun—Sun would still be 140 feet short of the 300 foot requirement.

Sun then urges that section 2401-6 creates an• unlawful delegation of legislative power. Section 106 of the ordinance sets forth its general purpose and intent: "* * The provisions of the ordinance shall be held to be the minimum requirements for the protection of the health and safety and welfare of the people at large * * *."In Archbishop O'Hara's Appeal, we upheld an ordinance containing almost identical language stating that it "provide (d) sufficient appropriate conditions and safeguards controlling the board's discretion to render valid the ordinance. (Citing cases.)" In the present ordinance, over and above the general purposes of the ordinance embodied in Section 106, the provision under attack provides that in considering a "site plan", "* * * the *Commission* shall endeavor to assure safety and convenience of traffic movement, both within the site covered and in relationship to access streets, and harmonious and beneficial relationship of *structures* and uses on the site as well as contiguous properties * * *." The legislative body—the Council of the City of Pittsburgh—both in Section 106 and Section 2401-6 has prescribed standards to control the determinations of the Commission which are adequate and sufficient. The ordinance does not constitute an unlawful delegation of legislative power.

Lastly, Sun urges that the Board abused its discretion. We have carefully examined this entire record and we are satisfied that the Board's conclusion that a building permit be denied Sun was arrived at without caprice and upon the basis of testimony which indicated that to permit use of this land under the circumstances as an automobile and gasoline service station would result in a hazard and danger to the public travelling on Saw Mill Run Boulevard.

Absent a commission of errors of law or an abuse of discretion, we must uphold the Board's decision.

Order affirmed. Costs on Sun.

McCRANN ET AL.

v.

TOWN PLAN AND ZONING COMMISSION

OF BLOOMFIELD

161 Conn. 65, 282 A.2d 900 (1971)

RYAN, Associate Justice.

The redevelopment agency of the town of Bloomfield, hereinafter referred to as the Agency, made application to the town plan and zoning commission of the town of Bloomfield for site plan approval for forty-six units of housing for the elderly which was proposed to be constructed on a 2.2-acre site by Interfaith Homes, Inc., hereinafter referred to as Homes. The plans submitted provided for the construction of four separate buildings facing an access road twenty-six feet wide, which begins at Mountain Avenue and terminates in a parking lot with two buildings on each side of the road. Thirty-one parking spaces are provided. On July 24, 1969, the commission held a public hearing on the application and on September 11, 1969, the commission denied it. Thereafter, the Agency applied for approval of the application on the basis of changes in the plans and on October 9, 1969, the commission held a public hearing on this application. On October 23, 1969, the commission approved the site plan. The plaintiffs, who own land abutting the subject property, appealed to the Court of Common Pleas which dismissed the appeal and rendered judgment for the defendants. The plaintiffs have appealed to this court. They have made numerous assignments of error and claim, in substance, that the site plan violated the Bloomfield zoning regulations and that improper procedures used by the commission render its approval of the site plan void.

The plaintiffs urge that proper notice of the public hearing on the site plan application was not given. Section 210(B) of the zoning regulations requires that such an application be "submitted to the Commission in the manner required for a change of zone" and that it include a site plan. Section 210(E) of the regulations provides that the commission "shall hold a public hearing * * * with due notice as provided by the General Statutes of the State of Connecticut for a change in the Zoning Regulations." Section 8-3 of the General Statutes provides the notice requirements for public hearings to consider changes in the zoning regulations. Advertisement in a newspaper is required to give notice of the time and place of the hearing, and there is a further proviso that "a copy of * * * (the) proposed regulation or boundary shall be filed in the office of the town, city or borough clerk." The plaintiffs do not claim that they failed to receive notice of the time and place of the hearing or that such notice was not properly advertised in a newspaper in accordance with the statute.

They urge that the agency failed to file the site plan with the town clerk of Bloomfield, and that this was a jurisdictional defect which rendered the actions of the commission void. The parties have stipulated that the proposed site plan was filed with the commission and the building inspector prior to October 9, 1969, the date of the hearing, and that it was not filed with the twon clerk.

Section 210(E) adopts the notice provisions for public hearings of § 8-3 of the General Statutes. The statute does not deal with site plans and there is nothing contained therein to indicate that site plans should be filed with the town clerk. The only requirement for filing documents with the town clerk under the provisions of § 8-3 is for a "proposed regulation or boundary." Since neither of these was involved in this hearing that portion of the statute was not applicable, nor was it the intention of § 210(E) of the regulations to require such a filing. The plaintiffs make no claim that they were unable to gain access to the site plan in time to contest its approval at the hearing on October 9, 1969. In fact, it is obvious from the manner in which the plaintiffs' attorney conducted himself at the hearing that he was thoroughly familiar with the site plan. The notice requirements of the zoning regulation were not violated.

* * *

The plaintiffs assign error in the conclusion of the trial court that the site plan was not a subdivision. It is their position that this permitted the Agency and Homes to ignore the subdivision regulations, thereby avoiding requirements which the proposed project would be unable to meet. Subdivision is defined in § 8-18 of the General Statutes. On analysis of the statute, it is clear and unambiguous language requires: (1) the division of a tract or parcel of land into three or more parts or lots, and (2) for the purpose, whether immediate or future, of sale or building development. The site in question was created by combining two lots to make one parcel of 2.2 acres. There was no division of a tract into three or more parts or lots and in the absence of this statutory requirement there was no subdivision. The conclusion of the trial court was correct.

The plaintiffs urge that the action of the commission was in violation of the zoning regulations in many respects. They claim that the site plan does not provide the requisite number of parking spaces in accordance with the regulations; that it provides for the construction of buildings with less than the rear-yard requirements of the regulations; that it fails to make adequate provision for the disposition of surface and flood waters; that it fails to provide for appropriate traffic circulation and access; and that it fails to provide adequate safeguards to adjacent properties. In applying their zoning regulations to a particular situation, the commission is endowed with a liberal discretion, and its action is subject to review by the courts only to determine whether it was unreasonable, arbitrary or illegal. This court cannot substitute its descretion for the discretion enjoyed by the commission. When reviewing the actions of the commission to determine if its findings complied with the standards set out in the regulations, we are not compelled to indulge in a microscopic search for technical infirmities. The determination of what the public interest requires is within the discretion of the commission. It is only where the local zoning authority has acted arbitrarily or illegally and thus abused the discretion vested in it that the courts can grant relief on appeal.

The site plan provides thirty-one parking spaces for forty-six dwelling units. Section 407(3) of the regulations requires one parking space for each dwelling unit for buildings used for residence. Section 407(8) allows a modification of this rule if the commission finds that the "proposed use is of such peculiar nature that the requirements for parking do not conform to the intent of the regulations and would clearly not require the parking spaces proposed." The commission heard evidence to the effect that thirty-one parking spaces would be more than adequate under both the F.H.A. requirements for housing for the elderly and the regulations of the state department of community affairs for housing. The finding of the commission that this type of housing does not require the same number of parking spaces normally required for residential housing, its modification of the parking rules and its acceptance of the proposed number of parking spaces in the site plan as adequate, were not unreasonable. In the minutes of the executive session of the commission there is a finding that "(i)t was generally agreed that there are more than sufficient parking spaces for the project." The claim of the plaintiffs that this finding lacked the specificity required by the regulations cannot be sustained.

Under the provisions of § 210(C) of the regulations a ten-foot side yard and a twenty-foot rear yard are required. The building nearest the plaintiffs' property complies with the side-yard requirement. The commission treated the rectangular piece of land as having a front yard along Mountain Avenue with side and rear yards determined accordingly. The easterly boundary abutting the plaintiffs' property would, therefore, be a side yard. The plaintiffs claim that this is a rear yard and that there is a twenty-foot requirement. It is their position that since the site plan calls for four buildings on the land, each building must have its own front, rear and side yards, determined, not by the existence of city streets, but by the location of each building on the parcel. The regulations contain the following definitions: A front yard is "an open space extending across the full width of the lot between the front wall of the principal building and the front lot line." § 104(30). A rear yard is "an open space extending across the full width of the lot, between the rear wall of the principal building and the rear lot line." § 104(32). A side yard is "an open space extending from the front to the rear yard, between the principal building and the side line of the lot." § 104(31). A lot is "a parcel of land occupied or to be occupied by a building or group of buildings and accessory buildings and including such open spaces as are required." § 104(17). From these definitions it appears that the property in question constitutes a lot and that this lot is to have one front yard and one rear yard. The contention of the plaintiffs that each of the buildings on the lot must have its own front, rear and side yards is not supported by the regulation. It remains to be determined what part of the lot is the front. In interpreting the language of the regulations, our function is to determine the expressed legislative intent. In constructing the meaning of a term, the enactment should be examined in its entirety and its parts reconciled so that a term has a consistent meaning throughout. The front part of a lot is referred to in the regulations. Section 104(18) defines a corner lot as one "fronting on two or more streets" and § 303 provides that buildings on a corner lot "shall be required to comply with the set back line on only one street front." In these regulations it seems clear that "front" refers only to the street side of the lot bordering Mountain Avenue and that the portion of the premises bordering the plaintiffs' property is a side yard. The conclusion of the trial court that the site plan satisfied the sideyard requirement of the regulation cannot be disturbed.

The plaintiffs claim that the site plan fails to provide for appropriate traffic circulation and access. The commission gave consideration to the traffic problem, in fact, one of the reasons for the denial of approval when the site plan was before the commission on a prior occasion in September, 1969, was because of safety problems regarding fire protection and snow removal due to the layout of the access road and the parking lot. The revised site plan contained an enlarged turn-around radius to accommodate fire and snow removal equipment. The burden of proving that the commission acted arbitrarily, illegally or in abuse of its discretion is on the plaintiffs. The plaintiffs point to no facts which would tend to show in what way circulation and traffic are impeded by the site plan. The commission did not abuse its discretion in this respect.

The plaintiffs also claim that the commission's approval of the drainage provisions of the site plan is arbitrary and in abuse of its discretion in that it permits occasional flooding of the parking lot and establishes drainage conditions detrimental to adjacent properties. A great deal of testimony was introduced before the commission at the public hearing in relation to the drainage problem. The evidence indicates that the parking lot is susceptible to flooding when the brook located on the western boundary of the subject plan is at flood level. The appropriate way to avoid flooding of the parking area is by filling it. The water resources commission did not authorize this, because it would increase flooding downstream. It required that the parking lot be maintained no higher than its present level so that its water-holding capacity will not be reduced. The site plan calls for a lowering of from two to three feet of the area where the parking lot is located but the plaintiffs have not demonstrated that this will create such a change in drainage conditions that surrounding properties will be adversely affected. The commission, in its executive session, found that if flooding did occur in the parking area those cars which might be located there could be temporarily parked along the drive which is twenty-six feet wide and which could accommodate parking on a temporary basis. Both the army corps of engineers and the water resources commission approved the drainage provisions of the site plan and there was no abuse of discretion on the part of the commission.

Section 210(D) (6) of the regulations requires that the commission consider "(s)afeguards to protect adjacent property, and the neighborhood in general, from detriment" when acting on a proposed sit plan. The plaintiffs claim that the site plan does not provide for protection of certain trees located on their property which have branches and roots extending onto the subject land, and that under the provisions of § 210(D) (6) the commission should have required safeguard for the trees. Where trees are located on the property of one party and their roots or branches extend onto the property of a second party, the latter may lop off the branches or roots up to the line of his land. We find nothing in the zoning regulations abrogating this right. This does not mean, of course, that complete disregard for the welfare of the trees is permitted. The site plan requires very little change in grade along the side yard of the subject land parallel to the trees in question. There was evidence before the commission that the defendant developers were concerned with preserving the trees and were going to give careful consideration to root structures. The plaintiffs have offered no evidence to show how the site plan will damage the trees. They ask safeguards for dangers which they cannot identify.

The commission approved the site plan "with the provision that every effort be made to obtain permission from the Water Rsources Commission to fill the parking area to a level which would make it less susceptible to flooding." Section 210(E) of the regulations requires that the commission, "after public hearing * * * approve, disapprove, or approve with modifications the proposed area." The proviso attached to the approval by the commission is not a condition nor does it render the meaning of its decision vague and ambiguous and, therefore, invalid. It is merely the expression of a hope that at some future time the water resources commission will permit the owners of the property to fill the parking area to a level which would make it less susceptible to flooding.

The plaintiffs also contend that they were deprived of "due process and a fair hearing" because of the participation of Dennis Brown, the planning consultant of the Commission, in the deliberations on the site plan. Brown was a consultant both to the commission and the town and in the latter capacity had worked with the redevelopment agency on the housing for the elderly project in question. He spoke five times at the first public hearing on the site plan, on July 24, 1969. On four occasions he gave short direct answers to questions from the commission or the plaintiffs' attorney, and once he made comments advocating the desirability of locating the project on the site in question. He also spoke at two other meetings, one on September 11, 1969, the other on October 23, 1969, which were held to decide on the disposition of the application in question. At the meeting on September 11, 1969, Brown said that the site plan met the requirements of the regulations and recommended approval. The commission at that time rejected Browns' advice and denied approval because of traffic circulation problems.

The proceedings before the commission are informal. "The only requirement is that the conduct of the hearing shall not violate the fundamentals of natural justice." In passing on the site plan in the present case the commission was acting in its administrative capacity. The fact that Brown acted as a consultant for the commission and advocated the cause of the applicant does not in itself indicate that the plaintiffs were not given a fair hearing. He was a mere technical adviser to the commission. Because the commission is composed of laymen it is entitled to professional technical assistance in carrying out its responsibilities. The presence of Brown in the executive session of the commission is not fully explained. The plaintiffs were aware of this at the time of the trial but made no effort to offer evidence to determine what, if anything, Brown said or did at that executive session. It was the right of the plaintiffs, if they saw fit, to offer evidence in the court below in order to determine what, if any, effect Brown's presence at the executive session might have had on the decision of the commission. No such effort was made and no evidence concerning this was introduced. The plaintiffs had a full opportunity to meet the issues with which they were confronted. There was no evidence that Brown had any personal or business interest in the matter. There is no showing of error or prejudice that would constitute a denial of due process. It cannot be said that the action of the commission in this regard was illegal, arbitrary or in abuse of the discretion vested in it, as claimed by the plaintiffs.

The claim that the commission acted illegally, arbitrarily or in abuse of its discretion is not supported by the record in this case. The commission had numerous problems to determine in the approval of the site plan and gave careful consideration to them. Courts do not substitute their own judgment for that of the commission so long as honest judgment has been reasonably and fully exercised after a full hearing. The plaintiffs failed to establish that the commission acted illegally, arbitrarily or in abuse of its discretion.

There is no error.

B. PLANNED UNIT DEVELOPMENT

(1) Introductory Description

Planned unit development (PUD) is a method of residential development in which an area with a specified minimum contiguous acreage is developed as a single entity according to a plan containing one or more residential clusters in which lot area, set-back and height restrictions may be waived and which may include commercial, public or quasi-public uses for the primary benefit of the residential development. By permitting the dwellings to be built close together in cluster, substantial land areas may be left in a natural state. Some PUD ordinances provide that the average density of dwelling units, or population, or cover of the land with buildings shall be no greater than is permitted in the district wherein the land lies.

A typical PUD ordinance will authorize the planning board to approve a planned unit development upon findings of specified facts and conclusions. The following provision from the New Jeresy Municipal Land Use Law is a good illustration of this requirement:

N.J. MUNICIPAL LAND USE LAW

C. 40:55D-45 Findings for planned developments.

33. Findings for planned developments. Every ordinance pursuant to this article that provides for planned developments shall require that prior to approval of such planned developments the planning board shall find the following facts and conclusions:

a. That departures by the proposed development from zoning regulations otherwise applicable to the subject property conform to the zoning ordinance standards pursuant to subsection 52 c. of this act;

b. That the proposals for maintenance and conservation of the common open space are reliable, and the amount, location and purpose of the common open space are adequate;

c. That provision through the physical design of the proposed development for public services, control over vehicular and pedestrian traffic, and the amenities of light and air, recreation and visual enjoyment are adequate;

d. That the proposed planned development will not have an unreasonably adverse impact upon the area in which it is proposed to be established;

e. In the case of a proposed development which contemplates construction over a period of years, that the terms and conditions intended to protect the interests of the public and of the residents, occupants and owners of the proposed development in the total completion of the development are adequate.

If the planning board makes the above findings and approves the proposed plan, it may also authorize waiver of the following types of bulk and use regulations that would otherwise have been applicable to development of that land:

(a) Bulk Regulations that may be Waived:

- lot sizes may be reduced
- set back requirements may be waived
- open-space may be distributed without regard to zoning lot lines.
- height regulations may be waived, subject to regulations governing the spacing of buildings.

(b) Use Regulations that may be Waived:

- convenience shopping, restaurants and certain other types of consumer services may be permitted within the development.
- recreational activities, such as swimming pools and tennis courts may be provided in the open space, subject to specified restrictions.
- industrial uses may be permitted in large developments (to provide employment and tax revenues).

There are many possible advantages to development under a PUD ordinance rather than the traditional zoning ordinance:

(a) Preservation of natural features

Instead of developing the area with uniform size lots and paved streets throughout the entire development, planned unit development permits a substantial proportion of the land area to remain in its natural state, including the preservation of such natural features as ponds, streams, large trees and rock out-croppings.

(b) Community Recreation Space

The land area accummulated from the reduction of size of individual lots can be used for recreation areas such as swimming pools, tennis courts, playing fields and other community facilities.

(c) Greater Housing Choice

Planned unit development encourages the construction of town-houses, garden apartments and semi-detached houses rather than single family dwellings on individual lots. This provides a greater choice of housing and provides an opportunity for the construction of housing to meet the needs of a variety of family size, age and income level.

(d) Safer Streets and Pedestrian Ways

The community open space may be used to create pedestrian walkways that avoid crossing streets with vehicular traffic. Traffic streets can be separated from neighborhood streets and the number of dangerous crossings can be reduced.

(e) Convenience Shopping

Unlike conventionally zoned residential districts, convenience shopping may be built in planned unit developments.

(f) Economic Advantages to the Developer

Planned unit development offers opportunities for reductions in development costs resulting from fewer and shorter streets, shorter and more efficient utility runs, less expensive site preparation and construction in concentrated areas.

(2) Legal Issues

**LEGAL PROBLEMS IN PLANNED
UNIT DEVELOPMENT:
UNIFORMITY, COMPREHENSIVE
PLANNING, CONDITIONS,
AND THE
FLOATING ZONE
FRANK A. ALOI**

1 REAL ESTATE LAW JOURNAL 5 (1972)

INTRODUCTION

Planned unit development (PUD), the balanced-community concept based upon a logical and coherent mixture of uses,[1] is a relatively new

---

1. See generally Krasnowiecki, "Legal Aspects of Planned Unit Residential Development," Technical Bull. 52 (Urban Land Inst. 1965); Krasnowiecki, "Planned Unit Development: A Challenge to Established Theory and Practice of Land Use Control," 114 U. Pa. L. Rev. 47 (1965); Mandelker, "Reflections on the

concept in land use and development which has begun to generate legal problems uniquely its own. Because planned unit development provides for a mixture of uses—residential, commercial, service, and even industrial in a single district—threshold questions arise with regard to compatibility with the traditional Euclidean rationale for zoning. Both large- and small-scale area developments can proceed only with substantial alteration of conventional use regulations and the inflexible dimensional standards of zoning. Since planned unit development requires the use of common elements for park and recreation areas, service areas, and transportation, traditional notions with regard to lot area requirements and density requirements are generally changed; cluster zoning and other modern land use techniques thus become a part of planned unit development implementation.

A planned unit development, even with a primitive mixture of uses, becomes a microcosm of the typical cumulative Euclidean ordinance.[2] To this extent, questions arise as to conformity with constitutional or statutory enabling provisions governing the delegation of legislative authority and requiring uniformity of regulation and compatibility of use districts. Further, questions arise with respect to the compatibility of the planned unit development district with the requirement of comprehensive planning as that term is ordinarily used.[3]

If these initial problems are favorably resolved, at least two serious questions remain during the implementation phase of planned unit development. Basic to the concept of planned unit development is the notion of phased or staged construction. While the entire plan is generally approved in concept, if not in detail, at the outset, specific building permit approvals together with various municipal and state departmental approvals are extended only to the particular phase under construction, for example, the single-family residential element. It is common practice for the municipality to use the device of conditional approval to insure proper completion of each phase and to prevent construction of any stage of the planned unit development inconsistent with adjoining elements and with

---

American System of Planning Controls: A Response to Professor Krasnowiecki," 114 U. Pa. L. Rev. 136 (1965). It should be noted that Professor Krasnowiecki's discussion in Technical Bulletin 52 and the PUD Symposium in 114 U. Pa. L. Rev. 3-170 (1965) are excellent starting points for a review of the area.

See also for material directed at the "area" and "density" requirements of planned unit developments Annot., "Zoning: Planned Unit, Cluster, Or Greenbelt Zoning," 43 A.L.R.3d 888 (1972); Lloyd, "A Developer Looks at Planned Unit Development," 114 U. Pa. L. Rev. 3 (1965); Hanke, "Planned Unit Development and Land Use Intensity," 114 U. Pa. L. Rev. 15 (1965); Goldston & Shuer, "Zoning of Planned Residential Developments," 73 Harv. L. Rev. 241 (1959).

2. Anderson, *American Law of Zoning* § 8.14 at 593-595 (1968); Anderson, *Zoning Law and Practice in New York State* §§ 8.97-8.10 (1963); Reps., "The Zoning of Undeveloped Areas," 3 Syracuse L. Rev. 292 (1952).

3. See generally Annot., "Requirement That Zoning Variances or Exceptions Be Made in Accordance With a Comprehensive Plan," 40 A.L.R.3d 372 (1971); Haar, "In Accordance With a Comprehensive Plan," 68 Harv. L. Rev. 1154 (1965).

the entire development. By reason of the necessity to rely heavily upon the use of conditions, problems arise in most jurisdictions with the inevitable conflict with the contract zoning prohibition.

Finally, the serious and most important question in implementation must be resolved with regard to the location of the planned unit development district; and amendment creating the typical stationary district is one which does not reserve to the municipality the flexibility which is indispensable to the rational pattern of land use development in the community consistent with the planned unit development. Resort is therefore had to the two-step amendment "floating zone" technique, the enactment of the planned unit development district without specific location on the zoning map, specific location being reserved for the particular development application.

It is the purpose of this article to explore in a summary fashion the threshold legal problems set forth above; compatibility with the Euclidean rationale, cluster zoning, delegation of legislative authority, districting and uniformity, and comprehensive planning. A more intensive review of the zoning problems in the implementation of a planned unit development district, the floating zone and conditional or contract zoning, will follow. All of the questions that arise with regard to these legal problems in planned unit development enactment and implementation must be favorably resolved before development can proceed.

THE CONCEPT

Planned unit development basically is designed to permit the development of small- to large-scale neighborhoods with a variety of uses including various residential types based upon unit area development; planned use of building sites and common property for recreation, parks, transportation, and service use are also included. Performance standards are used to facilitate this development; the traditional "use" and "bulk" requirements of zoning ordinances and "platting" and "design" requirements of subdivision provisions are not rigidly adhered to. Thus, a major effort is made to survey the metro community and available land to determine its physical, demographic, and environmental qualities so that (1) the most compatible type of occupancy housing, for example, individual ownership, condominium, cooperative, leasing, etc., can be constructed on lots of sufficient size with (2) incidental community facilities, service areas, and common elements being available to existing and future residents regardless of economic level. Convenience and compatibility are the principal concepts in the location of accessory, commercial, and service areas; the maximization of usable open space and recreation areas is likewise emphasized. The implementation of a planned unit development requires the development of a smaller network of utilities and streets than is ordinarily the case so as to preserve land for principal uses and prevent inordinate housing costs; the industrial and commercial use base of the community as well as demographic trends are also considered. Attention is given to the objective of preserving natural topography and geologic features; and every effort is made to achieve a physical development compatible with the environmental values in the area and which will permit an orderly transmission in development of land from rural or light urban to intensive urban uses.

The typical planned unit development is 100 acres, although developments of somewhat larger size (the new town concept) or lesser size are common. As indicated above, all uses are permitted, but accessory, commercial, service, and other nonresidential use are scaled primarily to meet the requirements of the residents of the planned unit development.

THRESHOLD QUESTIONS

Euclidean Zoning: The Cumulative Ordinance

At the outset, the notion of a mixture of uses and the compatibility of uses within a single district appears to run contrary to the traditional basis for cumulative zoning ordinances. Thus, the typical cumulative ordinance for residential, commercial, and industrial use is designed to preserve the single-family use as the highest use; under traditional learning, the single-family use is the use most directly related to the public welfare. The cumulative ordinance typically begins with an R-1 single-residence district and proceeds through an R-2 single- and double-residence district to an R-3 apartment or multiple-dwelling district. Each higher-zone permitted use drops into the succeeding lower zones as permitted uses, but single-family residence remains the only use permitted in the R-1 zone. There follow commercial districts, industrial districts and provisions for various service, public, and necessary uses for location in the various districts. While the highest-use districts remain inviolate from lower commercial or industrial uses on the theory that a lower use can be injurious to a higher use, the contrary is not true insofar as a cumulative ordinance generally permits residential use in a commercial zone, and both residential and commercial in an industrial zone.

While this pattern of development is consistent with the common law in terms of restrictive covenants and nuisances, i.e., the protection of residential use from the intrusion and interference of commercial and industrial use, it is inconsistent with the modern realization that the higher use can be just as injurious to the lower use.[4] For example, the location of residences in industrial zones may subject an industrial owner to restrictions upon normal industrial activity and expansion of his use; further, this kind of development may remove invaluable industrial land in economically depressed areas where such land is scarce. Likewise, commercial use may be incompatible with nearby residences by reason of pedestrian and vehicle traffic hazards, the inevitable drain on municipal services, and considerations of aesthetics and amenities in commercial use development.

The apparent inconsistency of the typical Euclidean cumulative ordinance with a planned unit development all but disappears upon considera-

---

4. See 1 Anderson, *American Law of Zoning* § 8.15 at 598-600 (1968). *See also* Annot., "Validity of Zoning Regulation Prohibiting Residential Use in Industrial District," 38 A.L.R.2d 1141 (1954).

tion of the often overlooked fact that mixture of use, even in the cumulative ordinance, is not only possible but also common in practice. In each zoned district, the municipality is always reserved the option of locating accessory commercial, service, and public uses through the special-permit device. Thus, it is not uncommon to find residential districts with gasoline stations, churches, schools, and police and fire station, as well as "ma and pa" commercial store facilities. Regulations protecting valid nonconforming uses likewise force a mixture of use in some neighborhoods. Further, the lowest zone in the cumulative ordinance, the last industrial zone, is itself a primitive PUD district insofar as all uses previously permitted in any district would be permitted in the lowest industrial district, in addition to whatever accessory and service uses the municipality chooses to locate in that district. The point is that formalistic adherence to the procedural concepts developed in the enactment and implementation of Euclidean cumulative ordinances, even within their own terms, do not provide any reason for a prohibition upon planned unit development districts.

Uniformity of Regulation

Single-use districting is typical in Euclidean cumulative zoning ordinances. Thus, it is common to find legislative enactments directing the division of municipalities into districts subject to uniform use, area, density, and bulk requirements. An example of this kind of enabling legislation is Section 262 of the Town Law of the State of New York.[5] That section provides:

> "Districts
>
> "For any or all of said purposes the town board may divide that part of the town which is outside the limits of any incorporated village or city into districts of such number, shape and area as may be deemed best suited to carry out the purposes of this act; and within such districts it may regulate and restrict the erection, construction, reconstruction, alteration or use of buildings, structures or land. All such regulations shall be uniform for each class or kind of buildings throughout such districts but the regulations in one district may differ from those in other districts."

Pursuant to this legislation, municipalities have generally zoned their entire area into single-use districts with fixed boundaries subject to uniform regulations and restrictions as to use and area, including height, density, bulk, and building setbacks. The question has arisen on occasion as to whether such statutory exactments mandate single-use districting as an

---

5. See generally Comment, "Planned Unit Development," 35 Mo. L. Rev. 27 (1970). In Green Point Sav. Bank v. Board of Zoning Appeals, 281 N.Y. 534, 24 N.E.2d 319 (1939), the New York Court of Appeals upheld special uses by permit in business districts; the uniformity provision did not prohibit the procedure since the owners in the district were treated equally in terms of the enumerated permitted uses and the permit procedure of the town board.

exclusive zoning pattern.[6] If so, the argument proceeds that the mixture of uses comtemplated in the typical planned unit development district is unlawful as ultra vires. As indicated above, this interpretation would be clearly contrary to the pattern of experience under the typical single-use district cumulative ordinance insofar as accessory and service uses result in a mixture of uses in most zones; also, a mixture of uses in the lower zones is an inevitable result of the cumulative-type ordinance. But even more basically, the single-use district argument must fail, since the statute itself does not state that each district be a single-use district. What the illustrative Section 262 of the New York Town Law provides is that "All such regulations shall be uniform for each class or kind of buildings throughout such districts but the regulations in one district may differ from those in other districts." The clear thrust of this provision is not to mandate single-use districts, but rather to insure that municipal restrictions and regulations have an equal and impartial impact upon owners of land similarly situated. The point is that regulations and restrictions can differ insofar as the owners at whom they are directed develop their property under differing circumstances; uniformity is required only to insure that owners having similar circumstances are not treated differently.[7]

The companion provision, Section 263 of the Town Law of the State of New York,[8] reinforces the conclusion stated above with respect to Section 262. Section 263 provides in relevant part that

"Such regulations shall be made with reasonable consideration, among other things, as to the character of the district and its peculiar suitability for particular uses, and with a view to conserving the value of buildings and encouraging the most appropriate use of land throughout such municipality."

The key to understanding Section 263 is compatibility; Section 263 seeks to avoid combinations of use which would result in a diminution in value to the respective uses. By direct inference, the combination of compatible uses, uses contributing to rational and harmonious development, is not prohibited; here, the selection of the phrase "particular uses" in the statute should be noted.

Interpreting a similar statute, the California court in *Orinda Homeowners Committee v. Board of Supervisors*[9] "uninformity" requirement

---

6. See, for example, Nappi v. LaGuardia, 184 Misc. 775, 55 N.Y.S.2d 80 (Sup. Ct. 1944), *aff'd* 269 App. Div. 693, 54 N.Y.S.2d 722 (1st Dep't), *aff'd* 295 N.Y. 652, 64 N.E.2d 716 (1945); Green Point Sav. Bank v. Board of Zoning Appeals, 281 N.Y. 534 24 N.E.2d 319 (1939). Cf. People v. Levine, 119 Misc. 766, 198 N.Y. Supp. 328 (Rensselaer County Ct. 1922). For a general discussion, see also 67 N.Y. Jur., "Zoning Planning Laws", § 72 at 637.
An attempt to clarify the misconceptions resulting from a restrictive reading of the "uniformity language" in some cases failed in the New York State Legislature. See the "Laverne Bill," S. 4579-A.

7. See, for example, Rodgers v. Village of Tarrytown, 302 N.Y. 115, 120-121, 96 N.E.2d 731, 734 (1951); Kensington Davis Corp. v. Council of the City of Buffalo, 239 N.Y. 54, 145 N.E. 738 (1925).

8. See Note, "Comprehensive Plan Requirement in Zoning," 12 Syracuse L. Rev. 342 (1961).

9. 11 Cal. App. 3d 768, 90 Cal. Rptr. 88 (1970).

was not inconsistent with a rezoning for planned unit development. There a rezoning of a 187-acre parcel from R-20, single-family, residential, to P-1, planned unit development with cluster residential areas, was challenged as being contrary to the "uniformity" provision of Section 65852 of the California Government Code. Section 65852 provided that "All such regulations shall be uniform for each class or kind of building or use of land throughout each zone, but the regulation in one type of zone may differ from those in other types of zones." Holding that the "uniformity" provision did not require the nullification of the PUD rezoning, the court stated:

"We hold that a residential planned unit development (a cluster development) does not conflict with Section 65852 merely by reason of the fact that the units are not uniform, that is, they are not all single family dwellings and perhaps the multi-family units differ among themselves. Section 65852 provides that the regulations shall be uniform for each class of kind of building or use of land throughout the zone. It does not state that the units must be alike even as to their character, whether single family or multi-family. In conventional zoning, where apartment houses are permitted in a particular zone, single family dwellings, being regarded (whether rightly or wrongly) as a 'higher' use, are also allowed. This causes no conflict with Section 65852." [10]

Enabling Legislation—Developmental Concept Gap

Another problem generated by the imposition of newly developed concepts for land use upon zoning ordinances ill drafted to accommodate them is the negative interpretation of particular legislative amendments. Again, sections of the New York Town Law will be used as illustrative examples. Drafted to permit local town zoning officials to utilize their planning boards to consider the PUD concept in the limited context of residential development, Section 281 [11] provides, in relevant part:

"*Approval of plats; conditions for changes in zoning provisions*
"The town board is hereby empowered by resolution to authorize the planning board, simutaneously with the approval of a plat or plats pursuant to this article, to modify applicable provisions of the zoning ordinance, subject to the conditions hereinafter set forth and such other reasonable conditions as the town board may in its discretion add thereto. Such authorization shall specify the lands outside the limits of any incorporated village to which this procedure may be applicable. The purposes of such authorization shall be to enable and encourage flexibility of design and development of land in such a manner as to promote the most appropriate use of land, to facilitate

---

10. *Id.* at 772, 90 Cal. Rptr. at 92.

11. Originally enacted in 1963 as Chapter 963 of the Law of 1963, Section 281 was designed to permit town governing bodies to consider residential planned unit developments. See also Van Deusen v. Jackson, 35 A.D.2d 58, 62, 312 N.Y.S.2d 853 859 (2d Dep't 1970).

the adequate and economical provision of streets and utilities, and to preserve the natural and scenic qualities of open lands. The conditions hereinabove referred to are as follows:

"(a) If the owner makes written application for the use of this procedure, it may be followed at the discretion of the planning board if, in said board's judgment, its application would benefit the town.

"(b) This procedure shall be applicable only to lands zoned for residential purposes, and its application shall result in a permitted number of dwelling units which shall in no case exceed the number which could be permitted, in the planning board's judgment, if the land were subdivided into lots conforming to the minimum lot size and density requirements of the zoning ordinance applicable to the district or districts in which such land is situated and conforming to all other applicable requirements. . . ."

Predictably, the "legislative preclusion" argument has been made to interpret the concern of Section 281 with residential development as an indication that the legislature intended by its limited response to go no further in authorizing a mixture of uses in a PUD. However, this provision in no way dilutes the broad power of the town board in New York to enact zoning ordinances, or to amend them. Thus Section 261 of the Town Law [12] provides:

"Grant of power; appropriations for certain expenses incurred under this article

"For the purpose of promoting the health, safety, morals, or the general welfare of the community, the town board is hereby empowered by ordinance to regulate and restrict the height, number of stories and size of buildings and other structures, the percentage of lot that may be occupied, the size of yards, courts, and other open spaces, the density of population, and the location and use of buildings, structures and land for trade, industry, residence or other purposes; provided that such regulations shall apply to and affect only such part of a town as is outside the limits of any incorporated village or city. . . ."

Section 281 as a limiting provision speaks only to the permissible area of delegated responsibility by the legislative body, the town board, to the administrative body, the planning board. [13] The prerogative to "district" remains solely that of the town board; conceptually, the PUD remains within that grant of power by direct implication, if not literally.

---

12. See generally Comment, "Zoning—A Comprehensive Study of Problems and Solutions," 14 N.Y.L.F. 79 (1968).

13. Orrell v. Planning Bd., 66 Misc. 2d 843, 322 N.Y.S.2d 444 (Sup. Ct. 1971). Cf. Hiscox v. Levine, 31 Misc. 2d 151, 216 N.Y.S.2d 801 (Sup. Ct. 1961). See also Orinda Homeowners Comm. v. Board of Supervisors, 11 Cal. App. 3d 768, 90 Cal. Rptr. 88 (1970).

Area Requirements

The multiple-use district essential to planned unit development has produced a corollary concept permitting relaxed area, density, bulk, and setback requirements in order to facilitate the most efficient and rational utilization of available land. The concept is, of course, cluster zoning, a device by which a number of area requirements may be relaxed to permit an otherwise desirable use in a particular district. The efficient utilization of limited land resources in the context of a planned unit development makes the use of this technique extremely important.

The planning board prerogative to vary regulatory area requirements in the context of the cluster concept, as distinguished from the town board's legislative districting function, is again illustrated by Section 281 of the New York Town Law.[14] That provision authorizes the planning board, upon the promulgation of an enabling resolution by the town board, "to modify applicable provisions of the zoning ordinance" in approving plats. The purpose of the planning board function is stated in the ordinance as "to enable and encourage flexibility of design and development of land in such a manner as to promote the most appropriate use of land, to facilitate the adequate and economical provision of streets and utilities, and to preserve the natural and scenic qualities of open lands."[15]

Applying this provision, the case of *Orrell v. Planning Board*[16] recognized setbacks, area coverage, sideline requirements, real-line requirements as making impossible the use of the particular parcel in question for residential development. The court approved the relaxation of these requirements by the Planning Board in order to permit the location of the housing units in a cluster on a portion of the property with the remainder being devoted to common recreational or park use. Significantly, the court distinguished the earlier case of *Hiscox v. Levine*[17] in avoiding the "invalid delegation of legislative authority" mire, in order to reach the issue of the planning board's application of the cluster zoning technique.

PROBLEMS IN IMPLEMENTATION

Although the foregoing discussion is summary in nature, it does identify several of the threshold objections to the legal validity of mixed-use planned unit development districts. The actual promulgation of a planned unit development ordinance raises additional questions in terms of the method of enactment and the method of implementation of the district:

At the outset, it must be recognized that most communities with existing zoning ordinances will be faced with the prospect of changing their ordinances by amendment to add a planned unit development district or

---

14. The 1969 revision of this section deleted the language "This procedure shall be applicable only to lands zoned for residential purposes. . . ."

15. N.Y. Town Law § 281.

16. 66 Misc. 2d 843, 322 N.Y.S.2d 444 (Sup. Ct. 1971). See also Op. N.Y.S. Comptroller 67-713 (1967).

17. 31 Misc. 2d 151, 216 N.Y.S.2d 801 (Sup. Ct. 1961).

districts. With the possible exception of a single state,[18] it is unquestioned that municipalities have the power to amend their zoning ordinances as they relate to particular owners or properties. The traditional amendment criteria require a showing that the original zoning classification is arbitrary and unreasonable; this test is usually satisfied by proving that the character of the area or neighborhood has so changed that the original classification is unreasonable. Alternatively, it is occasionally required that the applicant demonstrate that some mistake was made in the original zoning classifications.[19]

The Comprehensive Plan

Amendment can only take place if the redistricting is in accordance with the comprehensive plan for development in the community. Typically, enabling legislation contains provisions similar to those set forth in Section 263 of the New York Town Law:

"Such regulations shall be made in accordance with a comprehensive plan and designed to lessen congestion in the streets, to secure safety from fire, flood, panic and other dangers; to promote health and general welfare; to provide adequate light and air; to prevent the overcrowding of land; to avoid undue concentration of population; to facilitate the adequate provision of transportation, water, sewerage, schools, parks and other public requirements. Such regulations shall be made with reasonable consideration, among other things, as to the character of the district and its peculiar suitability of particular uses, and with a view to conserving the value of buildings and encouraging the most appropriate use of land throughout such municipality."

As distinguished from the master plan which is a plan in fact whether enacted into law by ordinance or not, the concept of comprehensive planning is one that requires development to be consistent with the pattern of land use in the community so that the most efficient utilization of land in the community is achieved to maximize benefits to area residents.[20] Thus, the comprehensive plan is not necessarily an actual documentary plan but may be perceived from the zoning ordinance itself, the pattern of development, the zoning map, and any documents or studies commissioned by the municipality to deal with the present and future requirements of the community in terms of land use and development. Planned unit development is by definition a concept designed to achieve the most rational utilization of available land resources for the benefit of area residents; as such, it must by definition promote the ends of comprehensive planning. Accordingly, any amendment of an existing zoning ordinance to

---

18. Cf. Pierson Trapp Co. v. Peak, 340 S.W.2d 456 (Ky. App. 1960).
19. See generally 1 Anderson, *American Law of Zoning* §§ 4.25-4.29 (1968).
20. Compare Lionshead Lake Inc. v. Wayne Township, 10 N.J. 165, 89 A.2d 693 (1952), *appeal dism'd* 344 U.S. 919 (1953), with Udell v. Haas, 21 N.Y.2d 463, 288 N.Y.S.2d 888, 235 N.E.2d 897 (1968); see also Annot., "Requirement That Zoning Variances or Exceptions Be Made in Accordance With Comprehensive Plan," 40 A.L.R. 3d 372 (1971).

facilitate such development must be in accordance with the requirement of comprehensive planning.

This conclusion, of course, presupposes the proper enactment of a planned unit development district setting forth·the objectives of the district and the appropriate use, area, bulk, density, and setback restrictions. Where the planned unit development district has been so enacted, after careful analysis and review of the community's land use requirements both in terms of the physical availability of land the demographic, economic, ecological, and aesthetic requirements of area residents, comprehensive planning has been achieved. As stated by the New York Court of Appeals in *Udell v. Haas*:[21]

> "Where a community, after a careful and deliberate review of the 'present and reasonably foreseeable needs of the community adopts a *general development policy* for the community' as a whole and amends its zoning law in accordance with that plan, Courts can have some confidence that the public interest is being served. Where, however, local officials adopt a zoning amendment to deal with various problems that have arisen, but give no consideration to alternatives which might minimize the adverse effects of a change on particular land owners, and then call in the experts to justify the steps already taken in contemplation of anticipated litigation, closer judicial scrutiny is required to determine whether the amendment conforms to the comprehensive plan."

The comprehensive plan as a continuum of community needs and land use responses over a period of time must be recognized if planned unit development is to proceed as a device to maximize land use benefits to the community at large. The language of the Pennsylvania Supreme Court in *Cheney v. Village 2 at New Hope, Inc.*[22] is particularly apropos:

> "The fallacy in the [lower] court's reasoning lies in its mistaken belief that a comprehensive plan, once established, is forever binding on the municipality and can never be amended. Cases subsequent to *Eves* have made it clear, however, that these plans may be changed by the passage of new zoning ordinances, provided the local legislature passes the new ordinance with some demonstration of sensitivity to the community as a whole, and the impact that the new ordinance will have on this community. . . . Presented as it was with evidence that the P.U.D. district has been under consideration by council for over six months by the Borough Planning Commission, a body specifically equipped to view proposed ordinances as they relate to the rest of the community, we hold that the board, within its sound discretion, could have concluded that council passed the ordinance with the proper overall considerations in mind."

21. 21 N.Y.2d 463, 469-470, 288 N.Y.S.2d 888, 893-894, 235 N.E.2d 897, 900-901 (1968). See also N.Y. Town Law § 272-a, dealing with the "master plan," and Walder v. Cook, 25 N.Y.2d 661, 306 N.Y.S.2d 471, 254 N.E.2d 772 (1969).
22. 429 Pa. 626, 631, 241 A.2d 81, 84 (1968).

The Floating Zone

General Considerations

If, then, the requirement of comprehensive planning is met, the municipality is faced with the particular decision as to the actual method of adopting the planned unit development district ordinance revision. Essentially, only two choices are available. The municipality can survey the available resources within its boundaries, make basic determinations as to the utility of unzoned or unused land for planned unit development, and amend its ordinance to specifically locate a planned unit development district or districts on the zoning map. While this technique has the advantage of certainty in terms of the location of the planned unit development district, it has two obvious shortcomings: First, by opting for a located district, the municipality may be imposing the planned unit development district on a land area wholly unsuitable for such development both in terms of the physical attributes of the land and the community interests to be served. Second, the municipality has abdicated a considerable amount of its flexibility in land use planning and development by restricting the planned unit development district to specific locations. Obviously, it may be wholly impossible for interested developers to acquire the planned unit development district property, and even if the property is available, its physical shortcomings may make actual implementation of any plan impossible.

As an alternative to the use of a stationary planned unit development district, municipalities have begun to explore the possibility of using the floating-zone technique in the implementation of planned unit development.[23] The legal requirements for such districts and the limitations on their use can best be illustrated by an examination of the case law in representative jurisdictions.[24] The New York cases illustrate the liberal use of the planned unit development technique, while the Pennsylvania cases illustrate what might be called an intermediate approach to the technique; on the other hand, the New Jersey cases are illustrative of a wholly restrictive view of the approach. While cases from other jurisdictions will be mentioned, the primary emphasis will be on these three.

---

23. On the floating-zone technique, see generally Reno, "Non-Euclidean Zoning: The Use of the Floating Zone," 23 Md. L. Rev. 105 (1963); Mosher, "The Floating Zone: Legal Status and Application to Gasoline Stations," 1 Tulsa L.J. 149 (1964); Platt, "Valid Spot Zoning: A Creative Tool for Flexibility of Land Use," 48 Ore. L. Rev. 245 (1969); Note, "Non-Euclidean 'Zoning': Its Theoretical Validity and Practical Desirability in Undeveloped Areas," 30 U. Cinc. L. Rev. 29 (1961). See also Vaughn, "Floating Zone or Planned Development," 1964 *Planning Inst.* 63 (N.Y.S. Fed'n Official Planning Orgs.); Reuter, "Modern Zoning Techniques," 27 N.Y.S. Planning News No. 3, p. 3 (1963); Annot., "Validity of Zoning Regulations With Respect to Uncertainty and Indefiniteness of District Boundary Lines," 39 A.L.R.2d 766 (1955).

24. See also the discussion in Krasnowiecki, "Legal Aspects of Planned Unit Residential Development," Technical Bull. 52, pp. 24-31 (Urban Land Inst. 1965); for a legislative approach, see Krasnowiecki, "Model Land Use and Development Code," 1971 Urban L. Ann. 101; Babcock, "An Introduction to the Model Enabling Act for Planned Residential Development," 114 U. Pa. L. Rev. 136 (1965).

The Conceptual Background

As a response to the necessity of building in flexibility to comprehensive zoning ordinances, and as a method for avoiding the spot-zoning prohibition against isolated amendments of the zoning ordinance, the device of the floating zone was developed and used by zoning authorities.[25] In general, floating zones are special-use districts, unlocated on the zoning map, for purposes consistent with the comprehensive plan for the development of the municipality, such as shopping centers, garden apartments, and light industry. This early emphasis on limited special-use districts is consistent with the broader mixture-of-use concept underlying planned unit development.

Uses designated in floating zones are subject to limitations designed to make them compatible with adjoining residential areas. The specific location of the floating zone is left for the particular application and use in question. Obviously, this device raises a number of questions with regard to threshold legality and legality in practice. Specifically, must zones be precisely located on the zoning map and in the zoning ordinance; can floating zones be consistent with and in accordance with the comprehensive plan of the community; is there an invalid delegation of the legislative authority to rezone and amend when applications for approval of floating zones are taken by and approved by an administrative body, usually the zoning board of appeals and has the zoning authority abdicated its planning function to the private developer who petitions for a floating-zone special-use district?

The New York Cases

Rodgers v. Village of Tarrytown,[26] decided by the New York Court of Appeal in 1951, remains the leading case. *Rodgers* involved an attack upon the validity of a Residence B-B floating zone for garden-type apartments. The zone contained limitations as to the spacing of buildings, minimum lot size (10 acres), and setbacks. The other zones in the community included a Residence A for single-family dwellings, a Residence B for two-family dwellings, and a Residence C for apartment houses. The court summarized the method selected by the board in utilizing the floating zone:[27]

> "The village's zoning aim being clear, the choice of methods to accomplish lay with the Board. Two such methods were at hand. It could amend the General Zoning Ordinance so as to permit garden apartments on any plot of ten acres or more in Residence A and B zones . . . or it could amend the Ordinance so as to invite owners of ten or more acres, who wished to build garden apartments or their properties, to apply for a Residence B-B classification. The Board

25. See Reno, *supra* note 23, at 105-107.
26. 302 N.Y. 115, 96 N.E.2d 731 (1951). This case is extensively discussed in Reno, *supra* note 23, at 108, 110-115, and Mosher *supra* note 23, at 150-156.
27. Rodgers v. Village of Tarrytown, 302 N.Y. at 122, 96 N.E.2d at 733-734.

chose to adopt the latter procedure. That it called for separate legislative authorization for each project presents no obstacle or
drawback—and so we have already held."

The court then addressed itself to the argument that the Board had abdicated its planning function to regulate future zoning with regard to garden
apartments by the use of the device. Rejecting this argument, the court
stated: [28]

> "The mere circumstance that an owner possesses a ten acre plot and
> submits plans conforming to the physical requirements prescribed by
> the 1947 amendment will not entitle him, ipso facto, to a Residence
> B-B classification. It will still be for the Board to decide in the exer-
> cise of a reasonable discretion, that the grant of such a classification
> accords with the comprehensive zoning plan and benefits the village
> as a whole."

Responding to the charge that the floating zone constituted illegal spot-
zoning, the court stated: [29]

> "Defined as the process of singling out a small parcel of land for a
> use classification totally different from that of the surrounding area,
> for the benefit of the owner of such property and to the detriment of
> other owners . . . 'spot zoning' is the very antithesis of planned zon-
> ing. If, therefore, an ordinance is enacted in accordance with a com-
> prehensive zoning plan, it is not "spot zoning" even though it (1)
> singles out in effect but one small plot . . . or (2) creates in the
> center of a large zone small areas or districts devoted to a different
> use."

Continuing, the court indicated that "the relevant inquiry is not whether
the particular zoning under attack consists of areas within larger areas of
different uses, but whether it was accomplished for the benefit of individual owners rather than pursuant to a comprehensive plan for the general welfare of the community." [30]

The court then considered the argument that the procedure adopted by
the board of trustees constituted an invalid method for granting a variance. Rejecting this argument, the court stated that "as we have already
shown, the village's zoning aim, the statute's purpose, was not to aid the
individual owner but to permit the development of the property for the
general welfare of the entire community. That being so, the Board of
Trustees followed approved procedure for changing the General Zoning
Ordinance itself. . . .[31] Accordingly, the court indicated that "when the
Board was called upon to consider the reclassification of the Ruben property under the 1947 amendment, it was concerned, not with any issue or
hardship, but only with the question of whether the property constituted
a desirable location for a garden apartment." [32]

---

28. *Id.* at 123, 96 N.E.2d at 734.
29. *Id.* at 123-124, 96 N.E.2d at 734-735. See also Note, "Spot Zoning and the
Comprehensive Plan," 10 Syracuse L. Rev. 303 (1958).
30. 302 N.Y. at 124, 96 N.E.2d at 735.
31. *Id.* at 124-125, 96 N.E.2d at 735.
32. *Id.* at 125, 96 N.E.2d at 735.

Last, the court considered the question whether the zone was invalid by reason of the fact that it was not definitely located within the community. Said the court:[33]

"The short answer is that, since the ordinance merely prescribed specifications for a new use district, there was no need for it to do either the one or the other [set boundaries for the new district or make changes on the building zone map]. True, until boundaries are fixed and until zoning map changes are made, no new zone actually comes into being, and neither property nor the rights of any property owner are affected. But it was not the design of the Board of Trustees by that enactment to bring any additional zone into being or to affect any property or rights; the ordinance merely provided the mechanics pursuant to which property owners might in the future apply for the redistricting of their property."

Subsequent New York cases illustrate the continuing willingness of the New York courts to utilize the floating-zone technique in the context of planned developments.

Rogers v. North American Philips Co.[34] permitted the enactment of a floating office building and laboratory district. The municipality first enacted a new master plan and implementing ordinance with the floating district in 1958; thereafter, upon an application for development in 1961, the owner of 91 acres in a residential zone requested rezoning for office building and laboratory use. After the required hearings, the municipality granted the permit for office and laboratory use for the specific parcel of land. Citing *Rodgers v. Village of Tarrytown*,[35] the court held that the two-step process was a permissible method of amendment stating, "(T)he two-step zoning, sometimes referred to as 'floating zone' is lawful and . . . the test of the lawfulness of the change of zone here questioned is whether the two steps 'read together as they must be, fully complied with the requirements of the Village Law.' "[36]

Thomas v. Town of Bedford,[37] decided by the New York Court of Appeals in 1962, involved the rezoning of areas in Residence 2-A and Residence 4-A districts to RO research office use, floating-use districts. The court held that the floating districts were consistent with the requirements of comprehensive planning; specifically, the court found that only 3

33. Rodgers v. Village of Tarrytown, 302 N.Y. at 125, 96 N.E.2d at 735. See also Nappi v. LaGuardia, 184 Misc. 775, 55 N.Y.S.2d 80 (Sup. Ct. 1944), *aff'd* 269 App. Div. 693, 54 N.Y.S.2d 722 (1st Dep't), *aff'd* 295 N.Y. 652, 64 N.E.2d 716 (1945).

34. 37 Misc. 2d 923, 236 N.Y.S.2d 744 (Sup. Ct. 1962), *aff'd* 19 A.D.2d 838, 245 N.Y.S.2d 995 (2d Dep't 1963).

35. 302 N.Y. 115, 96 N.E.2d 731 (1951).

36. Rogers v. North American Philips Co., 37 Misc. 2d at 930, 236 N.Y.S.2d at 751 (Sup. Ct. 1962).

37. 11 N.Y.2d 428, 230 N.Y.S.2d 684, 194 N.E.2d 285 (1962); see generally Annot., "Application of Zoning Requirements to Research and Laboratory Facilities," 98 A.L.R.2d 225 (1964).

percent of the land in the community was zoned commercial or industrial, while some 80 percent was residential. Further, the court found that the floating-zone district contained a complete pattern of restrictions on the use of property in the district including a 25-acre maximum provision, a 10 percent building area requirement, a three-story maximum-height requirement, screened parking, and a restriction of uses which would generate dust or smoke or result in excessive light, noise, or traffic congestion. Only incidentally did the court consider the floating-zone aspect of the case in summarily approving the two-step procedure: [38]

> "New studies and reports were made and hearings held and in October, 1959 the Town Board amended the 1946 zoning ordinance to establish an RO district, and the Planning Board recommended three areas, one of them being the subject property. Considerable opposition developed—part of it based on the incomplete status of a Town Development Plan which had been in progress for some years. However, the Town Board did no more than postpone decision on the matter in order to revise and make more strict the provisions relating to access and area requirements. Finally, on March 8, 1960, after a public hearing, the Town Board unanimously adopted a resolution rezoning the subject property for RO purposes."

Tata v. Town Babylon,[39] at 1967 New York Supreme Court decision, approved the enactment of a multiple-residence floating zone to rezone a 14-acre parcel from single-family residence to multiple use. Citing the enactment of the MR multiple-residence floating zone four years earlier, the court concluded that the ordinance was not confiscatory as regards adjoining owners; further, the court indicated that the existence of the floating zone for the prior four years, although not conclusive on the question of comprehensive planning, presented "strong evidence of planning."[40]

Again, in *Albright v. Town of Manlius*,[41] an intermediate New York appellate court approved a change in the zoning classification from residential shopping district to a previously enacted regional shopping district for a 50-acre tract. On the question of comprehensive planning, the court looked to the pattern of amendments previously enacted, as well as existing town studies, the zoning map, and the ordinance itself. Said the court:

---

38. Thomas v. Town of Bedford, 11 N.Y.2d 428, 430-433, 230 N.Y.S.2d 686-687, 184 N.E.2d 285, 287 (1962).

39. 52 Misc. 2d 667, 276 N.Y.S.2d 426 (Sup. Ct. 1967).

40. Tata v. Town of Babylon, 52 Misc. 2d 667, 670, 276 N.Y.S.2d 426, 429 (Sup. Ct. 1967); see also Fornaby v. Feriola, 18 A.D.2d 215, 219, 239 N.Y.S.2d 185, 189 (2d Dep't 1963) ("A master plan is to be distinguished from a zoning ordinance. The former is 'a long term, general outline of projected development,' while the latter 'is but one of the many tools which may be used to implement the plan' . . .").

41. 34 A.D.2d 419, 312 N.Y.S.2d 13 (4th Dep't 1970), *mdf'd* 28 N.Y.2d 108, 320 N.Y.S.2d 50, 268 N.E.2d 785 (1971).

"No New York case has defined the term 'comprehensive plan.' Nor have our courts equated the term with any particular document.' . . . What a comprehensive plan is not, however, has been considered. . . . [T]he 'comprehensive plan' requires that the rezoning should not conflict with the fundamental land use policies and development plans of the community. . . . These policies may be garnered from any available source, most especially the master plan of the community, if any has been adopted, the zoning law itself and the zoning map. . . . [T]he requisite 'comprehensive plan' (need not) be in writing . . . 'comprehensive plan' connotes, however, full consideration of the problems presented and reasonable and uniform provisions to deal with them, which tend to promote the general community welfare." [42]

Finally, in *Daum v. Meade*,[43] decided in 1971, a New York supreme court approved an amendment to rezone a previously enacted floating zone for planned industrial park use. The court specifically found compliance with the requirement of comprehensive planning; although no master plan had been promulgated, there was a comprehensive plan consisting of the existing map and ordinance and the various documents and studies previously made by the town, all of which, the court concluded, pointed to the present and future needs of the county and town to provide suitable industrial sites in the face of an increasing scarcity of land available for use use:

"There is no statutory or decisional requirement, and logic dictates that there not be, that a Town or Village Board adopt a master plan before enacting or amending a zoning ordinance, or that, having undertaken a study designed to lead to possible adoption of a master plan, that it leave uncorrected obviously unsuitable zoning, such as that which relegates the subject property to residential uses only . . . until the culmination of that study and/or adoption of a master plan." [44]

The liberality of the New York cases is matched in only one other jurisdiction and the leading case in that jurisdiction merits brief mention.

Huff v. Board of Zoning Appeals,[45] decided in 1961, involved a comprehensive ordinance which included one district, MR—manufacturing

---

42. *Id.* at 423, 312 N.Y.S.2d at 18.

43. 65 Misc. 2d 572, 318 N.Y.S.2d 199 (Sup. Ct.), *aff'd* 37 A.D.2d 691, 323 N.Y.S.2d 670 (2d Dep't), *motion for leave to appeal denied* 29 N.Y.2d 640, 325 N.Y.S.2d 463, 273 N.E.2d 315 (1971).

44. *Id.* at 576-577, 318 N.Y.S.2d at 204.

45. 214 Md. 48, 133 A.2d 83 (1957). See also discussion in Reno, "Non-Euclidean Zoning: The Use of the Floating Zone," 23 Md. L. Rev. 105, 108, 109, 111-119 (1963); Mosher, "The Floating Zone: Legal Status and Application to Gasoline Stations," 1 Tulsa L.J. 149, 156-157 (1964).

restricted—which was not specifically located on the zoning map. This floating zone required a minimum lot size of 5 acres to be located by the zoning commissioner upon an application by a property owner. The floating zone was restricted to light industrial uses that would not produce noise and odors and would not have a disturbing effect upon adjoining owners. An application was thereupon made by the owner of 18 acres of farmland zoned for residential use; the application requested a rezoning to the MR zone for the purpose of permitting construction of a precision instrument factory. Citing the *Rodgers* case, the Maryland Court of Appeals upheld the validity of the floating zone.

The Pennsylvania Cases

Perhaps the most famous case involving the validity of the floating-zone technique is *Eves v. Zoning Board of Adjustment*,[46] decided by the Pennsylvania Supreme Court in 1960. There, the town supervisors amended the general zoning ordinance to permit a floating zone for F-1, limited industrial; again, the purpose of the zone was to permit light industrial use in residential areas and such use was conditioned upon restrictions for setbacks, landscaping, and architecture. A minimum tract of 25 acres was required for reclassification, as well as prior review by the planning commission. An application was then made by an owner of a 103-acre tract in a Residential A district to use his land for light industrial purposes. After reducing the area to 86 acres, the supervisors approved the owner's request for an amendment to the general ordinance placing the subject tract in an F-1 limited industrial zone.

The adjoining owners challenged the validity of the floating-zone device, and the Supreme Court of Pennsylvania declared that the floating zone was an improprer zoning classification as being without the power of the municipality under the state enabling act; further, the court indicated that the floating-zone device in the ordinance was illegal because it failed to satisfy the requirement that it be in accordance with a comprehensive plan. Stating that the court below had confused "comprehensive planning with a comprehensive plan," the supreme court then indicated that a comprehensive plan "embodying resolutions of land use and restrictions" must be finally enacted at the time the ordinance is adopted.[47] Here, the Pennsylvania court appears to have confused the "enactment" aspects of the master plan with the essentially developmental basis in planning for the comprehensive-plan concept.

This question of planning versus comprehensive plan was also considered in the previously discussed *Huff* case, where the court commented that "the Legislative body determined that it was desirable and in the public interest that there be scattered about the undeveloped areas of the County tracts of 5 acres of more on which very light and unoffensive

---

46. 401 Pa. 211, 164 A.2d 7 (1960). For an extensive analysis of the *Eves* case, see Haar & Hering, "The Lower Gwynedd Township Case: Too Flexible Zoning or an Inflexible Judiciary," 74 Harv. L. Rev. 1552 (1961).

47. 401 Pa. at 217, 164 A.2d at 11.

manufacturing operations would be permitted. . . . These provisions are part of the general plan." [48]

The *Eves* holding regarding the requirement of the enactment of a master plan before the adoption of the ordinance raises an additional question previously touched upon in this article regarding the practical time of the enactment of a master plan, or whether a master plan is in fact literally enacted by most communities prior to the adoption and administration of their ordinances. Rather than require the formal adoption of the plan, many communities have been permitted to proceed with the adoption and implementation of their zoning ordinance so long as the ordinance itself discloses a pattern of land use that is reasonable and not arbitrary. Where this is the case, the argument made in *Eves* regarding the precondition of enacting a formal plan is without validity so long as the ordinance both literally and as applied is sufficiently specific in delineating the use pattern.

The *Eves* case further appears to have adopted a too-restrictive view of the language of the governing state enabling act which directed that town supervisors were required to "shape the land into districts." Reading this language literally, the court indicated that the supervisors had abdicated their duty to in fact "shape" the land into districts with respect to specific uses for which the land was adapted in utilizing the floating-zone technique. [49]

The language in *Rodgers v. Tarrytown*, some nine years earlier, in response to the same argument should again be reviewed. The *Rodgers* court indicated that

> "[I]n sum, the 1947 amendment was merely the first step in a reasoned plan of rezoning, and specifically provided for further action on the part of the Board. That action was taken by the passage of the 1948 ordinance which fixed the boundaries of the newly created zone and amended the zoning map accordingly. It is undisputed that the two amendments, read together as they must be, fully complied with the requirements of the Village Law and accomplished a rezoning of village property in an unexceptionable manner." [50]

In response to the argument in *Eves* that the prerogative to grant a floating zone used by an administrative zoning board is a usurpation of the legislative function of the governing authority of the municipality, the Maryland court in *Huff* analogized the floating-zone procedure to that of a

---

48. Huff v. Board of Zoning Appeals, 214 Md. 48, 133 A.2d 83 (1957). Cf. Carole Highlands Citizens Ass'n v. County Comm'rs, 222 Md. 44, 158 A.2d 663 (1960), and Overton v. County Comm'rs, 223 Md. 141, 162 A.2d 457 (1960), cases questioning the *Huff* special-exception analogy, with Board of County Comm'rs v. Tipon, 233 Md. 77, 222 A.2d 701 (1966), and Bigenho v. Montgomery County Council, 248 Md. 386, 237 A.2d 53 (1968), cases accepting the special-exception rationale.

49. Eves v. Zoning Bd., 401 Pa. 211, 216, 164 A.2d 7, 10 (1960).

50. Rodgers v. Village of Tarrytown, 302 N.Y. 115, 125, 96 N.E.2d 731, 736 (1951).

special exception.[51] If the analogy holds, the zoning authorities are merely exercising administrative duties in applying the standards contained in the ordinance governing the approval or disapproval of the application; further, the special-exception analogy depends upon whether the special use, a lower use, is consistent with a residential neighborhood and whether it can be implemented with special conditions so as not to interfere with the adjacent residential use. In determining the applicability of the special-exception argument as a justification for the floating zone, one must first determine whether the floating zone contains only specifically enumerated uses subject to conditions contained in the ordinance. If, for example, it is a light industrial zone permitting only specified kinds of industrial uses and nothing else, the special-exception analogy will apply since only development in accordance with a specific plan directed to complying with the conditions of the special zone is permissible; on the other hand, if the floating zone permits not only an enumerated use but in addition any authorized uses for other zones, the special-exception analogy breaks down and this rationale for the use of the floating zone becomes unavailable.

Certainly, where only garden apartments are involved, as in *Rodgers v. Tarrytown*, these conditions can be met. But when a floating zone for potentially unlimited industrial use is involved, as could have been the case in *Huff* and *Eves*, the analogy breaks down; likewise, for the mixture of uses required in a broad-based planned unit development. Again, however, caution is required to separate what may be the semantics of the special-exception argument from the indispensable prerequisites for a valid exercise of the power to zone in the floating-zone classification. If the amendment is in the first instance validly creating the floating zone, the inclusion of a multiplicity of uses in the zone does not reflect upon the validity of the floating zone but rather depends upon the enactment in the ordinance of sufficiently specific use regulations to serve as guidelines in implementation.

The unduly restrictive approach of the Pennsylvania court in *Eves* is nowhere better demonstrated than in a review of later cases in Pennsylvania which have tended to build in exceptions to the *Eves* holding; these exceptions have moved Pennsylvania from a negative floating-zone jurisdiction to what might be termed an intermediate floating-zone jurisdiction.

Donahue v. Zoning Board,[52] decided in 1963, was the first case to move significantly from the unequivocally negative holding of *Eves*. In *Donahue*, the floating-zone district was added to the ordinance with an actual application for such district granted six weeks laters. The time period in the *Eves* case between the enactment of the floating zone and the specific district amendment was ten months. Distinguishing *Eves* essentially by reason of the shorter period of time between the enactment of

---

51. See discussion of special-exception analogy in Reno, *supra* note 45, at 114-116. See also cases cited in note 48 for discussion of special exception analogy in later Maryland cases.

52. 412 Pa. 332, 194 A.2d 610 (1963).

the floating zone and the actual location of the zone on the map with a specific application, the court held in *Donahue* that the floating-zone procedure was lawful.

Some five years later, the Pennsylvania Supreme Court again had occasion to consider the floating-zone question as it applies to planned unit development in *Cheney v. Village 2 at New Hope, Inc.*[53] In *Cheney* a planned unit development district was added to the zoning ordinance on June 14, 1965; the district was unlocated on the zoning map; on that same day, a second ordinance was passed upon the application of a landowner rezoning his property from low-density residential to planned unit development. Neighboring property owners commenced a suit to challenge both the enactment of the planned unit development district as a floating zone and also the specific rezoning of the applicant's property. Again, the question was whether the holding in *Eves* required the court to strike down the planned unit development district and the amendment of the map upon the specific application. The language of the court merits close examination.

> "Closely tied to the comprehensive plan issue is the argument raised by Appellees that ordinances 160 and 161 constitute spot zoning outlawed by *Eves* . . . given the fact situation in *Eves*, however, as well as the post-*Eves* cases we do not believe that there is any spot zoning here. In *Eves*, the municipality created a limited industrial district, F-1, which, by explicit legislative pronouncement was not to be applied to any particular tract until the individual land owner requested that his own tract be so re-zoned. The obvious evil in this procedure did not lie in the fact that a limited industrial district might be placed in an area previously zoned, for example, residential. The evil was the pre-ordained uncertainty as to where the F-1 district would crop up. The ordinance all but invited spot zoning where the legislature could respond to private entreaties from landowners and re-zoned tracts F-1 without regard to the surrounding community. In *Eves*, it was impossible for the F-1 districts to conform to a comprehensive plan since tracts would be rezoned on a strictly ad hoc basis."[54]

Concluding that the *Donahue* case was controlling and required an affirmance of the actions by the planning and zoning board, the court stated:

> "Quite to the contrary, no such 'floating zone' exists in the present case. On the very day that the P.U.D. district was created by Ordinance 160, it was brought to earth by Ordinance 161; and . . . this was done 'in accordance with a comprehensive plan'."[55]

Quoting from the *Donahue* case, the court concluded:

---

53. 429 Pa. 626, 241 A.2d 81 (1968).

54. Cheney v. Village 2 at New Hope Inc., 429 Pa. 626, 633-634, 241 A.2d 81, 85 (1968).

55. *Id.* at 634, 241 A.2d at 85.

" 'It was this case by case review (in *Eves*) which demonstrated the absence of a comprehensive plan and which sought to enable the Board of Supervisors (the local legislative body) to exercise powers they did not statutorily possess.

" 'In the instant case, the new classification was established and the zoning map amended within a very short period of time (in the case at bar, on the same day). Under the rules of statutory construction which are likewise applicable to ordinances . . . these ordinances should be read together as one enactment. . . . So construed, ordinances 151 (creating new zone) and 155 (amending zoning map) do not create the "floating zone," anchored only upon case by case application by landowners, which we struck down in *Eves*. While it is true that the change here was made upon request of a particular land owner, this does not necessarily create the evils held invalid in *Eves* where the defects were specifically created by the very terms of the ordinances. It is not unusual for a zoning change to be made upon request of a landowner, and such change is not invalid if made in accordance with a comprehensive plan.' " [56]

Three years later, in 1971, the Pennsylvania Supreme Court was again presented with the question in *Marino v. Harrison Township*.[57] Relying upon the *Donahue* rationale, the court sustained an amendment of the ordinance for a shopping center district upon a specific application, despite the fact that the shopping center district had been added to the ordinances as a floating zone some four months earlier. The emphasis continued to be upon the relatively short period of time between the enactment of the floating zone and the specific rezoning for that use.

What we have seen in the Pennsylvania cases is a move away from the strict rule promulgated in *Eves* toward a somewhat more liberal approach based upon the determination whether the elapsed time between the enactment of the floating zone and the actual amendment of the map on a specific application is reasonable. If that time period is not inordinately long, the Pennsylvania courts will read the two enactments, the floating-zone and the specific map amendment, together as constituting but one rezoning; in this way, the floating-zone prohibition is avoided. This approach, of course, can be critizied as turning upon essentially artificial distinctions. For example, the crucial consideration is whether the amendment process is based upon sound municipal study of the demographic, economic, physical, and ecological problems of land use and adequate planning. The presumption is drawn in Pennsylvania that a relatively short period of time between the enactment of a floating zone and the actual map amendment upon application tends to indicate a fortiori that the process has been indeed in accordance with a comprehensive plan. It is submitted that the brevity or length of the elapsed time is not the significant fact. Proper municipal deliberations in the enactment pro-

---

56. *Id.* at 634-635, 241 A.2d at 85.
57. 1 Pa. Cmwlth. 116, 274 A.2d 221 (1971).

cedure for both the floating zone and the map amendment premised upon adequately detailed planning data should be the vital consideration regardless of whether the elapsed time is one month, six months, or a year.

The New Jersey Cases

New Jersey presents an example of an extremely restrictive approach to the floating zone in the context of a planned unit development. *Rudderow v. Township Committee*,[58] decided by a division of Superior Court in 1971, considered the issues. *Rudderow* involved, among other questions, the question whether an ordinance adopting a planned unit development district could do so without specifically amending the zoning map to locate the districts. The court first quoted from Section 6, Paragraph 2 in Article 4 of the New Jersey State Constitution:

> "The Legislature may enact general laws under which municipalities, other than counties, may adopt zoning ordinances limiting and restricting to specified districts and regulating therein, buildings and structures, according to their construction, and the nature and extent of their uses, and the nature and extent of the uses of land, and the exercise of such authority shall be deemed to be within the police power of the State. Such laws shall be subject to repeal or alteration by the Legislature."[59]

Continuing, the court indicated that the zoning enabling statute, Section 40:55-31 of the New Jersey Statutes Annotated, "follows the dictates of the constitutional mandate in providing that a municipality be divided into districts. . . ."[60] Citing additional language from the statute, the court stated:

> "One of the purposes outlined in our municipal Planned Unit Development Act provides:
> " 'To insure that the provisions of the Revised Statute 40:55-30 et seq., which direct the uniform treatment of dwelling type, bulk, density and open space within each zoning district, shall not be applied to the improvement of land by other than lot by lot development in a manner that would distort the objectives of Revised Statute 40:55-30 et seq. N.J.S.A. 40:55-30 provides in part:
> " ' "Any municipality may by ordinance, limit and restrict to specified districts and may regulate therein, buildings and structures according to their construction, and the nature and extent of their use, and the nature and extent of the uses of land, and the exercise of such authority, subject to the provisions of this article, shall be deemed to be within the police power of the State. . . ." ' "[61]

---

58. 114 N.J. Super 104, 274 A.2d 854 (1971).
59. Rudderow v. Township Comm., 114 N.J. Super. 104, 110-111, 274 A.2d 854, 858 (1971).
60. *Id.* at 111, 274 A.2d at 858.
61. *Id.*

Based upon the state constitution and the quoted portions of the enabling statute, the court concluded as follows:

"The above statute would seem to imply that the preparation of an ordinance under N.J.S.A. 40:55-54 would require some indication of a district or districts in which a planned unit development can be constructed. The ordinance of the defendant municipality declares that any district within the township may be used as sites for planned communities or planned unit developments. . . . This would appear to be in conflict with the constitutional requirements . . . and the provisions of N.J.S.A. 40:55-30, which refers to specified districts."[62]

In reaching its conclusion regarding the requirement of specific districting, the *Rudderow* court placed primary reliance on the 1957 opinion of the New Jersey Supreme Court in *Rock Hill v. Chesterfield Township*,[63] it is submitted, however, that this reliance was misplaced. Unlike *Rudderow*, *Rock Hill* involved an essentially unzoned community which provided for successive floating-zone overlays for a number of uses. All land in the community was zoned for residential and agricultural use; special uses, including shopping centers, restaurants, neighborhood businesses, gasoline stations, and light industrial, among others, could be located anywhere in the municipality upon the approval of the legislative body after a report from the planning commission. Holding that the ordinance flouted the "essential concept of district zoning according to a comprehensive plan,"[64] the court struck down the ordinance. *Rudderow* did not involve successive "floating use" overlays but rather was concerned with single planned unit development districts.

Where a single-use district is involved for planned unit development or any other use, reliance should have been placed upon authority involving single-use classification. One such case was decided by the Connecticut Supreme Court of Errors in 1962. *Summ v. Zoning Commission*[65] provided for the location of research laboratories in any zone upon issuance of a special permit, so long as the tract met a 40-acre minimum area. A suit was thereupon commenced to annul the ordinance before a specific application could be made. In dismissing a suit commenced to challenge the validity of the ordinance, the court disposed of the floating-zone argument as follows:

"The plaintiffs contend that § 9A violates the principles of zoning by creating what is known as a 'floating zone,' that is, a zone without boundaries. We are not unmindful of the conflicts which have arisen in other jurisdictions over the authority to establish floating zones [citing in support *Rodgers* and *Huff* and contra *Rock Hill* and *Eves*). *In all of the cited cases, the court was considering an actual change*

---

62. *Id.*

63. 23 N.J. 117, 128 A.2d 473 (1957).

64. Rock Hill v. Chesterfield Township, 23 N.J. 117, 127, 128 A.2d 473, 479 (1962).

65. 150 Conn. 79, 186 A.2d 160 (1962); see also De Meo v. Zoning Comm'n, 148 Conn. 68, 167 A.2d 454 (1961).

in zone. The principle involved in them has no application here, because § 9A does not affect zone district lines in any way. In the present case, there has been no change in the zoning of any particular property. Section 9A merely adds to the list of permissible uses in any zone a new use—that of research and development laboratories." [66]

The rationale of the *Rudderow* case, even when divorced from its reliance upon *Rock Hill,* is open to serious question. The contrary argument was succinctly stated in *Rodgers v. Village of Tarrytown,* cited above.

Said the court:

"We turn finally to the contention that the 1947 ordinance is invalid because, in proclaiming a Residence B-B district, it set no boundaries for the new district and made no changes in the building zone map. The short answer is that, since the ordinance merely prescribed specifications for a new use district, there was no need for it to do either the one or the other. True, until boundaries are fixed and until zoning map changes are made, no new zone actually comes into being, and neither property nor the rights of any property owner are affected. But it was not the design of the board of trustees by that enactment to bring any additional zone into being or to affect any property or rights; the ordinance merely provided the mechanics pursuant to which property owners might in the future apply for the redistricting of their property. In sum, the 1947 amendment was merely the first step in a reasoned plan of rezoning, and specifically provided for further action on the part of the Board. That action was taken by the passage of the 1948 ordinance which fixed the boundaries of the newly created zone and amended the zoning map accordingly. It is indusputable that the two amendments, read together as they must be, fully complied with the requirements of the Village Law and accomplished a rezoning of village property in an unexceptionable manner." [67]

What the New Jersey court failed to grasp in *Rudderow* was the essentially mechanical and procedural nature of the planned unit development floating zone in the first instance. The *Rodgers* court in New York was correct in focusing upon the completed legislative act in the amendment of the map after the approval of the specific application for the rezoning; the floating-zone enactment in the first instance was merely the enabling procedure.

The two-step procedure is not otherwise questionable as being contrary to the basic premise of comprehensive zoning generally, namely, rational development with the protection of property investment made in reliance upon the current provisions of the ordinance. The Connecticut court in *Summ* spoke to this issue:

---

66. Summ v. Zoning Comm'n, 150 Conn. 79, 90, 186 A.2d 160, 165 (1962).
67. Rodgers v. Village of Tarrytown, 302 N.Y. 115, 125, 96 N.E.2d 731, 735-736 (1951).

"The power of the zoning commission to grant a special permit even when the standards prescribed in § 9A have been satisfied is still subject to the additional conditions stated in the statute. It is true that the standards set forth in § 9A must be satisfied to obtain a permit, but it is also true that the permit is subject 'to conditions necessary to protect the public health, safety, convenience and property values'. These conditions must always be present, for the right to zone rests on the reasonable exercise of the police power in the public interest."[68]

Unzoned Use Overlays

The foregoing discussion should not be interpreted, however, as standing for the proposition that there are no legitimate restrictions upon the utilization of the floating-zone concept. Specific uses and restrictions and conditions upon those uses are generally the indispensable prerequisites for a finding of a valid floating zone. Where it possible to omit specific uses and conditions in the floating zone, a municipality might zone all of its territory into a single-use zone, a single-dwelling residential use, the highest use, with any number of floating zones for various other types of use. This is exactly the ploy struck down in the previously discussed *Rock Hill* case. There, the ordinance was struck down as ultra vires the state enabling act by reason of the fact that it could not meet the basic Euclidean comprehensive-zoning rationale which required territorial use districts based upon the peculiar use suitability of the land and structures in question; further, that ordinance was suspect insofar as it failed to perform the basic zoning function of stabilizing property uses so as to protect existing investments made on the basis of existing and established use districts. The Wisconsin case of *Town of Hobart v. Collier*[69] reached the same conclusion and emphasized the absence of standards for the guidance of the legislative body in passing upon the efficacy of particular applications. A later case in New York, *Marshall v. Village of Wappinger Falls*,[70] decided by an intermediate appellate court in 1967, struck down a planned residential district which stated no permitted uses but provided for use approvals only by permit. Citing *Rock Hill*, the court indicated that this enactment was invalid as being contrary to the requirement of comprehensive planning; further, the court indicated that since the board of appeals was granted permit authority, an invalid delegation of the legislative authority of the town board of trustees had occurred.

Floating Zone and the PUD: Prospects

The advantage of the floating zone over a piecemeal process of amendment is obvious upon a consideration of the amendment requirements; specifically, it is generally held that an applicant for an amendment must

---

68. Summ v. Zoning Comm'n, 150 Conn. 79, 91, 186 A.2d 160, 166 (1962).
69. 3 Wis. 2d 182, 87 N.W.2d 868 (1958.)
70. 28 A.D.2d 542, 279 N.Y.S.2d 654 (2d Dep't 1967).

show that the original zone classification was arbitrary and unreasonable, or that the character of the neighborhood has so changed that the original classification is unreasonable, or that some mistake was made in the original classification. The floating-zone device, of course, does not require either of these showings; the floating zone will be approved upon a showing that the particular application meets the standards set forth in the ordinance, standards enacted only after careful study by all competent municipal agencies of the overall land use and development requirements of the community.[71]

By removing the possible threefold requirements for an amendment, it can be argued, with some persuasiveness, that ordinances using the floating zones have in effect removed some protection from adjoining owners who argue that the floating zone is incompatible with the character of the neighborhood. As stated in *Summ v. Zoning Commission*,[72] however, this argument must fall by reason of the basic police-power rationale applied in all zoning cases that the classification protect the public health, safety, and convenience. Property values are conserved but only in the context of the legitimate development concerns of the community.

There remains, however, the undisputed fact that the jurisdictions are seriously split on the property of the floating-zone technique. The wave of the future in terms of planned unit development depends upon the continued expansion and acceptance of the floating-zone concept. The phrase "to shape land into districts," as it appears with variations in almost all enabling legislation and resultant zoning ordinances, is at the root of the difficulty. What the courts must accept is a modern interpretation of that phrase. While historic Euclidean comprehensive zoning undoubtedly used the phrase in the context of actual map-located districts, the planned unit development requires compatible mechanics in enactment—the floating zone—to achieve the same result, map-located districts. Actual map-located districts are the end to be achieved; they are not the required mechanics for development.

Conditions

Turning now to the implementation of a planned unit development application in the event final approval for the total development has been obtained, consideration must be given to the conditional and contract zoning devices often applied by municipalities. As indicated earlier, the implementation of a planned unit development district, the actual process of construction, is one of phased or staged development; thus, at any one time, the developer and the municipality may be directly involved with only one portion of the planned unit development plan. For example, of the municipality authorized the developer to first proceed with the commercial-service phase of the planned unit development, it might well

---

71. See Beall v. Montgomery County Council, 240 Md. 77, 212 A.2d 751 (1965), and discussion in Comment, "The Floating Zone: A Potential Instrument of Versatile Zoning," 16 Catholic L. Rev. 85, 93-95 (1966).

72. 150 Conn. 79, 186 A.2d 160 (1962).

require that the construction of that element proceed only with certain conditions designed to insure that later residential development in the same area would proceed without difficulty.[73] It is not uncommon for the municipality to require buffering with shrubbery, parking below grade, the reservation of parks and recreational areas, and pedestrian walkways as conditions to permitting the commercial development to proceed.

This procedure—a zoning approval with conditions—was considered in the leading case of *Church v. Town of Islip*.[74] *Church* involved the zoning of a corner lot from Residence A to Business B upon condition that the owners of the lot agree to perform conditions as follows:

"1. The building shall not total more than twenty-five percent of the area.

"2. An anchor post fence, or equal, six feet high, is to be erected five feet within the boundary line of the property.

"3. Live shrubbery, three feet high either within or outside the fence is to be planted, and allowed to grow to the height of the fence and after that, to be maintained at the height of the fence.

"4. The above must be performed or put in operation before carrying on any retail business on the property."[75]

Responding to the argument that the imposition of these conditions was invalid as contract zoning, the Court stated:

"Appellants' arguments all revolve about the idea that this is illegal as 'contract zoning' because the Town Board, as a condition for rezoning, required the owners to execute and record restrictive covenants as to maximum area to be occupied by buildings and as to a fence and shrubbery. Surely these conditions were intended to be and are for the benefit of the neighbors. Since the Town Board could have, presumably, zoned this Bay Shore Road corner for business without any restrictions, we fail to see how reasonable conditions invalidate the legislation. Since the owners have accepted them, there is no one in a position to contest them. Exactly what 'contract zoning' means is unclear and there is really no New York law on the subject. All legislation 'by contract' is invalid in the sense that a Legislature cannot bargain away or sell its powers. But we deal here with actualities, not phrases. To meet increasing needs of Suffolk's County's own population explosion, and at the same time to make as gradual and as little of an annoyance as possible the change from residence to business on the main highways, the Town Board imposes conditions. There is nothing unconstitutional about it."[76]

While conditional zoning is generally valid, contract zoning is not. Contract zoning involves an agreement by the municipality to rezone or authorize a particular use upon the owner covenanting to restrict the use;

---

73. See generally Shapiro, "The Case for Conditional Zoning," 41 Temple L.Q. 267 (1968); Comment. "The Use and Abuse of Contract Zoning and Conditional Zoning," 11 Prac. Law. 43 (1965); "Contract Zoning," 23 Md. L. Rev. 121 (1963).

74. 8 N.Y.2d 254, 168 N.E.2d 680 (1960).

75. Church v. Town of Islip, 8 N.Y.2d 254, 257, 168 N.E.2s 680, 681 (1960).

76. *Id.* at 259, 168 N.E.2d at 683.

alternatively, the rezoning may be adopted only after the owner files a covenant containing additional restrictions on the use. This device has been attacked primarily as an improper delegation by the zoning authority of its police power prorogative. Several courts have followed this argument in declaring contract zoning to be ultra vires. The New Jersey cases provide the clearest illustrative examples.

In *Midtown Properties Inc. v. Township of Madison,*[77] the New Jersey court was asked to review a contract between the municipality and the developer pursuant to which the municipality covenanted to adopt an ordinance with appropriate districts to permit development of a 1,475-acre subdivision; the municipality further contracted to refrain from passing any rules or regulations for seven years which would in any way jeopardize the implementation of the proposed subdivision. Also, the municipality agreed that the contract would govern over conflicting regulations and that the developer need not comply with the existing statutory procedure for obtaining subdivision approval. The Superior Court had no difficulty striking down the contract, holding that the municipality had unlawfully bargained away and surrendered its legislative power.

Similarly, in *Houston Petroleum Co. v. Automotive Products Credit Association,*[78] the New Jersey Supreme Court invalidated a contract pursuant to which the owner agreed to restrict the use of his land in consideration of the municipality agreeing to rezone it, the agreement to become effective upon rezoning; the contract providing in addition that the restrictions would remain effective only so long as the property remained rezoned and, further, that the restrictions could only be released by subsequent written agreement between the municipality and the owner or his successors in interest.

The New York cases generally, have reached the same result. In *Levine v. Town of Oyster Bay,*[79] the court declared invalid a zoning amendment reclassifying one parcel from residential to industrial use on condition that the owner lower the grade 15 feet to the grade of the road; the court emphasized that this lowering of the grade would require a public notice and hearing and permit pursuant to an excavation ordinance. As such, this procedure constituted invalid contract zoning as a present amendment purporting to change the zone in the future. Similarly, *Andgar Associates v. Board of Zoning Appeals*[80] held that a municipality is without authority to diminish its legislative power by entering into a settlement agreement in a zoning action which gave the owner a vested right to use his land in a specified way, without regard t subsequent changes in the zoning regulations.

---

77. 68 N.J. Super 197, 172 A.2d 40 (1961), *aff'd* 78 N.J. Super 471, 189 A.2d 226 (App. Div. 1963).

78. 9 N.J. 122, 87 A.2d 319 (1952).

79. 46 Misc. 2d 106, 259 N.Y.S.2d 247 (Sup. Ct. 1964), *aff'd* 26 A.D.2d 583, 272 N.Y.S.2d 171 (2d Dep't 1966).

80. 30 A.D.2d 672, 291 N.Y.S.2d 991 (2d Dep't), *motion for leave to appeal denied* 22 N.Y.2d 648 (1968).

The foregoing cases present rather clear-cut examples of invalid contract zoning. Other cases, however, reach results sometimes inexplicable on their facts. *Baylis v. City of Baltimore*[81] involved a rezoning from residential to commercial use on condition that a contract between the owner and municipality to executed and filed restricting the use of the property to funeral home use and providing for a return to residential zoning in the event the funeral home use was discontinued in the future. In striking down these conditions as contract zoning, the court drew the essentially artificial distinction that while administrative relief from the provisions of zoning ordinances by way of variances and special exceptions may be conditioned, legislative relief by way of amendments may not.

In *Sylvania Electric Products Inc. v. City of Newton,*[82] the owner voluntarily imposed restrictions to be effective upon the exercise of a thirty-year option to purchase a part of the property by the city; the city thereafter amended its ordinance to rezone the property. Although a close nexus was recognized between the self-imposed restrictions and the rezoning, the court held the two acts separable and unrelated. As such, the rezoning was deemed to be without condition and as such valid.

While *Baylis* and *Sylvania* may have reached questionable results, procedures which look suspiciously like contract zoning have been approved in other cases. For example, in *City of Greenbelt v. Bresler,*[83] the Maryland Court of Appeals required the specific performance of a contract between the municipality and developer for the conveyance of a tract for park and recreational purposes. Further, the developer had agreed, as an inducement to obtaining a favorable recommendation from the city for reclassification of property from rural-residential planned community to medium-density garden apartments, to limit the number of dwelling units to seven per acre. This agreement was enforceable upon breach by injunctive proceedings within thirty days after the city was notified that the developer had obtained a building permit for construction of the improvements in violation of the agreement. Where the municipality failed to seek relief within the thirty-day period, the court strictly enforced the agreement against the municipality; as a result, the municipality was estopped to challenge the granting of a building permit for construction of an eight-story apartment house containing 178 units on a 9-acre tract.

Funger v. Mayor & Council,[84] involved the interpretation of an agreement between the builder and the town obligating the town to recommend to the county council high-rise zoning for some 18 acres of an approximately 30-acre tract of land owned by the builder in consideration of the builder agreeing to enumerated conditions; the builder agreed to subject some 2 acres of the tract to a scenic and conservation easement, to

81. 219 Md. 164, 148 A.2d 429 (1959). See also discussion in Schaffer, "Contract and Conditional Zoning," 11 Prac. Law. 43 44-46 (1965).

82. 344 Mass. 428, 183 N.E.2d 118 (1962). See also Armstrong v. McInnis, 264 N.C. 616, 142 S.E.2d 670 (1965).

83. 248 Md. 210, 236 A.2d 1 (1967).

84. 249 Md. 311, 239 A.2d 748 (1968).

dedicate some 12 acres for use as a park, and to limit for a period of twenty years development of 16 acres to uses and density then permitted in a high-rise zone. In specifically enforcing the agreement, the court held that the town was obligated not to frustrate the builder's exercise of his rights after the rezoning of his property for high-rise use; further, the court held that the town's failure to perform constituted a substantial breach of contract, entitling the builder to a rescission on condition that he endeavor to return both parties to their status before the contract.

The cases discussed above are merely illustrative and are not intended to be exhaustive survey of the "conditional contract" zoning area. Suffice it to say that the case law going both ways tends to become hopelessly mired in the definition and redefinition of the two concepts; the process somewhat reminiscent of the difficulty in the law of contracts in distinguishing conditions precedent and conditions subsequent. Unfortunately, there is often little more than the catchword "contract" or "condition" to provide the basis for predicting the result in any particular fact situation.

Given the importance of the conditioned approval to the phased development of mixed uses common to the planned unit development, care must be taken by local governing bodies in implementing a planned development. Certainly, rezoning can proceed where the owner has fulfilled conditional requirements beforehand. Alternatively, the municipality is probably safe in adopting the amendment effective immediately but with automatic reversion to prior zoning in the event conditions are not fulfilled within a fixed time limit; less clear but likewise probably permissible is the practice of adopting the ordinance but postponing its effective date until conditions are performed within a specified time limit.[85]

CONCLUSION

This article has examined some of the threshold legal problems in enactment of planned unit development ordinances as well as the important problems in implementation—the floating-zone technique and conditional zoning. All these problems have been previously examined in the context of other problems in zoning classification and administration. It is of some importance, however, that they be reexamined both individually and as they relate to each other in the context of planned developments. If planned unit developments are to be fully exploited as a technique for solving some of the problems of urban land use and economic development, it is imperative that threshold questions of enactment be favorably resolved and that procedures be perfected to permit maximum utilization within the law of the floating-zone PUD and conditional PUD phase approvals.

C. THE OFFICIAL MAP

(1) Introductory Description

The **official map** is a technique of planning implementation by which a local government prepares, and files for public examination, a map showing existing

---

85. See Schaffer, *supra* note 81, at 48-50.

and *proposed* streets, and may or may not, include a designation of areas for proposed parks and other public facilities. The proposed streets designated on the official map are sometimes called **"paper streets"** because, until they are built, they exist only "on paper" and not in fact. The ordinance by which the official map is adopted will also provide that no building permits will be issued for construction on land lying in the bed of a proposed street, or on the site of proposed parks. The ordinance will usually contain provisions for a variance procedure to authorize construction where the enforcement of the ordinance would result in undue hardship or preclude a reasonable return to the owner of the property designated for streets or public areas.

The following provisions of the New Jersey Municipal Land Use Law is a good illustration of a modern enabling statute for official map ordinances:

N.J. MUNICIPAL LAND USE LAW

C. 40:55D-32 Establish an official map.

23. Establish an official map. The governing body may be ordinance adopt or amend an official map of the municipality, which shall reflect the appropriate provisions of any municipal master plan; provided that the governing body may adopt an official map or an amendment or revision thereto which, in whole or in part, is inconsistent with the appropriate designations in the subplan elements of the master plan, but only by the affirmative vote of a majority of its full authorized membership with the reasons for so acting recorded in the minutes when adopting the official map. Prior to the hearing on the adoption of any official map or any amendment thereto, the governing body shall refer the proposed official map or amendment to the planning board pursuant to subsection 17 a. of this act.

The official map shall be deemed conclusive with respect to the location and width of streets and public drainage ways and the location and extent of flood control basins and public areas, whether not not such streets, ways, basins or areas are improved or unimproved or are in actual physical existence. Upon receiving an application for development, the municipality may reserve for future public use, the aforesaid streets, ways, basins, and areas in the manner provided in section 32.
* * *

C. 40:55D-34 Issuance of permits for buildings or structures.

25. Issuance of permits for buildings or structures. For purpose of preserving the integrity of the official map of a municipality no permit shall be issued for any building or structure in the bed on any street or public drainage way, flood control basin or public area reserved pursuant to section 23 hereof as shown on the official map, or shown on a plat filed pursuant to this act before adoption of the official map, except as herein provided. Whenever one or more parcels of land, upon which is located the bed of such a mapped street or public drainage way, flood control basin or public area reserved pursuant to section 23 hereof, cannot yield a reasonable return to the owner unless a building permit is granted, the

board of adjustment, in any municipality which has established such a board, may, in a specific case, by an affirmative vote of a majority of the full authorized membership of the board, direct the issuance of a permit for a building or structure in the bed of such mapped street or public drainage way or flood control basin or public area reserved pursuant to section 23 hereof, which will as little as practicable increase the cost of opening such street, or tend to cause a minimum change of the official map and the board shall impose reasonable requirements as a condition of granting the permit so as to promote the health, morals, safety and general welfare of the public. Sections 59 through 62 of this act shall apply to applications or appeals pursuant to this section. In any municipality in which there is no board of adjustment, the planning board shall have the same powers and be subject to the same restrictions as provided in this section. ————————————

(2) Legal Issues

The legal issues that arise when the validity of an official map ordinance is challenged are: (1) Does the official map restriction on the use of the owner's property constitute an unreasonable deprivation of property in violation of the due process clause at any time *before* the owner is ready to build on the designated areas? See *Headley v. Rochester* and compare with *Miller v. City of Beaver Falls.* (2) Is the owner entitled to compensation for the temporary reservation and deprivation of use *when he is ready to build* and is denied a building permit because of official map restrictions. See *Lomarch v. Mayor of Englewood* and the provisions of the New Jersey Municipal Land Use adopted in response thereto.

(a) Is There a "Deprivation of Property?"

HEADLEY
v.
ROCHESTER
272 N.Y. 197, 5 N.E.2d 198 (1936)

LEHMAN, Judge.

The plaintiff since 1918 has been the owner of premises in the city of Rochester which are bounded on the south by East avenue and on the west by North Goodman street. East avenue and North Goodman street have been, for more than 20 years public streets or highways. In 1931, pursuant to article 3 of the General City Law (Consol. Laws, c. 21), the council of the city of Rochester passed an ordinance which amended, changed, and added to an official map or plan previously adopted by the council "so as to correct and revise said established Official Map or Plan and to lay out new streets and highways and to widen existing highways."

In that map or plan the southerly 25 feet of plaintiff's said premises are included in East avenue, as widened, and a strip of plaintiff's premises extending along its westerly edge is included in North Goodman street, as widened. The plaintiff has brought an action to obtain a judgment declaring "that the ordinance and map and plan adopted by the said City of Rochester as aforesaid is unconstitutional and void."At Special Term the complaint was dismissed. The Appellate Division reversed and granted judgment "declaring that the ordinance, map and plan herein involved, are void and ineffectual to create any limitations or restrictions upon the use or conveyance of plaintiff's property."

By chapter 690 of the Laws of 1926, the Legislature added article 3, entitled "Official Maps and Planning Boards," to the General City Law. That article empowers the legislative body of every city to establish an official map or plan of the city showing the streets, highways, and parts theretofore laid out and established by law. Section 26. It empowers such legislative body "whenever and as often as it may deem it for the public interest, to change or add to the official map or plan of the city so as to lay out new streets, highways or parks, or to widen or close existing streets, highways, or parks." d)—13 1/3 29. It further empowers the legislative body of the city to create a planning board of five members, and it requires that, before making any addition or change in an official map in accordance with section 29 "The matter shall be referred to the planning board for report thereon." The planning board is given "power and authority to make such investigations, maps and reports and recommendations in connection therewith relating to the planning and development of the city as to it seems desirable." Section 31.

The adoption or revision of a general map pursuant to the provisions of the General City Law does not have the effect of divesting the title of the owner of land in the bed of a street as shown on the map; it does not have the effect of placing upon the city a duty to begin, presently, condemnation proceedings to acquire such land. Article 3 of the statute provides the machinery for intelligent planning in advance for the needs of the city as the city is expected to grow in the future. Only time can prove whether the city has wisely guaged the future, and the city is under no compulsion to open any street shown on the map unless and until the legislative body of the city decides that it is actually needed.

The mere adoption of a general plan or map showing streets and parks to be laid out or widened in the future, without acquisition by the city or title to the land in the bed of the street, can be of little benefit to the public if the development of the land abutting upon and in the bed of the proposed streets proceeds in a haphazard way, without taking into account the general plan adopted and, especially, if permanent buildings are erected on the land in the bed of the proposed street which would hamper its acquisition or use for its intended purpose. So long as the owners of parcels of land which lie partly in the bed of streets shown on such a map are free to place permanent buildings in the bed of a proposed street and to provide private ways and approaches which have no relation to the proposed system of public streets, the integrity of the plan may be destroyed by the haphazard or even malicious development of one parcel or tract to the injury of other owners who may have developed their own tracts in a manner which conforms to the general map or plan.

A statutory requirement that a city must acquire title to the land in the bed of the streets shown on the general map or plan, and provide compensation for the land taken, would create practical difficulties which would drastically limit, if, indeed, they did not render illusory, any power conferred upon the city to adopt a general map or plan which will make provision for streets which will be needed only if present anticipations of the future development of the city are realized. On the other hand, to leave the land in private ownership, and, without compensation to the owner, incumber it with restrictions upon its use which would result in diminution in its value, might be inequitable and perhaps even beyond the power of the state. To meet the difficulty, the Legislature has provided in section 35 of the General City Law that, "for the purpose of preserving the integrity of such official map or plan no permit shall hereafter be issued for any building in the bed or any street or highway shown or laid out on such map or plan, provided, however, that if the land within such mapped street or highway is not yielding a fair return on its value to the owner, the board of appeals or other similar board in any city which has established such a board having power to make variances or exception in zoning regulations shall have power in a specific case * * * to grant a permit for a building in such street or highway which will as little as practicable increase the cost of opening such street or highway, or tend to cause a change of such official map or plan, and such board may impose reasonable requirements as a condition of granting such permit, which requirements shall inure to the benefit of the city." The sole complaint of the plaintiff is that, so long as that section remains in force, the effect of the ordinance adopted by the city is to restrict the use to which the plaintiff may put his land in the bed of the street, and to that extent constitutes a taking of his property, and that, since the city is not required to pay any compensation to him unless or until at some time in the indefinite future it may choose to take title to the land, the effect of the ordinance is to deprive him of his property without due process of law.

Not every restriction placed by authority of the state upon the use of property for the general welfare of the state, without payment of compensation constitutes a deprivation of property without due process of law. This court has sustained a reasonable restriction upon the height of signs on roofs, saying: "Compensation for such interference with and restriction in the use of property is found in the share that the owner enjoys in the common benefit secured to all." Under the provisions of the General City Law, the owner of land in the bed of the street shown in a map remains as free to alien the land or to use it as he sees fit as he was before the map was adopted, except in one respect. If he desires to improve the property by erecting a building for which a permit is required, the grant of such a permit is surrounded by drastic conditions or restrictions which will in many cases act as an obstacle to such use of the land.

In Junius Const. Co. v. Cohen, thought the appellant attempted to question the constitutionality of section 35 of the General City Law, we placed our decision on other grounds and said: "We find it also unnecessary to determine whether section 35 with its restrictions upon the enjoyment of the land within the boundaries of a mapped street is an unconstitutional interference with vested rights of property. Though the section has been on the statute books since 1926, its validity has not been challenged in any other case in this court. It is perhaps not without significance that during these years no owner has claimed that the statute has actually interfered with his enjoyment of the land, or has prevented him from obtaining a permit to improve the land in a manner which he deemed desirable.

The plaintiff in this case, too, makes no such claim. The complaint alleges only the conclusion of the pleader that, by reason of the filing of the ordinance and map or plan, "the plaintiff has been, and is, deprived of his property without the payment of compensation therefor." The complaint is silent as to how the plaintiff is injured by the ordinance and the map. The stipulation of facts upon which the case was submitted for decision again fails to indicate in what manner the ordinance has caused damage to the plaintiff or interferes with any use to which the plaintiff desires to put the land. On the contrary, it appears from the stipulated facts that "the plaintiff has at present no plans for the use of said premises nor any particular desire as to the purposes for which he expects to use the same" and "that the plaintiff, because of the claim of the defendant under said ordinance and map, is undecided as to whether he shall endeavor to build upon said premises or endeavor to sell the same." It may be added, incidentally, that the stipulated facts fail to show that there is at present any actual controversy with the city as to the use to which the property may be put, and it appears "that the plaintiff has made no application to the Planning Board, Board of Appeals or Supervisor of Zoning of the City of Rochester for a permit to use those portions of his property included in said map as widened streets or to build thereon or to alter any existing structures therein."

Regardless of the form of action in which relief is sought, the courts will not declare a statute unconstitutional unless and until such relief is necessary for the protection of some right of the suitor guaranteed by the Constitution. "The duty of this court, as of every judicial tribunal, is limited to determining rights of persons or of property, which are actually controverted in the particular case before it." "To complain of a ruling one must be made the victim of it. One cannot invoke to defeat a law an apprehension of what might be done under it and, which if done, might not receive judicial approval."

The courts have sustained, as a proper exercise of the police power, restrictions in zoning ordinances upon the use of land in defined districts which go so far as to require that all buildings be set back a specified distance from the street. There the restrictions were imposed to promote the general welfare and to protect the public health and safety. Here it may be urged that the restrictions, though less drastic, also affect less directly, if at all, the general welfare or the public health and safety. Even if some doubt may remain whether the state has power to impose present restrictions upon the use of land in the bed of a street as shown on an official map or plan, without compensation for the damage caused to the owner of land by reason of such restrictions, there can be no doubt that such restrictions are calculated to promote at least the public convenience if not the public health, and to benefit the district in which the land is situated, as well as the city itself; and that, in so far as such restrictions may constitute a taking of property, the taking would be for a public purpose and would accord with "due process of law," if compensation were paid for the consequent damage. Since the plaintiff's alleged grievance is that he has been deprived of his property without compensation, the grievance becomes illusory if it does not appear that damage has been done to him by the city's acts.

A statute cannot have the effect of depriving a person of his liberty or property unless it prevents such person from doing an act which he desires to do or diminishes the enjoyment of profit which he would otherwise derive from his property. There are approximately 19,000 feet in the plot owned by the plaintiff. The single dwelling house upon it is 95 years old and is now in course of demolition. By its adoption of the general map or plan, the city has given notice that at some future time, if present anticipations are realized, it intends to widen the two streets upon which the plaintiff's property abuts. If without building upon the strips of his land which may in the future be included in the widened streets, the plaintiff's property cannot be developed in manner which the plaintiff desires or which would best conduce to the enjoyment of profit which an owner might derive from his land, and, if it were shown that the statute, if valid, would require or even justify a denial of a permit for such development, the adoption of the map might constitute a grievance. In the absence of proof of such facts, it is difficult to see how the plaintiff has been deprived in any manner of the use of his property. Before the court should even consider the question of whether the Legislature could under the police power restrict, without compensation, the use of land in private ownership, there should be proof at least that the statute is in some manner interfering with or diminishing the value of the present property rights of the person complaining.

* * *

The statute here does not purport to give to the city the right to appropriate the plaintiff's land or any part of it for less than the full value of the lands with the improvements thereon erected at the time of such appropriation. The only restrictions upon the use of any part of the plaintiff's land while title thereto remains in the plaintiff result indirectly from the conditions which the statute attaches to the grant thereafter of a permit to erect a building upon the small portion of plaintiff's land, which, as shown on the map, will lie in the bed of the street on which the plaintiff's land abuts, if or when at some time in the future the city may desire to carry out its intention to widen the street. Since it is affirmatively shown that the plaintiff has no plans at present for the use of the premises, it seems plain that what this court said and decided in the case of Forster v. Scott, supra, cannot possibly be regarded as any precedent for the grant of a judgment declaring the statute invalid, unless from the facts here presented the court as matter of law would be constrained to draw the inference that the conditions which the Legislature has sought to impose upon the grant of a permit for the use of a small part of plaintiff's land creates a limitation upon its use "to the diminution of the value of the land."

No inference of law, indeed no inference of fact, that the attempted condition has affected or will affect the use to which the plaintiff's land will be put or has diminished the value of the land, may be drawn from the stipulated facts. There is no suggestion that a plot of 19,000 square feet cannot be suitably improved and put to the most profitable use by the erection of a building which does not encroach upon the small portions which may be used hereafter to widen the street. Sometimes landowners in a particular district assume mutual obligations to set back buildings some distance from the street. Sometimes such obligations are imposed by zoning ordinance. Sometimes an owner does so voluntarily because he believes that such a setback is the best use for the land immediately abutting on the street. The plaintiff or any successor in title to the property could use the land within the bed of the widened street for such purpose even without a permit. It may be the best use to which that land could be put, even if no map had been adopted, and there were no probability that the city would in time widen the street. Certainly it cannot be said that owners of property do not receive any benefit from the adoption of general maps or plans for the development of city streets, if they can develop their land with some assurance that other owners will not be permitted to frustrate the plan, maliciously or unreasonably. Whether the state may impose conditions for the issuance of permits in order to protect the integrity of the plan of a city where it appears that such conditions interfere with a reasonable use to which the land would otherwise be put or diminishes the value of the land should not now be decided. Without proof that the imposition of such conditions has deprived an owner of land of some benefit he would otherwise derive from the land, there can be no deprivation of property for which compensation should be made.

Solicitude for the protection of the rights of private property against encroachment by government for a supposed public benefit does not justify the courts in declaring invalid a public law which serves a public purpose, because 10 years after it has been on the statute books a single owner, without proof, or even claim, of actual injury, asserts that he has been deprived of his property.

The judgment of the Appellate Division should be reversed and that of the Special Term affirmed, with costs in this court and in the Appellate Division.

MILLER

v.

CITY OF BEAVER FALLS

368 Pa. 189, 82 A.2d 34 (1951)

BELL, Justice.

This appeal involves the constitutionality of an ordinance dated April 10, 1950 enacted pursuant to the Act of June 23, 1931, P.L. 932, known as the "Third Class City Law", art. XXXVII, §§ 3701, 3702, 53 P.S. §§ 12198-3701, 3702. Appellants purchased 16 acres of ground in the 6th Ward of the City of Beaver Falls on *April 8, 1950.* Either their predecessor in title or the holder of a mortgage on said property notified the City on *November 23, 1949* that the property had been purchased for immediate development; that the purchasers intended to erect 72 dwellings thereon; and requested City Council to install sewers in accordance with a plan and to connect the sewers with a public sewer. The property was on a *recorded plan* of lots, with streets and alleys laid out.

On *April 10, 1950,* the City Council—after notice (of November 23, 1949) of the owners' intention to erect houses on the land in question— passed an ordinance, No.960, adopting a *general plan for parks* and playgrounds of the City of Beaver Falls "including those which have been or may be laid out but not opened". A plan of the parks and the playgrounds was attached to and made a part of the ordinance. Appellants knew that such an ordinance had been introduced in Council and had passed first reading when they actually settled for the property. Several months prior to this time appellants' predecessor had begun the construction of 12 houses on a portion of the 16 acres of their land, but had not commenced the erection of any dwellings on the approximately 4½ acres of land which was covered by the above mentioned ordinance.

Section 3701 of the Act of June 23, 1931, supra, page 1084, reads: "* * * No person shall hereafter be entitled to recover any damages for the taking for public use of any building or improvements of any kind which may be placed or constructed upon or within the lines of any located park or playground, after the same shall have been located or ordained by council."

Section 3702 of said Act of June 23, 1931, is as follows: "Whenever any park or parkway may hereafter be superimposed upon the confirmed plan of the streets or parks of any city, in sections not entirely built up, by ordinance of council, unless an ordinance *actually appropriating the land*[1] within the lines of said park or parkway to public use is duly passed by council thereof, *or said land is acquired by council, within three years* from the passage of said ordinance superimposing said plan upon said land, said ordinance superimposing said plans upon said land shall be void and of no effect, * * *". The city has not condemned the property under its power of eminent domain nor made any appropriation of funds for the purpose of paying damages for any property which might be taken as a result of the aforesaid ordinance.

Plaintiffs filed a bill in equity for a decree declaring that Ordinance No. 960 was an encumbrance on their property and a cloud upon their title and was unconstitutional and void. The court, after hearing, found that parks and playgrounds are not only desirable but have become a modern necessity and that the establishment of a park and playground on the property here involved was desirable and necessary to the development, growth and expansion of the city, and dismissed plaintifs' bill.

The question raised is a very important one. Planning the future development or the building of a City Utilitarian and Beautiful, for present and future generations, has become the fashion of the day. There is no doubt that parks have a beneficial effect on public health and public welfare and their establishment and maintenance is certainly desirable. Moreover, the public interest should be favored over private interest whenever reasonably possible, if and when they conflict. However, it must not be forgotten that all acts of the legislature and of any govtal agency are subordinate to the Constitution, which is the Supreme Law of the land; and therefore no matter how desirable the act may appear or how worth the objective, it cannot be sustained if it is interdicted by the Constitution. It is well known that the Constitution of the United States and the Constitution of Pennsylvania provide for the protection and maintenance of Liberty, but it is not so well known or remembered that they likewise contain specific provisions for the protection of private property.

The Constitution of Pennsylvania provides in Article I, § 1, P.S.: "All men * * have certain inherent and indefeasible rights, among which are those of enjoying and defending life and liberty, *of acquiring, possessing and protecting property * * ." Article I, §* 10 provides: "* * * *nor shall private property be taken or applied to public use * * * without just compensation being first made or secured*".

Artical XVI, § 8 provides: "Municipal and other corporations and individuals invested with the privilege of taking private property for public use shall make just compensation for property taken, injured or destroyed by the construction or enlargement of their works, highways or improvements, which compensation shall be paid or secured before such taking, injury or destruction".

The Fourteenth Amendment to the Federal Constitution provides: "* * * nor shall any State deprive any person of life, liberty, or property, without due process of law".

The mandate of these constitutional provisions is clear: *Private property cannot be taken for or applied to public use without just compensation being first paid or secured.* It has long been well settled that the mere plotting of a *street* upon a city plan without anything more does not constitute a taking of land in a constitutional sense so as to give an abbuting owner the right to have damages assessed. The doctrine is said to be founded upon equitable considerations and a wise public policy.

Shall this principle relating to streets, which are narrow, well defined and absolutely necessary, be extended to parks and playgrounds which may be very large and very desirable but not necessary? The injustice to property owners of permitting a municipal body to tie up an owner's property for three years must be apparent to every one.[2] The city can change its mind and abandon or refuse to take the property at the end of three years; but in the meantime the owner has been, to all intents and purposes, deprived of his property and its use and the land is practically unsalable. He cannot build thereon because if he does the law is clear that he cannot recover damages for the loss of any building erected within the plotted line. At the present time there is a wide-spread demand for homes, but no one can foretell what conditions will exist at the end of or within the next three years. Our country may be at war or, because of the war effort or a scarcity of allocation of materials, the owner may not be able to erect dwelling houses at that time, and even if he can, there is the likelihood, because of mounting inflation, that the cost will be very greatly increased over the cost today and for this reason may be prohibitive.

The action of the City of Beaver Falls in plotting this ground for a park or playground and freezing it for three years is, in reality, a taking of property by possibility, contingency, blockade and subterfuge, in violation of the clear mandate of our Constitution that property cannot be taken or injured or applied to public use without just compensation having been first made and secured. The contention of the City in this case, if adopted, would make a travesty of the constitutional provisions protecting rights of property.

The law with respect to streets is too firmly esablished in Pennsylvania to be changed, but that is no reason or justification for extending it. In Harrison's Estate, the Court said: "It may be, as learned counsel for appellant so ably contend, that the profession have assumed the constitutionality of the acts of 1871 and 1891 [53 P.S. §§ 391 et seq., 7072, 7107, 7108, which relate to the right of municipal corporations to locate *streets* without compensation to the owner of the land until there is an actual taking] to be a settled question, *without giving due consideration to our Bill of Rights and the Fourteenth amendment of the Federal Constitution.* What was said by this court in *Bush* v. [*City of*] *McKeesport*, is applicable here: 'If the question, intended to be raised by appellants, were an open one, much might be said on both sides, but we think the underlying principle has been too long and firmly settled in this state, adversely to plaintiffs' contention, to justify us in holding that any new principle was introduced, or change in the law effected, by the clause quoted. * * The clause referred to is that provision of the act of 1891 which declares that damages cannot be recovered for any buildings or improvements 'placed or constructed-upon or within the lines of any located street or alley, after the same shall have been located or ordained by councils.' * * *It is true that the effect of the Bill of Rights, and of the Fourteenth amendment, was not discussed in that opinion, nor perhaps in the other cases in which the constitutionality of this and other similar acts, are involved;* but * * * we * * * must regard the question here raised as settled in our jurisdiction". See to the same effect. The *tendency to limit* this right to take private property or limit its deveopment or use without payment of compensation is indicated in In re Sansom Street, in City of Philadelphia. In that case a city ordinance forbade the erection of buildings on Sansom Street without recession to a new line which would have made it impossible for the plaintiff-relator to build on the remnant of his lot. The Court decided that in such case the rule that the mere plotting of a city street upon a city plan without anything more does not constitute a taking in the constitutional sense, did not apply, and held the property owner had been deprived of his property and was immediately entitled to damages. Mr. Justice, later Chief Justice Schaffer, in his opinion, after calling attention to the provisions of the Constitution of Pennsylvania, said, "The governing principle is accurately stated in 20 Corpus Juris, 666: 'There need not be an actual, physical taking, *but any destruction, restriction or interruption of the common and necessary use and enjoyment of property in a lawful manner may constitute a taking* for which compensation must be made to the owner of the property.'"

It follows that the aforesaid cases involving a plotting of streets should not and do not provide authority for an extension of the principle or doctrine therein enunciated. A principle of questionable constitutionality should not be extended beyond its present application or limitation especially if such extension would violate either the letter or the spirit of the Constitution. "The law as to what constitutes a taking has been undergoing a radical change during the last few years. Formerly it was limited to the actual physical appropriation of the property or a divesting of title, but now the rule adopted in many jurisdictions and supported by the better reasoning is that when a person is deprived of any of certain rights in and appurtenant to tangible things, he is to that extent deprived of his property, and his property may be taken, in the constitutional sense, though his title and possession remain undisturbed; 'and it may be laid down as a general proposition, based upon the nature of property itself, that, *whenever the lawful rights of an individual to the possession, use or enjoyment of his land are in any degree abridged or destroyed by reason of the exercise of the power of eminent domain, his property is, pro tanto, taken, and he is entitled to compensation*'," p. 312. As the Court of Appeals of New York, in Forster v. Scott, in a case involving a statute (very similar to Section 3701 of the Act of June 23, 1931, supra) which it held to be "in conflict with the provisions of the constitution for the protection and security of private property" so aptly said: "What the legislature cannot do directly it cannot do indirectly, as the Constitution guards as effectually against insidious approaches as an open and direct attack. Whenever a law deprives the owner of the beneficial use and free enjoyment of his property, or imposes restraints upon such use and enjoyment that materially affect its value, without legal process or compensation, it deprives him of his property, within the meaning of the Constitution. All that is beneficial in property arises from its use and the fruits of that use, and whatever deprives a person of them deprives him of all that is desirable or valuable in the title and possession. It is not necessary, in order to render a statute obnoxious to the restraints of the Constitution, that it must, in terms or in effect, authorize an actual physical taking of the property or the thing itself, so long as it affects its free use and enjoyment, or the power of disposition at the will of the owner."

As Mr. Justice Holmes said in his opinion in Pennsylvania Coal Co. v. Mahon: "The protection of private property in the Fifth Amendment presupposes that it is wanted for public use, but provides that it shall not be taken for such use without compensation. A similar assumption is made in the decisions upon the Fourteenth Amendment. When this seemingly absolute protection is found to be qualified by the police power, the *natural tendency of human nature is to extend the qualification more and more until at last private property disappears.* But that cannot be accomplished in this way under the Constitution of the United States".

While such regulations may not physically take the property, they do so regulate its use as to deprive the owner of a substantial right therein without compensation. '*We are in danger of forgetting that a strong public desire to improve the public condition is not enough to warrant achieving the desire by a shorter cut than the constitutional way of paying for the change*'. Pennsylvania Coal Co. v. Mahon.

The city is not without a remedy, but it cannot eat its cake and have its penny too. If it desires plaintiffs' land for a park or playground which it considers desirable or necessary for its future progress, it can readily and lawfully obtain this land in accordance with the Constitution which, we repeat, is the Supreme Law of the land. The Constitution of the United States and the Constitution of Pennsylvania empower the city to take and appropriate private land for public purposes. *All that is required is that just compensation be paid therefor.* We do not propose that our Federal or State Constitution shall be disregarded or nullified either directly or by subterfuge, even though the purposes and objectives of a legislative act are worthy and are sincerely believed to be in the best public interest.

Section 3702 of the Act of June 23, 1931, P.S. 932, which gives Councils in third class cities a three year locus penitentiae in taking private property for a park—three years to change their mind or pay—is hereby declared unconstitutional and the Ordinance of the City of Beaver Falls No. 960 is hereby declared unconstitutional and void.

Judgment reversed; costs to be paid by appellee.

(b). Compensation For Temporary Deprivation of Use

LOMARCH

v.

MAYOR OF ENGLEWOOD

51 N.J. 108, 237 A.2d 881 (1968)

HANEMAN, J.

This action in lieu of prerogative writs tests the constitutionality of N.J.S.A. 40:-55-1.32 and N.J.S.A. 40:55-1.38, a part of what is commonly known as the Offical Map Act, as well as an ordinance adopted by the Common Council of Englewood pusuant thereto. The Law Division found the Act unconstitutional and the defendant appealed to the Appellate Division. While pending there we certified the case on motion of both parties. R.R. 1:10-1A.

In April of 1967, plaintiff, who was and is the owner of some sixteen acres situate in Englewood, applied for approval of its plans to subdivide the property in order to construct single family dwellings. While consideration of the application was pending, the Common Council of Englewood adopted what is Ordinance ;1724 pursuant to N.J.S.A. 40:55-1.32 and N.J.S.A. 40:55-1.34 which placed the land on the Official Map of the City and designated it land reserved for use as a park.

N.J.S.A. 40:55-1.32 provides that a municipality may designate land uses upon an official map and that

"* * * Upon the application for approval of a plat, the municipality may reserve for future public use the location and extent of public parks and playgrounds shown on the official map, or any part thereof and within the area of said plat for a period of one year after the approval of the final plat or within such further time as agreed to by the applying party. Unless within such one year period or extension thereof the municipality shall have entered into a contract to purchase, or instituted condemnation proceedings, for said park or playground according to law, such applying party shall not be bound to observe the reservation of such public parks or playgrounds. During such period of one year or any extension thereof the applicant for the plat approval, and his assigns and successors in interest, may use the area so reserved for any purpose other than the location of buildings or improvements thereon, except as provided in [N.J.S.A. 40:55-1.38]."

Read in connection with N.J.S.A. 40:55-1.32, the practical effect of the ordinance was to "freeze", for a one year period, any attempt to develop the designated land.

On May 23, 1967 plaintiff's subdivision plan was granted initial approval. At the same time plaintiff was notified by letter that the land in question had been reserved for park land acquisition. Subsequently, the resolution granting final approval provided

> "The approval granted by this Resolution does not in any way obligate the City of Englewood, and the applicant is acting solely at its own peril since the applicant is on notice that this property has been reserved by the City of Englewood on the official map under the Green Acres Program and the applicable Statutes of the State of New Jersey."

Eight days before final approval was granted, plaintiff brought this suit to challenge the statutory authority by which it had been denied the right to develop its lands for a period of one year. Such a denial it argues constitutes a taking of property without compensation as the statute makes no provision for payment and therefore violates both the Fourteenth Amendment to the Federal Constitution and Art. I ¶ 20 of the State Constitution. The defendant denies that the statute violates the constitutional prohibitions and further argues that plaintiff is prevented from bringing the suit, since it has not availed itself of the relief provisions of the Act (N.J.S.A. 40:55-1.38) which provides:

> "For the purpose of preserving the integrity of the official map of a municipality, no permit shall be issued for any building in the bed of any street or drainage right of way shown on the official map, or on a plat filed pursuant to the Municipal Planning Act (1953) before adoption of the official map, except as herein provided. Whenever one or more parcels of land upon which is located the bed of such a mapped street or dranage right of way, or any park or playground location reserved pursuant to [N.J.S.A. 40:55-1.32] hereof, cannot yield a reasonable return to the owner unless a building permit be granted, the board of adjustment, in any municipality which has established such a board, may, in a specific case by the vote of a majority of its members, grant a permit for a building in the bed of such mapped street or drainage right of way or within such reserved location of a public park or playground, which will as little as practicable increase the cost of opening such street, or tend to cause a minimum change of the official map, and the board shall impose reasonable requirements as a condition of granting the permit so as to promote the health, morals, safety and general welfare of the public and shall inure to the benefit of the municipality. In any municipality in which there is no board of adjustment, the governing body shall have the same restrictions as provided in this section."

Plaintiff's answer is that this provision is inadequate and cannot serve to save the statutory scheme. We agree that the above provision pays but token service to the landowner's right to use his land and is of little practical value.

We come to the constitutional argument. In WHYY, Inc. v. Glassboro, this Court said:

> "* * * there is a strong presumption that a statute is constitutional, and a legislative act will not be declared void unless its repugnancy

to the Constitution is clear beyond a reasonable doubt. 'To declare a statute unconstitutional is a judicial power to be delicately exercised.' * * * "

In construing a statute the presumption is that the legislature acted with existing constitutional law in mind and intended the act to function in a constitutional manner. Thus, it follows, in light of our decision in Morris County Land Improvement Co. v. Parsippany-Troy Hills Tp., (1963), that the legislature understood that any attempt to deprive a land-owner of the use of his property for one year would be unconstitutional absent an intent to compensate the landowner.

The question now becomes whether that intent need be explicitly set forth in the statutory language. A statute often speaks as plainly by infer-ence as by express words. The details for the accomplishment of a statu-tory objective do not have to be specifically spelled out with particularity. It is not always essential in order to avoid unconstitutionality that provi-sions to insure compliance with the Federal or State constitution be spell-ed out in detail. Whenever the legislature authorizes municipal action which, if taken, would require, under the Constituion, that just compen-sation be paid, it follows that if the municipality wishes to exercise that power it must comply with the constitutional mandate and pay. The statute is not constitutionally defective for failure to expressly provide for com-pensation.

Consonant with the foregoing, we conclude that the "option" for the purchase of land upon the unilateral action of the municipality without any consensual action of the landowner, was statutorily granted to the municipality only upon the implied duty and obligation to make payment of adequate compensation to the landowner for the temporary taking and his deprivation of use.

Although question is not formally before us, in anticipation of further proceedings concerning the establishment of reasonable compensation to plaintiff for this taking and for future guidance of the parties, we suggest that fair compensation would be attained in the following manner: The landowner should receive the value of an "option" to purchase the land for the year. The "option" price should, among other features, reflect the amount of taxes accruing during the "option" period. This sum can be established by expert advice and opinion. If the municipality decides to purchase the lands, he shall be compensated, not only for the value of the land, but for reasonable amount of engineering expenses necessarily in-curred in connection with obtaining municipal approval of the plat. If the municipality does not eventually take title no compensation shall be made for such expenses as the landowner has the continued benefit thereof.

Judgment reversed. Costs to plaintiff.

NEW JERSEY MUNICIPAL LAND USE LAW
§ 40:55D-44

C. 40:55D-44 Reservation of public areas.

32. Reservation of public areas. If the master plan or the official map provides for the reservation of designated streets, public drainageways,

flood control basins, or public areas within the proposed development, before approving a subdivision or site plan, the planning board may further require that such streets, ways, basins, or areas be shown on the plat in locations and sizes suitable to their intended uses. The planning board may reserve the location and extent of such streets, ways, basins or areas shown on the plat for a period of 1 year after the approval of the final plat or within such further time as may be agreed to by the developer. Unless during such period or extension thereof the municipality shall have entered into a contract to purchase or institute condemnation proceedings according to law for the fee or a lesser interest in the land comprising such streets, ways, basins or areas, the developer shall not be bound by such reservations shown on the plat and may proceed to use such land for private use in accordance with applicable development regulations. The provisions of this section shall not apply to streets and roads, flood control basins or public drainageways necessitated by the subdivision or land development and required for final approval.

The developer shall be entitled to just compensation for actual loss found to be caused by such temporary reservation and deprivation of us. In such instance, unless a lesser amount has previously been mutually agreed upon, just compensation shall be deemed to be the fair market value of an option to purchase the land reserved for the period of reservation; provided that determination of such fair market value shall include, but not be limited to, consideration of the real property taxes apportioned to the land reserved and prorated for the period of reservation. The developer shall be compensated for the reasonable increased cost of legal, engineering, or other professional services incurred in connection with obtaining subdivision approval or site plan approval, as the case may be, caused by the reservation. The municipality shall provide by ordinance for a procedure for the payment of all compensation payable under this section.

Chapter Six

Eminent Domain

A. NATURE OF THE POWER

Eminent domain, also known as **condemnation,** is the power of government to take private property for a public use, without the owner's consent, on the payment of just compensation. Eminent domain is one of the **sovereign powers** that, together with the power of taxation and the police power, is inherent in every "sovereign" government. Both federal and state governments in the United States use the eminent domain power to acquire land for roads, schools, public buildings, urban renewal, parks, or other public uses. State governments can, and usually do, delegate this power to municipal governments. Under limited circumstances, public utilities and other private corporations may be authorized to exercise this power.

The power of eminent domain is similar to the **power of taxation** in that both impose an exaction upon, or demand a contribution from, someone within the jurisdiction. The powers are different in that the power to tax is based upon the right of the sovereign to raise funds for public purposes by requiring those within its jurisdiction to contribute thereto. When the taxing power is used, the burden is distributed in accordance with a politically and constitutionally acceptable system of apportionment. When the power of eminent domain is exercised, property is acquired for a public use but the burden falls most heavily upon a limited number of persons whose property is taken. Because of the uneven distribution of the public burden, the owners of property taken by eminent domain are compensated directly for their loss.

The power of eminent domain is similar to the **police power** in that the exercise of either power may result in a decrease in the value of the property left to the owner. For example, the police power may be exercised in the form of zoning laws that restrict the use of land and thereby reduce its value. When the power of eminent domain is exercised, part or all of the owner's land is actually *taken* from him. The power of eminent domain is different from the police power in that when eminent domain is exercised *title* to the property is *taken* from the owner by government and *compensation* is made; when the police power is exercised, title to the property *remains with the owner* but the *use of* the property is *restricted* by governmental regulations and *no compensation* is paid to the owner. Some legal scholars have argued that this difference in treatment of the owners of property is unfair and have suggested a principle of

compensatory regulation by which property owners would be compensated if the value of their property is decreased by government regulation. (See Krasnowiecki & Strong, "Compensable Regulation for Open Space: A Means of Controlling Urban Growth," 29 *J.Am. Inst. Planners* 87 (1963); Hagman, "Compensable Regulation: A Way of Dealing With Wipeouts From Land Use Control," 54 *J. of Urban L.* 45 (1975).) If the regulation is so onerous that the owner is deprived of its reasonable use, he may claim that his property has been **taken in fact** and that he should be compensated. The question is frequently referred to as "the taking issue." (See F. Bosselman, D. Callies & J. Banta, *The Taking Issue* (1973).)

The following statements indicate the kinds of problems that courts face in distinguishing the exercise of the police power and the power of eminent domain:

We assume that one of the uses of the convenient phrase, police power, is to justify those small diminutions of property rights, which, although within the letter of constitutional protection, are necessarily incident to the free play of the machinery of government. It may be that the extent to which such diminutions are lawful without compensation is larger than when harm is inflicted only as incident to some general requirement of public welfare. But whether the last mentioned element enters into the problem or not, the question is one of degree, and sooner or later we reach a point at which the Constitution applies and forbids physical appropriation and legal restrictions alike unless they are paid for.

Holmes, J. in *Bent v. Emery*, 173 Mass 495, 53 N.E. 910 (1899)

If the requirement is within the statutory grant of power to the municipality and if the burden cast upon the subdivider is specifically and uniquely attributable to his activity, then the requirement is permissible; if not, it is forbidden and amounts to a confiscation of private property in contravention of the constitutional prohibitions rather than reasonable regulations under the police power.

Pioneer Trust & Sav. Bank v. Village of Mt. Prospect, 22 Ill.2d 375, 380, 176 N.E.2d 799, 802 (1961).

For additional discussion and analysis of this topic, the following publications are suggested:

Anderson, "A Comment on the Fine Line Between 'Regulation' and 'Taking'," in *The New Zoning: Legal, Administrative and Economic Concepts and Techniques* 66 (N. Marcus and M. Groves eds. 1969).

Craig, "Regulation and Purchase: Two Governmental Ways to Attain Planned Land Use," in *Land and Law,* (C. Haar ed. 1964).

Netherton, "Implementation of Land Use Policy: Police Power Vs. Eminent Domain," 3 *Land & Water L. R.* 33 (1968).

Sax, "Takings and the Police Power," 74 *Yale L.J.* 36 (1964).

Sax, "Takings, Private Property and Public Rights," 81 *Yale L.J.* 149 (1971).

The federal and state constitutions contain provisions that impose limitations upon the power of government to take private property through the use of the eminent domain power. The following illustrate some of the differences in constitutional provisions:

. . . nor shall private property be taken for public use, without just compensation.

U.S. CONST. Amendment V.

Private property shall not be taken for public use without just compensation. Individuals or private corporations shall not be authorized to take private property for public use without just compensation first made to the owners.

N.J. CONST. Art. 1, Sec. 20.

Municipal and other corporations, and individuals invested with the privilege of taking private property for public use, shall make just compensation for property taken, injured or destroyed by them;. . . .

KENT. CONST. Art. 242.

Private property shall not be taken or damaged for public use without just compensation as provided by law. . . .

ILL. CONST. Art. 1, Sec. 15.

As a result of the wording of these constitutional provisions, the following legal issues arise when the power of eminent domain is exercised:

1. What is a **taking of property**?
2. What is **public use**?
3. What is **just compensation**?

B. WHAT IS A TAKING OF PROPERTY?

An analysis of what is a "taking of property" involves an examination of two sub-questions: (1) what is "property" and (2) under what circumstances is a person's property *taken in fact* by governmental action even though the governmental agency involved does not admit to a "taking."

When the property taken by governmental action is a *physical thing*, the legal issue is simple. Thus, if someone's house or land is taken for a highway or school, there is no question but that his "property" has been taken. However, when the "property" taken is a *legal right*, rather than a physical thing, then the legal issue becomes more complex. This problem arises because the *legal concept* of property assumes the existence of a **bundle of rights** that may be exercised by the owner to use, enjoy, control and dispose of the thing, called "property." The legal concept of property includes rights that: (1) can be divided *in time*, e.g., a tenant's term of years, a life estate, a reversionary interest; (2) can be divided *vertically*, e.g., mining rights, surface rights and air rights; (3) can be divided into *separate rights of interest or use*, e.g., joint tenancy, mortgage interests, liens, easements, development rights and deed restrictions. The following case illustrates the kind of problem that arises if someone claims separate ownership of one of the bundle of rights included in the concept of "property."

HORST

v.

HOUSING AUTHORITY OF COUNTY OF SCOTTS BLUFF

184 Neb. 215, 166 N.W.2d 119 (1969)

McCOWN, Justice.

The Housing Authority of the County of Scotts Bluff commenced condemnation proceedings to acquire 24 lots in Highland Park Second Addition, for the purpose of erecting multiple unit dwellings. Each of the appellants, some 40 in number, owned a lot in the addition. Their lots were not included in the 24 lots being acquired by condemnation. The appellants were joined as condemnees because of their interest in covenants affecting all lots in the addition and restricting each lot to single family residential use. In the condemnation proceeding, each of the 40 appellants received $200 damages. The award was signed by 2 of the 3 appraisers. In an appeal to the district court by the appellants, the Housing Authority filed a motion for summary judgment on the ground that the appellants did not own an interest in the property acquired by the Housing Authority, and were not entitled to compensation. The district court sustained the motion, entered judgment for the Housing Authority, and directed the damages awarded be returned.

The issue involved is whether a condemnation of real property, which extinguishes a covenant restricting the use of the property condemned, may constitute the taking or damaging of property of owners of other land for whose benefit the restrictions were imposed. The issue is one of first impression in this state. There is a direct conflict of judicial authority. See, Annotation, Eminent Domain: Restrictive Covenant or Right to Enforcement Thereof as Compensable Property Right, 4 A.L.R.3d 1137; 122 A.L.R. 1464; 67 A.L.R. 385, 17 A.L.R. 554.

Lines of decision are sufficiently extensive and contrasting that the positions of the courts are expressed as a majority view and a minority view. See 2 Nichols on Eminent Domain (3d Ed.), s. 5.73, p. 125, et seq. The position of the Housing Authority and the judgment of the lower court reflect the minority view. The Housing Authority contends that restrictive convenants are not enforceable against the government; that such covenants are made subject to the powers of government, including the power of eminent domain; and are, therefore, void as against the government and not compensable. It is also contended that the rights of the appellants arising from such restrictive covenants are negative rights not known at common law, and, therefore, not property rights in the lots being acquired.

On the technical issue of whether such a restriction is an interest in the land being taken and, therefore, compensable, Restatement, Property, is definitive. In 1944, Restatement adopted the view that such a restrictive covenant, insofar as it creates an obligation binding upon successors, constitutes an interest in land which is extinguished by the taking of the land by eminent domain to the extent to which the taking permits a use violative of the restriction. See Restatement, Property, s. 565, p. 3316. "Upon a condemnation of land subject to the obligation of a promise respecting its use in such manner as to extinguish the interest in the land created by the promise, compensation must be made to those entitled to the benefit of the promise." Restatement, Property, s. 566, p. 3320.

Housing Authority also contends that if such restrictive covenants are treated as property rights in the property actually condemned, eminent domain proceedings might involve many owners in a large subdivision and make the administrative and financial burden on condemning units excessive. It is also argued that since the landowners in an adjoining addition, which had no restrictive covenants, would not be entitled to compensation if the property being condemned was located in that addition, the appellants should be in no better position because of the existence of the contractual covenants.

Housing Authority relies on the rule that a landowner whose land is not being taken is not entitled to compensation for damages of the same kind as that suffered by the public in general, even though the inconvenience and the injury to the particular landowner may be greater in degree than that to others. This argument in effect, is that people should not be allowed to increase the value of their property by these covenants, or that the restrictive covenants here should be treated as though they did not exist, because the government is exercising its power of eminent domain. Such policy arguments are not impressive when weighed against the language of Article I, section 21 Constitution of Nebraska: "The property of no person shall be taken or damaged for public use without just compensation therefor."

It is tacitly conceded that these covenants could be enforced by the appellants against a private individual or corporation either by injunctive relief or by an action for damages for breach. It is also obvious that no injunctive relief is available against the governmental unit, and that the acquisition of the property by eminent domain extinguishes the restrictive obligation as to the land acquired. Under such circumstances, we cannot accept the premise that the government should be permitted to inflict damage without liability simply because it is the government. The constitutional language provides an effective shield. As Mr. Justice Holmes said in 1910: "It (the Constitution) does not require a parcel of land to be valued as an unencumbered whole when it is not held as an unencumbered whole. It merely requires that an owner of property taken should be paid for what is taken from him. It deals with persons, not with tracts of land. And the question is, what has the owner lost, not what has the taker gained."

The nature of some public works might ordinarily warrant little, if any, compensation. Even where substantial damages might be warranted to some owners, it would seem that the amount of damages would rapidly diminish as the distance of a claimant's lot from the condemned tract increased. See Aigler, Measure of Compensation for Extinguishment of Easement by Condemnation, 1945 Wis.L.Rev. p. 5, et seq.

Whether the interests involved here be treated as negative easements, equitable easements, equitable servitudes, or contractual covenants running with the land, they constitute property in the constitutional sense and must be compensated for if their extinguishment results in damage to the owners. We therefore hold that lawful covenants restricting the use of land and binding upon successors in title constitute an interest in the land, and property in the constitutional sense. Where the taking of the land by eminent domain permits a use violative of the restrictions and extinguishes such interest, there is a taking of the property of the owners of the land for whose benefit the restrictions were imposed, and such an owner is entitled to compensation for the damage, if any, to his property.

For the reasons stated, the judgment of the district court is reversed and the cause remanded for further proceedings in accordance with this opinion.

Reversed and remanded for further proceedings.

The second part of the question of what is a taking of property involves the issue of whether the "taking" of a person's property by governmental action *injures or damages* his property. The constitutions of Kentucky, Illinois (see excerpts above) and other states specifically provide for compensation when property is "injured" or "damaged" as well as "taken." However, the federal constitution and the constitutions of most other states do not have such provisions and it becomes necessary to determine at what point the action of government becomes so onerous and confiscatory as to constitute a "taking" of the property.

Where the action of a governmental agency results in a **de facto taking,** i.e., a taking, *in fact,* rather than by a legal proceeding, the owner of the property may in many states bring a law suit known as **inverse condemnation** for the purpose of requiring the governmental agency to make compensation as though the property had been taken by condemnation proceedings brought by the government. The *Washington Market Enterprises* case illustrates the legal issues raised by such a proceeding.

> ## WASHINGTON MARKET ENTERPRISES, INC.
> ### v.
> ### CITY OF TRENTON
> 68 N.J. 107, 343 A.2d 408 (1975)

MOUNTAIN, J.

This case presents the question of whether there can be a taking of property for which the Constitution demands just compensation, absent a physical invasion of the property or a direct legal restraint on its use. The suit arises out of the activities of the City of Trenton in first undertaking and then abandoning an urban redevelopment project for the business district of central Trenton. Plaintiff alleges that these activities resulted in the substantial destruction of the value of its property. It seeks to compel condemnation, or in the alternative, to be recompensed by way of damages for loss of value. At the trial level, defendant's motion for summary judgment was successful. We granted direct certification of plaintiff's appeal, R. 2:12-2, because of the importance of the issue presented.

The premises in question consist of a parcel of land upon which has been erected a large building designed for commercial use. Allegedly, what had been tenantable office and retail space is now largely vacant. It is contended that this is attributable, wholly or in large part, to the action taken by the City.

For reasons hereinafter set forth, we hold that where planning for urban redevelopment is clearly shown to have had such a severe impact as substantially to destroy the beneficial use which a landowner has made of his property, then there has been a "taking of property" within the meaning of that constitutional phrase.

As the matter is before us on appeal from a grant of summary judgment awarded the defendant, we must accept as true all record facts and reasonable inferences therefrom in the light most favorable to the plaintiff.

In 1958 Trenton undertook a feasibility study for the redevelopment of a considerable part of the downtown area of the municipality. From the very beginning a large shopping mall was planned which would require, were the project to come to fruition, the condemnation of plaintiff's property. After considerable study the city decided to proceed first with a smaller undertaking (the Fitch Way Project) immediately to the south of the planned mall area. The land for the Fitch Way Project was acquired and buildings thereon razed in 1963. In 1964 a public hearing was held on the question of whether the proposed mall area (now designated as the Center City South Project) should be declared "blighted," this being the first formal step looking to ultimate acquisition. For reasons not of record no declaration of blight was forthcoming at that time (apparently the City was experiencing difficulties in developing the Fitch Way Project). During this period and the ensuing years there were repeated newspaper accounts of the progress being made toward the creation of the proposed mall and officials of the City were making public statements describing the plans which had been made with respect thereto.

In 1967 another public hearing was held, and in September of that year the land encompassing the Center City South Project (including plaintiff's property) was declared a blighted area. Before the City moved to acquire the land, the Department of Housing and Urban Development of the federal government altered the designation of the project from a conventional Urban Renewal Program to a Neighborhood Redevelopment Program. The change meant that instead of receiving a block grant to acquire all of the properties at one time, the City would receive smaller grants in each of several successive years and only gradually come to acquire the entire tract. In the ordinary course plaintiff's property would have been one of the last taken, as it was large and in relatively good condition. The program continued for three years after the change mentioned above. During this time half of the properties in the project area were acquired by the City. In May of 1973 Trenton finally concluded that its redevelopment priorities lay elsewhere and notified the remaining property owners (including plaintiff) that the project was to be abandoned and that their lands would not be taken.

Plaintiff alleges that beginning in 1963 tenants began moving out in direct response to the threatened condemnation. After 1963 it was impossible to find a long-term tenant interested in the building. The space was finally rented to two temporary tenants whose rent barely met the expense of upkeep. After the declaration of blight in 1967 the area surrounding plaintiff's property markedly deteriorated and several buildings in the area were boarded up. Many neighboring properties were purchased or condemned. In 1972 the temporary tenants vacated and thereafter the building was for the most part vacant. Premises which had been generating $160,000 annually in 1963, were yielding $6,300 in rent in 1973.

The trial court, in deciding the motion for summary judgment, relied upon a section of the Blighted Area Act, N.J.S.A. 40:55-21.10, and upon our decisions in *Wilson v. City of Long Branch, Lyons v. City of Camden,* and *Jersey City Redevelopment Agency v. Kugler.* The trial judge concluded that under New Jersey law there can be no taking absent a physical invasion or a direct legal restraint on use. He felt that this was a "harsh" rule and was "completely unfair"; nevertheless, he felt bound by these precedents and entered judgment for the defendant. * * *

The foregoing cases and this statute, considered singly or together, do not establish the proposition that there can be no *de facto* taking absent a physical invasion or a direct restraint on use. Rather they stand for the principle that not every impairment of value establishes a taking. The question of whether a total or substantial destruction of the beneficial use of property amounts to a taking in the constitutional sense was previously before this Court in *Board of Educ. of Morristown v. Palmer,* 46 N.J. 522, 218 A.2d 153 (1966), *rev'g as premature,* 88 N.J.Super. 378, 212 A.2d 564 (App.Div.1965). There we expressly reserved the issue we decide today.

The general question as to when governmental action amounts to a taking of property has always presented a vexing and thorny problem. If there has been a taking, both Federal and State Constitutions require the payment of compensation: *U.S. Const. Amend. V; N.J. Const. art. 1,* ¶ 20. If there has not been a taking, any loss that may have been suffered in *damnum absque injuria;* there has been a noncompensable governmental exercise of the police power.

In partial taking cases, for instance in the construction of a highway, the landowner is entitled to be paid the value of the land taken, together with the diminution in value of the part that remains (severance value), *Village of Ridgewood v. Sreel Investment Corp.,* 28 N.J. 121, 125, 145 A.2d 306 (1958); *State v. Interpace Corp.,* 130 N.J.Super. 322, 329, 327 A.2d 225 (1974). Yet if no part of an adjoining property owner's land is taken, that neighbor will receive no compensation for the loss he may have suffered by virtue of his property now being close to a noisy expressway. *Beseman v. Pennsylvania R.R. Co.*, 50 N.J.L. 235, 13 A. 164 (Sup.Ct. 1888), *aff'd*, 52 N.J.L. 221, 20 A. 169 (E. & A.1889). While the results of these rules are sometimes harsh and seemingly inconsistent, it must be borne in mind that they represent pragmatic legislative and judicial responses to practical problems rather than being products of refined logic.

It was early held that actual appropriation or invasion might be deemed a compensable taking, although unrelated to any condemnation proceeding. From such cases there developed the idea of physical invasion or appropriation as the chief criterion for determining whether a "taking" had occurred. While the physical invasion standard has proven useful in singling out those occasions where compensation should clearly be forthcoming, it is obviously too narrow a standard to identify all instances of compensable taking. Such instances have been found where there had been no physical invasion, and indeed there have been rare occasions where despite physical invasion, no taking was found to have occurred, *National Bd. of YMCA v. United States*, 395 U.S. 85, 89 S.Ct. 1511, 23 L.Ed.2d 117 (1969).

The major departure from the physical invasion test is to be found in the cases dealing with direct restraints on the use of property. While the ultimate criterion for determining whether a taking has occurred in this context is still a subject of dispute, *e.g.*, Sax, "Takings, Private Property and Public Rights," 81 *Yale L.J.* 149 (1971), there is no doubt that land use restraints can amount to a taking of property, *Pennsylvania Coal Co. v. Mahon*, 260 U.S. 393, 43 S.Ct. 158, 67 L.Ed. 322 (1922) (Holmes, J.). We have held upon several occasions that depriving an owner of undeveloped land of all beneficial use of that land for a significant period of time was a "taking."

There is another context that has presented the issue anew as to whether there may be a taking without physical appropriation. The United States Supreme Court has held that low overflights of aircraft which make impossible the continuance of a business on premises adjoining an airport, *United States v. Causby*, (1946), or render living conditions intolerable in a home so located, *Griggs v. Allegheny County*, (1962) constitute compensable takings. Lower Federal courts have tended to limit these holdings to permit recovery only by property owners located directly below the flight path. *Batten v. United States*. But several state courts have rejected this narrow view and have allowed recovery upon the ground that there has been a taking, although the affected premises were close to, but not directly beneath, the flight path.. As the court said in *Martin*,

> We are unable to accept the premise that recovery for interference with the use of land should depend upon anything as irrelevant as whether the wing tip of the aircraft passes through some fraction of an inch of the airspace directly above the plaintiff's land. [391 P.2d at 545]

The case before us is yet another instance of a claim to compensation resting upon an alleged taking, where there is not, and will not be, any physical invasion of the plaintiff's land. It is asserted that the extensive loss of value which has been suffered is in large part attributable to the declaration of blight and to the related activities of the City of Trenton in and around the immediate vicinity of the property. This has had the effect, plaintiff argues, of substantially destroying the value of the property for the use to which it was adapted and to which it was being put.

A declaration of blight is one of the early steps in an urban renewal project. Experience had shown that there is generally a considerable interval of time between such an announcement and the eventual acquisition—whether by purchase or condemnation—of property located in the blighted area. Occasionally, as was the case here, the project will be entirely abandoned before completion. From the time it becomes generally known that an area has been selected as the site of an urban renewal project, as we have pointed out in earlier cases cited above, there ceases to be a ready market for premises within the area. It becomes difficult to find tenants and impossible to enter into long-term leases. Upkeep, maintenance and renovation cease; the value of the property tends constantly to diminish.

The statute adopted by our Legislature in 1967, to which reference is made above, decreed that a property owner would receive an award in condemnation no less than the value of his property on the date of the declaration of blight. This was an important legislative response to the problem, which had been identified and discussed in *Report of the Eminent Domain Revision Commission of New Jersey* 24-28 (1965). Where there eventually is a condemnation action resulting in an award to the landowner, the statute should go far to right what might otherwise be grave injustice. Here, however, there has been no condemnation action instituted by defendant. Hence the statute cannot help this plaintiff, or other property owners who may be similarly situated. This contrast between the unfortunate plight of the owner whose property has suffered the consequences of a declaration of blight, but has not been condemned, and the relatively fair treatment accorded a neighboring owner whose property has in fact been taken, strongly suggests that the treatment of the former has been arbitrary and unfair.

Courts have sought to meet the problem of condemnation blight in various ways. Many cases, while not finding any taking prior to a condemnation award or some form of physical appropriation, have nonetheless allowed the property owner to include the loss he has suffered in the determination of the damages to which he becomes ultimately entitled in eminent domain proceedings. But some courts have found, or have indicated a willingness to find, a compensable taking in this type of case, even though there has been no physical invasion nor any condemnation award. In *Foster v. City of Detroit*, (6th Cir. 1968), condemnation proceedings were commenced in 1950 only to be abandoned in 1960. A second proceeding, commenced a few years later, fixed the value of plaintiff's property as of the initiation of the second action. The court concluded that this did not constitute fair compensation. It said,

> [T]his court now holds that the actions of the defendant which substantially contributed to and accelerated the decline in value of plain-

tiffs' property constituted a "taking" of plaintiffs' property within the meaning of the Fifth Amendment, for which just compensation must be paid. [254 F. Supp. at 665-66]

The court further determined that the taking.actually took place in December, 1954, by which time the activities of the public agency had substantially destroyed the value of the property.

In *Howell Plaza, Inc. v. State Highway Comm'n,* although refusing to order inverse condemnation on the facts before it, the court nonetheless said:

> We have no doubt that there can be a cause of action for inverse condemnation if the facts alleged are sufficient to show that property owners so situated [in the path of a proposed freeway] have been deprived of all, or substantially all, of the beneficial use of their property. [226 N.W.2d at 189]

We hold that where the threat of condemnation has had such a substantial effect as to destroy the beneficial use that a landowner has made of his property, then there has been a taking of property within the meaning of the Constitution.

* * *

As mentioned above, the plaintiff requests relief by way of an order directing the defendant to condemn its property, or in the alternative that it be awarded damages for its loss in value. Generally speaking, condemnation should be ordered only where eventual acquisition appears inevitable, or where equitable considerations mandate that remedy. A private person is generally better able to develop and exploit a piece of real estate than is a municipality and as a matter of policy it is undesirable to remove ratables from the tax rolls. We think it inappropriate to grant this form of relief here.

If, however, the plaintiff is successful in its proofs, it should be entitled to damages. Upon remand the plaintiff will be required to show that there has been substantial destruction of the value of its property and that defendant's activities have been a substantial factor in bringing this about. It will be part of its burden of proof to identify the approximate time that this occurred; this will become the date of taking. Plaintiff will then be called upon to establish what the property would have been then worth had there been no declaration of blight and had the ensuing and related activities of the defendant not occurred. Finally, the value of the property as of the date the project was abandoned must be ascertained. This value should actually be determined as of a date somewhat subsequent to the date abandonment was announced so that the market's response to the lifting of the threat of condemnation can be better evaluated. Plaintiff will be entitled to the difference between these sums, with interest from the date of abandonment. It will also be entitled to interest on the value of its property determined as aforesaid as of the date of the hypothesized taking, calculated from that date to the date of the abandonment of the project, less the excess, if any, of rental receipts over actual disbursements made in maintaining the property for this period.

The judgment of the trial court is reversed and the cause remanded to that court for further proceedings consistent with this opinion.

For additional information on the subject of *de facto* takings and inverse condemnation, the following articles are recommended:

Gandel, "Governmental Liability for Nonphysical Damage to Land," 2 *The Urban Lawyer* 315 (1970).

Annot, "Plotting or Planning in Anticipation of Improvement—A Taking or Damaging of Property Affected," 37 *A.L.R.* 3d 127 (1971).

Mandelker, "Inverse Condemnation: The Constitutional Limits of Public Responsibility," 1966 *Wis.L.R.* 3.

Note, "Inverse Condemnation," 3 *Real Property, Probate & Trust J.* 173 (1968).

C. WHAT IS A PUBLIC USE

(1) Historic Development of the Expansive Definition

The power of eminent domain is the power of government to take private property for a **public use.** To the owner, whose property is taken, eminent domain is a very drastic exercise of governmental power. Historically, it was limited to situations where the property was needed for readily recognized public uses, such as roads, schools, parks, public buildings, etc. In addition, the eminent domain power was originally limited to takings for a public use because of the great danger of political abuse if governmental officials were permitted to take private property from one private person and then give or sell it to another private individual.

Starting in the 1930's the courts began to broaden the definition of "public use" to permit the taking of private property for uses that were not "public" in the traditional sense, i.e., where the *public at large* would use the property. Land taken for a road or a park would be used by the public at large; land taken for a low rent public housing project raised the question whether such a use is a "public use" within the meaning of the constitutional provision. In *United States v. Certain Lands in the City of Louisville*, 78 F.2d 684 (6th Cir. 1935) the United States Court of Appeals held invalid the condemnation of private property by the federal government for a low cost housing and slum clearance program administered by the federal government. The court held that the federal government has no express or implied power granted to it in the Constitution for such a program and consequently there is no "public use" to justify the exercise of the power of eminent domain. The appeal of this decision to the United States Supreme Court was withdrawn just before the oral argument because President Roosevelt feared that the entire New Deal Program could be jeopardized if the Supreme Court upheld the decision of the Court of Appeals. It is for this reason that subsequent federally financed programs of low income housing and urban renewal provided for the administration—including acquisition by eminent domain—by state and local governments.

The question of whether a taking by a local government for slum clearance and low income housing is for a "public use" was decided by the New York Supreme Court in *New York City Housing Authority v. Muller*, 270 N.Y. 333, 1 N.E.2d 153 (1936). In the *Muller* case the court upheld the use of the eminent domain power by the New York City Housing Authority for a public housing project by defining "public use" in terms of public benefits, such as the reduction in crime, the removal of health hazards and the increase in tax revenues that would result from the slum clearance and improvement of the neighborhood. Once having defined "public use" in terms of social and economic benefits the path was cleared for the courts to take the next step in the broadening of the concept of "public use," namely, to permit the taking of property *from one private onwer for the purpose of transferring ownership to another private owner* who would use it to achieve a social or economic public benefit. The validity of the urban renewal program required an affirmative answer to this question because this program involves the acquisition of properties in "blighted" areas and the transfer of those properties to a developer who agrees to demolish or rehabilitate them in accordance with an approved plan.

One of the first cases to uphold an urban renewal program that provided for an eminent domain taking of property and the transfer to a private, rather than a public, owner was *Murray v. LaGuardia,* 291 N.Y. 320, 52 N.E.2d 884 (1943). In this case the New York Court of Appeals upheld the taking of land, under a state urban renewal program, and the transfer of that land to a private company (the Metropolitan Life Insurance Company) for construction of low income housing. The court held that the elimination of substandard housing constitutes a benefit to the total population and is a "public use" even though the property is transferred to a private owner for development.

The principle of *Murray v. LaGuardia* was adopted in most other states, thereby providing the legal basis for the urban renewal programs of the 1950s and 1960s. It then became only a matter of time before the issue would be raised whether the power of eminent domain could be used whenever, in the judgment of governmental officials, private property should be acquired from one private owner and transferred to another private owner who would agree to use it for purposes that would best serve the interests of the community. This power was upheld by the New York Court of Appeals in *Cannata v. City of New York,* set forth below. The issue was resolved without much discussion in the majority opinion. Some of the implications of the decision are described vigorously, if not plaintively, in the dissent by Judge Van Vooris.

CANNATA

v.

CITY OF NEW YORK

11 N.Y.2d 210, 227 N.Y.S. 2a903, 182 N.E.2a395 (1962)

DESMOND, Chief Judge.

Sixty-eight home owners in the Canarsie section of Brooklyn bring this suit for a declaratory judgment that section 72-n of the General Municipal Law, Consol.Laws, c. 24 is unconstitutional on its face and as applied to the proposed redevelopment of the area in which these people live. Since

April, 1961 this statute, or one like it, has become part of article 15 of the General Municipal Law but at the times here in question it was section 72-n of that law (L. 1958, ch. 924). The section authorizes cities to condemn for the purpose of reclamation or redevelopment predominantly vacant areas which are economically dead so that their existence and condition impairs the sound growth of the community and tends to develop slums and blighted areas. There are in the statute declarations by the Legislature that such reclamation and redevelopment of such areas are necessary to protect health, safety and general welfare, to promote the sound growth of the community, etc. Recited by the Legislature were a number of conditions "or combinations thereof" which "with or without tangible physical blight" impair or arrest the sound growth of the community or tend to create slums or blighted areas. There are seven of these listed conditions as follows: subdivision of the land into lots of such form, shape or size as to be incapable of effective development; obsolete and poorly designed street patterns with inadequate access; unsuitable topographic or other physical conditions impeding the development of appropriate uses; obsolete utilities; buildings unfit for use or occupancy as a result of age, obsolescence, etc.; dangerous, unsanitary or improper uses and conditions adversely affecting public health, safety or welfare; scattered improvements. The statute then goes on to declare that land assembly by individual or private enterprise for purpose of redevelopment in such areas is difficult of attainment, that the conditions above listed create tax delinquency and impair the sound growth of the community, that there is a shortage of vacant land in such communities for residential and industrial development, that it is necessary to clear, replan and redevelop such vacant land, and that for such purposes it is necessary that municipalities be given the condemnation and other powers provided by the act. It is particularly to be noted that the statute, while it becomes applicable on the existence of certain listed factors or combination of factors, expressly requires that the area is "predominantly vacant." Of the area here involved at least 75% is vacant. Section 72-n, beginning at paragraph a of subdivision 3 thereof, describes the procedure. The Planning Commission, after public hearing, may designate an area for these purposes providing there are findings that the area is vacant or predominantly vacant, and, in addition, findings as to the existence of some or all of the seven conditions above listed and findings that those conditions impair or arrest the sound growth of the community or tend to create slums or blighted areas. The Planning Commission must then make a detailed statement of the existing physical, economical and sociological conditions in the project area and a general statement of the new project and there must be hearings on a preliminary plan and approval of the preliminary and final plan by the local legislative body, whereupon the municipality may acquire the property by condemnation or otherwise and may sell it for the purpose of clearing, replanning, redevelopment, etc., in accordance with the final plan.

This action came into Special Term on the city's motion for a dismissal of the complaint and for summary judgment and the court held that plaintiffs are not entitled to relief. On appeal to the Appellate Division, Second Department, that court modified only to the extent of directing that judgment go for defendant city, the court holding that in an action for declaratory judgment the granting of a motion by the defendant for judgment on the pleadings properly results not in a dismissal of the complaint but in a declaration on the merits in favor of defendant. The Appellate Division, as stated, modified by directing a declaratory judgment for the city.

This complaint does not allege any failure to carry out any of the statutory procedures. It points out that the Planning Board in this case made findings not only as to the vacancy of a large part of the area but also of these statutory factors: that the land is subdivided into plots of such form, shape and insufficient size as to prevent effective economic development, that the streets are obsolete and of poorly designed patterns, and that the improvements are scattered and incompatible with appropriate development. The real basis of the complaint is its statement that there is in the area no such "tangible physical blight" as to constitute the area of slum. Plaintiffs' argument, most simply put, is that this taking is not for a "public use" because it is a taking of nonslum land for development into a so-called "Industrial Park" or area set aside for new industrial development. We agree with the courts below that an area does not have to be a "slum" to make its redevelopment a public use nor is public use negated by a plan to turn a predominantly vacant, poorly developed and organized area into a site for new industrial buildings.

We see nothing unconstitutional on the face of this statute or in its proposed application to these undisputed facts. Taking of substandard real estate by a municipality for redevelopment by private corporations has long been recognized as a species of public use. The condemnation by the city of an area such as this so that it may be turned into sites for needed industries is a public use.

The judgment should be affirmed, with costs.

VAN VOORHIS, Judge (dissenting).

The appeal is from a declaratory judgment upholding the constitutionality of former section 72-n of the General Municipal Law. Pursuant to this section, which is now repealed and has been re-enacted in modified form in article 15 of the General Municipal Law, the City of New York proposes to condemn about 95 acres in the Canarsie section of Brooklyn to be resold to private developers—for a project to be known as "Flatlands Urban Industrial Park", which, in the opinion of the Board of Estimate and the City Planning Commission, will be more advantageous to the future of the city than the lawful uses to which the properties are being devoted by their present owners. There is no finding that any of this area is substandard or insanitary—i. e., slum. Plaintiffs are owners of 68 private residences which are not claimed to be physically deteriorated. The statute under which condemnation is undertaken authorizes acquisition by the city without physical blight of "vacant or predominately vacant areas". Vacant land comprises 75% of this area. The buildings are clustered together for the most part and not scattered through the vacant lands, nor is it necessary to condemn many of them in order to utilize the vacant lands except as the city planners deem it wise to enlarge the vacant area by converting residential to industrial purposes. This is not a case of slum clearance as the condemnation site was held to be in Kaskel v. Impellitteri. The present exercise of the power of eminent domain transcends anything involved therein. This kind of municipal redevelopment is not based on what was thought to have been the full scope of such enterprises by the New York State Constitutional Convention of 1938, for it goes beyond what is authorized by the housing article (N.Y.Const. art. XVIII) then added to the State Constitution, which provides only for low-rent housing or the reconstruction and rehabilitation of areas that are actually substandard and insanitary. This proceeding is not instituted on the basis that this area is substandard or insanitary but that the city will be improved if real property in good condition is transferred to other private owners who, in the judgment of city planners, will use it for more progressive purposes deemed to be more in accord with development of the municipality. Such a practice may bear hard on the owner, who loses the good will connected with his location (Banner Milling Co. v. State of New York), and, in a world where politics is seldom absent from municipal administration, runs the risk of having his property taken from him to be transferred to more deserving owners.

Matter of Murray v. La Guardia, and Kaskel v. Impellitteri (supra) marked a major step beyond what had theretofore been held to be public purposes in the exercise of the power of eminent domain. Property owners had been accustomed to parting with their real estate involuntarily where required for governmental uses such as highways, public buildings, parks, or for the use of transportation or public utility corporations deemed to be affected with a public interest. In 1936 it was held that substandard and insanitary real estate could be condemned to be replaced with public housing or limited dividend housing corporations. The Murray and Kaskel cases signified a departure in that there condemnation of real property was sanctioned for resale to other private owners, for ordinary private uses not affected with a public interest. The public purpose was conceived to be the elimination of slums to which resale of the subject property to other private owners was incidental. The difference of opinion on the court in Kaskel v. Impellitteri was confined to whether the site to be condemned in that case could be classified as being slum; the court was unanimous concerning the constitutionality of the statute there involved. Now we are faced with a further step in the socialization process. It does not necessarily follow that because the former statute was upheld this statute must be constitutional also. In ruling upon the validity of a statute like this, we are not to proceed upon the assumption that the Legislature has plenary power or none. "The state under the guise of paternal supervision may attempt covertly and gradually to mould its members to its will. The difference as so often is a difference of degree." (Cardozo: The Paradoxes of Legal Science, p. 111.) I see no escape from the duty and responsibility of courts in ruling upon the constitutionality of legislation of this kind to weight the social values which are involved, including the social value of ownership of private property, in order to determine whether the Legislature has exceeded its power under the Federal and State Constitutions.

Conceding that the power of eminent domain has been extended to the elimination of areas that are actually slum, the question here is whether this power can be further extended to the condemnation of factories, stores, private dwellings or vacant land which are properly maintained and are neither substandard nor insanitary, so that their owners may be deprived of them against their will to be resold to a selected group of private developers whose projects are believed by the municipal administration to be more in harmony with the times. It begs the question, in my judgment, merely to assert that such properties are to be taken to prevent them from becoming actually blighted at some future date. It is possible that there are certain definable situations where conditions can constitutionally be eliminated which tend to produce slums, before the properties have deteriorated to that level. It is possible that some of what is contemplated by this statute, including portions of this project, could be accomplished under more limited legislation. What has been attempted under a statute in a particular instance does not determine its constitutionality which is adjudged in the light of what could be done according to its terms. The 1958 statute *sub judice* is not satisfied by eliminating slums. It provides for the elimination of potential slums, which means anything that city planners think does not conform to their designs.

It might be thought, perhaps, that in the march of progress there is no limit to the power of the Legislature even short of authorizing municipal officials to determine, through zoning or eminent domain, who shall be permitted to own real estate in cities and to what purpose each separate parcel may be devoted. The sound view if still, however, that due process includes substantive as well as merely procedural limitations and that under the mores of the day there are substantive limits to what municipalities can do with private property, even by means of statutes enacted under the spur of single-minded city planners imbued with evangelistic fervor. At some stage the rights of private property owners become entitled to be respected, even if their use of their properties does not coincide with the ideas, however enlightened, of the *avant garde*. The public theorists are not always correct; if they had full sway a century and a quarter ago the country would have invested its substance in the construction of canals, which any intelligent theorist would have seen was the effective way to promote the economic development of the United States. The railroads were just around the corner, but their advent was obvious to nobody. Imposing some constitutional limit to the extremely wide scope of this statute would be a far cry from returning to the days of *laissez faire*. There are those among whom the writer is one who believe that, although the Constitution does not enact Mr. Herbert Spencer's *Social Statics*, it nevertheless holds substantive content in social matters and does mandate, at the minimum, some sort of economic or social middle way. It is not for the courts to question the wisdom of the Legislature in exercising the discretion which it has within constitutional limits, but there are limits to legislative power in dealing with private property and in my view they are exceeded by the breadth of the statute on whose constitutionality we are now ruling. The fundamental principle of government still applies which the mentor of the young Cyrus tried to implant in him in ancient Persia. When asked whether a ruler should compel a subject whose coat was too large for him to trade it with another whose coat was too small, if one of them objected to the exchange, the young future ruler replied in the affirmative, for the reason that then each would have a coat that fitted him. The mentor told him that he was wrong, since he had confused expediency with justice. The question here, it seems to me, is where to draw the line between supposed expediency and justice. In Berman v. Parker, the actual decision of the court did not go beyond what this court decided in Kaskel v. Impellitteri, supra, where it was recognized in both opinions that land, buildings or improvements, not in themselves insanitary or substandard, may be included in the condemnation site if necessary for the effective clearance, replanning, reconstruction or rehabilitation of the essentially slum area of which such land or property is a part. The question before the United States Supreme Court in the Berman case was whether a department store could be condemned which was so connected with a blighted area that the latter could not be rehabilitated without including the land occupied by the store. That was not a case, like this, of so-called "intangible blight." The principal area there was substandard and insanitary without dispute: 64.3% of the dwellings in it were beyond repair, 18.4% needed major repairs, only 17.3% were satisfactory; 57.8% of the dwellings had outside toilets, 60.3% had no baths, 29.3% lacked electricity, 82.2% had no wash basins or laundry tubs, 83.8% lacked central heating. All of those circumstances were noted in the opinion of the court by Mr. Justice Douglas, who recognized that there was a basis on which the municipal planning commission could determine that the subject property was so interrelated with the slum properties that the latter could not be effectively eliminated without the former. Although the opinion uses broad language in certain paragraphs, which do speak of unlimited power in the planning commission, these *obiter dicta* should be limited and construed by what the same Supreme Court Justice said in his dissenting opinion in United States v. Wunderlich: "Absolute discretion is a ruthless master. It is more destructive of freedom than any of man's other inventions." Nothing in the facts decided in Berman contravenes, it seems to me, the trenchant statements in the opinion in the same case of the three-Judge District Court (Schneider v. District of Columbia, D.C., 117 F.Supp. 705, 719–720), which are perhaps more applicable to this case than to that in which the words were spoken:

Even if the line between regulation and seizure, between the power to regulate and the power to seize, is not always etched deeply, it is there. And, even if we progress in our concepts of the 'general welfare', we are not at liberty to obliterate the boundary of governmental power fixed by the Constitution.

"The terms 'public use' and 'public purpose' have never been defined with precision, and cannot be. Localities, customs and times change, and with them the needs of the public may change. But even the most liberal courts have put boundaries upon the meanings. One eminent authority sums up the matter by saying that the courts which go furthest in sustaining the power of eminent domain hold that 'anything which tends to enlarge the resources, increase the industrial energies, and promote the productive power of any considerable number of the inhabitants of a section of the state, or which leads to the growth of towns and the creation of new resources for the employment of capital and labor' constitutes a public use. We think so unqualified a definition cannot be sustained, because every factory or mercantile house of any size meets that definition to some degree, and most certainly the Government has not an unrestricted power to seize one man's property and sell it to another for the building of a factory or a store. The decisions of the courts which used such sweeping language and which are cited to us fall far short of supporting the contention made to us in the present case. We shall discuss them in a moment.

"It is said that the established meaning of eminent demain includes measures for the 'general welfare' and that new social doctrines have so enlarged the concept of public welfare as to include all measures designed for the public benefit. The difficulty lies somewhat in the unqualified philosophical declaration, but it lies more in the practicality that some person or persons must determine, if that be the rule, what is the public benefit. Therein lies the insuperable obstacle, in the American view. There is no more subtle means of transforming the basic concepts of our government, of shifting from the preeminence of individual rights to the preeminence of government wishes, than is afforded by redefinition of 'general welfare', as that term is used to define the Government's power of seizure. If it were to be determined that it includes whatever a commission, authorized by the Congress and appointed by the President, determines to be in the interest of 'sound development', without definition of 'sound development', the ascendancy of government over the individual right to property will be complete. Such ascendancy would logically follow over the rights of free speech and press, it seems to us.

Few more persuasive illustrations could be found than the statute (not necessarily the particular project) now before us for decision of situations where "Absolute discretion", in the language of Mr. Justice Douglas, can be "more destructive of freedom than any of man's other inventions." I do not imply that this power necessarily would be used to that end, but potentially can be so employed. The constitutionality is to be tested by what can be done under this statute. If we uphold its validity, that means upholding everything which is an integral part of the act that can be done under its language.

Whether or not a proposed condemnation is for a public purpose is a judicial question. Perhaps the power of eminent domain might be invoked for the rehabilitation of vacant areas subdivided into lots of such irregular form and shape or insufficient size, depth, or width, as to render them incapable of effective or economic development; or rendered sterile by obsolete or poorly designed street patterns with inadequate access to such vacant areas rendering them unsuitable for appropriate development. It is possible that there are other conditions enumerated in former section 72-n of the General Municipal Law which could furnish a basis for condemnation. Nevertheless this act contains, in my judgment, fundamental defects which invalidate it. Thus it declares that in event of any of the factors existing which are enumerated in subparagraph a of subdivision 1, "with or without tangible physical blight," real property may be condemned if such areas impair or arrest "the sound growth of the community and tend to create slums and blighted areas." Among the factors enumerated are unsuitable topographical or other physical conditions *impeding the development of appropriate land uses*; an obsolete system of utilities serving the area, whatever that may mean; buildings and structures unfit for use and occupancy as a result of age, obsolescence, *improper uses and conditions which adversely affect the general welfare*; scattered improvements *which retard the development* of the land. When asked upon the argument of the appeal whether this means that the power of eminent domain may be invoked in any case of this nature where, in the judgment of municipal officers, the property should be acquired and sold to some other private owners who would agree to use it for purposes that would accord more nearly in their judgment with the progress of the municipality, the Corporation Counsel replied in the affirmative. He could hardly do otherwise, in view of the language of the statute.

Neither is it sufficiently clear or definite what constitutes a "predominantly" vacant area. In order that the power of eminent domain may be invoked for this purpose, under this statute the area to be condemned must be "vacant" or "predominantly vacant." In the case of this project it appears that the area is 75% vacant. We were told upon the argument that it would be enough if it were 50% vacant. The land which is occupied by buildings (plaintiffs' own 68 private residences which have not been found to be in inferior condition or improperly maintained) appears to be linked to the project for the reason that a larger area than the vacant land is needed for the proposed industrial park, rather than that it is an integral part of an "intangibly" blighted area. However, that may be in regard to this particular project, no such limitation is imposed by the statute itself whose constitutionality is being tested, which purports to render a finding by the governing body conclusive that an area to be condemned is "predominantly vacant" so as to enable almost any proportion of buildings to be condemned along with vacant land. On the basis of indefiniteness alone it seems to me that this statute fails to meet recognized constitutional requirements. Although the requirement of definiteness is most frequently presented in criminal cases, it has equal application to sumptuary statutes such as this depriving persons of property *in invitum*.

For the reasons stated, I dissent and vote to reverse the judgment appealed from and to grant to the plaintiffs the relief demanded in the complaint.

Judge Van Voorhis found the occasion to write another dissenting opinion on the same issue one year later in *Courtesy Sandwich Shop, Inc. v. Port of New York Authority*, 12 N.Y.2d 379, 240 N.Y.S.2d 1, 190 N.E.2d 402 (1963), where the New York Court of Appeals upheld an eminent domain taking of land for the World Trade Center as a "public use" even though portions of the proposed structures were to be devoted to purposes to be used for the production of revenue for expenses of the port development project. His argument is summarized in the following statement from his dissenting opinion in that case.

* * * To hold a purpose to be public merely for the reason that it is invoked by a public body to serve its ideas of the public good, it seems to me, can be done only on the assumption that we have passed the point of no return, that the trade, commerce and manufacture of our principal cities can be conducted by private enterprise only on a diminishing scale and that private capital should progressively be displaced by public capital which should increasingly take over. The economic and geographical advantages of the City of New York have withstood a great deal of attrition and can probably withstand more, but there is a limit beyond which socialization cannot be carried without destruction of the constitutional bases of private ownership and enterprise. It seems to me to be the part of courts to enforce the constitutional rights of property, which are involved here. * * *

In spite of the concerns and fears expressed by Judge Van Voorhis, the prevailing judicial definition of "public use" is the one offered by Mr. Justice Douglas in *Berman v. Parker.*

BERMAN

v.

PARKER

348 U.S. 26, 75S.Ct. 98, 99L.Ed. 27 (1954)

In this decision the United States Supreme Court upheld the use of the eminent domain power for an urban renewal program for the District of Columbia. The following paragraphs contain the most frequently cited statements from this landmark decision:

The power of Congress over the District of Columbia includes all the legislative powers which a state may exercise over its affairs. We deal, in other words, with what traditionally has been known as the police power. An attempt to define its reach or trace its outer limits is fruitless, for each case must turn on its own facts. The definition is essentially the product of legislative determinations addressed to the purposes of government, purposes neither abstractly nor historically capable of complete definition. Subject to specific constitutional limitations, when the legislature has spoken, the public interest has been declared in terms well-nigh conclusive. In such cases the legislature, not the judiciary, is the main guardian of the public needs to be served by social legislation, whether it be Congress legislating concerning the District of Columbia or the States legislating concerning local affairs. This principle admits of no exception merely because the power of eminent domain is involved. The role of the judiciary in determining whether that power is being exercised for a public purpose is an extremely narrow one.

Public safety, public health, morality, peace and quiet, law and order—these are some of the more conspicuous examples of the traditional application of the police power to municipal affairs. Yet they merely illustrate the scope of the power and do not delimit it. Miserable and disreputable housing conditions may do more than spread disease and crime and immorality. They may also suffocate the spirit by reducing the people who live there to the status of cattle. They may indeed make living an almost insufferable burden. They may also be an ugly sore, a blight on the community which robs it of charm, which makes it a place from which men turn. The misery of housing may despoil a community as an open sewer may ruin a river.

We do not sit to determine whether a particular housing project is or is not desirable. The concept of the public welfare is broad and inclusive. The values it represents are spiritual as well as physical, aesthetic as well as monetary. It is within the power of the legislature to determine that the community should be beautiful as well as healthy, spacious as well as clean, well-balanced as well as carefully patrolled. In the present case, the Congress and its authorized agencies have made determinations that take into account a wide variety of values. It is not for us to reappraise them. If those who govern the District of Columbia decide that the Nation's Capital should be beautiful as well as sanitary, there is nothing in the Fifth Amendment that stands in the way.

Once the object is within the authority of Congress, the right to realize it through the exercise of eminent domain is clear. For the power of eminent domain is merely the means to the end. Once the object is within the authority of Congress, the means by which it will be attained is also for Congress to determine. Here one of the means chosen is the use of private enterprise for redevelopment of the area. Appellants argue that this makes the project a taking from one businessman for the benefit of another businessman. But the means of executing the project are for Congress and Congress alone to determine, once the public purpose has been established. The public end may be as well or better served through an agency of private enterprise than through a department of government—or so the Congress might conclude. We cannot say that public ownership is the sole method of promoting the public purposes of community redevelopment projects. What we have said also disposes of any contention concerning the fact that certain property owners in the area may be permitted to repurchase their properties for redevelopment in harmony with the over-all plan. That, too, is a legitimate means which Congress and its agencies may adopt, if they choose.

In the present case, Congress and its authorized agencies attack the problem of the blighted parts of the community on an area rather than on a structure-by-structure basis. That, too, is opposed by appellants. They maintain that since their building does not imperil health or safety nor contribute to the making of a slum or a blighted area, it cannot be swept into a redevelopment plan by the mere dictum of the Planning Commission or the Commissioners. The particular uses to be made of the land in the project were determined with regard to the needs of the particular community. The experts concluded that if the community were to be healthy, if it were not to revert again to a blighted or slum area, as though possessed of a congenital disease, the area must be planned as a whole. It was not enough, they believed, to remove existing buildings that were insanitary or unsightly. It was important to redesign the whole area so as to eliminate the conditions that cause slums—the overcrowding of dwellings, the lack of parks, the lack of adequate streets and alleys, the absence of recreational areas, the lack of light and air, the presence of outmoded street patterns. It was believed that the piecemeal approach, the removal of individual structures that were offensive, would be only a palliative. The entire area needed redesigning so that a balanced, integrated plan could be developed for the region, including not only new homes but also schools, churches, parks, streets, and shopping centers. In this way it was hoped that the cycle of decay of the area could be controlled and the birth of future slums prevented. Such diversification in future use is plainly relevant to the maintenance of the desired housing standards and therefore within congressional power.

* * *

(2) Excess Condemnation

"Excess condemnation" describes the legal issue that arises if a governmental agency tries to acquire more land than is necessary for the specific public purpose it seeks to achieve. For example, the public purpose for the land taken for the bed of a road is clear. However, a legal issue arises relating to whether there is a sufficient public purpose to justify the taking of *land abutting the road* for the purpose of either (1) subsequent sale at a later date to help defray the costs of road construction, or (2) limiting its use to enhance the esthetic or environmental character of the adjoining area. The constitutions of California, New York, New Jersey and other states specifically authorize the taking of *excess land* abutting the land taken for a public use. The constitutions of other states do not provide such authorization and in those states it is not clear whether excess condemnation is valid. For additional information about this subject see:

Note, "Excess Condemnation–To Take or Not to Take–A Functional Analysis," 15 *N.Y.L.F.* 119 (1969).

Matheson, "Excess Condemnation in California: Proposals for Statutory and Constitutional Change," 42 *So. Cal.L.R.* 421 (1969).

Note, "Eminent Domain–The Meaning of the Term 'Public Use'–Its Effect on Excess Condemnation," 18 *Mercer L.R.* 274 (1966).

(3) Advance Acquisition: Land Banking

If a governmental agency seeks to use the power of eminent domain to **acquire property far in advance** of the time it expects to use it, a legal question will arise whether there is a "public purpose" to justify the taking. In *Grand Rapids Board of Education v. Baczewski,* 340 Mich. 265, 65 N.E.2d 810 (1954), the court held that the taking of property for school purposes thirty years before it was needed for that purpose is invalid. To justify the taking of property in condemnation proceedings the governmental agency must show that the property will either be immediately used for the purpose for which it is sought to be condemned or within the near future.

On the other hand, all of the details of the plans of the proposed use need not be completed before the time of the taking. For example, in *Carlor v. City of Miami,* 62 S.2d 897 (Fla. 1053), the court upheld a taking for airport facilities even though at the time of the taking the governmental agency did not have the plans or the funds for the construction of the airport. The court said: "It is not necessary that a political subdivision of the state have money on hand, plans and specifications prepared and all other preparations necessary for immediate construction before it can determine the necessity for taking private property for a public purpose."

The question whether there is a "public purpose" to justify the taking of land for purpose not specified at the time of the acquisition raises the issue of the validity of **land banking.** The term "land banking" is used to describe the program by which land is acquired and held in reserve for the purpose of achieving planning objectives whether or not any particular use is specified at the time of the acquisition. The National Commission on Urban Problems has recommended land banking programs for the purposes of: (1) controlling the timing, location, type and scale of future development; (2) assuring the continuing availability of sites for development; (3) reserving to the public the Increment in value of land resulting from government services and inflation, and (4) preventing urban sprawl. (For additional discussion, see *National Commission On Urban Problems, Building The American City* 251 (1968))

The constitutionality of land banking programs in the United States is still in doubt because of the limited number of judicial decisions on the subject. In *Commonwealth of Puerto Rico v. Rosso,* 95 P.R.R. 488 (1967), *appeal dismissed,* 393 U.S. 14 (1968), the Supreme Court of Puerto Rico upheld the Puerto Rican land banking program and found that "public use" for the taking is shown by the social benefit and common good to be derived from the program. In spite of the paucity of judicial decisions on this issue The American Law Institute has included land banking as a major provision of the *Model Land Development Code.* For additional information on the subject see:

Note, "Public Land Banking: A New Praxis For Urban Growth," 23 *Case W. Res. L. Rev.* 897 (1972).

Fitch & Mack, "Land Banking," in *The Good Earth of America* 134 (Harris ed. 1974).

K. Parsons, *Public Land Acquisition For New Communities and The Control of Urban Growth: Alternative Strategies* (1973).

S. Kamm, *Land Banking: Public Policy Alternatives and Dilemmas* (Urban Institute Paper No. 112–28, 1970).

(4) Open Space Preservation

Although there is some doubt about whether the acquisition of land for purposes not specified at the time of the taking is a "public use" within the meaning of eminent domain provisions in the federal and state constitutions, there is no doubt that public recreation and the conservation of natural resources constitute a "public use." Programs of **open space preservation** have been adopted in New Jersey (Green Acres Land Acquisition Act of 1961, N.J.S.A. 13:8A–1 et seq.), Connecticut, Illinois and other states. For additional information on this subject see:

Krasnowiecki & Paul, "The Preservation of Open Space in Metropolitan Areas," 110 *U.Penn.L.Rev.* 179 (1961).

S. Siegel, *The Law of Open Space* (Regional Plan Asso. 1960).

Evelett, "An Appraisal of Techniques to Preserve Open Space," 9 *Vill.L.Rev.* 559 (1964).

Note, "Techniques for Preserving Open Spaces," 75 *Harv.L.Rev.* 1622 (1962).

D. What is Just Compensation

The federal and state constitutions require governments to pay **just compensation** to the owner for the property taken by the power of eminent domain. **Just compensation** has been defined as the full equivalent in money for the value of the property taken. The "full equivalent in money" has been defined as the **market value** of the property. **Market value,** in turn, has been defined as the price that a buyer, willing and able, but not obliged to buy, would pay to a seller, willing and able, but not obliged to sell. Most eminent domain litigation involves the question of what is the market value of the property taken by governmental action.

Unfortunately, there is no one method of evaluation that can be used to determine the value of the many different types of property. For example, when a private house is taken by eminent domain, the usual method of evaluation used is **comparable sales.** On the other hand the value of an apartment house is usually best determined by **capitalization of income.** Buildings that have been constructed for a special purpose, such a brewery, have a very limited market and will be evaluated by the **cost less less depreciation** method. The value of vacant and undeveloped land will be based upon its **highest and best use.** The cases that follow illustrate each of these theories of valuation.

(1) Comparable Sales

Suppose that a single family house of the following description is taken by eminent domain to make way for a new highway: wood frame, two story, 1500 square feet of enclosed space, including four bedrooms and two bathrooms, on one half acre, part of a large development consisting of 250 similar houses. The original selling price, ten years ago was $40,000. What is just compensation for the taking of this house?

Under the general rule of valuation, just compensation would be the market value of the house, which in turn would depend upon the price that buyers would be willing to pay for such housing in the area. In most eminent domain proceedings it is usually not possible to provide evidence of a bona fide offer to buy that particular house to establish its market value. Under the **comparable sales method** the market value of the house in question would be determined by obtaining evidence of the selling price of similar or comparable houses in the area. The persuasiveness of the evidence that the selling price of other houses is an accurate indication of the market price of the house in question will depend upon whether the other houses are in fact comparable in (1) construction, (2) condition, (3) location and (4) time.

Where reliable evidence of comparable sales is available this method of determining market value may be the most accurate method of determining just compensation. However, as the *State of Louisiana Dept. of Highways v. Crow* indicates, evidence of other methods of evaluation may be considered also.

STATE OF LOUISIANA, DEPT. OF HIGHWAYS

v.

CROW

286 So.2d 353 (Louisiana, 1973)

SANDERS, Chief Justice.

Pursuant to the quick-taking statute, the Department of Highways expropriated four parcels of land from the Crow holdings in Slidell, Louisiana. Concomitant with the taking, the State deposited $135,425.00 in the registry of the court as compensation for the land and buildings taken and for severance damage to parts of the properties not taken.

Of the four parcels, the valuations of two were stipulated. The valuations of parcels 1–3 and 1–4 were placed at issue at trial. The trial court, after a hearing on the merits, rendered judgment fixing compensation for the property rights expropriated at the sum of $172,969.85 and granting severance damages in the amount of $10,117.10. The award totaled $183,086.95, subject to a credit for the $135,425.00 already withdrawn by the Crows from the registry of the court. The trial court, in reaching this award, evaluated the land and buildings taken by the so-called "income method."

The Court of Appeal for the First Circuit rejected the income method of valuation and reduced the compensation to the $135,425.00 already deposited plus $9,754.00, representing the additional compensation stipulated by the parties as due for the two parcels which were not at issue. 273 So.2d 721. In reducing the award, the Court of Appeal essentially held that, whenever sales figures of comparable tracts exist, valuations predicated upon the capitalization of income must, as a matter of law, be disregarded. We granted certiorari, primarily to review this rigid approach to valuation. We now reject the holding of the Court of Appeal.
* * *

Article I, Section 2 of the Louisiana Constitution provides:

"No person shall be deprived of life, liberty or property, except by due process of law. Except as otherwise provided in this Constitution, private property shall not be taken or damaged except for public purposes and after just and adequate compensation is paid."

In compliance with the constitutional mandate, this Court has long held that a landowner is entitled to the monetary equivalent of the property taken, or the market value.

All of the tools of evaluation, including the determination of highest and best use, the study of comparables, cost of structure and depreciation studies, and income analysis, are only means to fixing just and adequate compensation. No one of these tools is an end in itself.

It is true that, in the usual case, the study of comparables is the primary tool of analysis. This Court recognized that principle in State v. Tolmas, (1959). In that decision, however, we further noted:

"Plaintiff's evidence of comparable sales is not conclusive; neither is defendants, testimony as to one comparable sale. The determination of the market value of the instant property cannot, therefore, be limited to only a consideration of comparable sales."

What this means seems clear. If there is a priority attached to the study of comparables, it exists only because, in most cases, that approach is most likely to produce accurate results, insuring just and adequate compensation. When, however, the study of comparables does not, as a matter of fact, serve to best insure an accurate evaluation, the prime consideration of just and adequate compensation requires that courts be free to use any other method better suited to a correct assessment of value.
* * *
Here, the trial court used income analysis for reasons rooted in the facts of the case. These included the dissimilarities of the existing comparables, the inadequacy of the cost figures presented by the state, the use-division of parcel 1–3 which had been made by the landowners, and similar considerations. The Court of Appeal repudiated none of these factors. The reduction in the award was ordered only because of this holding:

"The adoption of the income approach in establishing value may be material in certain cases, but where they have been sales of comparable property, and improvements can be evaluated accurately by cost of reproduction new less depreciation, valuations arrived at by capitalization of rental value should be disregarded."

The holding is incompatible with the principle of just compensation and must be rejected. We hold, therefore, that, even when comparable sales are available courts are free to consider income studies if, on the facts of the case, these studies provide a substantial aid in evaluation. Our holding approves a similar decision of the First Circuit Court of Appeal in State v. Lewis, (1962). There, the Court of Appeal stated:

"The jurisprudence of this State recognizes that the best measure of compensation or market value is obtained through the use of comparable sales. However, in the absence of such comparable sales, a valuation based upon rental income from the property may be resorted to, and further, *even where there are comparable sales, utilization of the rental income may be resorted to for the purpose of supplementing the appraisal. . . .*" (Italics ours).

* * *

For the reasons assigned, the judgment of the Court of Appeal is reversed. The judgment of the trial court is reinstated and made the judgment of this Court.

---

(2) Capitalization of Income

Suppose that an apartment house of the following description is taken by eminent domain to make way for new municipal building: the net income (gross rental income, less expenses) from the building is $50,000; the rate of return expected by investors in apartment houses in this area is 15%; the original cost of construction 20 years ago was $100,000; the present cost of constructing a similar building is $500,000. What is just compensation for the taking of this building?

After considering all of the above information it is essential to remember that just compensation is to be measured by **market value,** i.e., the price that a willing and able buyer would pay to a willing and able seller after each has negotiated the best deal that he/she could make. For this reason the **rate of return** that investors in·this area would expect to receive from this type of investment becomes the critical fact in determining the price that a buyer would pay for the property, which in turn will determine its market value. In the illustration above investors in the area would expect a return on investment of fifteen (15%) percent; the net income of the building is $50,000; thus, it becomes possible to calculate the amount that an investor would pay for this building by **capitalizing the income. Capitalization of income** is a method of determining the value of income-producing property by dividing the dollar amount of net income by the expected rate of return, known as the **capitalization rate.** This simple arithmetic operation is derived from an elementary formula that expresses the relationship between Principal (or Capital Investment), Interest and Rate of Return:

Thus:

$$\text{Income} = \text{Principal} \times \text{Rate of Return}$$

$$\$50,000 = P \times .15$$

$$\frac{50,000}{.15} = P$$

$$333,333 = P$$

From this relationship it should be clear that once the dollar amount of the net income is determined, the value of the property will depend upon the rate of return that investors would expect from that kind of investment. The expected rate of return, known as the **capitalization rate,** or **cap rate** will vary depending upon the current rate of return from other investments and the comparative amount of risk of the investment. Thus an investor would expect a higher rate of return from an investment involving greater risk. Applying the above formula, the higher the expected rate of return, the lower will be the amount that the investor will pay. Consequently, with a specified amount of net income, riskier investments will have a lower market value than safer investments. For example, in the above illustration, if the building were subject to numerous housing code violations, an investor might insist upon a return of 20% rather than only 15% and consequently the prince he would pay (i.e., the market value) would be only $250,000:

Income = Principal × Rate of Return

$50,000 = P × .20

$$\frac{50,000}{.20} = P$$

250,000 = P

Although the theory and mathematics of the capitalization of income method are both forthright and simple, the application of this method of evaluation frequently raises litigable issues involving the details of the method of computing net income and the validity of the *cap rate* selected. Another cause of litigation is the attempt to use the capitalization of income method to determine the value of a business whose income depends more upon managerial skill than rental income of the premises. The following cases illustrate this problem.

DENVER URBAN RENEWAL AUTHORITY

v.

COOK

186 Colo. 182, 526 P.2d 652 (1974)

GROVES, Justice.

This case involves a condemnation action brought by the Denver Urban Renewal Authority (DURA). The property being condemned (at 1601 Larimer Street, Denver) was owned by the Cook family who leased it to a family-owned corporation, Dave Cook's Sporting Goods Inc. The corporation operated a retail sporting goods store at this location.

The court-appointed commission found that the value of the real estate and improvements was $467,000 and judgment was entered accordingly.

DURA appealed to the Court of Appeals, contesting the amount of the compensation award and claiming that in its determination of fair market value the commission was improperly permitted to consider evidence of the corporation's gross sales. We granted certiorari to the Court of Appeals as to Denver Urban Renewal Authority v. Cook, affirmed the award of the district court. We reverse.

Both parties' expert valuation witnesses agreed that the capitalization of income or rental value approach is a recognized method for determining the fair market value of property being condemned. In order to arrive at a fair market value under this method it is necessary to determine the reasonable rental value of the property. Valuation witnesses for both parties agreed that the actual amount of rent which the corporation paid to the Cook family was too low and did not fairly represent the property's reasonable rental value. The Cooks' appraisers arrived at a reasonable rental value by calculating a percentage of the corporation's gross sales. It is the use of the gross sales figure as a determinant of rental value to which DURA has taken issue.

It is well settled that when land occupied for business purposes is taken by eminent domain, the owner is entitled to compensation only for the value of the land and improvements but not for the value of any business conducted thereon. On the theory that profits derived from such a business are more a function of the entrepreneurial skills of management than the value of the land, evidence of business profits is not admissible as a determinant of the fair market value of the condemned property. *See* 4 Nichols on Eminent Domain, §§ 12.3121 and 13.3 (3rd ed. 1971). Under the business profits rule, evidence of the character and volume of business conducted on condemned property is admissible only for the limited purpose of showing a use for which the property may be utilized.

We have not previously ruled on the specific question of whether evidence of gross sales may be admitted for the purpose of determining the reasonable rental value of condemned property. Some jurisdictions have ruled that evidence of gross sales falls under the business profits rule and is therefore inadmissible. At least one jurisdiction has forbidden the specific valuation method utilized by the Cooks' experts in this case. "It is not proper in Maryland for an expert to arrive at fair market value by capitalizing gross sales since the nature and location of the property may be but a minor factor contributing to the establishment of a successful business." Other jurisdictions, however, do admit evidence of gross sales as a determinant of reasonable rental value.

We believe that gross sales like profits are more inextricably tied to the management and administration of a business than to the value of the property upon which the business is situated. The same reasons that cause the amount of profits to be an inappropriate measure of the value of the land are applicable to the use of gross sales figures, albeit to a lesser degree.

We hold that evidence of gross sales falls within the purview of the business profits rule and, therefore, is inadmissible as a determinant of a reasonable rental value.

The judgment of the Court of Appeals is reversed, and the cause is remanded to the Court of Appeals for return of the cause to the district court with directions to vacate the award and to order a new hearing to be conducted consonant with the views expressed herein.

STATE

v.

BARE

141 Mont. 288, 377 P.2d 357 (1962)

CASTLES, Justice.

This is an appeal from a judgment entered on a jury verdict in a condemnation action brought by the State, appellant here, to acquire Interstate Highway right-of-way. The defendants, respondents here, are the owners and operators of a 280 acre dairy farm in Park County.

Complaint seeking condemnation was filed. Necessity for the taking was found by the district court, and commissioners to appraise the property were appointed. The commissioners rendered their report, finding the value of the land and improvements taken to be $7,078 and the severance damages to the remainder at $33,105 for a total award of $40,183.

From the award the State appealed. Trial was had before a jury. The jury awarded $15,948.90 for the land and improvements taken and $26,297.50 for severance damages to the portion not taken for a total judgment of $42,246.40.

The Bare dairy farm consisted of 280 acres. It had been operated as a dairy farm for twenty-five years. It had somewhat over 100 acres of irrigated and subirrigated hay land and the balance was in dry land pasture. Bares had about 35 head of cattle and were licensed to milk 20 head. They had about 135 customers for their milk and sold $40 to $50 worth of milk a day. The raised their own hay and pasture and bought feed grain.

The Interstate Highway right-of-way runs almost through the middle of the farm, dividing it into two main parts and segregating another smaller part. The right-of-way went through several improvements, a small house, a root cellar, two wells, and covered several springs. The meandering creek channel was moved and straightened. Any practical access from one part to the other was cut off. All witnesses agreed that so far as dairying was concerned, Bares were out of business. The taking consisted of 30.81 acres of the heart of the farm.

The landowners testified and a real estate broker testified as to value as will be later discussed. * * *

At the trial, the landowners, Donald and Tam Bare testified. Donald did not testify as to value. Tam expressed an opinion as to value. On direct examination Mr. Bare stated the farm was worth $150,000, that the taking would require $80,000 to make him whole. He testified that the 30.81 acres taken were worth $250 per acre for a total of $7,702.50. Then he testified to the effect that, since the taking would put him out of the dairy business, the loafing shed was made worthless, the calving shed was rendered worthless, the dairy barn and milking equipment was worthless except as storage places. He placed values of $2,500 on the loafing shed, $1,500 on the calving shed, $7,000 on the value of the dairy barn, the purpose of which was destroyed.

On cross-examination, Mr. Bare testified that he and his borther made a net income of $5,000 on the place in 1959 on a gross income of about $15,000.

The next witness for the landowners, Mr. Paul Working, a real estate dealer in Livingston, was qualified as a land appraiser. He testified that he appraised the property here. On direct examination he was asked what method he used to appraise the property. He said, "I valued the place on income, and I adopted the final figure of the damges to the income of the Bare brothers, the damages of the Bare brothers, the damages to the damages they'd be entitled to. * * * I tried three methods. I used three methods one of which was comparable sales, another of which was a cost, that is, assume you go out and buy a piece of land, replace the buildings on it, and then depreciate them out to the present condition; and I didn't feel that either one of these other methods adequately represented the damage done to the Bare brothers. * * * I used the income method for my final result."

The capitalization of income method described by Mr. Working was applied as follows:

"I started by * * * using the Bare brothers' income tax statement [adjusted to a 12 month operation for a single year] * * *
"I started with an annual gross income * * * of $12,858."

The witness then described expense items of feed, seed, machine hire, supplies, repairs, veterinary charges, gas and fuel, taxes, insurance, utilities, freight, upkeep of machinery, depreciation on real estate, depreciation on livestock, replacement of livestock. He found a total expense item of $7,373.64 which he deducted from the gross of $12,858 leaving a net income (which would be net income for income tax purposes for the two men) of $5,494.67 before the taking.

Then Mr. Working estimated an income after the taking on what he termed the probable use of what was left. This probable use he based on 65 acres of irrigated land with production of 3 tons of hay per acre at an average price of $22.50 per ton for a figure of $4,387 for production of hay per year. Then as he described it: "Now then, since that [referring to the land above] cannot be operated as a unit, I assumed that the Bare brothers are landlords, as landlords they will get half of that hay production [50-50 share crop arrangement]. So their net from the hay production would be $2,193.75. Now there is a certain value in certain months of the year for pasture in this. * * * I assigned an animal use unit of 60, at a cost of $5.00 per unit, which would bring us $300 in this income figure." Then Working assigned a value of $900 per year income for the residence. Then he deducted certain items such as taxes, seed as sharecroppers, repairs to buildings, and depreciation on buildings representing a cost value of $1,180.34 annually. Thus he reasoned that the gross income after the taking was $3,393.75 with a net income of $2,213.41.

He then took:

The net income including labor before taking: $5,494.67

Minus net income without labor after taking: $2,213.41

Difference in income: $3,281.26

This latter figure he related: "I capitalized that figure at 5½ percent which means estimating the *amount of money that you would have to invest at 5½ percent to have an annual income of this amount,* and that figure is $59,471. I rounded that figure off to $59,500, which I estimate is the damage that has been done to the Bare brothers' operation." (There is a slight arithmetical error that appears here in the record, but it does not concern our discussion.)

Note the comparison of incomes used. The "before taking" income is income attributable to the land *plus* the labor involved. The estimated "after-taking" income is on a share-crop basis; that is, it is income attributable to the land itself *without* labor. Then note, that the capitalization rate is described as *money invested;* in other words, a rate figured on income attributable to investment in the land only. This is like deducting two heifers from five horses and getting three pigs to determine how much bacon is lost.

Continuing on with Mr. Working's testimony, on cross-examination, he testified that he only used figures for one year, viz., 1960, although he "thought" it represented an average year. He said he had used three methods in appraisal, cost approach, market data, and income, but he could not respond to any other method than the one above because, "I don't have that figure here." He could not give a value to the remaining land. He explained his use of the income approach to the income before taking by saying "Many people who like country living are satisfied with a greatly reduced income comparable to what they could have gotten from their money invested in some other way."

This statement does not coincide with the use of the so-called capitalization of income method. The very basis of the method, particularly as to the rate of capitalization, is on the basis of invested capital. * * *

In analyzing the capitalization of income approach, a discussion contained in the 1962 Report of Committee on Condemnation and Condemnation Procedure of the Section of Local Government Law of the American Bar Association commends itself to our quotation. There it is said at p. 34,

> "In the area of eminent domain as in other fields of law, concise, theoretical standards of valuation often are more effective in the abstract than when subjected to the rigors of practical application. In condemnation proceedings the yardstick used by the courts is 'market value' or 'fair market value.' The fictional representation of a willing buyer and a willing seller arriving at an agreed price in the open market employed by the courts, however, often does not provide just compensation." And in discussing the capitalization of *rental* income this statement was made at p. 38:
> "Admittedly the best method of arriving at market value is the use of recent sales of comparable property. Additionally, the 'income method' may be used to determine market value, where appropriate.

In fact the income producing capacity of real estate is one of the most, if not the most important consideration in determining the value of real estate. However, the majority of courts restrict this type of testimony. This stems in part from the principle that business profits are considered too speculative to be considered in determining value, and partly because courts view comparable sales as a more objective test. Rental property, however, is an exception to this rule. If the monthly or annual rental can be proved with a reasonable degree of certainty, in the absence of other evidence, courts will consider it as a factor in determining value. Normally the rental will be projected according to the going rate of interest in the financial community."

From what we have set out, in Mr. Working's application of the method it is patent that this is not an appropriate application. Further, in this case, none of the figures, being based on one year only, and in part pure estimates, have such degree of certainty as to be a credible factor. In the Heltborg case, supra, as our opinion reflects, very careful foundation for production figures, operation figures, and effect of the taking on those figures, were made before any effort was made to apply the capitalization of income method. In addition, in the Heltborg case the method used was not the key issue nor even seriously questioned.

While we do not reject the method in all cases, we believe for future guidance in eminent domain cases, the capitalization of income method should be carefully scrutinized even where it may be appropriate as one of the tools of the judicial workshop. We are aware that in some instances, where no comparable sales evidence is available or where it is shown to be not applicable for many reasons, the only useable method is the capitalization method. However, its use must be based on a foundation which minimizes to the extent possible conjecture and uncertainty.

Even though the appellant asserts that the owner's testimony should have been stricken also, by what we have already said, the cause must be retried, and we do not deem it necessary to discuss that feature. The judgment is reversed and the cause remanded for a new trial.

(3) Reproduction Cost Less Depreciation: Specialties

Suppose that an old brewery of the following description is taken by eminent domain to make way for an urban redevelopment project: the brewery was built 30 years ago at a cost of $200,000; although it is still in operation, there is no market for the building from other brewers because the equipment is old and out-of-date; the current cost of reproducing the building is estimated at $1,000,000. What is just compensation for the taking of this building?

The building in the above hypothetical illustration would be characterized as a **specialty** in eminent domain proceedings because it was designed to perform a very special and limited function. Because of the limited market for such a building the comparable sales method would not be a satisfactory method of determining its value. The profits made by the brewery would not be acceptable either because entreprenurial and managerial skill, rather than rental income from the property, would be the primary determinant of profits of the business. Because of these reasons, the value of specialties is determined by the **reproduction cost less depreciation** method. Under this method the cost of reproducing the building under current costs would be estimated. This amount would then be reduced to a fraction of that cost that reflects the depreciation of the existing building resulting from age. For example, if the existing building had a life expectancy of 40 years and had been used for 30 years, and if the reproduction cost of its replacement is $1,000,000, then the value of the building under the *reproduction cost less depreciation* method would be $250,000, i.e., $1,000,000 less $750,000 (30/40 of $1,000,000).

KEATOR

v.

STATE

23 N.Y.2d 337, 244 N.E. 248 (1968)

JASEN, Judge.

The State appropriated two pieces of claimants' land in Delaware County, located on both sides of State Route 30 and bordered on the East Branch of the Delaware River.

The property consisted of 0.267 acres and a wood-frame clubhouse, 52 feet long and 24 feet in depth, containing a meeting and dining room, together with a kitchen and sanitation facilities. The premises were used for meetings and social events sponsored by "The Isaac Walton League," an organization formed for "educational and conservation" purposes. The property was improved by the claimants for club use because of its unique location, as described in the record: "The land consists of about 0.42 acres, having 138 feet of frontage along the north side of Route 30, and 75 feet of frontage on the south side and along the East Branch of the Delaware River. The river, as it courses past the property, is a clear, fast running stream, 80 to a hundred feet in width, and at this point, just above the confluence of the Bush Kill stream, forms a deep and excellent pool for both swimming and trout fishing. * * * The East Branch of the Delaware River is considered one of the best trout streams by the Conservation Department of the State of New York, and it's also enjoyed many years of fame throughout the northeastern United States as being an excellent sports fishery. And, this property enjoyed frontage along one of the fine deep holes in this river."

The Court of Claims awarded $15,900 to the condemnees. The Appellate Division reduced the award to $12,000 holding that "[i]n arriving at damages so greatly in excess of the state's proof, the Trial Court necessarily relied to a great extent on the proof adduced from the claimants' expert, which incorrectly added building reproductions costs to land value, without any suggestion that the property was either unique or a specialty."

It is the general rule that "just compensation" is to be determined by reference to the fair market value of the property at the date of taking, and that the fair market value is the price for which the property would sell if there was a willing buyer who was under no compulsion to buy and a willing seller under no compulsion to sell. In the determination of the fair market value, the condemnee is entitled to have the appraisal based on the highest and best available use of the property irrespective of whether he is so using it. * * * That is, considering the best use to which the property could reasonably be put, what is its fair market value?

However, in some cases the use of the fair market value approach becomes unworkable. For such things as a church, school or clubhouse (generally referred to as specialty property) there is no readily recognizable market and testimony as to a fair market price is not usually available. While this property might be worth to the owners all that it cost, it would not be "marketable" in the accepted sense of the word because there is no similar group in the area which would offer to buy the clubhouse for its reproduction value. See discussion in 4 Nichols, Eminent Domain [3d ed., (1962), § 12.32.]

Since the character of the property is such as not to be susceptible to the rule of fair market value, an award based on the actual or intrinsic value would be proper, i.e., the current cost of reproduction less depreciation.

The crux of the question presented on appeal in whether this property was a specialty.

The condemnee's expert based his valuation of damages solely on reproduction costs less depreciation because he was of the opinion that the highest and best use of the property was for "a club type recreation property." The State's expert testified that the highest and best available use of the premises was "for the purpose to which it was being put, as a recreational hall and property." In determining the value of the property appropriated, he relied equally on the reproduction cost less depreciation and market data approaches.

We hold that the testimony of both experts clearly indicates that the highest and best use of the property was for the purpose to which it was being used as a clubhouse and recreational area which we find in this case was a specialty.

Accordingly, the order of the Appellate Division should be reversed and the judgment of the Court of Claims reinstated.

BURKE, SCILEPPI and BREITEL, JJ., concur with JASEN,J.

FULD, C. J., and BERGAN and KEATING, JJ., dissent and vote to affirm in the following memorandum: On the record before us, there is no basis for treating the claimants' property as a specialty and, as the Appellate Division noted, there was no indication or suggestion by the Court of Claims that the property was "either unique or a specialty." We would affirm on the very simple ground that the evidence supports the finding of value made by the Appellate Division rather than the finding made by the trial court.

BARTAGE, Inc.

v.

MANCHESTER HOUSING AUTHORITY

318 A.2d 152 (New Hamp. 1974)

GRIMES, Justice.

The main issue the court is asked to decide is whether evidence of reproduction cost is admissible as an element or circumstance to be considered in arriving at the fair market value of condemned property. This issue as well as defendant's exceptions to a failure to grant a requested instruction and to the exclusion of evidence of repairs after condemnation were reserved and transferred by *Dunfey*, J., after a jury trial with a view resulted in a $145,000 verdict for the plaintiff.

Plaintiff owned the Bartage Hotel which was situated on 10,350 square feet of land located on Pine Street in downtown Manchester. The Bartage, built in 1892, boasted a restaurant, lounge, and office space on the first floor and 52 rentable rooms for permanent and transient guests on the upper three floors, but had a high vacancy rate. It was located in a depressed area where other property had been taken over by the Manchester Housing Authority. On October 6, 1969, the Bartage was condemned by the authority in a petition for condemnation brought pursuant to RSA ch. 203, ch. 205 and 4:30–4:36.

At trial, one expert called by plaintiff valued the property at $130,000 and another expert valued it at $150,000. These estimates were arrived at by considering three standard approaches to valuation. The comparable sales method produces an estimate of value based on comparisons with and adjustments to sales and offerings for sale of similar properties in the area. The income approach is a determination of what value the property's net income will support based on a capitalization of net income. The cost approach, at issue on appeal, is figured by adding to the value of the land without buildings the cost of reconstructing the buildings as adjusted by subtracting an allowance for physical, economic and functional depreciation of the buildings. As applied to a valuation of the Bartage, these three factors depreciated the cost of reproduction an estimated 80% (T. 130). *See* American Institute of Real Estate Appraisers, The Appraisal of Real Estate 63–70 (4th ed. 1964).

Using these three methods, plaintiff's two appraisers arrived at six estimations of value ranging between $126,500 and $168,000. In choosing their best estimates, they arrived at the $130,000 and $150,000 figures respectively. Both experts considered the market data approach most accurate in valuing this property and one expert testified that the cost approach established merely the "upper limit" of what a buyer would pay for the property. All of the testimony on the methods and the values was introduced as a foundation to support the experts' final opinions.

In this State, the "rule of value permits all relevant factors to be received for the formation of the finding, in analysis an opinion, of the trier of fact."

The testimony objected to was offered by witnesses whose qualifications as experts were conceded by the defendant and accepted by the trial court. The testimony provided not the sole or primary basis for their opinion, but background information as to their appraisal techniques. It was subject to cross-examination. The jury was instructed that any method used which would not influence a willing buyer and not be reflective of market value should be rejected as not legally applicable to determining the issue of value. The cost of reconstruction figures were adjusted for three types of depreciation and were not inconsistent with estimates derived from other methods. The instructions to the jury emphasized and reemphasized that fair market value was the sole test to be applied. We hold it was not error for the trial court, in its discretion, to admit the testimony into evidence. * * *

Exceptions overruled.

All concurred.

---

(4) Highest and Best Use

If the property taken is vacant land or a building that is capable of more than one use, then the value attributed to such property in eminent domain proceedings must be its **highest and best use.** Suppose the property is zoned for one purpose but the owner argues that at the time of the taking the market value of the property reflects a probability of rezoning to permit a more valuable use within the reasonably foreseeable future. Should "just compensation" reflect this aspect of market value? The following case illustrates the nature of the problem.

MASHETER

v.

OHIO HOLDING CO.

38 Ohio App.2d 49, 313 N.E.2d 413 (1973)

WHITESIDE, Judge.

This is an appeal from a judgment of the Franklin County Court of Common Pleas in an eminent domain proceeding brought by the director of highways pursuant to R.C. Chapter 163, to appropriate the property of defendants needed in the construction and improvement of Route No. I–270 in Franklin County, Ohio. The case proceeded to a jury trial for the ascertainment of the compensation due defendants for the taking of their property. The jury returned a verdict assessing compensation for the land taken in the amount of $608,000 and an additional amount of $50,000 for damages to the residue.

* * *

This case involves a complex and difficult valuation issue in that the propery taken was zoned for single-family residential use but all of the expert witnesses, both those for the property owner and those for the director, testified that the highest and best use of the property would be to hold the property for future development under an anticipated change of zoning for commercial and apartment use. The residue of the tract had been rezoned to commercial use approximately a year before the date of take, and at the same time another portion of the original residue was zoned for apartment use, which portion was sold by the property owner prior to the date of take.

The record is replete with references to zoning requests and denials both as to the subject property and other properties in the area, coupled with the property owner's contention that a rezoning of the subject property taken had been denied solely because it was anticipated that it would be taken for highway purposes. Likewise, there are throughout the record contentions by the director that it was the policy of the city of Columbus to have no commercial zoning in this area, coupled with the contention that the rezoning of the residue which occurred was a result of the taking, although it occurred a year prior thereto. This inconsistency in the contentions of the parties created a difficulty for the trial court upon which he commented at length.

Compensation for land taken for public use is determined by the fair market value of the property on the date of taking unless for some unusual circumstance a different earlier date of valuation is ascertained. In this case, it was agreed that the date of take, and the date of valuation was July 14, 1969.

Fair market value is the amount of money which could be obtained on the open market at a voluntary sale of the property. It is the amount that a purchaser who is willing, but not required to buy, would pay and that a seller who is willing, but not required to sell, would accept, when both are fully aware and informed of all circumstances involving the value and use of the property. Market value is determined by the most valuable and best uses to which the property could reasonably, practically, and lawfully be adapted which is referred to as "the highest and best use."

The zoning of property is an important factor in determining highest and best use because an informed buyer would not pay more for property than it is worth for a use to which it can lawfully be put. Accordingly, evidence of the value of property for a use which is not permitted by the zoning of the property is inadmissible in an eminent domain proceeding. However, it is generally recognized that zoning laws are changed from time to time and that, especially with respect to undeveloped property, development of an area may result in a change of zoning from residential to apartments or to commercial. Both the evidence in this case, and general knowledge indicate that developers or investors buying such tracts of property anticipate a change of zoning and pay more for the property than it would be worth if devoted to the uses permitted by the existing zoning.

Holding property for future development in anticipation of a change of zoning to permit a more valuable use of the property to which it could reasonably and practically be adapted, if permitted by the zoning, is obviously a permitted use under existing zoning. How much an informed buyer would pay for property for that purpose is an issue of fact, and evidence may be admitted in an appropriation proceeding upon the issue. Obviously, the amount an informed buyer would pay under such circumstances depends upon his impression of the degree of probability of anticipated change of zoning and the length of time that he anticipates that the property must be held before such change in zoning occurs.

However, whether or not zoning authorities will in fact change the zoning is not an issue in appropriation proceedings; neither is the question of the validity of the existing zoning, which, if a question, must be determined by separate proceedings.

The zoning problem has been the subject of decisions in three other appellate districts: City of Euclid v. Lakeshore Co. (1956); In re Appropriation of Easement (1963), and Bd. of Edn. v. Graham (1968). *Graham* followed *Euclid* and *In re Appropriation* distinguished it. In *Euclid*, it is stated.

"* * * To speculate on what may be the legislative policy of a council of a city or village in the future in changing a particular zoning classification when considered for the purpose of fixing the value of land taken for public purposes is of such a speculative character that a court should not permit such evidence of value of the property to be presented in the trial of a condemnation proceeding."

In *In re Appropriation*, it is stated:

"Property admitted uncontroverted evidence in this record demonstrates that a reconsideration and amendment of the zoning applicable to this parcel was certain under conditions existing on the date of taking."

The zoning issue was also discussed in the unreported decision of this court in Masheter v. Mariemont. In that decision, Judge Troop stated:

"* * * the highest and best use is ordinarily one which is permitted by zoning regulations. * * * But buyers do buy and pay more for a given parcel of land than can be supported by a present legally permitted use, a possible highest and best use not in conformity to existing zoning limitations. Courts appear to permit such a situation to be considered and relax the rigid rule limiting testimony to the highest and best use permitted by present zoning regulations, but only within definite limitations."

Judge Troop further stated the rule to be applied, as follows:

"The determination of compensation cannot be dependent upon whether or not there will be a change of zoning of the property in the future. Compensation must be based upon the fair market value of the property for its highest and best use available within existing zoning regulations. The *possibility* of future rezoning may not be utilized to increase the fair market value over that which an informed willing purchaser would pay under existing zoning. If, however, such a purchaser would be presently willing to pay more than an amount justified by the uses permitted under existing zoning because of a general belief that there is a *probability* of a change in zoning, to permit a more valuable use within the reasonably foreseeable future, such evidence is admissible because it does reflect a factor in the present fair market value under existing zoning."

This court assumed that the rule so stated was sufficiently clear; however, the comments of counsel for both parties and the trial court indicate that this court was incorrect in this assumption.

We would thus attempt to clarify the issue and restate it as follows:

(1) Fair market value is not dependent upon whether there will or will not, in fact, be a change of zoning of that property in the future. Fair market value must be determined upon the basis of the highest and best use available within existing zoning. There should be no speculation as to what the future policy of the zoning authorities will be in regard to a zoning of the property, except to the extent, if any, it is shown by an expert appraiser's testimony that informed sellers and purchasers would so speculate.

(2) The mere possibility of future rezoning may not be utilized to increase fair market value to an amount over and above that which an informed willing purchaser would presently pay under existing zoning.

(3) It may, however, be shown by an expert appraiser's testimony that the highest and best use available, within existing zoning regulations, is to hold certain property for future development upon a generally held belief by informed purchasers and sellers that there is a probability of rezoning to permit a more valuable use within the reasonably foreseeable future.

(4) Further, where it is shown by such expert testimony that the highest and best use of property is to hold it for future development in anticipation of a future rezoning, the fair market value of the property is the amount that an informed willing purchaser would be presently willing to pay for the property, and an informed owner will to accept, with full knowledge of the existing zoning the probability of future rezoning, the difficulties attendant in obtaining such, and the reasonably foreseeable period of time necessary to hold the property before such change of zoning could be obtained, the adaptability of the property to the more valuable use, and the general development in the area involved, and evidence thereon may be presented by an expert appraiser's testimony.

Thus, as stated by Judge Troop in *Mariemont, supra:*

"Many factors enter into the consideration of buyers with respect to a given piece of land. Site analysis may be limited to present usage. It must be recognized, however, that a buyer may have in mind holding land out of use to await appreciation in value. The question is, narrowly and strictly, just what price would a willing purchaser pay an equally willing seller for the premises taken on a particular day * * *."

Thus, the issue remains, what is the fair market value of the property under existing zoning? This is the highest price that an informed willing buyer would pay and the lowest price that an informed willing seller would accept. It remains the price that the property would bring at a voluntary sale on the open market. But that price must be one uninfluenced by the existence of the improvement for which the property is being taken. In other words, in this case, the fair market value of the property taken is the amount that the property would bring in a voluntary sale on the open market on the date of take, July 14, 1969, assuming the property was not to be taken for highway purposes.

That the instant case is one where an informed willing buyer would anticipate a future change of zoning to a more valuable use is indicated by the testimony of all of the expert witnesses. * * *

(5) Partial Taking

Suppose that the city decides to widen a road adjoining a single family house on a 75 foot by 100 foot lot. The city takes a strip of land 20 feet x 75 feet. Before the road widening, the house had a market value of $75,000. After the road widening, because of the elimination of 20 feet of front lawn and the closeness of the traffic to the house, the market value of the house is only $40,000. What is just compensation for the **partial taking** of the 20 foot by 75 foot strip of land?

The usual method of determining just compensation for a partial taking is to apply the "**before and after rule**," by which the compensation is calculated as the difference between the value of the entire parcel of land before the taking and the value of the remainder of the land after the taking. Thus, in the illustration above, the owner of the property would receive the difference between $75,000 and $40,000, or $35,00. For an illustration of the application of this rule see *City of Pearland v. Alexander,* 483 S.W.2d 244 (Tex.Supp., 1972).

In some states, just compensation for a partial taking is calculated by a two step procedure in which the owner is compensated (1) for the market value of the land taken, and (2) the difference in the before and after value of the remainder of the property. For an illustration of the application of this rule see *City of Youngstown v. Thomas,* 97 Ohio App. 193, 124 N.E.2d 184 (1953). See also, 29 *C.J.S., Eminent Domain,* § 139, page 976.

(6) Consequential Damages

A difficult problem arises where the owner of land seeks compensation for the loss in market value resulting not from the taking of his/her land but rather from the taking of adjoining land owned by others. An even more troublesome issue arises where compensation is made for the taking of a building but no payment is made for the loss of goodwill or the destruction of a business conducted in the building, or the cost of moving fixtures and personal property from the building. These and similar losses to an owner are called *consequential damages.* Under the eminent domain provision of the federal constitution and many of the state constitutions, consequential damages, such as the destruction of an on-going business, the expense of moving machinery or furniture from the premises, or the loss of goodwill are not included in the definition of just compensation for the taking of the property. However, the constitutions or·statutes in other states provide for "just compensation for property taken, injured or destroyed" by governmental agencies. In these states many. types of consequential damages may be included in the award of just compensation.

The following case illustrates the type of legal issue that arises under the more restrictive eminent domain provision.

LUCAS

v.

STATE

44 A.D.2d 633, 353 N.Y.S.2d 831 (1974)

MEMORANDUM DECISION.

Cross appeals from a judgment in favor of the claimant, entered October 18, 1972, upon a decision of the Court of Claims.

Claimant is the owner of a house and lot on the corner of Sherman and Sheridan Avenues in the Chestnut Hill Park section of Mount Vernon, New York. In 1968, pursuant to section 30 of the Highway Law, the State appropriated certain portions of this property, namely, a temporary easement of 0.061 acre and, in fee, a triangular section of land from the corner, measuring 20 feet on Sherman Avenue and 20 feet on Sheridan Avenue taken for the purpose of reconstructing the adjoining street. The State also lowered the elevation of these two avenues by approximately seven feet and, in so doing, removed a hedge belonging to claimant and shade trees belonging to the City of Mount Vernon from the front of the subject property. In their place was erected a six-foot concrete retaining wall with a cyclone wire fence on top. While undoubtedly these takings and changes were made in connection with the reconstruction of the nearby Cross County Parkway, clearly neither said parkway nor any of its appurtenances intrude in any way upon claimant's land.

At trial, the court found, with both parties in agreement, that the subject property's highest and best use as a single family residence remained unchanged by the various takings. Similarly, the court's valuation of the temporary easement is well within the range established by the opposing appraisers and should not be disturbed. As to the award for the permanent appropriation, however,, wherein claimant seeks the adoption of her appraisal *in toto* and the State seeks a sharp reduction in the award for consequential damages, serious difficulties present themselves which make affirmance impossible.

The first problem concerns the after value of $50,415 which the court placed on claimant's property. This amount is higher than the corresponding figure of either appraiser, and the difference is neither supported by any other evidence nor sufficiently explained by the court. Accordingly, the decision is patently defective and will not be sustained.

Further error was committed in the determination of the consequential damages to claimant's fee. Thus, such factors as the increased noise and fumes and the loss of privacy and view resulting from the reconstruction of the Cross County Parkway on appropriated land directly across the street from claimant's property were considered by the court in making its award, as was the loss of shade trees planted by the City of Mount Vernon on city-owned property. These damages resulting from the taking of neighbors' lands are clearly not compensable, and claimant's recovery of consequential damages as limited solely to those damages which arise by reason of the use to which the State puts the property taken directly from her, i.e., the triangular section.

Judgment modified, on the law and the facts, without costs, so as to vacate the award of damages for the permanent appropriation, and a new trial ordered, limited to the issue of damages for the permanent appropriation, and, as so modified, affirmed.

E.   Acquisition Procedure and Policy

(1) Due Process Requirements

The due process clause of the federal constitution provides protection against a governmental taking of property without an opportunity to be heard. The due process requirements in eminent domain proceedings include the right of the owner to (1) receive *notice* of the proceedings, and (2) have a *hearing* on the issue of just compensation.

The **requirement of notice** is different for a resident and a non-resident. Where the owner is a resident and the ownership is recorded, the form of notice must be "reasonably calculated to inform" him/her of the time and place of the hearing to determine the amount of compensation. Publication in the local newspaper without written notice mailed to the owner is insufficient to satisfy this test. *Walker v. Hutchinson City*, 352 U.S. 112 (1956). On the other hand, where the owner of the property is a non-resident, or is unknown, personal notice is not required and service by publication is sufficient.

The due process protection of the **right to a hearing** does not include the right to a hearing on the issue of the propriety or wisdom of the taking of that property. However, federal and state statutes frequently require a public hearing when property is designated for condemnation. The only issue on which the owner is entitled to a hearing under the due process clause is the issue of the amount of the compensation to be paid. The due process clause does not require that the determination of just compensation be made by a jury. In most cases, the amount of the compensation is made by a judge, sitting without a jury, or by a court appointed master or panel.

The due process clause does not require that payment by made *before* the government takes possession of the property. It is possible for a governmental agency to "take-now-and-pay-later" if provision is made to assure payment of compensation without unreasonable delay. *Hays v. Port of Seattle*, 251 U.S. 233 (1920). A common method of fulfilling this requirement is for the governmental agency to deposit in court a sum of money equal to the amount of value of the property determined by its appraiser.

(2) Federal Acquisition Policy

The federal government (and some states) have established a policy and procedure for eminent domain takings to eliminate some of the harshness and inequities that can result when government takes private property from its owners. The Federal Uniform Relocation Assistance and Real Property Acquisitions

Policies Act of 1970, § 301, 42 U.S.C. 4651, set forth below illustrates one attempt to respond to some of the procedural problems of exercise of the power of eminent domain.

TITLE III—FEDERAL UNIFORM REAL PROPERTY ACQUISITION POLICY

Uniform Policy on Real Property Acquisition Practices

SEC. 301. In order to encourage and expedite the acquisition of real property by agreements with owners, to avoid litigation and relieve congestion in the courts, to assure consistent treatment for owners in the many Federal programs, and to promote public confidence in Federal land acquisition practices, heads of Federal agencies shall, to the greatest extent practicable, be guided by the following policies:

(1) The head of a Federal agency shall make every reasonable effort to acquire expeditiously real property by negotiation.

(2) Real property shall be appraised before the initiation of negotiations, and the owner or his designated representative shall be given an opportunity to accompany the appraiser during his inspection of the property.

(3) Before the initiation of negotiations for real property, the head of the Federal agency concerned shall establish an amount which he believes to be just compensation therefore and shall make a prompt offer to acquire the property for the full amount so established. In no event shall such amount be less than the agency's approved appraisal of the fair market value of such property. Any decrease or increase in the fair market value of real property prior to the date of valuation caused by the public improvement for which such property is acquired, or by the likelihood that the property would be acquired for such improvement, other than that due to physical deterioration within the reasonable control of the owner, will be disregarded in determining the compensation for the property. The head of the Federal agency concerned shall provide the owner of real property to be acquired with a written statement of, and summary of the basis for, the amount he established as just compensation. Where appropriate the just compensation for the real property acquired and for damages to remaining real property shall be separately stated.

(4) No owner shall be required to surrender possession of real property before the head of the Federal agency concerned pays the agreed purchase price, or deposits with the court in accordance with section 1 of the Act of February 26, 1931 (46 Stat. 1421; 40 U.S.C. 258a), for the benefit of the owner, an amount not less than the agency's approved appraisal of the fair market value of such property, or the amount of the award of compensation in the condemnation proceeding for such property.

(5) The construction or development of a public improvement shall be so scheduled that, to the greatest extent practicable, no person lawfully occupying real property shall be required to move from a dwelling (assuming a replacement dwelling as required by title II will be available), or to move his business or farm operation, without at least ninety days' written notice from the head of the Federal agency concerned, of the date by which such move is required.

(6) If the head of a Federal agency permits an owner or tenant to occupy the real property acquired on a rental basis for a short term or for a period subject to termination by the Government on short notice, the amount of rent required shall not exceed the fair rental value of the property to a short-term occupier.

7) In no event shall the head of a Federal agency either advance the time of condemnation, or defer negotiations or condemnation and the deposit of funds in court for the use of the owner, or take any other action coercive in nature, in order to compel an agreement on the price to be paid for the property.

(8) If any interest in real property is to be acquired by exercise of the power of eminent domain, the head of the Federal agency concerned shall institute formal condemnation proceedings. No Federal agency head shall intentionally make it necessary for an owner to institute legal proceedings to prove that fact of the taking of his real property.

(9) If the acquisition of only part of a property would leave its owner with an uneconomic remnant, the head of the Federal agency concerned shall offer to acquire the entire property.

Chapter Seven

Transfer of Development Rights (TDR)

A. INTRODUCTION TO THE CONCEPT OF TDR

> THE TRANSFER OF DEVELOPMENT RIGHTS:
> A PREVIEW OF AN EVOLVING CONCEPT,
> JEROME G. ROSE
> 3 REAL ESTATE LAW JOURNAL 330 (1975)

INTRODUCTION

Planners, attorneys and other real estate professionals have responded enthusiastically to the new technique of land-sue regulation—**transferable development rights.**[1] This rapidly emerging concept has received con-

---

1. In May 1974, at its Fortieth Annual National Planning Conference in Chicago, the American Society of Planning Officials selected the transfer of development rights (TDR) as the featured subject of discussion for its prestigious Alfred Bettman Symposia. The discussion served the twofold purpose of exposing the enthusiastic response of practicing planners to this new techniques of land-use regulation and also providing an opportunity for those who had been experimenting with the concept to share their findings and to reaffirm their initial observation that, as Audrey Moore put it, "Transferable development rights is an idea whose time has come!"

Participants in the discussion were Worth Bateman, The Urban Institute; Donald M. Carmichael, Associate Professor of Law, University of Colorado; Budd B. Chavooshian, Department of Environmental Resources, Rutgers University; John J. Costonis, Professor of Law, University of Illinois; Robert S. Devoy, Real Estate Research Corporation; Ellis Gans, Marin County Planning Department; James A. Graaskamp, Associate Professor of Real Estate, University of Wisconsin; Claude Gruen, San Francisco; David G. Heeter, Vermont Environmental Board; Daniel R. Mandelker, Professor of Law, Washington University; Norman Marcus, General Counsel, New York City Planning Commission; Richard A. Miller, General Counsel, Landmarks Preservation Service; Audrey Moore, Supervisor, Annandale District, Fairfax County Board of Supervisors; David Richards, Esq., Paul, Weiss, Goldberg, Rifkind, Wharton & Garrison, New York City; Jerome G. Rose, Professor of Urban Planning, Rutgers University; Jared Shlaes, Arthur Rub-

siderable exposure in a variety of journals.[2] The publicity has resulted in an influx of questions about the practical use of the technique, its underlying concepts, and the experience of communities that have proposed or adopted a TDR plan.

The basic concept underlying TDR is simple. It assumes that title to real estate is not a unitary or monolithic right, but rather is a "bundle of individual rights," each one of which may be separated from the rest and transferred to someone else, leaving the original owner with all other rights of ownership. This is not a new or novel idea. We have long been accustomed to the separation and alienability of such components of title as mineral rights and mortgage liens, to name just two rights. One of the components of this "bundle or rights" is the right to develop the land. In other than agricultural or mining areas, especially urban and suburban regions, the right to develop land tends to become the component of greatest value. In rural areas where there is little expectation of development in the foreseeable future, the right to develop has lower value. In either case, though, there is legal precedent for the transfer of just that one right, the development right, leaving the owner of the land with all other rights.

Each of the various TDR programs to be discussed seeks to use the transfer of development rights to achieve one or more specific goals:

- The New York and Chicago plans seek to preserve architectural and historical landmarks by transferring the right to develop that land to owners of other land.
- The New Jersey proposal seeks to preserve farmland and open space by transferring the right to develop that land to designated districts.
- The Maryland, Fairfax County, Virginia, and Sonoma County, California, plans seek to use TDR as a primary method of land-use regulation.
- The Southampton, New York, ordinance seeks to provide economic incentive to build low- and moderate-income housing.
- The British plan seeks to recover the increase in the value of private land that results from public investment.

Each of the proposals uses a variation of the transfer of development rights technique to accomplish its objective:

- The New Jersey proposal seeks to create a marketplace for the purchase and sale of development rights, subject to economic forces.
- The Chicago plan permits, with some limitations, landmark owners to sell development rights to owners of land in designated districts, subject to the power of the city to acquire those rights by

---

loff & Co., Chicago; and Sidney Willis, Assistant Commissioner, New Jersey Department of Community Affairs.

2. For example, *House & Home* 26 (June 1974); *Planning* 7-15 (July 1974); *The Urban Lawyer* (Fall 1974). For a recent bibliography on the transfer of development rights, see Helb, Chavooshian and Nieswand, *Development Rights Bibliography* (Cook College, Rutgers University, 1976).

condemnation proceedings for deposit in a "development rights bank."

- The Southampton ordinance authorizes the Town Board to transfer residential development rights pursuant to a prescribed procedure.
- The British system authorized the government in 1947 to acquire all development rights and under two programs (both now abandoned) an owner of land had to buy back his development rights before developing his property.

Under the plans that seek to create a free or partially free market for bringing or selling devlopment rights, the method of calculating the number of rights to which an owner is entitled varies:

- The Maryland proposal would distribute development rights on the basis of the *number of acres* of land owned, irrespective of value.
- The New Jersey proposal would dole out the development right on the basis of the *proportionate value* of the owner's land to the total value of all land preserved for open space use.
- The Sonoma County, California proposal, seeking a compromise between the *acreage method* and the *value method*, would create three concentric bands around the built-up area and would assign a value factor per acre that reflect the fact that the closer-in lands are more valuable because they are likely to be developed sooner than the farther-out lands.

We will examine the TDR concept in an orderly manner: *first*, by examining some of the legal precedents upon which it is based; *second*, by analyzing each of the TDR proposals; and *finally*, by evaluating the concept from a legal, administrative, economic, and practical perspective.

LEGAL ANTECEDENTS

Early American Precedents

Professor Donald M. Carmichael has recently described the early American precedents upon which TDR is based.[3] His article focuses on four ancestors of planning districts which involved the transfer of the development potential of privately owned properties to other property owners for the purpose of fulfilling a public need. Those precedents are (1) the early transportation systems; (2) the Milldam Acts; (3) major drainage and irrigation projects; and (4) oil and gas production regulations.

Early Transportation Systems

In the early 1800s it was common practice for the states to authorize private corporations to plan, construct, and maintain private toll roads. To avoid the problem of costly detours around the property of uncooperative landowners, the private corporations were given the power to acquire the necessary rights-of-way upon paying the landowner. This same power was

---

3. Carmichael, "Transferable Development as a Basis for Land Use Control," 2 Fla. State U.L. Rev. 55 (1974).

later given to private builders of canals and railroads. Thus, the practice was established for a system which transferred the right to develop some part of a person's property to another private owner, upon the payment of compensation, and where such transfer is designed to meet a public need.

Milldam Acts

In another practice dating back to early colonial days, the private owner of land through which a stream flowed could erect a dam to harness water power for the purpose of grinding grain. Damming the stream would invariably result in the flooding of the land of upstream landowners, thereby depriving them of their rights to develop that land. These rights could have been protected by requiring the millowner to tear down the dam. Instead, the millowner, under the Milldam Acts was permitted to maintain his dam and gristmill if he paid the upstream owner for the loss of his right to develop his flooded lands.

The Milldam statutes also authorized the miller to grind the the grain of all who requested the service and who paid a fee in the form of a share of flour produced. The courts upheld the Milldam statutes on the grounds that they were a reasonable police power regulation. Thus, the precedent was established for the involuntary transfer by the upstream owners of their right to develop their land, without the exercise of the power of eminent domain. The millowners, though, were required to submit to regulation of their operation for the protection of the public.

Drainage and Irrigation

Under the early American method of administering drainage and irrigation projects, the courts were authorized to oversee the administration of a drainage or irrigation district. A majority of the property owners in the district could vote to undertake an irrigation or drainage project and impose its costs upon the participating owners in accordance with benefits received from the project. Thus, some owners might be deprived of the right to develop or use their property so that the water resouces could be channeled to achieve the greatest benefit for the district. Those who received that benefit would provide the funds from which those who contributed would be compensated. Thus, a district was created in which the resources of all participants were pooled and the rights of development were reassigned within the district to achieve the maximum utilization of local resources.

Oil and Gas Production Regulations

The fourth precedent described by Professor Carmichael is the regulations on oil and gas production. They were designed to prevent each owner of property over a gas or oil "reservoir" or "field" from pumping as much oil and gas as he could, thereby draining the reserves under his neighbor's property. This practice caused rapid depletion of resources, waste, duplication, and over investment in drilling equipment. The states adopted statutes regulating the availability of the common fund of oil and gas resources for all of the owners of land overlying the reservoirs.

The United States Supreme Court upheld these regulations in a decision[4] that recognized the coequal right of all owners to share in common these resources. The decision confirmed the power of the legislature to prevent waste of resources and provide for a just distribution and enjoyment of those assets among the collective owners.

Professor Carmichael suggests that this precedent supports the transfer of development rights concept in that the potential for development within a planning or zoning district is similar to a reservoir of gas or oil resources. Regulating development density, type, and timing avoids waste and provides for a pooling of resources and an equitable system for distributing development rights among the co-owners.

British and Recent American Precedents

A recent article of my own reviewed the British and recent American precedents from which the transfer of development rights concept is derived. The British used the transfer of development rights technique in an attempt to establish a system by which increases in the value of real property resulting from public action would be recovered and in which property owners whose use of land was restricted would be compensated. In the Town and Country Planning Act of 1947, the British government acquired the development rights to all undeveloped land in the nation. This left the owners of land with all other rights of ownership, except the right to develop. When an owner wanted to develop his land he had to buy this right from the government by paying a development charge. The monies thus obtained went into a revolving fund that was used to compensate other owners of property who were denied the right to develop.

During the period from 1947 to 1971, as the governmental leadership alternated between the Conservative and Labour parties, the program was modified frequently. It was ultimately abandoned. At the present, the British government still owns the development rights to all land, but it has not been able to devise a politically acceptable system to utilize its development rights as an effective technique of land use regulation.

The recent American experience with the transfer of development rights, includes such programs as;

- eminent domain acquisition of less than a fee simple;
- landmark preservation transfer of. floor area ratio rights;
- incentive zoning transfer of floor area ration (FAR) bonuses.

There is ample judicial and legislative precedent for government acquisition of less-than-the-fee simple (that is, less than the full title). A typical illustration is the condemnation of a right of way for the purpose of installing utility poles. This concept has been extended to permit government acquisition (by condemnation or purchase) of only the right to develop the land, leaving the owner with all other rights of ownership. For example, the New Jersey enabling legislation authorizes the acquisition of a "restriction on the use of land"; the California statute authorizes the acquisition of a "lesser interest or right in real property . . . through limitation

---

4. Ohio Oil Co. v. Indiana, 177 U.S. 190 (1900).

5. Rose, "A Proposal for the Separation and Marketability of Development Rights as a Technique to Preserve Open Space," 2 Real Estate L.J. 635 (1974).

of their future use"; the Vermont statute is more explicit and authorizes the acquisition of "development rights."

There is, then, ample precedent for the transfer of development rights; the challenge now is to devise a technique, based on the TDR concept, which could be used effectively as a land-use control device.

Such a technique was attempted in New York City and Chicago. In those programs, the development rights would be transferred from landmark buildings to other lots. This transfer is made possible because urban landmark buildings usually do not have as much floor area as is authorized under the floor area ratio contained in zoning ordinances. The FAR is a zoning technique that regulates the physical volume (density) of a building by controlling the relation between the floor area of a building and the area of the lot on which the building stands. The consideration that the landmark owner receives for the sale of his excess FAR (that amount which is not built, although authorized), that is, his development rights, compensates him for preserving the landmark. We will return to this program later.

Under the plan adopted by the City of San Francisco involving the zoning transfer of FAR bonuses, the downtown is divided into four districts, each with a prescribed FAR. A builder may obtain a bonus of an increased FAR by providing such public benefits as pedestrian plazas, additional setbacks, observation decks, and the like. In a strict sense, the San Francisco plan and other programs of incentive zoning offering FAR bonuses are not examples of the transfer of development rights because part of the fee, the development right, is not separated from the owner's title and transferred to another property owner. Instead, the government, under its police power, artificially restricts development and then prescribes conditions under which those restrictions may be relaxed. On the other hand, these plans are similar to the transfer of development rights system in that the right to develop is specifically singled out, among the other rights of ownership, and manipulated as a device to control land use.

CURRENT PROGRAMS AND PROPOSALS

Planners and lawyers have begun to experiment with a variety of techniques to use the transfer of development rights for purposes of land-use regulation:

- New York City and Chicago used it for the preservation of landmarks.
- In New Jersey, legislation was proposed to use TDR to preserve open space.
- It was proposed as a technique to preserve the ecologically fragile Phosphorescent Bay in Puerto Rico.
- Legislation has been prepared in Maryland.
- Fairfax County, Virginia, and Sonoma County, California, are developing proposals to use TDR as a primary system of land use regulation.
- Southampton, New York, has adopted an ordinance using TDR to encourage construction of moderate- and low-income housing.

- St. George, Vermont, uses the transfer of development rights as a device for regulating community growth.
- TDR is being studied as one of the techniques for eliminating unconscionable profits (windfalls) or losses (wipeouts) to landowners resulting from government regulation of land use.

Landmark Preservation

Professor John J. Costonis, one of the leading authorities on development rights, wrote the definitive description of the Chicago plan in an article in the *Harvard Law Review* in 1972.[6] In that same year, David A. Richards described the New York City plan in a Note in the *Yale Law Journal*.[7] In 1973, Donald H. Elliott and Norman Marcus described the more recent use of the transfer of development rights in New York City.[8] The programs described in these articles seek to preserve urban landmark buildings by permitting the landmark owner to sell his authorized but unbuilt floor area to another landowner. These unused development rights may have substantial value when attached to the transferee parcel, particularly in high-density commercial zones. Once the excess floor area is transferred, the authorized floor of the landmark lot is exhausted and may no longer be used for higher density development. Thus, the landmark owner is compensated by the sale of a valuable asset—his development rights, as computed in terms of unused floor area ratio. Once the rights are sold, the economic incentive to demolish the landmark for higher density development is. removed.

Professor Costonis suggests that the Chicago plan is superior to the New York City program for a number of reasons. The primary weakness of the original New York City plan was that development rights could be transferred only to adjacent lots, whereas the Chicago plan permits the development rights to be transferred to designated transfer districts where increased density could be absorbed without serious effect. Second, the New York plan provides for only such compensation to the landmark owner as he may derive from the sale of his development rights in the open market. The Chicago plan, on the other hand, is designed to compensate the landmark owner for the actual loss incurred in retaining the landmark. A landmark commission is authorized to determine the amount of compensation and to devise a plan for payment of compensation, including development rights sale, real estate tax reduction, and additional subsidy, if necessary, funded out of a municipal development rights bank. Under the Chicago plan, the municipality would play an active role in making a market for development rights. The city would acquire de-

---

6. Costonis, "The Chicago Plan: Incentive Zoning and the Preservation of Urban Landmarks," 85 Harv. L. Rev. 574 (1972).

7. Note (Richards), "Development Rights Transfer in New York City," 82 Yale L.J. 338 (1972).

8. Elliott & Marcus, "From Euclid to Ramapo: New Directions in Land Development Controls," 1 Hofstra L. Rev. 56 (1973).

velopment rights by purchase and condemnation and would then sell them to owners of property where increased density would be appropriate.

In spite of the care with which the Chicago plan was devised and its apparent potential for providing a method of preserving historical landmarks, Chicago's commissioner of development and planning has indicated that the plan will not be used in Chicago.[9] Nor has the development rights techniques proven helpful in preserving landmarks in New York City.[10]

Open Space Preservation

The proposal to use TDR as a technique to preserve open space is the product of a committee made up of Rutgers University faculty and members of the New Jersey Department of Community Affairs. The committee's proposal has been described in two articles written by different members of the committee. One of the articles, written by Budd B. Chavooshian and Thomas Norman, appears in *Urban Land*.[11] The other article, written by this author, appears in the *Real Estate Law Journal*.[12]

The New Jersey scheme is designed to induce owners of undeveloped land to preserve their land as open space by compensating them through the sale of their development rights to developers of other land in the jurisdiction. To make such sales possible, a market would be created in which owners of developable land would have to buy development rights from owners of preserved open space land as a prerequisite for higher density development. The market would be created in the following way.

● Each local government would prepare a land-use plan that specifies the percentage of remaining undeveloped land in the municipality. The plan would also designate what land will be preserved as open space land. The land-use plan would also designate the land to be developed and would specify the uses to which the developable land may be put. A zoning law would be enacted or amended to implement this plan.

● The planning board of each local government would prescribe the number of development rights required for each housing unit to be developed. On the basis of this numerical assignment, the planning board would then compute the number of development rights which would be required to develop the municipality in accordance with the land-use plan. The local government would issue certificates of development rights (ownership of which would be recorded) in the exact amount so determined.

---

9. "Chicago Plan Ruled Out in Chicago," Planning 8 (July 1974).

10. Note, Yale L.J., note 7 *supra,* at 370. But see Elliott & Marcus, note 8 *supra* for a discussion of New York City programs administered with some success.

11. Chavooshian & Norman, "Transfer of Development Rights," Urban Land 12 (Dec. 1973).

12. Rose, Real Estate L.J., note 5 *supra.*

● Every owner of preserved open space land would receive certificates of development rights in an amount that represents the percentage of assessed value of his undeveloped land to the total assessed value of all undeveloped land to be preserved in open space in the jurisdiction.

● An owner of developable land, who desires to develop his land more intensively (for example, to build apartments instead of single-family residences) would have to buy additional development rights on the open market from those who have acquired such rights from either original distribution or subsequent purchase.

● Thus, owners of preserved open space would be able to sell their development rights to owners of developable land (or real estate brokers or speculators). What happens is that the land-owners have sold their rights to develop their land in the future. The money received from the sale is compensation for keeping the land undeveloped. Their land will thus be preserved in open space and the owners will have been compensated without any capital costs to government.

● Development rights would be subject to ad valorem property taxation as a component of the total assessed value of the developable real property in the jurisdiction.

The most notable characteristic of the New Jersey plan is that development rights in the form of certificates would be bought and sold on the open market in a manner similar to sales of registered bonds. The same economic forces that determine the value of land would also determine the value of the separated component of the value of land, namely, the right to develop. No governmental agency would be authorized to tinker with the interplay of economic forces. The goal of the plan is limited to the preservation of open space in accordance with sound planning principles. The plan does not purport to be a technique for recovering unearned increment in the value of land; nor does it seek to redistribute economic resources. By limiting its purposes, the proponents of the plan sought to make it more politically acceptable.

A second innovative characteristic of the New Jersey plan is that the certificates would be taxed, as a component of real estate value, in a manner similar to the other components of title. As a consequence, there would be an incentive for a farmer who, not wishing to speculate in real estate, would sell his certificates of development rights. He would then pay property taxes only on the reduced value of his land for farm purposes. Purchasers of development rights would also be motivated to use them quickly or sell them to long-term investors or speculators in real estate. The owner of the rights would pay property taxes as part of the cost of such investment. This provision would serve the same purpose as state farm assessment acts. The provision, though, would not contain the features of the farm assessment acts that have been criticized as being more beneficial to real estate speculators than to farmers.

Another characteristic of the New Jersey plan that distinguishes it from the Maryland and other proposals is that the number of development rights assigned to owners of restricted land would be based upon the land's *value* rather than the *number of acres* held. Each owner would receive a number of development rights in the same proportion to the total number of development rights as the value of his restricted land bears to the total value of all other land similarly restricted to open space use. Consequently, the owner of more valuable land, regardless of acreage, would receive a greater number of the total number of development rights than would the owner of a large tract of relatively worthless land. The value would be determined initially on the basis of assessed value with a procedure established to review the assessments based upon notice of the assessment of all other restricted land.

The fourth major characteristic of the New Jersey plan, one that distinguishes it from the Fairfax County, Virginia, and other proposals, is that the system relates only to the development rights for *residential* units. The New Jersey proposal does not purport to be a primary system of land-use regulation. It deals only with open space land and residential development. No development rights are required for *commercial* or *industrial* development. The drafters purposely did not extend the system to commercial and industrial development rights to avoid the complex calculations and difficulties of administration that would result. It was the consensus of the drafting committee that although there was no *logical* reason for not including commercial and industrial development rights, there were sufficient practical and *political* reasons why the proposal should be kept as simple and understandable as possible.

Preservation of Fragile Ecological Resources

Professor Costonis and Robert S. DeVoy of Real Estate Research Corporation have prepared a study for the Conservation Trust of Puerto Rico [13] in which the transfer of development rights is proposed as the technique for preserving ecologically sensitive areas from development. Under their plan, development rights are transferred from "Protected Environmental Zones" (PEZs) to sites in "transfer districts" where greater density would not only be unobjectionable but would tend to implement the island's comprehensive planning objectives.

The Puerto Rican plan has four basic components:

● *Preparation of a PEZ inventory.* The planning board would be authorized to prepare an inventory of the island's ecologically fragile areas, including but not limited to the dinoflagellates of the Phosphorescent Bay. The board would also establish criteria and procedures for the future designation of fragile areas. Regulations would be promulgated that would prescribe the types of development, if any, that would be permitted within those areas.

● *Identification of transfer districts.* The planning board would designate transfer districts where greater density development would be desirable. Such designation would be based upon both planning principles and

13. Costonis & Robert S. DeVoy, *The Puerto Rican Plan: Environmental Protection Through Development Rights Transfer* (The Conservation Trust of Puerto Rico and Real Estate Research Corporation, June 1974).

market demand. Property owners within the transfer districts would be able to develop their land up to specified densities. They would be able to increase this density by purchasing development rights at a price set either by open market public bid procedures or by negotiations with the government land administration authorized to administer the program.

● *Administration of the environmental trust fund.* The land administration would administer an environmental trust fund that would receive payments for development rights. It would use these funds for administrative expenses and to compensate owners who are denied a reasonable return on their land because of the restrictions.

● *Review and settlement of claims.* An aggrieved owner in a PEZ could challenge a denial of his application to develop his land asserting that the denial deprives him of a reasonable return from his land. Among the remedies available would be (1) compensation for his loss; (2) liberalization of the restriction on the use; or (3) agreement between the landowner and the land administration on some other alternative, such as an exchange of the owner's land for another parcel. Where compensation is made, the owner would be required to transfer his development right to the Commonwealth, thus eliminating all rights to develop at any time in the future.

Professor Costonis readily concedes that the transfer of development rights in the Puerto Rican plan is more metaphorical than real. He contrasts the transfers in the Puerto Rican plan to those in the Chicago plan, where there is a direct transfer of a specified quantity of development rights from one property to another property. Under the Puerto Rican plan, there is *no direct transfer* of the right to develop one property to another property. The Puerto Rican plan seeks to transfer the *dollar equivalent* of the loss of the right to develop in the PEZ. The land administration is not required to maintain a balanced amount of development rights; it is only required to balance the dollar amounts required for compensation awards and expenses of administration. There is no private market for development rights, as in the New Jersey and Maryland proposals. In fact, there is no market at all—but rather a program for funding the compensation of owners whose use of land is restricted to a public use.

The Puerto Rican plan is more like the British program under the Town and Country Planning Act of 1947 than any of the American programs. Although the ostensible purposes of the Puerto Rican plan is to preserve environmental resources, its most significant contribution may be in achieving other land-use regulation objectives. Similar to the British program, the Puerto Rican plan recovers for the public benefit the increase in land value that results from more intensive development; it addresses the other half of the windfall/wipeout inequity by compensating landowners whose use of land is restricted; and it directs attention to the fairness of programs that seek to charge to each development its share of the cost of environmental despoliation.

As a Primary System of Land-Use Regulation

The transfer of development rights may be used as the primary system of land-use regulation as a substitute for, or together with, the zoning power. Under such a system, the allocation and regulation of development rights would determine the use of land and the design and density of all development. To accomplish this, development rights for all types of private development—residential, commercial, and industrial—would be issued in amounts that would provide the prescribed measure of each type of development. Such proposals have been made in Maryland, in Fairfax County, Virginia, and in Sonoma County, California.

The Maryland proposal.

Maryland State Senator William J. Goodman introduced a bill[14] in the Maryland State Senate that would use the transfer of development rights as a primary technique of land use regulation. As Senator Goodman described his proposal,[15] the master plan in each political subdivision would designate the land to be developed and the use of such land. Development rights would be issued to all landowners for all private development permitted; no development would take place unless the owner has the requisite number of development rights. Once an owner of land sells all of his rights, he would no longer be able to develop his land unless he were to reacquire the requisite number of development rights.

The Maryland plan is similar to the New Jersey plan in that it contemplates a free market for the purchase and sale of development rights. It goes beyond the New Jersey plan by providing for the issuance of development rights for "commercial" uses, which are defined to include all private uses other than residential and agricultural. Thus, commercial and industrial development, as well as residential development, require development rights as a condition for governmental approval. Each owner of undeveloped land in the jurisdiction would receive a proportion of the total number of development rights that would be required for total development. Unlike the New Jersey proposal, the number of shares that each landowner would receive would depend upon the amount of acreage owned. Development rights would be traded, bought, and sold until they were no longer available, at which point no further development would be possible. Thus, the amount and type of development would be regulated.

The Fairfax County, Virginia proposal.

Audrey Moore, supervisor of Annandale District, Fairfax County, Virginia, has proposed the transfer of development rights as a substitute for zoning.[16] She proposes that each jurisdiction adopt a comprehensive plan that would establish the residential, commercial, and industrial needs of the community. Based upon these needs, the number of development rights necessary to fulfill those needs would be calculated. Every property

---

14. Maryland Senate Bill No. 254 (Jan. 1972).
15. Goodman, "Descriptive Material on Transfer of Development Rights," accompanying his proposed legislation (Mimeo 1972).
16. Moore, note 1 supra.

owner would receive his share of development rights based upon the proportion of the number of acres he owns to the total number of acres of land in the jurisdiction. To obtain permission to build, a landowner would have to submit, with his site plan or subdivision plan, development rights in the amount required for his proposed development.

The Fairfax County proposal has a number of interesting variations on the TDR theme: The basic features of the comprehensive plan, such as projected population, would require approval by referendum. This requirement is based upon the realization that all too frequently, fundamental policy decisions such as setting community population limits are based upon planners' statistical manipulations instead of the kind of democratic discussion and compromise upon which community support may be founded. By resolving these issues by referendum at an early stage of the planning process, it may be possible to obtain the community acceptance and continuing approval of the plan upon which the transfer of development rights implementation program depends.[17]

The Fairfax County proposal also addresses the problem of a subsequent revision of the comprehensive plan that requires an increase in the number of development rights. In such event, the revision of the comprehensive plan would require approval by referendum. If additional development rights were needed, they would be distributed to existing holders of development rights, similar to the distribution of a stock split.

One of the weaknesses of the Fairfax County proposal is the provision for allocation of development rights to landowners on the basis of acreage instead of value. The rationale for the proposed method of distribution is that "all land is buildable and eventually, given enough economic pressure, it will be developed." Nevertheless, it is easy to imagine circumstances in which the owner of large tracts of worthless swamp, mountainous, or otherwise "unbuildable" land would receive a disproportionate share of development rights while the owner of a smaller tract of more valuable land would receive less than his fair share. The obvious inequities that result therefrom pose serious constitutional questions under the due process and equal protection clauses.

The Sonoma County, California proposal.

Based upon a proposal originally expounded by County Supervisors Robert Theiller and Ig Vella, the Sonoma County Planning Department has prepared a pilot study of the use of "density transfer" for a 14-square-mile area west of Santa Rose, California.[18] In this study, a calculation was made of the number of "density units" (that is, development rights) needed for ultimate development within a prescribed area and for transfer from outlying areas. Purchase of development rights would be

---

17. This issue is discussed also in Rose, "Psychological, Legal and Administrative Problems of the Proposal to Use the Transfer of Development Rights (TDR) as a Technique to Preserve Open Space," J. Urban L. (Fall 1974).

18. *The Potential for Density Transfer in Sonoma County* (Sonoma County Planning Board, Mimeo, June 1974).

financed by a charge imposed upon developers who seek rezoning by increased density within the urban development area. By this system, it would become possible to "sell" zoning rights rather than allow windfall profits to developers who have been able to secure zoning changes for comparatively inexpensive raw land. In addition, development could proceed only within the limits of the prescribed number of development rights created. At the same time, the funds raised by the development charge would be used to purchase the development rights of land to be preserved in open space.

The study provides a detailed analysis of two major calculations upon which the proposal is based: (1) the number of density units that would be needed to achieve the desired mix of residential, commercial, and industrial uses; and (2) the number of development rights that would be available from the land suitable for open space preservation.

The calculation of the number of residential, commercial, and industrial development rights needed is based upon an in-depth analysis of each of nine districts into which the study area is divided. Within each district, optimum residential development is quantified in terms of residential units; optimum commercial and industrial development is quantified on the basis of trip (traffic) generation potential. The formula adopted is based upon the relationship of residential, commercial, and industrial uses and the extent to which they generate traffic, resulting in urban congestion, and how service needs are affected. After calculating the number of density units projected in each district, the number of density units existing under present zoning is subtracted. The difference is the number of development rights needed to achieve the desired mix of uses.

The calculation of the number of development rights that would be available from the land suitable for open space preservation is based upon the premise that only land capable of development should be allowed to sell development rights. Thus, land within the flood plain zone would have no development rights to sell under this proposal. Also in the absence of sewers in the area, land with hardpan soil conditions that could not support septic tanks would also be "undevelopable" and not entitled to development rights. The calculation is also based upon the determination that an "open space preserve" shall consist of no less than 25 contiguous acres.

The Sonoma County proposal then reviews each of three possible methods of calculating the number of development rights to which owners of open space land would be entitled. The New Jersey method, based upon the proportion of assessed value of the property to all open space property, is proposed as one possibility. The second method is a one-for-one exchange of density units. Under this method, each eligible parcel would be entitled to a share based upon the number of density units permitted under existing zoning. The third method in which three concentric bands would be designated around the built-up area of Santa Rosa, is premised upon the idea that closer-in lands are likely to be developed sooner than land further away and therefore would tend to have a higher present value. Thus, a value factor per acre would be assigned to each band that would reflect this difference in value. After analyzing each of the three methods, the study recommends a combination of the second and third as most appropriate for the study area.

The method proposed for the distribution of development rights is only one of the ways in which the Sonoma County proposal differs from the New Jersey and other proposals. Unlike the New Jersey proposal, a free market for the purchase and sale of development rights is not recommended. Although there is no explicit discussion of this issue, it would appear that the proposal contemplates a "development rights bank" operated by a governmental agency in which funds would be raised by development rights charges. The funds would finance the cost of purchasing the development rights from the owners of open space land. In addition, development rights would be required for commercial and industrial as well as residential development. The most significant contribution of the Sonoma County proposal would appear to be the care with which the calculations are made for determining the need for and distribution of development rights.

As a Method of Encouraging the Construction Of Moderate- and Low-Income Housing

In 1972, the Town of Southampton, Long Island, New York, amended its zoning ordinance.[19] The ordinance, as amended, provided for the transfer of development rights as a means of achieving elements of its "community planning objectives," which included the encouragement of a wide variety of housing types. More particularly, it sought to make available housing that residents who have low incomes or lower middle incomes could afford.

To achieve this objective, the town board was authorized to increase the permitted residential development density for a non-profit corporation that guaranteed to develop and maintain housing (sale and rental) at a cost within the means of the low- or lower-middle-income housing market. The ordinance established a procedure by which an application for increased residential development density is reviewed by the town board. Approval by the board would be subject to review by the Planning Board and contingent upon the execution of a contract designed to effect the purposes of the ordinance. The ordinance limits the number of low- and middle-income units which can be built under the plan to 4 percent of the total number of dwelling units of all types in the jurisdiction. It also limits the development site density to not more than twelve units per acre.

Admittedly, the Southampton ordinance does not involve a transfer of development rights in the strict sense because the right to develop land to a prescribed density is not in fact *transferred* from one property owner to another. Rather, the program is more like the San Francisco *bonus zoning* program in which a developer may obtain a bonus of increased floor area ratio (FAR) by providing such public benefits as pedestrian

19. The Town of Southampton Zoning Ordinance of 1971, adopted May 2, 1972, §§ 2-10-20, 2-10-30.

walkways and malls. Nevertheless, consideration of the Southampton ordinance is appropriate because the program is a variation on the basic technique by which the right to develop land is singled out from other ownership rights, and manipulated as a device to control land use. In addition, there is a great likelihood that, if the flow of federal financial assistance for housing diminishes, this technique will be considered seriously by communities as a possible method of economic assistance to provide housing for low and moderate income families.

An article in the Fall 1974 issue of the *Real Estate Law Journal* [20] discusses some of the problems involved in the use of the mandatory percentage of moderately priced dwellings (MPMPD) ordinance. Such an ordinance provides a housing developer with a bonus in terms of zoning density and relaxation of building code requirements in return for his agreement to build a proportion of the units within the range of the moderate or low income market. To create such a program, it is necessary to adopt guiding principles by which the following issues may be resolved: (1) What percentage of the total number of units built must be allocated to the moderate/low income market? (2) What range of tenant/purchaser income needs should the mandatory percentage units be designed to meet? (3) What kind of administrative machinery is necessary to adjust rents to changing economic circumstances? (4) If dwelling units are to be sold, what administrative mechanism is necessary to retain the economic advantages for future low/moderate income purchasers?

In addition to the administrative problems, MPMPD ordinances face questions of statutory authorization and constitutional validity. In the only case to date in which these issues have been raised,[21] the Virginia Supreme Court has held a Fairfax County MPMPD ordinance invalid on the grounds that the ordinance is both outside the scope of statutory authority and also violates the state constitutional provision protecting private property. Nevertheless, proponents of MPMPS ordinances have urged that the validity will be upheld in other jurisdictions.

As a Method of Regulating the
Location and Timing of Community Growth

All of the TDR programs already mentioned have at least one significant characteristic in common: They all use the transfer of development rights in a *negative* way. That is, all of the programs are designed primarily to prevent development of specified areas by directing development elsewhere. However, it is also possible to use the TDR technique to achieve the *affirmative* objective of directing development to a specified area and regulating the timing of each phase of development.

Leonard U. Wilson has described the program that St. George, Ver-

---

20. Rose, "The Mandatory Percentage of Moderate Priced Dwellings (MPMPD) Ordinance Is the Latest Technique of Inclusionary Zoning," 3 Real Estate L.J. (Fall 1974).

21. Board of Supervisors of Fairfax County v. DeGroff Enterprises, Inc., 214 Va. 235, 198 S.E.2d 600 (1973).

mont, has adopted to control the location and rate of its development.[22] St. George is a small town with a population under 500 and total size of 2,300 acres. It is located in the path of Vermont's largest and fastest growing urban area, Burlington. Rather than allow the town to grow in a haphazard, sprawling manner, the people of St. George have adopted a plan to achieve orderly growth. They purchased 48 acres of land on a site which will become the center of a projected village where all future growth will be focused.

The town intends to use its ownership of that parcel, together with the transfer of development rights technique, to concentrate all development in the prescribed area and to regulate the pace of development. To achieve this objective, the town will require a developer to transfer to the town the development rights which the developer purchased from owners of land within the town but outside the project area. In exchange for these development rights, the town will authorize equivalent development within the core village. Under the plan, the number of development rights assigned to each property equals the number of dwelling units that may be built on the property under existing zoning. Thus, for example, a developer could purchase the development rights assigned to 10 acres of land, zoned one dwelling unit per acre, and exchange these ten development rights for authorization to build ten dwelling units on land within the core village.

The net effect of this plan is that development will be concentrated in the designated area and the owners of land outside the village will be compensated by the sale of their development rights for the loss of their right to develop their own land. The rate of development of the village will be regulated by the rate at which the town issues the certificates of development rights.

Some of the problems involved in regulating the location and timing of development by the distribution of development rights are discussed in a paper by Professor Kevin Lynch.[23] Professor Lynch notes that local government must make two political determinations: (1) the desired locations for development, and (2) the rate of growth. The first is a more stable decision, not unlike the exercise of the zoning power where areas are designated for development and restricted development. However, under the TDR system, development can be prohibited in certain areas without outright confiscation. In addition, the more equitable distribution of the rights of development within the jurisdiction should make such locational decisions easier and less prone to corruption, political pressures, and charges of inequity.

The determination of the *rate of growth* involves a more difficult political and planning decision. Professor Lynch suggests that to achieve both public flexibility and private predictability, the growth rate might be set

22. Wilson, "Precedent-Setting Swap in Vermont," 61 American Inst. of Architects J. 51 (1974).

23. Kevin Lynch, *Controlling the Location and Timing of Development by the Distribution of Marketable Development Rights* (Unpublished Mimeo, June 1973). Professor Lynch wrote this paper with the understanding that it would be considered to be a tentative statement subject to modification.

annually for three to five years in the future. In addition, it might be necessary for the state to regulate the local government decision with respect to residential development to assure that such decision is reasonably related to ecological, fiscal, and social constraints, and particularly to the planned and budgeted expansion of public services.

Once the growth rate is determined in terms of the number of residential units, Professor Lynch suggests that some amount be subtracted from that total and held by the government to be given or sold to developers of low income housing. The remainder would then be distributed annually to landowners in the jurisdiction in proportion to the number of acres they own. The recommendation to distribute solely on the basis of acreage rather than development potential under existing zoning is justified on the grounds of administrative simplicity and the desire to reduce the pressures and opportunities for windfall profits from the zoning process.

The proposal to authorize an annual distribution of development rights in accordance with rational and comprehensive planning principles might be even more useful at the regional level, Lynch suggests, where a governmental entity could set growth rates for the entire region. In addition to the planning advantages that would accrue from such allocation at a regional level, the marketability of development rights would be enhanced. The paper does not address the sticky problem of virulent political opposition to any proposal involving a diminution of home rule prerogatives.

As a Method of Avoiding the Windfalls and Wipeouts Syndrome

Professor Donald Hagman's study for the Department of Housing and Urban Development, with the catchy title *Windfalls and Wipeouts Project*, directs attention to the double-edged problem of whether (1) the owners of real estate should be able to keep increases in the realty's value which were created by society; and (2) society should be able to impose losses on the owners of real estate without paying damages. In one of the many publications to be produced in that study,[24] Professor Hagman suggests that the answer to both questions should be "no," and he proposes a number of mechanisms for recapturing windfalls or avoiding wipeouts.

The mechanisms he proposes for windfall recapture are (1) special assessments; (2) subdivision permission exactions; (3) subdivision cash fees in lieu of dedications; (4) development permission exactions; (5) development taxes; (6) capital gains tax; (7) transfer taxes; (8) unearned increment tax; and (9) single tax.

Mechanisms to avoid wipeouts include (1) damages for public improvement; (2) damages in nuisance; and (3) compensable regulation. Suggested as the most exciting techniques that simultaneously deal with both windfalls and wipeouts problems are (1) zoning by eminent domain; (2)

---

24. Hagman, "Windfalls and Wipeouts," in *The Good Earth of America: Planning Our Land Use* (C. Harriss, Ed. 1974).

transfer of development rights; and (3) public ownership. Thus, although the transfer of development rights is only a small part of the *Windfalls and Wipeouts* study, TDR is recognized as a mechanism that holds great potential for resolving both aspects of the problem.

Ellis Gans has proposed[25] a plan in which the transfer of development rights is combined with a "windfall tax" similar to the one used by the British in their Town and Country Planning Act of 1947. The purpose of this proposed "tax" is to recover some of the public investment that makes high density development possible.

Under Gans's plan, the local government would play an active role in the process: Government would help create a market for development rights by keeping a file on willing buyers and sellers and putting them in touch with each other; it would also buy and sell development rights in competition with other purchasers; government would set the windfalls tax in an amount high enough to recover part of the increment in value while leaving sufficient profit for the developer to have an incentive to produce a better product. By "fine tuning" of both the price for development rights and the amount of the "windfalls tax," government would be able to manipulate the economic forces of the marketplace to regulate development in the public interest. Mr. Gans does not address the legal problems involved in the manipulation of a "tax" or other charge.

Evaluations of the Proposals

Many of the proposals for the use of the transfer of development rights as a technique of land-use regulation have come forth during the brief period of 1972 to 1974. It is still too early for a definitive evaluation of these proposals. Nevertheless an interim evaluation of the psychological, legal, administrative, economic, and practical problems raised by TDR would be appropriate.

Psychological, Legal, and Administrative Issues

A recent article of mine[26] suggests that the introduction of TDR proposals—a "strange" new concept in the body of property law—may evoke a form of intellectual xenophobia, that is, fear of a stranger, at least in the beginning. There is a rational basis for concern on the part of planners, attorneys, and government officials about the effect of creating a separate market and conveyance system for development rights. Consequently, a better understanding of the concept and greater knowledge of its effect upon the existing system is essential for the adoption and success of the proposal.

The article also discusses some of the legal problems raised by TDR. A conceptual problem arises because the TDR proposal does not fit unambiguously into the definition of either the police power or the power of

---

25. Gans, *Saving Valued Spaces and Places Through Development Rights Transfer* (Mimeo, 1974).
26. Rose, J. Urban L., note 17, *supra*.

eminent domain. It has some of the characteristics of both traditional governmental powers. The TDR proposal involves something more than police power regulation of property because the right to develop land is taken away from some owners of land. On the other hand, if it is the power of eminent domain that is being exercised, it would be necessary to comply with the well-established principles by which "just compensation" is defined. One such principle requires that compensation be in *money*. It is unclear whether certificates of development rights for use on other property will be held by the courts to be "compensation" within the meaning of the constitutional requirement. One recent decision held that a transfer of zoning density in New York City was not just compensation under the facts of that case.[27]

However, there are sufficient differences between the TDR proposal and the traditional exercise of the power of eminent domain to preclude a blind application of the tranditional principles that limit eminent domain compensation. As a result, the validity of the TDR proposal, when challenged for failure to meet the requirements of just compensation, may very well depend upon the ability of counsel to explain and the ability of the court to understand the unique nature of the TDR proposal.

The criticism to which the TDR proposal is most vulnerable, the article suggests, is that the success of the program depends upon the proficiency of the planners and the integrity of the governing body responsible for its administration. To the extent that either group falters, the program may be jeopardized. The planners' projection of future market demand for land development must be reasonably accurate and the designation of sites for specified land uses must be skillfully performed if there is to be, in fact, a market for development rights. After the planners have performed their role successfully, the governing body must withstand political pressures to modify the planners' recommendations. It will also be necessary for the governing body to persuade the real estate industry of its intention to provide long-term support of the program. The belief that the program will be abandoned at any time in the future would become a self-fulfilling prophecy because it would destroy the market for development rights.

Professor Costonis, in his excellent analysis of the legal issues involved in the transfer of development rights,[28] notes that challenges to TDR are based upon the uniformity provisions of state zoning acts and equal protection substantive due process clauses of state and federal Constitutions. The "uniformity" issue arises out of the provision in most zoning enabling acts that all zoning regulations "shall be uniform for each class of kind of buildings throughout each district." The question is whether different treatment of lots within a transfer district violates this provision. Professor Costonis suggests that the uniformity requirement is not violated because the courts have begun to recognize that the *individual lot* is not the most appropriate unit of development control. When cluster zoning and plan-

---

27. Fred F. French Investing Co. v. City of New York, 352 N.Y.S.2d 762 (N.Y. 1973).

28. Costonis, note 6 *supra*. See also Costonis, *Space Adrift: Saving Urban Landmarks Through the Chicago Plan* 145-166 (1974).

ned unit development ordinances were challenged, courts held that these ordinances met the uniformity requirement if all owners *within the district* are entitled to develop their parcels in accordance with the flexible density or use provisions of the law. That is, if the same options are available to all developers within the district, there is no violation of the uniformity clause. It is generally believed that if the transfer of development rights to a developer within a transfer district does not violate the uniformity provision, it will also not violate the equal protection clause.

The legal challenge to the TDR proposal based upon substantive due process is that a program that imposes density restraints upon most landowners in a district and at the same time relaxes them for some who purchase development rights, sacrifices long-term public objectives for short-term fiscal advantages. Therefore, it is an arbitrary exercise of the police power violating the due process clause of the Fourteenth Amendment. Professor Costonis believes that this argument "misconceives the process by which bulk levels are determined and [the] functions that they serve. As a result, it invests the numbers in the zoning code with an aura of scientific exactitude that is largely without foundation in fact." He argues that density limitations are based upon both fact determination and political judgment and that reasonable variations from the prescribed density within a prescribed range would not undermine the integrity of the planning process. It is not, therefore, an arbitrary exercise of the police power, nor is it a violation of substantive due process.

Economic Issues

Jared B. Shlaes has written an article appearing in *Planning*, a publication of the American Society of Planning Officials, that discusses some of the economic issues raised by TDR. More specifically, the question raised is: Who, if anyone, pays the costs of the transfer of development rights to other sites? Owners of property from whom development rights are taken do not pay the costs because they are compensated by the sale of such rights. The developers who purchase the rights do not pay the costs because as long as there is sufficient market demand for development at higher densities, those costs will be included in the rental or sales charges of the new units. The purchasers or renters of the new units do not pay the costs because they will pay no more for such space than they would pay for equivalent space either inside or outside the district. Whether that space exists by virtue of development rights or because of additional land purchase is immaterial to them.

It has been suggested that it is the owners of property adjacent to the higher-density development who pay the costs of TDR because they must endure larger structures within the community than would otherwise be possible without a zoning change. Mr. Shlaes argues against this position for a number of reasons. First, he asserts, such claims are speculative because in the typical urban situation entire districts are already grossly overzoned. Consequently, the TDR process that permits a slight overreach of permissible densities at specific locations merely redistributes the density within the district. Furthermore, Shlaes argues, the increase in value of property adjacent to high density structures may more than offset any such costs.

He also argues that the general public does not pay the costs because tax revenues are in no way diminished; landmarks and open spaces are preserved; and the community benefits from improved planning. And so it appears to Mr. Shlaes that the benefits of a TDR program may be achievable without any costs other than the costs of administration.

Practical Planning Issues

Audrey Moore, in her evaluation of the Fairfax County, Virginia proposal,[29] calls attention to some of the disadvantages and advantages of that proposal. The Fairfax County plan is based upon a free market for development rights. Consequently, that program does not deal with the windfalls/wipeouts problem with the effectiveness possible under the Puerto Rican or Chicago plans, where the governmental agency acquires and sells development rights at prices that recover the windfalls and compensate owners whose land use is restricted. Ms. Moore also expresses her concern for the inequities that may result if the planners err in their projections of future populations: If their populations projections turn out to be lower than actual growth, then astute speculators will reap large profits; if their population projections turn out to be higher than actual growth and economic demand for land, then there will be an insufficient market demand for development rights. (It is just for this reason that the Sonoma County, California, proposal is based upon an in-depth analysis of (1) the number of density units needed for planned development, and (2) the number of development rights to be issued.) But the greatest problem that Audrey Moore recognizes is the lack of public understanding of the TDR concept and the fear that a change from the existing system will have an adverse effect upon their rights.

On the other hand, Ms. Moore argues that the potential advantages of the TDR proposal far outweigh its disadvantages. The system can provide a more effective control of the use of land and the timing of development than zoning; it can provide compensation to owners of land whose use is restricted; it can provide an effective mechanism for monitoring and controlling total planned growth; it can save time and expense for developers by providing certainty in the rules that determine where and how development can take place; it can preserve open space and farmland; *and it can do all of these things without any direct cost to government.*

Because of this wide array of opportunities and advantages, it is easy to understand why planners, lawyers, and public officials have indicated a growing interest in the transfer of development rights as a new technique of land-use regulation.

---

29. Moore, note 1 *supra*, at 23-31.

A PROPOSAL FOR THE SEPARATION
AND MARKETABILITY OF DEVELOPMENT RIGHTS
AS A TECHNIQUE TO PRESERVE OPEN SPACE
JEROME G. ROSE
2 REAL ESTATE LAW JOURNAL 635 (1974)

INTRODUCTION: ALTERNATE TECHNIQUES OF PRESERVING OPEN SPACE

The history of American land-use policy has been a history of land *development*.[1] From the Northwest Ordinance of 1787 to the Homestead Act of 1862 to the large-scale FHA mortgage insurance programs in aid of home ownership after World War II, the objective of land-use policy has been the *development* of land to meet the shifting patterns of national migration. During the nineteenth century, opportunities for land ownership and development were used to encourage the migration to the Western states. During the last half of the nineteenth century, intensive land development was encouraged to provide for the aggregations of population in the cities. In the middle of the twentieth century, our land-use policy encouraged the development of land to create suburban communities around those cities. Currently a new migration of population appears to be emerging from metropolitan areas to nonmetropolitan areas in Vermont, Virginia, Colorado, California, Washington, and attractive regions of other states.[2] Encouraged by manufacturers of second homes, the recreation industry, the hotel-motel industry, the road-builders[3] and real estate industry, this migration may create a surge of demand for land development beyond the regulating ability of existing techniques of land-use control.

An examination of existing techniques of regulating land development to preserve open space is useful to determine the limits of effectiveness of those techniques.[4] Some techniques are in general use; others are proposals that have not been widely adopted. Considered together, the fol-

---

1. Two notable exceptions to this generalization are the Conservation Movement during the administration of Theodore Roosevelt and the Greenbelt Movement during the administration of Franklin D. Roosevelt.

2. *See* Note, "Protection of Environmental Quality in Nonmetropolitan Regions By Limiting Development," 57 Iowa L. Rev. 126 (1971), particularly footnotes 4 to 14 for citations of articles describing this migration in different regions.

3. *Id.* at 127.

4. In general *see* Note, "Techniques for Preserving Open Spaces," 75 Harv. L. Rev. 1622 (1962); Eckert, "Acquisition of Development Rights: A Modern Land Use Tool," 23 U. Miami L. Rev. 347 (1969); Eveleth, "Appraisal of Techniques to Preserve Open Space," 9 Vill. L. Rev. 559 (1964); Beuscher, "Some Legal Aspects of Scenic Easement," 1 Land Use Controls 28 (1967); Krasnowiecki and Paul, "The Preservation of Open Space in Metropolitan Areas," 110 U. P. L. Rev. 179 (1961).

lowing constitute the current state of the art of open space preservation: (1) police power regulation (e.g., zoning and subdivision control); (2) compensable regulation; (3) public acquisition of the fee; and (4) public acquisition of less than the fee (e.g., conservation easements).

Police Power Regulation

Police power regulation is based upon the principle that, in a society governed by law, everyone must submit to reasonable regulation of his liberty and property to prevent the abuse of these rights by those who are unskillful, careless or unscrupulous.[5] The police power is exercised by the government "to promote and protect the health, safety, morals, comfort and general welfare of the people."[6] Based upon this power, states have delegated to local government the power to regulate the use of property and "to impair the owner's rights therein to some *reasonable extent* without compensation because the legislature, acting under the police power of the state, deems the free exercise of such rights detrimental to the public interests." [Emphasis added.][7]

The difficulty in relying upon the police power to preserve open space is the lack of objective standards for determining whether the property use restriction is reasonable under the circumstances.[8] In determining the reasonableness (and therefore the validity) of a land-use regulation, a court must weigh the evidence relating to the public interest and the rights of the property owner. As a result of this comparative evaluation, the court may determine that the public interest is so slight or the deprivation of the owner is so great that the regulation is unreasonable under the circumstances and therefore is invalid as a violation of substantive due process.[9] Based upon this reasoning, courts have held invalid zoning ordinances restricting land use to flood storage and open space,[10] parking lot purposes,[11] school and recreational use,[12] and greenbelt and park pur-

---

5. Fruend, *The Police Power* (1904).

6. La Salle Nat'l Bank v. Chicago, 5 Ill. 2d 344, 350, 125 N.E.2d 609, 612 (1955).

7. Robinson v. Town Council of Narragansett, 60 R.I. 422, 434, 199 A. 308, 313 (1938).

8. For a general discussion of this topic *see* Heyman & Gilhool, "The Constitutionality of Imposing Increased Community Costs on New Suburban Residents Through Subdivision Exaction," 73 Yale L.J. 119 (1964) Sax, "Takings and the Police Power," 74 Yale L.J. 36 (1964); Netherton, "Implementation of Land Use Policy; Police Powers vs. Eminent Domain," 3 Land and Water L. Rev. 33 (1968); Comment, "Control of Urban Sprawl or Securing Open Space: Regulation by Condemnation or Ordinance?" 50 Calif. L. Rev. 483 (1962).

9. *See* Rose, *Legal Foundations of Urban Planning: Cases & Materials on Planning Law* 46 (1973).

10. Morris County Land Improvement Co. v. Parsippany-Troy Hills Tp., 40 N.J. 539, 193 A.2d 232 (1963).

11. Vernon Park Realty v. Mount Vernon, 307 N.Y. 493, 121 N.E.2d 517 (1954).

12. City of Plainfield v. Borough of Middlesex, 69 N.Y. Super. 136, 173 A.2d 785 (L. Div. 1961).

poses.[13] Similarly, subdivision regulations have been held invalid, in spite of a substantial public interest, where the owner is denied reasonable use of his property.[14]

In *Morris County Land Improvement Co. v. Parsippany-Troy Hills Tp.*,[15] a leading case on the issue of zoning regulation for flood-detention purposes, the court conceded that the determination of whether the ordinance is a valid regulation or an invalid taking is always a matter of degree. It stated, however, that "there is no question that the line has been crossed when the purpose and practical effect of the regulation is to appropriate private property for a flood-water basin or open space."[16] The court stated that public *acquisition* (with compensation) rather than *regulation* (without compensation) was required to provide land for open space.

To the extent that this principle continues to be adopted by the courts, police-power regulation will not provide an effective technique for preserving open space.

Compensable Regulation

To overcome the constitutional objection to the harsh effect of depriving an owner of the use of his property restricted to open space purposes, Professors Jan Krasnowiecki and James Paul proposed a system by which owners would be compensated for part of their losses.[17] Under their proposal, an owner would be compensated for the loss of the development value of his property at the time the controls were imposed. For example, an owner of agricultural land with a market value of $1,000 before it is restricted to open space use would be entitled to compensation of $400 if the market value of his land is reduced to only $600 when restricted to agricultural or other open spaces use. The proposed compensation represents the development value of the property "taken" from the owner by the police-power restriction upon the use of his property. The owner would not be eligible for compensation until he sells the property because, until the sale, he would have not incurred any loss. To prevent fraudulent claims for excessive compensation, the proposal includes a requirement for an administratively controlled public sale.

The Krasnowiecki and Paul proposal is based upon a skillful and imaginative combination of the police power and the eminent domain power. The harshness of police-power restriction is softened by compensa-

---

13. Greenhills Home Owners Corp. v. Village of Greenhills, 202 N.E.2d 192 (Ohio Ct. App. 1964), rev'd 5 Ohio St. 2d 207, 215 N.E.2d 403 (1965), *cert. denied* 385 U.S. 836 (1967); *see* Kusler, "Open Space Zoning: Valid Regulations or Invalid Taking," 57 Minn. L. Rev. 1 (1972).

14. Baker v. Planning Board, 353 Mass. 141, 228 N.E. 831 (1967). The court held that a planning board could not disapprove a subdivision plan so that the town could continue to use the owner's land as a water storage area.)

15. Note 10 *supra*.

16. *Id.* at 555.

17. Krasnowiecki and Paul, note 4 *supra*; see also Krasnowiecki and Strong, "Compensable Regulations for Open Space," 29 Journal of the American Institute of Planners 87 (1963).

tion for the loss of the development value. The high cost of acquisition under the eminent domain power is reduced by limiting the public cost to the development value at the time of regulation. In spite of these advantages, compensable regulation has not been utilized as an effective technique for preserving open space for a number of reasons. The primary reason is that the American public does not seem prepared to accept a program that denies a property owner the speculative value of his property; i.e., the value based upon the expectation, whether real or fancied, that the value will continue to increase with time. Secondly, the public and the legal profession are not sufficiently comfortable with the concept of development rights and are fearful of unknown consequences of the concept upon the real estate market. Thirdly, the proposal requires a relatively complex system of governmental administration that would tend to impede the alienability of property. Consequently, the effectiveness of compensable regulation as a technique for preserving open space remains untested.

Public Acquisition of the Fee

The power of the federal and state governments to acquire property for park and recreational purposes is well established.[18] A number of states, including New Jersey,[19] New York,[20] Massachusetts,[21] California,[22] and Wisconsin[23] have authorized state or local government acquisition of land for recreational, conservation, or open-space purposes. There is little doubt about the effectiveness of this technique to preserve open space—when it can be implemented. The primary impediment to the use of public acquisition of the fee is the lack of funds available for this purpose. Voter reluctance to approve programs or bond issues that will result in increased taxation is a serious obstacle. The numerous federal programs of financial assistance for local government acquisition of land[24] have not overcome this problem because the federal appropriations under these programs can fill only a very small portion of the need.

In addition to the lack of financial resources, there are other objections to the public acquisition of lands for open-space preservation: (1) When title is transferred from private to public ownership, the property is removed from the tax rolls and the remaining property owners in the jurisdiction must bear a proportionately larger share of the tax burden. (2) There exists in many areas of the nation strong political opposition to government ownership and management of land. (3) Many farmers and

---

18. Shoemaker v. United States, 147 U.S. 282 (1893).

19. N.J. Stat. Ann. § 13:8A-1 (1961).

20. N.Y. Conservation Law §§ 1-701, 1-0708 (1960 as amended 1964).

21. 1B Mass. Laws. Ann. Ch. 40 § 8(c) (1961).

22. Calif. Gov't Code 12 §§ 6950-6954 (1959), § 7000 (1963).

23. Wisc. Stat. Ann. § 23.09(16).

24. E.g., the Open Space Program in Title VII of the Housing Act of 1961, §§ 701-06, 42 U.S.C.A. §§ 1500-1500(e) (Supp. 1961); the Federal Land and Water Conservation Program, 16 U.S.C. §§ 4601-5 (Supp. V. 1970); the Cropland Adjustment Act, 7 U.S.C. § 1838 (1971); the Watershed Protection and Flood Prevention Act, 16 U.S.C. §§ 1001-09 (1964) as amended (Supp. V. 1970).

other landowners are unwilling to relinquish possession of their land even for a fair consideration. (4) Although preservation of open space is a commendable objective, the high costs of land acquisition would divert substantial public resources from other objectives of higher priority, such as education and housing. Taken together, these factors have created a formidable obstacle to the widespread use of public acquisition of land for open space preservation.

Public Acquisition of Less Than the Fee: Conservation Easements

In 1959, William H. Whyte, Jr. proposed a method of preserving open space by authorizing governments to acquire only the owner's right to develop the land, leaving him with all other rights of ownership, including the right of continued possession.[25] Whyte called this right a "conservation easement" because the purpose of its acquisition by government is to conserve the environmental amenities of land, air, soil, open space, and historic areas. After acquisition of the conservation easement by the government, the owner continues to own and use his land, subject only to the right of the government to prevent its development. The easement runs with the land and binds all subsequent purchasers.

Public acquisition of the conservation easement rather than the fee simple (entire title) has a number of advantages: (1) The cost of acquisition of a conservation easement is less than the cost of the fee. The value of a conservation easement would be the difference between the value of the land restricted to agricultural or other open space uses. Consequently, in rural areas, outside the influence of demand for urban development, the conservation easement could be acquired at very low cost. (2) There would be less opposition from farmers to the acquisition of conservation easements because they would be able to remain in possession and use their land for farming purposes. (3) The land would remain on the tax rolls and, at the time of acquisition, would not impose any appreciable burden upon other property owners. The property tax would be imposed upon the assessed value of the land restricted to agricultural or open space use. Therefore, property taxes would not increase as development values rise and would not make the land too costly to maintain for farming purposes. As the demand for development in the area increases, the owners of developable land will reap the benefits of increased value and will pay taxes upon a higher assessed value.

In spite of these apparent advantages, public acquisition of conservation easements has not been an effective technique of preserving open space. As one critic put it, "A policy of taking conservation easements is undesirable, potentially unfair, and legally dangerous."[26] It has been argued that conservation easements are not effective where they are used to

---

25. Whyte, Securing Open Space For Urban America: Conservation Easements (Urban Land Inst. Tech. Bull. No. 36, 1959).

26. N. Williams, Land Acquisition For Outdoor-Recreation—Analysis of Selected Legal Problems, 48 (U.S. Outdoor Recreation Resources Review Comm. Study Report No. 16, 1963).

make significant changes in existing land use or where real estate speculation has affected the market value of the land.[27]   Because of these difficulties, the National Park Service discontinued the acquisition of scenic
easements and reported: "On the basis of 20 years of experience, such
easements breed misunderstandings, administrative difficulties, are difficult to enforce, and cost only a little less than the fee."[28]

Thus, it seems clear that each of the existing techniques of preserving
open space has one or more serious limitations that makes it incapable of
preventing the development of land in the amount and locations necessary
to enhance the quality of life in metropolitan areas. New and imaginative
techniques must be devised, refined, and perfected for this purpose. It is
the thesis of this report that the separation and marketability of development rights may provide the legal instrumentality by which open space
may be preserved in a manner that is consistent with constitutionally protected property rights and the realities of municipal finance.

Precedent for Transferability of Development Rights

The transfer of development rights as a means of controlling the use
and development of land is not without precedent. Almost three decades
of British experimentation in land-use control has been based upon this
concept. In the United States, there are numerous illustrations of judicial
recognition of its existence and sanction of its validity. Examination of
these precedents will be useful to an understanding of the concept.

The British Experiment [29]

In the late 1930s and early 1940s, the British Parliament, concerned
with the need to decentralize and disperse industries and industrial population, redevelop congested urban areas, and decrease the vulnerability of
population and industry to air attack, created three committees to study

27. *Id.* at 45.
28. H. R. Rep. No. 273, 87th Cong. 1st Sess. 1961, as cited in Eveleth, note 4
supra, at 566-567.
29. American students of British land-use planning have observed and reported
on developments in the British experiment in land-use planning over the years.
The following, in chronological sequence, is a bibliography of those reports: D.
Pooley, The Evolution of British Planning Legislation (Legislative Research
Center, University of Michigan Law School, 1960); Mandelker, "Notes from the
English: Compensation in Town and Country Planning," 49 Calif. L. Rev. 699
(1961); D. Heap, An Outline of Planning Law (4th ed. 1963); D. Heap, Introducing the Land Commission Act (1967); Heap, "The Taxation of Development Value
in Land: The English Bill for a Land Commission," Trends (ASPO 1967); Thomas,
"Land Planning and Development Values in Postwar Britain," Trends (ASPO
1967); Garner, "Introduction to English Planning Law," 24 Okl. L. Rev. 457
(1971); Garner & Callies, "Planning England the Wales and in the United States,"
1 Anglo-American L. Rev. 434 (1972); Hagman, "Planning Blight, Participation
and Just Compensation: Anglo-American Comparisons," 4 The Urban Lawyer 434
(1972); Moore, "Planning in Britain: The Changing Scene," 1972 Urban Law Annual 89.

and report on these problems and their solution. Extensive studies by these committees resulted in three now famous reports: (1) the *Barlow Report*,[30] (2) the *Uthwatt Report*,[31] and (3) the *Scott Report*.[32] Together, these reports proposed land-use planning on a national scale, recommended that private rights in land be subjected to the public welfare, and that the use of land by private owners be restricted to accomplish this objective.[33]

Of the three reports, the *Uthwatt Report* made the most significant contributions to the field of land use regulation in its conceptualization of the problem and its recommendations for solution. The *Uthwatt Report* defined and emphasized the importance of several new land-use concepts, including (1) *betterment* and (2) *floating value*.

Betterment is defined as an increase in the value of land that results when government undertakes public works or other improvements on adjacent or nearby land. This concept includes "the principle that persons whose property has clearly increased in market value by an improvement effected by local authorities should specially contribute to the cost of the improvement."[34] *Betterment charge* is the term describing the exaction by which government recoups this increment in market value.

Floating value is defined as the potential increase in value of all undeveloped land in an area. In the early stages of development of an area, it is practically impossible to predict with any certainty the exact parcels of land upon which the floating value will settle. However, public control of land use results in shifting of floating value from some land to other land.

After analyzing the nature and implications of these concepts the Uthwatt committee recommended, inter alia, that:

(1) A system be established to "recoup the betterment" from landowners who are "unjustly enriched" by increases in value of their land resulting from government action and to compensate landowners from whose land the "floating value" had been shifted by governmental action; and

(2) The rights of development in all land lying outside built-up areas (with certain exceptions) be vested immediately in the government and that fair compensation be paid for those rights. Thereafter the land could not be developed without the consent of the government and the repurchase of the development right.

The *Uthwatt* committee believed that these (and other) recommendations would achieve the benefits of government control of land use without government nationalization (i.e., ownership) of the land. The device proposed to accomplish this objective was the separation of the develop-

---

30. Royal Commission on the Distribution of the Industrial Population, Report Cmd. No. 6153 (1940).

31. Expert Committee on Compensation and Betterment, Final Report, Cmd. No. 6386 (1942).

32. Committee on Land Utilization in Rural Area, Report Cmd. No. 6378 (1942).

33. *See* Pooley, *supra*, note 29 at 27.

34. House of Lords Paper (159) at 1894 quoted in the Uthwatt Report, ¶ 259 at 104; *see* Pooley, note 29 *supra*, at 17.

ment right from the other rights of ownership of land and the transfer of that right to government.

Parliament adopted these recommendations in the Town and County Planning Act of 1947[35] (hereinafter called the 1947 Act). Under this law, the British government took over the development rights of all undeveloped land. This left the owners of land with all other rights of ownership, except the right to develop.[36] When an owner wanted to develop his land he had to buy back the right to develop from the government by paying a development charge.

The 1947 Act provides for compensation to landowners for the value of the development right at the time of the taking in 1947. The amount of the compensation was set at the value of the land in excess of "existing uses" as defined in the statute. A 300-million-pound revolving fund was created from which compensation would be paid and into which the betterment charges would be deposited.

In spite of the hopes and best intentions of planners and legislators, it is generally conceded that the system did not work well in practice,[37] primarily because owners "refused to develop their land or sell it for anything less than its full market value."[38] Buyers, who would have to pay a development charge in an amount equal to the difference between the current market value and the 1947 "existing-use" value would be willing to pay for land no more than the 1947 "existing-use" value. It soon became apparent that the price that sellers demanded and the price that developers could pay for land was so far apart that the marketability of land had been destroyed. Consequently, Parliament abolished the development charge in the Town and Country Planning Acts of 1953 and 1954.[39] This legislation did not return the development rights to the land owners. The law only eliminated the charge previously exacted for permission to develop. The development rights remained separated from the rest of the rights of land ownership.

Then in 1967, in an extremely intricate and complex[40] piece of legislation,[41] the development charge was reinstated at 40 percent of the development value (not unlike our capital gains tax) and remained in effect until 1971 when it was abolished once again.[42]

---

35. 10 & 11 Geo. 6, c. 51.

36. "Indeed, after July 1, 1948, ownership of land carries with it nothing more than the bare right to go on using it for its existing purpose. The owner has no right to develop it, that is to say, has no right to build on it and no right to change its use." Heap, *An Outline of Planning Law* 12 (1963).

37. Town and Country Planning in Britain (Central Office of Information Reference Pamphlet No. 9, 1962).

38. Pooley, note 29 *supra*, at 84.

39. 1 & 2 Eliz. 2, c.16; 2 & 3 Eliz. 2, c.72.

40. "I would be the last person to say I understand the Bill," a statement made by the Lord Chancellor on December 6, 1966 during the House of Lords debate on the Land Commission Bill, as cited in D. Heap, Introducing the Land Commission Act (1967).

41. Land Commission Act, 1967, c.1.

42. Land Commission (Dissolution) Act of 1971; see Moore, note 29 *supra*, at 91, 93.

The British experience with development rights has been something less than a resounding success. The development rights are still separated from the balance of the title and have been retained by the British government. Thus far, the British have been unable to devise an effective system by which the separation and marketability of development rights may be used as a land use control device.

American Experience

American experience with development rights transfer is less specific, more diverse, less systematized, and more recent than the British. Nevertheless, the development rights transfer concept has been used in the United States in the following programs: (1) eminent domain acquisition of less than a full fee; (2) landmark preservation transfer of FAR rights; (3) incentive zoning transfer of FAR bonuses.

Eminent Domain Acquisition of Less Than the Fee

There are both judicial and legislative precedents for government acquisition of less-than-the-fee simple.[43] One of the original proponents of government acquisition of less-than-the-fee simple used the phrase "conservation easement" to describe the part of the title acquired by government.[44] The use of the word easement to describe this legal right was an unfortunate choice of nomenclature because of numerous technical common law restrictions on easements. For example, there are the following common law principles: (1) The law will not recognize the creation of new kinds of easements.[45] (2) The benefits of easements are generally not assignable.[46] Where assignable may not be separated from the land benefited therefrom.[47] In spite of these common law rules, American courts have recognized the right of government agencies to acquire less than the full fee under varied circumstances. For example, the Minnesota Supreme Court upheld the "taking" of the right to build certain classes of buildings in areas where such restriction was necessary to assure a fit and harmonious surrounding for residential use.[48] In California, a court upheld the condemnation of the right of joint use of utility line poles. The court conceded that there was no precise legal designation for the right being acquired but said that, wherever a substantial right of use exists,

---

43. Weissburg, "Legal Alternatives to Police Power: Condemnation and Purchase, Development Rights, Gifts," in *Open Space and The Law* (F. Herring ed. 1965); N. Williams, *Land Acquisition for Outdoor Recreation—Analysis of Selected Legal Problems* (U.S. Outdoor Recreation Resources Review Comm. Study Report No. 16, 1963).

44. Whyte, note 25 *supra*.

45. Keppell v. Bailey, 2 Myl. & K. 517, 535, 39 Eng. Rept. 1042, 1049 (Ch. 1834).

46. 2 American Law of Property §§ 8.78-8.83 (Casner ed. 1952).

47. 2 American Law of Property *supra* at § 8.73; see Eveleth, note 4 *supra*, at 568 for additional authorities cited therein.

48. *See* State *ex rel.* Twin City Bldg. & Inv. Co. v. Houghton, 144 Minn. 1, 174 N.W. 885 (1919), 176 N.E. 159 (1920).

that right is subject to the power of eminent domain.[49] In New York, a court upheld the condemnation of interests in strips of land next to a highway that left the owner of the fee with little more than the right to use the land for ornamental courtyards only. The court held that the city could limit its taking to only that legal interest required to meet the public need.[50]

The legislatures of several states have begun to recognize the advantage of acquiring interests in land less than the full fee. The New Jersey Green Acres Land Acquisition Act of 1961 provides:

> "Without limitation of the definition of 'lands' herein, the commissioner may acquire, or approve grants to assist a local unit to acquire . . . (b) an interest or right consisting, in whole or in part, of a *restriction on the use* of land by others including owners of other interests therein. . . ."[51] (Emphasis added.)

Notice that the New Jersey statute describes the right to be taken in negative terms, i.e., authorization is granted to acquire a "restriction on the use of land." This self-conscious discomfort with the concept also appears, but to a lesser extent, in the wording of the California statute:

> "Any county or city may acquire, by purchase, gift, grant, devise, lease or otherwise, and through the expenditure of public funds, the fee, *or any lesser interest or right* in real property in order to preserve, *through limitation of their future use,* open spaces and areas for public use and enjoyment."[52] (Emphasis added.)

On the other hand, authors of the Vermont statute seems to have overcome any insecurity with this new concept and have expressly recognized development rights in their eminent domain enabling legislation:

> "The legislative body of a municipality or a department, as the case may be, shall determine the types of rights and interests in real property to be acquired, including licenses, equitable servitudes, profits, rights under covenants, easements, *development rights,* or any other rights and interests in real property of whatever character."[53] (Emphasis added.)

As American planners and attorneys became familiar with the concept of the transferability of development rights, they began to experiment with techniques by which the concept may be used as a land-use control device. This effort has moved in two directions to date: (1) preservation of landmarks and (2) incentive or bonus zoning.

Transfers of FAR Rights to Preserve Historic Landmarks

One student of urban affairs has compared urban landmarks to the

---

49. Sacramento Municipal Util. Dist. v. Pacific Gas & Elec. Co., 72 Cal. App. 2d 638, 165 P.2d 741 (Dist. Ct. App. 1946).

50. In the Matter of the City of New York, 57 App. Div. 166, 68 N.Y. Supp. 196, *aff'd. mem.* 167 N.Y. 624, 60 N.E. 1108 (1901).

51. N.J. Stat. Ann. § 13:8A-12 (1961).

52. Cal. Gov't. Code § 6950.

53. Vt. Stat. Ann. tit. 10, § 6303(b) (Supp. 1971).

ocelot and the snow leopard because all are "imperiled species."[54] Attempts to preserve urban landmarks by police-power prohibition of their demolition have been held to violate the constitutional protection against unreasonable deprivation of property.[55] On the other hand, municipal resources are chronically insufficient to fund the acquisition of urban landmarks through the eminent domain power. This dilemma has provided the incentive for some cities, including New York City and Chicago, to experiment with the transfer of development rights as a means of preserving urban landmarks.[56]

The New York City ordinance provides:

"The City Planning Commission may permit *development rights* to be transferred to adjacent lots from lots occupied by landmark buildings . . . and may permit in the case of residential developments or enlargements, the minimum required open space or the minimum lot area per room to be reduced on the basis of such transfer of development rights."[57] (Emphasis added.)

The New York City transfer of development rights system is based upon the fact that the value of real estate in many parts of the city depends upon the intensity of development permitted under the zoning law and the fact that urban landmarks usually have an excess of authorized but unbuilt floor area under the floor area ratio (FAR) provisions. The FAR is a zoning technique to regulate the physical volume (density) of a building by controlling the relation between the floor area of a building and the area of the lot on which the building stands.[58]

Expressed as a formula:

$$\text{FAR (5)} = \frac{\text{Floor Area (50,000 sq. ft.)}}{\text{Lot Area \quad (10,000 sq. ft.)}}$$

Thus, a building to be constructed in a zoning district with a FAR of five could have five times more floor space than lot area. Consequently, an owner of a lot of 10,000 square feet could build no more than 50,000 square feet of floor space. If that parcel happens to be in an area with sufficient economic demand for more intensive development, e.g., high-rise office construction, the owner would seek to find ways to increase the floor area of his proposed building. The New York City ordinance permits landmark owner to sell the authorized but unused floor area of their landmark site to adjacent lotowners. Consequently, the owner of an adja-

---

54. Costonis, "The Chicago Plan: Incentive Zoning and the Preservation of Urban Landmarks," 85 Harv. L. Rev. 574 (1972).

55. *See* People *ex rel.* Marbro Corp. v. Ramsey, 28 Ill. App. 2d 252, 171 N.E. 246 (1960); *In re* Opinion of the Justices, 333 Mass. 773, 128 N.E.2d 557 (1955).

56. See Costonis, note 54 *supra; see* also Note, "Development Rights Transfer in New York City," 82 Yale L. J. 338 (1972).

57. New York City Zoning Ordinance, art. VII, ch. 4, §§ 74-79 (1971).

58. For a more detailed discussion of the system, *see* Note, "Building Size, Shape and Placement Regulations: Bulk Control Zoning Reexamined," 60 Yale L. J. 506 (1951).

cent lot may purchase the unused floor area from the landmark owner. The consideration for this transfer of development rights compensates the landmark owner for preserving the landmark. Once the landmark owner transfers the development rights (i.e., authorized but unused floor area), the incentive to demolish the landmark is reduced because of the limited floor area authorization still remaining for use on the landmark site.

The New York City system of development right transfer has been neither widely used nor successful in preserving the city's landmarks.[59] The Chicago ordinance seeks to improve upon this system by a more ambitious and comprehensive program. Under the Chicago plan:[60] (1) Transfers of development rights are not limited to adjacent properties. Transfers are permitted to any property within specially created development rights transfer districts. (2) An attempt is made to compensate the landmark owner for the actual cost of preserving the landmark structure, including the right to transfer up to 100 percent of the FAR, and real estate tax reduction and special municipal subsidies, where necessary. Nevertheless, the primary incentive is the transfer of development rights from one land owner to another. The Chicago plan stops short of a general bonus system for favored improvements.

Incentive (Bonus) Zoning

The logical extension of the New York City and Chicago programs, where development rights are transferred from one owner to another, is a general bonus system where an FAR bonus is created by the municipality. The City of San Francisco has adopted this system. Under the plan, the downtown is divided into four districts, each with a prescribed FAR. A builder may obtain a bonus of an increased FAR, within prescribed limits, by providing public benefits such as: (1) improved accessibility (e.g., rapid transit access; rapid transit proximity; parking access); (2) improved pedestrian movement (e.g., multiple building entrances, sidewalk widening, shortening walking distances); (3) pedestrian amenities (e.g., a plaza); (4) light and air for streets (e.g., additional setbacks or low coverage on upper floors); or, (5) view enhancement (e.g., an observation deck).[61]

In a strict sense, the San Francisco plan and other programs of incentive zoning offering FAR bonuses are not examples of the transfer of development rights because a part of the fee is not separated from the title of one landowner and transferred to another landowner. Instead, the government, under its police power, artificially restricts development and then prescribes conditions under which those restrictions may be relaxed. On the other hand, the San Francisco plan is similar to the transfer of

---

59. For a discussion of the reasons for its failure see Costonis, supra, note 54 and Note, "Development Rights Transfer in New York City," note 56 supra.

60. San Francisco Planning Code, §§ 122-122.4.

61. See Sversky, "San Francisco: The Downtown Development Bonus System," and Ruth, "Economic Aspects of the San Francisco Zoning Ordinance Bonus System," both in The New Zoning: Legal Administrative and Economic Concepts and Techniques, N. Marcus & M. Grove, Eds. (1970).

development rights system in that the right to develop is specifically sing-led out, among the other rights of ownership, and manipulated as a de-vice to control land use. For this reason, awareness of the incentive bonus system, as well as the landmark preservation system and the British ex-periments is helpful in understanding the newer proposals to use the transfer and marketability of development rights as a means of preserving open space.

PROPOSED LEGISLATION TO UTILIZE DEVELOPMENT RIGHTS
MARKETABILITY AND TRANSFERS TO PRESERVE OPEN SPACE

The first legislative attempt to create a comprehensive system in which the marketability and transfer of development rights are used to regulate land use was introduced in the Maryland Senate in 1972 by State Senator William Goodman.[62] At the same time, in New Jersey, a committee made up of Rutgers University faculty and members of the New Jersey Department of Community Affairs were independently engaged in a simi-lar project.[63] The provisions set forth below are excerpts, *with modifica-tions* of the legislative proposal that emerged from that committee.[64] This draft does not purport to be a complete or final draft of a legislative proposal. It is designed primarily as a device to draw attention to the possibilities for the use of the concept and to the problems which require solution.

Summary of the Legislative Proposal[65]

The proposed legislation seeks to utilize the separability and transfer-ability of development rights as the basis of a technique to induce owners of undeveloped land to preserve their land in open space. The owners of preserved open space are compensated for their deprivation of use by the sale of development rights to developers of other land in the jurisdiction. To make these sales possible, it is necessary to establish a system that creates a market for development rights in which owners of developable land must buy development rights from owners of preserved open space land as a prerequisite for development.

---

62. S. 254, Senate of Maryland; introduced, read first time and referred to the Committee on Economic Affairs, January, 1972.

63. Members of this committee were: T. Airola, R. Binetsky, B. Chavooshian, R. Ginman, T. Hall, J. Jager, T. Norman, E. Reoch and J. Rose.

64. Many of the provisions set forth herein contain modifications made by this author and may not be in accord with the corresponding provisions in the final draft submitted by the committee. For a more detailed report of the work of this committee, *see* B. Chavooshian and T. Norman, Transfer of Development Rights; A New Concept in Land Use Management (Mimeo, Leaflet No. 492, Cooperative Extension Service, Cook College, Rutgers University, 1973).

65. *See* Rose, "Proposed Development Rights Legislation Can Change the Name of the Land Investment Game," 1 Real Estate L. J. 276 (1973).

The legislation is designed to create such a market in the following manner:

(1) Each local government would prepare a land-use plan that specifies the percentage of remaining undeveloped land in the jurisdiction and that designates the land to remain undeveloped as preserved open space land. The land-use plan would also designate the land to be developed and would specify the uses to which the developable land may be put. A zoning law would be enacted or amended to implement this plan.

(2) The planning board of each local government would prescribe the number of development rights required for each housing unit to be developed. On the basis of this numerical assignment, the planning board would then compute the number of development rights required to develop the jurisdiction in accordance with the land-use plan. The local government would issue certificates of development rights (ownership of which would be recorded) in the exact amount so determined.

(3) Every owner of preserved open space land would receive certificates of development rights in an amount that represents the percentage of assessed value of his undeveloped land to the total assessed value of all undeveloped land in the jurisdiction.

(4) An owner of developable land, who desires to develop his land more intensively (e.g., apartments instead of single family residence) would have to buy additional development rights, on the open market, from those who have acquired such rights from either original distribution or subsequent purchase.

(5) Thus, owners of preserved open space would be able to sell their development rights to owners of developable land (or real estate brokers or speculators). In return for the compensation derived from this sale, owners of preserved open space land will have sold their rights to develop their land in the future. Their land will thus be preserved in open space and the owners will have been compensated without any capital costs to government.

(6) Development rights will be subject to ad valorem property taxation as a component of the total assessed value of the developable real property in the jurisdiction.

Legislative Provisions With Commentary

Grant of Power to Local Government

The power of zoning granted by the provisions in (State Enabling Legislation) shall include the power to provide for open space preservation districts wherein the use of land may be restricted to agriculture, conservation or recreation or any combination thereof and only such buildings or structures which are incidental to the permitted

Any municipality may by ordinance amend its zoning regulations to provide for an open space preservation district, subject to the provisions of this act. The enactment of an ordinance or amendment thereto pursuant to the powers granted herein shall be in accordance with the procedure required for the adoption of an amendment to the zoning ordinance as provided in (applicable provision of State Enabling Legislation).

Commentary:

This legislation does not disturb the existing allocation of the power of land-use regulation to local governments. Some members of the committee urged that regulating authority be vested in a state agency rather than in local governments. However, the limited political feasibility of approval of this proposal was the primary reason for retaining local control. The last paragraph seeks to retain the existing procedure in most states by which the Planning Board participates in the process for amending the zoning ordinance.

Creation of Open Space Preservation Districts

(a) *The governing body may create an open space preservation district of such numbers, shapes and areas as it may deem necessary to carry out the purposes of this act, provided that (i) all land in each district is substantially undeveloped farmland, woodland, flood plain, swamp, marsh, or land of steep slope, and that farmland or woodland, or a combination thereof shall constitute more than 60 percent of all the land in the open space preservation district; (ii) the location of each district is consistent with and corresponds to the master plan of the municipality; (iii) the aggregate size of the districts bears a reasonable relationship to the present and future patterns of population growth set forth in the zoning ordinance and master plan; and, (iv) the land in each district is not less than 25 contiguous acres.*

Commentary:

Subsection (a) makes it clear that the open-space preservation plan must be based upon the municipal master plan with particular reference to studies of future population projections and topographical, soil and other land use studies. In the process of computing the amount of land required to meet various municipal needs and designation of land most appropriate to meet those needs, land will be designated for open-space preservation. To avoid the designation of open-space districts too small to be effective, a minimum size of 25 contiguous acres is prescribed. The land in any open space preservation district may be comprised of any combination of the enumerated types of undeveloped land but must contain at least 60 percent farmland, woodland, or a combination thereof. The purpose of this provision is to preserve land that might otherwise be developed in addition to swamp, marsh, flood plain, and other land of limited utility for development.

(b) *Land zoned exclusively for commercial, industrial or other non-residential use at the time of the adoption of an ordinance pursuant to this act shall not be included in an open-space preservation district.*

Commentary:

Subsection (b) is intended to exclude land zoned for commercial or industrial uses from open-space preservation districts. There are two reasons for this exclusion. The primary reason is based upon the committee's determination to limit the application of the program to *residential* development. The committee concluded that, if development rights are issued for commercial and industrial development, the program would become too complex to administer. The second reason for the exclusion of commercial and industrial property is that land zoned for those purposes may be too expensive or otherwise inappropriate for open space preservation. The committee was mindful of the fact that some municipalities zone unrealistically large proportions of undeveloped land for commercial and industrial uses as an extra-legal technique of retarding residential development.[66] In this case, a realistic rezoning of the areas will be required before adopting an ordinance pursuant to the provisions of this act.

(c) *Any nonconforming use or structure existing in the open-space preservation district at the time of adoption thereof may be continued and in the event of partial destruction of such nonconforming use or structure it may be restored or repaired.*

Commentary:

Subsection (c) is intended to particularly protect the right of farmers and others who have existing structures that do not conform to the restricted use on open-space preservation land.

(d) *Subject to subsections (e) and (f) of this section, all proposals for the construction or enlargement of a building, or other structure in an open-space preservation district shall be made to the planning board for review and recommendation after a public hearing and shall be submitted to the governing body for approval after favorable referral by the planning board.*

Commentary:

Subsection (d) is intended to require all proposals for construction in open-space preservation districts to be subjected to the scrutiny of the planning board and the governing body. It is contemplated that farm residences, agricultural buildings, stables, and other structures not inconsistent with open-space preservation will be permitted, but only with the approval of both governmental bodies.

(e) *Land within the open space preservation district may be subdivided pursuant to [Subdivision Enabling Legislation] only for the purpose of transferring ownership of the subdivided parcel for farming purposes and a residential dwelling may be constructed on the subdivided parcel only if the parcel contains at least 25 acres.*

---

66. *See* Cutler, "Legal and Illegal Methods for Controlling Community Growth on the Urban Fringe," 3 Wisc. L. Rev. 370 (1961).

Commentary:

Subsection (e) is intended to restrict the subdivision of land in open-space preservation districts. The only exception permitted is subdivision of farmland into a parcel of not less than 25 acres. This exception was made to accommodate the practice of some farmers to subdivide their land among children.

(f) *A variance for a use of land not otherwise permitted in an open-space preservation district may be granted by the governing body after favorable referral by the local planning board and by the appropriate state agency only for a development proposal which is reasonably necessary to protect public health or safety and no practical alternative to the proposed development is available. Otherwise no variance for a change of use or zoning amendment shall be approved to permit development in an open space preservation district other than for uses which conform to the provisions of Section 1 of this act.*

Commentary:

Subsection (f) transfers the power to grant a variance in an open-space preservation district from the zoning board to the governing body, which in turn must obtain the approval from both the planning board and the appropriate state agency. This provision is intended to protect the integrity of the program from the kind of influences often exerted upon zoning boards.

Certificates of Development Rights

(a) *The ordinance creating an open-space preservation district shall also provide for the establishment and distribution of certificates of development rights by the municipality and the transferability of certificates of development rights by the owners of land in the open-space preservation district and shall further provide that an increase in the density of the development hereinafter provided for in Section (b) shall not be permitted unless the applicant therefor submits for cancellation the required number of certificates of development rights.*

Commentary:

This subsection authorizes the creation of an innovative legal instrument never used before, i.e., the certificate of development rights. Certificates will be inscribed in specific denominations and will be transferable by endorsement and registration as provided in Subsection (b). Certificates will be issued to owners of land designated for open space. Owners of developable land will have to purchase these certificates to increase the density of development of their land. Thus, both a supply of and demand for certificates is created.

(b) *Certificates of development rights, issued by the municipality pursuant to the provisions of this act, shall be recorded in the office of the County Clerk of the county in which the municipality is located. The sale and transfer of certificates of development rights shall be regulated and recorded in the same manner as the sale and transfer of real property. Upon exercise of certificate of development right pursuant to Section 6(b) herein and upon the issuance of a building permit therefor, the certificate of development right shall be cancelled by the municipal official designated for that purpose. Notice of cancellation shall be given by said municipal official to the County Clerk, who shall record the cancellation of the certificates.*

Commentary:

This subsection authorizes the creation of a recording system for certificates of development rights similar to the recording system for other instruments of real estate conveyancing. When an owner of land designated for open space sells his certificates to an owner of developable land (or to anyone else, such as a broker or speculator), the transfer will be recorded by the county clerk. When the development rights are used to obtain a building permit, the certificates are cancelled. When all the authorized certificates are cancelled, the remaining owners of developable land will be limited to the restricted use designated in the zoning ordinance, i.e., single-family residences. These constraints will tend to keep the certificates marketable as long as there is demand for residential development at increased densities. The market value of development rights will respond to the same economic forces as the market value of developable residential land. If an owner of development rights holds out for too high a price, the owners of developable land will tend to buy the rights from someone else or will use their land for single-family residences.

Establishment of Development Rights

(a) The planning board, after public hearing with personal notice to all owners of land in the proposed open-space preservation districts, shall recommend to the governing body for adoption the total number of units of development rights for distribution to all owners of property in the proposed open-space preservation districts.

Distribution of Residential Development Rights

(a) The total number of certificates of development rights determined pursuant to section 4 herein shall be distributed in accordance with subsection (b) of this section to all owners of land in the open space preservation district. For purposes of distribution of certificates of development rights ownership of land shall be determined as of the date of the adoption of the ordinance creating the open space preservation district.

Commentary:

This provision calls for the distribution of the development rights to the owners of open-space land. The certificates of development rights they receive provide the compensation for their loss of the right to develop their land. The right to receive development rights vests at the time of adoption of the local ordinance. As a result, when enactment of a development rights ordinance is anticipated the market value of open-space land will reflect the value of the development rights attached to it.

(b) *To provide a just and equitable distribution of certificates of development rights the number of such certificates distributed to an individual property owner shall be equal to a percentage calculated by comparing the market value of the individual's property to the market value of all property in the open-space preservation district on the date of adoption of the open space preservation district.*

Commentary:

This subsection provides the method of allocation of the previously determined total of development rights in the jurisdiction to the owners of open-space land. Each owner is entitled to the same proportion of the total number of development rights as the value of his open space land bears to the total value of all land designated for open-space preservation. This method of allocation is based upon the recognition that acreage alone is an insufficient basis of allocation of development rights because some land has greater value than other land because of its development potential prior to adoption of the development rights ordinance. Under this provision, the owner of the more valuable land will receive a greater proportion of the total number of development rights.

(c) *To implement this section, the planning board shall review the assessed value of all property in the open-space preservation district in order to establish market value on an equalized basis for the purpose of ensuring just distribution of certificates of development rights. The planning board shall hold special hearings with personal notice to all owners of property in the proposed open space preservation district to review all appraisals and consider such objections as may be presented, and shall take such action as it deems necessary to ensure the just distribution of development rights.*

Commentary:

This subsection is intended to provide an open procedure to assure a fair distribution of development rights among owners of open-space land. Notice of all appraisals of land in the open space preservation districts will be given to all owners of open space land. Open hearings on the issue of value will allow each owner to compare the assessed value of his property with the assessed value of all other open space land.

(d) *Any owner of property in the open space preservation district may appeal any determination made under this section to the (appropriate court).*

Commentary:

This subsection provides a judicial remedy for owners of open-space land who feel aggrieved by the allocation of development rights.

Marketability of Residential Development Rights

(a) *To create an incentive for the purchase of development rights, the governing body, by amendment to the zoning ordinance, shall designate specific zoning districts wherein the permissible residential dwelling-unit density may be increased to a specified range of densities. Such zoning districts shall be designated for use and densities consistent with the master plan to create a greater incentive to develop land in such districts with certificates of development rights than without such certificates.*

Commentary:

This subsection provides for the designation of zoning districts in which higher densities will be permitted if the owner acquires development rights. Increased density is to be authorized only (1) where such density would be appropriate as determined by the land-use plan and (2) where there would be market demand for development at higher densities. The existence of this economic incentive is critically important because, unless there is a market for housing at higher densities in the district so designated therefor, there will be no market for the development rights and no compensation for the owners of land preserved for open space. On the other hand, if there is no market for housing at higher densities anywhere in the jurisdiction, then the claim of compensation by owners of open space land is probably equally remote and premature.

(b) *Development of prescribed higher densities shall be permitted as a matter of right if the applicant proposing such higher density owns development rights certificates in an amount equal in number to the increase in dwelling unit density above the number of dwelling units permitted under the zoning regulations.*

Commentary:

This is the provision that authorizes higher densities in designated districts to the extent permitted by the zoning ordinance if the owner has a sufficient number of development rights for the increased density. This provision presupposes the existence of height and bulk regulations in other sections of the zoning ordinance to the extent that such regulations are necessary to prevent overcrowding of the area and overutilization of neighborhood facilities.

(c) *Development proposals consistent with the residential density requirements of the zoning regulations may be approved at such lower density without the requirements of certificates of development rights. However, if development proposals are approved at the lower density and as a result thereof an imbalance is created whereby the number of uncancelled certificates of development rights exceeds the amount of undeveloped land upon which certificates of development rights may be exercised, the governing body may amend the zoning*

*ordinance to rectify the imbalance to maintain the marketability of
the outstanding development rights certificates.*

Commentary:

The first sentence of this subsection authorizes the development of land
in developable districts at the lower authorized density. For example, an
owner of an acre of land on which one residential unit per acre is permitted may build that one unit without the use of development rights. This
provision is designed to overcome objection to the plan by owners of developable land who are content with that restricted use. An owner of
developable land has a number of choices: (1) He can build in accordance
with the lower authorized density. (2) He can purchase development
rights and build at a higher density. (3) He can sell his land to others for
development at higher densities.

The last sentence of this paragraph is intended to deal with the unlikely
possibility that most owners of developable land will act against their
economic self-interest and develop their land at the lower density in spite
of market demand for more intensive use of their land. In this event,
owners of open-space land would not be compensated because the demand for their development rights requires the existence of land developable at higher densities. Under these circumstances, the governing body
is authorized to designate additional districts of developable land for
which the development rights may be used to meet a projected housing
need and the market demand based thereon.

(d) *No variance for residential use at increased densities shall be
granted pursuant to [appropriate section of state enabling legislation]
unless the applicant provides evidence of ownership of certificates of
development rights in an amount sufficient to authorize a higher density under the provisions of this act. No building permit shall be
issued upon such variances unless the requisite number of certificates
of development rights are attached to said application for cancellation.*

Commentary:

This provision is designed to protect the integrity of the plan from derogation by the variance procedure. Without this provision, the entire plan
could be frustrated by use variances for residential development. A use
variance for residential units, under this provision, can be issued only if
the applicant owns a sufficient number of development rights and is prepared to surrender them for cancellation when application is made for a
building permit.

Taxation

(a) *Certificates of development rights shall be taxed in the same manner as real property is taxed. The assessed value of each uncancelled
certificate, in the year of adoption of a development rights ordinance, shall be equal to the difference between the aggregate value*

of all undeveloped land zoned for restricted residential use and the aggregate value of said land if developed with the use of all development rights issued, divided by the total number of development rights issued. Thereafter, current sales, of certificates of development rights in that jurisdiction shall constitute evidence of market value for tax assessment purposes.

Commentary:

This subsection provides the basic guidelines for the taxation of development rights. Because they represent a substantial part of the value of undeveloped land, development rights are to be taxed as real property. When the ordinance is first enacted, the aggregate value of all outstanding development rights will be the difference between the value of all residential land if fully developed with development rights and the value of the same land for restricted residential development. This is illustrated by the following example:

	Aggregate value of the land only
200 acres developed with 1,000 residential units (with development rights).................	$5,000,000
200 acres developed with 200 residential units (restricted use)	1,000,000
Value of 800 development rights............	$4,000,000
Value of 1 development right	$ 5,000

The underlying assumption of this calculation is that an owner would be willing to pay for a development right an amount of money equal to the increment in value of the land resulting from the use of that development right (in the above illustration, $5,000). As soon as a market for development rights is established in the jurisdiction, actual sales will provide evidence of value for assessment purposes.

(b) *Land in the open-space preservation district shall be assessed at its value for agricultural or other open space use.*

Commentary:

This subsection gives effect to the fact that, once the development right is removed from the land in open-space preservation districts, the value of that land is limited to its agricultural or other open-space use.

(c) *Tax exemption—DELETED.*

Commentary:

The original draft of the proposed New Jersey legislation contains a provision exempting development rights from taxation if issued to and held by an owner of land qualified for tax exemption under the New Jersey Farmland Assessment Act. This provision is not recommended because these tax exemption (1) would tend to discourage the marketability of development rights while held by farmers; (2) would impose an unnecessary tax burden on other taxpayers; and (3) would give an unjustified advantage to owners of farmland who may thereby continue to use the land for farm purposes and reap the advantages of increasing value of development rights without corresponding tax liability.

Effective date

This act shall become effective 12 months after enactment thereof and during the said 12-month period the [appropriate state agency] shall conduct such studies as may be necessary to prepare model ordinances, suggested rules and regulations and other studies that will assist municipalities in the adoption and implementation of the powers granted herein. An appropriation of [$-------] is authorized for this purpose.

Commentary:

The last provision conveys the unanimous opinion of the members of the drafting committee that there are still undiscovered implications and effects of this proposal that require additional investigation and study.

B. SOME UNRESOLVED LEGAL PROBLEMS

FRED F. FRENCH INV. CO., INC.
v.
CITY OF NEW YORK
39 N.Y.2d 587, 385 N.Y.S.2d 5, 350 N.E.2d 281 (1976)

BREITEL, Chief Judge.

Plaintiff Fred F. French Investing Co., purchase money mortgagee of Tudor City, a Manhattan residential complex, brought this action to declare unconstitutional a 1972 amendment to the New York City Zoning Resolution and seeks compensation as for "inverse" taking by eminent domain. The amendment purported to create a "Special Park District," and rezoned two private parks in the Tudor City complex exclusively as parks open to the public. It further provided for the granting to the defendant property owners of transferable development (air) rights usable elsewhere. It created the transferable rights by severing the above-surface development rights from the surface development rights, a device of recent invention.

Special Term, in a studied and painstaking opinion, declared the amendment unconstitutional and restored the former zoning classification, R-10, permitting residential and office building development. The Appellate Division, 47 A.D.2d 715, 366 N.Y.S.2d 346 unanimously affirmed, without opinion. By its appeal, the city seeks review of the declaration of unconstitutionality and the denial of its summary judgment motion on the issue of damages. By their cross appeals, plaintiff mortgagee and defendants, owners and mortgage interest guarantor, seek review of the denial of their summary judgment motions for compensation based on an "inverse" taking.

The issue is whether the rezoning of buildable private parks exclusively as parks open to the public, thereby prohibiting all reasonable income productive or other private use of the property, constitutes a deprivation of property rights without due process of law in violation of constitutional limitations.

There should be an affirmance. While the police power of the State to regulate the use of private property by zoning is broad indeed, it is not unlimited. The State may not, under the guise of regulation by zoning, deprive the owner of the reasonable income productive or other private use of his property and thus destroy all but a bare residue of its economic value. Such an exercise of the police power would be void as violative of the due process clauses of the State and Federal Constitutions (N.Y.Const., art. I, § 6; U.S.Const., 14th Amdt., § 1). In the instant case, the city has, despite the severance of above-surface development rights, by rezoning private parks exclusively as parks open to the public, deprived the owners of the reasonable income productive or other private use of their property. The attempted severance of the development rights with uncertain and contingent market value did not adequately preserve those rights. Hence, the 1972 zoning amendment is violative of constitutional limitations.

Tudor City is a four-acre residential complex built on an elevated level above East 42nd Street, across First Avenue from the United Nations in mid-town Manhattan. Planned and developed as a residential community, Tudor City consists of 10 large apartment buildings housing approximately 8,000 people, a hotel, four brownstone buildings, and two 15,000 square-foot private parks. The parks, covering about 18½% of the area of the complex, are elevated from grade and located on the north and south sides of East 42nd Street, with a connecting viaduct.

On September 30, 1970, plaintiff sold the Tudor City complex to defendant Ramsgate Properties for $36,000,000. In addition to cash, plaintiff took back eight purchase money mortgages, two of which covered in part the two parks. Payment of the mortgage interest for three years was personally guaranteed by defendant Helmsley. Ramsgate thereafter conveyed, subject to plaintiff's mortgages, properties including the north and south parks to defendants, North Assemblage Co. and South Assemblage Co. Each of the mortgages secured in part by the parks has been in default since December 7, 1972.

Soon after acquiring the Tudor City property, the new owner announced plans to erect a building, said to be a 50-story tower, over East 42nd Street between First and Second Avenues. This plan would have required New York City Planning Commission approval of a shifting of development rights from the parks to the proposed adjoining site and a corresponding zoning change. Alternatively, the owner proposed to erect on each of the Tudor City park sites a building of maximum size permitted by the existing zoning regulations.

There was immediately an adverse public reaction to the owner's proposals, especially from Tudor City residents. After public hearings, the City Planning Commission recommended, over the dissent of one commissioner, and on December 7, 1972 the Board of Estimate approved, an amendment to the zoning resolution establishing Special Park District "P." By contemporaneous amendment to the zoning map, the two Tudor City parks were included within Special Park District "P."

Under the zoning amendment, "only passive recreational uses are permitted" in the Special Park District and improvements are limited to "structures incidental to passive recreational use." When the Special Park District would be mapped, the parks are required to be open daily to the public between 6:00 a.m. and 10:00 p.m.

The zoning amendment permits the transfer of development rights from a privately owned lot zoned as a Special Park District, denominated a "granting lot," to other areas in midtown Manhattan, bounded by 60th Street, Third Avenue, 38th Street and Eighth Avenue, denominated "receiving lots." Lots eligible to be receiving lots are those with a minimum lot size of 30,000 square feet and zoned to permit development at the maximum commercial density. The owner of a granting lot would be permitted to transfer part of his development rights to any eligible receiving lot, thereby increasing its maximum floor area up to 10%. Further increase in the receiving lot's floor area, limited to 20% of the maximum commercial density, is contingent upon a public hearing and approval by the City Planning Commission and the Board of Estimate. Development rights may be transferred by the owner directly to a receiving lot or to an individual or organization for later disposition to a receiving lot. Before development rights may be transferred, however, the Chairman of the City Planning Commission must certify the suitability of a plan for the continuing maintenance, at the owner's expense, of the granting lot as a park open to the public.

It is notable that the private parks become open to the public upon mapping of the Special Park District, and the opening does not depend upon the relocation and effective utilization of the transferrable development rights. Indeed, the mapping occurred on December 7, 1972, and the development rights have never been marketed or used.

Plaintiff contends that the rezoning of the parks constitutes a compensable "taking" within the meaning of constitutional limitations.

The power of the State over private property extends from the regulation of its use under the police power to the actual taking of an easement or all or part of the fee under the eminent domain power. The distinction, although definable, between a compensable taking and a noncompensable regulation is not always susceptible of precise demarcation. Generally, as the court stated in *Lutheran Church in Amer. v. City of New York.* "[G]overnment interference [with the use of private propety] is based on one of two concepts—either the government is acting in its enterprise capacity, where it takes unto itself private resources in use for the common good, or in its arbitral capacity, where it intervenes to straighten out situations in which the citizenry is in conflict over land use or where one person's use of his land is injurious to others. (Sax, Taking and the Police Power, 74 Yale L.J. 36, 62, 63.) Where government acts in its enterprise capacity, as where it takes land to widen a road, there is a compensable taking. Where government acts in its arbitral capacity, as where it legislates zoning or provides the machinery to enjoin noxious use, there is simply noncompensable regulation."

As noted above, when the State "takes," that is appropriates, private property for public use, just compensation must be paid. In contrast, when there is only regulation of the uses of private property, no compensation need be paid. Of course, and this is often the beginning of confusion, a purported "regulation" may impose so onerous a burden on the property regulated that it has, in effect, deprived the owner of the reasonable income productive or other private use of his property and thus has destroyed its economic value. In all but exceptional cases, nevertheless, such a regulation does not constitute a "taking," and is therefore not compensable, but amounts to a deprivation or frustration of property rights without due process of law and is therefore invalid.

True, many cases have equated an invalid exercise of the regulating zoning power, perhaps only metaphorically, with a "taking" or a "confiscation" of property, terminology appropriate to the eminent domain power and the concomitant right to compensation when it is exercised. Thus, for example, in *Arverne Bay Constr. Co. v. Thatcher*, the court stated "An ordinance which *permanently* so restricts the use of property that it cannot be used for any reasonable purpose goes, it is plain, beyond regulation, and must be recognized as a taking of the property." Similarly, in *Pennsylvania Coal Co. v. Mahon*, a police power and not an eminent domain case, Mr. Justice Holmes stated: "while property may be regulated to a certain extent, if regulation goes too far it will be recognized as a taking."

The metaphor should not be confused with the reality. Close examination of the cases reveals that in none of them, anymore than in the *Pennsylvania Coal* case *(supra)*, was there an actual "taking" under the eminent domain power, despite the use of the terms "taking" or "confiscatory." Instead, in each the gravamen of the constitutional challenge to the regulatory measure was that it was an invalid exercise of the police power under the due process clause, and the cases were decided under that rubric. As has been cogently pointed out by Professor Costonis: "the goal of [challenges to regulatory measures] in conventional land use disputes is to preclude application of the measure to the restricted parcel on the basis of constitutional infirmity. What is achieved, in short, is declaratory relief. The sole exception to this mild outcome occurs where the challenged measure is either intended to eventuate in actual public ownership of the land or has already caused government to encroach on the land with trespassory consequences that are largely irreversible." (Costonis, "Fair" Compensation and the Accommodation Power: Antidotes for the Taking Impasse in Land Use Controversies, 1975 Col.L.Rev. 1021, 1035.

In the present case, while there was a significant diminution in the value of the property, there was no actual appropriation or taking of the parks by title or governmental occupation. The amendment was declared void at Special Term a little over a year after its adoption. There was no physical invasion of the owner's property; nor was there an assumption by the city of the control or management of the parks. Indeed, the parks served the same function as before the amendment, except that they were now also open to the public. Absent factors of governmental displacement of private ownership, occupation or management, there was no "taking" within the meaning of constitutional limitations. There was, therefore, no right to compensation as for a taking in eminent domain.

Since there was no taking within the meaning of constitutional limitations, plaintiff's remedy, at this stage of the litigation, would be a declaration of the amendment's invalidity, if that be the case. Thus, it is necessary to determine whether the zoning amendment was a valid exercise of the police power under the due process clauses of the State and Federal Constitutions.

The broad police power of the State to regulate the use of private property is not unlimited. Every enactment under the police power must be reasonable. An exercise of the police power to regulate private property by zoning which is unreasonable constitutes a deprivation of property without due process of law.

What is an "unreasonable" exercise of the police power depends upon the relevant converging factors. Hence, the facts of each case must be evaluated in order to determine the private and social balance of convenience before the exercise of the power may be condemned as unreasonable.

A zoning ordinance is unreasonable, under traditional police power and due process analysis, if it encroaches on the exercise of private property rights without substantial relation to a legitimate governmental purpose. A legitimate governmental purpose is, of course, one which furthers the public health, safety, morals or general welfare. Moreover, a zoning ordinance, on similar police power analysis, is unreasonable if it is arbitrary, that is, if there is no reasonable relation between the end sought to be achieved by the regulation and the means used to achieve that end.

Finally, and it is at this point that the confusion between the police power and the exercise of eminent domain most often occurs, a zoning ordinance is unreasonable if it frustrates the owner in the use of his property, that is, if it renders the property unsuitable for any reasonable income productive or other private use for which it is adapted and thus destroys its economic value, or all but a bare residue of its value.

The ultimate evil of a deprivation of property, or better, a frustration of property rights, under the guise of an exercise of the police power is that it forces the owner to assume the cost of providing a benefit to the public without recoupment. There is no attempt to share the cost of the benefit among those benefited, that is, society at large. Instead, the accident of ownership determines who shall bear the cost initially. Of course, as further consequence, the ultimate economic cost of providing the benefit is hidden from those who in a democratic society are given the power of deciding whether or not they wish to obtain the benefit despite the ultimate economic cost, however initially distributed (Dunham, Legal and Economic Basis for Planning, 58 Col.L.Rev. 650, 665). In other words, the removal from productive use of private property has an ultimate social cost more easily concealed by imposing the cost on the owner alone. When successfully concealed, the public is not likely to have any objection to the "cost-free" benefit.

In this case, the zoning amendment is unreasonable and, therefore, unconstitutional because, without due process of law, it deprives the owner of all his property rights, except the bare title and a dubious future reversion of full use. The amendment renders the park property unsuitable for any reasonable income productive or other private use for which it is adapted and thus destroys its economic value and deprives plaintiff of its security for its mortgages. Indeed, as Rathkopf has characterized it, the case is an "extreme example" of a deprivation (1 Rathkopf, *op. cit.*, at p. 6-55; contra Marcus, Mandatory Development Rights Transfer and the Taking Clause: The Case of Manhattan's Tudor City Parks, 24 Buffalo L.Rev. 77, 93-94, 105).

It is recognized that the "value" of property is not a concrete or tangible attribute but an abstraction derived from the economic uses to which the property may be put. Thus, the development rights are an essential component of the value of the underlying property because they constitute some of the economic uses to which the property may be put. As such, they are a potentially valuable and even a transferable commodity and may not be disregarded in determining whether the ordinance has destroyed the economic value of the underlying property.

Of course, the development rights of the parks were not nullified by the city's action. In an attempt to preserve the rights they were severed from the real property and made transferable to another section of mid-Manhattan in the city, but not to any particular parcel or place. There was thus created floating development rights, utterly unusable until they could be attached to some accommodating real property, available by happenstance of prior ownership, or by grant, purchase, or devise, and subject to the contingent approvals of administrative agencies. In such case, the development rights, disembodied abstractions of man's ingenuity, float in a limbo until restored to reality by reattachment to tangible real property. Put another way, it is a tolerable abstraction to consider development rights apart from the solid land from which as a matter of zoning law they derive. But severed, the development rights are a double abstraction until they are actually attached to a receiving parcel, yet to be identified, acquired, and subject to the contingent future approvals of administrative agencies, events which may never happen because of the exigencies of the market and the contingencies and exigencies of administrative action. The acceptance of this contingency-ridden arrangement, however, was mandatory under the amendment.

The problem with this arrangement, as Mr. Justice Waltemade so wisely observed at Special Term, is that it fails to assure preservation of the very real economic value of the development rights as they existed when still attached to the underlying property. By compelling the owner to enter an unpredictable real estate market to find a suitable receiving lot for the rights, or a purchaser who would then share the same interest in using additional development rights, the amendment renders uncertain and thus severely impairs the value of the development rights before they were severed (see Note, The Unconstitutionality of Transferable Development Rights, 84 Yale L.J. 1101, 1110-1111). Hence, when viewed in relation to both the value of the private parks after the amendment, and the value of the development rights detached from the private parks, the amendment destroyed the economic value of the property. It thus constituted a deprivation of property without due process of law.

None of this discussion of the effort to accomplish the highly beneficial purposes of creating additional park land in the teeming city bears any relation to other schemes, variously described as a "development bank" or the "Chicago Plan" (see Costonis, The Chicago Plan: Incentive Zoning and the Preservation of Urban Landmarks, 85 Harv.L.Rev. 574; Costonis, Development Rights Transfer: An Exploratory Essay, 83 Yale L.J. 75, 86-87). For under such schemes or variations of them, the owner of the granting parcel may be allowed just compensation for his development rights, instantly and in money, and the acquired development rights are then placed in a "bank" from which enterprises may for a price purchase development rights to use on land owned by them. Insofar as the owner of the granting parcel is concerned, his development rights are taken by the State, straightforwardly, and he is paid just compensation for them in eminent domain. The appropriating governmental entity recoups its disbursements, when, as, and if it obtains a purchaser for those rights. In contrast, the 1972 zoning amendment short-circuits the double-tracked compensation scheme but to do this leaves the granting parcel's owner's development rights in limbo until the day of salvation, if ever it comes.

With respect to damages caused by the unlawful zoning amendment the issue is not properly before the court. The owner never made such an unequivocal claim and still does not. Instead, it claims compensation for value appropriated as for an "inverse" taking in eminent domain. The mortgagees and personal guarantor make parallel claims. That view of the invalid amendment is not adopted for the reasons discussed at length earlier. The city, on the other hand, seeks a declaration with respect to such damages, but in the absence of allegation or proof that such damages lie, are claimed, or how they have been incurred, there can be no abstract declaration, and therefore there is none.

It would be a misreading of the discussion above to conclude that the court is insensitive to the inescapable need for government to devise methods, other than by outright appropriation of the fee, to meet urgent environmental needs of a densely concentrated urban population. It would be equally simplistic to ignore modern recognition of the principle that no property has value except as the community contributes to that value. The obverse of this principle is, therefore, of first significance: no property is an economic island, free from contributing to the welfare of the whole of which it is but a dependent part. The limits are that unfair or disproportionate burdens may not, constitutionally, be placed on single properties or their owners. The possible solutions undoubtedly lie somewhere in the areas of general taxation, assessments for public benefit (but with an expansion of the traditional views with respect to what are assessable public benefits), horizontal eminent domain illustrated by a true "taking" of development rights with corresponding compensation, development banks, and other devices which will insure rudimentary fairness in the allocation of economic burdens.

Solutions must be reached for the problems of modern zoning, urban and rural conservation, and last but not least landmark preservations, whether by particular buildings or historical districts. Unfortunately, the land planners are now only at the beginning of the path to solution. In the process of traversing that path further, new ideas and new standards of constitutional tolerance must and will evolve. It is enough to say that the loose-ended transferable development rights in this case fall short of achieving a fair allocation of economic burden. Even though the development rights have not been nullified, their severance has rendered their value so uncertain and contingent, as to deprive the property owner of their practical usefulness, except under rare and perhaps coincidental circumstances.

The legislative and administrative efforts to solve the zoning and landmark problem in modern society demonstrate the presence of ingenuity. That ingenuity further pursued will in all likelihood achieve the goals without placing an impossible or unsuitable burden on the individual property owner, the public fisc, or the general taxpayer. These efforts are entitled to and will undoubtedly receive every encouragement. The task is difficult but not beyond management. The end is essential but the means must nevertheless conform to constitutional standards.

Accordingly, the order of the Appellate Division should be affirmed, without costs, and the certified question answered in the affirmative.

THE FRENCH CASE AND THE FUTURE OF TDR PROGRAMS
JEROME G. ROSE
5 REAL ESTATE LAW JOURNAL 374 (1977)

In *Fred F. French Investing Co. v. City of New York*,[1] the New York Court of Appeals invalidated a New York City zoning ordinance designed to preserve park space through the transfer of development rights (TDR). The issues raised in the *French* case will have an impact upon the validity of existing TDR programs in such diverse places as Collier County, Florida,[2] Buckingham Township, Pennsylvania,[3] Montgomery County, Maryland,[4] Sunderland, Massachusetts,[5] Chesterfield Township, New Jer-

---

1. 39 N.Y.2d 587, 385 N.Y.S.2d 5, 350 N.E.2d 281 (1976).
2. Collier County, Fla. Comprehensive Zoning Ordinance § 9 (1974).
3. Buckingham Township, Pa. Zoning Ordinance (1975).
4. Montgomery County, Md. Ordinance No. 7-24 (1972).
5. Town of Sunderland, Mass. Zoning Bylaw § 4400 (1974).

sey,[6] Hillsborough, New Jersey,[7] and as far away as Matanuska-Susitna Borough, Alaska.[8] The *French* case will also have an impact upon TDR proposals currently pending in New York,[9] New Jersey[10] and California.[11]

The basic principles, mechanics, and variations of TDR programs have been described at length in prior issues of the *Real Estate Law Journal*.[12] The underlying principle of the TDR system is that the right to develop land may be separated from the other components of title, thereby permitting it to be transferred from land to be restricted in use to other land where a higher density of development is acceptable. A basic premise of the concept is that the value of "developable" land will be enhanced by the increased density resulting from the transfer of development rights to it and that this increase in land value will provide economic incentive for the purchase of development rights from owners of "restricted" land. The remuneration received by owners of "restricted" land will provide compensation to them or at least remove the harshness of the restriction on the use of their land. The TDR program is proposed as a method to preserve historic sites, agricultural land, park land, and ecologically fragile areas.

The *French* case involves a New York City zoning ordinance that re-zoned privately owned property, previously used as a *private* park in a residential complex, for *public* park use. The effect of this zoning designation was to prohibit development on this land. In return for this restriction of development, the corporate owner was permitted to convey development rights from this land to land not owned by it in a designated commercial area in the vicinity. The New York Court of Appeals held the zoning ordinance to be an invalid exercise of the police power under the due process clauses of the New York State and Federal Constitutions.

"TAKING" ISSUE IS CRUCIAL

The first issue that the court was called upon to determine was whether the change of use of the property by zoning ordinance from *private* park,

---

6. Chesterfield Township, N.J. Zoning Ordinance (1975). In July 1976, an action was brought challenging the validity of this ordinance. Chesterfield Associates v. Township of Chesterfield, Dkt. No. L45806-75 P.W. (N.J. Super. Ct. L. Div. Burlington County 1976).

7. Hillsborough, N.J. Ordinance No. 75-13 (1975).

8. Matanuska-Susitna Borough, Alaska Ordinance No. 75-15 (1975).

9. The College of Environmental Science and Forestry, State University of New York-Syracuse has undertaken a study, directed by Robert D. Hennigan and Robert M.I. Bellandi, to propose enabling legislation for a TDR program in New York State.

10. The Cooperative Extension Service, Cook College, Rutgers University, has sponsored an extensive investigation of TDR proposals, by a team, including B. Budd Chavooshian, George N. Nieswan, and Thomas Norman, that has produced state enabling legislation for New Jersey.

11. Sedway/Cooke, *Central Sonoma County Density Transfer Project* (County of Sonoma, Cal. 1976).

12. Rose, "The Transfer of Development Rights: A Preview of an Evolving Concept," 3 Real Est. L.J. 330 (1975); Rose, "A Proposal for the Separation and Marketability of Development Rights as a Technique to Preserve Open Space," 2 Real Est. L.J. 635 (1974).

limited to the use by residents of the residential complex, to *public* park, open to the use by the public at large, constitutes a "taking" of property under the eminent domain power, for which compensation is required. The court held that there was no "taking" of property involved. The language of the opinion is particularly significant on this issue:

"In the present case, while there was a significant diminution in the value of the property, there was no actual appropriation or taking of the parks by title or governmental occupation. The amendment was declared void at Special Term a little over a year after its adoption. There was no physical invasion of the owner's property; nor was there an assumption by the City of the control or management of the parks. Indeed, the parks served the same function as before the amendment, except that they were now also open to the public. Absent factors of governmental displacement of private ownership, occupation or management, there was no 'taking' within the meaning of the constitutional limitations (see City of Buffalo v. J.W. Clements Co., 28 N.Y.2d 241, 255-257). There was, therefore, no right to compensation as for a taking in eminent domain." [13]

This analysis of the court is likely to produce a great deal of critical comment from legal scholars. The effect of this holding is that a municipal ordinance that permits the general public to use a person's private property does not constitute a "taking" of the property without the consent of the owner for a public use for which compensation is required under the eminent domain power. It is difficult to distinguish this case from an ordinance that designates private property for highway use and that permits the general public to use that private property for purposes of transportation. In both cases, it would seem that there has been an expropriation of private property for a public use that should constitute a "taking" of property and compensation therefor.

In spite of the questionable theoretical basis of this holding, the *French* case can be used to support the argument, with respect to the TDR proposal, that the inclusion of property in a "restricted" district which may be limited to conservation or environmental protection purposes, does not constitute a "taking" under the eminent domain power. This is a critical issue because if the restriction of the use of property under the TDR proposal is deemed to constitute a "taking," then a serious legal issue arises because of a long line of decisions that have held that compensation must be in *money* and not in other forms of substituted *property*. Consequently, with respect to the "taking" issue, the *French* case can be cited to support the TDR proposal.

DOES A TDR PROGRAM VIOLATE DUE PROCESS RIGHTS?

A more complex issue arises with respect to the court's holding that the New York City TDR program is invalid under the due process clauses of the State and Federal Constitutions. Such a holding is based upon a judicial finding that there is no reasonable relation between the end sought to

---

13. Fred F. French Investing Co. v. City of New York, note 1 *supra*, at 385 N.Y.S.2d at 9.

be achieved by the legislation and the means used to achieve that end. This, in turn, involves a weighing, by the court, of the relative importance of the objective sought to be achieved for the general welfare on one hand, and the extent of the deprivation or harshness as applied to the owner of property, on the other. As a general rule, "a zoning ordinance is unreasonable if it frustrates the owner in the use of his property, that is, if it renders the property unsuitable for any reasonable income productive or other private use for which it is adapted and thus destroys its economic value, or all but a rare residue of its value."[14]

This holding is important in determining the validity of the TDR proposal because it raises the issue of the extent to which the granting of transferable development rights to owners of "restricted" land overcomes the harshness of depriving them of the use of their property for development purposes. In the *French* case, the court held that the granting of the transferable development rights did *not* overcome the harshness of the deprivation of the owner's rights because the value of the development rights was "so uncertain and contingent, as to deprive the property owner of their practical usefulness, except under rare and perhaps coincidental circumstances."[15]

At first glance, this holding might appear to be a very discouraging prognosis for the TDR proposal. However, this need not be the case. The court has said no more than that which students and proponents of TDR proposals have long recognized, namely, that the viability, as well as the legality, of a TDR program depends upon "the assumption that the owners of preserved open space land will be compensated for the deprivation of the use of their land by the sale of certificates of development rights to owners of developable land. This relationship is predictable in theory and workable in practice only to the extent that the planners' projection of future economic demand for land is accurate and their designation of sites for specified land use is skillfully performed."[16] In the *French* case, the court was not persuaded (either because of insufficient evidence or insufficient factual material on which such evidence could be based) that the transferable development rights, characterized by the court as "disembodied abstractions of man's ingenuity [that] float in a limbo until restored to reality by reattachment to tangible real property" could, in fact, be sold. The court was concerned that the prospect of sale of the development rights was too uncertain and speculative because it was "subject to the contingent future approvals of administrative agencies, [and] events which may never happen because of the exigencies of the market and the contingencies and exigencies of administrative action."[17]

---

14. *Id.* at 10.

15. *Id.* at 13.

16. See Rose, "Psychological, Legal and Administrative Problems of the Proposal to Use the Transfer of Development Rights as a Technique to Preserve Open Space," in *Transfer of Development Rights: A New Technique of Land Use Regulation* at 297 (Rutgers University Center for Urban Policy Research 1975).

17. Fred F. French Investing Co. v. City of New York, note 1 *supra*, at 385 N.Y.S.2d at 11.

TDRs MUST BE MARKETABLE

There is a lesson to be learned from this judicial declaration: The validity of the TDR proposal may very well depend upon the extent to which the development rights are made marketable *in fact*. This will involve careful consideration of the technical and administrative impediments to alienability, as well as the creation, of conditions that create and enhance market demand for the rights. This evaluation should also consider the possibility of creating an effective and workable development rights bank.

A discussion of the *French* case would be incomplete without mention of the tone of encouragement contained in the last paragraphs of the otherwise negative decision. The court indicated its awareness of the ingenuity with which the complex problems of landmark preservation and land-use regulation were being addressed by recent innovative proposals. The court then suggested:

> "That ingenuity further pursued will in all likelihood achieve the goals without placing an impossible or unsuitable burden on the individual property owner, the public fisc, or the general taxpayer. These efforts are entitled to and will undoubtedly receive every encouragement. The task is difficult but not beyond management. The end is essential but the means must nevertheless conform to constitutional standards." [18]

With this encouragement from the New York Court of Appeals, land-use lawyers and planners will continue to explore ways to make the TDR program comform to statutory and constitutional standards.

C. VARIATIONS ON THE TDR THEME

TRANSFER OF DEVELOPMENT CREDITS (TDC): A NEW FORM OF CLUSTER ZONING WILLIAM QUEALE, JR. N.J. FEDERATION OF PLANNING OFFICIALS PLANNING INFORMATION REPORT (1976)

Initially, the Report of the Blueprint Commission [1] drew wide attention to the increasingly serious need to preserve farmland. The contribution of New Jersey agriculture to food production is significant. The employment it offers as well as the aesthetic calm it provides are also interwoven considerations in an urbanized area such as New Jersey. The Transfer of De-

---

18. *Id.* at 13.

---

1. *Report of the Blueprint Commission on the Future of New Jersey Agriculture*, N.J. Department of Agriculture, April, 1973.

velopment *Rights* (TDR) concept[2] continues to be discussed at considerable length around the state. Other articles and issues published by the N.J. Federation of Planning Officials, the Center for Analysis of Public Issues, and the American Institute of Planners have outlined problems, pointed to opportunities, and offered suggestions for farmland and open space preservation, with proper land use relationships in the process. The Blueprint and TDR concepts as well as other articles contain a common theme of an interest in preserving agricultural land and other critical areas. All have done much to generate grass roots understanding and support for one or more preservation programs. This TDC concept is yet another approach.

Over the past few years, several of our municipalities have been concerned about the loss of valuable farmland as well as past development that had encroached upon environmentally critical areas. These same communities are also concerned with accepting their share of development at a rate and in a location consistent with regional growth patterns. Such was the dilemma in 1973-74 in Chesterfield and Hillsborough. Both groups of officials discussed the problems at length and both requested alternate proposals to preserve farmland and critical areas while still providing the opportunity for reasonable development in concert with regional trends. Of interest may be the fact that these questions and the solutions were raised and considered prior to the *Mount Laurel* decision. The result in both town was a TDC Ordinance. The same basic approach was used in each case, but with variations suited to the particular planning and zoning needs of each town.

THE BASIC CONCEPT

Working within the existing planning and zoning statutes, the Transfer of Development Credits (TDC) concept was conceived as an extension of cluster zoning and planned unit development. The rational was that the traditional cluster or PUD proposal begins with one tract and is subsequently subdivided into major parcels consisting of public open space, common property, apartments, townhouses, or single family homes. The

---

2. B. Budd Chavooshian, AIP, PP, Thomas Norman, Esquire, Dr. George H. Nieswand, *Transfer of Development Rights: A New Concept in Land Use Management*, Leaflet 492-A, Rutgers University, June 1973, (Reprinted July, 1974), Reprinted in the Federation Planning Information Report, Vol. VIII, No. 4, Winter 1973.

B. Budd Chavooshian, AIP, PP, Dr. George H. Nieswand, and Thomas Norman, *Growth-Management Program . . . A Proposed New Approach to Local Planning and Zoning*, Esquire, Leaflet 503, Cooperative Extension Service, Cook College, Rutgers University, June 3, 1974.

Prof. John J. Costonis, *Development Rights Transfer, Description & Perspectives for a Critique, Volume III, Management & Control of Growth*, The Urban Land Institute, 1975.

Jerome G. Rose, *The Transfer of Development Rights: A Preview of an Evolving Concept, Real Estate Law Journal*, Vol. 3, No. 4, Spring 1975.

Transfer of Development Rights Bibliography, Division of Information and Research, Legislative Services Agency, State House, Trenton, N.J. November 1975 (to be revised February/March, 1976).

basic concept, however, remains the same; namely, one tract becomes fragmented into non-contiguous properties serving different functions and owned by different individuals or corporations. The question raised and subsequently answered by the TDC approach was, "If you can end up with parcels fragmented in a logical design, why can't you start out with fragmented parcels?" The TDC concept has become more easily envisioned as a community-wide cluster zoning concept. As in a traditional cluster zoning proposal, the TDC approach also requires the applicant to control all the land for which he is seeking "credit" - either as owner, holder of an option, or holder of a contract of sale. This is the major difference between this concept and the Transfer of Development Rights (TDR). Under TDR the development rights can be sold separately from the land. Under TDC both the land and the credits remain intact until approval of the development proposal by the municipality, the same as practiced now with the traditional cluster development proposal.

CONSIDERING USE OF THIS CONCEPT

As with cluster zoning, PUD, average lot sizes in industrial areas, and other zoning concepts, the TDC concept may not be advisable in every community. It is, however, a means to broaden the cluster concept to provide a measurable impact on preserving agricultural areas, environmentally critical land or generating open space. Preserved areas under the TDC concept appear to present the opportunity to assemble major tracts suited to agricultural use or to preserve major areas having environmental limitations than would normally result by an accumulation of preserved areas from individual cluster designs.

The concept is also seen as receiving impetus from the new *Municipal Land Use Law*'s definition and use of the term "planned development," (40:550-1). In addition, the new law speaks to the preservation of agricultural land and natural resources in the Master Plan section and calls for zoning ordinances to be adopted either "substantially consistent with the· land use plan element of the master plan or designed to effectuate such plan element."

PRESERVING AGRICULTURE

There are different approaches to be considered in using the TDC concept, some urban, some rural. If agricultural preservation is the goal, designating an agricultural district could be considered. The minimum permitted tract size for a farm might be established at 25 acres or larger. A distinction is made between an agricultural use (acreage for crops or pastures) and a farm (the crop land plus a residence). The minimum tract size for an agricultural use might be as small as 10 acres to permit convenient subdivision of crop land and exchanges of land for growing purposes. When a residence is included, requiring a larger lot size is important in order to preserve the agricultural purpose and not have it weakened by a pattern of 10-acre, single-family lots in the name of agriculture.

A key factor when creating an agricultural district with ±25 acre lots relates to the question of the municipality taking property without just

compensation. The TDC approach provides for the development value of
the land to be received, it's just that the buildings are erected elsewhere.
For example, a developer who owns land that qualifies for development
can purchase a farm or agricultural tract elsewhere, receive credit for the
farm acreage (spelled out in the ordinance at so many units per acre), and
submit a proposal for the receiving tract. The proposal would consist of
the number of units generated by the acreage of the receiving tract *plus*
the number of units generated by the acreage of the farm. Concurrent
with final approval, the farm would either be dedicated to the community
for public purpose or have a deed restriction placed on the property to
assure its continued agricultural use. With the imposition of the agricultural deed restriction, the developer could re-sell the property to the
farmer at an agricultural price. In theory, then, a developer will pay a net
price related to the value he receives for usable construction sites. That is
very close to a definition of the speculative value the farmer had in his
land before he gave up the right to develop it. By receiving the development value for the land, the residual, agricultrual value is lower which
should permit entry into farming at a smaller investment in land. This is
an important consideration if farming is to continue in New Jersey and
other urbanizing centers. The key to the TDC concept is that a developer
must control all the land either as the owner, or through an option, contract of sale or similar mechanism. The development credits only become
separated as the result of the municipal approval of the proposal, the
same as under present cluster zoning projects.

The concept can also be used in a rural community without necessarily
imposing a restricted agricultural district in its zoning scheme. In this
instance, the same concept would apply except that the receiving tract
could be located anywhere in the community, not just in a designated
area. More than likely, however, the concentration of units on the receiving tract should be expected to require sewage treatment facilities, not
septic systems, and probably some central water supply system. From a
practical point of view the location of the receiving lots would therefore
be in the vicinity of existing sewage treatment facilities and water systems.

PRESERVING OPEN SPACE AND
ENVIRONMENTALLY CRITICAL AREAS

Beyond the purpose of agricultural preservation is the applicability of
the TDC concept to preserve environmentally critical areas and generate
open space and recreation areas. In the context of the new *Municipal
Land Use Law* the TDC concept would apply to the implementation of a
"recreation plan" or a "conservation plan" as delineated under the Master
Plan portion of that law. By having preservation of these areas as a major
policy in the TDC approach, it is important that the community outline
the policies and/or delineate designated areas in its Master Plan and/or a
Natural Resources inventory prepared by the Environmental Commission.
Adoption of a Master Plan and/or NRI would remove arbitrariness when
considering the merits of accepting lands offered for preservation.

An important aspect of the TDC concept is that farmland, open space and critical area preservation takes place in direct proportion to the level of development. In a sense, the concept relies on development to preserve these areas. While sounding contradictory, it is actually very sensible. After all, if there is no development, the land remains open due to the lack of market pressures for development. Without development there is no need to preserve the open space or farmland through public acquisition or other implementing measures. On the other hand, when development pressures mount, it is the threatned loss of farmland, open spaces, or critical areas needed to serve increased population that mandates governmental response. The TDC concept relates the two and ties the rate of land preservation to the rate of development. The guide is the market place, not artificially imposed timing. By thinking out the pattern of land preservation, total population and service needs in advance of development pressures, the planning process is made an integral part of the concept.

BENEFITS TO THE DEVELOPER, PROPERTY OWNER, AND PUBLIC-AT-LARGE

The opportunities to properly use the TDC concept are as limitless as the number of zones one would consider for a municipality. The location of the sending and receiving districts and whether they are restricted to specified areas or permitted throughout the community will depend on the development characteristics of the community, the intensity of the existing development, and the long-range goals of the community with respect to population growth, housing needs, and community facilities; the same considerations given under present zoning deliberations. Likewise, the credits to be received for the "sending" properties and the maximum densities permitted on the "receiving" property are also a matter related to existing conditions and long-range planning. In short, the TDC approach does not lower or increase the ultimate population in a community. It offers the opportunity to equalize the market pressures and allow the development design to relate more directly to natural features and broader community needs including farmland, open space and critical areas while encouraging development in areas served by roads and facilities. Significant opportunities can be afforded through this concept to property owners as well as the general public. First, properties eligible to "send" credits are on an immediate equal basis with all other properties for development purposes, regardless of their location. This is so because the actual construction will not take place on that site even though it may be a good, developable site. Because the development will take place on another "receiving" lot, all land becomes a potential "sending" lot, not just those convenient to highways and utilities.

Depending on the language of the ordinance, the potential also exists for undevelopable land to be marketable under this concept whereas it had little or no value before. Swamps and streams, for example, may be established as a critical area to be preserved for flood control, a natural habitat or other environmental purposes, or as sources of water supply for the preserved agricultural uses. Their preservation may be a significant public purpose for which some development credits might be granted under the ordinance, even though not as high a credit perhaps as developable land. With this approach, the property can assume a value for development which, without this concept, would be minimal due to either the cost of improvements or the prohibition of development on those properties.

The TDC approach also offers flexibility to the owner of a receiving property. Under traditional zoning and development concepts, the owner would be required to negotiate with adjoining properties in order to assemble an adequate sized, contiguous tract. With the TDC approach, all property owners in the community are potential sellers, not just the adjoining owners.

Finally there is also value to the public-at-large. The municipality can accept a fair share of growth, but preserve crop producing land, open space, critical areas and potential public land in the process. Where farmland is dedicated, it remains on the tax roles—taxed at farm value. Through the clustering techniques, the mileage of streets, utilities, curbs, drainage structures and sidewalks to be maintained can be reduced and the reduction in roofs and other hard surfaces minimizes other related problems such as storm water run-off. The TDC concept is also an approach which removes the town from the individual negotiating process in determining sales prices.

RESPONDING TO MOUNT LAUREL

Adequate housing is another major item in municipal planning. It is felt, first, that the TDC concept increases the potential for development initially (all lands are potentially marketable, not just those convenient to highways and utilities). However, this should settle down after some initial applications and once other communities begin implementing the concept. Second, coupled with the TDC concept (community-wide clustering), clustering on the receiving lot can also be permitted. Depending on the tract size of the receiving lot, it can allow a mixture of housing types—single family, townhouse and apartment. Generally speaking the larger the tract, the more flexibility for housing mix. The clustering on a community-wide basis offered by TDC combined with clustering on the receiving lot significantly reduces the improvement costs for the developer. The mileage of streets, utilities and similar elements of the infrastructure are cut considerably on a per unit basis. From the municipal point of view, this whole concept not only permits a mixture of housing types, but with reduced streets, etc. long-term municipal service costs are reduced while an additional opportunity is offered the developer to have savings on improvements which can theoretically be passed on to the home purchaser. If it is, and if a proper mix of housing units is allowed, a significant joint effort by the citizens of a municipality and a builder will have resulted in a major step in the direction of sensible, long-range planning to provide opportunities for "least cost" housing to meeting a portion of the housing needs of a region.

To aid in assuring proper site aesthetics, permitting clustering on the receiving lot offers greater opportunities to provide recreational facilities, preservation of stream and drainage rights-of-way, and similar open space within the complex itself. Further, by permitting a mixture of housing types, including townhouses and/or apartments with single family units on a variety of lot sizes, more units can be properly designed for accommodation on the site while still preserving open space and an aesthetic environment. Through the use of a fixed density per gross acre, the number of units is not increased. It is only the mixture of housing types that might change. Such subtleties as senior citizens housing with lower parking requirements, or garages within or under structures can further reduce the amount of paving and total land coverage (including costs) and reduce the rate of storm water run-off. Also, a mixture of housing types provides a greater housing choice aiding the ability of the community through its zoning to provide the opportunity for a variety of housing needs for different age and economic groups.

ALTERNATIVES IN TDC PROVISIONS

The TDC concept involves more individual decisions because of the broader application it has in the community. Generally, the old cluster concept is based on a residential density on one lot with some percentage of the tract being set aside in open space. Most tracts are in one zone. Under the TDC concept, the decisions are not necessarily complicated, but there are more of them. The "sending" lot should have a minimum size. In Chesterfield and Hillsborough, this was 25 acres. For additional flexibility, a provision in both ordinances permits a lot as small as 5 acres to be a "sending" lot provided it is attached to an already dedicated parcel of 25 or more acres to increase its size; hopefully enlarging a dedicated farm area, flood hazard area, park or similar use.

The receiving lot requires two considerations: 1) that the zoning on the property meet the test of reasonableness without the use of TDC and, 2) with TDC, that the receiving property not be so intensely developed that the scale of human living, site aesthetics, and ultimate utility and highway capacities are exceeded upon completion of the community development.

If the community establishes an agricultural preserve, or other significant areas in which development is prohibited, the ratio of the land area that can "receive" development should be carefully evaluated in light of the acreage in the preserves, e.g. the "sending" areas. In short, there should be sufficient capacity in the receiving land to accommodate any credits generated by all land placed in a preserve. A 50 percent margin of error was anticipated in some of our initial discussions in Chesterfield to make allowances for non-participants or partial participants in an area originally contemplated as a receiving district. A preserve was not considered in Hillsborough. Ultimately, the creation of a delineated preserve and development district was deleted from the Chesterfield ordinance. However, in the initial discussions with Chesterfield a 50 percent factor was felt to offer reasonable assurances that all land could be sold for "credit" purposes. With this margin of assurance, if all property owners on receiving tracts did participate in the concept, demand for land in the "sending" district would exceed supply. But in all cases, the owner of a receiving lot is permitted a reasonable use of his land by the zoning on that tract alone plus the ordinance's allowance to cluster that development. In addition, if demand did exceed the supply, the community may or may not want to consider amending the ordinances to allow new density levels on the remaining receiving lots under some bonus zoning concept, a general change in density levels throughout the community, or other land development mechanism. The major concern would have to be an assurance that these modifications were related to an overall planning program like any zoning change today. Also, because dedicated land under this concept is perpetual, it does not mean that the language of the ordinance must also be perpetual. As conditions change and new ideas in land development emerge, zoning amendments should be evaluated and adopted if appropriate.

It is also recommended that any land dedicated to the township for public purpose incorporate broad language in the deed. The land for public purpose should not be artificially restricted so that a legitimate public use at some future date is preempted. Designating a property for open space purposes, for example, may be too restrictive when school sites, a municipal, complex, drainage detention basin, or other purpose may be more a desired use in the future. Likewise, the restriction should not be limited to one public agency such as the governing body. The public purpose might provide flexibility for another public agency such as the school board, municipal utilities authority, county park commission, State Department of Environmental Protection, or other public agency to assume ownership and maintenance responsibilities for a public purpose consistent with the objectives of the local Master Plan or the Natural Resources Inventory.

Further flexibility can be added to the ordinance by allowing dedicated land to be undedicated and developed. Permitting this should be based on such conditions as 1) the lot not already being improved for public purposes; 2) a major public improvement having resulted which directly improves the developability of the lot; 3) equal or greater land area will be dedicated elsewhere in exchange for the area undedicated, but with no acreage credit for the previously dedicated lands; and 4) the replacement land offers the same opportunity to serve the intended purpose as the originally dedicated area including such characteristics as convenient location to population being served, accessibility, topography, soil conditions, lot configuration, and agricultural suitability in cases involving land dedicated to agricultural use. The most significant aspect of the TDC concept is broader than its specific design criteria or its application to a specific tract. It permits municipal planning efforts to be more concerned with the ultimate impact of land development. The officials can concentrate more on the concepts of total population growth and densities, public services, farmland zoning to preserve agriculture while allowing farmland to participate in the development market, preserving critical areas, and relating land preservation to the rate of development and the increased need for land preservation caused by the development.

As in the delineation of any zoning districts under the traditional concepts, the physical characteristics and existing development patterns together with the Master Plan are important in creating a TDC ordinance.

Reasonable use of the land, ultimate population, preventing development in critical areas, utility service areas, job opportunities, housing and similar considerations are necessary, but to varying degrees depending on each community. As with traditional zoning, the TDC concept can also be applied in several reasonable ways to the same community. The true test is that the particular configuration and interrelationships are not unreasonable.

With the TDC concept, the density of the lots should be permitted to be increased to a level appropriate for proper design. For example, in suburban or rural areas the basic density on a tract might be 0.5-1.0-1.5 units per "gross" acre; meaning that swamps, steep slopes, and water areas as well as good land is used to calculate the number of units even if these critical areas might be calculated at a reduced rate because of their environmental limitations. By using the credits generated by other tracts under the TDC concept, the receiving lot might be allowed to be increased to an average density not exceeding four units per acre. For example, four separate tracts of 100 acres each zoned at one unit per acre would generate 400 dwelling units. These 400 units could be located on one of the 100 tracts since the density would equal 4 units per acre. Then if cluster zoning and mixture of housing types is allowed on the receiving lot, the portion of the lot designed for garden apartments might have a permitted density of 8-9-10 units per acre while portions dedicated to townhouse development might be 5-6-7 units per acre. Lots for detached or zero-lot-line single family homes might be 40-50-60 feet in width. But regardless of the type units or their individual design densities, no more than 400 units would be erected on the 100 acre tract in the above example. Such relationships permit a reasonable use of the land without using the TDC concept while also permitting an increase in density where the TDC concept is used. Yet the rise in density on the receiving lot is still at a level allowing on-site aesthetics without imposing tight building design, crammed parking, and poor internal circulation. For ease of administration and flexibility, this concept is best used when based on a density concept of "X" units per gross acre. But the density concept should be understood. For example, a density of one unit per acre is not the same as zoning for one acre lots. With minimum one acre lots, land needed for streets and other site inefficiencies due to topography, swamps and other problems reduce the "density" to 0.75 units per gross acre or less if site conditions are poor. In agricultural areas, with all land receiving some credit, even a density of one unit per gross acre may be high, particularly if one considers potable water resources and the potential population impact contained in the million or so acres of farmland in the state.

INDUSTRIAL POSSIBILITIES

Since most land development is related to residences, it is expected that the TDC concept will have its greatest application with residential development. In Chesterfield, though, the preservation of agricultural land was offered additional stimulus by allowing industrial owners to purchase and dedicate agricultural land in exchange for an increase in the floor area ration, building height, and total lot coverage in the industrial district. The ability to use the.TDC concept in conjunction with industrial development may, however, have limited application in industrialized or essentially developed communities. In agricultural areas, more potential exists for using the TDC concept beyond its residential application. When used in conjunction with industrial development, flexibility can also be added to the "receiving" industrial lot by allowing "average" lot sizes and relating the increased floor area ratio, lot coverage and heights to a percentage of the lot and a setback envelope. These provisions will assure some proportionate relationships even though the intensity of development on any one lot is increased.

ADMINISTERING THE ORDINANCE

Finally, once a TDC ordinance is adopted, the community should carefully establish a record-keeping system to prevent "sending" lots from being used more than once. The system can be simple and straight forward. A map (perhaps a set of tax maps) showing all lots involved would not only indicate the patterns that evolve (helpful in giving priority to subsequent sites to be dedicated), but the subdivision or site plan application number could be recorded on the appropriate lots on the map. This reference would enable the complete file on the original application to be retrieved for more detailed review if necessary. For a convenient code, a parcel receiving subdivision approval might be identified by a prefix "SUB" ("SITE" for site plan) and the application number, e.g., 1-76 for the first such application in 1976. A suffix of "R" (receiving lot) and "S" (sending lot) could be added. Hence, a code of *SUB: 1-76-S* would identify the first subdivision application in 1976 identifying it also as a "sending" lot under the TDC concept. If the sending lot is dedicated to the community, no ownership or other notation would appear critical, but if it is retained in private ownership and restricted to agricultural use, a further suffix of "Ag" would be appropriate. The above example would then be noted as *SUB: 1-76-S-Ag*. The "Receiving" lot for that same application would also be identified by the code *SUB: 1-76-R*. If the second subdivision application avoids the TDC approach, it would merely be identified as *SUB: 2-76*. This method of recording is also easily added to computer records in towns using computers.

Index

531